I0868878

# Computational and Cognitive Approaches to Narratology

Takashi Ogata
*Iwate Prefectural University, Japan*

Taisuke Akimoto
*The University of Electoro-Communications, Japan*

A volume in the Advances in Linguistics and Communication Studies (ALCS) Book Series

Information Science REFERENCE
An Imprint of IGI Global

Published in the United States of America by
Information Science Reference (an imprint of IGI Global)
701 E. Chocolate Avenue
Hershey PA, USA 17033
Tel: 717-533-8845
Fax: 717-533-8661
E-mail: cust@igi-global.com
Web site: http://www.igi-global.com

Copyright © 2016 by IGI Global. All rights reserved. No part of this publication may be reproduced, stored or distributed in any form or by any means, electronic or mechanical, including photocopying, without written permission from the publisher. Product or company names used in this set are for identification purposes only. Inclusion of the names of the products or companies does not indicate a claim of ownership by IGI Global of the trademark or registered trademark.

Library of Congress Cataloging-in-Publication Data

Names: Ogata, Takashi, 1958- editor. | Akimoto, Taisuke, 1984- editor.
Title: Computational and cognitive approaches to narratology / Takashi Ogata and Taisuke Akimoto, editors.
Description: Hershey, PA : Information Science Reference, [2016] | Includes bibliographical references and index.
Identifiers: LCCN 2016010967| ISBN 9781522504320 (hardcover) | ISBN 9781522504337 (ebook)
Subjects: LCSH: Discourse analysis, Narrative. | Narration (Rhetoric)--Data processing. | Narrative inquiry (Research method) | Natural language processing (Computer science) | Computational linguistics.
Classification: LCC P302.7 .C657 2016 | DDC 401/.41--dc23 LC record available at https://lccn.loc.gov/2016010967

This book is published in the IGI Global book series Advances in Linguistics and Communication Studies (ALCS) (ISSN: Pending; eISSN: Pending)

British Cataloguing in Publication Data
A Cataloguing in Publication record for this book is available from the British Library.

All work contributed to this book is new, previously-unpublished material. The views expressed in this book are those of the authors, but not necessarily of the publisher.

For electronic access to this publication, please contact: eresources@igi-global.com.

# Advances in Linguistics and Communication Studies (ALCS) Book Series

Abigail G. Scheg
*Western Governors University, USA*

ISSN: Pending
EISSN: Pending

Mission

The scope of language and communication is constantly changing as society evolves, new modes of communication are developed through technological advancement, and novel words enter our lexicon as the result of cultural change. Understanding how we communicate and use language is crucial in all industries and updated research is necessary in order to promote further knowledge in this field.

The **Advances in Linguistics and Communication Studies (ALCS)** book series presents the latest research in diverse topics relating to language and communication. Interdisciplinary in its coverage, ALCS presents comprehensive research on the use of language and communication in various industries including business, education, government, and healthcare.

Coverage

- Cross-Cultural Communication
- Graphic Communications
- Sociolinguistics
- Media and Public Communications
- Semantics
- Language acquisition
- Language in the Media
- Non-Verbal Communication
- Forensic Linguistics
- Computer-Mediated Communication

IGI Global is currently accepting manuscripts for publication within this series. To submit a proposal for a volume in this series, please contact our Acquisition Editors at Acquisitions@igi-global.com or visit: http://www.igi-global.com/publish/.

The Advances in Linguistics and Communication Studies (ALCS) Book Series (ISSN Pending) is published by IGI Global, 701 E. Chocolate Avenue, Hershey, PA 17033-1240, USA, www.igi-global.com. This series is composed of titles available for purchase individually; each title is edited to be contextually exclusive from any other title within the series. For pricing and ordering information please visit http://www.igi-global.com/book-series/advances-linguistics-communication-studies/78950. Postmaster: Send all address changes to above address. Copyright © 2016 IGI Global. All rights, including translation in other languages reserved by the publisher. No part of this series may be reproduced or used in any form or by any means – graphics, electronic, or mechanical, including photocopying, recording, taping, or information and retrieval systems – without written permission from the publisher, except for non commercial, educational use, including classroom teaching purposes. The views expressed in this series are those of the authors, but not necessarily of IGI Global.

## Titles in this Series

*For a list of additional titles in this series, please visit: www.igi-global.com*

*Analyzing Language and Humor in Online Communication*
Rotimi Taiwo (Obafemi Awolowo University, Nigeria) Akinola Odebunmi (University of Ibadan, Nigeria) and Akin Adetunji (Emmanuel Alayande College of Education, Nigeria)
Information Science Reference • copyright 2016 • 324pp • H/C (ISBN: 9781522503385) • US $185.00 (our price)

*Discourse Analysis as a Tool for Understanding Gender Identity, Representation, and Equality*
Nazmunnessa Mahtab (University of Dhaka, Bangladesh) Sara Parker (John Moores University, UK) Farah Kabir (Action Aid, Bangladesh) Tania Haque (University of Dhaka, Bangladesh) Aditi Sabur (University of Dhaka, Bangladesh) and Abu Saleh Mohammad Sowad (University of Dhaka, Bangladesh)
Information Science Reference • copyright 2016 • 323pp • H/C (ISBN: 9781522502258) • US $185.00 (our price)

*Revealing Gender Inequalities and Perceptions in South Asian Countries through Discourse Analysis*
Nazmunnessa Mahtab (University of Dhaka, Bangladesh) Sara Parker (John Moores University, UK) Farah Kabir (Action Aid, Bangladesh) Tania Haque (University of Dhaka, Bangladesh) Aditi Sabur (University of Dhaka, Bangladesh) and Abu Saleh Mohammad Sowad (University of Dhaka, Bangladesh)
Information Science Reference • copyright 2016 • 286pp • H/C (ISBN: 9781522502791) • US $185.00 (our price)

*Interdisciplinary Perspectives on Contemporary Conflict Resolution*
Paulo Novais (University of Minho, Portugal) and Davide Carneiro (University of Minho, Portugal)
Information Science Reference • copyright 2016 • 363pp • H/C (ISBN: 9781522502456) • US $185.00 (our price)

*Handbook of Research on Effective Communication, Leadership, and Conflict Resolution*
Anthony H. Normore (California State University Dominguez Hills, USA & International Academy of Public safety, USA) Larry W. Long (Illinois State University, USA & International Academy of Public Safety, USA) and Mitch Javidi (North Carolina State University, USA & International Academy of Public Safety, USA)
Information Science Reference • copyright 2016 • 733pp • H/C (ISBN: 9781466699700) • US $315.00 (our price)

*Handbook of Research on Cross-Cultural Approaches to Language and Literacy Development*
Patriann Smith (University of Illinois at Urbana-Champaign, USA) and Alex Kumi-Yeboah (University at Albany–State University of New York, USA)
Information Science Reference • copyright 2015 • 567pp • H/C (ISBN: 9781466686687) • US $305.00 (our price)

*Communication and Language Analysis in the Corporate World*
Roderick P. Hart (University of Texas - Austin, USA)
Information Science Reference • copyright 2014 • 435pp • H/C (ISBN: 9781466649996) • US $215.00 (our price)

IGI GLOBAL
DISSEMINATOR OF KNOWLEDGE
www.igi-global.com

701 E. Chocolate Ave., Hershey, PA 17033
Order online at www.igi-global.com or call 717-533-8845 x100
To place a standing order for titles released in this series, contact: cust@igi-global.com
Mon-Fri 8:00 am - 5:00 pm (est) or fax 24 hours a day 717-533-8661

## Editorial Advisory Board

Akinori Abe, *Chiba University, Japan*
Akihito Kanai, *Hosei University, Japan*
Yoji Kawamura, *Kinki University, Japan*
Yukiko Ogawa, *Hosei University, Japan*
Koichi Takeuchi, *Okayama University, Japan*
Akira Utsumi, *The University of Electro-Communications, Japan*

## List of Reviewers

Shinichi Asakawa, *Tokyo Woman's Christian University, Japan*
Stefano Calabrese, *University of Modena and Reggio Emilia, Italy*
Tüge T. Gülşen, *Istanbul Bilgi University, Turkey*
Shun Ishizaki, *Keio University, Japan*
Ryota Nomura, *The University of Tokyo, Japan*
Akira Ohtani, *Osaka Gakuin University, Japan*
Takeshi Okada, *The University of Tokyo, Japan*
Kai Seino, *National Institute of Vocational Rehabilitation, Keio Research Institute at SFC, Japan*
Tohru Seraku, *Hankuk University of Foreign Studies, Korea*
Yoko Takeda, *Yokohama National University, Japan*
Gen Tsuchiyama, *Doshisha University, Japan*
Sara Uboldi, *University of Modena and Reggio Emilia, Italy*
Miki Ueno, *Toyohashi University of Technology, Japan*

# Table of Contents

# Detailed Table of Contents

The objective of this chapter is to develop a method for generating and analyzing creative work by using computers. In this chapter, novels, comics, and animations are considered representative creative work because the main method for representing creative work is the use of natural language and pictures. These works focus on interesting issues, which can be explained by computational approaches to narratology. In this chapter, the authors discuss the following three topics. First, a method of semi-automatic story generation by agent-based simulation is presented. Second, methods of generating and analyzing comics on the basis of the features of pictures and stories used are described. Third, the authors introduce a method of estimating the difficulties of translating a storyboard into original pictures in the process of creating animations.



The goal with this chapter is to discuss the possibility of language resources in determining the states, actions, and change-of-states of characters in narratives. An overview of previous work on linguistic theory and language resources is given then the Predicate-Argument Structure Thesaurus (PT), a Japanese language resource constructed based on the extended framework of the Lexical Conceptual Structure (LCS), is proposed. The PT provides hierarchical clusters of synonyms for 11,900 predicates and 22,000 example sentences annotated with semantic role labels. Each concept has an abstracted LCS, and example sentences are attached to each concept. By virtue of the structure, a correlation of the arguments between other clusters can be determined. The semantic structure of the PT is investigated to enrich generated texts of narratives, and the high possibility of lexical semantics contributing to narrative processing is revealed.



In Japanese, whose basic word-order is S(ubject)-O(bject)-V(erb), non-verbal elements may be permuted with the restriction that such elements cannot occur post-verbally. This restriction, however, does not apply to narrative discourse, especially conversations in novels. This discourse phenomenon with post-verbal elements is called "postposing." This chapter reveals several grammatical properties of postposing based on Japanese novels, and present an explicit account in an integrated theory of grammar. More precisely, the narrative data indicate that the syntactic type of postposed element is quite diverse and that, contrary to the prevalent, opposing view, Japanese postposing is not restricted to a matrix clause. These issues are addressed within Dynamic Syntax, a cognitively realistic grammar formalism which specifies a set of constraints on building up a structure online. This architectural design formalises the incremental process of how the reader gradually updates an interpretation by parsing a postposing sentence in narrative discourse.



This paper has two objectives: (1) to describe the significance and applicability of narratology, which features computational and cognitive approaches, in the field of interpersonal relationship supports for persons with disabilities, and (2) to determine effective work supports by analyzing the narratives of the persons with disabilities. In this chapter, the narratives were operationally defined as free-expression answers obtained from mail-survey questionnaires from people with various disabilities describing their work and work life. The questionnaires were sent to 14,448 people and, of these, 4,546 responded. The survey items included their employment status, problems they encountered before employment, problems in their working life, support required in their working life, and opinions regarding disability employment. The results suggested that employment status and problems at work depended on their disability type and the presence of effective supports.



Stylometry is the application of quantitative analysis, primarily to written language, to identify variations in style. Statistical analysis of linguistic characteristics is applied to identify authorship, creation period, and creation order. This study involves stylometric research into "The Tale of Genji," which is a Japanese classical literary work. "The Tale of Genji" is a long story consisting of 54 volumes. However, in the last 13 volumes, the content is different from that in the other volumes, and the writing quality differs from that of the previous 41 volumes; thus, it has long been theorized that the 13 volumes was written by a different author. The result of an analysis using the word frequency for auxiliary verbs found no evidence that positively support the theory of separate authorship. Therefore, the results indicate that the possibility that there are multiple authors of "The Tale of Genji" is low.

In this chapter, the authors showed that eyeblink synchronization enables researchers to investigate the appeal power of narrative performance empirically. The proposed method relies on the ability of audience members as epistemic agents to recognize and understand the performance. As spontaneous eyeblinks loosely co-vary with individual's allocation and release of attentions, the timings of eyeblinks could be entrained by the details of narrative performances as the common inputs. Thus, the standard basis accumulated by the collective eyeblink responses enables experimenter to judge whether or not a particular performance contains universal appeal to sense-making. Here, the authors introduced that the empirical studies to assess the appeal power of Rakugo (a traditional narrative performance). An expert artist, compared to a novice performer, created implicit breakpoints on participants' attentional process. It were discussed that the applicable scopes of the eyeblink relevant indices, upcoming research on eyeblink synchronization, and new research on human collective behaviors.

**Chapter 12**
The Dilemma of Suspense: Neuronarratology, Cognitive Neurosciences, and Computer Technology ............ 322
*Sara Uboldi, University of Modena and Reggio Emilia, Italy*
*Stefano Calabrese, University of Modena e Reggio Emilia, Italy*

The new generation Narratology shows a renewed heuristic scenario, involving an intense dialogue among Humanities, Cognitive Neuroscience and Computer Technology. The case of suspense is emblematic: the pleasure that suspense exercises on the human mind can be precisely explained by identifying the mechanisms of reward provided by neurological and imaging studies. At the same time, patterns of automatic generation of narrations highlight the profound implications of a heated debate between Narratology and Computer Technology, in order to understand the processes of reception and inference during the narrative immersion in storyworlds. At the end of their overview on of a cross-disciplinary approach to suspense analysis, the authors report a case study considered of interest, by a group of researched, called Liquid Narrative Group, of North Caroline State University.

**Chapter 13**
Fact, Narrative, Visualization as Fiction, and Love: Analysis of the Japanese Film *The Land of Hope* ............ 333
*Yukiko Ogawa, Hosei University, Japan*

This chapter's subject matter is "The Land of Hope", a Japanese film inspired by facts. The primary aim is to apply structural analysis of narrative, a method commonly used for natural language text, to film, which is an audiovisual text. This research will adopt methods for decomposing the film into component units and rules for linking them that are appropriate to the physical/representational characteristics of the medium, and propose a procedure for visualizing the narrative structure using a single diagram. The second aim is to sketch the aspects of narrative content that structural analyses – which only regard its formal aspects – overlook, supporting the argument with knowledge from film cognition research and by focusing on particular themes. This chapter's research deals with a practical simulation that analyzes a film's form and content with an integrated approach, and advocates the methodology that is applicable to any film in principle.

# Preface

Studying narratives is often the best way to gain a good understanding of how various aspects of human information are organized and integrated—the narrator employs specific informational methods to build the whole structure of a narrative through combining temporally constructed events in light of an array of relationships to the narratee and these methods reveal the interaction of the rational and the sensitive aspects of human information. Therefore, a wide variety of narrative contents has been created so far, along with many types of media. We are now in a position to expect that the concept and methods of narrative, which have been explored by narratology and literary theories, are to be connected in the future with contemporary information studies—including those in computational fields, such as artificial intelligence (AI), and in cognitive fields, such as cognitive science—which will then bring about the emergence of a significant conceptual and methodological foundation for various technologies of novel contents, media, human interface, and so on. This book explores new possibilities and directions of narrative-related technologies and theories and their implications for the innovative design, development, and creation of future media and contents, such as automatic narrative or story generation systems, through interdisciplinary approaches to narratology that are dependent on computational and cognitive studies, i.e., "computational and cognitive approaches to narratology."

## OBJECTIVE

Based on the abovementioned idea, this book simultaneously discusses issues of narrative-related information and computational technologies, cognitive mechanisms and analyses, and theories as the context of technology, particularly those from humanities and social sciences. This book especially focuses on the systems or analysis of narrative or story generation process and its applications to advertisement, management, welfare, literature, and art (movie, *rakugo* [a form of Japanese verbal entertainment], and *kabuki* [a form of traditional Japanese dance-drama]), which has within its scope narratology, literary theories, poetics, semiotics, rhetoric, philosophy, linguistics, psychology, marketing and advertisement, etc. Media and genres to be examined in the narrative analysis and the applications cover a very broad range. A significant characteristic of this book that distinguishes it from other books in similar fields is the introduction of narratological knowledge or theories into actual system design and development and actual text analysis through computational and cognitive methods.

The following groups will find this text useful in furthering their research exposure to pertinent and interdisciplinary topics in "computational and cognitive approaches to narratology" and also in furthering their own research efforts in this field.

1. Researchers and advanced-level students of information technologies and cognitive studies (including AI, cognitive science, narrative or story generation, natural language comprehension and generation, computational creativity, communication study, media study, neuroscience, etc.)
2. Researchers and advanced-level students of literary studies (including narratology, discourse theory, rhetoric, poetics, semiotics, linguistics, film theory, etc.)
3. Designers, creators, developers, researchers, and advanced-level students of advanced digital content design and development (including computer game, interactive storytelling, automated content generation, human interface, the Web design, etc.)

## BOOK ORGANIZATION

The chapters compiled in this book involve a variety of studies based on diverse backgrounds, objectives, and methodologies and across the three phases of narrative phenomenon, i.e., generation, text, and reception. In the organizational level, they correspond to production, content, and consumption. They also examine various narrative genres including novel (classical and contemporary), poem, film, comic, advertising film, business communication, diary or personal narrative, *rakugo*, *kabuki*, *emoji*, etc. Moreover, they include various objectives and research approaches: technological studies including computational modeling and implementation of narrative processing, empirical studies on human narrative reception based on techniques of cognitive or psychological studies, conceptual thought, design, and criticism on narrative phenomenon, qualitative or quantitative analysis of narrative text, etc.

Although it is difficult to clearly categorize these studies, the editors organized them into the following four sections: (1) "Introduction"; (2) "Generation and Creation of Narratives": Five chapters contain discussions centered on generative, creative, or productive aspects of narrative; (3) "Language and Narrative": The book contains four papers primarily relevant to the fields of linguistics and natural language processing; (4) "Cognition, Culture, and Narrative": This section explores topics about the aspects of reception and cultural nature of narrative (one of the characteristics in this book is that the sections occasionally also include Japanese cultural elements).

### Section 1: Introduction

The first chapter by Takashi Ogata that comes before the start of the abovementioned sections serves as an introduction to the entire book. This chapter surveys and discusses interdisciplinary approaches to primarily AI-based computational narrative or story generation systems by way of introducing cognitive science and narratology and related literary theories. This is also an expansion of ideas, theories, and systems of the "Informatics of narratology" presented by Ogata and Kanai (2010). The first part of this chapter provides a general description of narrative or story generation from the perspective of the framework for narrative-related research and the second part presents the research process, theoretical concepts, designs, and implementations of narrative generation. The first part particularly seeks to provide a comprehensive overview of narratology and the relevant literary theories, computational and cognitive theories and techniques related to narratology and narrative generation, and narrative generation systems. Readers will be able to comprehensively understand the overview of computational and cognitive approaches to narratology and to aim at the extension of this novel research area in the future. The second part presents an example of the practices of computational approach to narratology through narrative generation studies and also presents, in relative detail, the components that constitute a systematic study for narrative generation and an "Integrated Narrative Generation System: INGS" of all of the previous attempts by the author.

The remaining part overviews the background and the chapters contained in each section.

## Section 2: Generation and Creation of Narratives

This section consists of studies centered on generative or creative aspects of narrative. The methodology and fundamental mechanism of narrative or narrative generation are major subjects in works from Aristotle's (1895) "Poetics" to modern narratology or literary studies. The computational or cognitive modeling of narrative generation and narrative ability is also a major and crucial subject in the fields of AI and cognitive science, including the interdisciplinary studies with narratology and literary theories. For instance, Propp's (1968) "Morphology of the folktale" and Genette's (1980) "Narrative discourse theory" have influenced the fields of AI and cognitive science. From the perspective of application, computational or formalized narrative generation technologies will enable the automation or support of human narrative creation processes or creative activities in the real world. The chapters contained in this section are outlined below.

Chapter 2 by Akinori Abe discusses the possibility of literary work generation by computer. The chapter introduces the literary concept of "intertextuality" proposed by Kristeva (1980) as a key idea for the computational modeling of literary work generation. After reviewing several related studies in the "language sense processing engineering," which is an original idea of an AI-based research field by the author and the research group, and computational creativity of literature, the chapter discusses a new type of computational method for generating various literary works including *waka* and *haiku* [forms of Japanese traditional short poem], contemporary poem, and novel.

Chapter 3 by Taisuke Akimoto and Takashi Ogata proposes the design plan, partially and experimentally implemented as computer program, of a "Socially Open Narrative Generation System: SONGS" that co-creates a collection of diverse narratives from the interaction between a narrative generation program and people. This challenge aims at both a kind of social level application of narrative generation technology and a computational approach to narratology as a model for the social or collaborative process of narrative production.

Chapter 4 by Yoji Kawamura shows a generative technology of narrative for the field of advertising. In particular, the chapter presents the concepts and technologies behind a "Commercial Film Production Support System: CFPSS" in which image editing techniques and rhetorical knowledge based on structural analyses of TV commercial films are implemented. The chapter also presents the result of an experiment for investigating how an advertising story influences viewers, using commercial films generated by CFPSS.

Chapter 5 by Yoko Takeda provides an empirical discussion for exploring factors or methodologies of effective digital storytelling in the context of business planning. By using the data, including narrative or story texts, collected through a workshop on business planning using digital storytelling with six participants (creators) and thirty-five audience members (evaluators), the chapter analyzes the relationship between the structure and content of each work and the evaluation by the human audience.

Chapter 6 by Miki Ueno, Kiyohito Fukuda, and Naoki Mori presents three narrative-related studies on computational implementations of generation or analysis of story, comic, and animation storyboard. The first part presents a method of semi-automatic story generation based on agent-based simulation. The second part describes methods of generating and analyzing comics. The third part shows a method of estimating the difficulty of translating a storyboard into original pictures for supporting an animation creation process.

## Section 3: Language and Narrative

Section 3 contains studies primarily relevant to the fields of linguistics and natural language processing. Language is one of the major media for narrative representation. In addition, both narrative and language are closely related as the fundamental natures that characterize human intelligence and cognition. From a broader perspective, the chapters contained in this section are divided into two categories. First, chapter 7 and chapter 8 approach narrative from the standpoints of linguistics and linguistics-based natural language processing. They deal with the relationship between narrative and language based on the formal and computational studies on semantics and syntax of language. These challenges will be connected to the technology of computational narrative processing—e.g., generation, analysis, understanding, interpretation, etc.—in the future. Second, Chapters 9 and chapter 10 analyze human created/told narratives for understanding the author/tellers, by using techniques of natural language processing. In particular, they apply natural language processing to the effective employment support for people with disabilities and the authorship identification problem of a classical literary work. The chapters contained in this section are outlined below.

Chapter 7 by Koichi Takeuchi discusses the possibility or availability of language resources, semantic dictionaries of language, mainly constructed in the field of natural language processing, on narrative comprehension and generation processing. In particular, the chapter considers availability of the "Predicate-argument structure Thesaurus: PT," a Japanese language resource constructed by the author, for various narrative processing, including the determinations of states, actions, and change-of-states of characters in human- or computer-generated narrative texts.

Chapter 8 by Tohru Seraku and Akira Ohtani reveals several grammatical properties of "postposing" based on Japanese contemporary novels and presents an explicit account of an integrated theory of grammar. In Japanese, non-verbal elements may be permuted with the restriction that such elements cannot occur post-verbally. This restriction, however, does not apply to dialogues or conversations, especially in novels. The chapter addresses this syntactic flexibility within "Dynamic Syntax: DS", a cognitively realistic grammar formalism that specifies a set of constraints on building up an online structure.

Chapter 9 by Kai Seino, Yuichiro Haruna, and Shun Ishizaki describes clinical knowledge for the effective employment support for people with disabilities through a computer-based analysis of the many narratives obtained from mail survey questionnaires from people with various disabilities who described their work and work life. The chapter presents the mixed analytical method of text mining as a topic in recent natural language processing field and narratological language analysis for examining effective employment support.

Chapter 10 by Gen Tsuchiyama involves stylometric research of "The Tale of Genji," one of the greatest novels in the world penned by Murasaki Shikibu (1973) in the middle age of the Heian era (794-1185 or 1192), which consists of 54 volumes. "Stylometry" is the application of quantitative analysis to identify variations in style and is applied to identify authorship, creation period, and creation order. The chapter especially addresses authorship identification—the theory that "The Tale of Genji" was written by different authors—by the stylometric method.

## Section 4: Cognition, Culture, and Narrative

This last section mainly deals with the aspects of reception and cultural nature of narrative. In the literary field, the reception aspect of narrative is mainly discussed or thought in the reception theories or reader-centric criticisms of Iser (1978), Jauss (1982), and others. The studies in this section empirically address the issues of narrative reception based on the methodologies of cognitive science, neuroscience, information technology, etc. In addition, based on the obtained knowledge, several studies discuss rhetorical techniques for computational narrative generation. On the other hand, from the cultural perspective, the chapters particularly examine the genres or narrative systems rooted in the Japanese culture, including *rakugo*, *kabuki*, and *emoji* communication. The chapters contained in this section are outlined below.

Chapter 11 by Ryota Nomura and Takeshi Okada presents an empirical method for assessing the appeal power of narrative performance by using "eyeblink synchronization" as an objectively observable feature of the human audience. The chapter applies the method to empirical studies to assess the appeal power of performance in *rakugo*, a Japanese traditional narrative performance based on one sitting artist's direct narration and body language on the stage. The chapter also discusses the applicable scope of the eyeblink relevant indices, upcoming research on eyeblink synchronization, and new research on human collective behaviors.

Chapter 12 by Sara Uboldi and Stefano Calabrese introduces "neuronarratology," an emergent perspective that includes linguistic and cognitive contributions to the cognitive poetics and neurological studies of human mind's structure and function. The chapter addresses the issue around suspense effect in a narrative reception process. After overviewing cross-disciplinary studies on suspense analysis, the chapter reports a case study on human cognitive responses using the result of a study on narrative generation system.

Chapter 13 by Yukiko Ogawa proposes a combined method for film analysis that connects structural analysis of the overall narrative and cognitive analysis of the narrative effect of the expression in a specific image of a characteristic part. The chapter applies the method to "The Land of Hope" (2012) by Shion Sono, a fictional film that is based on an actual event, the 2011 Great East Japan Earthquake. The chapter mainly takes the following two perspectives in the film analysis: how the facts are dramatized in the fictional narrative film and how enjoyment is obtained from the themes of love and death.

Chapter 14 by Tüge T. Gülşen discusses the nature and mechanism of new communication modes that have emerged from digital platforms, especially *emojis* as a new language system of daily narratives. Through reviewing related studies in the fields of communication study, linguistics, narratology, semiotics, etc., the chapter explores how computer users integrate *emojis* in their daily narrative practices and how *emojis* create a new mode of language to communicate stories on digital platforms.

Chapter 15 by Akihito Kanai deals with the aspects of non-story narrative—in which discourse is considered more important than story or a clear story does not exist—and nostalgia effect in the cognition of film reception, in addition to the story aspect of narrative. In particular, the chapter analyzes film cognitive effects related to nostalgia through the method of narrative rhetoric of "cutting techniques" (for a flow of a story), which the author has been studying, and "defamiliarization" in literary theories.

The knowledge derived from the analysis is applied to a computational modeling for composing films or images of nostalgia-based narrative rhetoric, based on his non-story narrative concept.

Chapter 16 by Takashi Ogata seeks to undertake the problem of a narrative generation-reception and narrative production-consumption modeling of *kabuki* from the viewpoint of an information system, and in particular, a narrative generation system. A fundamental concept of the modeling is "multiplicity," or "multiple narrative structures" in narrative. Therefore, the direct objective of this chapter is to propose a first approach to a narrative generation-reception and production-consumption model of *kabuki* based on the above concepts. In addition, this chapter associates the model to the concept of the "Geino Information System: GIS," representing a system model in which multiple narrative generation and production mechanisms or processes, i.e., narrative multiple structures, are included. Introductory knowledge on *kabuki*, including the history and basic terms, is also mentioned as background for the discussion. The next main objective of the chapter is to phenomenally describe the aspects of *kabuki*'s multiple narrative structures with actual examples. Although only indicated in this chapter, the ultimate goal of the author is to conduct social distribution experiments of the "Integrated Narrative Generation System: INGS," which the author has been developing as a synthesis of previous studies. By social distribution, the author means a new type of business model for social applications using the Web, etc., for the narrative generation system itself, or for a content system including narrative generation systems. Finally, the chapter anticipates directions for future research on social distribution of INGS through a greater understanding of *kabuki* and its multiple narrative structures model. This topic will be one of the central issues of the following book.

*Takashi Ogata*
*Iwate Prefectural University, Japan*

*Taisuke Akimoto*
*The University of Electro-Communications, Japan*

## REFERENCES

Aristotle. (1895). The poetics of Aristotle (S. H. Butcher, Trans.). London, UK: Macmillan; Retrieved from https://archive.org/details/poeticstranslate00arisuoft

Genette, G. (1980). *Narrative discourse: An essay in method* (J. E. Lewin, Trans.). Ithaca, NY: Cornell University Press. (Original work published 1972)

Iser, W. (1978). *The act of reading: A theory of aesthetic response*. Baltimore, MD: Johns Hopkins University Press.

Jauss, H. R. (1982). *Toward an aesthetic of reception* (T. Bahti, Trans.). Minneapolis, MN: University of Minnesota Press. (Original work published 1970)

Kristeva, J. (1980). *Desire in language: A semiotic approach to literature and art*. New York, NY: Columbia University Press. (Original work published 1969)

Murasaki Shikibu. (1978). *Geiji monogatari* [The tale of Genji]. (E. G. Seidensticker, Trans.). New York, NY: Knopf. (Original work published in the middle age of the Heian era)

Ogata, T., & Kanai, A. (2010). *Monogatariron no johogaku josetsu-Monogatari seisei no shiso to gijutsu wo megutte* [An introduction to informatics of narratology: About the thoughts and technologies of narrative generation]. Tokyo, Japan: Gakubunsha.

Propp, V. Y. (1968). *Morphology of the folktale* (L. Scott, Trans.). Austin, TX: University of Texas Press. (Original work published 1928)

# Acknowledgment

The editors would like to acknowledge the help of all the people involved in this project. Without their great contributions, this book would not have been completed. First, the editors wish to thank all the authors for their high quality contributions and the reviewers for their valuable advices in improving the quality of the book. Second, the editors acknowledge the comprehensive support of the editorial advisory board members—Akinori Abe (Chiba University, Chiba, Japan), Akihito Kanai (Hosei University, Tokyo, Japan), Yoji Kawamura (Kinki University, Osaka, Japan), Yukiko Ogawa (Hosei University, Tokyo, Japan), Koichi Takeuchi (Okayama University, Okayama, Japan), and Akira Utsumi (The University of Electro-Communications, Tokyo, Japan). Finally, the editors thank IGI Global, particularly Ms. Jan Travers, for their assistance in the entire process.

*Takashi Ogata*
*Iwate Prefectural University, Japan*

*Taisuke Akimoto*
*The University of Electro-Communications, Japan*

# Section 1
# Introduction

# Chapter 1
# Computational and Cognitive Approaches to Narratology from the Perspective of Narrative Generation

**Takashi Ogata**
*Iwate Prefectural University, Japan*

## ABSTRACT

*This chapter surveys and discusses interdisciplinary approaches to primarily Artificial Intelligence (AI)-based computational narrative or story generation systems by way of introducing cognitive science, and narratology and related literary theories. The first part of this chapter provides a general description (from the perspective of the research framework of the author) and the second part presents processes, theories, designs, and implementations of narrative generation by the author. In particular, the first part includes an overview of narratology and the relevant literary theories, computational and cognitive theories and techniques related to narratology and narrative generation, and narrative generation systems. The second part presents, in relative detail, components that constitute a systematic study for narrative generation by the author and an integrated narrative generation system of all of the previous attempts.*

## INTRODUCTION

This first chapter surveys and discusses interdisciplinary approaches primarily to Artificial Intelligence (AI)-based computational and cognitive narrative generation systems, including cognitive science as the scientific background, by way of introducing narratology and related literary theories. Narrative or story generation is a basic software technology for human-like communication or interaction using language or other media, including images and music. It is a challenging issue in AI and cognitive science. Research in narrative generation has great academic value in blending different genres, i.e., narratology as an area of the humanities, and information theories and techniques, such as AI and cognitive science, as parts of

DOI: 10.4018/978-1-5225-0432-0.ch001

Copyright © 2016, IGI Global. Copying or distributing in print or electronic forms without written permission of IGI Global is prohibited.

science proper. At the same time, it contributes content to the industry at the intersection of information technology and a variety of actual narratives, such as those in entertainment, art, and literature.

Although they are not explicitly titled, this chapter is divided into PART I, which comprises the next section, and PART II, which includes the following two sections.

PART I surveys aspects of computational and cognitive approaches to narratology from the author's perspective of narrative generation, but with a general viewpoint. The content is structured as follows. The author devotes the first portion of PART I to a presentation of the fundamental framework of narrative generation research that the interdisciplinary computational narrative generation researchers should survey from the macroscopic perspective. The core of PART I is formed from Narratology and Literary Theories and Computational Theories and Techniques Related to Narratological Knowledge. The next section, Narratology and Literary Theories, explains computational theories and techniques related to narrative generation that are employed in AI and cognitive science studies. The following section, Computational Theories and Techniques Related to Narratological Knowledge, is dedicated to an overview of several important narratological and literary theories, and their relationships to AI and cognitive science. Then, Narrative generation Systems introduces a few narrative generation systems that borrow techniques and methods from AI and cognitive science. Finally, Future Research Directions in this Section suggests future research issues related to the topics in PART I.

PART II subsequently presents a history, concepts, and implementations of the author's narrative generation research. It consists of two large sections, A Synthetic Approach To Narrative Generation And An Integrated Narrative Generation System: INGS. In the former, some topics from the narrative generation research by the author are described in Two Frameworks of Narrative Generation, Development of each Mechanism of Narrative Generation, Narrative Analyses, and Application Systems, while Theoretical Concepts details the design and development of the author's narrative generation systems. The latter section introduces an attempt at a synthesized narrative generation system called the "Integrated Narrative Generation System: INGS" through the subsections: An Overview of INGS, INGS as ELT: Narrative generation Mechanisms using Three Literary Theories, Theoretical Concepts in the Expanded ELT and INGS, and Future Plans for INGS. The descriptions of the previous subsections result in the presentation of INGS. The final section of this chapter offers the CONCLUSION.

PART I of this chapter is an extended version of (Ogata, 2011) and the survey portion of (Akimoto & Ogata, 2014a). PART II of this chapter partially utilizes the description of the INGS system implementation in (Akimoto & Ogata, 2014a), as well as the theoretical concepts of narrative generation in (Ogata, 2014). Furthermore, a systematic and comprehensive description of the author's conceptions and plans concerning narrative generation is provided in (Ogata & Kanai, 2010).

## TOWARD A NARRATOLOGY FOR/FROM NARRATIVE GENERATION

This section provides an explanation of narratology, computational narrative knowledge, and narrative generation systems according to a research framework at the macro level.

### Research Framework

From the viewpoint of narrative generation, the author surveys a novel area of computational and cognitive narratology to give a large sketch, plan, or framework for the overview in the next subsection.

What is narrative? The term "narrative" is ordinarily interpreted as a type of linguistic representation in which two or more events are temporally combined. However, according to narratology, a discipline that explores characteristics, forms, and functions common to narratives (Prince, 1982, 2003), we can also understand narrative as a special form of language, based on a variety of rhetorical devices, involving multiple relationships between a narrator and a narratee. This interpretation of narrative is based on a view of narratology that considers complex relationships between a narrator and a narratee. As indicated above, a narrative text consists of two aspects: that of a sequence of events, and that of communication. Broadly speaking, the former and the latter correspond to the story, referring to what is narrated, and the discourse or narration, which is how the story is narrated, respectively.

A story is defined as a temporal sequence of events, while a discourse is related to the various ways in which a story can be edited and narrated. In this sense, a story has a structural and abstract aspect, whereas a discourse contains a structural and abstract aspect, as well as surface linguistic aspects. The co-existence of these aspects never leads to a contradiction, nor is it a consequence of the ambiguity of definition. A narrative work is a mixed language presentation or system consisting of these two aspects, and the ratio between them is variable. In the most extreme cases, if only a story or only a discourse exists, a narrative can still be formed. In other cases, the story and the discourse are the two essential elements. The various adjustments form a narrative.

Furthermore, from a broader perspective, the term "narrative" has been used in the fields of philosophy and thought. For example, the term "large narratives" introduced by Lyotard (1979) means a collection of systematic ideas or notions that are dominant in a society or age. The "communal fantasy" introduced by Yoshimoto (1968), which is a philosophical idea regarding human society that forms a set with other categories, e.g., pair illusion and personal illusion, is a pioneering and more comprehensive proposition. If narrative generation can deal with collective organization of information through social communication, it will be strongly related to the above broad ideas of narrative. On the contrary, the narratological approaches to human history proposed by Danto (1965) and White (1980) considered narrative a necessary concept for the interpretation of the human world and historical construction. Concepts also exist to deal with narrative from the point of view of its effects on the receiver and broader social functions. The main social functions of narrative proposed by Ogata and Kanai (2010) include aesthetic, political, agitating, brainwashing, persuasive, institutional, normative, educational, religious, etc. From the standpoint of AI research, Nakashima (2006) proposed that the value of constructive studies, such as AI, could be evaluated through a persuasive function as a consistent narrative or story. These examples show the wide variety of meanings assumed by the word "narrative."

What are narratology and literary theories? The largest overview of narratology is attempted. The major studies relevant to narratology and contemporary literary theories are Russian formalism, English literary theories such as the New Criticism, and literary and cultural theories based on structuralism and post-structuralism. On the periphery, but in close connection with the above theories, are a variety of literary theories, including Marxist criticism, psychoanalytical criticism, feminist criticism, cultural studies, post-colonialism, and so on (Compagnon, 1998). Barry (2009) provides a list of literary and cultural studies. From a broader perspective, one of the first studies containing material that was called narratology was "Poetics" by Aristotle (1895).

The following part deals with narrative generation system research as a synthetic framework from which to comprehensively treat narratives. Based on the recognition of multiplicity or plurality of narratives, the narrative generation research described in this chapter was conducted according to a broad framework, including a wide range of narratives, from narrative generation systems in a narrow sense, i.e., systems as computer programs, to narrative generation systems in a wide sense, i.e., systems as a method of dealing with collective societies of humans as a symbolic narrative generation system. As shown in Figure 1, Ogata (1995), and Ogata and Kanai (2010) divided this comprehensive framework for research in narrative generation into five fields. The core portion of this diagram covers narrative generation systems as computer programs. Beyond this are two types of interdisciplinary areas: literary studies (primarily narratology and literary theories) and information studies (mainly AI and cognitive science). A new narratological area, created by blending both of these areas, has been called "Expanded Literary Theory: ELT" (Ogata, 2002, 2014). The next level contains a variety of narratological approaches to a number of fields, such as folklore, cultural anthropology, history, sociology, philosophy, psychology, marketing and advertising, business administration, architecture, biology, and so on. The outermost level consists of spaces occupied by various fields relevant to narrative. Although this chapter is primarily related to narrative generation systems as computer programs, its description here is founded on this overall and comprehensive perspective of narrative studies. Additionally, the author needs to describe where the content of this book is covered (relating to the Preface of this book).

Historically, human narrative generation, such as art, music, drama, novels, and films, has been closely connected to various technologies and media. The most recent point of connection is its relationship to AI and cognitive science. Prior to proceeding to examine narrative generation in AI and cognitive science, the author refers to the problem of media and narrative. For example, the generation and development of modern novels were associated with the popularization of books by the invention of type printing technology. In addition, *kabuki* and *ningyo-joruri* are special, but universal examples of narrative. For instance, innovations in the stage settings in *kabuki*, which is a synthetic dramatic form, have contributed to the improvement of dramatic production. Literature and narrative are also not the exceptions. Equally novel, in the narrow sense, was the literary genre associated with the rise of the letterpress. Likewise, machinery or mechanical style itself in the arts and literature are not necessarily a drawback. *Ningyo-joruri* (Japanese puppet show) is an example in which artistic value is enhanced by using mechanical constraints in an underhanded manner, while *kabuki* borrows its scenarios and depicts extraordinary representative beauty based on the imitation of mechanical and artificial motions by human actors. For

*Figure 1. A comprehensive framework for research in narrative generation*

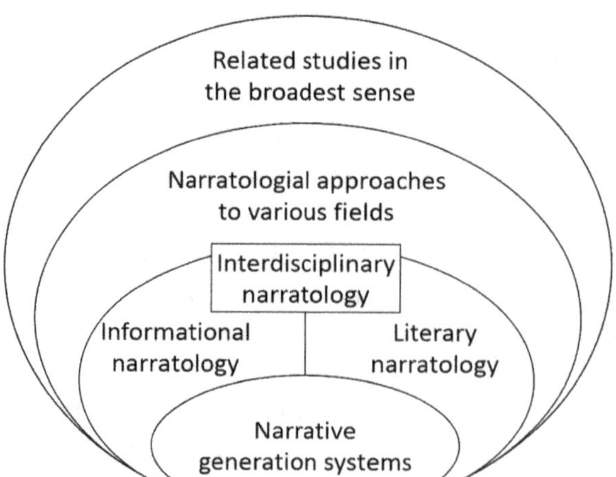

instance, in a scene from *Sugawara Denju Tenarai Kagami* ("Sugawara's Secrets of Calligraphy"), a work in *ningyo-joruri* tradition from 1746, an animated wooden puppet moves and, in the transfer to *kabuki*, a human actor plays the puppet through the use of machinery and artificial motion. Therefore, technological characteristics contribute to beauty in literature and the arts. However, narrative generation systems have a feature that renders them different from past participants in relationships between narrative and media technologies–the mechanization and automation of the process of creating narrative content. In the conventional methods of narrative generation from the past, humans conceived of and created narratives. In contrast, narrative generation systems think and create each narrative as an AI-based "thinking machine."

AI and cognitive science are the most important areas in the field of informatics. AI is a branch of computer science that aims to design and develop intelligent software systems. Research in this area includes theories, technologies, and core and applicable systems. If AI is a field of constructive engineering, cognitive science is a scientific approach that researches the principles of intelligence in human beings, animals, and machines in order to provide basic design knowledge for AI. In this sense, AI and cognitive science are complementary. The design and implementation of narrative generation systems that can automatically generate narrative texts has long been a well-known issue in AI and cognitive science.

As mentioned above, the concept of narrative has different meanings, owing to which research on narrative generation is necessarily interdisciplinary. In particular, research in AI-based narrative generation has a high affinity with narratology and literary theories, as this chapter will show here. Although previously narratology and a group of literary theories were often called "the science of literature," this practice was problematic in the context of traditional literary studies because of the absence of systematic methods for precise and detailed analyses and experiments. By contrast, the practice of "the science of literature" is easy and natural from the point of view of using computational methods, such as AI and cognitive science, because this involves presenting systematic technologies for investigation or simulating narrative analyses and theories.

The following section describes various studies of interdisciplinary narratology in AI and cognitive science, emphasizing the interdisciplinary narrative study and the ELT by Ogata as pioneering attempts. With few exceptions, such as the narrative grammar proposed by Prince (1982), the field of literary research has witnessed few attempts at a conscious blend of informatics and literature. Although still emerging in the field of informatics, various approaches to such a combination have gradually appeared. Ryan (1991) explained the first narrative generation systems and related technologies in detail. Mateas and Sengers (2003) proposed the concept of "narrative intelligence" from a literary, interdisciplinary point of view, combined with AI. Stockwell (2002), Herman (2003), and Gavins and Steen (2003) presented methods to assimilate narrative theories to cognitive science, and Meister (2003) proposed a computational model that applied narratology to narrative action. Research by Ogata and Kanai (2010) provided a systematic and comprehensive description of the expanded literary theory of narratology and AI, the integrated narrative generation system, and other related issues. As stated above, researchers in AI and cognitive science have primarily been extending this interdisciplinary direction of research. This chapter reviews related research genres for more productive uses of narratological knowledge that have been accumulated by narratology and literary theories. The ELT will be intimately described in a later section, A Synthetic Approach to Narrative Generation.

## Narratology and Literary Theories

This subsection presents a simple overview of narratology and related literary theories as a background for narrative generation systems research. It is necessary to refer to the systematic collection and systematization of references relating to narratology, including the newest books, English versions, management sciences, advertising, and other major related areas.

Narratology, in the narrow sense, structural narratology, is introduced here. Narratology, in the narrow sense, is "the (structuralist-inspired) theory of narrative. Narratology studies the nature, form, and functioning of narrative (regardless of medium of representation), and tries to characterize narrative competence" (Prince, 2003). Although contemporary narratology covers a wide range of materials, its chief and original characteristics are structural, and involve a formal approach to texts in various narrative genres. Many researchers have developed great eminent and productive theories, such as, the "polyphony" by Bakhtin (1984), the "mythology" by Lévi-Strauss (1964), the "characters' relationships and story structures" by Greimas (1966), the "morphology of a folktale" by Propp (1968), the "narrative discourse theory" by Genette (1972), the "narrative structural analysis" by Barthes (1975), the "narrative grammar" by Prince (1982), etc.

Before proceeding, the author would like to introduce a very brief overview of modern and contemporary Japanese narratology, including the English versions of Kojin Karatani's works, as well as others. In modern Japan, many works, including *Bungaku ron* (1907) by Natsume Soseki (1867-1916), *Kyodo genso ron* (1968) by Yoshimoto Takaaki (1924-2012), *Monogatari hihan josetsu* (1985) by Hasumi Shigehiko (1936-), "Origins of modern Japanese literature" (1993) by Karatani Kojin (1941-), and *Nihon shousetsu gijutsu shi* (2012) by Watanabe Naomi (1952-), have proposed original theoretical literary studies by blending Japanese and European literary traditions. Oe Kenzaburo (1935-) published experimental novels, such as *Dojidai ge-mu* (1979), to introduce narratology and literary theories.

A systematic anthology of narratology by Bal (2004) covers the full scope of contemporary narratology in the following contents: Vol.1) Major Issues in Narrative Theory (Preposterous beginnings; Plot, Representing speech; Believe it or not), Vol.2) Special Topics (Deixis; Time; Character/plot; Paradigmatic case studies; The ethics of narrative truth; Against wholeness), Vol.3) Political Narratology (Where is the political?; Understanding ideology; The politics of desire; Time.), Vol.4) Interdisciplinarity (Law, justice, history, truth; Social narrative; Subjectivity; Music and film; Science and/as Narrative?)

As shown above, narratology already forms a discipline covering various related topics. Through narratology, the word "narrative" has been treated as an important term, primarily in literature and the humanities. Narratology considers narrative to be the conscious or unconscious mental framework that supports and directs human thinking and culture from the background. Narratology also focuses on the general characteristics of narrative, and its basic orientation is to pursue common narrative mechanisms. Although, as mentioned above, the first representative narratologists held forth on a variety of themes, the characteristics common to their approaches were the coexistence of an extremely macroscopic and interdisciplinary humanistic orientation, and a microscopic and precise analysis or modeling of narrative mechanisms. As a whole, they commonly contained outstanding systematic intentionality. In addition to the above description, the author would like to include advertising, marketing, management, and so on.

The following discussion defined the main components of narrative generation. The classification by Aristotle (1895) should first be recalled. He divided the constituents of a tragedy into Plot (*mythos*), Character (ethos) and Thought (dianoia), Diction (lexis) and Song (melos), and Scenery (opsis). He claimed that the plot is the most important element. His theory had a massive influence on narratology.

At the same time, this idea was not necessarily universal. For instance, the kabuki does not accept a hierarchy in which plot is supreme. However, if this hierarchical feature is eliminated, the effective use of the theoretical framework is possible. It becomes a synthetic modeling of various narrative elements based on a Greek drama for future narrative-generative architectures. Focusing on a sequence of events, Russian formalism divided it into fabula (corresponding to story or narrative content) and sjuzet (corresponding to plot). This basic idea was inherited by narratology. Moreover, Genette (1972) proposed a highly organized narrative model with three elements: story or narrative content, narrative discourse, and the act of narration.

Today, there are four commonly accepted constitutional elements in narratology. Based on these ideas, narrative mechanisms are overviewed, as shown in Table 1. Although such computational theories and technologies as AI and cognitive science, as well as narratology and literary theories, have been independently studied, Table 1 shows possible correlations between the elements of narrative generation stated above and the available implementation technologies or theories from AI and cognitive science. The narrative generation research by the author is based on this narratological model. The author would like to further consider how to utilize this table.

The author now presents the major narratological theories relevant to narrative generation studies, first from the standpoint of an overview and then related narrative generation studies. The selection and description of these theoretical themes are dependent upon the author's framework of narrative generation research, shown in Figure 1. Although many topics are focused on the theoretical frameworks proposed by a particular author, some topics in the last half correspond to particular academic fields.

## Poetics by Aristotle

As mentioned earlier, "Poetics" by Aristotle, based on a Greek tragedy, is clearly considered the origin of narratological study from the viewpoint of a structural or systematic analysis of a narrative work. The analysis is dependent upon the idea that the aspect of plot or sequence of events is more important than the other elements: the characters and thoughts of the dramatic characters, the music and songs, the rhetorical representation of language, and costumes. His theory indicates a kind of hierarchical production process in which a constructed plot determines all of the other components or elements of the dramatic work, from the selection of actors to the stage directions.

Concerning the narrative generation of the author, Aruga and Ogata (1998) defined a hypothetical pattern for dramatic stories by re-analyzing the description by Aristotle:

1. The occurrence of a problem,
2. The setting of a goal,
3. Actions,
4. Results,
5. Reversal and cognition, and
6. Unhappiness.

In the first problem occurrence, a hero faces a fundamental problem, namely the narrative theme or the most significant problem. In phase (2), the hero sets an actual goal to cause unfolding or problem solving, thinks of means of achieving the goal, and then executes them in (3). In phase (4), if the hero fails in his attempts, secondary problems are often generated. If the goal is achieved, this narrative is

*Table 1. Narrative elements and related computational techniques*

| Narrative Element | Overview | Detailed Elements | Computational Techniques |
|---|---|---|---|
| The generation of the story or the narrative world to be narrated | A mechanism is necessary for generating the content or story to be narrated in the final narrative work. In general, this is understood to be the most important part of the narrative generation process. The mechanism generates characters, events, episodes, and so on. A character has such external features as a face and a body, along with internal features, such as a personality and manner of thinking. In many cases, events and episodes are constructed and developed by the actions and interactions of the characters. Furthermore, a story contains physical and mental objectives. The characters and the objectives form a narrative world, and these elements interact with one another to form a sequence of events. The whole is called a story. A story often has one or more narrative theme(s) or narratological meaning(s) to form strong consistency. | • Character: external and internal features<br>• Event, episode<br>• World: physical and abstract objects, their relation<br>• Story: Narrative content<br>• Theme, topic | • Frame<br>• Semantic network<br>• Rule base<br>• Story grammar<br>• Knowledge base<br>• Agent<br>• Conceptual system, Ontology<br>• Problem solving, planning, inference<br>• Case-based reasoning<br>• Case grammar<br>• Discourse theory |
| The manner of narrative discourse (A: deep structure generation) | Another chief narrative element is the manner in which a story or narrative content is narrated. This element is divided into an abstract and structural level, and a concrete representational level using a medium or media. (Category (A) corresponds to the former level.) Narrative discourse at the deep and abstract level represents a kind of adaptation of a story to form a plot indicating the construction, order, and organization of events and other narrative elements based on the narrator perspectives, tempo, and so on. Narrative genres are defined more concretely by the level of narrative discourse than at the level of the story. For example, the same event of murder produces genres of work as diverse as detective novels and psychological novels, based on the differentiated plots of the narrative discourse. | • Plot, construction<br>• Narrative discourse techniques<br>• Genre | • Structure transformation<br>• Grammatical and rhetorical knowledge structure |
| The manner of narrative discourse (B: surface level generation) | This level is directly associated with surface media for representation or expression, and contains language, image, and music. Body representation may be possible. The idea in Barthes (1975) indicates that narrative is a linguistic or semiotic medium, but actual representation is not limited to language. Therefore, in narratological meaning, the manner of narrative discourse (A) is more significant than that of (B). However, the surface generation level is connected to various rhetorical techniques that significantly affect narrative impression. | • Linguistic representation<br>• Image representation<br>• Musical representation | • Natural language generation<br>• Image processing technology<br>• Automatic composition and variation |
| Narrator or sender, and narratee or receiver | A narrative work is organized by communication between narrators and narratees on multiple levels. As stated by Booth (1983), a basic standpoint in narratology shows that narrators and narratees have multiple existences. This means that one or more narrators in a narrative work are internal virtual agents who are differentiated from the actual author. Likewise, one or more narratees are also at the level of virtual agents involved in the narrative that are different from the actual readers. These agents for narration and reception multiply control of a narrative generation process for the story, the narrative discourse, and the surface expression. | • Narrator, author, sender<br>• Narratee, reader, receiver<br>• Voice | • Agent<br>• Knowledge representation<br>• Generation control technique |

not a tragedy. (However, surface success often results in final failure.) Phase (5) involves the hero realizing that his attempt at problem solving is useless by recognizing a traumatic fact, and in (6) the hero becomes unhappier than in the initial situation. This skeleton of a story is a special example pertaining to a tragic work in ancient Greece, but it is a fundamental pattern according to which various stories are generated. The story theory by Propp corresponds to a detailed version of the above summary, and contains a basic problem-solving unit similar to Aristotle's story pattern.

## Defamiliarization by Shklovsky

The idea of"defamiliarization" by Shklovsky (1990) involves describing a familiar object using strange and extraordinary language in such a way that recognition of it may change. It also indicates the effect of changing the receiver's recognition. Although all literary acts themselves can be interpreted as a type of defamiliarization, some literary artists consciously utilized the idea of defamiliarization to literary practices in poem and drama, so this theory could be associated with various artistic practices. For example, Breton (1969) and other surrealists created strange poems driven by intentional unconsciousness, so to speak, and Brecht (1964) performed experimental dramas that artificially or intentionally exposed the feature of drama for the defamiliarization of drama itself.

In the author's view, this may be positioned as a meta-level technique or strategy to apply to various elements or phases of a narrative generation process. Various techniques have been employed to differentiate a commercial product by analyzing television commercials and developing rhetorical rules of defamiliarization to generate similar short scenarios (Kayamori & Ogata, 2003; Abe, Ogata, & Onodera, 2009; Zhang, Ono, & Ogata, 2011, 2012), and attempts are being made to expand these results to develop a general, norm-deviation mechanism (Kurisawa & Ogata, 2013).

## Narrative Morphology of a Folktale by Propp

Vladimir Propp was a Russian folklorist. He proposed a general theory about narrative structure (Propp, 1968), which has become one of the foundations of narratology and modern literary theories, especially the structural approaches, although the original article had been published in 1928. He considered folktales to be a symbol of people's collective mentality, and investigated their common structure and cultural characteristics. According to the analysis of about 100 Russian fairy tales, Propp called the most important units for defining a common structure of the stories "functions." In short, the central argument of Propp's theory is a structural method based on certain "functions." He defined 31 functions, including "villainy or lack," "struggle," "wedding," and others. Each of the functions corresponds to one event, or a sequence of events, seen from the result.

However, his overall accomplishments included the discovery of knowledge related to various aspects of folktales and general narratives. The central core of this knowledge is certainly the aspect of structuralism, but the research essentially identified the other elements as an entire theory. Propp, for example, presented plural examples or techniques for realizing the functions in the comparatively lower level of the collected folktales.

Additionally, Greimas and Dundes inherited and extended the above theory. Greimas (1966) remade Propp's theory through an abstract operation based on the unique semiotics, structural semantics, while Dundes (1965) applied Propp's theory to his analysis of Native American folktales to define a newly transformed function chain.

Propp's theory has been introduced to areas such as AI and cognitive science, and has been applied to story-generation systems. Narrative and story have also been interpreted as schemata for human cognition in the world. Propp's theory has influenced story schema and story grammar. Propp's narrative model deals not only with aspects of story, but also with a variety of aspects in narrative. Thus, it has the potential to contribute to narrative generation studies in a different manner from Aristotle's "Poetics." Approaches have already been proposed to introduce narratological theories into narrative generation. Based on Propp's theory, Lakoff (1972) described a set of grammatical rules in the form of generative grammar to define structures for fairy tales. Klein et al. (1974) used the same theory to propose a story-generation system. The use of narratology has increased in computational narrative models. Gervás, Lönneker-Rodman, Meister, and Peinado (2006) claimed that an interdisciplinary approach to computational modeling could yield great strides in both AI and narratology. Szilas (2010) referred to narratological theories as a requirement for narrative structural elements in his list of needs for computational models of interactive narratives. Many recent generation system architects have used the parameters of narratology to reflect on the distinction between story and discourse. Grasbon and Braun (2001) already proposed a framework for an interactive storytelling system in which plots were managed based on Propp's functions. Peinado and Gervás (2005) used Propp's theory to define the ontology of fairy tales. Their findings resulted in the Knowledge-Intensive Interactive Digital Storytelling (KIIDS) generation system capable of using case-based reasoning to building stylized Russian fairy tales. Gervás (2013b) derived concepts and terms from Propp's work, and proposed the framework of a story-generation system to achieve a comprehensive formalization of the theory. His system architecture had three particular aims: it generated a sequence of functions, transformed the sequence into a series of actions, and replaced all variables in the sequence with constants. His paper showed the implementation of the first two goals.

Previously, in many cases only the functions were treated in the applications of Propp's theory in informatics, but his theory was supported by the study of an enormous number of actual folktales, since he was originally a folklorist. However, Propp presented an array of examples and techniques at a lower level, in order to materialize functions as abstract definitions, by analyzing collected folktales. The author has formed the main part of Propp's theory into a type of story grammar to generate hierarchical story structures according to several types of processors. Ogata and Terano (1991, 1992) have already implemented a story-generation system using story grammar based on Propp's theory and character action based on AI planning methods. After using Propp's theory in the first attempt at a story-generation system, the research shifted to generating a general narrative into which narratological knowledge could be introduced. However, even when exploring this alternate direction, they have maintained a continuing study of Propp-based mechanisms. A design has been created for techniques utilizing the combination of several stories or moves, as well as for the narrative creation aid (Hosaka & Ogata, 2002; Ogata & Hosaka, 2004). Ogata (2007) summarized these studies to help with future development of the idea. Imabuchi and Ogata (2012) analyzed Propp-based story grammar (PBSG), which is rooted in the reorganization of Propp's original theory, and is divided into four hierarchical levels. Although Imabuchi and Ogata (2013, 2014) revised the work by adding a fifth level, the two models are more or less identical. For details of its use in INGS, see Propp-based Mechanism in the section, An Integrated Narrative Generation System: INGS.

## Bakhtin's Theory of Polyphony

Bakhtin (1984) understood that multiple narrators exist in Dostoyevsky's novels, and compared this type of novel to a kind of polyphonic music. By contrast, he claimed that Tolstoy's novels were monophonic, and only one narrator controlled the entire world of the novel. By Bakhtin's polyphonic theory, a narrator and other characters simultaneously exist in the worlds of Dostoyevsky's novels, each with an uncontrolled "voice." Therefore, each world involves contradictions and confusion. Conversely, the polyphonic disorder generates a narrative dynamism. In other words, Bakhtin's theory of polyphony argues that characters in a narrative, including the author, are all independent subjects with their personal attributes beyond the author's unified control. Based on this theory, a literary work is a world in which the voices of a variety of characters are blended.

Although immediate introduction of this theory into the author's narrative generation research, including INGS, is difficult, this is very attractive idea. One potential plan has been to design an artificial society simulation or agent-based simulation mechanism with narrative generation by simplifying and limiting each character's definition. Ogata and Yazawa (1999) explored ways of applying this theory to narrative generation, and proposed a conceptual model in which a narrator's function in a novel is distributed to many characters, including the narrator. This model may correspond to a type of multi-agent narrative model. Furthermore, this insight by Bakhtin could help develop such new research issues in narrative generation as deeper modeling of a character and a narrator in a multiple recognition model. Oikawa and Ogata (2012) have analyzed the characters and their mutual relationships in a novel by Mishima (1963). These attempts by a sort of re-interpretation of the Bakhtin's theory are intended to be applied to the future expansion of INGS.

## Intertextuality by Kristeva

Bakhtin's theory of polyphony led to the theory of intertextuality by Kristeva (1980). Bakhtin indicated that the polyphonic characteristic of a novel is based in part on various voices from other works by the novelist, and that fragments within the literary space outside the novel add to the diversity of characters' voices inside the novel's world. Kristeva extended this idea to a general theory of intertextuality, arguing that a literary text is positioned as an organization and citation of related preceding texts, which include the author's subsequent works. This theory claims that a narrative text is formed through the usage and transformation of existing narrative texts, and that narrative creativity appears during the usage and transformation.

Intertextuality can be associated with the idea of case-based reasoning (Riesbeck & Schank, 1989) found in AI with the claim that it indicates the usage and editing of existing works. In the context of the author's narrative generation, this study potentially presents a framework of knowledge acquisition that includes a text-mining narrative generation system to which the concept of intertextuality is applied. Nakashima and Ogata (2006) and Ono and Ogata (2013) divided a narrative text into elements to generate a new narrative through reconstruction, while Tsuchihashi and Ogata (2009) generated a narrative by the citation and transformation of existing narratives.

## Reception Theory by Jauss

The central concept underlying traditional literary studies was that of an author, that is, a standpoint from which the reading and interpreting of literary works are attempted based on an author's autobiographical facts, the social and cultural situations, and the psychological features and intentions. By contrast, since the last half of the 20$^{th}$ century, reception theory and reader-centric criticism have focused on the reader and the receiving process of literary works. In these theories, readers are interpreted as existences positively related to the production of literary works and are placed at the core of the creative process. Similar to this, reception theory is an important standpoint in contemporary literary theories and narratology, which focuses on the reception or reading process of literary texts. Readers or receivers strongly contribute to the production process of literary texts in this theory. H. R. Jauss was a typical researcher in this area. Jauss (1970) proposed an idea to characterize literary histories based on the concept of "horizon of expectation," referring to a kind of framework of previous knowledge used for positioning a new literary work in the context of the reader's experiences of reading. The artistic characteristics of a new literary work can be grasped according to the disparity between the given horizon and the work, and the appearance of a new work may result in the change of an existing horizon.

The author expanded the theory to a computational model, in which literary works are continuously changing through the interaction between an author or narrator and a reader or narrate, for a narrative discourse control mechanism in our narrative generation system. Akimoto and Ogata (2012, 2014a) mixed the Jauss-based mechanism with the following Genette-based mechanism to form a model and system controlling the deviation of narrative discourse mechanism based on the interaction between a narrator mechanism and a narratee mechanism within a narrative. In system modeling, Jauss's reception theory is simply interpreted as a mechanism to control the discourse construction process through the interaction between a narrator mechanism with generative parameters and a narratee mechanism with expectation parameters. In the most recent implementation, the two mechanisms do not define an existence beyond the system, but are instead virtual agents that are individual models within the system. The Genette portion uses structural processing and the Jauss portion controls it. For details of its use in the INGS, see the subsection, Jauss-based Mechanism.

## Narrative Discourse Theory by Genette

G. Genette is a French literary theorist and narratologist associated primarily with structuralism. His "Narrative Discourse" (Genette, 1972) clearly categorized various classes of discourse strategies through the analysis of an actual novel, *À la recherche du temps perdu* ("In Search of Lost Time" or "Remembrance of Things Past") (1913-1927) by Marcel Proust (1871-1922).

His theory consists of the following three broad categories: "tense," relevant to the relationship between the story's time and the discourse's time in a narrative, "mood," equal to the modality for regulating narrative information, and "voice," treating the relationship among narration, story, and discourse. Each of the categories is further divided into many detailed subcategories. For instance, "focalization" is a subcategory of mood. The technique of focalization was derived from the concept of narrative "perspective," which has been defined as "the second mode of regulating information, arising from the choice (or not) of a restrictive 'point of view'." Genette described the following three basic types of focalization: "zero focalization" or nonfocalized narrative, "internal focalization" or narrative focalized by one character's perspective (This is further divided into three variations: "fixed," "variable," and "multiple."), and "external focalization" or narrative that presents only the external behavior of characters.

From the perspective of narrative generation, Genette's theory consists of both the concrete means of transforming the structure of a story into the structure of narrative discourse (i.e., the ways that we can label narrative discourse techniques), and the description of the classification of the features of narrative discourse. The former corresponds to the categories of time and mood. Since Ogata (1999) reorganized Genette's entire theory to design narrative discourse techniques for a narrative generation architecture, the research group has continued system design and development: temporal order (Mukoyama, Shinohara, Kanai, & Ogata, 2002), perspective (Ueda & Ogata, 2004; Akimoto & Ogata, 2015b), and distance (Ogata & Yamakage, 2004). Although Genette never commented on narrative generation, these studies changed the theory's context by using a computational perspective to create a technological method for designing or formalizing a narrative-discourse-generation process. This allows for each of the classified techniques applied by Genette to be used as a rule for associating an input structure with a transformed output discourse structure. An input structure is equivalent to a complete story, the partial structure of a story, or a part of the discourse structure. Although other researchers have presented plans for such a mechanism as an integrated whole (Ogata 1999, 2004), experimental systems have been developed independently to verify a single narrative discourse technique. Later issues arose from attempting to incorporate a systemized narrative discourse mechanism based on Genette's theory and other knowledge into INGS (Akimoto & Ogata, 2010). For details in INGS, see the subsection, Genette-based Mechanism.

Whereas many narrative generation systems have focused primarily on methods for generating stories, only recently have a small group of researchers introduced the idea of a narrative discourse that utilizes Genette's theory. Lönneker-Rodman (2005) presented a conceptual design for introducing voice into a natural-language-generation system. Montfort (2007) developed an interactive fiction system in which the progression of a story could be managed through natural language interaction with the user. This exchange contains a function for producing variations within the discourse. These rules are based on Genette's categorization. Jhale and Young (2010) proposed a camera-work operation system for creating a discourse of visual narratives in a three-dimensional (3-D) virtual environment. Moreover, several studies address focalization. Bae, Cheong, and Young (2011) proposed a system that generates different stories based on various types of planning. Such planning is based on character perspectives of the same events by using multiple internal focalizations. A simulation of the movie *Rashomon* (1950) by Akira Kurosawa (1910-1998) was provided as an example. Gervás (2013a) proposed a system that simulates narrative compositions based on focalization in a simplified story of a chess game. His system composes narratives from the log of a chess game, i.e., the player moves of chess pieces on the board. The game log corresponds to a story, and a narrative is composed based on the experience (i.e., perspective) of a particular chess piece.

## Dream Interpretation by Freud, Narrative Approaches to Psychology

This subsection does not rely on the chronological order of the work of researchers. Rather, the author attempts a comprehensive description of primarily mental analysis, narrative therapy, clinical psychology, etc.

"Censorship agents" based on the dream theory by Freud were placed in the mechanisms for "not thinking" in the mind society modeled by Minsky (1988), who is a researcher within AI. For Freud (1900), a dream was a narrative in which a human mind tries to satisfy its desire. Human desire was divided into a direct type, in which a sleeping person tries to respond to any stimulus to his or her body, and an indirect type, in which a sleeping person wants the unconscious satisfaction of the suppressed desire inside his or her mind. In the latter type, we cannot easily determine the satisfied desire from the content of the dream. The theory claims that "censorship" is the reason. This is the mind's function of blocking the satisfaction of the relevant desire. Censorship functions between consciousness and unconsciousness, and only the elements that pass censorship appear in the content of the dream. However, although this apparent content is associated with satisfying the desire, which is the original objective, it is camouflaged and distorted to hide the true desire. Freud called the operations involved in this process "dream works." The "manifest content" of a dream represents the dream that a sleeping person has, while the "latent content" or the "thought" of a dream corresponds to the actual dream representing the true desire before being distorted.

Saito and Ogata (1998) presented preliminary research for associating the manifest content and the latent content with story and narrative discourse, respectively, to apply to the design of a narrative generation system.

Since Freud, mental analysis and psychology have been strongly connected with narrative. For example, narrative therapy (Freedman & Comb, 1996) is a pragmatic field of psychotherapy that placed the concept of narrative as a theoretical foundational principle. Some types of psychology (Bruner, 2003) have also dealt with the problem of the mental functions of narrative.

### Folklore and "Geino"

Narrative is not necessarily a concept that is equivalent to a particular literary genre such as novels and folktales. It is a universal concept within which diverse content genres are contained. For example, the Japanese word geino has a complex meaning that includes elements of shrine rituals, entertainment, and amusement. The geino is a representative field to be treated by folklore and strongly related to narrative. For instance, kabuki (Kawatake, 2003) can also be located as a geino genre as a collection of multiple narratives built around original scenarios, authentic related histories, the actors' private scenes, and so on.

The idea of the "Geino information system (GIS)" was considered by Kawamura and Ogata (1997, 2000, 2002) and Amino, Kawamura, and Ogata (2002) based on the survey and analysis of Japanese folklore, performing arts (such as kabuki), and features of the modern entertainment business. The GIS has been considered a framework in which various levels of narrative generation processes were driven by authors, receivers, characters, actors, and actresses. The construction is connected with the author's plan for a future narrative generation system comprising several narrative generation systems. This concept led to the rejection of a unified interpretation of a narrative. See Chapter 16 in this book regarding the survey and analysis of *kabuki* and the concept of GIS.

## Computational Theories and Techniques Related to Narratological Knowledge

In addition to automatic generation systems and related interactive storytelling systems (Magerko, 2006; Montfort, 2007) and interdisciplinary approaches to narratology and literary theories Gervás et al. (2006), narrative-related information studies include the following themes: narrative-making support (Bers, 1999), representation technologies for images (Jhale & Young, 2010), narrative prose generation (Callaway & Lester, 2002), narrative understanding, such as narrative extraction and summary (Elson & McKeown, 2007; Mueller, 2007), database, knowledge base, and ontology for narrative generation

(Peinado & Gervás, 2005), evaluation and verification (Rowe, McQuiggan, Robison, Marcey, & Lester, 2009), cognitive modeling (Herman, 2000), and so on. Moreover, in new workshops and recent research meetings, such as "Workshop on Computational Models of Narrative," active discussions on this topic have taken place. In this workshop, narrative generation is one of the major topics and themes related to narrative theories are also treated.

Application studies have also been conducted on narratives: applications to computer games with interactive narrative technologies, education and learning environments with narrative functions (Hecht, Starosielski, & Dora-Abrams, 2007), human-computer interaction related to narrative (Riedl, Saretto, & Young, 2003; Riedl & Young, 2010), WEB-based narrative representation (Alani, Kim, Millard, & Weal, 2003), and advertising generation and production (Ogata, Hori, & Ohsuga, 1995). Regarding application, from a broad perspective, Ogata (1995) discussed the possibilities of covering human interfaces, multimedia interfaces, gaming and simulation, education, idea formation and thinking support, decision-making support, social planning, creation support for various types of texts, entertainment such as games, novel book media such as electronic publishing, narrative creation process support, etc. These partially overlap with the discussion of "narrative intelligence" by Mateas and Sengers (2003).

Various aspects of information research relating to narrative are introduced in this subsection. These narrative-based approaches, including narrative generation systems, commonly use theories and techniques developed by past research in AI and cognitive science. Knowledge representations and computational techniques to be used for text comprehension and generation include story grammar (Rumelhart, 1975), script and goal planning (Schank & Abelson, 1977), frame theory (Minsky, 1975), semantic networking (Quillian, 1968), ontology (Mizoguchi, 2005), etc. These theories and techniques are closely related to analytical studies in narratology and literary theories for story, discourse, and communication between a narrator (or author or sender) and a narratee (or reader or receiver).

In the following description, narrative-related approaches and attempts will be presented according to some topics regarding computational and cognitive approaches. In the future, various elemental technologies, including various recent and new directions such as brain science, cognitive science, management science, etc., will be addressed by these theories and techniques.

## Problem Solving and Planning

Problem solving by reduction and planning according to a goal was a central issue in classical or traditional AI (Newell & Simon, 1972). These have been among the most important technical engines driving narrative generation systems. In the main direction, the problem-solving behaviors of one or more characters form the structure of an event sequence as a story. Another method defines the narrative generation model based on the problem-solving process of an author or narrator. Case-based reasoning (Riesbeck & Schank, 1989), which is an expansion of problem solving and planning, has been applied to generate narratives by transforming existing narratives and partial fragments.

## Schema

The theory of schema or schemata, originally proposed in cognitive psychology, often uses narratives as one of the study materials (Bartlett, 1923). The schema theory represents the framework of knowledge preliminarily held by humans, and controls cognition. When people try to recognize an (abstract or concrete) object, they intuitively extract and use schemata in a top-down manner of cognition of sorts.

The schema theory has been applied to human narrative comprehension, and the researchers reported that typical or common structural patterns were applicable to many stories. Story schema or grammar by Rumelhart (1975) proposed a schema for folktales. Although studies on story schema are similar to the theory by Propp (1968) in narratology, which is detailed in the next section, many story schemata have formalized descriptions that employ the idea of generative grammar, whereas Propp's theory is valuable in its fullness of narrative information. In the theory of script by Schank and Abelson (1977), a script is a type of schemata used to represent a temporal event sequence. Scripts are used to define relatively microlevel event sequences, such as those for constituting a scene. By contrast, story schemata are suitable for defining more macrolevel event sequences, such as an entire story.

## Knowledge Representation

The schema theory proposed a method for explicitly studying human mental processes, and these attempts were tied AI to cognitive psychology. The assignment of a computational description to each of the various types of schemata is called knowledge representation. The schema theory was the headstream of knowledge representation in AI. Well-known theories of knowledge representation include the semantic network theory by Quillian (1968), rule-based systems or production systems (Davis & Lenat, 1982), and frame theory by Minsky (1975). A system constructed using knowledge representation(s) is called a knowledge-based system. Knowledge representation techniques are often used to implement various components in narrative generation systems. A group of frames can be used as a data structure to describe the attribute knowledge used to represent features of concepts to be defined in a story, such as characters, events, concrete or physical objects, abstract or psychological objects, and so on. A semantic network is a method of flexibly representing the relationships among such concepts. In an extension of knowledge representation, studies of deep knowledge representation structures, such as the "Thematic Abstraction Unit: TAU" (Dyer, 1983), were intended to be applied directly to narrative or story comprehension.

## Conceptual Dictionaries and Ontology

Forms of knowledge representation, like semantic networks and frames, are necessary for many narrative generation systems, in order to describe objectives in story worlds. However, we can systematically define wider-ranging and more detailed descriptions of objectives by using conceptual dictionaries and ontological knowledge bases. A conceptual dictionary and an ontological knowledge base are too general and large to describe a limited story world, and hence the development can be difficult. However, these are effective approaches for developing a general and versatile narrative generation system, in which genres, themes, and contents are not narrowly restricted. Their essential use in narrative generation systems is quite primitive. For example, the narrative generation system proposed by Okada and Endo (1992) was organized as an application of a large-scale conceptual dictionary, but used a few narrative themes. Mizoguchi (2005) discussed an ontological model using "The Tale of Genji" by Murasaki Shikibu, but its actual implementation will be very challenging. By contrast, Ogata (2015) aimed at the development of an integrated narrative generation system, described in the section, An Integrated Narrative Generation System: INGS, based on conceptual dictionaries.

## Natural Language Processing/Generation, Discourse Theory

In the qualitative processing of natural language, prior to quantitative and statistical natural-language processing, many narrative comprehension studies were attempted, and the outcomes have often been applied to narrative generation (Schank, 1982, 1986, 1990). In particular, the generation processing of deep level language structures was associated with narrative generation (Ishizaki, 1988; Hovy, 1993), and discourse comprehension attempted to analyze the structures of complex novels (Hobbs, 1990). In contrast to the processing of the deep structural level of language, the new trend of natural-language processing was dealing with language by surface information using techniques of information retrieval and linguistic characteristics, such as word frequency and co-occurrence. For narrative that originally needs deep knowledge, an important direction in the information processing is to introduce the surface processing into the deep approaches. Natural language generation (Reiter & Dale, 2006) is a current field of research and development. The general approach divides a language-generation process into the following two phases: the deep generation phase, which generates a conceptual structure of the meaning to be described, and the surface generation phase, which transforms the semantic structure into a surface language structure. Although the macro framework is similar to the generation process of narrative generation systems, narrative generation is a rather comprehensive and complete framework, since it should include the textual knowledge concerning ordinary description in addition to narrative-oriented textual knowledge. Furthermore, regarding the role of surface language generation, narrative generation needs many more style texts, including description, dialogue, monologue, and so on.

## Cognitive Poetics/Narratology, Narrative Rhetoric

Cognitive poetics and cognitive narratology, which have been proposed by Stockwell (2002), Herman (2003), etc., aim to analyze narrative texts using theories developed in the field of cognitive science to show formal, cognitive, or rhetorical structures in the texts. A series of cognitive science studies about the phenomenon of narrative rhetoric by Kanai et al. (Kanai & Ogata, 2004a, 2004b; Kanai, 2006; Kanai & Kodama, 2010) aimed to develop the cognitive science of imagery that focused on relationships between and aspects of story and non-story, or discourse, in films by blending narratology and film theory. This consideration gestured toward the strategic aspect of the control mechanisms of narrative generation. These are considered moving from a story-centered narrative style to a discourse-centered style using film narratology and an original picture analysis. For bridging the gap between narrative analysis and narrative generation, Kanai and Ogata (2004a, 2004b) conducted an experiment of an image-generation system having rhetorical techniques for cutting a story's continuity, in order to introduce the technique as a narrative generation method. The "cognitive rhetoric of metaphor" by Utsumi, Nakamura, and Sakamoto (2012) was also related to the problem of narrative comprehension. Furthermore, many attempts were made to develop affective inference models using narrative texts based on various forms of knowledge representations, such as problem solving by goal-planning (Tokosumi, 2007). These pioneering narrative studies in AI and cognitive science will likely prove significant for the future progress of narrative generation systems.

## Human Creativity Aid

The study of human creativity aid by Hori (2005) and other researchers can be related to narrative generation at various junctures. Akaishi (2006) proposed a system that interpreted stories in a document based on surface language analysis and context transformation. according to points of view. In his general discussion regarding creativity, Hori (2007) pointed out why contemporary narrative generation systems are not narrative "creation" systems. This, he said, is because such systems generate narratives only within the thinking space in the knowledge base preliminarily created by the system designer. Therefore, these systems cannot create novel thinking space beyond that prepared by the system designer. However, he said that if a narrative generation system could generate results predictable by the system designer, and a user could create new thinking space using a stimulus, such a system could be said to have some function as a creativity "support" system. This insight will probably be very important in the development or use of future narrative generation (or creation) systems. Recently, Sakuma and Ogata (2005) presented a method of narrative generation support and Chapter 3 in this book by Akimoto and Ogata proposed a socially open narrative generation model applying human creativity aid to the task of narrative generation.

## Media and Hypertext

The new concept proposition on human interface by Laurel (2013) relies on the "Poetics" by Aristotle that was described above. She modeled the process of a user involved in the system through good human interfaces in computational systems dependent upon Aristotle's plot theory, in which a sequence of events is constructed and structured in the relationship with effects on the audience. Matsuoka (1992), based on a more comprehensive narrative viewpoint, attempted to analyze the mechanisms and structures common to many narratives according to the idea that narratives are strong human knowledge media, but this plan has not been implemented. Smith and Bates (1989) attempted a narratological discussion for interactive fiction or interactive storytelling through the actual implementation of the OZ system. The media for surface narrative representation in narrative generation systems is not limited to language. As approaches to narrative representation media, many studies have been conducted, including computer graphics and comic generation by Hoshino (2004) and Thawonmas, Oda, and Shuda (2009), and the bridging of music representation and narrative generation by Akimoto, Endo, and Ogata (2013a). However, many of these systems do have an automatic generation function — hyper-text novels that use multiple links of fragments of texts to present new possibilities from which the reader can proceed and control the progression of a narrative work (Bolter, 1991; Morita, 2006). Endo and Ogata (2002), by way of a similar approach, proposed a hyper-comic that was a hyper-text-based *manga* (comic) system with a partially automatic generation function. The idea underlying hyper-text novels and similar approaches can be positioned in an exploration of reception theory or reader-oriented criticism in narratology, because a reader is actively involved with narrative progression by selecting one of several subsequent narrative possibilities. Further, in the context of narrative generation, Riedl and Young (2006) provided an approach of branching stories.

Consideration was also given to changing from a story-centered narrative style to a discourse-centered style using film narratology (Chatman, 1980) and picture analysis (Kanai & Ogata, 2004a, 2004b). The latter experiments performed using an image-generation system that contained rhetorical techniques for cutting a story's continuity in order to introduce the techniques as a method of narrative generation. On the other hand, "musical narratology" has been attempted since Tarasty (1994) based on the semiotic method.

### Computer Game Technologies

Computer game technologies are closely related to narrative and narrative generation, which includes various interesting technologies more than interactive storytelling. Recently, IRIS is the architecture of non-interactive text adventure game (Fendt & Young, 2014). Li and Riedl (2010) presented an offline planning plot generation mechanism and Hartsook, Zook, Das, and Rield (2011) showed game worlds generation mechanism. "Suspenser" by Cheong and Young (2015) is an interactive storytelling system based on the reader's cognition of suspense. As a relating direction, Barber (2008) already presented an idea of interactive narrative generation system based on dilemma ("Generator of Adaptive Dilemma-based Interactive Narratives": GADIN) Further, Min, Ha, Rowe, Mott, and Lester (2014) applied a new AI technology, deep learning, to the world of digital game.

## Narrative Generation Systems

In the first part of this section, a simple history of science fiction related to narrative generation is given. Devices or systems to automatically create documents and narratives have long existed in the human imagination. Ramon Llull (or Raimundus Lullus (1232-1315)) wrote "Ars Magna Generalis et Ultima" (1305-1308) to show mechanisms of generating words and sentences with philosophical meanings by using a *Lullian circle* (Oda, 2007). In Part III of "Gulliver's Travels" (1726) by Jonathan Swift (1667-1745), the narrator introduces an invention in the *Grand Academy* that can be called an "automatic document production device," which enabled people to write various genres of documents, including literary poems, without effort or thought. More recently, in his "An Imaginary Number" (1973), Stanislaw Lem (1921-2006) narrated fictional histories of computational literature ("bit literature"); in his "Galatea 2.2" (1995), Richard Powers (1957-) described in detail the design and development of a fictional narrative generation system using neural network technology.

However, automatic document production has partially reached the stage of actual business. For example, the "Wordsmith" system by Automated Insights, Inc. (https://automatedinsights.com/) transforms structured data in industrial genres, such as ecommerce, financial services, real estate, media, entertainment, personal fitness, business intelligence, etc., into story forms. The "Qull" system by Narrative Science, Inc. (https://www.narrativescience.com/) is a data-driven storytelling system for business fields. Narrative generation and story generation relevant to human creativity have also been important and major theme for automatic document production.

As a guideline, the author divided the majority of past narrative generation systems into two approaches, based on the AI techniques supporting their development: a problem-solving approach and a structural approach.

A chief strategy of the former is planning, or having a goal-plan strategy (Schank & Abelson, 1977). For example, TALE-SPIN (Meehan, 1980) applied this method to a system that automatically generated different stories from a story world based on characters' actions to achieve specific goals. Although more comprehensive and complicated, DAYDREAMER (Mueller, 1990) and MINSTREL (Turner, 1994) are also classified in this group. The system based on the Aesop World series (Okada & Endo, 1992) utilized large-scale conceptual dictionaries that employed the goal-plan mechanisms of characters as the basic method for story generation.

By contrast, the structural approach involves a narrative generation process based on narrative structural formalizations, such as story grammar and story schema. GESTER (Pemberton, 1989) and JOSEPH (Lang, 1999) are both narrative generation systems consisting of an interpreter with both a story grammar and a world model. The story grammar in each system defines the abstract structure of the stories, and the world model contains elements embodied within the story structure: actors or characters, objects, and causal relations between events. BRUTUS (Bringsjord & Ferrucci, 1999) employs a blended approach by using various problem solving and planning narrative methods, and such structural techniques as story grammar and theme structure. Such synthetic systems may be grouped into a third approach.

Examples of some narrative generation systems are provided in the following pages.

## TALE-SPIN

This story-generation system is the most famous study from the early stage of research in this field (Schank & Riesbeck, 1981). The system, which Meehan (1980) called TALE-SPIN, is theoretically simple and clear. It involves a character (animal) and interactions that form a sequence of events based on goal-oriented problem-solving planning. The flow results in a story of success (goal achievement) or failure. Each event is described or defined using the conceptual dependency theory by Schank and Abelson (1977). This theory classifies a large number of verbs into a limited number of categories by, for instance, such descriptions as the transposition of physical and mental objects. The mechanism implies a kind of higher ontology of verb concepts. Therefore, the TALE-SPIN system has various interesting narrative generation methods, such as character interactions, semantic natural language processing, and simple sentence generation, in addition to the planning approach. The methods proposed by the system, particularly the planning method, were inherited by the following narrative generation systems.

## DAYDREAMER

This system by Mueller (1990) is among the most synthetic of narrative generation systems using the planning method. DAYDREAMER is a computer program that simulates the consciousness of daydreaming, with a consistent character and a narrator. The goal of the system is to compensate for and rationalize a negative mental state, based on the failure of external actions (for instance, lost love), into a positive mental state through planning. The continuous simulation and narration of the wandering flow of consciousness in the process is equivalent to daydreaming. Therefore, although this system is not a narrative generation system, strictly speaking, it synthetically implements various interesting mechanisms and techniques related to AI and cognitive science that include, in addition to goal-oriented planning associated with emotional states, the generation of external stories (occurring in the external world), creativity processing by serendipity, scripts for detailed expansion of an episode, various narrative knowledge representation techniques using semantic networks and frames, and so on. Lebowitz (1985) also proposed a synthetic narrative generation framework involving character planning as well as the author's goals and planning, but its implementation has not been considered thus far.

## A Story Generation System Based on Aesop's World

This system by Okada and Endo (1992) generates stories of the animal world, similar to Aesop's fables, based on problem-solving or goal-oriented planning methods, according to the goals of specific characters. One of the characteristics of this system is processing based on a mind model comprising both intelligent processing, such as recognition and understanding, and sensitive processing, such as emotional inference. Another significant merit of this system is its use of conceptual dictionaries for verb concepts, noun concepts, and adjective concepts to describe the story's world and define the rules of goal planning. Yet another feature is that the system is multi-modal, with a computer-generated-based animation mechanism in addition to natural language processing (Noma, Kai, Nakamura, & Okada, 1992).

## MINSTREL

The MINSTREL system by Turner (1994) is a problem-solving program that automatically generates stories according to material in the narrative of "King Arthur and the Knights of the Round Table". The system contains a function for a character's problem solving, while it prepares a different type of problem-solving function for the author. This is based on the important idea that the task of narrative generation is a comprehensive problem-solving activity trying to satisfy different goals using multiple planning through a generation process. In this sense, this research is a synthetic consideration and result of narrative generation using the problem-solving method. The use of case-based reasoning in AI as a means of driving goal-oriented planning is a distinctive feature in the system, and is a mechanism for implementing a form of creativity in the sense that new narratives are generated by the use and transformation of existing narratives and fragments. The mechanism based on case-based reasoning is also related to intertextuality (Kristeva, 1980; Genette, 1982) in the literary context.

## BRUTUS

The BRUTUS system by Bringsjord and Ferrucci (1999) has a synthetic narrative generation system architecture, like MINSTREL, and deals with a consistent narrative generation process. In the generation process, the system first creates a story, which is the material to be narrated, using a theme structure. It then extends the story into a plot based on the goal-based problem-solving simulation of characters. Following this, based on the created plot, the system generates a text structure using story grammar, and finally carries out natural-language generation using literary rhetoric. As stated above, the outstanding merit of such a system is that the narrative generation process is clearly divided into three stages or modules of story, plot, and text. The system adequately applies different and corresponding methods and techniques to process each stage. In previous narrative generation studies, only the aspect of story generation was treated, or the division between aspects was very vague when multimodule programming was attempted. The partition of narrative generation in BRUTUS reflects the basic framework of story and discourse (deep and surface).

## MEXICA

This system (Pérez & Pérez, 1999; Pérez y Pérez & Sharples, 2001) generates stories from Native Mexican folktales. Based on the engagement-reflection theory by Sharples (1996), they modeled a narrative generation process as a creation process of construction and revision based on constraints (constraint conditions). The system uses case-based reasoning to implement the narrative generation framework for exploring existing narratives and revising the explored fragments into a novel form using the rules of the theory. Incremental and repetitive revision and extension of the first existing narrative fragment correspond to a narrative generation process. Therefore, this is also related to intertextuality in the literary context, and deals with the general problem of incremental creation by revising existing materials.

### IF

This "interactive fiction" system by Montfort (2007) realizes narrative variations. One of the characteristics of the system is introducing the narrative discourse theory proposed by Genette (1972) for introducing techniques of "how to narrate" into the system. Narrative discourse techniques contain exchanges of temporal orders to narrate events and viewpoints to view an event or the sequence from multiple perspectives. In processing, a simulator in the system generates a world model at the specified time according to the user's input information, and a narrator narrates the world model using the narrative discourse techniques. It is a narrative generation system focusing on a variety of narratives of the same event.

In addition, recently, for instance, Swartjes (2010) provided a multi-agent narrative generation system Si (2010) developed a narrative generation system by the interaction between characters and the user Liedl and the group have conducted the Scheherazade project (Li & Riedl, 2015).

## Future Research Directions

Selected future research and development directions or issues relating to the preceding PART I are as follows:

- **Computational and Cognitive Approaches to Narratology:** At the current stage of the approaches from the side of narratology, cognitive approaches have mainly focused on linguistic or rhetorical analysis of narrative texts. However, relatively computational methods from the side of narratology, such as the narrative grammar by Prince (1982), also exist. Computational studies that have deep and large literary knowledge will be expected in the future. Constructive approaches beyond analytical tactics will be possible as the cognitive approach and practice will enable revisiting the area of the previous narratology. On the other hand, from the sides of computational and cognitive sciences, narratological studies need to be updated to deal with narrative or literary phenomena and texts in actual society and diverse themes covered by contemporary narratology.
- **Narrative Generation Systems Based on an Interdisciplinary Narratology:** One of the most pressing issues is the approach to narrative generation as an integrated intelligent and knowledge system for computational and cognitive approaches to narratology. A major method in previous similar studies was narrative analysis, while narrative constructive studies, such as narrative generation, creation, and production, will become important by using computational approaches to narratology for new content creation and invention. The problem of narrative generation, including its creation and production, should be located as a central position in the area of computational and cognitive approaches to narratology.

The author's research framework and practice of interdisciplinary narratology and narrative generation systems will primarily be described in the following two sections.

## A SYNTHETIC APPROACH TO NARRATIVE GENERATION

The themes related to the author's research and development are treated in the following two sections, which correspond to PART II of this chapter. The first section mainly deals with background information and the chief concepts of a narrative generation study by the author, which are discussed in six subsections. At first, the author shows the temporal flow of his previous studies on narrative generation, which aims to synthesize the integrated narrative generation system (INGS) described in the next section. Although the description in this section partly overlaps with the previous one, it is arranged from the viewpoint of the author's research.

In addition, the author has strategically divided the previous narrative generation research into a "paper" and a "book." The book is a tool that will be utilized to describe the comprehensive results and plans of the research and development, whereas the paper will be used to provide a detailed description of the various research issues. In this sense, this paper as a chapter in a book aims at a comprehensive discussion of a variety of themes.

### Two Basic Narrative Generation Architectures

The author developed experimental systems that show the following two aspects in narrative generation: (1) an interdisciplinary approach to narratology and literary theories, and (2) an organic integrality of various modules.

- **A Story Generation System Based on the Theory by Propp:** An experimental system was implemented based on the theory by Propp (1968), which mixes story grammar with characters' actions (Ogata & Terano, 1991, 1992). A "function," which is a central concept in the theory, means "an action of a character seen from the result." Propp showed 31 kinds of functions to show a structural feature in a genre of Russian folktales. This system grammatically forms the functions and the lower level events for representing more concrete possibilities as a set of basic knowledge for the story generation. Moreover, hierarchical planning, which is sometimes used as a basic method of story generation in artificial intelligence (AI) systems, was utilized to generate the action sequences by a character. This system mixes two types of representative methods in AI, story grammar and hierarchical planning, and corresponds to the first concrete example of the ELT.
- **A System Based on Narrative Techniques and Strategies:** The aforementioned system bridges the implementation and experimentation of an integrated framework of narrative generation based on narrative techniques, narrative strategies, and other knowledge bases (Ogata, Hori, & Ohsuga, 1994, 1995, 1996a). This system is a generalized framework for organically collecting a variety of narrative generation methods and knowledge instead of performing a narrative generation by using only a particular method. A story and a plot constitute each tree structure, which has events as the terminal nodes. The constitutional elements in each event are associated to an element in conceptual dictionaries and to their instance. Narrative techniques are a set of rules for making such a tree structure, whereas narrative strategies have various rules for controlling the generation

using the narrative techniques. Additionally, narrative techniques need knowledge for a particular narrative expansion. They contain concrete descriptive contents including many types of sequence patterns of narrative events, such as causal relationships and scripts.

## Development of Each Mechanism of Narrative Generation and the Integration

The author has designed developed, and experimented with narrative generation systems according to several large modules based on the basic frameworks of the aforementioned narrative generation systems. The following themes show the macro level mechanisms that the author has been attempting to do, each of which is aimed at integrating them into an INGS.

- **Story Generation Mechanism:** Redesigning and re-implementing the Propp-based story generation mechanism have been continued from the viewpoint of integrating it into an entire system, and then it was expanded to use conceptual dictionaries for the event generation. The author has also prepared a "story content knowledge base" to store the content knowledge to be used in the story techniques. The part of grammatical description in the Propp-based mechanism, the Propp-based story content grammar, is also considered as a kind of knowledge that can be stored. An important topic or a non-achievement point in story generation is that event sequence knowledge or event structural knowledge has not been considered systematically. Future studies need to be approached based on, for instance, text analyses, such as folktales based on Propp's theory, and on the automatic acquisition of event sequence knowledge including scripts.
- **Narrative Discourse Mechanism:** The author has studied the following individual theoretical components according to the narrative discourse theory by Genette (1972): "temporal order" transformation (Mukoyama et al., 2002), "viewpoint", "focalization", or "perspective" (Ueda & Ogata, 2004; Akimoto & Ogata, 2015b), "speed" or "tempo", "distance" (Ogata & Yamakage, 2004), and "voice". However, currently, only a part of the temporal order transformation has been integrated. For the purpose of introducing them into the integrated system, more systematic considerations of some narrative discourse techniques will be needed in the future. In contrast, the reception theory by Jauss (1970) has also been adapted for the mechanism to control the use of narrative discourse techniques (Akimoto & Ogata, 2014a).
- **Music Generation Mechanism:** The narrative generation concept by the author does not fix the generation order among the modules. This concept has been experimented mainly through music generation mechanisms. The original and essential idea is that music can be generated by using narrative methods; by contrast, a narrative can be generated by using musical methods. The author has considered different ways to achieve knowledge blending from mutual knowledge transformation. The author has set correspondence relationships between a story and a piece of music to come up with a basic mechanism for transforming a story into a piece of music (Akimoto et al., 2013a). Although the "Generative Theory of Tonal Music: GTTM" (Lerdahl & Jackendoff, 1983) has been used partially, musical theories concerning composition and variation have not been fully introduced.
- **Knowledge Mechanism:** Conceptual dictionaries of linguistic semantic knowledge and other types of knowledge were developed individually as various small-scale systems according to each of the purposes. Based on these ideas, for an integrated narrative generation system, the author has developed relatively large-scale conceptual dictionaries mainly for noun and verb concepts

(Ogata, 2015); the constituent elements in the structures of a story and a discourse are intended to connect to the elements of these conceptual dictionaries, such as the values of the case structure for an event. A group of these conceptual dictionaries is a fundamental part for basically supporting the system. The proper noun conceptual dictionary and attribute information are also significant knowledge that will be added to the existing noun conceptual dictionary. The role of the attribute information is to store the properties that each noun concept includes. Moreover, a state-event transformation knowledge base (Onodera, Akimoto, & Ogata, 2012) was necessary to generate states based on a generated event. States should be placed in the lowest level in a story tree structure.

- **Generation Control Mechanism:** For a narrative discourse, a control mechanism by a virtual narrator and narratee (Akimoto & Ogata, 2012, 2014a) applying the reception theory by Jauss (1970) was proposed. However, previously, the problem of narrative control was generally treated without deep consideration. Although the following may overlap with future issues in the INGS in the next section, the author, for example, needs to consider collecting and acquiring the parameters for the narrative generation and how a narrative author should utilize the rules for linking the parameters to conduct concrete tasks for more strategic mechanisms of narrative generation.
- **Language Generation Mechanism:** For generating a sentence from the conceptual representation of an event, templates for sentences were prepared and various mechanisms, including the procedures of word representation using inflection, multiple sentences generation method, Japanese representation method using language notation dictionaries for nouns and verbs, etc., were attempted. For the improvement, it is necessary to fundamentally consider the problem of the boundary between conceptual representation level and language expression level. In addition, in the level of each word, there is the problem of readability or comprehensibility. In developing conceptual dictionaries and language notation dictionaries, elements with a variety of features about them are mixed.
- **Image Generation Mechanism:** Current image processing is based on a primitive method that represents a simple image by mapping the conceptual representation of events to an image database and simple image scripts. At present, previous image-related studies, such as rhetorical analyses of image techniques (Kanai et al., 2002; Kanai & Ogata, 2004a, 2004b) and a camera-work analysis of a movie (Ogata, Tachibana, & Tomite, 2009), are not considered in the system development.

As shown previously, Ogata, Hori, and Ohsuga (1994, 1995, 1996a) proposed a basic narrative generative framework developed from a variety of stories based on narrative techniques, narrative strategies, and other knowledge bases. One direction of study is to integrate narrative knowledge and various techniques into an organically integrated generation system (INGS). Previously, some conceptual and basic design (and the following narrative analyses) implemented an experimental integrated mechanism by using an organic combination in a consistent architecture based on past independent programs. The fundamental structure was centered on earlier methods proposed, but the discourse and expression were expanded. The eventual goal was to develop a "versatile" narrative generation system grounded on an integrated architecture. Versatility here means that the system will be applicable to any purpose relevant to narrative generation without genre limitations. The theory by Propp (1968) was used as a mechanism, but its purpose was beyond the creation of folktales. Revisions of structural techniques and narrative content will enable a transformation of the genre. This involves the integration of certain elements: story phase, narrative discourse phase (using the theory by Genette (1972) and the reception theory by Jauss (1970)), expression media, literary theories and informatics, and other diverse narrative techniques. The system is knowledge based with different steps of discourse and several expressions of language, music, and imagery. At each point, the process is executed with a variety of narrative techniques equivalent to functions used to construct various types of narrative structures. The INGS will be explained in detail in the next section.

## Narrative Analyses

The author has analyzed narratives in the following genres to develop individual narrative mechanisms and application systems, before finally introducing them into the INGS. They partially overlap with the theoretical frameworks of narratology and literary theories.

- **Folktale:** The theory by Propp (1968) has been adapted to the analysis of Japanese folktales, aiming at developing grammatical knowledge of stories that was extended and generalized beyond Propp's theory.
- **Novel:**
    - An analysis of the story and plot in a detective story (Ogata, Hori, & Ohsuga, 1996b) showed a relationship between mutual structural transformation and acquired knowledge being applied to the first fundamental narrative generation architecture (Ogata, Hori, & Ohsuga, 1994, 1995, 1996a).
    - An analysis of the hyper-text structure in a detective story showed that some different stories could be generated according to the viewpoints of several characters (Ishii & Ogata, 1998). Although the method by hyper-text structure has not been used on purpose in the author's previous narrative generation systems, its use will be made into a topic in the future, especially in the INGS.
    - An analysis of the mutual cognitive structures of the characters in *Gogo no Eiko* (1963) by Mishima Yukio (1925-1970) indicated that one of the dramatic features in the novel was a result of the correspondence and contradiction (Oikawa & Ogata, 2012). The characters have each of the recognitions of the world, and an actual narrative is constituted depending on the various techniques for multiple syntheses by each character. Introducing knowledge into the INGS may be too difficult an issue at present.
- **Advertisement:**
    - In an analysis of story structures in TV commercial films, the author showed that many scenarios in TV commercial films could be analyzed by using the same knowledge used in analyzing folktales and novels (Ogata, Watanabe, Hori, & Ohsuga, 1995); hence generation of advertising scenarios was achieved as an application of general narrative generation.
    - Analysis of rhetorical techniques for introducing a product into a TV commercial-like story showed techniques for differentiating a product in various methods (Abe et al., 2009). A part of the narrative rhetorical techniques has been experimented as a mechanism of narrative generation.
- **Movie:**
    - For an analysis of the narrative discourse, the author analyzed movie works made by a complicated temporal progression of events, especially the rhetoric that intentionally cuts the

consistent flow of a story (Kanai & Ogata, 2004a, 2004b). Rhetoric here means a type of technique used for transforming a story into a narrative discourse.
    - An attempt to analyze the original camerawork in *Tokyo Monogatari* ("Tokyo Story") (1953) by Ozu Yasujiro (1903-1963) showed a rhetorical movement by the machinery repetition of a normal pattern and the interference (Ogata, Tachibana, & Tomite, 2009).
- **Comic or *Manga*:** In the analyses of a Japanese *manga* (comic) work, *Mezon Ikkoku* ("Maison Ikkoku") (1980-1987) by Rumiko Takahashi (1957-):
    - The author showed a hyper-textual space for representing several possibilities of a story using the theory by Genette (1972) and implemented the idea as an experimental system. Moreover,
    - With the same theory, a rhetorical method was discovered in which different narrative discourse techniques, "multiple narrative discourse in *manga*," were simultaneously represented in one frame (Endo & Ogata, 2004b).
- **Dream:** As mentioned in Dream Interpretation by Freud, Narrative Approaches to Psychology in the previous section, the author preliminarily reinterpreted a dream interpretation by Freud (1900) as a kind of narrative discourse technique for transforming real materials into a story (Saito & Ogata, 1998). The author considers that a variety of narratological and literary techniques are involved in his description of dream interpretation.
- **Drama:** As described in Poetics by Aristotle in the previous section, the author preliminarily attempted a reinterpretation of an analysis of a tragedy by Aristotle (1895) using a set of techniques for developing a story, namely, a kind of story grammar (Aruga & Ogata, 1998). Similar to the story grammar by Propp's theory, such story grammar can also be considered as a type of narrative technique that can be used as a whole or in part.

## Application Systems

This part shows various experimental applicable systems of narrative generation that apply literary theories and other methods.

- **KOSERUBE:** This is a picture-story-show-like application system using the theory by Propp that generates a story and the expression with primitive moving and still images, music, and simple natural language. The system uses the whole of the INGS, in particular the part of the Propp-based story generation mechanism, to generate stories with the style or structure of a folktale (Imabuchi, Akimoto, Ono, & Ogata, 2012; Akimoto et al., 2013b). In addition, this system especially treats the places in and the cultural objects and culture of the Iwate Prefecture of Japan. This feature is related to the use of proper noun concepts and words in a noun-oriented dictionary.
- **Hyper-Comic (an Application of the Theory by Genette):** This is an application of the theory by Genette and of the comic or *manga* system using semi-automatic narrative generation with a hyper-text structure. Each of the frame images in the hyper-comic is multiply linked to the other frames. Moving from a frame to another frame is partially based on an automatic method. The system also has another automatic function for completing a frame by the synthesis of the components or parts. Genette's theory can be applied to reorganize in different ways a sequence of frame images with a story based on various narrative discourse techniques (Endo & Ogata, 2002, 2003, 2004a, 2004b).

- **Musical Variation Mechanisms:** This mechanism performs musical variation using the narrative discourse techniques that apply Genette's theory. In particular, Genette-based narrative discourse techniques for a narrative conceptual structure transform a part of a narrative structure into a new structure. The musical version also applies the techniques to a musical structure to transform it. The semantic processing in the former is changed to purely formal processing in the musical version. The mechanism has been expanded to a module of the expression phase in the INGS (Akimoto et al., 2013a; Akimoto & Ogata, 2014b). The essential role and purpose of the mechanism are that a narrative conceptual structure and a musical structure can be transformed into each other through the same framework. This characteristic enables various flexible and free narrative generation processes, such as the route to a conceptual narrative from music, in addition to the common one, which is to music from a conceptual narrative (Kobayashi & Ogata, 2004a, 2004b; Akimoto et al., 2013a; Akimoto & Ogata, 2014b).
- **Narrative Forest (NF):** NF is an application system using the INGS that consists of a narrative generation part and a user interface part. The former automatically and repeatedly generates narrative conceptual structures and the surface expressions in natural language texts and music, whereas the latter displays the growing process of a narrative tree structure as the corresponding visual image of a tree with music. The user can see the narrative generation process through a figurative user interface with a metaphorical image. At the same time, the user can intervene in the narrative generation process using several types of functions represented by icons in an interface window and appreciate the generated narrative sentences and the corresponding music (Akimoto, Ono, & Ogata, 2012).
- **Advertising Rhetorical Mechanisms and Norm-Deviation Mechanisms:** These projects employed various defamiliarization techniques designed to differentiate a commercial product by analyzing television commercials. The author then analyzed them to develop experimental systems and has generalized or expanded the attempts to a general "norm-deviation mechanism" in which defamiliarization techniques are used to adjust the narrative deviation from a realistic standard(Kayamori & Ogata, 2003; Abe et al., 2009; Zhang et al., 2011, 2012; Kurisawa & Ogata, 2013). These techniques are related to Shklovsky's (1990) concept of "defamiliarization." In particular, the norm-deviation mechanism was used in experiments in which the system operates the generation of many narratives, with the parameters changing according to the degree of defamiliarization.
- **Others:** User interfaces for the aforementioned *KOSERUBE* and *NF* applications are aimed at considering the potentialities of information visualization for narrative generation: "narrative interfaces" (Ogata & Ono, 2013; Akimoto & Ogata, 2015c). Story-cutting mechanisms, based on cognitive experiments that consider the relationship between a story and a discourse, were also included in the applicable system for the INGS (Kanai & Ogata, 2004a, 2004b).

## Theoretical Concepts

This subsection presents various fundamental and philosophical considerations and concepts for the research on narrative generation and on the synthesis of the INGS.

## Expanded Literary Theory

The author presents a new concept called ELT (Ogata, 2002, 2004, 2014, etc.). ELT is a concept for a research field in which narratology and literary theories are organically introduced into computational and cognitive approaches, such as AI and cognitive science, or into narrative generation systems. The author also aims at an extended narratology for developing digital narratives or information contents in ELT. In particular, ELT has the following two features: (1) developing and analyzing narratives as information contents (in the wide sense) and (2) developing narrative generation systems (in the narrow sense). The second aspect is related to the point that a narrative work as an information content has an automatic narrative generation mechanism as a narrative engine. It will be associated with the author's research plan as represented by "an information content including or using a narrative generation system." ELT is related to the creation of literary or entertaining narrative works over existing styles that either use a narrative generation function or are supported by it. In these viewpoints, ELT is the most significant concept for pursuing the INGS project. Actually, by proposing the concept of ELT, the author is presenting several attempts at mixing informatics and literature to design and develop narrative generation systems and its applicable mechanisms.

Originally, the author's familiarity with narratology and literary theories was related to or dependent on his strong interest in narratives themselves, such as novels, dramas, films, comics, folktales, histories, etc. The study of automatic narrative generation systems by applying computational and cognitive technologies is also connected to narratological approaches for narratives themselves. Narratological and literary knowledge correspond to the so-called domain knowledge for computational technologies, which is an important factor for the final product to be associated with literary or narrative fields.

The following describes the characteristics of ELT using three criteria—object, direction or concern, and method—as compared to previous approaches to narratology. In the previous narratology, non-digital texts were studied, and the analysis and interpretation were the main directions or concerns. And a variety of methods were proposed based on very rich literary knowledge. By contrast, ELT deals with narratives and literary works using information media including automatic narrative generation systems. The major objects are narrative generation systems and narratives or literary works using/including them. The narrative generation systems need to be opened toward a variety of applications and should work to achieve such purpose. Next, the primary direction or concern is the generation or creation of texts, as well as the invention or development of new genres and styles in narratives or literary works. One of the reasons for the invention or development of narrative innovation is as follows. Previous narratology has dealt with narratives and literary works that had a very long history; therefore, the analysis and interpretation were primarily the important issues. In contrast, the history of narratives or literary works using information technologies is currently very short and this new narratology does not fully accumulate a wealth of knowledge on works and theories. ELT is necessary to create a theoretical framework for generation and production through narrative innovation. Finally, as stated previously, ELT with only a short history has not acquired a wealth of theoretical and experiential knowledge and methods. The current important topic is to introduce the experiential knowledge of previous narratology and literary theories into ELT to effectively adapt to the new field for the future expansion of target texts and for the constitution of an expanded original narrative theory.

One of the current goals of ELT is the synthesis of literary theories in the INGS. The current experimental version of the INGS also mixes organically and partially three literary theories: the story structure theory by Propp (1968), the narrative discourse theory by Genette (1972), and the reception theory by Jauss (1970). These will be described in the next section.

## GIS and the Multiple Narrative Structures Model

As shown in the previous section, the "*Geino* Information System: GIS" (Kawamura & Ogata, 1997, 2000; Amino et al., 2002, etc.) was based on the survey and analysis of Japanese folklore, performing arts (such as the *kabuki*), and angles of the modern entertainment business. The GIS corresponds to an actual example of the next multiple narrative structure model.

This model is partially related to the theory of polyphony by Bakhtin (1984) and to the theory of inter-textuality by Kristeva (1980). As stated previously, Bakhtin calls such types of novels that are not integrated by the author's single voice as polyphony novels. Kristeva proposed an idea that a document exists in a network having many documents or fragments including novels and other genres, whether or not the author is aware of the fact. In the contemporary situation, this idea on literature is strongly originally related to the documents and narratives produced by people on the Web.

These literary ideas show multiplicities in a literary work and networking relations. However, the multiple narrative structure model is more of a comprehensive research plan, including its methods. For the author, the basis of narrative generation is set on "multiplicity" and it is necessary that his narrative generation systems be designed and developed based on this model. Although the basic concept of multiplicity is based on the complexity of structures and representations of narratives that have a folkloric typical communication structure, it was extended to the level of elements or components such as the story, character, and so on. For instance, an actor who appears in a kabuki play demonstrates multiplicity. He plays one or more characters in the drama, is a person with a real body and a personal life history, as well as plays an actor with a name inherited historically in many cases.

That kind of phenomenon indicates that a narrative, a kabuki play in the aforementioned example, has multiple structures. Although it is similar to the multiplicity of voices by Bakhtin, the author clearly divides the phenomenon of narrative generation into the following two levels for designing and developing narrative generation systems that cover multiple structures with a wider range: (1) the level of the generation (and reception) process of a single narrative work and the work itself, and (2) the level of the production (and consumption) process of two or more narrative works and the sequential narrative including each of the narrative works. Multiple voices and structures are derived in each of the narratives. Of course, each of the narratives has various relationships with the narrative works by other authors. However, a narrative also has diverse associations with a sequence of narratives as the historical and social process in the production and consumption level or the organizational level. The production and consumption level or the organizational level contains the generation and reception level of a single narrative work.

GIS is a synthetic system model that integrates both levels. GIS is intended to perform a sequential narrative generation in organizational and social mechanisms, such as entertainment production organizations and publishing companies.

## Circular Narrative Control

This concept is related to some developed mechanisms, although it is incomplete. A recent attempt is seen in the narrative discourse phase of the INGS (more detailed explanation will be provided in a subsection of the next section). The control mechanism, which applies the reception theory by Jauss (1970), iteratively repeats the narrative discourse generation according to the interaction between a narrator and a narratee involved in the system. It is a mechanism that embodies the concept of circular narrative control. Although this mechanism is for a particular generation part, this concept originally aims to perform a free and flexible narrative ordering control for which the sequence or order of the operating modules or phases is not preliminarily decided. The INGS in the current step partially achieves the concept in the aforementioned sense by introducing a music generation and transformation mechanism that the author has been developing in piecemeal fashion. The original idea asserted not only that music is the accompanied expressive medium of semiotic narrative representation, but that its input-output relations can be very flexible and diverse. This idea has been generalized to the relationship between music and narrative as a basic concept for narrative generation as an appearance of circular narrative control.

The circular narrative control is a design plan of narrative generation systems by the author, in particular in current INGS. The first meaning is iterative narrative generation, as shown in the aforementioned experimentally implemented mechanism for the narrative discourse phase. It will be connected to a method through which a narrative generation cycle is continued to get many generated results, and it will be synthesized to an edited and individual narrative work. In contrast, the second meaning is the part of a free and flexible control of the applicable order of narrative generation phases. For example, the INGS should not fix the generation order among all modules or generation units including conceptual structure generation and surface expression generation. It should be designed to enable various and diverse generation courses and repletion. Furthermore, GIS is also a medium for the circular narrative control in the sense that the narrative production and consumption mechanism repeat the various levels of narratives, such as individual narrative works, an actor's authentic narratives, an entire narrative of a sequence of each productive narrative, etc.

## Fluidity and Fixation

The concept of "fluidity and fixation" (Ogata, 2014) was adopted as a concept to design and use various information contents, including narrative contents generated by the INGS, related to narrative generation. Information contents have the following characteristics: capacities of free compilation, self-organization, and automatic generation. The concept of fluidity and fixation involves these characteristics. In the cases of previous and traditional contents, the author may consider these kinds of floating characteristics of contents in a human brain (through written texts) and in a social process of a human group or an organization to create fixed contents outside. In contrast, information contents enable the fluidity itself to be brought out. A novel that an author has written is equivalent to a work in the world of traditional contents, whereas the writing or creating process involved in writing a novel can be considered as a work in the world of information contents and narrative generation. The creation by a narrative generation system will enable the representation and visualization of the narrative content generation at any stage of the narrative generation process. It may be regarded as a literary or artistic work.

This idea will open the possibilities of a variety of narrative representation forms, creation styles, and novel experiments. The following two types of forms are considered from the author's viewpoint on work as an information content: (1) the style in which the fluidity itself is equivalent to a work (the fixation), and (2) the form in which various means of processing are used to fix one or more works based on many or a huge number of works and the fragments generated through a fluid narrative generation process. One of the significant characteristics of information contents compared to traditional contents is that the fluidity of the information itself can be considered as a work. It results in the diversity of the forms or methods for fixing floating information. With few exceptions, a main research objective in traditional literary theories was the consideration of fixed works in the aforementioned sense. As an exception, generative criticism has dealt with the creation process of a literary work or an author's work based on the analysis of incomplete or ongoing manuscripts, etc. Also, in human authors, for instance, Miyazawa Kenji (1896-1933), an excellent Japanese poet and author, was known as a writer who wrote many incomplete and on-going works. The final works were not necessarily truly completed works or final works either, which were clearly intended by the author himself. Different works also exist with the same title, and these may be considered as fluid works. The concept of fluidity and fixation will help to treat consciously and expressly such literary situations. Simply, a narrative generation process corresponds to a fluidity process, whereas a resulting work (content) is the fixation. Narrative generation systems enable representing the process itself, as well as transform the process into a narrative work (content). They also open the door to experimenting with possibilities different from previous forms and styles, such as various representation forms of narrative contents, many kinds of creation styles of narrative contents, etc.

*Narrative Forest (NF)* (Akimoto et al., 2012), as stated in the previous subsection, has been developed in connection with the concept of fluidity and fixation. In this visualized system, a changing and fluid narrative generation process is represented as a tree and a forest, and the user can see a fixed narrative in a certain moment. A tree corresponds to a narrative, and a collection of trees is regarded as a forest. The forest world changes according to a continuous narrative generation process. Although this is a representation of the fluidity process of a narrative, it is not merely a visualization or explanation. The true aim was that such a mechanism in which a generation process is equal to the fluidity process itself corresponds to the content of a work. The process of writing a novel itself can now be considered as a form of fluidity, in addition to the previous method in which an author's work itself can be considered as a form of fixation. Various possibilities can be imagined. For example, in the content generation in a generation process, a reader can cut and edit only the part that he/she likes or feels beautiful to make a fixed work.

## Norm and Deviation

The concept of norm and deviation is a narrative control method based on norm, the standard framework by which a narrative generation process should be performed, and on the deviation from the norm. This is related to the concept of "defamiliarization" by Shklovsky (1990). The defamiliarization techniques were originally acquired by analyzing television commercials. In television commercials, various techniques for defamiliarizing and deviating from realistic events are employed to differentiate a commercial product. A television commercial scenario structurally has a narrative structure. The author applied the acquired rhetorical rules of defamiliarization to generate similar short scenarios (Zhang et al., 2011, 2012).

The author has attempted to employ and generalize the concept of norm and deviation in the INGS. One of the methods used was the rhetorical defamiliarization rules in the INGS. In relation to the attempt, the circular control based on Jauss's (1970) theory was associated with the concept of norm and deviation through the development of a mechanism that repeats the process of deviating from a current narrative. Currently, attempts are being made to introduce the concept into the development of a general framework of norm-deviation mechanism (Kurisawa & Ogata, 2013; Akimoto & Ogata, 2015a) as small-scale and exploratory systems.

The other method used is related to the conceptual dictionaries in the INGS. From an overall viewpoint, conceptual dictionaries and other knowledge in the INGS are basically described based on "realistic standard," which means that realistic possibilities in the real world and canonical narrative generation functions generate narratives according to this standard. In contrast, to apply the techniques of deviation, defamiliarization techniques enable the systematic generation of narratives that deviate from the norm. In particular, the mechanism provides the constraint information set in the noun conceptual dictionary with a function for changing the definition of the range to adjust the range of the possible noun concepts in a generated event.

From a more general viewpoint, this concept is associated with narrative transformation techniques from a story to a discourse, if a story is equal to a norm and the discourse corresponds to the deviation.

## Toward a Comprehensive Expansion of ELT

The author has presented four concepts related to narrative generation for shaping the design and development of the INGS. The ELT reinterpreted some of the traditional literary theories from the viewpoint of informatics and experimentally implemented programs for the mechanisms of narrative generation. Although four concepts have been independently developed from ELT, they can be regarded as a group of concepts that correspond to the subcategories of ELT. They are also related to literary theories; at the same time, they are concepts geared toward the original directions of information contents and narrative generation. Positioning them as subcategories of ELT is related to the aim of incorporating previous literary theories into a conceptual framework geared toward an original literary theory or narratology for information contents and narrative generation. This entire or "expanded" ELT is substituted for the previous ELT.

GIS and the multiple narrative structure model involve literary theories by Bakhtin and Kristeva. They are also closely related to the Japanese *geino* such as the kabuki. Circular narrative controls were implemented in the INGS according to Jauss's reception theory and music composition functions. The concept of norm and deviation made from analyzing television commercials and the defamiliarization techniques by Shklovsky was also included in the reception theory in the INGS. This concept was associated with the theories of Genette and Propp in relation to the narrative transformation techniques. Finally, the concept of fluidity and fixation strongly reflects the characteristics of information contents and narrative generation. It is related to generative criticism in existing literary theories, but using different texts and methods will produce a new generative criticism based on the concept of fluidity and fixation. As remarked previously, the expanded ELT enables to consider discrete literary theories under the meta-level concepts.

ELT is a theoretical concept used in the development of the author's narrative generation systems. And it was applied to the current INGS, which uses a mix of three literary theories. The Propp-based mechanism was used to generate relatively long and macro stories or the skeletons, and the Genette-based mechanism was used to systematically implement the discourse techniques. The Jauss-based mechanism processes a discourse generation control under the interaction between a narrator and a narratee within the system. An important result was that the theories of previous narratologies were effectively reinterpreted from the viewpoint of an integrated practical method.

On the basis of the technological result, the author proposes a framework for further expanding ELT. The main future issues are divided into theoretical and practical aspects. One of the former themes is to associate various literary theories to the sub-concepts in ELT. An important theme of the latter is to implement a particular literary theory interpreted under the framework of a proposed concept as a mechanism in the INGS.

## AN INTEGRATED NARRATIVE GENERATION SYSTEM: INGS

This section describes the detailed mechanisms of INGS. The following two sub-sections present the overview and mechanisms, respectively, that introduce three types of literary theories.

### INGS Overview

Figure 2 shows the overall INGS architecture. The main generation modules are for story, narrative discourse, and expression, including language, music, and picture images. The story and narrative discourse are represented by respective conceptual representation forms. All modules are controlled by each local control mechanism under the global control. Story and discourse generation are performed using story and discourse techniques, respectively. Furthermore, INGS has dictionaries, including conceptual and language, and various knowledge, including story content and state-event transformation knowledge bases. In addition, as stated in the previous section, several literary theories are incorporated into INGS for ELT practice.

All the program components of the implementation in the current version are listed in Table 2. The main development program language is Common Lisp, but several types of development tools are also used partially for particular purposes.

*Figure 2. INGS architecture*

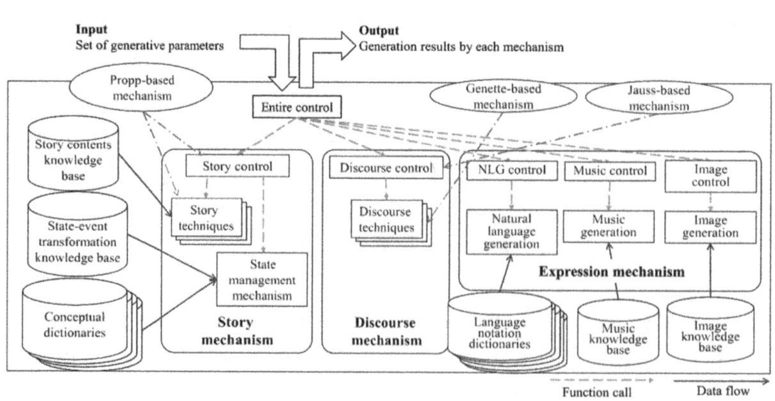

*Table 2. Components of the current version of INGS*

| Program Structure/Data | | | Function | Data |
|---|---|---|---|---|
| Main functions | | | 12 | - |
| Common library | | | 61 | - |
| **Conceptual Structures Generation Mechanism** | | | | |
| Story generation mechanism | Main functions | | 11 | - |
| | Control functions | | 17 | - |
| | Story techniques selection functions | | 19 | - |
| | Event concepts generation | Event generation functions based on verb concept | 1 | - |
| | | Event generation functions based on instance | 1 | - |
| | Story techniques | Story techniques application functions | 18 | - |
| | | Story content grammar | 38 | - |
| | | Pair relationships | 18 | - |
| | | Defamiliarization rhetoric | 4 | - |
| | States generation rules | States generation rules based on event | 18 | - |
| | | Event complement functions based on states | 9 | - |
| Narrative discourse generation mechanism | Main functions | | 13 | - |
| | Control functions | | 16 | - |
| | Narrative discourse techniques selection functions | | 9 | - |
| | Narrative discourse techniques application functions | | 10 | - |
| | Narrative discourse techniques | | 21 | - |
| | Evaluation functions | | 19 | - |
| | Discourse generation functions based on variation music | | 17 | - |
| | Common library | | 9 | - |
| **Surface Expression Generation Mechanisms** | | | | |
| Control functions | | | 3 | - |
| Sentence generation mechanism | Main functions | | 23 | - |
| | Single sentence generation mechanism | Basic form generation functions | 7 | - |
| | | Name generation functions for instances | 7 | - |
| | | Location addition functions | 1 | - |
| | | Conjugation decision functions | 9 | - |
| | | Word order transformation function | 1 | - |
| | | Language notation decision functions | 3 | - |
| | | Basic form transformation functions | 2 | - |
| | Complex sentence generation mechanism | Application rules | 37 | - |
| | | Connection rules | 142 | - |
| | Structural transformation functions from narrative relationships to language relationships | | 3 | - |

*continued on following page*

*Table 2. Continued*

| Program Structure/Data | | | Function | Data |
|---|---|---|---|---|
| Music generation mechanism | Original music generation mechanism | Main functions | 1 | - |
| | | Transformation functions from story to original music | 14 | - |
| | | Transformation functions from original music to original music | 13 | - |
| | | Transformation functions from variation music to original music | 4 | - |
| | Variation music generation mechanism | Main functions | 2 | - |
| | | Transformation functions from narrative discourse to variation music | 15 | - |
| | | Transformation functions from narrative discourse to variation music | 6 | - |
| | | Transformation functions from original music to variation music | 17 | - |
| | Midi generation functions (including "Text music SAKURA") 5 mm | | 15 | - |
| | Common library | | 14 | - |
| Image generation mechanism | Main functions | | 2 | - |
| | Animation generation functions | | 8 | - |
| | Image expression interface (by HSP: Procedural programming language) | | 31 | - |
| **Dictionaries** | | | | |
| Conceptual dictionaries | Noun conceptual dictionary | | - | 115765 |
| | Verb conceptual dictionary | | - | 23978 |
| | Adjective conceptual dictionary | | - | 1428 |
| | Adjective verb conceptual dictionary | | - | 2382 |
| Language notation dictionaries | Noun notation dictionary | | - | 70079 |
| | Verb notation dictionary | | - | 4920 |
| | Adjective notation dictionary | | - | 12 |
| | Adjective verb notation dictionary | | - | 20 |
| | Particle notation dictionary | | - | 40 |
| Paraphrase dictionaries | Dialect transformation dictionaries (Iwate) | Noun dialect transformation dictionary | - | 11 |
| | | Verb dialect transformation dictionary | - | 31 |
| | | Adjective dialect transformation dictionary | - | 22 |
| | | Adjective verb dialect transformation dictionary | - | 3 |
| | | Particle dialect transformation dictionary | - | 1 |
| | Verb paraphrase dictionary | | - | 45 |
| Name dictionary | | | - | 45093 |
| **Knowledge Bases** | | | | |
| State-event transformation knowledge base | | | - | 5241 |

*continued on following page*

*Table 2. Continued*

<table>
<tr><th colspan="4">Program Structure/Data</th><th>Function</th><th>Data</th></tr>
<tr><td rowspan="20">Story content knowledge bases</td><td rowspan="6">Story content grammar</td><td rowspan="2">Propp-based story content grammar</td><td>Functions</td><td>-</td><td>32</td></tr>
<tr><td>Sub-functions</td><td>-</td><td>271</td></tr>
<tr><td rowspan="2">Story content grammar based on "Introduction- development-turn-conclusion"</td><td>Functions</td><td>-</td><td>6</td></tr>
<tr><td>Sub-functions</td><td>-</td><td>13</td></tr>
<tr><td rowspan="2">Story content grammar based on "The Story of the White Crane"</td><td>Functions</td><td>-</td><td>7</td></tr>
<tr><td>Sub-functions</td><td>-</td><td>7</td></tr>
<tr><td colspan="3">Cause-effect knowledge base</td><td>-</td><td>17</td></tr>
<tr><td colspan="3">Villainy-liquidation knowledge base</td><td>-</td><td>3</td></tr>
<tr><td colspan="3">Interdiction-violation knowledge base</td><td>-</td><td>3</td></tr>
<tr><td colspan="3">Lack-liquidation knowledge base</td><td>-</td><td>1</td></tr>
<tr><td colspan="3">Order-obey knowledge base</td><td>-</td><td>2</td></tr>
<tr><td colspan="3">Pursuit-rescue knowledge base</td><td>-</td><td>1</td></tr>
<tr><td colspan="3">Reconnaissance-delivery knowledge base</td><td>-</td><td>3</td></tr>
<tr><td colspan="3">Struggle-victory knowledge base</td><td>-</td><td>5</td></tr>
<tr><td colspan="3">Transfer-return knowledge base</td><td>-</td><td>1</td></tr>
<tr><td colspan="3">Trickery-complicity knowledge base</td><td>-</td><td>4</td></tr>
<tr><td colspan="3">Theme knowledge base</td><td>-</td><td>10</td></tr>
<tr><td colspan="3">Script knowledge base</td><td>-</td><td>60</td></tr>
<tr><td colspan="3">Noun-verb relationship knowledge base</td><td>-</td><td>6</td></tr>
<tr><td rowspan="4">Musical knowledge base</td><td colspan="3">Motif knowledge base</td><td>-</td><td>2</td></tr>
<tr><td colspan="3">Scale knowledge base</td><td>-</td><td>12</td></tr>
<tr><td colspan="3">Instruments knowledge base</td><td>-</td><td>3</td></tr>
<tr><td colspan="3">Narrative structure-music structure transformation knowledge base</td><td>-</td><td>8</td></tr>
<tr><td colspan="4">Animation knowledge base</td><td>-</td><td>170</td></tr>
<tr><td colspan="4">Picture knowledge base</td><td>-</td><td>53520</td></tr>
<tr><td colspan="4">Total</td><td>721</td><td>323238</td></tr>
</table>

## Conceptual Narrative Representations Using Conceptual Dictionaries

"Conceptual dictionaries" consist of hierarchical structures that range from higher to lower concepts by "is-a" relationships for verb and noun concepts mainly (Ogata, 2015). Figure 3 shows the portion of a story structure in these terms. Conceptual dictionaries are for verb and noun concepts, although INGS includes other conceptual dictionaries (for adjective and adjective verb concepts). A story is a hierarchical structure whose basic unit is an event or event concept, and whose lower level corresponds to two states. The constitutional elements of an event and state refer to the adequate elements in the conceptual dictionaries.

In particular, a story event is described as a case structure, and the value in each case is an instance of the corresponding noun concept in the noun conceptual dictionary. For example, "obj%Apple#1" indicates an instance or concrete object of the noun concept, "Apple." INGS automatically makes the

*Figure 3. Story structure and related conceptual dictionaries*

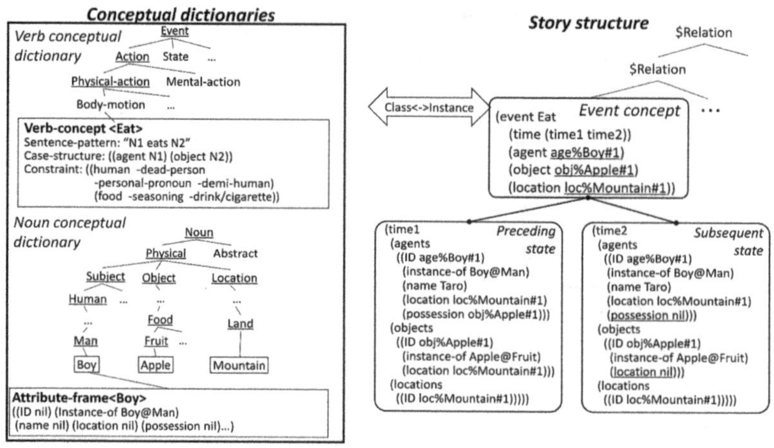


corresponding instance when an event is produced during the story generation phase. An important role of the verb concept in an event ("eat" in this example) is to provide constraint conditions for the case values. The constraint information for "eat" in Figure 3 is "human," with the exception of "dead-person," "personal-pronoun," and "semi-human" for "agent," and "food," with the exception of "seasoning" and "drink/cigarette" for "object."

A terminal verb concept also fits the description: a basic sentence pattern for natural language generation and one or more case structures. The case structure is comprised of several noun concepts required by the case of a verb concept. Figure 3 also shows both the precedent and subsequent states that define those preconditions that allow an event and its results. They also manage the instances and any changes according to the progression of events. At the same time, an instance is further expanded into a set of the attributes (called an "attributes frame") generated based on the noun conceptual dictionary.

## Process and Control

INGS provides mechanisms for controlling the overall generation and level of each point in a narrative process. The major function for each phase of the control mechanisms is to direct the use of techniques, namely those involving story and discourse, to manipulate characteristics of the generated narrative texts; a relatively full-fledged Jauss-based control mechanism is currently being used entirely within the discourse phase.

### Circulative Generation Control for the Entirety of INGS

One of the characteristics of narrative generation control in INGS is circulative control based on the use of one of the basic concepts of the narrative generation by the author. INGS aims to implement a form of the concept of circular control. The mechanisms are partially developed through the diversity of generation routes. Ideally, this mechanism means that all of the generation mechanism can receive any type of input information. The current version of INGS partially implements the generation routes shown in Figure 4. The user can select the generation route at the starting time in a session in any of the following ways:

*Figure 4. Possible generation routes in INGS*

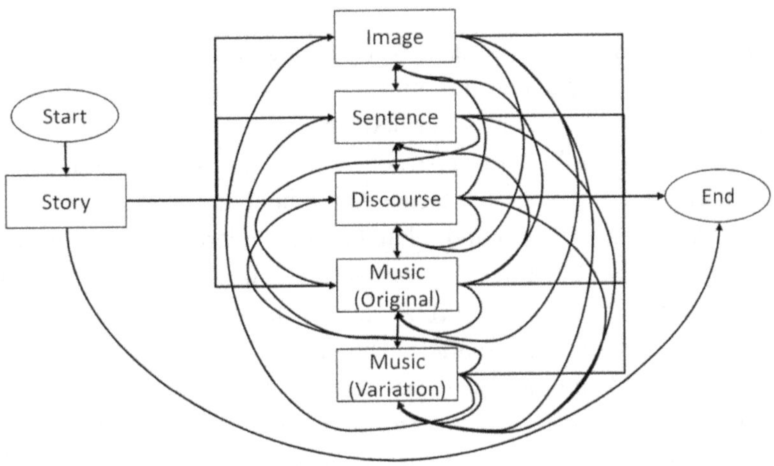


1. The user selects a possible route (a free combination of "story, narrative discourse, sentence, visual image, original music, variation music"),
2. The system automatically determines a route, and
3. The system automatically determines the next module at the ending time of a generation module. Furthermore,
4. If the user does not select any of the previous ways, the system determines the order "story -> narrative discourse -> sentence -> visual image -> variation music."

Table 3 lists the input information of each generation module and the corresponding output information. In general, a generation module uses the previous output data as the input data. However, for example, in the case of the order "story -> sentence -> discourse," the discourse module takes the output data from the story module as the input data. Such details are explained in the respective subsections.

*Table 3. Input and output information in each module*

| Generation Mechanism (Module) | Input | Output |
|---|---|---|
| Story generation | Generation parameters | Story structure |
| Narrative discourse generation | • Generation parameters<br>• Story structure or variation music structure | Discourse structures |
| Sentence generation (expression) | • Generation parameters<br>• Story structure or narrative generation structure | Sentences (text file) |
| Original music generation (expression) | • Basic setting data<br>• Story structure, narrative discourse structure, original music structure, or variation music structure | Original music structure (MIDI files) |
| Variation music generation (expression) | • Basic setting data<br>• Discourse structure, original music structure, or variation music structure | Variation music structure (MIDI file) |
| Image generation (expression) | Story structure or narrative discourse structure | Command file |

## Story Generation and Control

The story generation module involves methods to be applied to a structure and selected conceptual units in the events. It also includes a state generation mechanism for each generated event.

A story produced by such mechanism is defined by either the content of a narrative or temporal sequence of events. It is represented by a tree structure that consists of the three types of basic units: event, relationship, and state. An event is described in conceptual representation form as a frame or case structure that includes a verb concept and related noun concepts. It is the principal combination of preceding and subsequent states. A relationship semantically combines events or sub-structures (such as "cause-effect," "continuation," and "script"). A state is the static information within a story, while "event" corresponds to the dynamic information. The chief functions of the state are to maintain the knowledge about a story's world and manage the coherency of the flow of events.

The input data is listed in Table 4. These are set as global parameters through each generation session. Using values between one and three, a user can input parameters to provide the direction for a story. The mechanism manipulates the different entered techniques in order to generate a story structure through the process flow. In addition, the mechanism necessarily uses a story technique from previously prepared candidates at the starting point to generate a first story structure.

## Narrative Discourse Generation and Control

The discourse mechanism is composed of narrative discourse techniques applied to its developing structure. The module has implemented generation and circular control mechanisms that use the narrative discourse theory by Genette and reception theory by Jauss, respectively. The latter mechanism shows a possible implementation of narrative generation control in various possibilities.

A narrative discourse generated or changed by the Genette-based mechanism translates to the structural aspect of story narration, namely by a sequence or series of events. The discourse structure to be narrated and its required surface media (such as language and image) are points distinguished within the system, and are described accordingly in conceptual representation form; the discourse should correspond to a transformed story structure. In the main portion of the process, Genette's theory develops a set of discourse techniques as the root for the narrative techniques; the Genette and Jauss-based control mechanisms are related to this phase. A detailed description is provided in Genette-based Mechanism and Jauss-based Mechanism.

*Table 4. Input data to story generation module*

| Parameter | Meaning | Procedure |
|---|---|---|
| Length | The length of a story | Accounts for the number of events |
| Macro-structure | The degree of macro structure in the entire story | Accounts for the number of the following events: "$Theme", "$Villainy-liquidation", "$Order-obey", "$Interdiction-violation", "$Russian_forktail", "$Reserve_portion", "$Beginning", "$Reserve_trial", "$Strugle_and_victory", "$Task_and_solution", "$Solution_of_problem", "$Arrival_and_trial", and "$End" |
| Unreality | The degree of unreal events | Accounts for the number of "$Defamiliarization-scenario" events |
| Repetition | The degree of appearance of similar event patterns | Accounts for the number of "$Repetition" and "$Defamiliarization-scenario" events |

## Natural Language Expression and Control

Used in the last phase, "expression" refers to the aspect of narrative representation composed of various surface media that include natural language (Kumagai, Funakoshi, Akimoto, & Ogata, 2012) and such visual media as animation, still image, and music. The first natural language mechanism defines the syntax in each of the sentences, selected vocabularies, and their letters of notation. This module uses language notation (or representation for the Japanese language) dictionaries for the constituent elements in events generated in the story and discourse modules, and states generated in the story module. The structures of the dictionaries correspond to the conceptual dictionaries. For a terminal concept in the conceptual dictionaries, the language notation dictionary can provide the following four types of word representations:

1. That which includes one or more Kanji,
2. That by only Hiragana,
3. That by only Katakana, and
4. That by only Roma-ji.

In addition, each concept in the conceptual dictionaries is described using the most popular representation. Naturally, the concept representation is also included in the corresponding language notation dictionaries (Figure 5).

The natural language generation mechanism transforms all events in the structure of a generated narrative conceptual representation into a sequence of sentences through the following flow:

1. Generating basic forms of intermediate representation using the sentence patterns in the verb conceptual dictionary (the recursive form of a sentence is also treated here),
2. Transforming the basic forms of intermediate representation into the changed forms using various linguistic elements, such as word order and tense,
3. Transforming the intermediate form into the surface sentence forms, and
4. As optional processing, the generated simple sentences are transformed into one or more complex sentences partially or as whole.

Figure 6 shows examples of an intermediate sentence and its transformed form.

*Figure 5. The descriptive form of a word in language notation dictionary*

| *Description form* | *Example* |
|---|---|
| (<終端概念名> ; Concept name | (男[man] |
| (<漢字を含んだ言語表記>) ; Kanji | (男) |
| (<ひらがなのみ言語表記>) ; Hiragana | (おとこ おおのこ) |
| (<カタカナのみ言語表記>) ; Katakana | (オトコ オオノコ) |
| (<アルファベット（ローマ字）のみ言語表記>)) ; Roma-ji | (otoko o onoko)) |

*Figure 6. Examples of intermediate sentence and transformed form*

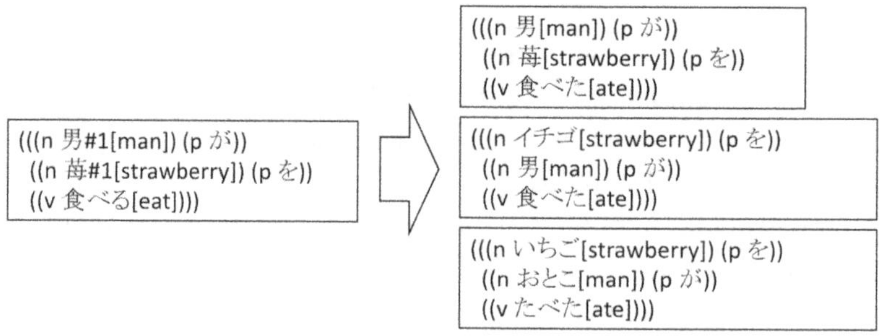


### Parallel Control by KOSERUBE

The standard processing in INGS is sequential; namely, a generation or expression module is executed at one generation timing. However, the author seeks to explore parallel narrative generation processing. An experimental system called KOSERUBE, intended to be an application system for INGS, is an example of parallel narrative generation. Figure 7 shows the overall architecture of KOSERUBE. The system is mainly divided into narrative generation and interface parts. The system has an "Iwate region database" related to Iwate prefecture and the near area in Japan. The database contains conceptual data that includes characters (34), objects (21), places (85), explanation sentences, and other data. First, the user selects the characters, story type, narrator, etc. Seven types of narrators are prepared in order to change the narration style.

The generation flow is as follows:

1. Generating a story structure:
   a. Expanding the story content grammar by top-down method,
   b. Generating states,
   c. Generating scripts of the particular events using a script technique, and
   d. Complimenting the states;
2. Generating a narrative discourse structure:
   a. Generating a first narrative discourse structure,
   b. Inserting descriptions, and
   c. Using discourse techniques according to a selected narrator;
3. Generating a musical structure;
4. Generating visual image expression.

## Techniques and Knowledge

### Story Techniques and Story Content Knowledge

A story structure that consists of events and relationships can be generated using story techniques as part of the applicable narrative techniques, and any states associated with the created events are developed according to another mechanism. Figure 8 shows the expansion process using a story technique. The concrete content knowledge for expanding "E5" to add "E6" is kept in the story content knowledge base.

*Figure 7. Overall architecture of KOSERUBE*

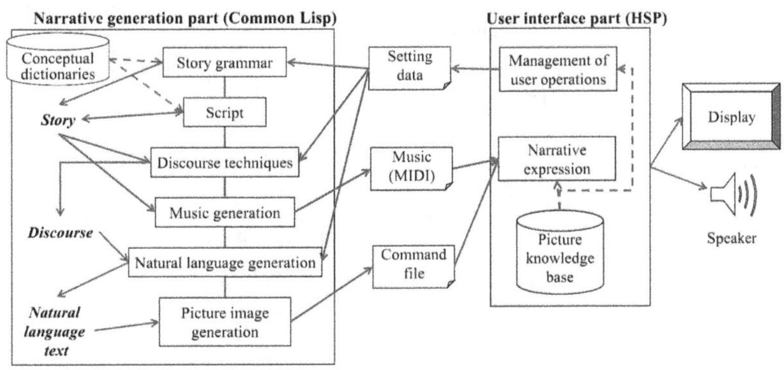


The Propp-based mechanism is also a type of both the story technique and story content knowledge. In other words, stories are represented by a tree structure with events bound by various relationships, and it is gradually expanded using rules composed of differing functions of structural transformation; each technique uses the information stored in a story content knowledge base. Figure 9 is the description form of a story technique and example. Table 5 lists story techniques and story content knowledge.

*Figure 8. Story structure's transformation using story technique*

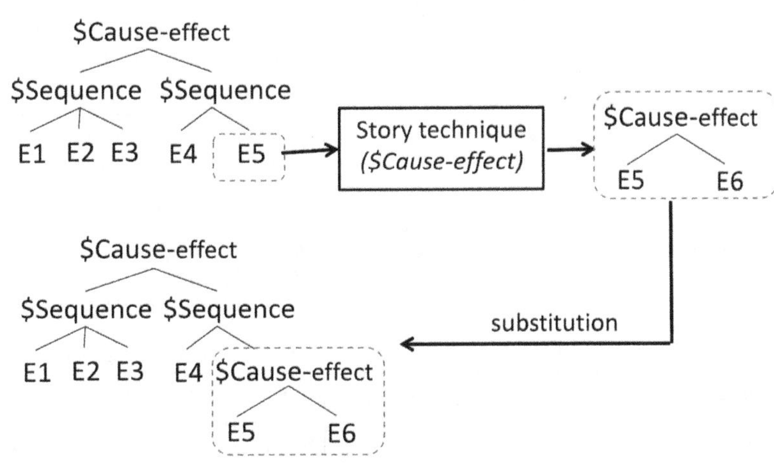


*Figure 9. Description form of story technique and example*

<u>Description form</u>

((relationship {story-technique-name})
  (eve-pos {pair; 1|2|3| pattern; 'root | 'leaf}); Type of story content
  (relationship-type {'rel | 'pat}); Pair type or pattern type
)

<u>Example</u>

((relationship '$原因-結果); Cause-effect
  (eve-pos 2); "Pair 2 content" type
  (type 'rel); "Pair relationship" type
)

*Table 5. Story techniques and story contents*

| Type | Technique | Knowledge Base | Example |
|---|---|---|---|
| Pair type | Effect | Cause-effect knowledge base | ((event 飲む2[drink] (agent (&v age1)) (object (&v obj1) (&sc 酒[liquor]))) (event 酔う2[get-drunk] (agent (&v age1)) (object (&v obj1)))) |
| | Cause | | |
| | Villainy-liquidation | Villainy-liquidation knowledge base | ((event 略奪する2[plunder] (agent (&v age1)) (counter-agent (&v age2)) (object (&v obj1))) (event 奪還する1[recapture] (agent (&v age2)) (object (&v obj1)) (from (&v age1)))) |
| | Lack-liquidation | Lack-liquidation knowledge base | ((event 欠如する1[be-lacking] (agent (&v age1)) (counter-agent (&v age2))) (event 出会う1[meet] (agent (&v age2)) (counter-agent (&v age1)))) |
| | Struggle-victory | Struggle-victory knowledge base | ((event 戦う1[fight] (agent (&v age1)) (counter-agent (&v age2))) (event 敗れる2[be-defeated] (agent (&v age2)) (counter-agent (&v age1)))) |
| | Trickery-complicity | Trickery-complicity knowledge base | ((event 使う3[spend] (agent (&v age1)) (object (&sc 錠剤[tablet]@薬品類{医用}[medicine])) (to (&v age2))) (event 眠る1[sleep] (agent (&v age2)))) |
| | Transfer-return | Transfer-return knowledge base | ((event 移動する1[move] (agent (&v age1)) (from (&v loc1)) (to (&v loc2))) (event 脱出する2[escape] (agent (&v age1)) (from (&v loc2)))) |
| | Reconnaissance-delivery | Reconnaissance-delivery knowledge base | ((event 捜す2[look-for] (agent (&v age1)) (counter-agent (&v age2))) (event 示す2[indicate] (agent (&sc 人間[human])) (object (&sc 噂[gossip]@噂[gossip])))) |
| | Repetition | - | - |
| Pattern type (sequence) | Pursuit-rescue | Pursuit-rescue knowledge base | ((event 妨げる2[disturb] (agent (&v age1)) (object (&sc 道[road]@道路[street]))) (event 退ける3[refuse] (agent (&v age2)) (object (&sc 誘惑[temptation]@勧誘[invitation])))) |
| | Interdiction-violation | Interdiction-violation knowledge base | ((event 禁じる1[forbid] (agent (&v age1)) (counter-agent (&v age2)) (object (&v-eve 2))) (event 食べる2[eat] (agent (&v age2)) (object (&sc 果樹[fruit-tree]))) (event 罹る1[suffer] (agent (&v age2)))) |
| | Order-obey | Order-obey knowledge base | ((event 命令する1[order] (agent (&v age1)) (counter-agent (&v age2)) (object (&v-eve 2))) (event 食べる2[eat] (agent (&v age2))) (event 回復する3[recaover] (agent (&v age2)))) |

*continued on following page*

## State-Event Transformation Knowledge Base

This knowledge base is used to generate states for a generated event in the story generation phase (Onodera et al., 2012; Akimoto, Kurisawa, & Ogata, 2013c). Each of the 5241 stage-event transformation rules corresponds to a verb concept. Figure 10 shows the description form and example of a rule.

*Table 5. Continued*

| Type | Technique | Knowledge Base | Example |
|---|---|---|---|
| Pattern type (inclusion) | Script (inclusion) | Script knowledge base | (script0001 (働く1[work] ((or 焼く3[burn] 茹でる1[boil]) 盛る2[serve] 渡す2[give])) ((event 働く1[work] (agent (&v age1)) (location (&v loc1) (&sc 飲食店[restrain])))<br>((or (1a (event 焼く3[burn] (agent (&v age1)) (object (&v obj1) (&sc 食料[food])) (location (&v loc1))))<br>(1b (event 茹でる1[boil] (agent (&v age1)) (object (&v obj1) (&sc 食料[food])) (location (&v loc1)))))<br>(2 (event 盛る2[serve] (agent (&v age1)) (object (&v obj1) (&sc 食料[food])) (location (&v loc1))))<br>(3 (event 渡す2[give] (agent (&v age1)) (object (&v obj1) (&sc 食料[food])) (location (&v loc1))))))) |
| | Theme (inclusion) | Theme knowledge base | (theme0002 (刑事[police] (殺す1[kill] 発見する2[discover] 捜査する1[investigate] 発見する1[find] 逮捕する1[arrest]))<br>((theme 刑事[police])<br>((1 (event 殺す1[kill] (agent (&v age1)) (counter-agent (&v age2)) (location (&v loc1))))<br>(2 (event 発見する2[discover] (agent (&v age3)) (counter-agent (&v age2)) (location (&v loc1))))<br>(3 (event 捜査する1[investigate] (agent (&v age4) (&sc 刑事[police]@警官[police-officer])) (counter-agent (&v age1))))<br>(4 (event 発見する1[find] (agent (&v age4)) (object (&sc 証拠[evidence]@証拠[evidence]))))<br>(5 (event 逮捕する1[arrest] (agent (&v age4)) (counter-agent (&v age1))))))) |
| Pattern type (expansion) | Script (expansion) | Same as "Script (inclusion))" | |
| | Theme (expansion) | Same as "Theme (inclusion))" | |
| ' | - | Noun-verb relationship knowledge base) | ((食料[food]) (食べる2[eat] 試食する2[taste] 料理する2[cook] 調理する1[cook])) |
| Defamiliarization type | Character defamiliarization | - | - |
| | Object defamiliarization | - | - |
| | Location defamiliarization | - | - |
| | Defamiliarization scenario | - | - |
| Macro type | Propp-based story techniques (for story content grammar) | Propp-based Story content grammar | See "Propp-based Mechanism" |

- **INGS as ELT:** Mechanisms that Introduce Three Literary Theories.

The INGS system is an ELT practice, and currently incorporates three types of literary theories—Propp's story structure theory, Genette's narrative discourse theory, and Jauss's reception theory—mainly into several parts, although other literary theories are also partially considered.

## Propp-Based Mechanism

The central argument of Propp's theory is a structural method based upon certain "functions", but the overall accomplishment includes other knowledge related to various aspects of folktales and general

*Figure 10. Description form and rule example*

*Description form*

```
(
 (Changing state condition <Case frame to be changed>)
 (Precondition
  (Condition1s <Case frame before changing>))
 (Case frame
  <Case frame of corresponding verb concept>)
 (Name of verb concept
  (<Verb concept name>))
```

*Example*

```
(
 (変化内容 [Changing state condition]
  ((actor agent) (slot 所持[Possession]) (op nil) (order (del counter-agent))))
 (前提条件 [Precondition]
 (条件1 [Condition1] (条件名[Name] 所持[Possession]) (op nil) (actor agent)
                     (slot 所持 [Possession]) (val (contain counter-agent))))
 (格フレーム [Case frame] ((agent N1) (counter-agent N2)))
 (動詞概念名 [Verb concept name]
  (食べる2 [eat])))
```

narratives. Most of the generation systems that use Propp's theory focus only on these functions, but the theory includes productive and theoretical ideas that could contribute to story creations. Propp presented an array of examples and techniques in the lower level for materializing the functions as abstract definitions by analyzing collected folktales. The two methods he used are "interdiction" and "order or a suggestion," and correspond to the description for materializing the former abstract "functions"; these levels of analysis are known as "sub-functions."

In his studies, Propp noted that specific functions have a strong tendency to be combined with other specific functions in order to form different pairs. For example, "inhibition and the violation" are strongly connected in many narratives. Likewise, a specific function can include heroes, villains, victims, helpers, dispatchers, and princesses. Such parts can be abstracted simply to advance smaller story functions, and others are formed as a specific role that becomes a major agent for driving a group of functions.

## Propp-Based Story Grammar (PBSG)

As shown in Figure 11, Propp-based story grammar (PBSG) is rooted in the reorganization of the theory and is divided into four hierarchical levels. This figure shows a portion of Common Lisp's actual description of PBSG, which has five levels in the hierarchical structure, as listed in Table 6.

PBSG opens to different types of operational methods: top-down, bottom-up, and hybrid. The top-down method is the standard and simply expands PBSG from higher to lower levels by the automatic choice of subsequent options using a random function. When the process reaches the lowest level in the

*Figure 11. PBSG hierarchical structure*

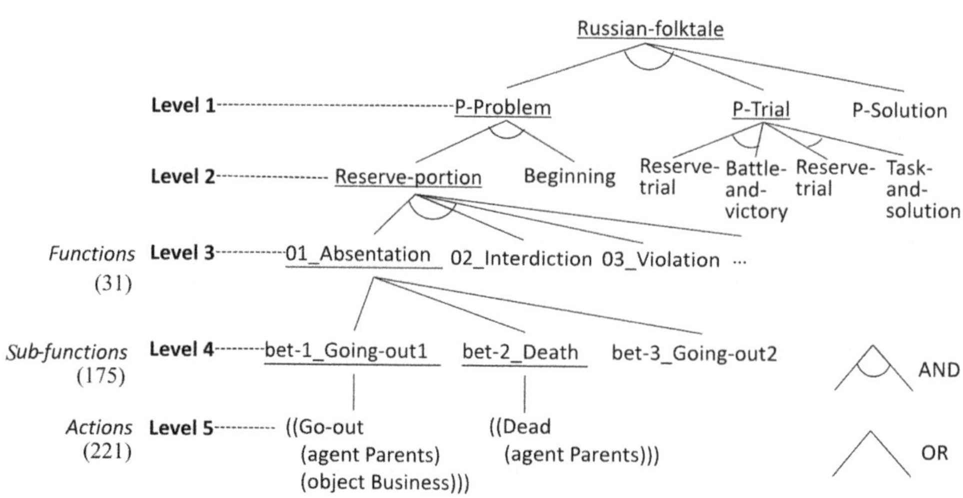

*Table 6. PBSG hierarchical structure*

| Level | Definition |
|---|---|
| Level 1 | Definition of a macro or entire story structure (1). |
| Level 2 | Definition of a macro or entire story structure (2). |
| Level 3 | Division of 31 "functions" into several parts. |
| Level 4 | Generation of "sub-functions" from "functions": A "function" means the abstract and comprehensive definition of an actor's action, while a sub-function corresponds a concrete way to actualize a "function". PBSG also implements "pairs of functions" to connect two distant functions (pairs between sub-functions are actually used). |
| Level 5 | Actualization of each sub-function to an action or a sequence of actions: Each action is described as a case structure including a verb concept and necessary noun concepts. |

grammar's description, the operation generates an event concept using conceptual dictionaries in INGS and develops a PBSG tree structure using depth-first search and constructs the overall structure of a story. In this process, if a sub-function is selected as an element in a pair, the corresponding sub-function is selected automatically. The pairs contribute to maintain a story's consistency and its comparatively natural flow. Although Propp prepared both pairs of functions and sub-functions, this method uses only the latter.

The bottom-up method ascends the levels of a hierarchy within a story from the lowest level of its PBSG case structure as determined by the user. The generated result is often a collection of fragmented parts. The hybrid method is a blending of the two methods and completes a story structure by expanding the results of a bottom-up operation using sub-function pairs and PBSG.

### Generation Example

Box 1 and 2 in the Appendix show a generated story according to the top-down method. The upper conceptual structure is the actual output description of the generated story, and the lower text is an English translation of the Japanese text generated from the conceptual structure using a natural language generation mechanism in INGS.

One of the basic standards used for evaluating the Propp-based system is the coherence of a story or resulting sequence of events. One system used for breakdown and interpretation is KOSERUBE (Imabuchi et al., 2012; Akimoto et al., 2013b), an application that uses the Propp-based system as its mechanism for story generation, and can clarify problems relevant to a story's cohesion. By finding most of the results that overlap with the problems of the Propp-based system, we prepared natural language sentences generated by the mechanism within KOSERUBE. The experimenter asked the subjects (including eight university students) to identify and describe coherence problems according to categorized questions. The object of the evaluation is not the aspect of natural language description, but the aspect of logical development. The results showed problems such as "hard to understand; the meaning of an event; the reason of a character's action; the relationship between an event and the entire story." These indicate future studies.

### Incorporating into INGS

Although the Propp-based mechanism can function as an independent system, INGS can also use it as a part. PBSG and the structure generation function correspond to a story technique and its content knowledge base. This collection of information exists to define micro-story structures (such as the causal relationship) and promote the continuing relationships between events to form a partial story structure. Adversely, the Propp-based mechanism constructs macro-story structures where the names of the "functions" and other elements (with the exception of events in the PBSG hierarchy) are equivalent to the names of the relationships. Three types of method development that concern content grammar correspond to a group of story techniques capable of retrieving a tree structure from the input information. A structure built by the Propp-based mechanism can be the portion of an overall story structure that uses other approaches. Story techniques based on Propp include the top-down process, bottom-up process, and hybrid processing methods. PBSG corresponds to the knowledge to be contained in the story content knowledge base.

The Propp-based mechanism is designed to be combined simultaneously with INGS through the conceptual dictionaries. Stories in the system essentially amount to sequential events linked hierarchically by story relationships. Each event is described with a frame representation, including a verb concept and case elements with a variety of noun concepts (agent, object, and location), and is associated with conceptual hierarchy dictionaries for both verbs and nouns. Using this mechanism, the lowest level of the story content grammar addresses the same event structures.

### *Generation Example in INGS*

Incorporation of the Propp-based mechanism into INGS allows the creation of stories where the macro-development (using Propp-based story generation) and micro-development (based on other story techniques) are mixed. As indicated in Box 3 in the Appendix, such macro-story can be refined by other story techniques as the higher level of the hierarchy. Box 4 in the Appendix, shows a Propp-based macro-story inserted into the portion of a micro-sequence that does not belong to a larger structure.

## Genette-Based Mechanism

In his work on narrative discourse theory, Genette (1972) never commented on narrative generation. This study changed the theory's context using a computational perspective to create a technological method for designing or formalizing the narrative discourse generation process. This allows each of the classified techniques applied by Genette to be used as a rule for associating an input structure with a transformed output discourse structure. An "input structure" is equal to a complete story, the partial structure of a story or part of the discourse structure. Figure 12 shows an example where a story structure

*Figure 12. Transformation from story structure to discourse structure*

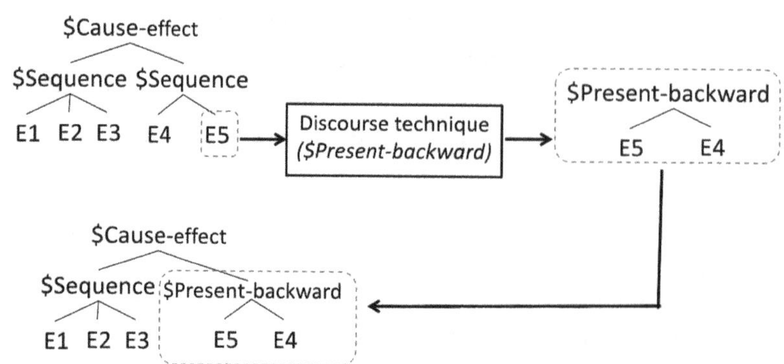

is transformed into a discourse structure; a relationship specified to discourse, "present-backward", is added to the structure. Both structures for story and discourse have similar tree forms. Each leaf node in a story's tree corresponds to an event described with conceptual representation, which is further described by a case structure that consists of one verb concept and eight types of cases, such as "agent" and "object". Each internal node in the tree is equivalent to a "relationship" such as "cause-effect" and "serial" combined with the child nodes.

A total of 13 types of discourse techniques are used currently (Table 7). Because they are related mainly to tense, the results of the narrative discourse techniques are not fully introduced. However, this research is developing a new possible direction of narratological approach to our narrative generation through connection to a Jauss-based control mechanism.

The seven types of relationship used for discourse trees are: "recall," "present-backward," "prophecy," "present-feature," "episode," "description," and "repetition_discourse." In addition, five types of procedural primitives were prepared for defining narrative discourse techniques in order to operate the internal or terminal nodes in an input structure: deletion, copy, conjunction, substitution, and creation. For example, in the operation process of the "complementary analepsis_ellipsis" technique. A past event in a discourse structure is moved to a position different from its original point in the input story.

Nine types of input parameters (satisfaction point, generation cycle, complexity, suspense, length, hiding, description, repetition, diffuseness, and implication) are prepared for the narrative discourse module (one of the major mechanism is the Genette-based mechanism). The Genette-based mechanism plays the part of discourse structure generation, and the Jauss-based mechanism controls the processing. The above parameters in are used to make one discourse structure, whereas the Jauss-based part performs circulative generation based on another control mechanism (it controls the parameters' changes).

*Table 7. Used narrative discourse techniques*

| Name | Meaning |
|---|---|
| External analepsis | Narration of past events positioned outside a story's temporal range (i.e., the events are not included in the story). |
| Complementary analepsis_ellipsis | Narration of past events lacking from the original position in a story. |
| Complementary analepsis_ paralipsis | Narration of past events lacking partially from the original position in a story. |
| Repetitive analepsis | Narration of past events repeatedly. |
| External prolepsis | Narration of prospective events positioned outside a story's temporal range (i.e., the events are not included in the story). |
| Complementary prolepsis_ellipsis | Narration of prospective events resulting in a lack from the original position in a story. |
| Complementary prolepsis_ paralipsis | Narration of prospective events resulting in partial lack from the original position in a story. |
| Repetitive prolepsis | Narration of prospective events at the original position repeatedly. |
| Achronie | Narration of events that cannot be positioned in the temporal range of a story. |
| Pause | Pause of temporal progress in a story by inserting descriptions. |
| Implicit ellipsis | Omission of one part of a story. |
| Repeating | Narrating the same events twice. |
| Paralipsis | Narration of less information than the original sequence of events that a story has. |

Boxes 5 and 6 in the Appendix show execution examples with input data. All 13 types of discourse techniques are applied. These examples commonly used a generated story in the Appendix (Box 1 and 2). Box 5 in the Appendix is a discourse that was automatically generated completely, while Box 6 is an example that was generated based on the partial intended application of techniques. Figure 13 illustrates the temporal structures with the horizontal axis corresponding to the temporal progress events ordered from 1 to 16. Connecting nodes allow the order of the discourse to be narrated. Six events not included in the input story are inserted by the discourse techniques of "external analepsis," "external prolepsis," and "achronie."

## Jauss-Based Mechanism

The application of Jauss is intended to work along with the Genette-based mechanism. Several discourse categories by Genette are elaborately formalized for transforming a story structure into a discourse structure. Jauss's reception theory is simply interpreted as a mechanism for controlling the circulative discourse construction process through the interaction between a narrator mechanism with generative parameters and narratee mechanism with expectation parameters. The two mechanisms do not define an existence beyond the system, but are virtual agents within it and are individual models in the current

*Figure 13. Temporal structure of generated discourse*

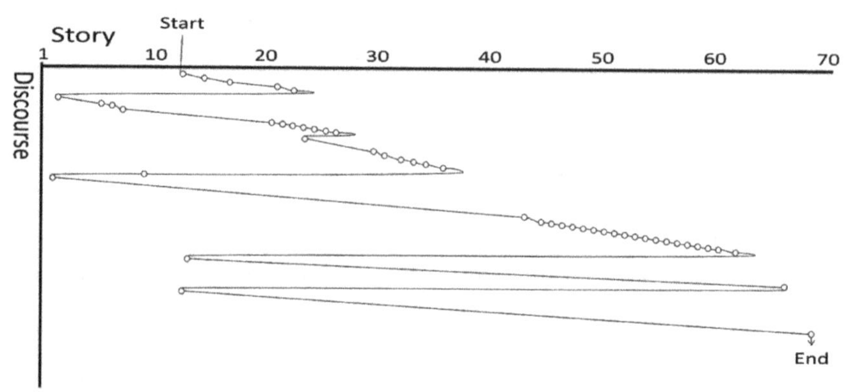


*(1) Completely automatic generation*

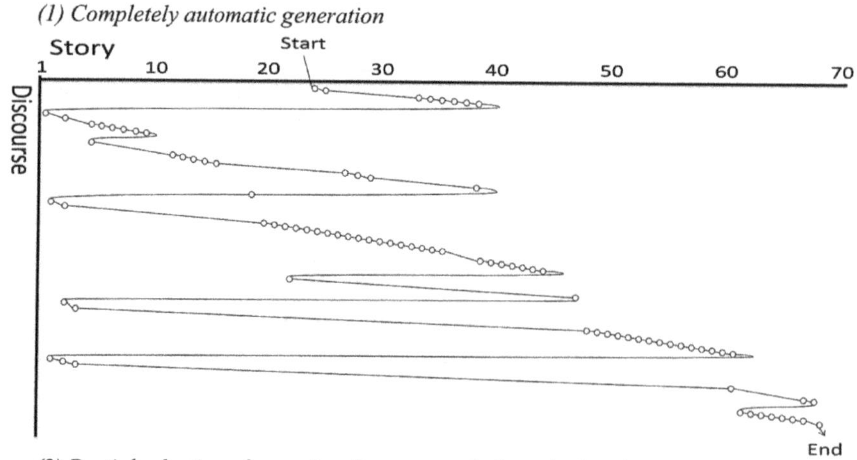


*(2) Partial selection of narrative discourse techniques by hand*

implementation. Therefore, the Jauss-based mechanism is essentially different from the Propp-based mechanism because the Genette portion uses structural processing and the Jauss section controls it. The Jauss-based control mechanism is currently applied only to the narrative discourse phase in INGS, but a future goal is the expansion of a similar mechanism to the entire range.

One of Jauss's aims was to present a new idea concerning the history of literature (Jauss, 1970). He criticized the literary theory of evolution as being dependent upon the dynamism of change in narrative techniques and descriptions. He sought to center his literary design on the dynamism of the mutual relationship between a literary work/author and the readers. Jauss developed seven types of *these* (thesis) for the essence of his reception theory. His idea involved designing the literary history of various relationships between a reader's "horizon of expectation" and literary works, including those estrangements, and the change of expectation through a continual reception process.

The Jauss-based mechanism focuses on *these II* and *these III* for describing the horizon of expectation and changing catalyst to design a Jauss-based mechanism. His *these II* describes the "horizon of expectation" as being the reader's preliminary knowledge for ranking a literary work in the context of reading experience, and it can be acquired by known genres and exposure to famous literary works. In *these III,* Jauss proposed that readers understand literary artistic features as the distance between the work and their horizon of expectation. If the distance is small, the work has strong recreational purpose and a familiar beauty. Those with a large distance have various and distinguished influences on the readers: to some the work might be highly regarded creative work, but might be a waste of time for other readers. The horizon of expectation can change so that the impression of a work becomes ordinary for a particular reader.

The author created a model of Jauss's reception theory where literary works are repeatedly produced according to a reader's expectations and the corresponding responses from an author; the interaction can continuously or historically change a literary work. In particular, texts of narrative discourse are repeatedly produced through a process according to parameters for a reader (or narratee) as the expectation and using the same parameters for an author (or narrator) as the generative goals. These parameters are same as those in the Genette-based mechanism.

The cycle continues according to the interaction between a narrator and narratee. A narrator mechanism has a set of rules for controlling the application of discourse techniques based on the generative parameters to transform a discourse structure. The direct transformation of a discourse structure is conducted using techniques defined by Genette's theory. A narratee mechanism evaluates the results by comparing the narratee's expectation parameters with the narrator's generative parameters. In the next cycle, the narrator applies corrections according to the narratee's evaluation in order to achieve reader satisfaction. The process, however, eventually reaches a point where the narratee becomes tired or his/her satisfaction begins to fall. When this happens, "deviation" occurs and the narrator abandons a portion of the old generative parameters and moves to a new cycle of discourse grounded on the newly found strategy. The narratee's expectations change according to the reconstruction.

Figure 14 is a detailed process flow of the narrative discourse control based on the interaction between the narrator and narratee mechanisms. As seen in (1), the system selects the corr esponding techniques according to the parameter values. In (2), the Genette-based techniques fulfill the functions in the context of the Jauss-based control. In (3), higher satisfaction can be obtained when a more strongly desired parameter is satisfied. The narratee indicates one parameter with the lowest satisfaction. In (4), the narratee rewrites an expectation parameter through two different procedures. The first rewrites the

*Figure 14. Overview of interaction between narrator and narratee*

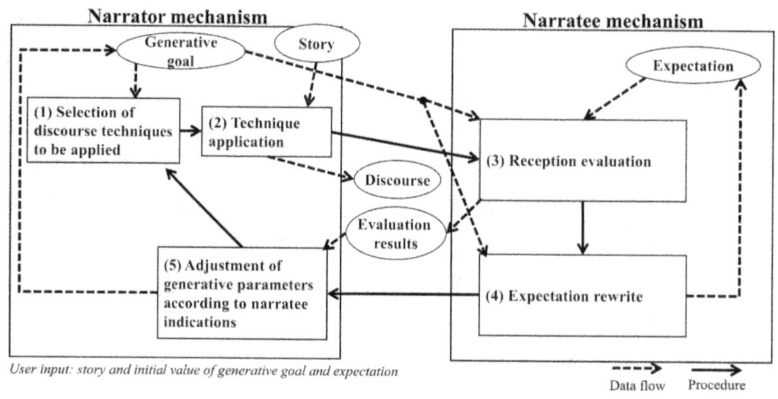


sufficiency number and degree of desire. The former is increased each time the narratee receives the sufficed discourse. Finally, (5) includes "deviation" from the expectation. See (Akimoto & Ogata, 2012, 2014a) in detail.

## Future Plans for INGS

The design and development of INGS will continue in the following directions:

- **Continual System Development for INGS:**
    1. **Direction to Narrative Generation Control:** The basic orientations are that the system admits various types of input information for each generation module, and allows the flexible flow of generation order in connection to the concept of "circulative control".
    2. **Content Knowledge for Generation:** A central work in the next step is related to the aspect of content, which is the knowledge to be used, especially outside of the dictionaries for concepts and words. The main parts contain narrative paternalized knowledge, such as scripts and story grammar for story generation and property knowledge for the noun conceptual dictionary. This knowledge acquisition is related to the next automatic functions.
    3. **Knowledge Acquisition and Learning Mechanisms:** As the content knowledge becomes large, it is particularly necessary to automatically acquire knowledge using formal and semantic methods. This theme also includes automatic data acquisition using statistical analysis methods to control or adjust the use of conceptual knowledge.
    4. **Natural Language Generation:** This includes formal processing and semantic processing. The latter needs the previous various content knowledge. In INGS, the property knowledge for the noun conceptual dictionary provides the main content knowledge for the natural language generation. Hence, this topic is associated to points (b) and (c).
    5. **GIS or Web Business-Like Narrative Interface and Distribution System:** GIS is not only an application system of INGS, but it is also an extension of INGS to connect it to a social framework for the production and distribution of generated narratives; GIS is designed to contain one or more INGS.

- **ELT:** This part should discuss to introduce the previous narratology and literary theories into the INGS system. First, previously analyzed literary theories, such as Bakthin, Freud, Kristeva, or intertextuality, will be applied into various sides of the narrative generation. In addition, other important literary theories, such as Barthes, Levi-Straus, and especially Japanese theories and narratology, will be incoprated as a cultural approach into INGS.
- **Extending ELT:**
    1. **Circulative Narrative Control:** The author will extend and elaborate this concept and more concretely apply it to the INGS system. Perfectly free processing order among the modules will also be related to *fluidity and fixation.*
    2. **Norm–Deviation:** In the relative sense, each cycle of narrative generation corresponds to a system of the deviation from the current state (norm). In particular, preliminarily constructed scripts and dictionaries correspond to the norm, whereas various rhetorical techniques perform the deviation. For the entire INGS, the author seeks to consider the application of this concept.
    3. **Fluidity–Fixation:** For instance, the Jauss-based mechanism indicates one of the future directions. Namely, the circulative process that corresponds to the fluidity and user-viewing of one or more generated results is equivalent to fixation.
- **Multiple Narrative Structures:** The current INGS does not reflect the concept of multiple narrative structures model. Although the model has various aspects, the author, as stated in Narrative Analyses, has considered model-making through a novel by Mishima (1963). In order to introduce INGS, the system requires each character agent to be actualized as a system, and the entirety of the narrative generation system should be actualized as the synthesis of each narrative generation system.
- **Plans for Social and Individual Development:**
    1. **Social Narrative Distribution:** This topic means that narratives produced by a narrative generation system, which include narratives by the collaboration with humans, and the narrative generation system itself are connected to society—the outside of the system. Although one of the typical forms is business, there are other possibilities. "Virtual publishing" and "virtual entertainment production" (by GIS) also show images for introducing the aspect of business into narrative generation systems. This is at the most outside field of a multiple narrative generation framework by the author.
    2. **"My (the Author's)" Narratives Creation:** This concept means narratives based on one's private themes and materials. The INGS system introduces private content into the knowledge content. In particular, INGS introduces private knowledge content into the story content knowledge base and other content knowledge bases.
- **Evaluating Narrative Generation Systems:** The author draws attention to the problem of evaluating narrative generation systems. As a general tendency, the evaluation of narrative generation systems has consisted of quantitative and qualitative evaluations. Quantitative evaluation, in the major methods, is based on certain standards. The evaluator shows the generation results to the subjects, obtains answers, and adds the score. For instance, Peinado and Gervás (2006), in the evaluation of a story generation system based on case-based reasoning, proposed three types of stories to their subjects: an example, story where the example is transformed randomly, and story where the example is transformed using the proposed method. The evaluator added the scores for linguistic quality, consistency, interestingness, and novelty using a number from zero to ten for

each. By contrast, in the major method of qualitative evaluation, users (subjects) utilize the system or see the generated results, and describe their opinions. The evaluator then discusses the results with them based on their opinions. Sharma, Ontañón, Mehta, and Ram (2007), in an interactive storytelling system, discussed acquired descriptions, such as "[t]he system can improve the experience of unskilled players", according to the description of players' actions and interviews that concerned the proposed system. That which is evaluated in narrative generation systems or generated narratives is too difficult to accurately answer. First, evaluating narrative, literature, and arts related to narrative generation systems is extremely difficult because of the difficulty involved in finding or deciding upon a universal or versatile standard of values. In literary history, for example, we often see the phenomenon whereby a literary work previously overlooked because of the popularity of contemporary works is subsequently highly regarded. However, yet another different evaluation of the work may appear and gain influence. We can thus safely claim that evaluation standards are pluralistic. Moreover, if we evaluate each narrative generation system and its generated narratives by making clear an effective standard from the perspective of a specified aim, we will be able to acquire meaningful results and insights. Rowe et al. (2009) considered the problem of the evaluation of narrative generation systems and proposed a multiple-evaluation framework that consists of the following four perspectives:

1. Narrative metrics,
2. Director-centric studies,
3. Cognitive-affective studies, and
4. Extrinsic narrative evaluations. The framework contains standards that concern both generated narrative content and methods and techniques of the target narrative generation system. This proposal also suggests that evaluative components for artistic and literary aspects are necessary in addition to academic aspects in future narrative generation systems.

The study of narrative generation systems is a proper field of research and development. However, this field does not form an established technology. The author ought to avoid the prediction and assertion from a perspective according to simple and monistic standards. For instance, the author can image that both the direction and possibilities of "a narrative generation system creates narratives in itself" and "a narrative generation system supports our narrative creation", but does not necessarily think that these are completely antinomy. The author will be able to generate stories of the sublation and unification of both direction and concept. For example, the author can design narrative works by blending the parts of automatic generation by a system with parts of human creation. Likewise, it is possible to design an integrated system of art and business, such as an artistic practice supported by narrative generation systems for a publishing business. As the author has seen in this article, future possibilities for narrative generation connected with human vision, imagination, and creativity are necessary for truly interesting progress in the field.

## CONCLUSION

This chapter introduced interdisciplinary approaches to primarily AI-based computational narrative generation systems by way of introducing cognitive science, narratology, and related literary theories. First, the author presented an original research framework for narrative and narrative generation to explain narratological theories, computational and cognitive narrative-relating theories and systems, and previous narrative generation systems. The last half of the paper described, in relative detail, a systematic approach to narrative generation by the author. Fundamental ideas and concepts for narrative generation research were described, as well as an overall architecture of the current ongoing version of an integrated narrative generation system called INGS. One of the aims of INGS is to incorporate narratological theories and methods into several parts, and is in this sense, a practice of ELT, which is one of the fundamental concepts.

## ACKNOWLEDGMENT

This work was supported by JSPS KAKENHI Grant Number 26330258.

## REFERENCES

Abe, H., Ogata, T., & Onodera, K. (2009). An analysis of products introducing rhetoric in advertising and the prototype system implementation. In *Proceedings of the 23rd Annual Conference of the Japanese Society for Artificial Intelligence* (1J1-OS2-4). Takamatsu, Japan: Academic Press.

Akaishi, M. (2006). A dynamic de-composition/re-composition framework for documents based on narrative structure model. *Transactions of the Japanese Society for Artificial Intelligence*, *21*(5), 428–438. doi:10.1527/tjsai.21.428

Akimoto, T., Endo, J., & Ogata, T. (2013a). The expansion of paths in the mutual transformation mechanism of music and narrative. *International Journal of Cognitive Informatics and Natural Intelligence*, *7*(4), 44–63. doi:10.4018/ijcini.2013100103

Akimoto, T., Imabuchi, S., Endo, J., Ono, J., Kurisawa, Y., Kamada, M., & Ogata, T. (2013b). Development of a generation/expression system of narratives in the style of a folk tale, KOSERUBE Version 1. *Transactions of the Japanese Society for Artificial Intelligence*, *28*(5), 442–456. doi:10.1527/tjsai.28.442

Akimoto, T., Kurisawa, Y., & Ogata, T. (2013c). A mechanism for managing the progression of events by states in integrated narrative generation system. In *Proceedings of the 2nd International Conference on Engineering and Applied Science* (pp. 1605-1614). Tokyo, Japan: Academic Press.

Akimoto, T., & Ogata, T. (2010). Implementing a narrative discourse system as a mechanism in narrative generation: A hybrid approach of AI and narratology. In *Proceedings of the 7th International Conference on Cognitive Science* (pp. 359-360). Beijing, China: Academic Press.

Akimoto, T., & Ogata, T. (2012). A narratological approach for narrative discourse: Implementation and evaluation of the system based on Genette and Jauss. In *Proceedings of the 34th Annual Conference of the Cognitive Science Society* (pp. 1272-1277). Sapporo, Japan: Academic Press.

Akimoto, T., & Ogata, T. (2014a). An information design of narratology: The use of three literary theories in a narrative generation system. *The International Journal of Visual Design*, *7*(3), 31–61.

Akimoto, T., & Ogata, T. (2014b). Circulative narrative generation based on the mutual transformation between narrative conceptual structures and music in the integrated narrative generation system. *Journal of Robotics. Networking and Artificial Life*, *1*(3), 198–202. doi:10.2991/jrnal.2014.1.3.6

Akimoto, T., & Ogata, T. (2015a). Evaluation of a narrative discourse generation system based on the concept of "norm and deviation". *Journal of Robotics. Networking and Artificial Life*, *2*(1), 50–53. doi:10.2991/jrnal.2015.2.1.12

Akimoto, T., & Ogata, T. (2015b). Experimental development of a focalization mechanism in an integrated narrative generation system. *Journal of Artificial Intelligence and Soft Computing Research*, *5*(3), 177–188. doi:10.1515/jaiscr-2015-0027

Akimoto, T., Ono, J., & Ogata, T. (2012). Narrative Forest: An automatic narrative generation system with a visual narrative operation mechanism. In *Proceedings of the 6th International Conference on Soft Computing and Intelligent Systems & the 13th International Symposium on Advanced Intelligent Systems* (pp. 2164-2167). Kobe, Japan. doi:10.1109/SCIS-ISIS.2012.6505319

Alani, H., Kim, S., Millard, D. E., & Weal, M. J. (2003). Automatic ontology-based knowledge extraction and tailored biography generation from the Web. *IIIE Intelligent Systems,* 14-21.

Amino, T., Kawamura, Y., & Ogata, T. (2002). Hierarchical generation of *geino*-idol stories: Toward *geino* information system and narrative marketing. In *Proceedings of 17th Congress of the International Association of Empirical Aesthetics* (pp. 549-552). Takarazuka, Japan: Academic Press.

Aristotle. (1895). The poetics of Aristotle (S. H. Butcher, Trans.). London, UK: Macmillan; Retrieved from https://archive.org/details/poeticstranslate00arisuoft

Aruga, H., & Ogata, T. (1998). Structural analysis of tragic story and formalization of general rules. In *Proceedings of the 12rd Annual Conference of the Japanese Society for Artificial Intelligence* (pp. 697-700). Tokyo, Japan: Academic Press.

Bae, B. C., Cheong, Y. G., & Young, M. R. (2011). Automated story generation with multiple internal focalization. In *Proceedings of 2011 IEEE Conference on Computational Intelligence and Games* (pp. 211-218). Seoul, South Korea. doi:10.1109/CIG.2011.6032009

Bakhtin, M. (1984). *Problems of Dostoevsky's poetics* (C. Emerson, Trans.). MN: University of Minnesota Press. (Original work published 1963)

Bal, M. (2004). *Narrative theory: Critical concepts in literary and cultural studies* (Vol. I-IV). Routledge.

Barber, H. (2008). *Generator of adaptive dilemma-based interactive narratives* (Thesis). Department of Computer Science. The University of York, York, UK.

Barry, P. (2009). *Beginning theory: An introduction to literary and cultural theory* (3rd ed.). Manchester, UK: Manchester University Press.

Barthes, R., & Duisit, L. (1975). An introduction to the structural analysis of narrative (L. Duisit, Trans.). *New Literary History*, *6*(2), 237–272. doi:10.2307/468419

Bartlett, F. C. (1923). *Psychology and primitive culture.* London: Cambridge University Press.

Bers, M. U. (1999). Narrative construction kit: "Who am I? Who are you? What are you?". *Narrative Intelligence: Papers from the 1999 AAAI Fall Symposium, Technical Report* (FS-99-01, pp. 44-52), North Falmouth, Massachusetts.

Bolter, J. D. (1991). *Writing space: The computer, hypertext and the history of writing*. Lawrence Erlbaum.

Booth, W. C. (1983). *The rhetoric of fiction*. Chicago: University of Chicago Press. doi:10.7208/chicago/9780226065595.001.0001

Brecht, B. (1964). *Brecht on theatre: The development of an aesthetics* (J. Willett, Trans. & Ed.). London: Methuen. (Original work published 1950)

Breton, A. (1969). *Manifestoes of surrealism*. Ann Arbor, MI: University of Michigan Press. (Original work published 1924)

Bringsjord, S., & Ferrucci, D. A. (1999). *Artificial intelligence and literary creativity: Inside the mind of BRUTUS, a storytelling machine*. Lawrence Erlbaum.

Bruner, J. (2003). *Making stories: Law, literature, life*. Cambridge, MA: Harvard University Press.

Callaway, C. B., & Lester, J. C. (2002). Narrative prose generation. *Artificial Intelligence*, *139*(2), 213–252. doi:10.1016/S0004-3702(02)00230-8

Chatman, S. (1980). *Story and discourse: Narrative structure in fiction and film*. Cornell University Press.

Cheong, Y. G., & Young, R. M. (2015). Suspenser: A story generation system for suspense. *IEEE Transactions on Computational Intelligence and AI in Games*, *7*(1), 39–52. doi:10.1109/TCIAIG.2014.2323894

Compagnon, A. (1998). *Le demon de la theorie: Litterature et sens commun*. Paris: Seul.

Danto, A. C. (1965). *Analytical philosophy of history*. London: Cambridge University Press.

Davis, R., & Lenat, D. B. (1982). *Knowledge-based systems in artificial intelligence*. New York, NY: MkGraw-Hill.

Dundes, A. (1965). *The study of folklore*. Prentice Hall.

Dyer, M. G. (1983). *In-depth understanding: A computer model of integrated processing for narrative comprehension*. Cambridge, MA: MIT Press.

Elson, D. K., & McKeown, K. R. (2007). A platform for symbolically encoding human narratives. In *Intelligent Narrative Technologies: Papers from the 2007 AAAI Fall Symposium, Technical Report* (FS-07-05).

Endo, Y., & Ogata, T. (2002). Hyper-comic system as representation field of narrative discourse. In *Proceedings of 17th Congress of the International Association of Empirical Aesthetics* (pp. 555-558). Takarazuka, Japan: Academic Press.

Endo, Y., & Ogata, T. (2003). Hyper-comic system as consideration of rhetoric. In *Proceedings of The 4th International Conference on Cognitive Science* (pp. 111-116). Sydney, Australia: Academic Press.

Endo, Y., & Ogata, T. (2004a). A rhetorical analysis of a Japanese comic for hyper-comic system. In *Proceedings of 18th Congress of the International Association of Empirical Aesthetics* (pp. 502-508). Lisbon, Portugal: Academic Press.

Endo, Y., & Ogata, T. (2004b). Multilayered discourse in hyper-comic. In *Proceedings of the Ninth International Symposium on Artificial Life and Robotics* (*Vol.1*, pp. 49-52). Beppu, Japan: Academic Press.

Fendt, M. W., & Young, R. M. (2014). Adapting IRIS, a non-interactive narrative generation system, to an interactive text adventure game. In *Proceedings of the 27th International Florida Artificial Intelligence Research Society Conference* (pp. 244-249). Pensacola Beach, CA: Academic Press.

Freedman, J., & Comb, G. (1996). *Narrative therapy: The social construction of preferred realities*. Haddon Craftsmen.

Freud, S. (1900). *Die traumdeutung*. Leipzig, Wien: Franz Deuticke.

Gavins, J., & Steen, G. (Eds.). (2003). *Cognitive poetics in practice*. Routledge. doi:10.4324/9780203417737

Genette, G. (1972). Narrative discourse: An essay in method (J. E. Lewin, Trans.). Cornell University Press.

Genette, G. (1982). *Palimpsestes: la littérature au second degré*. Paris: Seuil.

Gervás, P. (2013a). Stories from games: Content and focalization selection in narrative composition. In *Proceedings of I Spanish Symposium on Entertainment Computing*. Madrid, Spain: Academic Press.

Gervás, P. (2013b). Propp's morphology of the folk tale as a grammar for generation. In *Proceedings of 2013 Workshop on Computational Models of Narrative* (pp. 106-122). Hamburg, Germany: Academic Press.

Gervás, P., Lönneker-Rodman, B., Meister, J. C., & Peinado, F. (2006). Narrative models: Narratology meets artificial intelligence. In *Proceedings of Satellite Workshop: Toward Computational Models of Literary Analysis, 5th International Conference on Language Resources and Evaluation* (pp. 44-51). Genoa, Italy: Academic Press.

Grasbon, D., & Braun, N. (2001). A morphological approach to interactive storytelling. In *Proceedings of CAST 2001, Living in Mixed Realities: Conference on Artistic, Cultural and Scientific Aspects of Experimental Media Spaces* (pp. 337-340). Sankt Augustin, Germany: Academic Press.

Greimas, A. J. (1966). Sémantique structurrale: recherché de method. Paris: Larousse.

Hartsook, K., Zook, A., Das, S., & Riedl, M. O. (2011). Toward supporting stories with procedurally generated game worlds. In *Proceedings of 2011 IEEE Conference on Computational Intelligence and Games* (pp. 297-304). Seoul, South Korea. doi:10.1109/CIG.2011.6032020

Hasumi, S. (1985). *Monogatari hihan josetsu* [An introduction to narrative criticism]. Tokyo: Chuokoronsha.

Hecht, B., Starosielski, N., & Dora-Abrams, D. (2007). Generating educational tourism narratives from Wikipedia. In *Intelligent Narrative Technologies: Papers from the 2007 AAAI Fall Symposium, Technical Report* (FS-07-05, pp. 37-44), Arlington, Virginia.

Herman, D. (2000). Narratology as a cognitive science. *Image and Narrative, 1*(1).

Herman, D. (2003). *Narrative theory and the cognitive sciences*. CSLI.

Hobbs, J. R. (1990). *Literature and cognition*. CSLI.

Hori, K. (2005). Do knowledge assets really exist in the world and can we access such knowledge?: Knowledge evolves through a cycle of knowledge liquidization and crystallization. *Lecture Notes in Computer Science, 3359*, 1–13. doi:10.1007/978-3-540-32279-5_1

Hori, K. (2007). *Sozo katsudo shien no riron to oyo* [Theories and applications of creativity support]. Tokyo: Ohmsha.

Hosaka, Y., & Ogata, T. (2002). Story generation based on narratology and representation with CG animation. In *Proceedings of 17th Congress of the International Association of Empirical Aesthetics* (pp. 561-564). Takarazuka, Japan: Academic Press.

Hoshino, J. (2004). Storytelling and AI. *Transactions of the Japanese Society for Artificial Intelligence, 19*(1), 29–34.

Hovy, E. H. (1993). Automated discourse generation using discourse structure relations. *Artificial Intelligence, 63*(1-2), 341–386. doi:10.1016/0004-3702(93)90021-3

Imabuchi, S., Akimoto, T., Ono, J., & Ogata, T. (2012). KOSERUBE: An application system with a Propp-based story grammar and other narrative generation techniques. In *Proceedings of the 6th International Conference on Soft Computing and Intelligent Systems & the 13th International Symposium on Advanced Intelligent Systems* (pp. 248-253). Kyoto, Japan. doi:10.1109/SCIS-ISIS.2012.6505320

Imabuchi, S., & Ogata, T. (2012). *A story generation system based on Propp theory: As a mechanism in an integrated narrative generation system. Lecture Notes in Artificial Intelligence* (Vol. 7614, pp. 312–321). Berlin, Germany: Springer.

Imabuchi, S., & Ogata, T. (2013). Lecture Notes in Computer Science: Vol. 8210. *Methods for generalizing the Propp-based story generation mechanism* (pp. 333–344). Berlin, Germany: Springer. doi:10.1007/978-3-319-02750-0_36

Imabuchi, S., & Ogata, T. (2014). Integrating the event generation mechanism in the Propp-based story generation mechanism into the integrated narrative generation system. *Journal of Robotics. Networking and Artificial Life, 1*(2), 164–168. doi:10.2991/jrnal.2014.1.2.14

Ishii, K., & Ogata, T. (1998). A study on the methodology of hypertext novels based on a prototyping. In *Proceedings of the 12th Annual Conference of the Japanese Society for Artificial Intelligence* (pp.701-702). Tokyo, Japan: Academic Press.

Ishizaki, S. (1988). Generating Japanese text from conceptual representation. In D. D. McDonald & L. Bole (Eds.), *Natural language generation system* (pp. 256–279). Springer-Verlag. doi:10.1007/978-1-4612-3846-1_7

Jauss, H. R. (1970). Literaturgeschichte als provokation. Frankfurt am Main: Suhrkamp Verlag.

Jhale, A., & Young, M. R. (2010). Cinematic visual discourse: Representation, generation, and evaluation. *IEEE Transactions on Computational Intelligence and A.I. in Games, 2*(2), 69-81.

Kanai, A. (2006). Reality of unfamiliar situations on moving image. In *Proceedings of 19th Congress of the International Association of Empirical Aesthetics* (pp. 800-803). Avignon, France: Academic Press.

Kanai, A., & Kodama, K. (2010). Film edit design: Story and irrational cutting. *Cognitive Studies, 17*(3), 444–458.

Kanai, A., & Ogata, T. (2004a). Aspect of non-story processing and film rhetoric composition in the narrative generation mechanism. In *Proceedings of the Ninth International Symposium on Artificial Life and Robotics* (pp. 162-165). Beppu, Japan: Academic Press.

Kanai, A., & Ogata, T. (2004b). Non-story processing on the film rhetoric composition system. In *Proceedings of 18th Congress of the International Association of Empirical Aesthetics* (pp. 433-436). Lisbon, Portugal: Academic Press.

Kanai, A., Ogata, T., & Shinohara, K. (2002). Film rhetoric generation system for intensive cognitive system. In *Proceedings of IEEE International Conference on Systems, Man and Cybernetics (CD-ROM)*. Yasmine Hammamet, Tunisia: IEEE.

Karatani, K. (1993). *Origins of modern Japanese literature*. Durham, UK: Duke University Press. (Original work published 1980)

Kawamura, Y., & Ogata, T. (1997). The generation process of entertainment character image. In *Proceedings of the International Conference on Cognitive Science* (pp. 293-294). Seoul, South Korea: Academic Press.

Kawamura, Y., & Ogata, T. (2000). A conceptual framework on *geino* organization model for artificial *geino* performers with lives. In *Proceedings of the Fifth International Symposium on Artificial Life and Robotics* (pp. 793-796). Oita, Japan: Academic Press.

Kawamura, Y., & Ogata, T. (2002). A Trial on Narrative Interpretation of Geino Information System. In *Proceedings of IEEE, International Conference on Systems, Man and Cybernetics (CD-ROM)*. Yasmine Hammamet, Tunisia. doi:10.1109/ICSMC.2002.1175727

Kawatake, T. (2003). *Kabuki: Baroque fusion of the arts (F. & J., Connel Hoff, Trans.)*. Tokyo, Japan: The International House of Japan.

Kayamori, O., & Ogata, T. (2003). Analysis and scenario generation of TVCFs based on the relations between story and brand. In *Proceedings of the 17th Annual Conference of the Japanese Society for Artificial Intelligence* (2G2-06). Niigata, Japan: Academic Press.

Klein, S., Aeschlimann, J. F., Appelbaum, M. A., Balsiger, D. F., Curtis, E. J., Foster, M., & Salsieder, D. F. etal. (1974). *Modeling Propp and Levi-Strauss in a meta-symbolic simulation system. Computer Sciences Technical Report, 226*. Madison, WI: University of Wisconsin.

Kobayashi, F., & Ogata, T. (2004a). Narrative and music as variation: Transformation of musical structure based on narrative discourse theory. In *Proceedings of the Ninth International Symposium on Artificial Life and Robotics* (*Vol.1*, pp. 170-173). Beppu, Japan: Academic Press.

Kobayashi, F., & Ogata, T. (2004b). A musical variation system by the structural correspondence between music and narrative. In *Proceedings of 18th Congress of the International Association of Empirical Aesthetics* (pp. 555-559). Takarazuka, Japan: Academic Press.

Kristeva, J. (1980). *Desire in language: A semiotic approach to literature and art.* NY: Columbia University Press. (Original work published 1969)

Kumagai, S., Funakoshi, S., Akimoto, T., & Ogata, T. (2012). Development of a language dictionary and a simple narrative sentence generation mechanism. In *Proceedings of the 26th Annual Conference of the Japanese Society for Artificial Intelligence* (1N1-OS-1a-3). Yamaguchi, Japan: Academic Press.

Kurisawa, Y., & Ogata, T. (2013). A consideration of a norm-deviation mechanism in the integrated narrative generation system. *Proceedings of Language Sense Engineering Research Group in Japanese Artificial Intelligence Society, 44*, 25–35.

Lakoff, G. P. (1972). Structural complexity in fairy tales. *The Study of Man, 1*, 124.

Lang, R. R. (1999). A declarative model for simple narratives. In *Narrative intelligence: Papers from the 1999 AAAI fall symposium, Technical Report* (FS-99-01, pp. 134-141), North Falmouth, Massachusetts.

Laurel, B. (2013). *Computers as theatre* (2nd ed.). Boston: Addison-Wesley Professional.

Lebowitz, M. (1985). Story-telling as planning and learning. *Poetics, 14*(6), 483–502. doi:10.1016/0304-422X(85)90015-4

Lerdahl, F., & Jackendoff, R. (1983). *A generative theory of tonal music.* Cambridge, MA: MIT Press.

Lévi-Strauss, C. (1964). *Mythologiques 1: Le cru et le cuit.* Paris: PLON.

Li, B., & Riedl, M. O. (2010). An offline planning approach to game plotline adaptation. In *6th Conference on Artificial Intelligence for Interactive Digital Entertainment* (pp. 45-50). Stanford, CA: Academic Press.

Li, B., & Riedl, M. O. (2015). Scheherazade: Crowd-powered interactive narrative generation. In *Proceedings of the 29th AAAI conference on artificial intelligence* (pp. 4305-4306). Austin, TX: Academic Press.

Lönneker-Rodman, B. (2005). Narratological knowledge for natural language generation. In *Proceedings of the 10th European Workshop on Natural Language Generation* (pp. 91-100). Aberdeen, Scotland: Academic Press.

Lyotard, J-F. (1979). *La condition post moderne.* Paris: Les edition de Minuit.

Magerko, B. S. (2006). *Player modeling in the interactive drama architecture.* (Ph.D. thesis). University of Michigan, Ann Arbor, MI.

Mateas, M., & Sengers, P. (Eds.). (2003). *Narrative intelligence.* Amsterdam: John Benjamins Publishing. doi:10.1075/aicr.46

Matsuoka, S. (1992). Narrative archetypes and media. In *Proceedings of Interactive AI Symposium 92 Nagoya: New Paradigm for Artificial Intelligence-AI in Media Space-* (pp. 61-66). Nagoya, Japan: Academic Press.

Meehan, J. R. (1980). *The metanovel: Writing stories by computer.* Garland Publishing.

Meister, J. C. (2003). *Computing action: A narratological approach.* Walter de Gruyter.

Min, W., Ha, E. Y., Rowe, J., Mott, B., & Lester, J. (2014). Deep learning-based goal recognition in open-ended digital games. In *Proceedings on 10th Annual Conference of Artificial Intelligence and Interactive Digital Entertainment* (pp. 27-43). Santa Cruz, CA: Academic Press.

Minsky, M. (1975). A framework for representing knowledge. In P. H. Winston (Ed.), *The psychology of computer vision*. McGraw-Hill.

Minsky, M. (1988). *The society of mind.* Touchstone Books.

Mishima, Y. (1963). *Gogo no eiko* [The sailor who fell from grace with the sea]. Tokyo: Kodansha.

Mizoguchi, R. (2005). *Ontoroji kogaku* [Ontology engineering]. Tokyo: Ohmsha.

Montfort, N. (2007). *Generating narrative variation in interactive fiction.* (Doctoral dissertation). University of Pennsylvania, Philadelphia, PA.

Morita, H. (2006). Literary hyper-text conversion: Applications of comuter aided text analysis. In *Proceedings of the 19th Congress of the International Association of Empirical Aesthetics* (pp. 401-405). Avignon, France: Academic Press.

Mueller, E. T. (1990). *Daydreaming in humans and machines.* Ablex.

Mueller, E. T. (2007). Understanding goal-based stories through model finding and planning. In *Intelligent Narrative Technologies: Papers from the 2007 AAAI Fall Symposium, Technical Report* (FS-07-05, pp. 95-101), Arlington, Virginia.

Mukoyama, K., Shinohara, K., Kanai, A., & Ogata, T. (2002). Rhetorical analysis and automatic editing of the film. In *Proceedings of 17th Congress of the International Association of Empirical Aesthetics* (pp. 571-574). Takarazuka, Japan: Academic Press.

Nakashima, H. (2006). Constructive informatics and AI. *Transactions of the Japanese Society for Artificial Intelligence, 21*(6), 502–513. doi:10.1527/tjsai.21.502

Nakashima, M., & Ogata, T. (2006). Narrative generation system and intertextuality: A consideration on the concept and prototype systems. In *Proceedings of the 20th Annual Conference of the Japanese Society for Artificial Intelligence* (2E2-2). Tokyo, Japan: Academic Press.

Natsume, S. (2007). *Bungaku ron (I, II)* [Literary theory]. Iwanami Shoten. (Original work published 1907)

Newell, A., & Simon, H. A. (1972). *Human problem solving*. Prentice Hall.

Noma, T., Kai, K., Nakamura, J., & Okada, N. (1992). Translating from natural language story to computer animation. In *Proceedings of First Singapore International Conference on Intelligent Systems 92* (pp. 475-480). Singapore: Academic Press.

Oda, J. (2007). Re-reinvestigation of Raimundus Lullus on creativity. *Proceedings of Language Sense Engineering Research Group in Japanese Artificial Intelligence Society, 26*, 47–51.

Oe, K. (1979). *Dojidai ge-mu* [The game of contemporaneity]. Tokyo: Shinchosha.

Ogata, T. (1995). *Narrative generation: An approach based on techniques and strategies for narrative.* (Ph.D thesis). The University of Tokyo, Tokyo, Japan.

Ogata, T. (1999). An attempt for systematization of narrative discourse theory from the viewpoint of narrative generation system. *Proceedings of IPSJ SIG Computers and the Humanities*, *99*(85), 31–38.

Ogata, T. (2002). Expanded literary theory: Cognitive/computational expansion of literary theories and narratology. In *Proceedings of 17th Congress of the International Association of Empirical Aesthetics* (pp. 163-166). Takarazuka, Japan: Academic Press.

Ogata, T. (2004). A computational approach to literary and narrative production: Toward computational narratology. In *Proceedings of 18th Congress of the International Association of Empirical Aesthetics* (pp. 509-516). Lisbon, Portugal: Academic Press.

Ogata, T. (2007). To the rhetoric of story from Propp: Centering around the rhetoric of de-composition and re-composition. *Cognitive Studies*, *14*(4), 532–558.

Ogata, T. (2011). Narrative generation system as the practice of "informatics of narratology.". *Journal of Japan Society for Fazzy Theory and Intelligent Informatics*, *23*(5), 14–24.

Ogata, T. (2014). Expanded literary theory for automatic narrative generation. In *Proceedings of Joint 7th International Conference on Soft Computing and Intelligent Systems and 15th International Symposium on Advanced Intelligent Systems* (pp. 1558-1563). Kitakyushu, Japan: Academic Press.

Ogata, T. (2015). Building conceptual dictionaries for an integrated narrative generation system. *Journal of Robotics. Networking and Artificial Life*, *1*(4), 270–284. doi:10.2991/jrnal.2015.1.4.6

Ogata, T., Hori, K., & Ohsuga, S. (1994). Towards narrative text generation based on narrative techniques and strategies. In Proceedings of International Federation for Information and Documentation (pp. 296-300). Saitama, Japan: Academic Press.

Ogata, T., Hori, K., & Ohsuga, S. (1995). A basic framework of narrative generation system as creative interface. In Y. Anzai, K. Ogawa, & H. Mori (Eds.), *Symbiosis of human and artifact (20A)* (pp. 679–684). Elsevier. doi:10.1016/S0921-2647(06)80107-3

Ogata, T., Hori, K., & Ohsuga, S. (1996a). A basic framework for narrative conceptual structure generation based on narrative techniques and strategies. *Journal of the Japanese Society for Artificial Intelligence*, *11*(1), 148–159.

Ogata, T., Hori, K., & Ohsuga, S. (1996b). An analysis of narrative structure and generation process for narrative generation system. *Cognitive Studies*, *3*(1), 72–109.

Ogata, T., & Hosaka, Y. (2004). Transformation of story in the story generation system based on narratology. In *Proceedings of the Ninth International Symposium on Artificial Life and Robotics* (*Vol. 2*, pp. 593-596). Lisbon, Portugal: Academic Press.

Ogata, T., & Kanai, A. (2010). *An introduction to informatics of narratology: Towards the thoughts and technologies of narrative generation*. Tokyo, Japan: Gakubunsha.

Ogata, T., & Ono, J. (2013). Designing narrative interface with a function of narrative generation. In *Proceeding of the 2013 International Conference on Cyberworlds* (pp. 214-221). Yokohama, Japan. doi:10.1109/CW.2013.74

Ogata, T., Tachibana, S., & Tomite, S. (2009). Animated movie generation from narrative conceptual representation and the automatic camerawork: Analysis and simulation of "Tokyo Story." In *Proceedings of the 26th Annual Meeting of the Japanese Cognitive Science Society* (P2-32). Yokohama, Japan: Academic Press.

Ogata, T., & Terano, T. (1991). Explanation-based narrative generation using semiotic theory. In *Proceedings of Natural Language Processing Pacific Rim Symposium* (pp. 321-328). Singapore: Academic Press.

Ogata, T., & Terano, T. (1992). Plot generation and expansion in explanation-based narrative generator. In *Proceedings of First Singapore International Conference on Intelligent Systems* (pp. 549-554). Singapore: Academic Press.

Ogata, T., Watanabe, K., Hori, K., & Ohsuga, S. (1995). A basic framework of the application of narrative generation system for integrated support of marketing/advertisement. *Journal of the Japan Society for Management Information*, *4*(1), 19–42.

Ogata, T., & Yamakage, S. (2004). A computational mechanism of the "distance" in narrative: A trial in the expansion of literary theory. In *Proceedings of the 8th World Multiconference on Systemics, Cybernetics and Informatics* (pp. 179-184). Orlando, FL: Academic Press.

Ogata, T., & Yazawa, K. (1999). Bakhtin literary theory and structure of novels as artificial society simulation. In *Proceedings of the 2nd International Conference on Cognitive Science and the 16th Annual Meeting of the Japanese Cognitive Science Society Joint Conference* (pp. 950-953). Tokyo, Japan: Academic Press.

Oikawa, H., & Ogata, T. (2012). On the narrative generation as a mutual cognition mechanism among characters. In *Proceedings of the 29th Annual Meeting of the Japanese Cognitive Science Society* (pp. 540-549). Sendai, Japan: Academic Press.

Okada, N., & Endo, T. (1992). Story generation based on dynamics of the mind. *Computational Intelligence*, *8*(1), 123–160. doi:10.1111/j.1467-8640.1992.tb00341.x

Ono, J., & Ogata, T. (2013). A framework of the inter-textual knowledge acquisition and creation mechanism for an integrated narrative generation system. In *Proceedings of Forum on Information Technology 2013* (*Vol.2*, pp. 201-204). Tottori, Japan: Academic Press.

Onodera, K., Akimoto, T., & Ogata, T. (2012). A state-event transformation mechanism for generating micro structures of story in an integrated narrative generation system. In *Proceedings of the 34th Annual Conference of the Cognitive Science Society* (pp. 2150-2155). Sapporo, Japan: Academic Press.

Peinado, F., & Gervás, P. (2005). Creativity issues in plot generation. In *Workshop on Computational Creativity, Working Notes, 19th International Joint Conference on A.I.* (pp. 45-52). Edinburgh, UK: Academic Press.

Peinado, F., & Gervás, P. (2006). Evaluation of automatic generation of basic stories. *New Generation Computing*, *24*(3), 289–302. doi:10.1007/BF03037336

Pemberton, L. (1989). A modular approach to story generation. In *Proceedings of the Fourth Conference on European Chapter of the Association for Computational Linguistics* (pp. 217-224), Manchester, UK. doi:10.3115/976815.976845

Pérez, R. (1999). *A computer model of creativity of writing.* (Ph.D. Thesis). The University of Sussex, Brighton, UK.

Pérez y Pérez, R., & Sharples, M. (2001). MEXICA: A computer model of a cognitive account of creative writing. *Journal of Experimental & Theoretical Artificial Intelligence*, *13*(2), 119–139. doi:10.1080/09528130010029820

Prince, G. (1982). *Narratology*. Walter de Gruhter. doi:10.1515/9783110838626

Prince, G. (2003). *A dictionary of narratology* (Revised ed.). University of Nebraska Press.

Propp, V. Y. (1968). *Morphology of the folktale* (L. Scott, Trans.). Austin, TX: University of Texas Press. (Original work published 1928)

Quillian, M. (1968). Semantic memory. In M. Minsky (Ed.), *Semantic information processing* (pp. 227–270). Cambridge, MA: MIT Press.

Reiter, E., & Dale, R. (2006). *Building natural language generation systems: Studies in natural language processing*. London: Cambridge University Press.

Riedl, M., Saretto, C. J., & Young, R. M. (2003). Managing interaction between users and agents in a multi-agent storytelling environment. In *Proceedings of the Second International Joint Conference on Autonomous Agents and Multiagent Systems* (pp. 741-748). Melbourne, Australia. doi:10.1145/860575.860694

Riedl, M. O., & Young, R. M. (2006). From linear story generation to branching story graphs. *IEEE Computer Graphics and Applications*, *26*(3), 23–31. doi:10.1109/MCG.2006.56 PMID:16711214

Riedl, M. O., & Young, R. M. (2010). Narrative planning: Balancing plot and character. *Journal of Artificial Intelligence Research*, *39*, 217–267.

Riesbeck, C. K., & Schank, R. C. (1989). *Inside case-based reasoning*. Lawrence Erlbaum.

Rowe, J. P., McQuiggan, S. W., Robison, J. L., Marcey, D. R., & Lester, J. C. (2009). STORYEVAL: An empirical evaluation framework for narrative generation. In *Intelligent Narrative Technologies II: Papers from the 2009 AAAI Spring Symposium, Technical Report* (SS-09-06, pp. 103-110), Palo alto, California.

Rumelhart, D. E. (1975). Notes on a schema for stories. In D. G. Bobrow & A. Collins (Eds.), *Representation and understanding: Studies in cognitive science*. Academic Press. doi:10.1016/B978-0-12-108550-6.50013-6

Ryan, M. L. (1991). *Possible worlds, artificial intelligence, and narrative theory*. Bloomington, IN: Indiana University Press.

Saito, Y., & Ogata, T. (1998). On the computational modeling of Freud's dream theory. In *Proceedings of the 12rd Annual Conference of the Japanese Society for Artificial Intelligence* (pp. 706-706). Tokyo, Japan: Academic Press.

Sakuma, T., & Ogata, T. (2005). Story generation support system used the story theory of Propp. In *Proceedings of the 19th Annual Conference of the Japanese Society for Artificial Intelligence* (3D3-04). Kitakyushu, Japan: Academic Press.

Schank, R. C. (1982). *Dynamic memory: A theory of learning in computers and people*. Cambridge, UK: Cambridge University Press.

Schank, R. C. (1986). *Explanation patterns: understanding mechanically and creativity*. Lawrence Erlbaum.

Schank, R. C. (1990). *Tell me a story*. Scribners.

Schank, R. C., & Abelson, R. P. (1977). *Scripts, plans, goals, and understanding: An inquiry into human knowledge structures*. Lawrence Erlbaum.

Schank, R. C., & Riesbeck, C. K. (1981). *Inside computer understanding*. Lawrence Erlbaum.

Sharma, M., Ontañón, S., Mehta, M., & Ram, A. (2007). Drama management evaluation for interactive fiction games. In *Intelligent Narrative Technologies: Papers from the 2007 AAAI Fall Symposium, Technical Report* (FS-07-05, pp. 138-145), Arlington, Virginia.

Sharples, M. (1996). An account of writing as creative design. In C. M. Levy & S. Ransdell (Eds.), *The science of writing: Theories, methods, individual difference and applications* (pp. 127–148). Lawrence Erlbaum.

Shklovsky, V. (1990). *Theory of prose* (B. Sher, Trans.). Dalkey Archive Press.

Si, M. (2010). *Thespian: a decision-theoretic framework for interactive narratives.* (Ph.D thesis). Faculty of the USC Graduate School, University of Southern California, Los Angeles, CA.

Smith, S., & Bates, J. (1989). Towards a theory of narrative for interactive fiction. *Technical Report CMU-CS-89-121*. Pittsburgh: Carnegie Melllon University.

Stockwell, P. (2002). *Cognitive poetics: An introduction*. Routledge.

Swartjes, I. (2010). *Whose story is it anyway? How improve informs agency and authorship of emergent narrative.* (Ph.D thesis). University of Twente, Enschede, Netherlands.

Szilas, N. (2010). Requirements for computational models of interactive narrative. In *Computational Models of Narrative: Papers from the 2010 AAAI Fall Symposium, Technical Reports* (FS-10-04, pp. 62-68), Arlington, Virginia.

Tarasti, E. (1994). *A theory of musical semiotics*. Bloomington, IN: Indiana University Press.

Thawonmas, R., Oda, K., & Shuda, T. (2009). Camerawork editor for automatic comic generation from game log. In NICOGRAPH International 2009 (V-3).

Tokosumi, A. (2007). *Computational theories of mind: New edition*. Tokyo, Japan: Tokyo University Press.

Tsuchihashi, S., & Ogata, T. (2009). Toward the narrative generation by quotations and anagram. In *Proceedings of the 23rd Annual Conference of the Japanese Society for Artificial Intelligence* (1J1-OS2-2). Takamatsu, Japan: Academic Press.

Turner, S. R. (1994). *The creative process: A computer model of storytelling and creativity*. NJ: Lawrence Erlbaum.

Ueda, K., & Ogata, T. (2004). A computational modeling of perspective and voice in the narrative rhetoric. In *Proceedings of 18th Congress of the International Association of Empirical Aesthetics* (pp. 480-486). Lisbon, Portugal: Academic Press.

Utsumi, A., Nakamura, K., & Sakamoto, M. (2012). Effects of discourse goals on the process of metaphor production. In *Proceedings of the 34th Annnual Meeting of the Cognitive Science Society* (pp. 2475-2480). Sapporo, Japan: Academic Press.

Watanabe, N. (2012). *Nihon shosetsu gijutsu shi* [A history of techniques in Japanese novels]. Tokyo, Japan: Shinchosha.

White, H. (1980). The value of narrativity in the representation of reality. W. J. T. Mitchell (Ed.), On narrative. Chicago: The University of Chicago Press.

Yoshimoto, T. (1968). *Kyodo genso ron* [The theory of communal fantasy]. Tokyo, Japan: Kawade Shobo Shinsha.

Zhang, Y., Ono, J., & Ogata, T. (2011). An advertising rhetorical mechanism for single event combined with conceptual dictionary in narrative generation system. In *Proceedings of 7th International Conference on Natural Language Processing and Knowledge Engineering* (pp. 340-343). Tokushima, Japan. doi:10.1109/NLPKE.2011.6138221

Zhang, Y., Ono, J., & Ogata, T. (2012). Single event and scenario generation based on advertising rhetorical techniques using the conceptual dictionary in narrative generation system. In *Proceedings of the Fourth IEEE International Conference on Digital Game and Intelligent Toy Enhanced Learning* (pp. 162-164). Takamatsu, Japan. doi:10.1109/DIGITEL.2012.46

## KEY TERMS AND DEFINITIONS

**Circular Narrative Control:** A design plan of narrative generation systems including mainly both an iterative narrative generation concept and a free and flexible control concept of the applicable order of narrative generation phases.

**Expanded Literary Theory (ELT):** A concept for a research field in which narratology and literary theories are organically introduced into computational and cognitive approaches.

**Fluidity and Fixation:** A concept for design and development of narrative generation systems. In particular, it means capacities of free compilation, self-organization, and automatic generation that information contents have.

**Geino Information System (GIS):** A system model of *geino* production and consumption. GIS has been considered a framework in which various levels of narrative generation processes were driven by authors, receivers, characters, actors, and actresses.

**Genette-Based Narrative Discourse Mechanism:** A narrative discourse generation mechanism in INGS based on the narrative discourse theory by Genette.

**Integrated Narrative Generation System (INGS):** A synthetic narrative generation system architecture integrating the previous studies by the author.

**Jauss-Based Narrative Discourse Control Mechanism:** A narrative discourse generation process control mechanism in INGS based on the reception theory by Jauss.

**Multiple Narrative Structures (Model):** A conceptual model by which a narrative text is multiply constituted and the narrative generation process is also multiply executed.

**Norm and Deviation:** A narrative control method based on norm, the standard framework by which a narrative generation process should be performed, and on the deviation from the norm.

**Propp-Based Story Generation Mechanism:** A story generation mechanism in INGS based on the narrative morphology theory by Propp.

## APPENDIX

*Box 1. The conceptual representation of a generated story (partially omitted)*

```
Input:
(st-propp '((イワン[Ivan] 勇士[warrior]@勇者[warrior]) (蛇[snake] 蛇[snake]@爬虫類{蛇}[reptiles{snake}]) (マリア)[Mary] 皇女[princess]@女[woman]) (魔法の杖[Magic-wand] 杖[wand]@棒{杖}[rod{wand}]) (王様[king] 王様@君主{王}[monarch{king}]) (バーバ・ヤガー[Baba-Yaga] 老婆[older-woman]@女[woman]) (メロス[Melos] 男[man]@男[man])) 'PROPP 'topdownC 0 '(ロシア民話[Russian-folktale])))
Output:
($ロシア民話[Russian-folktale]
 ($問題[P-Problem]
  ($予備部分[Reserve-potion]
   ($01_留守[Absentation]
    (event 出かける1[go-out] (type action) (ID 1) (time (time1 time2)) (agent age%子供[child]#2) (location loc%自然[nature]#1) (object (event 摘む1[gather] (type action) (ID 2) (agent age%子供[child]#1) (location loc%京師[imperial-capital]#1) (object age%苺[strawberry]#1)))
   ($06_謀略[Trickery]
    (event 混入する2[mix] (type action) (ID 3) (time (time2 time3)) (agent age%蛇[snake]#1) (location loc%自然[nature]#1) (object obj%プトマイン[ptomaine]#1) (to obj%錠剤[tablet]#1)) / (event 与える1[give] (type action) (ID 4) (time (time3 time4)) (agent age%蛇[snake]#1) (counter-agent age%皇女[princess]#1) (location loc%自然[nature]#1) (object obj%錠剤[tablet]#2)))
   ($07_幇助[Complicity]
    (event 眠る1[sleep] (type action) (ID 5) (time (time4 time5)) (agent age%皇女[princess]#1) (location loc%自然[nature]#1))))
  ($発端[Beginning]
   ($08_加害[Villainy-or-lack]
    ($一
     (event 赴任する1[assume-office] (ID 2) (time (time5 time5-1)) (agent age%皇女[princess]#1) (location loc%自然[nature]#1) (object age%国[country]#1)) / (event 追い出す1[drive] (type action) (ID 6) (time (time5-1 time6)) (agent age%列侯[many-daimyo]#1) (counter-agent age%皇女[princess]#1) (location loc%抜け道[secret-path]#1) (from age%国[country]#1))))
   ($09_仲介[Mediation]
    (event 挟む8[happen-to-hear] (type action) (ID 7) (time (time6 time7)) (agent age%勇士[warrior]#1) (location loc%曲浦[winding-coast]#1) (object obj%噂[gossip]#1)) / (event 知る1[know] (type action) (ID 8) (time (time7 time8)) (agent age%勇士[warrior]#1) (location loc%曲浦[winding-coast]#1) (object obj%被害[damage]#1)))
   ($10_対抗開始[Beginning counter-action]
    (event 決意する2[determine] (type action) (ID 9) (time (time8 time9)) (agent age%勇士[warrior]#1) (location loc%曲浦[winding-coast]#1) (object obj%冒険[adventure]#1)))
   ($11_出立[Departure]
    (event 出国する1[depart] (type action) (ID 10) (time (time9 time10)) (agent age%勇士[warrior]#1) (location loc%外堀[outer-moat]#1) (from loc%曲浦[winding-coast]#1) (to loc%登山鉄道[mountain-railway]#1)))))

------------------------------ <Omission> ------------------------------
   ($30_処罰[Punishment]
    ($一
     (event 止まる2[stop] (ID 18) (time (time50 time50-1)) (agent age%蛇[snake]#1) (location loc%地方事務所[local-office]#1) (to loc%曲浦[winding-coast]#1)) / (event 射殺する1[shoot] (type action) (ID 57) (time (time50-1 time51)) (agent age%王様[king]#1) (counter-agent age%蛇[snake]#1) (location loc%曲浦[winding-coast]#1)))
    (event 射殺する1[shoot] (type action) (ID 58) (time (time51 time52)) (agent age%王様[king]#1) (counter-agent age%男[man]#1) (location loc%曲浦[winding-coast]#1)))
   ($31_結婚[Wedding]
    ($一
     (event はびこる1[spread] (ID 19) (time (time52 time52-1)) (agent age%皇女[princess]#1) (location loc%曲浦[winding-coast]#1) (to loc%リンク[rink]#1) (adverb nil)) / (event 婚約する1[get-engaged-to] (type action) (ID 59) (time (time52-1 time53)) (agent age%勇士[warrior]#1) (counter-agent age%皇女[princess]#1) (location loc%リンク[rink]#1)))))))
```

*Box 2. The sentences by the conceptual representation in Box 1*

{t1}子ども[child]が「子ども[child]が苺[strawberry]を摘む[gather]」ことに出かける[go-out]。{t2}蛇[snake]がプトマイン[ptomaine]を錠剤[tablet]に混入する[mix]。{t3}蛇[snake]から錠剤[tablet]を皇女[princess]へ与える[give]。{t4}皇女[princess]が眠る[sleep]。{t5}皇女[princess]が邦[country]へ赴任する[assume-office]。{t6}列侯[many-daimyo]が皇女[princess]を邦[country]より追い出す[drive]。{t7}勇士[warrior]が噂[gossip]を小耳に挟む[happen-to-hear]。{t8}勇士[warrior]が被害[damage]を知る[know]。{t9}勇士[warrior]が冒険[adventure]を決意する[determine]。{t10}勇士[warrior]は曲浦[winding-coast]から登山鉄道[mountain-railway]に出国する[depart]。{t11}老婆[older-woman]が「勇士[warrior]が残飯[leavings-of-a-meal]を食べる[eat]」ことを勇士[warrior]に命じる[order]。{t12}勇士[warrior]が命令[command]に従う[be-engaged]。{t13}勇士[warrior]が残飯[leavings-of-a-meal]を食べる[eat]。{t14}老婆[older-woman]が勇士[warrior]を樫[oak]へ連れる[take]。{t15}勇士[warrior]が杖[wand]を発見する[discover]。{t16}勇士[warrior]が杖[wand]に乗る[ride]。{t17}杖[wand]が浮かび上がる[come-to-the-front]。{t18}杖[wand]が地方事務所[local-office]より下級裁判所[lower-court]まで飛ぶ[jump]。{t19}勇士[warrior]が地方事務所[local-office]を来訪する[visit]。{t20}勇士[warrior]が地方事務所[local-office]より下級裁判所[lower-court]へ移動する[move]。{t21}蛇[snake]が下級裁判所[lower-court]を独走する[have-a large-lead]。{t22}勇士[warrior]が蛇[snake]と戦う[fight]。{t23}蛇[snake]が暴れる[act-violently]。{t24}勇士[warrior]に傷が付く[get-hurt]。{t25}蛇[snake]が勇士[warrior]に敗れる[be-defeated]。{t26}皇女[princess]が下級裁判所[lower-court]を散策する[take-a-walk]。{t27}皇女[princess]に羽[wing]が生える[cut]。{t28}皇女[princess]が浮かび上がる[come-to-the-front]。{t29}弓取[archer]が強弓[tightly-drawn-bow]を皇女[princess]に射る[shoot]。{t30}皇女[princess]が空[sky]にぶら下がる[hang-on]。{t31}皇女[princess]が空[sky]より池[pond]へ落ちる[fall]。{t32}皇女[princess]が池[pond]に潜入する[sneak]。{t33}黄犬[yellow-colored-dog]が皇女[princess]を池[pond]より地面[ground]に引き上げる[pull-up]。{t34}皇女[princess]が下級裁判所[lower-court]を来訪する[visit]。{t35}勇士[warrior]が皇女[princess]を蛇[snake]から取り戻す[get-back]。{t36}勇士[warrior]が下級裁判所[lower-court]から脱出する[escape]。{t37}蛇[snake]が地方事務所[local-office]に埋まる[be-buried]。{t38}蛇[snake]が「蛇[snake]がピン[pin]を勇士[warrior]に杖[wand]で刺す[stab]」ことを計画する[plan]。{t39}勇士[warrior]が下級裁判所[lower-court]から地方事務所[local-office]に転じる[be-transferred]。{t40}蛇[snake]がピン[pin]を勇士[warrior]に奴豆腐[cubes-of-tofu]で刺す[stab]。{t41}三従姉妹[second-cousin]が勇士[warrior]へ近付く[approach]。{t42}三従姉妹[second-cousin]が地方事務所[local-office]に参拝する[worship]。{t43}三従姉妹[second-cousin]がピン[pin]を勇士より抜く[pull]。{t44}勇士[warrior]が息を吹き返す[come-to-life]。{t45}勇士[warrior]が蛇[snake]とぶつかる[bump-into]。{t46}勇士[warrior]が蛇[snake]から曲浦[winding-coast]まで逃げる[escape]。{t47}勇士[warrior]が曲浦[winding-coast]より下級裁判所[lower-court]に近道する[take-a-shortcut]。{t48}勇士[warrior]が下級裁判所[lower-court]から曲浦[winding-coast]へ到着する[arrive]。{t49}男[man]が言い張る[insist]。{t50}男[man]が報酬[reward]を王様[king]に要求する[demand]。{t51}王様[king]が勇士[warrior]と会う[meet]。{t52}皇女[princess]が勇士[warrior]と会う[meet]。{t53}勇士[warrior]が傷[injury]を顔[face]に持つ[have]。{t54}皇女[princess]が曲浦[winding-coast]に舵を取る[be-at-the helm-to]。{t55}皇女[princess]が「勇士[warrior]に傷が付く[get-hurt]」ことを思い出す[remember]。{t56}皇女[princess]が真実[truth]を知る[know]。{t57}王様[king]が曲浦[winding-coast]に乗る[get-onto]。{t58}皇女[princess]が真実[truth]を命令[command]に伝える[convey]。{t59}王様[king]が真実[truth]を知る[know]。{t60}王様[king]が「男[man]が王様[king]に「令姉[your-elder-sister]が子ども[child]を助ける[help]」ことと嘘を言う[lie-to]」ことに気付く[notice]。{t61}男[man]の錠剤[tablet]が嘘偽り[lie]が露見する[come-to-light]。{t62}勇士[warrior]が耳[ear]を探訪する[investigate]。{t63}勇士[warrior]が杖[wand]を耳[ear]から内部[inside]へ通り抜ける[pass-through]。{t64}勇士[warrior]がリンク[rink]で釣りをする[fish]。{t65}勇士[warrior]が評議員[councilor]に昇格する[be-promoted]。{t66}蛇[snake]が曲浦[winding-coast]に止まる[stop]。{t67}王様[king]が蛇[snake]を射殺する[shoot]。{t68}王様[king]が男[man]を射殺する[shoot]。{t69}皇女[princess]がリンク[rink]にはびこる[spread]。{t70}勇士[warrior]が皇女[princess]と婚約する[get-engaged-to]。

*Box 3. Underlined parts are refined by other story techniques*

子ども[child]が「子ども[child]が苺[strawberry]を摘む[gather]」ことに出かける[go-out]。蛇[snake]がプトマイン[ptomaine]を錠剤[tablet]に混入する[mix]。蛇[snake]から錠剤[tablet]を皇女[princess]へ与える[give]。皇女[princess]が眠る[sleep]。皇女[princess]が邦[country]へ赴任する[assume-office]。**列侯[many-daimyo]が皇女[princess]を叱る[scold]。列侯[many-daimyo]が皇女[princess]を押す[push]。皇女[princess]が列侯[many-daimyo]に抵抗する[resist]。列侯[many-daimyo]が皇女[princess]を押す[push]。列侯[many daimyo]が皇女[princess]を突き放す[thrust]**。勇士[warrior]が噂[gossip]を小耳に挟む[happen-to-hear]。勇士[warrior]が被害[damage]を知る[know]。勇士[warrior]が冒険[adventure]を決意する[determine]。勇士[warrior]は曲浦[winding-coast]から登山鉄道[mountain-railway]に出国する[depart]。老婆[older-woman]が「勇士[warrior]が残飯[leavings-of-a-meal]を食べる[eat]」ことを勇士[warrior]に命じる[order]。勇士[warrior]が命令[command]に従う[be-engaged]。勇士[warrior]が残飯[leavings-of-a-meal]を食べる[eat]。老婆[older-woman]が勇士[warrior]を樫[oak]へ連れる[take]。勇士[warrior]が杖[wand]を発見する[discover]。勇士[warrior]が杖[wand]に乗る[ride]。杖[wand]が浮かび上がる[come-to-the-front]。杖[wand]が地方事務所[local-office]より下級裁判所[lower-court]まで飛ぶ[jump]。勇士[warrior]が地方事務所[local-office]を来訪する[visit]。勇士[warrior]が地方事務所[local-office]より下級裁判所[lower-court]へ移動する[move]。蛇[snake]が下級裁判所[lower-court]を独走する[have-a-large-lead]。**蛇[snake]が勇士[warrior]を襲う[attack]。勇士[warrior]が蛇[snake]を避ける[avoid]。勇士[warrior]が武器[weapon]を引き抜く[pull-out]。勇士[warrior]が蛇[snake]を突く[attack]。蛇[snake]が勇士[warrior]を避ける[avoid]。蛇[snake]が勇士[warrior]に反撃する[make-a-counterattack-upon]**。**蛇[snake]が勇士[warrior]を殴る[strike]。蛇[snake]が勇士[warrior]を蹴る[kick]。蛇[snake]が騒ぐ[make-a-noise]**。勇士[warrior]に傷が付く[get-hurt]。蛇[snake]が勇士[warrior]に敗れる[be-defeated]。**蛇[snake]が落ち込む[be-depressed]**。皇女[princess]が下級裁判所[lower-court]を散策する[take-a-walk]。皇女[princess]に羽[wing]が生える[cut]。皇女[princess]が浮かび上がる[come-to-the-front]。弓取[archer]が強弓[tightly-drawn-bow]を皇女[princess]に射る[shoot]。皇女[princess]が空[sky]にぶら下がる[hang-on]。皇女[princess]が空[sky]より池[pond]へ落ちる[fall]。皇女[princess]が池[pond]に潜入する[sneak]。黄犬[yellow-colored-dog]が皇女[princess]を池[pond]より地面[ground]に引き上げる[pull-up]。皇女[princess]が下級裁判所[lower-court]を来訪する[visit]。**勇士[warrior]が駆け付ける。皇女[princess]が勇士[warrior]に安心する。皇女[princess]が蛇[snake]から離れる。勇士[warrior]が蛇[snake]から離れる。蛇[snake]が勇士[warrior]に憤る。勇士[warrior]が助け[help]を喜ぶ[be-glad]**。勇士[warrior]が下級裁判所[lower-court]から脱出する[escape]。蛇[snake]が地方事務所[local-office]に埋まる[be-buried]。蛇[snake]が「蛇[snake]がピン[pin]を勇士[warrior]に杖[wand]で刺す[stab]」ことを計画する[plan]。勇士[warrior]が下級裁判所[lower-court]から地方事務所[local-office]に転じる[be-transferred]。蛇[snake]がピン[pin]を勇士[warrior]に奴豆腐[cubes-of-tofu]で刺す[stab]。三従姉妹[second-cousin]が勇士[warrior]へ近付く[approach]。三従姉妹[second-cousin]が地方事務所[local-office]に参拝する[worship]。三従姉妹[second-cousin]がピン[pin]を勇士より抜く[pull]。勇士[warrior]が息を吹き返す[come-to-life]。勇士[warrior]が蛇[snake]とぶつかる[bump-into]。勇士[warrior]が蛇[snake]から曲浦[winding-coast]まで逃げる[escape]。勇士[warrior]が曲浦[winding-coast]より下級裁判所[lower-court]に近道する[take-a-shortcut]。勇士[warrior]が下級裁判所[lower-court]から曲浦[winding-coast]へ到着する[arrive]。男[man]が言い張る[insist]。男[man]が報酬[reward]を王様[king]に要求する[demand]。王様[king]が勇士[warrior]と会う[meet]。皇女[princess]が勇士[warrior]と会う[meet]。勇士[warrior]が傷[injury]を顔[face]に持つ[have]。皇女[princess]が曲浦[winding-coast]に舵を取る[be-at-the helm-to]。皇女[princess]が「勇士[warrior]に傷が付く[get-hurt]」ことを思い出す[remember]。皇女[princess]が真実[truth]を知る[know]。王様[king]が曲浦[winding-coast]に乗る[get-onto]。皇女[princess]が真実[truth]を命令[command]に伝える[convey]。王様[king]が真実[truth]を知る[know]。王様[king]が「男[man]が王様[king]に「令姉[your-elder-sister]が子ども[child]を助ける[help]」ことと嘘を言う[lie-to]」ことに気付く[notice]。男[man]の錠剤[tablet]が嘘偽り[lie]が露見する[come-to-light]。勇士[warrior]が耳[ear]を探訪する[investigate]。勇士[warrior]が杖[wand]を耳[ear]から内部[inside]へ通り抜ける[pass-through]。勇士[warrior]がリンク[rink]で釣りをする[fish]。勇士[warrior]が評議員[councilor]に昇格する[be-promoted]。蛇[snake]が曲浦[winding-coast]に止まる[stop]。王様[king]が蛇[snake]を射殺する[shoot]。王様[king]が男[man]を射殺する[shoot]。皇女[princess]がリンク[rink]にはびこる[spread]。勇士[warrior]が皇女[princess]と婚約する[get-engaged-to]。

*Box 4. Underlined portion is Propp based macro-story*

肉牛[beef-cattle]がシェパード[german-shepherd]と競走する[compete]。肉牛[beef-cattle]がシェパード[german-shepherd]に敗れる[defeated]。肉牛[beef-cattle]が下水[sewer]を独走する[have-a-large-lead]。肉牛[beef-cattle]が堕落する[degenerate]。肉牛[beef-cattle]が復調する[recover]。肉牛[beef-cattle]が駆けっこ[race]を修行する[be-trained]。シェパード[german-shepherd]が村村[villages]を回転する[rotate]。肉牛[beef-cattle]が村村[villages]を荒らす[rob]。**子ども[child]が「子ども[child]が苺[strawberry]を摘む[gather]」ことに出かける[go-out]。肉牛[beef-cattle]がプトマイン[ptomaine]を錠剤[tablet]に混入する[mix]。肉牛[beef-cattle]から錠剤[tablet]を皇女[princess]へ与える[give]。皇女[princess]が眠る[sleep]。皇女[princess]が邦[country]へ赴任する[assume-office]。列侯[many-daimyo]が皇女[princess]を邦[country]より追い出す[drive]。シェパード[german-shepherd]が噂[gossip]を小耳に挟む[happen-to-hear>。シェパード[german-shepherd]が被害[damage]を知る[know]。シェパード[german-shepherd]が冒険[adventure]を決意する[determine]。シェパード[german-shepherd]は曲浦[winding-coast]から登山鉄道[mountain-railway]に出国する[depart]。老婆[older-woman]が「シェパード[german-shepherd]が残飯[leavings-of-a-meal]を食べる[eat]」ことをシェパード[german-shepherd]に命じる[order]。シェパード[german-shepherd]が命令[command]に従う[be-engaged]。シェパード[german-shepherd]が残飯[leavings-of-a-meal]を食べる[eat]。老婆[older-woman]がシェパード[german-shepherd]を樫[oak]へ連れる[take]。シェパード[german-shepherd]が杖[wand]を発見する[discover]。シェパード[german-shepherd]が杖[wand]に乗る[ride]。杖[wand]が浮かび上がる[come-to-the-front]。杖[wand]が地方事務所[local-office]より下級裁判所[lower-court]まで飛ぶ[jump]。シェパード[german-shepherd]が地方事務所[local office]を来訪する[visit]。シェパード[german-shepherd]が地方事務所[local office]より下級裁判所[lower-court]へ移動する[move]。肉牛[beef-cattle]が下級裁判所[lower-court]を独走する[have-a-large-lead]。シェパード[german-shepherd]が肉牛[beef-cattle]と戦う[fight]。肉牛[beef-cattle]が暴れる[act-violently]。シェパード[german-shepherd]に傷が付く[get-hurt]。肉牛[beef-cattle]がシェパード[german-shepherd]に敗れる[be-defeated]。皇女[princess]が下級裁判所[lower-court]を散策する[take-a-walk]。皇女[princess]に羽[wing]が生える[cut]。皇女[princess]が浮かび上がる[come-to-the-front]。弓取[archer]が強弓[tightly-drawn-bow]を皇女[princess]に射る[shoot]。皇女[princess]が空[sky]にぶら下がる[hang-on]。皇女[princess]が空[sky]より池[pond]へ落ちる[fall]。皇女[princess]が池[pond]に潜入する[sneak]。黄犬[yellow-colored-dog]が皇女[princess]を池[pond]より地面[ground]に引き上げる[pull-up]。皇女[princess]が下級裁判所[lower-court]を来訪する[visit]。シェパード[german-shepherd]が皇女[princess]を肉牛[beef-cattle]から取り戻す[get-back]。シェパード[german-shepherd]が下級裁判所[lower-court]から脱出する[escape]。肉牛[beef-cattle]が地方事務所[local-office]に埋まる[be-buried]。肉牛[beef-cattle]が「肉牛[beef-cattle]がピン[pin]をシェパード[german-shepherd]に杖[wand]で刺す[stab]」ことを計画する[plan]。シェパード[german-shepherd]が下級裁判所[lower-court]から地方事務所[local-office]に転じる[be-transferred]。肉牛[beef-cattle]がピン[pin]をシェパード[german-shepherd]に奴豆腐[cubes-of-tofu]で刺す[stab]。三従姉妹[second-cousin]がシェパード[german-shepherd]へ近付く[approach]。三従姉妹[second-cousin]が地方事務所[local-office]に参拝する[worship]。三従姉妹[second-cousin]がピン[pin]を勇士より抜く[pull]。シェパード[german-shepherd]が息を吹き返す[come-to-life]。シェパード[german-shepherd]が肉牛[beef-cattle]とぶつかる[bump-into]。シェパード[german-shepherd]が肉牛[beef-cattle]から曲浦[winding-coast]まで逃げる[escape]。シェパード[german-shepherd]が曲浦[winding-coast]より下級裁判所[lower-court]に近道する[take-a-shortcut]。シェパード[german-shepherd]が下級裁判所[lower-court]から曲浦[winding-coast]へ到着する[arrive]。男[man]が言い張る[insist]。男[man]が報酬[reward]を王様[king]に要求する[demand]。王様[king]がシェパード[german-shepherd]と会う[meet]。皇女[princess]がシェパード[german-shepherd]と会う[meet]。シェパード[german-shepherd]が傷[injury]を顔[face]に持つ[have]。皇女[princess]が曲浦[winding-coast]に舵を取る[b-at-the-helm-to]。皇女[princess]が「シェパード[german-shepherd]に傷が付く[get-hurt]」ことを思い出す[remember]。皇女[princess]が真実[truth]を知る[know]。王様[king]が曲浦[winding-coast]に乗る[get-onto]。皇女[princess]が真実[truth]を命令[command]に伝える[convey]。王様[king]が真実[truth]を知る[know]。王様[king]が「男[man]が王様[king]に「令姉[your-elder-sister]が子ども[child]を助ける[help]」ことと嘘を言う[lie-to]」ことに気付く[notice]。男[man]の錠剤[tablet]が嘘偽り[lie]が露見する[come-to-light]。シェパード[german-shepherd]が耳[ear]を探訪する[investigate]。シェパード[german-shepherd]が杖[wand]を耳から内部[inside]へ通り抜ける[pass through]。シェパード[german-shepherd]がリンク[rink]で釣りをする[fish]。シェパード[german-shepherd]が評議員[councilor]に昇格する[be-promoted]。肉牛[beef-cattle]が曲浦[winding-coast]に止まる[stop]。王様[king]が肉牛[beef-cattle]を射殺する[shoot]。王様[king]が男[man]を射殺する[shoot]。皇女[princess]がリンク[rink]にはびこる[spread]。シェパード[german-shepherd]が皇女[princess]と婚約する[get-engaged-to]。**肉牛[beef-cattle]がシェパード[german-shepherd]と勝負する[have-a-game]。肉牛[beef-cattle]がシェパード[german-shepherd]に勝つ[victory]。肉牛[beef-cattle]が学園[school]へ埋まる[be-buried]。肉牛[beef-cattle]が駆けっこを祝う[celebrate]。シェパード[german-shepherd]が村村[villages]から片側町[street-with-houses-lined-up-only-on-one-side]に沈下する[sink]。シェパード[german-shepherd]が落ち込む[be-depressed]。

*Box 5. Completely automatic generation (the result by 200 cycles)*

**Input**

(B-np20-cyc200
(generative-goal ((長さ[Length] 2) (複雑性[Complexity] 3)))
(expectation ((長さ[Length] 2) (複雑性[Complexity] 1) (暗示性[Implication] 3) (冗長性[diffuseness] 3) (隠蔽性[Hiding] 2)))
(np[Satisfaction point] 20) (end-condition (cycle-num[Generation cycle] 200)))

**Output**

{t13}勇士[warrior]が残飯[leavings-of-a-meal]を食べる[eat]。{t14}老婆[older-woman]が勇士[warrior]を樫[oak]へ連れる[take]。{t15}勇士[warrior]が杖[wand]を発見する[discover]。{t25}蛇[snake]が勇士[warrior]に敗れる[be-defeated]。{t26}皇女[princess]が下級裁判所[lower-court]を散策する[take-a-walk]。{t2}蛇[snake]がプトマイン[ptomaine]を錠剤[tablet]に混入する[mix]。{t7}勇士[warrior]が噂[gossip]を小耳に挟む[happen-to-hear]。{t8}勇士[warrior]が被害[damage]を知る[know]。{t10}勇士[warrior]は曲浦[winding-coast]から登山鉄道[mountain-railway]に出国する[depart]。{t28}皇女[princess]が浮かび上がる[come-to-the-front]。{t29}弓取[archer]が強弓[tightly-drawn-bow]を皇女[princess]に射る[shoot]。{t30}皇女[princess]が空[sky]にぶら下がる[hang-on]。{t31}皇女[princess]が空[sky]より池[pond]へ落ちる[fall]。{t33}黄犬[yellow-colored-dog]が皇女[princess]を池[pond]より地面[ground]に引き上げる[pull-up]。{t35}勇士[warrior]が皇女[princess]を蛇[snake]から取り戻す[get-back]。{t36}勇士[warrior]が下級裁判所[lower-court]から脱出する[escape]。勇士[warrior]が「{t28}皇女[princess]が浮かび上がる[come-to-the-front]。」を回想する[look-back-on]。{t39}勇士[warrior]が下級裁判所[lower-court]から地方事務所[local-office]に転じる[be-transferred]。{t46}勇士[warrior]が蛇[snake]から曲浦[winding-coast]まで逃げる[escape]。{t47}勇士[warrior]が曲浦[winding-coast]より下級裁判所[lower-court]に近道する[take-a-shortcut]。{t48}勇士[warrior]が下級裁判所[lower-court]から曲浦[winding-coast]へ到着する[arrive]。{t49}男[man]が言い張る[insist]。{t50}男[man]が報酬[reward]を王様[king]に要求する[demand]。{t8}勇士[warrior]が被害[damage]を知る[know]。勇士[warrior]が「{t2}蛇[snake]がプトマイン[ptomaine]を錠剤[tablet]に混入する[mix]」を回想する[look-back-on]。{t51}王様[king]が勇士[warrior]と会う[meet]。{t52}皇女[princess]が勇士[warrior]と会う[meet]。{t53}勇士[warrior]が傷[injury]を顔[face]に持つ[have]。{t54}皇女[princess]が曲浦[winding-coast]に舵を取る[be-at-the helm-to]。{t55}皇女[princess]が「勇士[warrior]に傷が付く[get-hurt]」ことを思い出す[remember]。{t58}皇女[princess]が真実[truth]を命令[command]に伝える[convey]。{t59}王様[king]が真実[truth]を知る[know]。{t60}王様[king]が「男[man]が王様[king]に「令姉[your-elder-sister]が子ども[child]を助ける[help]」ことと嘘を言う[lie-to]」ことに気付く[notice]。{t61}男[man]の錠剤[tablet]が嘘偽り[lie]が露見する[come-to-light]。男[man]が「{t12}勇士[warrior]が命令[command]に従う[be-engaged]。」を回想する[look-back-on]。{t69}皇女がリンクにはびこる。{t11}老婆[older-woman]が「勇士[warrior]が残飯[leavings-of-a-meal]を食べる[eat]」ことを勇士[warrior]に命じる[order]。{t70}勇士[warrior]が皇女[princess]と婚約する[get-engaged-to]。

*Box 6. Partial selection of narrative discourse techniques by hand*

勇士[warrior]が「{t23}蛇[snake]が暴れる[act-violently]。{t24}勇士[warrior]に傷が付く[get-hurt]。{t25}蛇[snake]が勇士[warrior]に敗れる[be-defeated]。{t35}勇士[warrior]が皇女[princess]を蛇[snake]から取り戻す[get-back]。{t36}勇士[warrior]が下級裁判所[lower-court]から脱出する[escape]。{t37}蛇[snake]が地方事務所[local-office]に埋まる[be-buried]。{t38}蛇[snake]が「蛇[snake]がピン[pin]を勇士[warrior]に杖[wand]で刺す[stab]」ことを計画する[plan]。{t39}勇士[warrior]が下級裁判所[lower-court]から地方事務所[local-office]に転じる[be-transferred]。{t40}蛇[snake]がピン[pin]を勇士[warrior]に奴豆腐[cubes-of-tofu]で刺す[stab]。」を予言する[foretell]。{t1}子ども[child]が「子ども[child]が苺[strawberry]を摘む[gather]」ことに出かける[go-out]。{t4}皇女[princess]が眠る[sleep]。{t5}皇女[princess]が邦[country]へ赴任する[assume-office]。{t6}列侯[many-daimyo]が皇女[princess]を邦[country]より追い出す[drive]。{t7}勇士[warrior]が噂[gossip]を小耳に挟む[happen-to-hear]。{t8}勇士[warrior]が被害[damage]を知る[know]。{t9}勇士[warrior]が冒険[adventure]を決意する[determine]。{t10}勇士[warrior]は曲浦[winding-coast]から登山鉄道[mountain-railway]に出国する[depart]。{t11}老婆[older-woman]が「勇士[warrior]が残飯[leavings-of-a-meal]を食べる[eat]」ことを勇士[warrior]に命じる[order]。{t12}勇士[warrior]が命令[command]に従う[be-engaged]。{t13}勇士[warrior]が残飯[leavings-of-a-meal]を食べる[eat]。勇士[warrior]が「{t6}列侯[many-daimyo]が皇女[princess]を邦[country]より追い出す[drive]」を回想する[look-back-on]。{t14}老婆[older-woman]が勇士[warrior]を樫[oak]へ連れる[take]。{t15}勇士[warrior]が杖[wand]を発見する[discover]。{t16}勇士[warrior]が杖[wand]に乗る[ride]。{t17}杖[wand]が浮かび上がる[come-to-the-front]。{t18}杖[wand]が地方事務所[local-office]より下級裁判所[lower-court]まで飛ぶ[jump]。{t19}勇士[warrior]が地方事務所[local-office]を来訪する[visit]。{t20}勇士[warrior]が地方事務所[local-office]より下級裁判所[lower-court]へ移動する[move]。老婆[older-woman]が「{t29}弓取[archer]が強弓[tightly-drawn-bow]を皇女[princess]に射る[shoot]。{t30}皇女[princess]が空[sky]にぶら下がる[hang-on]。{t31}皇女[princess]が空[sky]より池[pond]へ落ちる[fall]。」を予言する[foretell]。老婆[older-woman]が「{t40}蛇[snake]がピン[pin]を勇士[warrior]に奴豆腐[cubes-of-tofu]で刺す[stab]。」を予言する[foretell]。{t21}蛇[snake]が下級裁判所[lower-court]を独走する[have-a large-lead]。蛇[snake]が「{t2}蛇[snake]がプトマイン[ptomaine]を錠剤[tablet]に混入する[mix]。{t3}蛇[snake]から錠剤[tablet]を皇女[princess]へ与える[give]」ことを回想する[look-back-on]。{t22}勇士[warrior]が蛇[snake]と戦う[fight]。{t23}蛇[snake]が暴れる[act-violently]。{t24}勇士[warrior]に傷が付く[get-hurt]。{t25}蛇[snake]が勇士[warrior]に敗れる[be-defeated]。{t26}皇女[princess]が下級裁判所[lower-court]を散策する[take-a-walk]。{t27}皇女[princess]に羽[wing]が生える[cut]。{t28}皇女[princess]が浮かび上がる[come-to-the-front]。{t29}弓取[archer]が強弓[tightly-drawn-bow]を皇女[princess]に射る[shoot]。{t30}皇女[princess]が空[sky]にぶら下がる[hang-on]。{t31}皇女[princess]が空[sky]より池[pond]へ落ちる[fall]。{t32}皇女[princess]が池[pond]に潜入する[sneak]。{t33}黄犬[yellow-colored-dog]が皇女[princess]を池[pond]より地面[ground]に引き上げる[pull-up]。{t34}皇女[princess]が下級裁判所[lower-court]を来訪する[visit]。{t35}勇士[warrior]が皇女[princess]を蛇[snake]から取り戻す[get-back]。{t36}勇士[warrior]が下級裁判所[lower-court]から脱出する[escape]。{t37}蛇[snake]が地方事務所[local-office]に埋まる[be-buried]。{t38}蛇[snake]が「蛇[snake]がピン[pin]を勇士[warrior]に杖[wand]で刺す[stab]」ことを計画する[plan]。{t39}勇士[warrior]が下級裁判所[lower-court]から地方事務所[local-office]に転じる[be-transferred]。{t40}蛇[snake]がピン[pin]を勇士[warrior]に奴豆腐[cubes-of-tofu]で刺す[stab]。{t41}三従姉妹[second-cousin]が勇士[warrior]へ近付く[approach]。{t42}三従姉妹[second-cousin]が地方事務所[local-office]に参拝する[worship]。{t43}三従姉妹[second-cousin]がピン[pin]を勇士より抜く[pull]。{t44}勇士[warrior]が息を吹き返す[come-to-life]。{t45}勇士[warrior]が蛇[snake]とぶつかる[bump-into]。{t46}勇士[warrior]が蛇[snake]から曲浦[winding-coast]まで逃げる[escape]。{t47}勇士[warrior]が曲浦[winding-coast]より下級裁判所[lower-court]に近道する[take-a-shortcut]。{t48}勇士[warrior]が下級裁判所[lower-court]から曲浦[winding-coast]へ到着する[arrive]。皇女[princess]が「{t3}蛇[snake]から錠剤[tablet]を皇女[princess]へ与える[give]。{t4}皇女[princess]が眠る[sleep]」を回想する[look-back-on]。{t49}男[man]が言い張る[insist]。{t50}男[man]が報酬[reward]を王様[king]に要求する[demand]。{t51}王様[king]が勇士[warrior]と会う[meet]。{t52}皇女[princess]が勇士[warrior]と会う[meet]。{t53}勇士[warrior]が傷[injury]を顔[face]に持つ[have]。{t54}皇女[princess]が曲浦[winding-coast]に舵を取る[be-at-the helm-to]。皇女[princess]が「勇士[warrior]に傷が付く[get-hurt]」ことを回想する[look-back-on]。{t55}皇女[princess]が「勇士[warrior]に傷が付く[get-hurt]」ことを思い出す[remember]。{t56}皇女[princess]が真実[truth]を知る[know]。{t57}王様[king]が曲浦[winding-coast]に乗る[get-onto]。{t58}皇女[princess]が真実[truth]を命令[command]に伝える[convey]。{t59}王様[king]が真実[truth]を知る[know]。{t60}王様[king]が「男[man]が王様[king]に「令姉[your-elder-sister]が子ども[child]を助ける[help]」ことと嘘を言う[lie-to]」ことに気付く[notice]。皇女[princess]が「{t2}蛇[snake]がプトマイン[ptomaine]を錠剤[tablet]に混入する[mix]。{t3}蛇[snake]から錠剤[tablet]を皇女[princess]へ与える[give]。{t4}皇女[princess]が眠る[sleep]」を回想する[look-back-on]。{t61}男[man]の錠剤[tablet]が嘘偽り[lie]が露見する[come-to-light]。王様が[king]「{t67}王様[king]が蛇[snake]を射殺する[shoot]。{t68}王様[king]が男[man]を射殺する[shoot]」を予言する[foretell]。{t62}勇士[warrior]が耳[ear]を探訪する[investigate]。{t63}勇士[warrior]が杖[wand]を耳[ear]から内部[inside]へ通り抜ける[pass-through]。{t64}勇士[warrior]がリンク[rink]で釣りをする[fish]。{t65}勇士[warrior]が評議員[councilor]に昇格する[be-promoted]。{t66}蛇[snake]が曲浦[winding-coast]に止まる[stop]。{t67}王様[king]が蛇[snake]を射殺する[shoot]。{t69}皇女[princess]がリンク[rink]にはびこる[spread]。{t70}勇士[warrior]が皇女[princess]と婚約する[get-engaged-to]。

Section 2

# Generation and Creation of Narratives

# Chapter 2
# The Possibility of the Literary Work Generation by Computer

**Akinori Abe**
*Chiba University, Japan*

## ABSTRACT

*Recently the importance of entertainment for senior citizens and children has been pointed out. Accordingly, it is necessary to develop robots who can write poems, compose music, paint pictures, etc. For that, for instance, an automatic poem or story generation system will be necessary. This chapter will show the possibility of literary-work (poem, story, novel etc.) generation. First, the author introduces the research field, "Language-Sense Processing Engineering (LSE)" where the affective or psychological aspects of language is focused on. The author defined "language sense (the key concept in LSE)" as affective or psychological aspects of language. One of the features can be used for literary work generation is the "intertextuality" proposed by J. Kristeva. The possibility of the automatic literary work generation will be shown by the strategy to generate waka (Japanese poem). In addition, several strategies to generate literary works will be shown to illustrate the possibility of the automatic literary work generation.*

## INTRODUCTION

Recently the importance of entertainment for senior citizens and children has been pointed out. It is rather difficult to maintain staff that can perform such entertainment as writing and reading poems. Accordingly, it is necessary to develop robots who can write poems, compose music, paint pictures, etc. An automatic poem- or story-generation system is one way to achieve this. This chapter will show the possibility of literary-work (poems, stories, novels, etc.) generation.

First, the author introduces the research field, "Language-Sense Processing Engineering (LSE)." The key concept in LSE is language sense. The author defines "language sense" as affective or psychological aspects of language, to analyze and show several types of literary-work generation. For instance, the author analyzes the emotional and technical part of waka generation to generate new waka (Japanese poems). One feature that can be used for literary-work generation is "intertextuality" proposed by J.

DOI: 10.4018/978-1-5225-0432-0.ch002

Copyright © 2016, IGI Global. Copying or distributing in print or electronic forms without written permission of IGI Global is prohibited.

Kristeva. Below, the possibility of the automatic literary-work generation will be shown using a strategy to generate waka. In addition, several strategies to generate literary works will be shown to illustrate the possibility of automatic literary-work generation.

## BACKGROUND: LANGUAGE-SENSE PROCESSING ENGINEERING (LSE)

Since the very end of the 20th century, the author has been studying language-sense processing engineering (LSE). This is a specialized language processing where KANSEI[1] (the affective or psychological aspects of human activity) can be considered and dealt with. Of course, this is not proposed only for the computational generation of literary work. The concept of language sense can be applied to various other language applications. In this section, the author will illustrate language-sense engineering with several examples.

### Definition of Language Sense

The key concept in LSE (Language-Sense Processing Engineering) is "language sense." The author hereby defines the concept of language sense to show affective, emotional, or psychological aspects of language (Abe, 2002). In fact, language is used as a tool for communication. Accordingly, as Grice pointed out (Grice, 1957), language should correctly transfer the speaker's or writer's intention to the listeners or readers. However, sometimes we add effects to language, or intentionally remove certain information. These can sometimes become humor, a joke, ésprit, or pun. These types of phenomenon cannot be logically explained, because they are a mental or intellectual human activity. By language sense, the author would like to express and explain a type of non-logical feeling in language. Therefore, some of the targets of language sense are to analyze, entertain, or automatically generate literary works, such as poems, humor, jokes, ésprit, conversation, etc.

### Tools Dealing with Language Sense

This section shows one of the tools for dealing with language sense. As shown above, a tool that can deal with the non-logical aspects of language is necessary to deal with language sense. The author believes that one of the non-logical aspects of language comes from ambiguity, or multiple meanings for words. This language feature causes various word effects. Next, the author will illustrate one of the tools used to achieve LSE.

#### Conceptual Base

A conceptual base (Kasahara, Matsuzawa, Ishikawa, & Kawaoka, 1996) is a type of dictionary that can express words (concepts) by a vector and calculate the similarity or associativity between words. A concept in the conceptual base represents the meaning of a word. Each concept, $Concept_i$, in the conceptual base is defined by a list of weighted attributes: an attribute $p_{ij}$ of $Concept_i$ and an importance $q_{ij}$ of $p_{ij}$, where

$$Concept_i = \{(p_{i1}, q_{i1}), (p_{i2}, q_{i2}), \ldots, (p_{in}, q_{in})\}. \tag{1}$$

All of $q_{ij}$ and $p_{ij}$ are retrieved automatically from the explanation of $Concept_i$ in some language dictionaries. For example, if one dictionary says that a horse is "a type of animal that has a tail, a mane on its neck, runs fast …," the knowledge about a "horse" can be represented as

$$Horse = \{(Mane, 1), (Tail, 1), (Animal, 2), \ldots)\}, \tag{2}$$

where the importance come from the number of attributes in the explanation. Then, the concept, which has various weighted attributes, is mapped into an $n$-dimensional vector space. Each dimension corresponds to a keyword (vectorized concept). For instance, the vectorized-concept $Word_i$ can be expressed as follows:

$$Word_i = (Q_{i1}, Q_{i2}, \ldots, Q_{ij}, \ldots, Q_{ik}), \tag{3}$$

where

$$Q_{ij} = \sum_{l=1\ p_l \in c_j}^{n} q_{il} \,. \tag{4}$$

Then, the vectorized concept, whose weights are normalized, is as follows:

$$Word\_N_i = (\hat{Q}_{i1}, \hat{Q}_{i2}, \ldots, \hat{Q}_{ij}, \ldots, \hat{Q}_{ik}), \tag{5}$$

where

$$\hat{Q}_{ij} = \frac{Q_{ij}}{\left\| Word_i \right\|} = \frac{Q_{ij}}{\sqrt{\sum_{m=1}^{k} Q_{im}^2}} \,. \tag{6}$$

## Associativity or Similarity Between Words

Since the conceptual base is developed using concepts, as shown above, the similarity between two words can be shown by the cosine of the angle between two vectorized concepts. The similarity between two words, $Word_a$ and $Word_b$, can be calculated as:

$$Sim\,(Word_a, Word_b) = Word_a \bullet Word_b = \sum_{J=1}^{k} \hat{Q}_{aj} \cdot \hat{Q}_{bj} \,. \tag{7}$$

In addition, the meaning of a word sometimes changes according to the context or viewpoint. Thus, in (Kasahara et. al, 1996), viewpoints (context) are also considered when calculating the similarity between two words. To consider the viewpoint, attributes in words should be emphasized according to the viewpoint. In this paper, a detailed explanation of viewpoint consideration is omitted, due to lack of space.

The associativity between words that can be calculated using the conceptual base can be regarded as one of the affective or psychological aspects of language. We can say that such aspects come from patterned, not symbolic, language features. Therefore, the author uses the associativity that can be calculated using the conceptual base to deal with language sense. This sense is similar to using a rhyme dictionary while writing poems.

## LSE Applications

In this section, several LSE applications will be reviewed, including our research.

### Automatic Pun or Joke Generation

Puns and jokes are rather classical applications. However, the following applications can be reviewed because they deal with the affective or psychological aspects in language use. These language uses are not logical. JAPE (Binsted & Ritchie, 1994; Binsted, 1996), BOKE (Binsted & Takizawa, 1998), and the B-class machine (Matsuzawa, Kanasugi, & Abe, 1998) are reviewed next.

These applications automatically generate puns or jokes. For example, JAPE (Joke Analysis and Production Engine) is a system that can generate a pun by constructing a word or phrase using one of three mechanisms: juxtaposition, substitution, or comparison. JAPE mainly uses word substitution to produce puns. BOKE is a Japanese version of JAPE. One of the puns generated by BOKE is "通常残業省 [tsuujouzangyousyou] (Ministry where the staff always overworks)." This pun comes from "通商産業省 [tsuusyousangyousyou] (The Ministry of International Trade and Industry)."

The B-class machine generates jokes (*dajare* in Japanese) based on proverbs or celebrity names. One of the jokes generated by the B-class machine is "腐ってもタイソン [kusattemo Tyson][2]." This joke comes from "腐っても鯛 [kusattemo tai] (A sea bream is a precious fish, even if it decays.)." The author used a very simple algorithm to generate the joke.

This type of word-play was analyzed by Takiura (Takiura, 2002). He pointed out that we usually utilize context deviation when doing a word-play. However, we can notice what is interesting about the word-play by re-recognizing the context. The author focused on this type of gap to generate jokes computationally (Matsuzawa et al., 1998). The author adopted a very simple method to generate such jokes. For instance, the author used a proverb to generate jokes, where the last word was exchanged for a new word that includes the same or a similar sound.

Ritchie's group studies pun-generation mechanisms and the computational generation of puns and humor (Manurung et al., 2008; Ritchie, 2005, 2008; Ritchie et al., 2007). In addition, as members of the Joking Computer Project, they developed an automatic riddle-generation system called STANDUP (System To Augment Non-speaker's Dialogue Using Puns) (http://www.abdn.ac.uk/jokingcomputer/). Their recent research on computational humor is available (Ritchie, 2009).

### Computational Word-Play: Associative Shiritori

Associative shiritori (Matsuzawa, Abe, Kanasugi, & Nagamori, 1997) continuously generates words that have a certain associative relationship with the previous word. For example, if we give the word "sugar," the next word could be "rabbit." Since both sugar and rabbits are white, they have a certain relationship. Similarly, the word after rabbit could be frog (from the viewpoint of jumping), etc. The conceptual base (Kasahara et al., 1996) shown below is applied to this application. That is, to generate the next word (concept), we search for concepts similar to the current word. In fact, a rather deviated concept seems to apply better. The most similar concept is generally not interesting. The author usually used the second or third best concept.

## Computational Riddle Solving

The author proposed a computational riddle-solving system (Kanasugi, Matsuzawa, & Kasahara, 1996). The system computationally solves types of rebus riddles (as shown by Thaler (1987)). For instance, if the question is, "What kind of KURI comes out of the mouth?" then the answer "SYAKKURI (a hiccup)" is returned. In this system, 'KURI' is for the phonology and morphology shown by hiragana or katakana. In fact, 'KURI' usually implies a chestnut; however, it is not the correct answer because it does not come out of the mouth. SYAKKURI has the same sound as KURI and comes out of the mouth; therefore, it is the correct answer. The conceptual base (Kasahara et al., 1996) is also applied to riddle solving.

Following is the generalized riddle-solving algorithm:

1. A query can be represented as follows:

*Query* (*w*, *f*(*x*)),

where *f*(*x*) is a phrase that shows a feature or function of *w*.

The above example can be expressed as:

*Query* (*chestnut*, << *mouth*, *come out of*>>).

2. We can express the phonology and morphology shown by hiragana or katakana. That is, in *Query* (*w*, *f*(*x*)), *w* can function as both a phonological and morphological hint. Accordingly, the word set *W*, which includes the same or similar sound as *w*, is extracted from the knowledge base. For instance, since the word in the query has the key sound *w* = *'Kuri,'* the word set includes 'Ku[ra–ro][3]' or 'Gu[ra–ro][4].' In this case, W can be described as follows:

*W* = {*AmaGuri* (*sweet chestnut*), *SyattKuri* (*hiccup*), *Kurikaeshi* (*repeat*),…}.

3. The word set that can be generated from *C* (*mouth*, *come_out_of*) is << *mouth*, *come_out_of*>>.

Our strategy is a very simple method.

*C* (*f*(*x*)) = {*words in f*(*x*)}.

For instance,

*C* (<<*mouth*, *come_out_of*>>) = {*mouth*, *come_out_of*}.

4. Then, referring to the knowledge base, a word relating to $C(f(x))$ is searched from $W$. Then, from the previously searched $C(f(x))$, the most similar word is selected as an answer. For instance, '*Amaguri* (*sweet chestnut*)' and '*Kurikaeshi* (*repeat*)' cannot come out of the mouth, but '*Syakkuri* (*hiccup*)' can come out of the mouth. [5] Accordingly, '*Syakkuri* (*hiccup*),' which has the best relationship with *C* (<<*mouth, come_out_of*>>) is selected as the answer. JAPE, shown above, can also generate this type of question.

## THE ROLE OF INTERTEXTUALITY IN LITERARY-WORK GENERATION

In this section, the author will discuss the possibility of computationally generating literary work.

### Intertextuality

Kristeva proposed the intertextuality of literary work as follows:

*The word's status is thus defined horizontally (the word in the text belongs to both writing subject and addressee) as well as vertically (the word in the text is oriented towards an anterior or synchronic literary corpus).... Each word (text) is an intersection of words (texts) where at least one other word (text) can be read.... Any text is constructed as a mosaic of quotations; any text is the absorption and transformation of another. (Kristeva, 1980)*

According to Kristeva's definition, it is possible to generate literary work from fractions extracted from existing literary work. This type of strategy is very suited to computational generation. Accordingly, this feature was adopted for literary-work generation. As an example, the author will show automatic waka generation from existing waka (short Japanese fixed-type poems).

### Automatic Waka Generation

The author utilized this feature of intertextuality to generate literary work. One-hundred waka, included in the Hyakuninisshyu (an waka anthology), were divided into several parts and then rebuilt to generate new waka. It would be better to introduce a random-generation method. However, since only 100 poems were used, a simpler method was introduced. For each part of the clusters (5-7-5-7-7), 300 sets of seven letters (in kana) were sorted following the あいうえお order (alphabetical) and 200 sets of five letters (in kana) were sorted following the reversed あいうえお order (reverse alphabetical). The first hundred five-letter groups (in kana) were the first cluster. The first hundred seven-letter groups (in kana) were the second cluster. The second hundred five-letter groups (in kana) were the third cluster. The second hundred seven-letter groups (in kana) were the fourth cluster. The third hundred seven-letter groups (in Kana) were the fifth cluster.

For instance, the following waka could be generated (in Japanese[6]).

鳴く鹿の 尾上の桜 命にて ながながし夜を 山の奥にも

*A bleating deer, cherry blossoms in Ogami, it may be our fatal, in a long long night, deep in the mountain.*

初霜の 衛士のたく火の 奥山に つらぬきとめぬ 紅葉なりけり

*The first frost, fire given by guardians, in the secluded mountain, cannot penetrate, red leaves.*

These waka are generated by combining several phrases from the existing waka. They are not fluently composed, and different seasons are included. For instance, in the first poem, spring (cherry blossoms) and fall (a long long night) are both included. In fact, the author introduced a very simple method to generate Japanese poems, but it shows very interesting results. Thus, we can say that, by introducing intertextuality, we can generate short poems. If we do not include different seasons, it will be necessary to label seasonal information for each phrase.

In the above experiments, a very simple method, which can be regarded as random generation, was applied. It can be concluded that, even with a simple method, if we collect appropriate phrases or words, good poems can be generated. If we extend the method to longer poems, the result will be the same. Of course, not all of the generated poems are good. It is necessary to select the better ones. Since readers are human beings, the generated poems can be read according to human interpretation. In addition, a honkadori (quotation) can be naturally included during the generation. Thus, the generated poems can inherit the meaning and atmosphere of the "quoted" poems without any intent.

## Automatic Haiku Generation

For a haiku, which is also a short Japanese poem (shorter than waka), Rzepka and Araki proposed the haiku generator (Rzepka & Araki, 2015). It can analyze blog entry input and use nouns and adjectives for web-mining. The haiku generator utilizes grammar templates automatically generated from poems written by Japanese poets, and a lexicon of 2,473 kigo (seasonal) words from an online haiku repository.

First, a haiku theme is chosen from a list of frequent nouns (in the input blog contents), and the system tests the importance of one of these against the others by searching the web for co-occurrences. Then, the most appropriate seasonal-word kigo is chosen from a kigo database by considering the probability of co-occurrences of the kigo and the theme word. Then, the system adopts a haiku-generation mechanism, as follows:

- Theme word + possessive particle "no" (first line).
- Three-syllable kigo + possessive particle "no" + three-syllable noun (second line).
- Five-syllable noun or noun phrase (third line).

For instance, the following haiku was generated:

*Mount Moiwa/ is this the view of yellow/ gingko leaves?*

もいわ山 見える黄葉(こうよう) いてふかな (Author's translation)

The author simply applied random generation. However, Rzepka and Araki adopted an algorithm for haiku generation. The styles of waka and haiku are rather different. In addition, a haiku needs a seasonal keyword (kigo). Sometimes, such a restriction can function as better guidance. However, for waka generation, such an algorithm can be considered. A more difficult task is kyoka (short humorous Japanese poem) generation.

## Cutup Method

The cutup method has possibilities for computational literary-work generation. It randomly assembles words to generate poems. Sometimes, the source of the cutup poem is a newspaper or original poem. The poem-generation system seems to follow Kristeva's intertextuality.

For instance, "Poem Rocket" by Allen Ginsberg will be re-composed using the cutup method.

*Moon politicians earth-weeping and warring in eternity*
*tho not one star disturbed by screaming madmen from*
*Hollywood*
*Oil tycoons from Romania making secret deals with flabby green*
*Plutonians—*

This method is rather simple, and easy to implement on a computer. Below are other waka, generated using the cutup method.

## Cutup in E-Mail Generation

When generating spam e-mail texts, randomly generated texts are used not to outsmart spam-detection strategies using a Bayesian filter. The most famous production is shown below:

*The first question of course was, how to get dry again: they me as I walked, the remembrance of my churlishness and that I must confidence between himself and Mrs. Micawber. After which, he for his dagger till his hand gripped it. Then he spoke. I kissed her, and my baby brother, and was very sorry then; but not*

Thus, it is sometimes possible to generate a grammatically correct sentence.

*Then, from sea to shining sea, the God-King sang the praises of teflon, and with his face to the sunshine, he churned lots of butter.*

Such texts are called "spampetry (spam poetry)" or "spam art." The original texts are chosen from existing books[7]. Therefore, they can be regarded as the cutup method.

## Generating Literary Work Using the Cutup Method

Above, the author introduced Allen Ginsberg's "(perhaps)" cutup poem. As shown above, the cutup method may generate a good poem that is better than one made with human intention or desire. In musical composition, composers such as John Cage and Ionius Xenakis use the chance-operation system or probabilistic music composition to compose music. They can also be composed above human intention or expectations.

In most musical compositions, the player changes the order of the musical score. Thus, composers compose music. In the literary-work cutup method, a source, such as an article in a newspaper, is cut and the fragments are randomly synthesized. The source can be an existing article or an original (self-composed) article. If we consider the intertextuality of Kristeva (Kristeva, 1980), all literary works can be regarded as a mosaic of quotations. Accordingly, works composed by the cutup method can be regarded as such by intertextuality. The difference between a cutup work and human-made (beautiful) work is caused by the human's proper control and evaluation. Otherwise, the work will be an accidental product, like the cutup.

## Waka Generation Revisited

In the above waka-generation case, the author used the original words. However, for this case, the author did not use original words. Instead, the author cut the waka into four-letter clusters (kanji and kana are included). Then, the four-letter clusters form a 5 × 133 matrix. They can be regarded as 133 waka. Afterward, the composition/sort was performed with a system similar to the one above.

For each part of the clusters (4-4-4-4-4), the first 100 sets of four letters (in kana) are sorted following the あいうえお order (alphabetically), the second 100 sets of four letters (in kana) are sorted following the reversed あいうえお order (reverse alphabetically), the third 100 sets of four letters (in kana) are sorted following the あいうえお order, and so forth. Then, the following poems are generated. (It is rather difficult to translate these poems into Japanese. Accordingly, the reading is added.)

淡路島か くに君が 知る忘れ くなりぬ 昔なりけ

*(Awaji-shima Ka kuni kimiga Shiru wasure Kunarinu Mukashi narike)*

三笠の山 じ今はた 山の峰に せもが露 山おろし

*(Mikasano yama Ji imahata Yamano mineni Semoga tsuyu Yamaoroshi)*

祈らぬも とづれて 関わたの て若菜つ を命にて

*(Oramumo Tozurete Sekiwatano Te wakanatsu Wo inochinite)*

るらむ誰 に雲がく る人にせ に朽ちな るも別れ

*(Ruranu dare Ni kumogaku Ru hitonise Ni kuchina Rumo wakare)*

な小倉山 らけかな なぎに焼 る白菊の に匂ひぬ

*(Na Ogurayama Rakekana Nagini yaki Ru shirakikuno Ni nioinu)*

かりほの 白妙の衣 がむれば 暮るるも がれつつ

*(Karihono Shirotaeno koromo Gamureba Kururumo Garetsutsu)*

あらねど 龍田の川 あぢきな 猪名の笹 あだ波は

*(Aranedo Tatsutano kawa Ajikina Tyonano sasa Adanamiha)*

A strange division such as "るらむ誰" appears, but the last poem can be regarded as a poem composed by a (novice?) human. The phrases in the waka are computationally divided. Therefore, the generated poem is rather difficult to understand, compared with a poem composed of meaningful phrases. However, it is obviously composed with very exciting "Japanese" phrases. That is, the combination without consciousness and intention can generate exciting works.

This might be related to the "Descriptions automatiques," which were performed in the age of Dada and Surrealism. Although it will be difficult to extend the above method to the generation of general literary work, it is possible to generate literary work using the feature of intertextuality.

## Literary-Work Generation Using the Cutup Method

The cutup method was applied to "Konjiki Yasya (金色夜叉)" by Koyo Ozaki (尾崎紅葉). Following is the beginning of the novel:

未だ宵ながら松立てる門は一様に鎖籠めて、真直に長く東より西に横はれる大道は掃きたるやうに物の影を留めず、いと寂くも往来の絶えたるに、例ならず繁き車輪の轆は、或は忙かりし、或は飲過ぎし年賀の帰来なるべく、疎に寄する獅子太鼓の遠響は、はや今日に尽きぬる三箇日を惜むが如く、その哀切に小き腸は断れぬべし...[8]

Here is its application result:

疎に寄する獅子太鼓の遠響は、或は忙かりし、例ならず繁き車輪の轆は、いと寂くも往来の絶えたるに、未だ宵ながら松立てる門は一様に鎖籠めて、或は飲過ぎし年賀の帰来なるべく、はや今日に尽きぬる三箇日を惜むが如く、真直に長く東より西に横はれる大道は掃きたるやうに物の影を留めず、その哀切に小き腸は断れぬべし...[9]

In the above text, the cutup method is used for the phrases. Phrases are simply exchanged. Therefore, the generated text will be grammatically correct, but it may be difficult to understand. However, it might be possible to understand, if we try. This is an entertaining activity, but the possibility of generating a good novel is low. The cutup method is easy to apply to computers. Therefore, it will be better to generate as many novels as possible and select the best one.

## Computational Generation of a Poem or Story

Ito proposed a method to semi-automatically generate poems that appeared to be written by Yuming (Japanese Pop singer) (Ito, 1999). His method is based on the concept of intertextuality. It generates quasi-Yuming poems using words that Yuming used in her poems. Accordingly, the generated poems seem to be composed by Yuming.

Ogata proposed Computational Narratology (Ogata, 1998). His method is based on the narratology of Propp (Propp, 1968) and Genette (Genette, 1972). Based on these theories, the system automatically generates a story, such as a legend. Moreover, he developed a system to automatically generate image works (films, etc.). He is still developing a story-generation system. Currently, it can generate a story outline. From the outline, we can build a story or a pastiche. Ogata's current work is included in this book.

Ontañón and Zho proposed the SAM (Story Analogies through Mapping) algorithm for analogy-based story generation (Ontañón & Zho, 2011). SAM performs as follows:

1. Generate all possible phase mappings.
2. Find the analogical mappings.
3. Construct a story *R*.
4. Transform *R* using the analogical mappings.

This system can generate a story using an analogical mapping from a source story. In addition, it can modify the generated story to a different story.

## Possibility of Literary-Work Generation as LSE

In the above sections, the author discussed the possibility of literary-work generation. This section will discuss the integrated literary-work generation as LSE. As a very small literary work, an automatic waka-generation strategy is illustrated, which utilizes the concepts of intertextuality and the cutup method. In addition, an automatic haiku-generation system was introduced, which uses sentences from blogs. From the above examples, the author believes we can perform automatic poem generation using the concept of intertextuality.

A strategy based on the concept of intertextuality is suitable for computational generation. Thus, as shown above, several systems are proposed for automatic novel or story generation, and the cutup method was introduced. In fact, the shown strategies show great possibilities for literary-work generation. Of course, they do not always generate good work. However, from many generated works, it is possible to select good works. Computers can be used in such a way.

In addition, Geravás et al. discussed the *Story Generator Project*. In the paper, they reviewed many story-generation systems based on artificial intelligence (AI):

*Neither the under-defined nor the over-specific concepts developed in literary theory and Narratology seem good choices for AI formalizations. In the same vein, the limited scope of predominantly descriptive linguistic models renders these unsatisfactory. Conversely, Artificial Intelligence approaches in Story Generation are generally based on a highly reductionist concept of 'story,' which ignores the Humanities' disciplines' insights into the complexity and dynamics of narrative....*

*In our view, a methodological combination of description, analysis, and generation—in other words: an inter-disciplinary approach—holds the potential for a mutually beneficial qualitative breakthrough in research on Story Generation, and on narrative models in general. This inter-disciplinary approach might start by identifying those existing narrative models in the Humanities whose set of ontological commitments is better suited for the Story Generation task, and by searching for (or producing) computationally oriented implementations of these models. (Gervás, Lönneker-Rodman, Meister, & Peinado, 2006)*

The author has been studying literary-work generation as a part of LSE. In fact, several approaches can or should be applied to this field. First, we had to remove or limit the emotional part of the literary work. However, we will currently be able to focus on such affective or psychological parts of literary works in their generation.

## FUTURE RESEARCH DIRECTIONS

In the above text, the author illustrated the possibility of literary-work generation from the aspect of intertextuality. Although rather random generation is focused on above, our final direction should deal with the affective aspects of literary-work generation. Currently, the above applications deal only partially with the affective aspect. In fact, such technologies are not sufficient to deal with these aspects. For future directions, it will be necessary to focus on more affective aspects of literary-work generation. Therefore, it will be necessary to develop strategies to feel and generate human-type emotional activities.

In addition, Ryan and Thon replaced "narrative" with "storyworld" and pointed out:

*Nowadays, we have not only multimodal representations of storyworlds that combine various types of signs, and virtual online worlds that wait to be filled with stories by their player citizens, but also serial storyworlds that span multiple installments, and transmedial storyworlds that are deployed simultaneously across multiple media platforms, resulting in a media landscape in which creators and fans alike constantly expand, revise, and even parody them. (Ryan & Thon, 2014)*

In the future, such media-conscious narratologies can be considered to create better literary works.

## CONCLUSION

In this chapter, the author reviewed several works that were studied as LSE and other works as literary-work generation. For literary-work generation, the author focused on the concept of intertextuality. This is a very simple concept, but is suitable for computational operation. In fact, novelists and poets frequently select good and proper quotations from existing works. It is rather difficult for computers to understand which phrases are good or proper when constructing novels and poems. However, computers can generate many novels and poems in a short time. Accordingly, the proper selection of phrases is not a serious problem. After the generation of novels and poems, the better works can be selected by humans.

In addition, for affective or psychological aspects of language, the author developed and introduced the conceptual base, which can calculate the relationship or similarity of objects. Using the conceptual base and the concept of intertextuality, the author studied a riddle-solving system and an automatic waka-generation system. From the experience, it may be possible to build a certain literary-work-generation system. In addition, the author introduced several literary-work generation methods, such as the cutup method, and story-generation systems. Artificial intelligence systems, such as abduction and analogical mapping, can be added to literary-work generation. For that purpose, Abe (1998) discussed the generation of humorous conversation using abduction and analogical mapping. The author also introduced context changes to generate humorous conversations. Such a strategy can also be adopted for a literary-work generation system.

## REFERENCES


Abe, A. (1998). Applications of abduction. In *Proceedings of the ECAI98 Workshop on Abduction and Induction in AI* (pp. 12-19). Academic Press.

Abe, A. (2002). Computational generation of affective phrase. In *Proceedings of SCI2002*, (vol. 16, pp. 261-266). Academic Press.

Binsted, K. (1996). *Machine humour: An implemented model of puns.* (Ph. D. Thesis). University of Edinburgh.

Binsted, K., & Ritchie, G. (1994). An implemented model of punning riddles. *Proceedings of, AAAI94*, 633–638.

Binsted, K., & Takizawa, O. (1998). BOKE: A Japanese punning riddle generator. *Journal of the Japanese Society for Artificial Intelligence, 13*(6), 920–927.

Genette, G. (1972). *Discours du récit, essai de methode, Figures III.* Paris: Seuil.

Gervás, P., Lönneker-Rodman, B., Meister, J. C., & Peinado, F. (2006). Narrative models: Narratology meets Artificial Intelligence. In *Proceedings of International Conference on Language Resources and Evaluation* (pp. 44-51). Academic Press.

Grice, H. P. (1957). Meaning. *The Philosophical Review, 66*(3), 377–388. doi:10.2307/2182440

Ito, M. (1999). Sakushi Android Yuming [Poem making Android Yuming]. *JSAI SIG Report, SIG-LSE-9903-S2.*

Kanasugi, T., Matsuzawa, K., & Kasahara, K. (1996). ABOUT suiron no "kotoba asobi" heno tekiyou [Application of ABOUT Reasoning to solving Wordplays]. *Technical Report of IEICE, NLC96-31.*

Kasahara, K., Matsuzawa, K., Ishikawa, T., & Kawaoka, T. (1996). Viewpoint-based measurement of semantic similarity between words. In *Proceedings of the 5th International Workshop on Artificial Intelligence and Statistics (LNS112)* (pp. 433-442). doi:10.1007/978-1-4612-2404-4_41

Kristeva, J. (1980). *Desire in language: A semiotic approach to literary work and art.* Columbia University Press.

Manurung, R., Ritchie, G., Pain, H., Waller, A., O'Mara, D., & Black, R. (2008). The construction of a pun generator for language skills development. *Applied Artificial Intelligence, 22*(9), 841–869. doi:10.1080/08839510802295962

Matsuzawa, K., Abe, A., Kanasugi, T., & Nagamori, C. (1997). Gainen-base wo mochita network-kata "kotoba asobi" no teian [Proposal of wordplays on the network using the conceptual base]. In *Proceedings of the 3rd Annual Meeting of the ANLP*, E5-4 (pp. 577-580).

Matsuzawa, K., Kanasugi, T., & Abe, A. (1998). Computer jou no gengo kankaku jitsugen ni mukete: B-kyu machine [Computational language sense: Perpetual word-playing machine]. In *Proceedings of the JSAI Annual Meeting*, 37-11 (pp. 685-686).

Ministry of Economy, Trade, and Industry. (Eds.). (2007, May). "KANSEI" Initiative—Suggestion of the Fourth Value Axis. *Ministry of Economy, Trade, and Industry Press Release*. Retriever from http://www.meti.go.jp/english/information/downloadfiles/PressRelease/080620KANSEI.pdf

Ogata, T. (1998). A proposal of computational narratology. *PSJ SIG Notes Computer and Humanities Abstract* No. 041 - 008.

Ontañón, S., & Zho, J. (2011). The SAM algorithm for analogy-based story generation. In *Proceedings of the 7th AAAI Conference of Artificial Intelligence and Interactive Digital Entertainment* (pp. 67-71). Academic Press.

Propp, V. Y. (1968). *Morphology of the folktale* (2nd ed.). (L. A. Wagner, Trans.). University of Texas Press. (Original work published 1928)

Ritchie, G. (2005). Computational mechanisms for pun generation. In *Proceedings of the 10th European Natural Language Generation Workshop* (pp. 125-132). Academic Press.

Ritchie, G. (2008). Uninformed resource creation for humour simulation. In *Proceedings of the 5th International Joint Workshop on Computational Creativity* (pp. 147-150). Academic Press.

Ritchie, G. (2009). Can computers create humor? *AI Magazine*, *30*(3), 71–81.

Ritchie, G., Manurung, R., Pain, H., Waller, A., Black, R., & O'Mara, D. (2007). A practical application of computational humour. In *Proceedings of the 4th International Joint Conference on Computational Creativity* (pp. 91-98). Academic Press.

Ryan, M.-L., & Thon, J.-N. (Eds.). (2014). *Storyworlds across media*. University of Nebraska Press.

Rzepka, R., & Araki, K. (2015). Haiku generator that reads blogs and illustrates them with sounds and images. *Proceedings of, IJCAI2015*, 2496–2502.

Takiura, M. (2002). Kotoba asobi ha nani wo tsutaeruka?—Jakobson no shiteki kinou to Gris no kaiwa riorn wo baikai to shite[Wordplay and communication—from the viewpoint of poetic function by Jakobson and conversation theory by Gris]. *Nihongo Kagaku*, *11*, 79–96.

Thaler, M. (1987). *Jokes, riddles and activities*. Modern Publishing.

## KEY TERMS AND DEFINITIONS

**Conceptual Base:** A type of dictionary that can express a word (concept) using vector and calculates the similarity or associativity between words.

**Intertextuality:** Concept proposed by Kristeva. It means that any text is constructed as a mosaic of quotations; any text is the absorption and transformation of another.

**Language Sense:** Affective or psychological aspects of language.

**Waka:** Short Japanese poem.

## ENDNOTES

1 KANSEI is an original Japanese concept. KANSEI is defined as "a high-order function of the brain, including inspiration, intuition, pleasure and pain, taste, curiosity, aesthetics, emotion, sensitivity, attachment, and creativity" (Ministry of Economy, Trade, and Industry, 2007).

2 This phrase can be interpreted as, for instance, "Tyson is a strong boxer even though he had several problems."

3 The last vowel can be changed.

4 The last vowel can be changed.

5 This relationship between 'Syakkuri (hiccup)' and 'come out of mouth' can be calculated using the similarity determination algorithm (Kasahara et al, 1996). Then, the relationship between 'Syakkuri (hiccup)' and 'Kuchi (mouth),' that between 'Amaguri (sweet chestnut)' and 'Kuchi (mouth),' and that between 'Amaguri (sweet chestnut)' and 'Deru (come out of),' etc. can be calculated.

6 I offer an English translation, but it is not complete because it is not a complete poem. Accordingly, it will be difficult to understand.

7 For details, please refer to Wikipedia or http://www.synthtopia.com/content/2008/09/22/cutup-generator-creates-aleatory-text/.

8 It is rather difficult to translate the novel into English.

9 It is more difficult to translate the novel into English, and meaningless.

# Chapter 3
# Designing a Socially Open Narrative Generation System

**Taisuke Akimoto**
*The University of Electro-Communications, Japan*

**Takashi Ogata**
*Iwate Prefectural University, Japan*

## ABSTRACT

*The authors propose the design of a Socially Open Narrative Generation System (SONGS) that co-creates a collection of diverse narratives from a narrative generation program and people. This is a challenge of the social application of narrative generation technology used for vitalizing the social activity of producing and sharing narratives. The key idea is to connect and unify individual narrative productions by many agents, including a computer program and many humans, via a collection of narratives produced and accumulated by these agents. At the same time, SONGS is the practice of a computational approach to narratology as a model for the social process of narrative production. This chapter describes the key concepts and mechanism design of SONGS with several experimental programs.*

## INTRODUCTION

Narrative is a universal form of human knowledge and memory, and a strong way for people to communicate knowledge and information in their society. The computational modeling for narrative generation and understanding is a key topic for the next information society. Such modeling will contribute to the creation of human-friendly information technology and culture development. The fundamental interest of this study is to explore the possibilities of the social application of narrative generation technologies.

This chapter proposes the design of a Socially Open Narrative Generation System (SONGS) that will run on the Web as a space for co-creating a collection of diverse narratives from a narrative generation program and many humans. The ultimate goal of this study is to vitalize the social activity of producing and sharing narratives. Its long-term vision includes, in particular, the creation of a new type of platform

DOI: 10.4018/978-1-5225-0432-0.ch003

Copyright © 2016, IGI Global. Copying or distributing in print or electronic forms without written permission of IGI Global is prohibited.

for expanding and supporting creative activity and a content industry with computational narrative creativity. At the same time, SONGS is the practice of a computational approach to narratology as a model for the social narrative production process.

The remaining part is organized as follows. First, the authors provide background information on intelligent information technologies for narrative. Second, the authors propose the basic design of SONGS. Third, in the subsequent two sections, the authors describe the two main components of the narrative generation and interface parts. Finally, the authors discuss future works and conclude the chapter.

## BACKGROUND

This section takes two perspectives for providing background information. The first subsection reviews the history of the studies on narrative generation systems. For further information in this area, refer to the "Introduction" chapter of this book by Ogata or other surveys, such as Gervás (2009). The second subsection discusses the significance of narrative and narrativity for artificial intelligence (AI) and informatics.

### Narrative Generation System

Narrative generation systems, or the computational modeling of narrative creativity, are a challenging AI topic. The fundamental objectives include the computer implementation of narrative creativity and elucidation of the human narrative ability or narrative nature. In the early stage, since approximately 1970s to 1990s, researchers attempted to apply AI methods to narrative generation models. These studies are broadly divided into three approaches. First, several researchers attempted to model the story generation process as the planning of character actions directed by goals, emotions, or other bases (Meehan, 1980; Okada & Endo, 1992; Riedl & Young, 2010). Second, the formulation of generative rules or schemes for narrative structures were addressed (Pemberton, 1989; Lang, 1999; Bringsjord & Ferrucci, 1999). These are mainly rooted in a cognitive model of the story scheme (Rumelhart, 1975). The third approach was derived from the framework of case-based reasoning (CBR) (Riesbeck & Schank, 1989). In this approach, narrative generation is formalized as the transformation or adaptation of a previous narrative or case to fit the current problem (Turner, 1994; Peinado & Gervás, 2005; Swanson & Gordon, 2012).

Since approximately 2000s, several researchers have introduced narratology—the theory of narrative mainly inspired by structuralism—to narrative generation studies. Ogata (2002, 2004a) proposed a research methodology called "expanded literary theory" that aims to create synergy between narrative generation technologies and narratology. Gervás, Lönneker-Rodman, Meister, and Peinado (2006) also discussed the importance of interdisciplinary approaches for both disciplines of AI and narratology. In this movement, the morphology of the folktale by Propp (1968) has been applied to several studies as a model or schematic knowledge of story composition (Ogata & Terano, 1991; Peinado & Gervás, 2005; Imabuchi & Ogata, 2012; Gervás, 2015). In addition, narratology provided a distinction between story—"[t]he [content] plane of [narrative]" (Prince, 2003, p. 93)—and discourse—"[t]he [expression] plane of [narrative]" (Prince, 2003, p. 21)—to narrative generation studies. Whereas most of the early systems focus primarily on the story aspect, several recent studies have applied the narrative discourse theory by Genette (1980) to the modeling of narrative discourse composition (Ogata, 2004b; Montfort, 2007; Bae, Cheong, & Young, 2011; Akimoto & Ogata, 2012, 2013).

For the past few years, Ogata and colleagues have been developing an integrated narrative generation system (INGS) where the three generative modules for story structure, discourse structure, and surface expression are connected (refer to the "Introduction" chapter by Ogata for further information). This includes three narratology-based mechanisms that apply the theories of Propp (1968), Genette (1980), and Jauss (1982) as central elements for the story and discourse generation (Akimoto & Ogata, 2014). Although INGS is in an ongoing process of the research project, this systematic framework provides a solid foundation for the narrative generation mechanism of SONGS.

Meanwhile, narrative generation studies have great application potential for advanced information technologies, but this is almost unexplored. A possibility is to expand the creative activities of people or society. Narrative or narrativity is a common and core element of various artistic or entertainment works, such as novels, film, drama, manga (comic), anime (animation), video games, and commercial films. Narrative generation technologies can create new forms of expression and a creation method for the narrative. Interactive narrative systems are already a major genre of narrative content that uses computer technologies (Riedl & Bulitko, 2013), but this is based only on a semi-automatic narrative generation, and most content is designed by the human creators. Because of technological difficulties, there are very few applied studies on fully automatic narrative generation. However, the authors propose two exploratory applied narrative generation systems: "KOSERUBE," which automatically generates multimedia narrative expressions in the style of a folk tale (Akimoto et al., 2013), and "Narrative Forest," which figuratively expresses the floating narrative generation process within the system using the image of growing trees (Akimoto, Ono, & Ogata, 2013).

## Narrative as Information, Knowledge, and Intelligence

Narrativity is a fundamental nature of the human mind that forms memory or knowledge. From the psychological perspective, Bruner (1991) discussed that the human experience and cognition of the real world is based on narrativity and is formed as narratives. In addition, a narrative contextually integrates a variety of things or knowledge and effectively provides rich information to people. From such nature, narratives provide different values to people and society. People tell and receive narratives in various scenes of daily life. Narrative is commonly involved in various genres of art and entertainment. People develop knowledge or cultural literacy and cultivate sensitivity through the accumulation of such artistic experiences. Narrative is an effective and versatile communication tool for various business fields. Quesenbery and Brooks (2010) described practical methods of storytelling for improving the design processes of services or artifacts. Information technology has great potential to expand human activities in a broad range of fields.

Meanwhile, narrative is an essential research subject for the computational implementation of intelligence, a common goal of AI. Schank and colleagues have addressed the story nature of human intelligence and proposed several key AI frameworks, including Conceptual Dependency, script, plan, goal, and CBR (Schank & Abelson, 1977; Riesbeck & Schank, 1989; Schank, 1990). These ideas have significant influence on narrative generation studies.

Several researchers have addressed the construction of large-scale commonsensical knowledge bases mainly based on the concept of script. Singh, Barry, and Liu (2004) designed StoryNet as a database of scripts constructed through crowdsourcing. Chambers and Jurafsky (2010) presented a database of narrative schemas that consists of the semantic knowledge of events and their temporal relationships. This was constructed with their knowledge acquisition algorithms for learning narrative schemas from texts (Chambers, Wang, & Jurafsky, 2007; Chambers & Jurafsky, 2008, 2009). This type of knowledge is applicable to various tasks of natural language processing, such as understanding and summarization, and also provides a basic knowledge for narrative generation. McIntyre and Lapata (2009) and Li, Lee-Urban, Appling, and Riedl (2012) proposed a story generation method based on script similar to chains of events. The case base in the CBR-based narrative generator is also narratives.

Another important research topic is to explore how narrative-based knowledge works in a cognitive system. Although CBR provides a reasonable model, in recent years, several researchers have addressed modeling narrative-centered cognitive architecture and knowledge systems (Szilas, 2015; Anderson, 2015). From the perspective of cognitive systems, a role of narrative creativity is to construct internal narratives as knowledge or episodic memory from external information.

Similar to the topics discussed above, narrative computational modeling is a crucial problem for future intelligent information technology. First, it will expand the creation and sharing of narratives in society. Second, it is necessary for true intelligent systems that construct knowledge through interaction with the real world, subjectively cognize things, create new narratives or knowledge, and effectively communicate with others.

## BASIC DESIGN OF SONGS

Figure 1 shows the overall structure of SONGS, which co-creates a collection of narratives (CNs) through the continual interaction of produced narratives from a narrative generation program and many human users. The central idea of the narrative generation program is to model narrative generation as a cyclic process for composing new narratives in relation to previously generated narratives. The authors call this narrative-based narrative generator (NBNG). CNs provide NBNG with comprehensive knowledge for composing new narratives. In addition, SONGS involves an interface that opens CNs to individual humans (users). The design for SONGS assumes that users will access CNs based on their values or objectives, and appreciate contained narratives or create new ones by recomposing those that already exist. Moreover, user-created narratives are added to CNs. In order to allow such usage, the interface provides multiple perspectives on CNs, in particular:

1. Collective view on CNs for exploring valuable narratives,
2. Surface view on a narrative for appreciating it, and
3. Internal view on a narrative structure for creating a new narrative by recomposing the structure.

*Figure 1. Overall structure of SONGS*

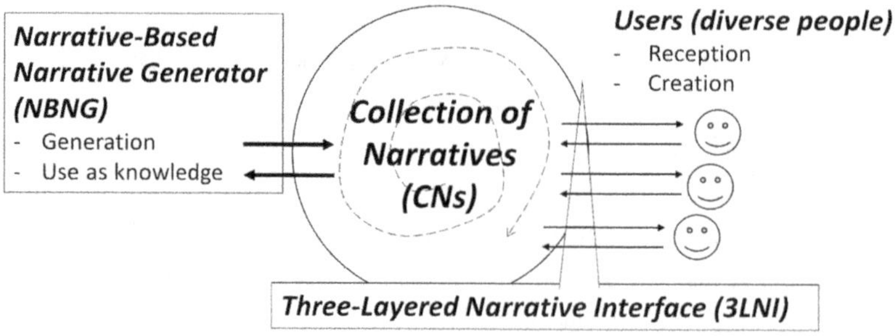

We call the interface that is based on the above framework a three-layered narrative interface (3LNI). The following four subsections describe the key concepts of SONGS.

## Narratives as Comprehensive Knowledge for Narrative Generation

Narrative is a type of comprehensive knowledge structure that contains various types of information or knowledge. A narrative can contain a variety of things, including events, humans, objects, abstract concepts, time, space, and so on, within its contextual information or meaning. In addition, the composition of a narrative implicitly includes such abstract or ill-defined information as emotion, sense of value, and aesthetic, which are crucial aspects for generating valuable narratives for people.

By focusing on the above narrative nature, SONGS positions CNs as the central knowledge for producing new narratives. The basic principle of using narratives as generative knowledge is to formalize a narrative generation process as recomposition of an existing narrative through structural operations, such as decomposition, transformation, and synthesizing with other narratives.

The point that SONGS positions individual and concrete narratives as the central knowledge is different from a major approach that generalizes narrative structures as a set of abstract rules or schemes—e.g., schematic methods based on Propp's morphology of the folktale (Ogata & Terano, 1991; Imabuchi & Ogata, 2012; Gervás, 2015). However, such abstract knowledge is essentially acquired empirically and dynamically from many narratives, similar to Propp (1968) deriving his morphological knowledge from the analyses of approximately 100 Russian fairy tales. An essential question is to explore a unified framework of the individuality/concreteness and generality/abstractness of narrative knowledge.

On the other hand, NBNG is partially similar to CBR-based narrative generators. Riesbeck and Schank (1989) described the basic procedure of CBR as "[finding] those cases in memory that solved problems similar to the current problem, and [adapting] the previous solution or solutions to fit the current problem, taking into account any difference between the current and previous situations" (p. 25). CBR-based narrative generators basically follow this procedure. However, NBNG uses CNs in flexible ways as types of materials for composing new narratives. In addition, narrative generation in NBNG is directed not as problem solving, but as the production or exploration of some differences and novelty from prior narratives. This concept is discussed in the next subsection.

## Narrative Generation in Relation to Prior Narratives

Because the macroscopic goal of SONGS is to accumulate a wealth of narratives through the continual generation cycle, the microscopic goal in each generation process is to produce a narrative that has some novelty or difference from prior narratives. Namely, the prior narratives are not only material knowledge for narrative generation, but basing points for creating new narratives. CNs have a higher-level structure for organizing the narratives, and by using it, NBNG systematically controls the narrative production.

A relationship among narrative works is a crucial aspect for the process of producing narratives in the real world. Several literary models of relative narrative production have discussed in the field of narratology. In early twentieth century, the movement of Russian formalism discussed a model for the evolution of literature as a continual cycle of "automatization" of human perception and alternation of the immanent laws of a particular genre (Tynyanov, 1982). Jauss (1982) presented a new idea concerning the history of literature. Although he respected the previous research regarding Russian formalism, he criticized the literary theory of evolution as being dependent upon the dynamism of change in narrative techniques and descriptions. He sought to center his literary process model in the dynamism of the mutual relationship between a literary work/author and the readers. His idea involved modeling the literary history of various relationships between a reader's "horizon of expectation" and literary works, including those estrangements and the change of horizon through a continual reception process.

In another context, Kristeva (1980) described the theory of "intertextuality," arguing that a literary text is positioned as an organization and citation of related preceding texts, and also included subsequent works for the reader. There exist few studies that apply the concept of intertextuality to narrative generation methods. Nakashima and Ogata (2006) proposed several experimental programs that generate new stories through elemental substitution or associations of an input story.

## Collective Narrative Generation

The co-creation in SONGS refers to the collective creation process as a continual chain reaction of narrative productions among different types of generative agents—i.e., NBNG and the users—via produced narratives or CNs. Narrative generation in SONGS is basically formalized as the recomposition or derivation of prior narratives. Computers where basic principles of narrative generation are programed can systematically produce a large number of different narratives in order to not be tied to commonsensical or stereotyped constraints on narratives. The distinct narrative creativity will bring inspiration or surprising ideas to the users. On the other hand, the cooperation of diverse users is important for both increasing the diversity of narratives and the generation ability of NBNG. How to attract and activate user creation activity is a key issue in designing SONGS.

Meanwhile, because SONGS aims to create new values for people or society, the problem is similar to the one for artifact design. Co-creation is an important approach in designing complex artifacts that involve pluralistic values related to various people (Fujita & Ota, 2015). Internet technology has expanded co-creation by many people. Tanaka (2011) introduced a novel design method called "Design as Re-Design." This refers to the continual upgrading and remixing of existing open data on the Web through "editing, reforming, or deriving" as a type of collective creation.

Collective creation is traditionally embedded in Japanese culture, and it is a distinguishing feature of contemporary subculture in Japan. Information technologies—e.g., online community spaces such as "Nico Nico Douga" (Niwango, n.d.) and "VOCALOID," a technology for singing voice synthesis (Yamaha, n.d.)—are increasing collective creation activity through "N-th order derivative creation" (Hamano, 2008). This activity is building a singular and rich culture. Co-creation is a valid approach for the problem of narrative generation, and SONGS aims to drive such type of activity by the computational narrative creativity.

## Providing Diverse Values to Diverse People

The authors broadly categorize types of users as readers, those who appreciate narratives, and authors, those who use SONGS for creating original narratives. For instance, potential uses of SONGS include the following situations: a manga (comic) artist searches/makes primitive materials for his/her work, a commercial planer searches/makes ideas of scenario for advertising a product, an amateur author creates derivative works of computer-generated narratives, and a student learns multiple perspectives on a social issue from different narratives relevant to the issue.

SONGS should provide some type of value to diverse users. The authors assume that narrative values include the following two aspects: giving some type of cognitive effect to readers—e.g., impression, surprise, and knowledge discovery—and giving some type of effect to the author's creation process or the result—e.g., inspiration, augmentation, extension, amplification, constraint, and inducing. In the above sense, narrative values vary depending on various factors, such as individual value, purpose or use situation, and historical or cultural background. Hence, it is difficult to computationally define and control narrative values.

The authors apply the computational design methodology called "Design as Search" introduced by Tanaka (2011) to the above problem. In the methodology, "design" refers to a process where the user searches or explores a preliminary modeled solution space for finding a solution that meets his/her need or purpose. In SONGS, the user searches valuable narratives from CNs. This is an application of the concept of "Design as Search." The system will be useful for individual users when there exist few valuable narratives for them, and they can find them. A central problem is designing an interface that allows the user to find valuable or desired narratives, including cases where the user has no explicit narrative needs. This is a common problem with general information retrieval. Although there is another method as a type of on-demand narrative generation, in many cases, users cannot represent their needs or have no clear narrative needs. In addition, it is difficult task to generate narrative that is suitable to the user's needs.

## NBNG: NARRATIVE-BASED NARRATIVE GENERATOR

In designing NBNG, the authors start with by modifying and expanding a Jauss-based narrative discourse generation system proposed by Akimoto and Ogata (2012, 2013). A central idea of the system is to model a generative process of historical or continual literature changes based on the reception theory by Jauss (1982). Although the implemented system has many theoretical problems, the fundamental idea is applicable to NBNG. After an overview of the Jauss-based system, the authors describe the NBNG design.

### Narrative Discourse Generation System

This subsection outlines the Jauss-based system based on Akimoto and Ogata (2012, 2013) and discusses the issues from the perspective of SONGS. The system was developed as a prototype version of the discourse generation part of INGS. The system generates a series of different "discourse" structures from an input "story" structure. A story represents the content information of a narrative. In particular, it represents the temporal sequence of events. A discourse means the structural aspect of how a story is expressed. Discourse generation refers to structural transformations from a story structure to a discourse one, and it is modeled based on the narrative discourse theory by Genette (1980). Jauss's theory is applied to the controlling model of continual discourse generation.

#### Modeling of Discourse Generation Based on Genette's Theory

Both story and discourse are described through the conceptual representation of a tree that consists of "events" and "relations." Figure 2 shows diagrams of story and discourse structures. An event is the basic unit of constituting a story or discourse, whereas a relation semantically combines the child nodes, i.e.,

*Figure 2. Story and discourse structures*

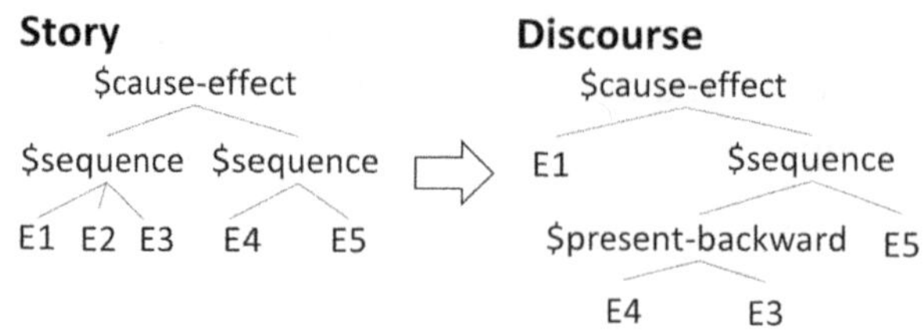


the events or sub-structures. In the figure, events and relations are indicated by "E*" and "$*", respectively. An event is represented with a case structure of verb concept. Figure 3 is an example of event representation. The system includes a simple natural language generator for transforming a conceptual representation to Japanese text. For instance, the event representation in Figure 3 is transformed into the sentence "蛇が皇女を誘拐した" ("a snake abducted a princess").

Structural transformation techniques, or "discourse techniques," are defined by applying the narrative discourse theory by Genette (1980). He categorized various classes of discourse structures through the analysis of a novel. His discourse classes consists of the following three broad categories: "tense," which concerns the relationship between the time of the story and that of the discourse; "mood," which concerns the modality for regulating narrative information; and "voice," which concerns the relationship among narration, story, and discourse. Each category is further divided into subcategories.

Through the computational formalizations of part of Genette's subcategories, the authors implemented the following 13 discourse techniques: "external analepsis," "complementary analepsis_ellipsis," "complementary analepsis_paralipsis," "repetitive analepsis," "external prolepsis," "complementary prolepsis_ellipsis," "complementary prolepsis_paralipsis," "repetitive prolepsis," "achronie," "pause," "implicit ellipsis," "repeating," and "paralipsis." In general terms, they include the following transformation types: temporal ordering of events, adding supplemental events for the story, omitting events, repeating events, and inserting descriptions of characters, objects, or locations. For instance, in the discourse structure of Figure 2, E2 is omitted by "implicit ellipsis" and E3 is reordered by "complementary analepsis_ellipsis."

*Figure 3. Representation of an event (the words in angle brackets are English translations)*

(event 誘拐する(1) <abduct>
(*type* action)
(*ID* 1)
(*time* (1 2))
(*agent* 蛇<snake>)
(*counter-agent* 皇女<princess>)
(*object* nil)
(*instrument* nil)
(*location* 庭<garden>)
(*from* nil)
(*to* nil))

One or more discourse techniques can be used in combination with generating a discourse structure. Different discourse structures are generated depending on the selected techniques and target part—i.e., a node of the tree structure—of each technique. Because each target part is determined randomly with several conditions, output structures by the same combination of techniques have relatively small differences.

## Continual Discourse Generation Based on Jauss's Reception Theory

Jauss (1982) developed seven theses for the essence of his reception theory. The authors focus mainly on theses II and III in modeling the continual generation process. Jauss's thesis II describes the "horizon of expectation" as being the reader's preliminary knowledge for ranking a literary work in the context of reading experience, and this can be acquired by known genres and exposure to famous literary works. In thesis III, Jauss proposes that readers understand literary artistic features as the distance between the work and their "horizon of expectation." If the distance is small, the work has strong recreational purpose and a familiar beauty. Those with large distances have various and distinguished influences for the reader: to one reader the work may be highly regarded creative work, but it could be a waste of time to another reader. The horizon can change so that the impression of a work becomes ordinary for a reader.

The authors modeled Jauss's historical view as an iterative mutual action, referred to as "generation cycle," between the two mechanisms of narrative generator, or "narrator," and evaluator, or "narratee." Figure 4 outlines the process flow. In the system, authors and readers in Jauss's theory respectively correspond to the narrator and narratee mechanisms. The notion of "horizon of expectation" is objectivized as the narratee's expectation represented as a set of parameters.

The input consists of a story, initial parameters of the narrator's generative goal and the narratee's expectation, total number of generating discourses, and other configurations. The parameters for the generative goal and expectation commonly consist of the following ten structural features: "supplement," "complexity," "suspense," "length," "hiding," "descriptiveness," "repetition," "diffuseness," "implication," and "temporal-independency." Each parameter takes a value of 1 (small), 2 (medium), or 3 (large). Through an iterative generation process, the system outputs a series of discourses. A text by the natural language generator and log data accompany each discourse.

The generation cycle continues according to the interaction between the narrator and narratee. First, the narrator generates discourse from the input story based on the generative goal. The narrator has a

*Figure 4. Jauss-based narrative discourse generation system*

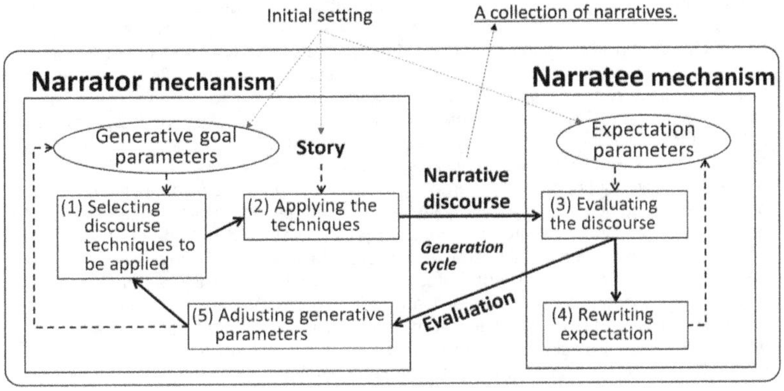

set of rules for controlling the application of discourse techniques based on the generative parameters. The narratee then evaluates the results by comparing his/her expectation parameters and the narrator's generative ones. In the next cycle, the narrator applies corrections according to the evaluation in order to achieve the narratee's satisfaction. The process, however, eventually reaches a point where the narratee becomes tired or his/her satisfaction begins to fall. When this happens, "deviation" occurs and the narrator abandons a portion of the old generative parameters and moves to the generation of a discourse with the new generative goal. The narratee's expectations also change according to the reconstruction.

## System Behavior

The authors show an example of executing the system for 10,000 steps. In Figure 5, the upper and lower texts respectively show the input story and generated discourse by English translations of Japanese sentences by the natural language generator. The authors added explanations on the discourse structure in angle brackets.

In order to analyze all generated discourses, the authors defined metrics to quantify the structural features of each discourse, referred to as discourse feature values (DFVs) (see Table 1). These features correspond to the aforementioned ten parameters in the system. These metrics are incorporated in the above system, and DFVs for each generated discourse are automatically logged in the generation cycle. Figure 6 shows the transitions of each DFV from step 1 to 1000. There are two types of changing patterns: micro level changes based on the same generative parameters that occur in each step, and macro level changes caused by the narrator's deviations.

## Issues

The central problem of the above model is that the narrator and narratee mechanisms are disconnected from accumulated discourses through the generation cycle. In each step, the narrator generates a discourse from the input story according to a set of absolute parameters represented in three-point scale.

Potential narratives to be generated are prelimited depending on finite combinations of parameters, independently of the past history of the system actions. Actually, the authors observed that the difference

*Figure 5. Generation example*

Natural language expression of the input story (English translation):
A snake abducted a princess at a garden. An older woman sang a grief-stricken song at the garden. Ivan resolved to search the princess at a town. Ivan departed from the town. Ivan battled with the snake at the snake's land. Ivan injured his arm by the snake at the snake's land. Ivan won against the snake at the snake's land. Ivan abducted the princess at the snake's land. Ivan departed from the snake's land. The snake flied at the snake's land. The snake chased Ivan at the snake's land. Ivan hid himself on the back of a rock at the snake's land. The princess knew Ivan's wound at the snake's land. Dwarfs built a palace at the town. Ivan lived at the palace. Ivan married with the princess at the palace.

Natural language expression of a generated discourse (English translation):
A snake abducted a princess at a garden. [<future> The princess divorced with Ivan. The princess returned home from a palace.] An older woman sang a grief-stricken song at the garden. Ivan resolved to search the princess (at a town). Ivan departed from the town. [<future> Ivan won against the snake at the snake's land. [<future> Ivan lived at a palace.]] Ivan battled with the snake (at the snake's land). Ivan injured his arm by the snake. Ivan won against the snake. Ivan abducted the princess. The princess knew Ivan's wound. Dwarfs built a palace at the town. Ivan lived at the palace. Ivan married with the princess. [<backward> Ivan battled with the snake (at the snake's land). Ivan injured his arm by the snake. Ivan won against the snake.]

*Table 1. DFVs metrics*

| DFVs | Metrics |
|---|---|
| **DFV$_1$:** Supplement | Number of "events" positioned outside the story's temporal range that provide complementary information. |
| **DFV$_2$:** Complexity | Number of "relations" required to define temporal order transformations. A relation nested under one or more relations of temporal ordering is additionally weighted in proportion to the depth of nesting. |
| **DFV$_3$:** Suspense | Number of "events" moved from a backward position in the story and not accounted for before. |
| **DFV$_4$:** Length | Total number of "events" and "descriptions." |
| **DFV$_5$:** Hiding | Number of "events" contained in the story, but not accounted for in the discourse. |
| **DFV$_6$:** Descriptiveness | Number of "descriptions." |
| **DFV$_7$:** Repetition | Sum of the numbers of repetition of each "event." |
| **DFV$_8$:** Diffuseness | Subtraction of DFV$_5$ ("hiding") from DFV$_7$ ("repetition"), i.e., "diffuseness" is increased by "repetition" and decreased by "hiding." |
| **DFV$_9$:** Implication | Number of "relations" required to define the prospective temporal order transformation. |
| **DFV$_{10}$:** Temporal-independency | Number of "relations" using the "achronie" technique, which inserts events that do not have any temporal connection with the story. |

*Figure 6. Change of generated discourses through generation cycle*

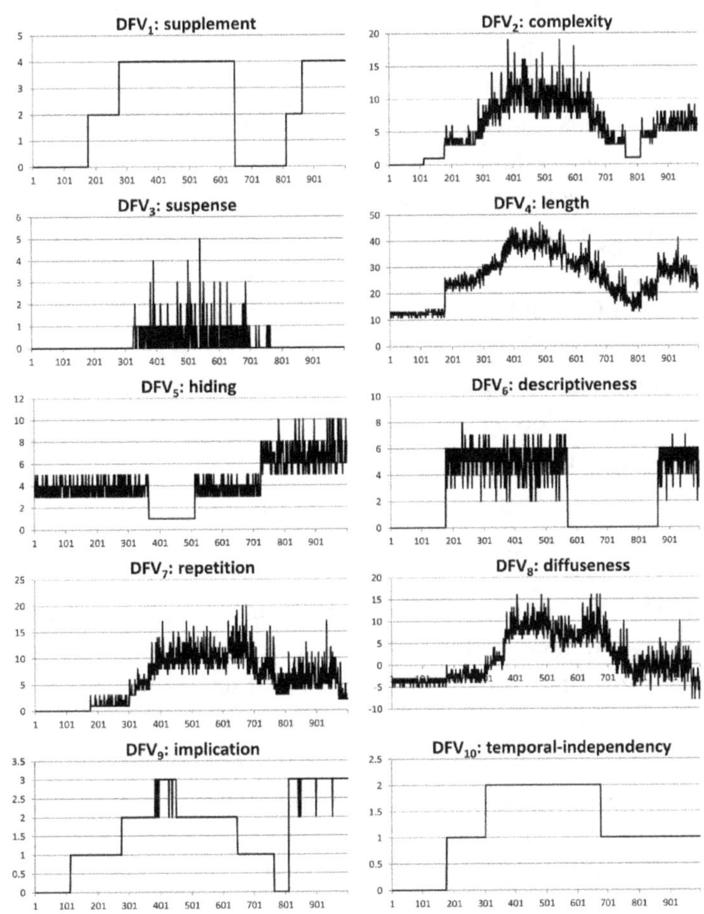

or novelty of the generated narrative from those prior, based on DFVs, decreases gradually through the generation cycle. Because the primary goal of NBNG is to continually increase narrative diversity, this model is not adequate for NBNG.

A root cause of the above problem is in the functional relationship between the narrator and narratee, i.e., the modeling of how the generation and reception interact in a continual narrative production process. The above system is implemented as the direct interaction of the generation and evaluation of the two agents. This is a personal interaction, rather than a social or historical process. However, the point of Jauss's theory is to provide the role of dynamically forming the "horizon of expectation" to the reception side (i.e., readers) and construct a literary history based on the historical change of the horizon. Namely, each work is historically positioned based on the relationship to the horizon at the time. In this manner, the reception side plays a central role in the construction of literary history. This idea is applicable to the model of production and organization of narratives in SONGS, but is missed in the above model. The authors designed a new model for NBNG mainly by modifying this problem.

## Designing NBNG

A main modification from the previous model is to place the recipient side not as the direct evaluation mechanism for the narrative, but as the mechanism for organizing narratives in CNs. In particular, the recipient side attaches external attribute information to a generated narrative in order to position the narrative into the organization of CNs. On the other hand, the generation side generates new narratives with reference to CNs, based on a relative goal as difference from prior narratives. This way, an indirect interaction between the narrative generation and reception arise via CNs. In addition, the authors mainly apply the following modifications. First, the users are explicitly associated with the model. Second, the system treats the total process of narrative generation, not only discourse generation, but also story generation. Third, the authors completely revise the terms from the previous model. In particular, because the mechanisms of narrative generation and reception in SONGS are positioned as being the outside agents of a narrative text, the authors change the names narrator—"[t]he one who narrates, as inscribed in the text" (Prince, 2003, p. 66)—and narratee—"[t]he one who is narrated to, as inscribed in the text" (Prince, 2003, p. 57)—to "generator" and "recipient," respectively. Figure 7 shows the overall architecture of NBNG, including the relationships to CNs and users. In the figure, "N" indicates a narrative and "N*" means a narrative accompanied by the external attribute information by the recipient. The rest of this section describes the main elements of NBNG.

### Narrative (N)

In CNs, each N corresponds to a conceptual representation as the formal description of content and structure of a given narrative. In the development of INGS, the authors defined a structural framework of narrative that consists of the three dimensions of story structure, discourse, and expression. A story represents the content information of a narrative and discourse is the structural aspect of how a story is expressed. A story is further divided into two types of structures: a temporal sequence of events and the background states. The latter corresponds to the structure of the story world that defines the information of characters, objects, and locations in a story.

According to the above framework, the authors defined a frame format, referred to as N-frame, for representing N in CNs (see Figure 8). Each italic element in the figure indicates a slot, a composing

*Figure 7. NBNG architecture*

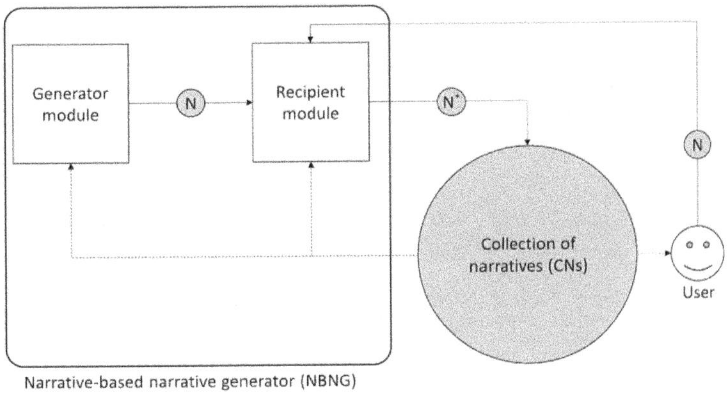


*Figure 8. N-frame*

N (
*StoryWorld* (conceptual representation of story world),
*Story* (conceptual representation of chronologically structured events),
*Discourse* (conceptual representation of discourse structure) )

element of N. Namely, N is composed of conceptual representations of the story world (*StoryWorld*), chronologically structured events (*Story*), and discourse structure (*Discourse*). The representation method of each element is basically defined based on that in INGS. Note that in SONGS, the narrative expression generation is a function of the interface part.

## Collection of Narratives (CNs)

CNs are organized based on the two substructures of "N*" and "Norm." Each element is defined by a frame format referred to as N*-frame, Norm-frame, and CNs-frame (see Figure 9). In the figure, each italic element indicates a slot, tailing plus ("+") means "one or more," and a period (".") between two elements means "of"—e.g., ID.N* means *ID* of N*.

In N*-frame, the *NarrativeStructure* slot contains N, and other slots correspond to the external attributes. *ID* indicates the unique number for N. *Time* marks the actual date when N is generated. It means the temporal position on the timeline of the continual production process. *BackgroundNorm* indicates the Norm in which N* is placed. *DerivedFrom* links prior N(s) used in generating N. *Feature* takes a set of feature values of N. It is similar to DFVs for the Jauss-based system.

Each Norm forms a subset of N*s that have some commonality in their features. In other words, it is an intermediate unit of CNs that corresponds to the notion of "horizon of expectation" in Jauss's theory. A Norm is used as the basis for both processes of the generator's narrative production and the recipient's narrative positioning. Norms and CNs are automatically updated when a new N* is added to CNs. In Norm-frame, *ID* and *Time* respectively indicate the unique number and temporal position. *Member* lists the contained N*s. *DerivedFrom* links the prior Norm(s) from which the Norm is derived. *NormSpace* represents the ranges of the feature values in the member N*s. CNs are only a set of all Norms.

*Figure 9. N*-frame, Norm-frame, and CNs-frame*

**$N^*$** (
*ID* (ID-number),
*Time* (time-number),
*NarrativeStructure* (N-frame),
*BackgroundNorm* (ID.Norm),
*DerivedFrom* (ID.$N^*$+),
*Feature* ($v_1$, $v_2$, …, $v_i$) )

**Norm** (
*ID* (ID-number),
*Time* (time-number),
*Member* (ID.$N^*$+),
*DerivedFrom* (ID.Norm+),
*NormSpace* ({min($v_1$), max($v_1$)}, {min($v_2$), max($v_2$)}, …, {min($v_i$), max($v_i$)}) )

**CNs** (
*Member* (ID.Norm+) )

Overall, CNs are organized based on the following four formation principles:

- **Timeline:** N*s and Norms are placed on a timeline (*Time*).
- **Norm-Based Hierarchy:** CNs are hierarchically grouped by Norms, in particular, *Member* in Norms and CNs and *BackgroundNorm* in N*s.
- **Derivative Network:** N*s and Norms are respectively linked based on their derivative relationships, in particular, *DerivedFrom* in N*s and Norms.
- **Feature Space:** N*s and Norms are positioned in a feature space based on their feature values, in particular, *Feature* in N*s and *NormSpace* in Norms.

## Process Flow

Figure 10 shows a total picture of the system actions through generator to recipient.

The generator produces a new N through the following procedure:

**G1 - Setting a Basing N*:** The generator selects N* for the basing point of generating a new N.

**G2 - Planning a Generative Strategy:** The generator makes a plan for how to recompose the basing N*. First, with reference to the *BackgroundNorm* of the basing N*, the generator sets a basic objective of either normative generation or deviation from the Norm. Deviation means an action to attempt to produce a new type of N by breaking the existing Norm. Based on the basic objective, the generator makes the following two choices: *what*, or target elements in the basing N*—i.e., constituents of *StoryWorld*, *Story*, and *Discourse*—and *how*, or operations for each target—e.g., transformation, deletion, addition, substitution, abstraction, concretization, and synthesizing with other N*s.

**G3 - Generating N:** The generator recomposes the basing N* in order to generate a new N based on the generative strategy.

The new N is sent to the recipient. In addition, the generator may send additional information to the recipient on background information of the generation process, i.e., the basing N* or *BackgroundNorm*. This helps the recipient to position N into CNs.

Next, the recipient composes N* through the following procedure:

*Figure 10. Total picture of system action*

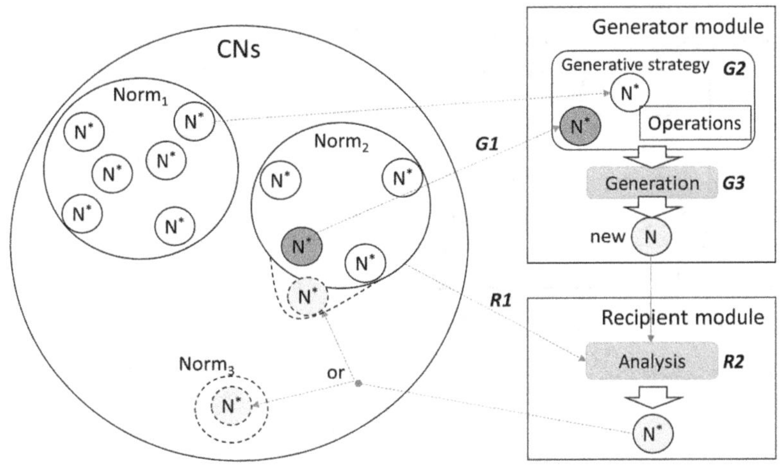


**R1 - Setting a basing Norm:** The recipient selects a basing Norm in receiving the N based on the generator's additional information.

**R2 - Composing N*:** The recipient analyzes N and fills the slots of N*-frame. The values of *ID*, *Time*, and *NarrativeStructure* are simply determined. *DerivedFrom* is determined by the Generator's additional information. The values of *Feature* are calculated by analyzing the structure of N. *BackgroundNorm* is determined based on *Feature*. When N is located near the basing Norm or the inside, based on the features, it is incorporated in the basing Norm—i.e., *BackgroundNorm* is the basing Norm. Otherwise, N is regarded as a deviation from the basing Norm and is positioned as a new Norm—i.e., *BackgroundNorm* is a new Norm to be created. Finally the composed N* is sent to CNs.

After the process, CNs and Norms are updated. When N* is placed in an existing Norm, the latter is expanded. Otherwise, a new Norm is created. The above process is iteratively executed at a regular time interval—e.g., once a minute. On the other hand, the user also can create a new N.

## 3LNI: THREE-LAYERED NARRATIVE INTERFACE

In this section, the authors propose the basic framework of 3LNI by considering a basic scenario for the use of SONGS. The central method is to visualize the following three aspects of CNs: organization of narratives, surface expressions of a narrative, and internal structures of a narrative. The authors also present a partial prototyping of 3LNI.

### Basic Scenario of SONGS Usage

Figure 11 shows a basic scenario of user actions. This consists of the following three phases:

- **Exploration Phase:** First, users explore CNs to find a valuable narrative for their value or objective. In particular, users repeat the following two actions until a valuable narrative is found. First,

*Figure 11. Basic scenario of SONGS usage*

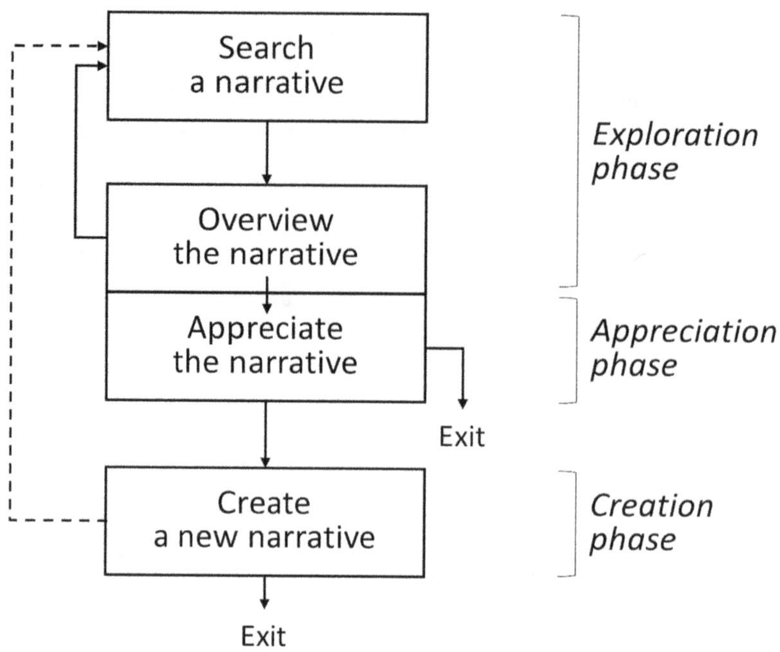


the users search and select a narrative from CNs. Second, they overview the narrative in a short time. If the narrative seems valuable, the users proceed to the appreciation phase. Otherwise, they search another narrative.

- **Appreciation Phase:** The users closely read or see the selected narrative. This phase is always performed regardless of whether the user's objective is appreciation or creation. Subsequently, when the users have an objective or motivation of narrative creation, they proceed to the creation phase. Otherwise, the users exit from SONGS.
- **Creation Phase:** The users create an original narrative using the selected narrative as the material or draft. In the process, the users can obtain additional narratives or materials from CNs, as indicated by the dotted arrow line in Figure 11. Finally, the created narrative is added to CNs via the NBNG recipient module.

## 3LNI Framework

As the authors indicate in the above scenario, the interface needs to provide mainly the three functions of exploration, appreciation, and creation. The framework of 3LNI is designed to integrate these functions and the authors employ visualization—a well-known technique for providing human-friendly expressions in order to understand a huge amount of data or complex objects—for the central interface method. In particular, 3LNI divides and connects the following three perspectives on CNs: *CNs layer*, or collective view on whole and parts of CNs; *NE layer*, or surface view on a narrative expression; and *NS layer*, or internal view on a narrative structure. Via the above views, individual users share CNs, i.e., the object of co-creation, with NBNG and other users. Figure 12 shows the above concept of 3LNI.

The basic functions of each layer are as follows:

*Figure 12. 3LNI basic concept*

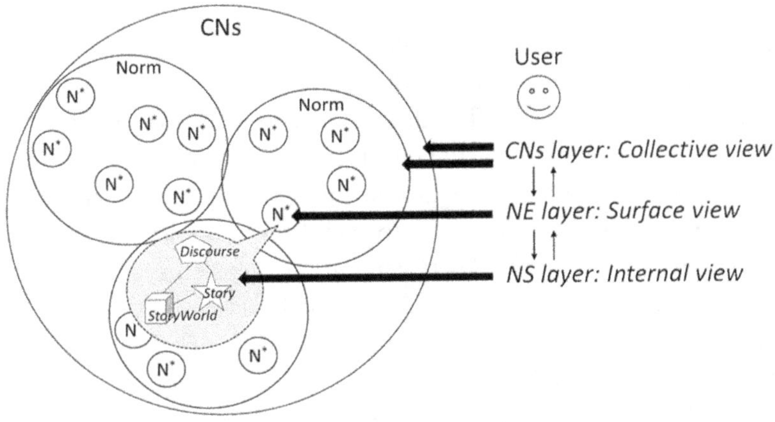


- **CNs Layer (Collective View):** This visualizes the organization of CNs into a two-dimensional space. Narratives or norms are represented as visual objects in the space. This includes various visualization methods depending on the CNs aspect or formation principle that is focused, in particular, timeline, norm-based hierarchy, derivative network, or feature space. The user explores and selects narratives with this macroscopic perspective.
- **NE Layer (Surface View):** This provides the surface expressions of a narrative. Because each narrative in CNs corresponds to a conceptual representation, surface expressions are generated in this layer. Natural language is a basic expression form. However, a narrative potentially allows various expressions depending on media—e.g., natural language, still or moving image, and music—and styles of expression. The user appreciates a narrative selected from the CNs layer.
- **NS Layer (Internal View):** This visualizes the internal structure of a narrative from multiple perspectives of the story world (*StoryWorld*), organization of events (*Story*), and discourse structure (*Discourse*). In addition, this layer includes editing functions that allow the user to visually recompose a narrative structure. The user sees the internal structures of a narrative from an analytical perspective and creates a new narrative by recomposing the visualized narrative structure.

In the exploration phase, the user mainly employs the CNs layer to search a narrative, and the NE layer to overview it. In addition, the NS layer may provide multifaceted summaries of a narrative structure and help the user understand it quickly. Meanwhile, keyword retrieval is a popular method for searching information or content. However, the authors assume that, in many cases, the user has no clear requirement for narratives or cannot adequately represent the requirement through language. The authors will apply keyword retrieval methods as a subsidiary function for the exploration phase in the CNs layer.

The above design positions the user creation phase in the NS layer. Although it is possible to design the creation phase at the surface expression level or NE layer, in order to share user-created narratives with NBNG, surface narratives must be transformed into a conceptual representation. This is a very difficult task for a computer. In addition, editing narrative expressions requires significant time and effort from the user. Hence, designing editing functions in the NS layer is a key issue for smoothly circulating the collective creation process between NBNG and users.

## VISUAL INTERFACE FOR COMPUTER-GENERATED NARRATIVES

As a preceding idea for 3LNI, Akimoto and Ogata (2015a) proposed a visual interface for exploring narratives generated by the Jauss-based narrative discourse generation system introduced in the section "Narrative Discourse Generation System." The design concept partially overlaps the 3LNI framework. This subsection outlines the implemented visual interface in order to provide the readers with a concrete image of a part of 3LNI. The basic idea of the interface is to arrange and visualize many narratives into a two-dimensional space that allows users to explore and browse narratives based on their values or objectives. Figure 13 shows the relationship between the Jauss-based system and the visual interface.

The composition of a series of narratives produced by the Jauss-based system is summarized in Figure 14. Such composition consists of a number of groups or subsets of narratives respectively formed by the same set of generative parameters. Namely, each group contains one or more narratives with similar features. In terms of the SONGS design, the entire set of narratives and groups correspond to CNs and norms, respectively. The number of narratives in each group is indefinite, but loosely controlled depending on the initial configurations of the Jauss-based system. A new group is produced via the narrator's deviation process that changes a parameter value. In Figure 14, "N" refers to a set of discourse structure, the natural language expression, and DFVs. Although the design of 3LNI includes the function of narrative expression generation in the NE layer, in this version, this is embedded in the Jauss-based system.

The preprocessing part in Figure 13 calculates the statistics—minimum, maximum, and average for each DFV—of each narrative group and the entire set of narratives. The visual interface uses the group-based hierarchy and feature spaces to organize the narratives into a two-dimensional space. In particular, this consists of the following three perspectives:

**V1:** This plots the visual objects of the groups.
**V2:** This plots the visual objects of the narratives in a group.
**V3:** This represents a narrative by a natural language text and diagram of the structure.

*Figure 13. Process flow through narrative generation to visual interface*

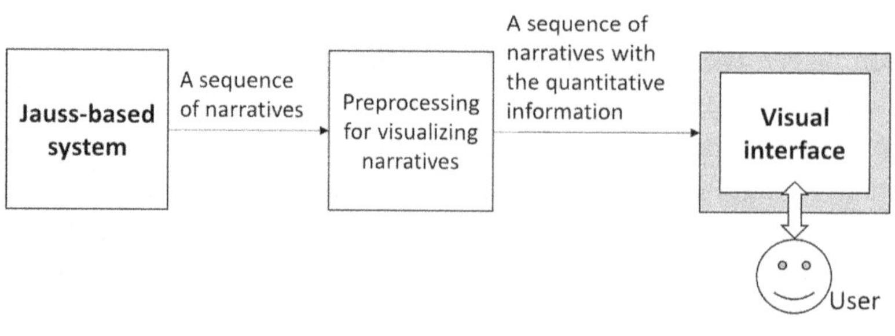


*Figure 14. Composition of a series of generated narratives*

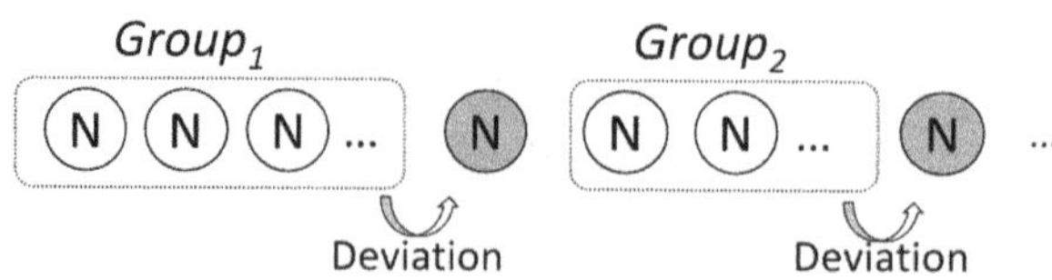

In terms of the 3LNI framework, V1 and V2 correspond to the CNs layer, and V3 includes the NE and NS layers. Each perspective corresponds to an interface window, and these are mutually connected via the visual objects. Figures 15–17 show screenshots of each window for a series of 10,000 generated narratives with 271 groups. The input story is equal to that shown in Figure 5. In V1 and V2, two of the DFVs are used to arrange the discourses into a two-dimensional space. We indicate the features of the horizontal and vertical axes as $DFV_x$ and $DFV_y$, respectively. Choosing different features for these axes results in different narrative arrangements. In Figures 15 and 16, $DFV_x$ and $DFV_y$ are $DFV_4$ (length) and $DFV_2$ (complexity), respectively. The user can change $DFV_x$ and $DFV_y$ using the "up"/"down" and "left"/"right" arrow keys, respectively.

In the V1 window, each group is represented by a blue rectangle with the group number. In the space, the left/lower ends and right/upper ends correspond to the minimum and maximum of $DFV_x$/$DFV_y$ in the entire set of narratives, respectively. The area of a rectangle represents the ranges of $DFV_x$ and $DFV_y$ in the corresponding group. The users can move to the V2 window by clicking the left mouse button on a group number.

In the V2 window, each discourse is represented by a small yellow circle. The center of the space—i.e., the intersection of the horizontal and vertical axis lines—corresponds to the average of each $DFV_x$ and $DFV_y$. Discourse objects are positioned based on their distance from the center, i.e., the averages. In addition, the deviated discourse is positioned as a small red circle. The user can move to the V3 window by clicking the left mouse button on a small circle. When the user clicks the right mouse button on a small circle, a sub-window for the miniature window L3 is displayed. In Figure 16, a sub-window of $Discourse_{3507}$ is shown. The user can return to the V1 window by clicking the "back" button.

The V3 window expresses a narrative using Japanese text and a diagram of the structure. The text in Figure 17 corresponds to the English expression of the generation example in Figure 5. The diagram

*Figure 15. V1 window that contains 271 groups*

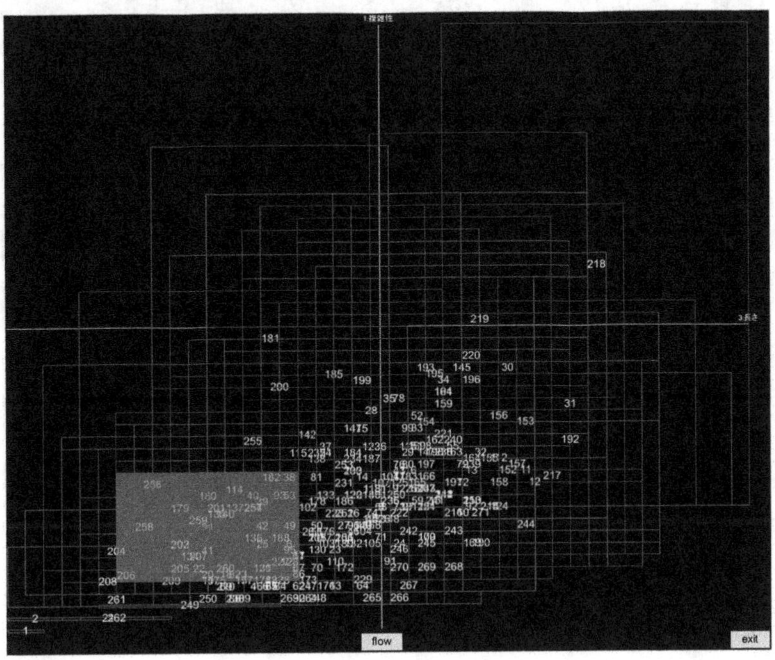

*Figure 16. V2 window of group$_{94}$ that contains 37 narratives*

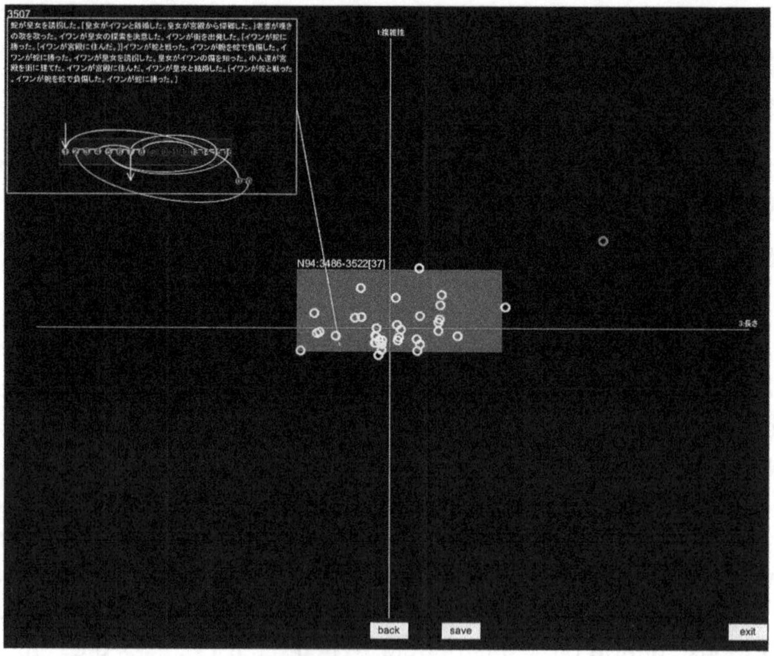


*Figure 17. V3 window of narrative$_{3507}$*

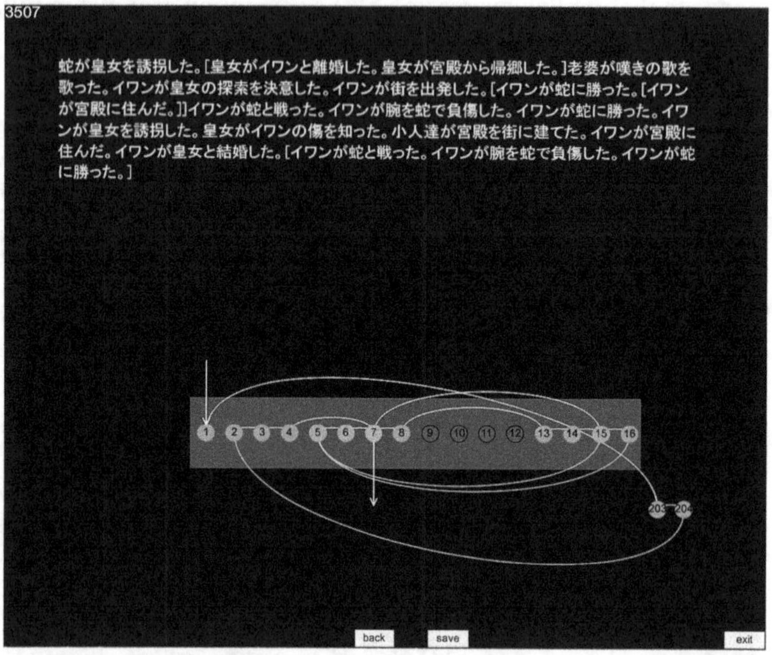

represents the discourse structure using a graph. Each node (numbered circle) corresponds to an event, and the edges show the flow of the narration (for more detail, refer to Akimoto and Ogata (2015a)). The user can save the narrative text to a file by clicking the "save" button and return to the V2 window by clicking the "back" button.

## FUTURE RESEARCH DIRECTIONS

This chapter presented the core concepts and basic mechanism design of SONGS. The next challenge is to concretize the system design through the constructive cycle of experimental developments and the verifications or considerations of mechanisms. A main focus is to design a method for strategically triggering various types of creative interactions between NBNG and human users. At the same time, it is important to discuss a macroscopic vision on the social impact of SONGS for determining the correct direction of system development. In the following subsections, first, the authors describe a plan for designing interaction between NBNG and human users. Second, the authors draw several long-term visions toward relating SONGS to the real world.

### Toward Interaction Design between Generative Program and People

In order to produce a wealth of CNs, SONGS needs to be able to originate various types or modes of creative interactions between the generative program (i.e., NBNG) and many humans in the collective creation process. For this, it is important to design not only the mechanism of the program side, but also the behavior of the human side. If the program's narratives have an expansionary effect on human narrative creations—e.g., increasing the diversity of created narratives or triggering unique ideas—this will be a positive aspect of SONGS. In contrast, if the program's narratives do not give rise to such positive phenomena, the authors should consider the causes and redesign the system.

From the above perspective, the authors have conducted an experiment to investigate the effects of computer-generated narratives on human narrative creation using a narrative generation system that consists of the Jauss-based system and visual interface, i.e., preceding versions of NBNG and 3LNI (for details of the experiment, refer to Akimoto and Ogata (2015b)). In the experiment, 14 human subjects were divided into two groups: A and B. Each subject in group A used the system and created a variety of scenarios by obtaining narrative texts on the interface and then editing them to make them unique. Each subject in group B performed the same creation task, but without using this system. The authors then analyzed the structures of created scenarios and compared the differences between the scenarios created by both groups. From the experiment results, the authors found a type of creation mode where humans strengthen the weakness of structural organization of computer-generated narratives. From a cognitive perspective, it seems that blanks or disconnections from the flow of a narrative text generated by the program strongly induce human creation in order to cause the narrative to be organized logically. This way, many scenarios were created that have unique storylines. A direction of future development is to design functions of the NS layer of 3LNI that allow this type of creation. However, the authors also need to consider strategies for triggering more diverse modes of the human creation processes.

## Toward Relating SONGS to Real World

Next the authors take a long-term view and discuss possible impacts of SONGS to the real world. First, the central goal of SONGS is to activate creative activity and content industry in the real world. In order to consider this possibility, the authors discuss the relationship between the characteristics of the Japanese content industry based on Koyama (2009) and those of the SONGS design. Koyama described the characteristics and strengths of the Japanese-style content industry model by comparing with the Hollywood style. According to Koyama, the characteristics of the Hollywood style model can be summarized as follows: Groups of many professionals mass-produce huge works and maximize the benefits that arise from "hits." In this type of model, because the professionals excessively pursue the maximization of benefits while avoiding risks, diversity of subjects or narratives in the works tend to decrease. In contrast, the Japanese style model has the following characteristics: a) the boundary between professionals and amateurs is vague and there are many and diverse creators, b) the boundary of creators and consumers is vague and derivative, or collective creation activity is lively, c) the market consists mostly of small to medium-scaled works, d) there is a high degree of freedom for creation/expression activity, and so on. The unique and diverse creative culture in Japan is underpinned by these types of characteristics.

These characteristics of the Japanese style model are, at a fundamental level, largely similar to the design concepts of SONGS. In addition, SONGS drives the co-creative cycle through the computer program with a distinguishing narrative creativity. It has the potential of creating a new platform for expanding the creative culture and content industry. In order to obtain several users and gain powerful influence on the real world, it is naturally important to enhance the system's basic performance, such as the quality of produced contents, interface usability, degree of freedom for user creation, etc. The accumulation of steady efforts to achieve these is required.

Another possibility or secondary application of SONGS is for CNs to be a type of knowledge resource for intelligent information technologies in various fields. As described in the background section, narrative or story-based knowledge is focused as an important aspect of intelligence. Because each narrative in CNs consists of conceptual information by formal descriptions, CNs have high availability for computers or AI systems. For instance, lately, humanoid robots or AI applications have been active in various fields, such as entertainment, nursing care, education, etc. CNs can help the dialogue or storytelling tasks of such AI systems in various situations by providing diverse narratives. In addition, narrative knowledge or creativity is necessary for human-like intelligent machines. For instance, CNs or NBNG can be applicable to robots that compose high-level future goals or action plans, similar to the way in which humans makes decisions or life plans based on their narrative knowledge, such as past experiences, history, and so on.

## CONCLUSION

In this chapter, the authors proposed a design of SONGS that continually co-creates a wealth of narratives between a narrative generation program and many human users. This is based on the following four design concepts:

- SONGS uses narratives as comprehensive knowledge for producing new narratives.
- SONGS controls the continual narrative production process with relation to prior narratives.

- The generative program and many humans collectively produce narratives through the interaction of produced narratives.
- SONGS provides diverse narratives for people with diverse values or objectives.

In the next study stage, through experimental developments, the authors will elaborate the designs of NBNG for the narrative generation engine, and 3LNI for the visual interface. An important basis for the narrative co-creation is to formalize the narrative structure and its operations. The authors will apply their fundamental study of INGS to the modeling of structural representation and operations of narrative in SONGS. Although this chapter focused on a particular system, the basic framework or idea can be applicable to other creative activities of structural artifacts, such as music, architecture, and graphic arts. SONGS can be a form of connection between computational creativity and the real world.

## REFERENCES


Akimoto, T., Imabuchi, S., Endo, J., Ono, J., Kurisawa, Y., Kamada, M., & Ogata, T. (2013). Development of a generation/expression system of narratives in the style of a folk tale, KOSERUBE Version 1. *Transactions of the Japanese Society for Artificial Intelligence*, *28*(5), 442–456. doi:10.1527/tjsai.28.442

Akimoto, T., & Ogata, T. (2012). A narratological approach for narrative discourse: Implementation and evaluation of the system based on Genette and Jauss. In *Proceedings of the 34th Annual Conference of the Cognitive Science Society* (pp. 1272-1277), Austin, TX: Cognitive Science Society.

Akimoto, T., & Ogata, T. (2013). Towards a discourse mechanism in narrative generation system: Proposal of a system introducing narrative discourse theory and reception theory. *Cognitive Studies*, *20*(4), 396–420.

Akimoto, T., & Ogata, T. (2014). An information design of narratology: The use of three literary theories in a narrative generation system. *The International Journal of Visual Design*, *7*(3), 31–61.

Akimoto, T., & Ogata, T. (2015a). A visual interface for a collection of computer-generated narratives. *Information Engineering Express*, *1*(4), 43–52.

Akimoto, T., & Ogata, T. (2015b). An investigation of effects of computer-generated narratives on humans' narrative creations. In *Proceedings of 32nd Annual Meeting of the Japanese Cognitive Science Society* (pp. 462-471). Chiba, Japan: Academic Press.

Akimoto, T., Ono, J., & Ogata, T. (2013). Designing information contents with automatic narrative generation system. In *Proceedings of the 5th International Conference of International Association of Societies of Design Research* (pp. 5424-5435). Tokyo, Japan: Academic Press.

Anderson, T. S. (2015). From episodic memory to narrative in a cognitive architecture. In *Proceedings of 6th Workshop on Computational Models of Narrative* (pp. 2-11). Atlanta, GA: Academic Press.

Bae, B. C., Cheong, Y. G., & Young, M. R. (2011). Automated story generation with multiple internal focalization. In *Proceedings of 2011 IEEE Conference on Computational Intelligence and Games* (pp. 211-218). Seoul, South Korea. doi:10.1109/CIG.2011.6032009

Bringsjord, S., & Ferrucci, D. A. (1999). *Artificial intelligence and literary creativity: Inside the mind of BRUTUS, a storytelling machine*. Mahwah, NJ: Lawrence Erlbaum.

Bruner, J. (1991). The narrative construction of reality. *Critical Inquiry, 18*(1), 1–21. doi:10.1086/448619

Chambers, N., & Jurafsky, D. (2008). Unsupervised learning of narrative event chains. In *Proceedings of 46th Annual Meeting of the Association for Computational Linguistics: Human Language Technologies* (pp. 789-797). Columbus, OH: Academic Press.

Chambers, N., & Jurafsky, D. (2009). Unsupervised learning of narrative schemas and their participants. In *Proceedings of Joint Conference of the 47th Annual Meeting of the Association for Computational Linguistics and the 4th International Joint Conference on Natural Language Processing of the Asian Federation of Natural Language Processing* (pp. 602-610). Suntec, Singapore. doi:10.3115/1690219.1690231

Chambers, N., & Jurafsky, D. (2010). A database of narrative schemas. In *Proceedings of Seventh International Conference on Language Resources and Evaluation* (pp. 1614-1618). Malta: Academic Press.

Chambers, N., Wang, S., & Jurafsky, D. (2007). Classifying temporal relations between events. In *Proceedings of the 45th Annual Meeting of the ACL on Interactive Poster and Demonstration Sessions* (pp. 173-176). doi:10.3115/1557769.1557820

Fujita, T., & Ota, J. (2015). *Jinkoubutsu kougaku nyuumon* [Introduction to artifact engineering]. Tokyo, Japan: University of Tokyo Press.

Genette, G. (1980). *Narrative discourse: An essay in method* (J. E. Lewin, Trans.). Ithaca, NY: Cornell University Press. (Original work published 1972)

Gervás, P. (2009). Computational approaches to storytelling and creativity. *AI Magazine, 30*(3), 49–62.

Gervás, P. (2015). *Computational drafting of plot structures for Russian folk tales*. Cognitive Computation;

Gervás, P., Lönneker-Rodman, B., Meister, J. C., & Peinado, F. (2006). Narrative models: Narratology meets artificial intelligence. In *Proceedings of Satellite Workshop: Toward Computational Models of Literary Analysis, 5th International Conference on Language Resources and Evaluation* (pp. 44-51). Genoa, Italy: Academic Press.

Hamano, S. (2008). *A-kitekucha no seitaikei* [Ecosystem of architecture]. Tokyo, Japan: NTT Publishing.

Imabuchi, S., & Ogata, T. (2012). A story generation system based on Propp theory: As a mechanism in an integrated narrative generation system. In H. Isahara & K. Kanzaki (Eds.), *Advances in Natural Language Processing: Proceedings of the 8th International Conference on Natural Language Processing (LNAI)* (*vol. 7614*, pp. 312-321). Berlin, Germany: Springer. doi:doi:10.1007/978-3-642-33983-7_31 doi:10.1007/978-3-642-33983-7_31

Jauss, H. R. (1982). *Toward an aesthetic of reception* (T. Bahti, Trans.). Minneapolis, MN: University of Minnesota Press. (Original work published 1970)

Koyama, Y. (2009). Futatsu no kontentsu sangyou sisutemu [Two content industrial systems]. In H. Deguchi, H. Tanaka & Y. Koyama (Eds.), Kontentsu sangyou ron: Konkou to denpa no Nippon gata moderu [Studies of content industries: Mixture and diffusion of Japanese content] (pp. 61-90). Tokyo, Japan: University of Tokyo Press.

Kristeva, J. (1980). *Desire in language: A semiotic approach to literature and art*. New York, NY: Columbia University Press. (Original work published 1969)

Lang, R. R. (1999). A declarative model for simple narratives. In *Narrative Intelligence: Papers from the 1999 AAAI Fall Symposium* (Technical Report FS-99-01, pp. 134-141), North Falmouth, MA.

Li, B., Lee-Urban, S., Appling, D. S., & Riedl, M. O. (2012). Automatically learning to tell stories about social situations from the crowd. In *Proceedings of the Third Workshop on Computational Models of Narrative* (pp. 142-151). Istanbul, Turkey: Academic Press.

McIntyre, N., & Lapata, M. (2009). Learning to tell tales: A data-driven approach to story generation. In *Proceedings of Joint Conference of the 47th Annual Meeting of the Association for Computational Linguistics and the 4th International Joint Conference on Natural Language Processing of the Asian Federation of Natural Language Processing* (pp. 217-225). Suntec, Singapore. doi:10.3115/1687878.1687910

Meehan, J. R. (1980). *The metanovel: Writing stories by computer*. New York, NY: Garland Publishing.

Montfort, N. (2007). *Generating narrative variation in interactive fiction* (Doctoral dissertation). Available from ProQuest. (AAI3271851)

Nakashima, M., & Ogata, T. (2006). Narrative generation system and intertextuality: A consideration on the concept and prototype systems. In *Proceedings of the 20th Annual Conference of the Japanese Society for Artificial Intelligence* (2E2-2). Tokyo, Japan: Academic Press.

Niwango. (n.d.). *Niconico*. Retrieved from http://www.nicovideo.jp/

Ogata, T. (2002). Expanded literary theory: Cognitive/computational expansion of literary theories and narratology. In *Proceedings of 17th Congress of the International Association of Empirical Aesthetics* (pp. 163-166). Osaka, Japan: Academic Press.

Ogata, T. (2004a). A computational approach to literary and narrative production: Toward computational narratology. In *Proceedings of 18th Congress of the International Association of Empirical Aesthetics* (pp. 509-516). Lisbon, Portugal: Academic Press.

Ogata, T. (2004b). Toward the consistent simulation of narrative discourse based on narratology. In *Proceedings of the Ninth International Symposium on Artificial Life and Robotics* (*Vol. 2*, pp. 579-584). Oita, Japan: Academic Press.

Ogata, T., & Terano, T. (1991). Explanation-based narrative generation using semiotic theory. In *Proceedings of Natural Language Processing Pacific Rim Symposium 1991* (pp. 321-328). Academic Press.

Okada, N., & Endo, T. (1992). Story generation based on dynamics of the mind. *Computational Intelligence*, *8*(1), 123–160. doi:10.1111/j.1467-8640.1992.tb00341.x

Peinado, F., & Gervás, P. (2005). Creativity issues in plot generation. In *Workshop on Computational Creativity, Working Notes, 19th International Joint Conference on A.I.* (pp. 45-52), Scotland, UK: Academic Press.

Pemberton, L. (1989). A modular approach to story generation. In *Proceedings of the Fourth Conference on European Chapter of the Association for Computational Linguistics* (pp. 217-224). doi:10.3115/976815.976845

Prince, G. (2003). *A dictionary of narratology* (Revised Ed.). Lincoln, NE: University of Nebraska Press.

Propp, V. Y. (1968). *Morphology of the folktale* (L. Scott, Trans.). Austin, TX: University of Texas Press. (Original work published 1928)

Quesenbery, W., & Brooks, K. (2010). *Storytelling for user experience: Crafting stories for better design.* New York, NY: Rosenfeld Media.

Riedl, M. O., & Bulitko, V. (2013). Interactive narrative: An intelligent systems approach. *AI Magazine, 34*(1), 67–77.

Riedl, M. O., & Young, R. M. (2010). Narrative planning: Balancing plot and character. *Journal of Artificial Intelligence Research, 39*, 217–267.

Riesbeck, C. K., & Schank, R. C. (1989). *Inside case-based reasoning*. Mahwah, NJ: Lawrence Erlbaum.

Rumelhart, D. E. (1975). Notes on a schema for stories. In D. G. Bobrow & A. Collins (Eds.), *Representation and understanding: Studies in cognitive science*. Waltham, MA: Academic Press. doi:10.1016/B978-0-12-108550-6.50013-6

Schank, R. C. (1990). *Tell me a story: Narrative and intelligence*. Chicago, IL: Northwestern University Press.

Schank, R. C., & Abelson, R. P. (1977). *Scripts, plans, goals, and understanding: An inquiry into human knowledge structures*. Mahwah, NJ: Lawrence Erlbaum.

Singh, P., Barry, B., & Liu, H. (2004). Teaching machines about everyday life. *BT Technology Journal, 22*(4), 227–240. doi:10.1023/B:BTTJ.0000047601.53388.74

Swanson, R., & Gordon, A. S. (2012). Say Anything: Using textual case-based reasoning to enable open-domain interactive storytelling. *ACM Transactions on Interactive Intelligent Systems, 2*(3), Article 16.

Szilas, N. (2015). Towards narrative-based knowledge representation in cognitive systems. In *Proceedings of 6th Workshop on Computational Models of Narrative* (pp. 133-141). Academic Press.

Tanaka, H. (2011). A-kitekuchuraru ko-dingu. [Architectural coding]. In Y. Karasawa, H. Tanaka, C. Dominick, R. Fujimura, & S. Matsukawa (Eds.), *Sekkei no sekkei* [Design of design] (pp. 53–110). Tokyo, Japan: INAX Publishing.

Turner, S. R. (1994). *The creative process: A computer model of storytelling and creativity*. Mahwah, NJ: Lawrence Erlbaum.

Tynyanov, Y. (1982). Bungaku no sinka. [Evolution of literature]. In *Rosia forumarizumu bungaku ronshuu 2* [A collection of literary essays in Russian formalism 2] (T. Kodaira, Trans.) (pp. 104–130). Tokyo, Japan: Serika Shobo. (Original work published 1929)

Yamaha. (n.d.). *What is VOCALOID*. Retrieved from http://www.vocaloid.com/en/about/

## KEY TERMS AND DEFINITIONS

**3LNI:** Three-layered narrative interface, the user interface for accessing CNs. 3LNI provides multiple perspectives on CNs: collective, surface, and internal.

**CNs:** Collection of narratives. Narratives produced in SONGS are accumulated in this part and shared by the narrative generation program (NBNG) and human users.

**Co-Creation:** Cooperative process for producing novel and valuable artifacts or information through mutual action among two or more agents.

**Computational Creativity:** Research field that addresses computer-based modeling, design, simulation, and implementation of creativity. Research subjects include various creative areas, such as arts, entertainment, artifacts, content, ideas, and knowledge.

**Narrative:** Product that represents one or more events by some media for humans, or some formal descriptions for computers. In our study, a narrative is constructed as the totality of a story, discourse, and expression.

**Narrative Discourse:** The structural aspect of how a story is expressed. In our study, a discourse is represented not as surface expression, but as a formal description.

**Narrative Expression:** Surface expression of a narrative by a medium such as natural language, still or moving image, and music, or their combination.

**Narrative Generation System:** Computer program that produces some types of narratives.

**NBNG:** Narrative-based narrative generator, the generative program in SONGS. The narrative generation is modeled as a cyclic process for composing new narratives in relation to previously generated narratives in CNs.

**Story:** The content information of a narrative, in particular, a chronologically ordered sequence of events.

**Story World:** The background world information of a story, including characters, objects, places or spaces, timelines, etc.

# Chapter 4
# An Attempt of the Commercial Film Production Support System Based on the Image Rhetoric of Commercial Film

**Yoji Kawamura**
*Kindai University, Japan*

## ABSTRACT

*This chapter describes the concepts behind a Commercial Film Production Support System (CFPSS) in terms of related studies in the areas of advertising, image techniques and rhetoric, cognitive science, and information engineering. The chapter then analyzes the structure of commercial films to establish and describe an information system that is tested with a viewing experiment. The proposed system reflects the environment by implementing basic image techniques to create commercial films through an interaction between the users and the system. The experiment uses commercial films for beer with 55 participants. The results show that evaluations for image types related to the advertising story generate the most interest and high evaluations for the provider type of rhetoric stimulates willingness to buy. In terms of technique, mise-en-scène and editing attracts interest, and the advertising story associated with the product function and the supporting production and distribution stimulates willingness to buy.*

## INTRODUCTION

### Narrative and Advertising

This chapter considers narrative from the business point of view. For novels, movies, theater shows, and so on, the narrative itself is the product and service, and the consumer pays a fee to use the service. The narrative must be good enough that consumers are willing to pay these fees; if consumers are satisfied, the writer can then create narratives with any content. The contents of the narratives vary, as does the structure of narrative expressions. The writer builds the narrative world and provides it to consumers.

DOI: 10.4018/978-1-5225-0432-0.ch004

Copyright © 2016, IGI Global. Copying or distributing in print or electronic forms without written permission of IGI Global is prohibited.

On the other hand, the narrative within an advertisement is not the product or service, but rather acts as a means to trigger consumers to pay for the products and services presented in the narrative. Advertisements are profitable when they successfully convince consumers to pay for the products and services presented through the narrative. The writer creates a narrative about the contents and features of products and services while considering consumer behavior. Since consumer behavior varies, narratives with various contents are created, though they all maintain the basic communication structure between businesses and consumers through the products and services. The creator always assumes a consumer's status (awareness of products, understanding, interest, willingness to buy, purchase results, etc.) and drafts a story according to that status. Providing this narrative to consumers builds the relationship between the consumer and products and services.

This chapter takes the view that the basic structure of the advertising story is the communication structure between businesses and consumers through products and services, and attempts to analyze advertising image techniques and build an information system to generate commercial films.

## Characteristics of Commercial Films

A commercial film lasting roughly 15 to 30 seconds is complex in terms of the information it contains because the film itself (shots or cuts) includes various information and because the chronological editing shots allow viewers to envision different images. For instance, a film with numerous shots shown within a short time frame quickly provides viewers with an image. The following characteristics of a commercial film are especially interesting:

1. The film is short and embraces only a brief advertising story selected from among the various characteristics of the product and its consumption.
2. Despite its brevity, the film comprises broken information elements that constitute the shot. The audience perceives these expressed elements to have the potential to invoke ideas.
3. When the film is edited chronologically, the tempo created from the series of shots and the shot-to-shot relationship may give the audience different images. The audience may also perceive any image related to the event (and information elements) of a series of shots.
4. The audio produced throughout a film with the components of sounds and events also invokes ideas in the mind of the audience.

## Current State of Commercial Film Production

It is the creative groups in advertising companies who produce this complex medium of information. To produce a commercial film, the groups analyze information about the product (concept, characteristics, appeal, etc.), company (concept, characteristics, history, etc.), consumers (target, characteristics, needs, etc.), and society (popularity, social conditions, competition, etc.). The groups take advantage of their skills to produce advertising stories, storyboards, and commercials. The commercial film should fulfill both its economic function of promoting the product and fulfill its cultural function of stimulating consumers' attention within their daily lives (entertainment, providing food for thought, and encourage lifestyle changes, etc.) (Kobayashi & Shimamura, 1997). Therefore, much of the production process depends upon each group members' subliminal sensitivity. Furthermore, most of the nature and artistic quality of entertainment depends on the creative group's sensitivity.

When mass marketing focused on the television, mainstream advertising companies embraced commercial film creators demonstrating sensitivity, and have thus provided sophisticated commercial films to the mass media. However, with the advent of one-to-one marketing, there is now an expectation of advertisements appealing to individual consumer preferences, potentially leading to an era of "individual advertisement" (KOKOKU) instead of merely "advertisement" (KOUKOKU). Nevertheless, commercial films for the individual advertisement era also have a cultural function. Thus, advertising agencies must welcome numerous film creators to produce individual advertisements, which is practically impossible. It may be possible to address this issue using Information Technology to support the production of "Individual Advertisements" serving a cultural function.

## Commercial Film Production Support System (CFPSS)

The cultural function of commercial film includes image rhetoric, the combination of image techniques such as mise-en-scène (direction), editing shots, and so forth (Kawamura, 2003, 2004). In line with this concept, the Information System aims to support the following production processes based on image rhetoric (Figure 1):

1. Creator's production of commercial film.
2. Joint production by both creators and marketers.
3. Joint production by advertising creators, marketers, and consumers.

Information systems converge with research areas such as image theory, marketing communication, and database management, yielding a type of database system in terms of sensitivity processing (information processing that incorporates sensitivity processing) that includes image rhetoric.

The system's current objective is to help the creator produce commercial films, though eventually the system is expected to aid production as a joint effort of both the creators and marketers along with advertising companies and consumers.

*Figure 1. Commercial film production support system (CFPSS) plan*
*Kawamura, 2003.*

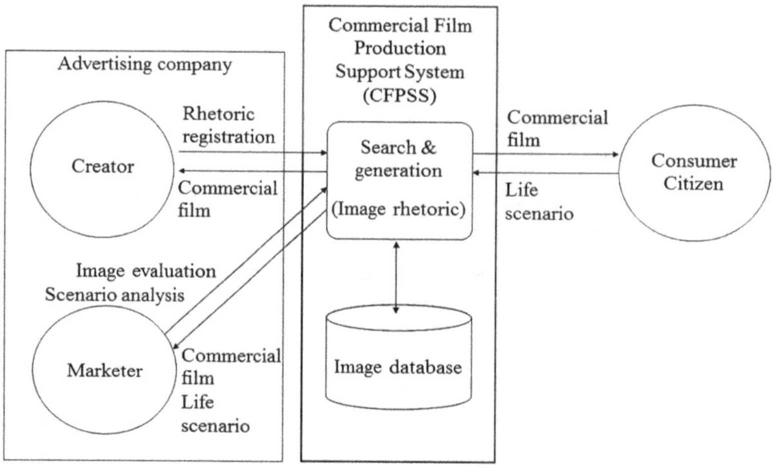

## Chapter Objective

This chapter describes the concept of the CFPSS in terms of the current state of related studies in areas including advertising research, image techniques and rhetoric, cognitive science, and information engineering. The chapter then analyzes the structure of commercial films to aid in establishing an information system. It subsequently explains the CFPSS functions developed based on the results of this analysis and examines the results of a viewing experiment using the CFPSS.

## BACKGROUND

### Image Techniques and Rhetoric

Film directors, writers, and critics have addressed the methods and techniques of producing images and the grammar of image language (Whitaker, 1970; Monaco, 1977; Deleuze, 1983; Bordwell, 1985; Asanuma, 1990). Film production occurs in the following steps: create a scenario (film script), create a storyboard, shoot images, edit shots of images, and add sound. Thus, there are four views related to image techniques:

1. **Story (Content):** How is the content expressed through a structured film? This considers topics such as love and hate, conflict or separation (or keywords). Genres such as romance, comedy, or historical drama may be another perspective for examination. Based on the selected topic, a story (events and a group of events) is configured to visualize images. The title of the work frequently represents the theme, while stories are expressed through a scenario.
2. **Mise-en-Scène:** How are the shots of images (information elements and screen layout, etc.) laid out? Shots, age, film characters, and scripts are translated into specific images. Prior to shooting, images are often expressed using storyboards before ultimate expression through a series of shots.
3. **Editing:** How are shots placed in a series? Images are either placed chronologically or the order is reshuffled. Finally, a series of shots are arranged to constitute the image work.
4. **Sound:** What type of sound is incorporated into the work? Script speech, narration, sound effects, and music, etc., are recorded as a series of images. Sound may be recorded while filming, or it may be recorded after filming and is attached as a sound track in the film.

However, this framework to create images alone does not always produce the image that fulfills the cultural function. In the past, image techniques and the rhetoric of the movies or commercial films produced have been studied extensively from the perspective of criticism and analysis.

### Advertising Research

There are case studies into effective commercial films with a focus on marketing and advertisement (Stewart & Furse, 1986). Some of these studies include elements of advertising expression that have been classified and extracted to enhance advertising effects. Alternatively, other studies classifying advertising expressions according to the nature of the information (comparative, unique selling proposition, preemptive, hyperbole, generic-informatic), and the nature of transformation (user image, brand image, use occasion, generic-transformatic) examine the ideas of advertising expressions (Laskey, Day, & Crask, 1989). Similarly, other researchers have classified and organized advertising expressions (Shimp, 1976; Crask, & Laskey, 1990; Laskey, Fox, & Crask, 1994, 1995). However, these studies provide insight into advertising expressions from a particular vantage point, and are not conducive to developing specific rules for creating images at the microcosm level. This chapter aims to extract rules to create more specific expressions of commercial films considering the results of those case studies.

Related to print advertisements (text, photo, poster etc.), studies examine an interpretation and analysis of the effect of advertising rhetoric on viewers (Scott, 1994; McQuarrie & Mick, 1996, 1999, 2003; Phillips, 1997; Mothersbaugh, Huhmann, & Franke, 2002; McQuarrie & Phillips, 2005; Stathakopoulos, Theodorakis, & Mastoridou, 2008; Huhmann & Albinsson, 2012; Theodorakis, Koritos, & Stathakopoulos, 2015). However, these studies do not include analyses related to commercial films. Moreover, as these research approaches aim to interpret and analyze existing advertisements, these studies also exclude information systems to generate specific advertisements according to operating rhetoric. Under such circumstances, Kawamura (2009) provided one of the few studies aiming to build an information system that analyzes the advertising image techniques (advertising story, editing). In this chapter, the systems are analyzed as commercial film techniques constituting the rhetoric of the commercial film, concentrating on the advertising story and editing based on Kawamura's (2009) research. The information system developed herein stores these to test tests the effects of the advertising story on consumers.

## Cognitive Science

In the field of cognitive science, many studies examine advertising expressions based on cognitive psychology, wherein elements expressing advertisements are classified and extracted to enhance advertising effects. Furthermore, researchers examined themes such as the cognitive processing of image techniques and rhetoric and consumers' process of recognizing a commercial film (Kanai, 2001; Kanai & Kato, 2001). Thus, the area includes an active research stream related to how specific expressions in commercial films influence consumers' minds and emotions. This study provides guidelines for selecting elements of commercial expressions as commercial effects when producing commercial image rhetoric. However, this paper presents the elements of commercial expressions included in the study in parts for further structuring. This chapter examines image expressions in a relatively organized manner while considering the results of cognitive psychology.

## Information Engineering

Some search systems for commercial films exist for private commercial research firms. One system employs the date of film production, the name of an advertiser, the name of the product, the name of a performer, or the first phrase of the scenario text as a tag to search for a commercial film.

Very few studies examine information systems based on image rhetoric, which is the central theme of this paper. One study involved support for commercial production (planning of an advertising story) with the use of artificial intelligence (Ogata, Watanabe, Hori, & Ohsuga, 1995). While this chapter fundamentally follows from research by Ogata et al. (1995) and Kanai (2001), this study focuses on commercial film rhetoric in a more structured and organized manner.

## AN ATTEMPT OF CFPSS BASED ON IMAGE RHETORIC

### Structural Analysis of Commercial Films

Kawamura (2009) provides an analysis of commercial films for 140 pieces of high involvement products (61 mobile phones, 79 personal computers (PC)), and 140 pieces of low involvement products (36 coffee, 64 bottles of beer, 40 tea).

This section summarizes Kawamura's (2009) analysis to aid in developing a CFPSS.

#### Advertising Story

An analysis of 280 commercial films reveals four types of advertising stories. These are described below and summarized in Table 1, with the system and number of films indicated in Figure 2.

1. **Provider Story Type (PT):** The primary structure expresses the provider's story (production and distribution, product function, effect on company). This is the "story of the product" and "story of the company."
2. **Consumer Story Type (CT):** This primary structure expresses consumers' stories (consumption situation, product acceptance, consumption effect). This is the "story of consumption."
3. **Overall Type (OT):** This structure generally expresses both the provider's and consumer's stories. This is represented as PT + CT.
4. **Image Type (IT):** This structure expresses images related to the consumer situation, though does not express product acceptance and consumption effects in the film. Rather this structure represents a product function. This category also includes structures expressing an image that does not belong to the consumer, provider, or product function.

*Table 1. Advertising story structure*

| Story Type | Provider Story Phase | | | Consumer Story Phase | | | Other |
|---|---|---|---|---|---|---|---|
| | Production and Distribution | Product Function | Effect on Company | Consumption Situation | Product Acceptance | Consumption Effect | |
| PT | + | + | + | | | | |
| CT | | + | | + | + | + | |
| CT-S | | + | | ++ | + | | |
| CT-A | | + | | + | ++ | + | |
| CT-E | | + | | | + | ++ | |
| OT | + | + | + | + | + | + | |
| IT | | + | | + | | | |
| | | + | | | | | + |

+: Expressed ++: Mainly Expressed

*Figure 2. System and number of advertising stories*
*Kawamura, 2009.*

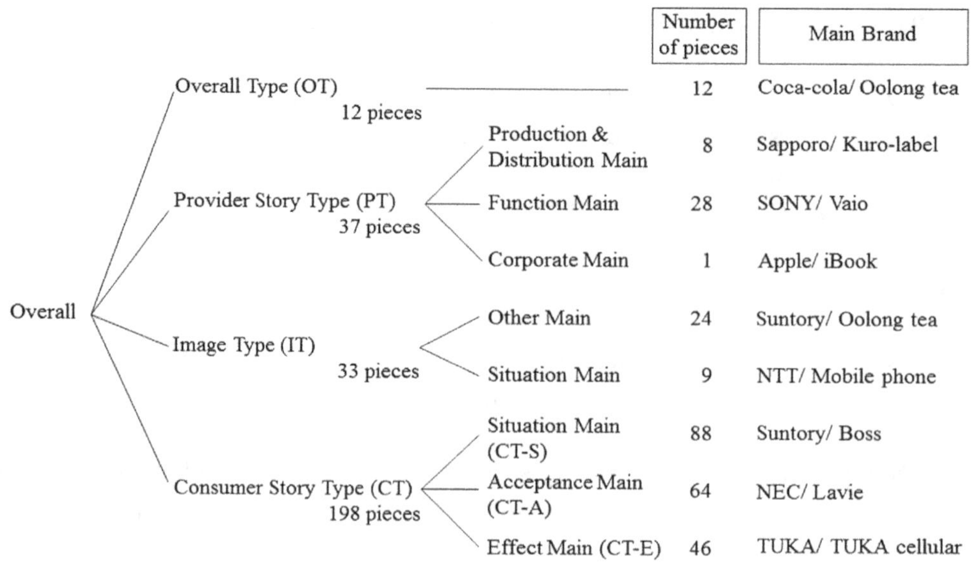


Among the 198 films (71%) in the consumer type category, those that emphasize the consumption situation (situation main: CT-S), product acceptance (acceptance main: CT-A), and consumption effect (effect main: CT-E) were 88 (31%), 64 (23%), and 46 (16%) films, respectively. Over 70% of the commercial films had an advertising design in which the consumer appeared and that appealed to consumers.

## Editing

Figure 3 illustrates the time-series and editing manipulation type, ranging from the Time-Series Type (TST) on the left to the manipulation type on the right. The figures indicate a pattern where the product function shot is manipulated. As connections of scenes constituting the advertising story, the TST type represents the flow of production and distribution to the consumption situation, the product function, product acceptance, consumption effect, and the effect on the company, while the manipulation type of editing employs production and distribution, product function, product acceptance, and effect on the company inserted into the time series flow. Among the manipulation types, the structures use Production and Distribution Shots (PDIT), Product Function Shots (PFIT), the effect on the company shots (effect on company insertion type), Other Shots (OIT), consumption situation shots (consumption situation insertion type), Product Acceptance Shots (PAIT), and consumption effect shots (consumption effect insertion type). Figure 4 notes the system and number of films for the 280 commercial films. Among the 244 (87%) within the manipulation type, most (205, 73%) belong to PFIT. Most of the commercials had some time order manipulation including many that manipulated the product function.

## Relationship between Advertising Story and Editing

There are four relationships between the advertising story and editing as a structure:

*Figure 3. Time-series and manipulation type*
*Kawamura, 2009.*

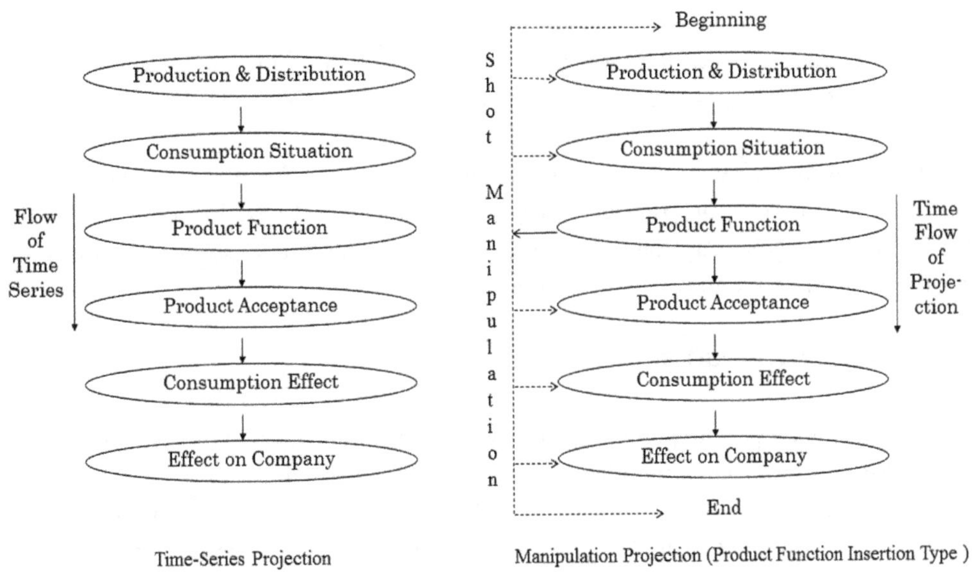


*Figure 4. Film editing system and number of films*
*Kawamura, 2009.*

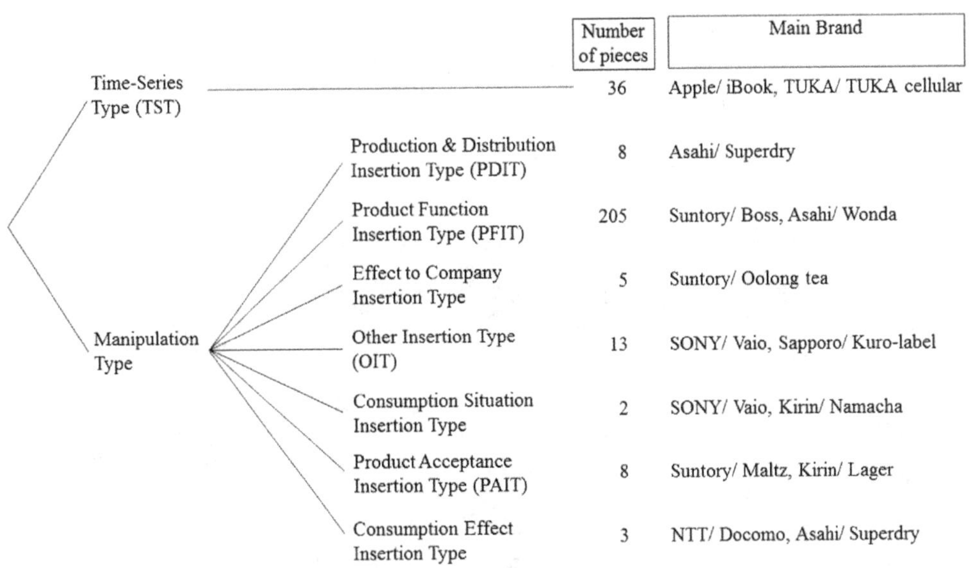


1. OT uses fewer average seconds for the shots and inserts the production and distribution shot into the consumer flow (consumption situation, product acceptance, consumption effect) two to three times.
2. PT extends the average seconds for shots and edits by time series. When manipulating the temporal order, the product acceptance shot is inserted into the provider flow (production and distribution, product function) one to two times.

3. CT uses fewer average seconds for the shots and inserts the consumer product function shot into the consumer flow (consumption situation, product acceptance, and consumption effect) one to two times.
4. IT uses more average seconds for shots and inserts the product function shot into others (consumption situation without others and product acceptance) one to two times.

In the "story of products" and "story of the company," there is limited time manipulation and the central theme included a structure that carefully represents the advertising concept in a time series. Conversely, the "story of consumption" manipulates time and uses a structure that inserts the product function into the consumer scene with a good tempo.

## Structure by Product Category

Figure 5 summarizes the aggregate percentage of the advertising story by product category. Coffee used the maximum consumer type, accounted for over 90% of the advertising story. Beer, tea, mobile phones, and PCs also demonstrated the consumer type most frequently, and OT stories, including the consumer story showing the consumer accounted for between 70-80%. Low-involvement products (coffee, beer, tea) among the consumer types indicated many CT-S and high-involvement products (mobile phone, PC) indicated many CT-A. For tea, there were numerous ITs and OTs. Furthermore, there were many PTs for beer and PCs. Table 2 provides a summary of the structural features by product category. The number of shots in the table was calculated considering that structures by product category were 15–30 seconds. Low-involvement products (coffee, beer, tea) had numerous time order manipulations, with fewer seen in high-involvement products (mobile phone, PC).

*Figure 5. Advertising story type by product category*
*Kawamura, 2009.*

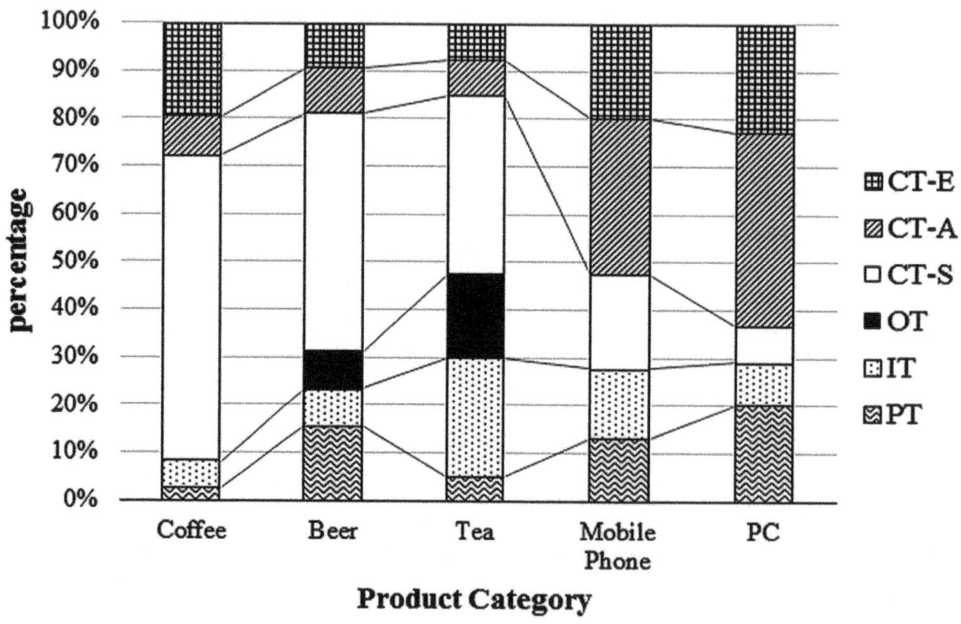

*Table 2. Summary of structural characteristics by product category*

| Item | | Coffee | Beer | Tea | Mobile Phone | PC |
|---|---|---|---|---|---|---|
| Number of shots | | 6 - 12 | 6 - 13 | 5 - 9 | 5 - 11 | 5 – 9 |
| Advertising Story | | • CT-S<br>• CT-E | • CT-S<br>• PT | • CT-S<br>• OT<br>• IT | • CT-A<br>• CT-S<br>• CT-E | • CT-A<br>• CT-E<br>• PT |
| Editing | OT or PT | | PAIT | PDIT | TST | • TST<br>• OIT |
| | CT or IT | PFIT | PFIT | PFIT | PFIT | PFIT |
| | Landing Story Phase | • Consumption effect<br>• Product acceptance | • Consumption situation<br>• Product acceptance | • Consumption situation<br>• Product acceptance | • Product acceptance<br>• Consumption effect | • Product acceptance<br>• Effect on company |
| | Frequency of Insertion | 1 | 1 - 3 | 1 - 3 | 0 - 1 | 0 - 1 |

Kawamura, 2009.

## Proposed CFPSS

### Functional Overview of the System

Based on these characteristics, Table 3 lists the specifications for when a CFPSS automatically generates commercial films. The system includes a database of 3643 image shots converted to a commercial film, that searches and classifies image shots based on keywords and sentences, and includes a function to generate the storyboard and playback in the order arranged in the storyboard.

### System Functions

#### *Image Database*

One commercial (15 or 30 seconds) is composed of an average of 13 image shots. The existing 280 commercials (beer, 64; coffee, 36; tea, 40; mobile phones, 61; and PCs, 79) were divided into 3,643 image shots and filed in the database as image files. Indexes were added to each image file for easy search. The search index comprises 54 categories of items related to image techniques and style as follows:

1. **Advertising Story:** Data for events that the image shot focuses on.
2. **Mise-en-Scène Technique:** Information elements that constitute the image shot.
3. **Editing Technique:** Data related to the number of seconds and the order-connection for the image shot.
4. **Sound Technique:** Data related to the sound elements added to the image shot.
5. **Rhetoric:** Data to combine and manipulate image techniques 1 to 4.
6. **Effect:** Effect data for the image shot.

*Table 3. Specifications for CFPSS use to automatically generate commercial films*

| | Item | | | Specification |
|---|---|---|---|---|
| Database | Number of Shots (Movies) | | | 3,643 |
| | Number of Indexes | | | 3,643 |
| | Product Categories | | | Coffee, Beer, Tea, Mobile Phone, PC |
| User Input | Selection of Category | | | Coffee, Beer, Tea, Mobile Phone, PC |
| | Input Information | | | Keyword or Sentences |
| | Selection of Advertising Story | | | OT, PT, CT, IT |
| | Selection of Editing | | | TST, PFIT, PAIT |
| Generation | Search of Image Shots | | | Extraction of image shots with high similarity between index and query (keywords or sentences) |
| | Storyboard Generation | | | Generation based on selection of advertising story and editing rules |
| | Number of Shots | | | 10 |
| | Story and Editing Rules | OT | TST* | Production & distribution, 2 shots → consumption situation, 2 shots → product function, 2 shots → product acceptance, 2 shots → consumption effect, 1 shot → effect on company, 1 shot |
| | | | PFIT** | Product function shot inserted between product acceptance and consumption effect |
| | | | PAIT** | Product acceptance shot inserted between production and distribution and consumption situation |
| | | PT | TST* | Production & distribution, 5 shots → product function, 4 shots → effect on company, 1 shot |
| | | | PFIT** | Product function shot inserted between production and distribution |
| | | | PAIT** | Product acceptance shot inserted between production and distribution and product function |
| | | CT | TST* | Consumption situation, 4 shots → product function, 1 shot → product acceptance, 3 shots → consumption effect, 2 shots |
| | | | PFIT** | Product function shot inserted between production acceptance and consumption effect |
| | | | PAIT** | Product acceptance shot inserted between consumption situations |
| | | IT | TST* | Consumption situation, 8 shots → product function, 2 shots |
| | | | PFIT** | Product function shot inserted between consumption situations |
| | Frequency of Insertion | | | 1 |
| Playback | Image Playback | | | Playback in the order of the image shots arranged in the storyboard |
| | Number of Sound Tracks | | | 2 |

*: Shot arrangement in the storyboard. **: Manipulation rule for TST arrangement.

### *Input and Retrieval Screen*

Figure 6 shows a screen capture of the input and retrieval screen. The system receives the product category selection from the user through inputs such as keywords and sentences on the left of the screen, with a set of search methods.

*Figure 6. System input and retrieval screen*

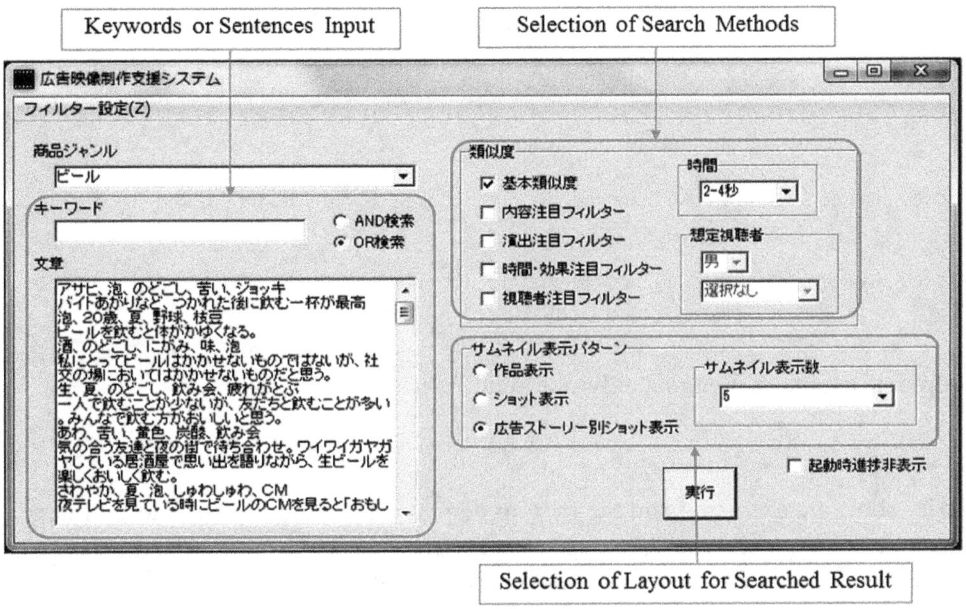


## *Morphological Analysis of the Input Information*

Figure 7 illustrates an abstract process using the CFPSS. Based on input keywords or sentences, the system extracts items using the natural language processing software ChaSen (Matsumoto et al., 1999), and makes the nouns, adjectives, and verbs a query. For example, if the input information "Beer turned his tears into a smile" is entered, it extracts "beer," "tear," "smile," and "turn" and uses these as queries.

*Figure 7. Abstract CFPSS process*

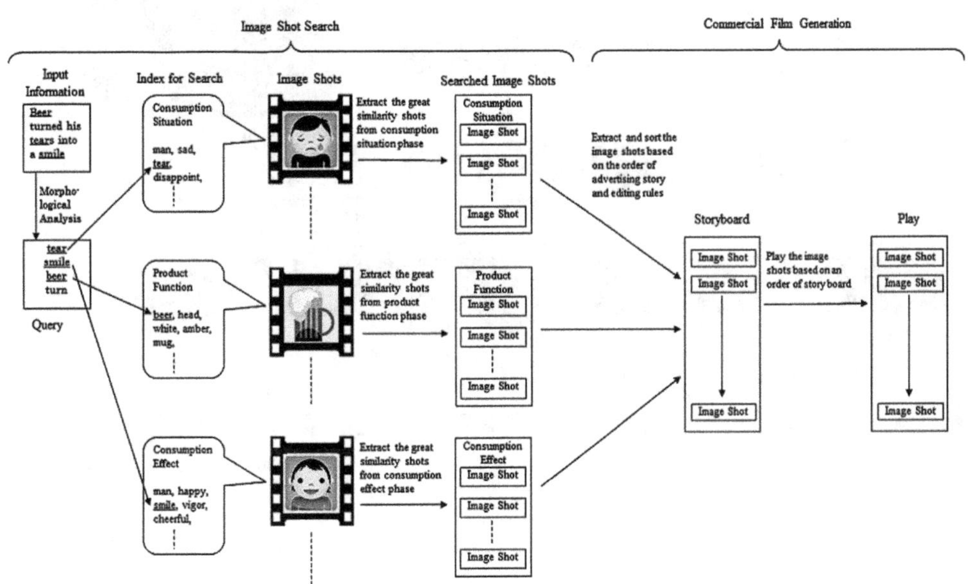

### Calculating Similarity

The query Qi (i=1~n) and the index Ij (j=1~m) are used to calculate the similarity S.

$$S = \sum_{i=1}^{n}\sum_{j=1}^{m} S\left(i, j\right)$$

$$S\left(i, j\right) = \begin{cases} 1, & Qi = Ij \\ 0, & Qi \neq Ij \end{cases}$$

For example, if the index contains only one "tear," the similarity is 1.

### Image Extraction

High similarity shots are extracted and the system displays thumbnails with 5 to 10 image shots as the search results for each stage of the advertising story. Figure 8 shows the system's storyboard and playback screen illustrating an advertising story by shot. The system displays a thumbnail of search result image shot groups in the upper left corner of the screen.

*Figure 8. Storyboard and playback screen*

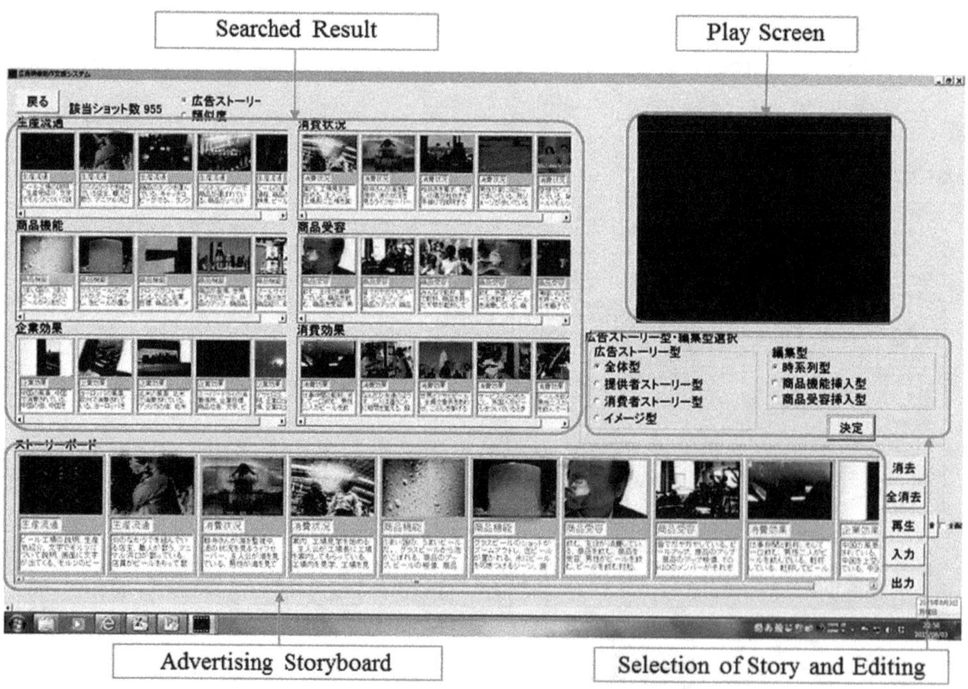

### *Generating Storyboards Based on Advertising Stories and Editing Method*

Based on the rules for the selected advertising story and editing types, thumbnails of 10 image shots with a high degree of similarity are arranged into a storyboard. The system includes OT, PT, CT, and IT story types with editing types TST, PFIT, and PAIT (Table 3). For example, when the advertising story type is CT and the editing type is TST, the system provides a sequential arrangement of 4 shots with consumption situations, 1 shot with product functions, 3 shots with product acceptance, and 2 shots with consumption effects.

### *Commercial Film Playback*

Clicking on playback plays the commercial film in the order of the thumbnails (left to right) of the image shots arranged in the storyboard.

## Experiment

This experiment aims to show how an advertising story influences viewers using commercial films derived from the four types of advertising stories generated from the image shots that were likely related to the viewer's associations and experiences.

### Data and Method

For the study, 55 viewers provided four to five associated keywords about beer and simple sentences (approximately one to two lines) about the relationship between beer and the viewer. The sample included 28 male and 27 female participants between from 20 to 23 years of age. The input from the viewers included such keywords and statements as:

- Asahi, foam, throat, bitter, mug.
- A glass to drink when tired, such as after working a part-time job, is the best.
- Foam, twenty, summer, baseball, green soybeans.
- The body gets itchy after drinking a beer.
- Alcohol, throat, bitter, taste, foam.
- For me, beer is not something necessary, but I think it is necessary on social occasions.

The database was then searched for images using a summary of the viewers' sentences as input. An advertising story was selected from the OT, PT, CT, and IT types with TST editing, and the generated image shot shown to viewers who provided their evaluations and feedback (films of primary interest, areas of interest, films with the highest stimulation of willingness to buy, areas stimulated, gender, beer drinking frequency) for each.

### Results

Table 4 summarizes the image shot composition and order of the generated commercial film. The numbers in the advertising story columns indicate the order of the shots. Figure 9 illustrates the continuity for OT in the generated commercial film. In this experiment, commercial films have no sound.

*Table 4. Image shot composition and order of the generated commercial film*

| Advertising Story Phase | Advertising Story | | | | Abstract of Shots |
|---|---|---|---|---|---|
| | OT | PT | CT | IT | |
| Production and Distribution | 1 | 1 | | | Introduction of the production area of the beer |
| | | 2 | | | Production process of the beer (low-temperature aging) |
| | | 3 | | | Transporting the beer tank |
| | 2 | 4 | | | The cook sings a song while cooking |
| | | 5 | | | The products are being transported on the belt conveyor |
| Consumption Situation | 3 | | 1 | 1 | A lifesaver monitoring the sea |
| | | | 2 | 2 | A man walking toward home |
| | | | | 3 | Appear to drink a beer, even without a glass |
| | | | | 4 | People talking to the camera man |
| | 4 | | 3 | 5 | The consumers asked to tour the factory |
| | | | | 6 | People talking at the stock exchange |
| | | | | 7 | People preparing meal at the poolside |
| | | | 4 | 8 | Attempting to borrow a bottle opener for beer at a seaside house |
| Product Function | | 6 | | | Catch the copy of a product "All for Delight" |
| | | 7 | | | Promotion of urban scenery and the product |
| | 5 | 8 | 5 | 9 | Foam spilling from the beer mug |
| | 6 | 9 | | 10 | Canned beer breaking the ice |
| Product Acceptance | 7 | | 6 | | Consumer drinking beer in the cup |
| | 8 | | 7 | | Drinking beer while socializing |
| | | | 8 | | Making a toast with a large number of people |
| Consumption Effect | | | 9 | | Making a mysterious face |
| | 9 | | 10 | | Drinking beer and recounting funny stories |
| Effect on Company | 10 | 10 | | | Urban (overseas, China) scenery |

Figure 10 reports the viewer evaluations of interest and willingness to buy related to the four types of commercial films. IT has a greatest evaluation for interest, while PT has a greatest evaluation for willingness to buy.

The summary below shows the consolidated contents for films that stimulate interest and willingness to buy for items with responses in more than two cases. The frequency of comments is indicated in parentheses.

### Areas of Interest

Primarily related to the advertising story (including advertising concept):

- **Copy Added:** "All for the customer's 'delight'!!" (4)
- **Acceptance Added:** Demonstrations of an energetic way of drinking (2)
- **Production Added:** When the provider's efforts to provide delicious beer is apparent (3)

*Figure 9. Generated film continuity for OT*

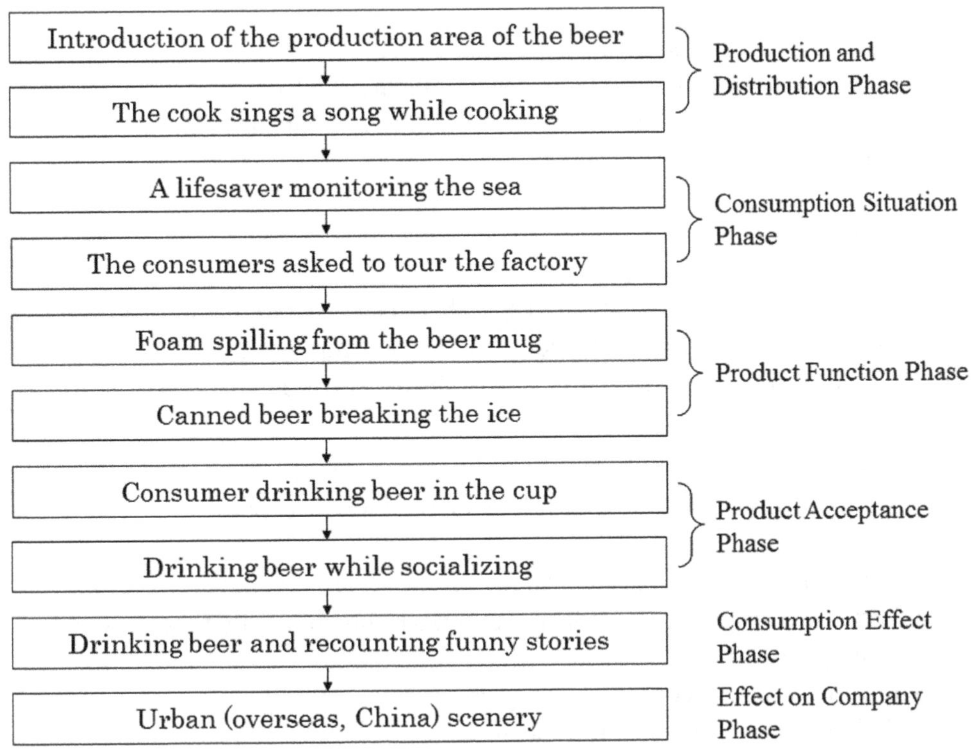


*Figure 10. Interest and willingness to buy by advertising story type*

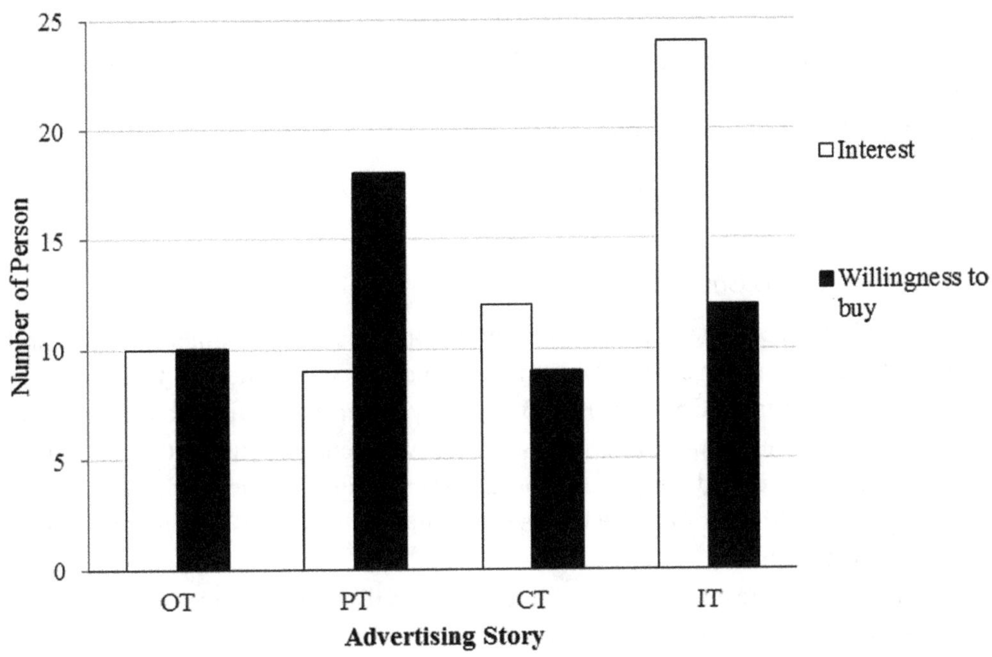

Primarily related to mise-en-scène:

- **Product:** When the beer is widely zoomed in (2)
- **Buddy Added:** Where there are many people are having fun (6)
- **Scene Added:** Scene showing that the beer is actually consumed with a gesture, even in the absence of a glass (14)

Primarily related to editing:

- **Connection:** The plot unravels gradually (2) / There is a perceived association from the creation of a professional story extending to the consumer's consumption (2)
- **Irregularity:** The type of commercial message was initially unknown (2)

### *Willingness to Buy*

Primarily related to the advertising story (including advertising concept):

- **Copy Added:** Deceived by the phrase "All for the customer's 'delight'!!" (7)
- **Situation Added:** A scene depicting drinking in a bar, imagining that the cuisine was easy (3)/A scene of a man going home (2)
- **Acceptance Added:** Many scenes indicating product consumption (7)
- **Effects Added:** The beer was consumed with zest (4)
- **Production Added:** The story clearly shows the producer's efforts to provide delicious beer (2)

Primarily related to mise-en-scène:

- **Product:** The beer overflows from the cup (2) / The beer package in ice representing the chill and delight (3)
- **Scene Added:** Drinking beer with a gesture is impressive (2)

## Discussion

### *Interest and Willingness to Buy*

The image shots behind the commercial films are divided into multiple commercial films and compiled into a database. There were many cases where the sequence of image shots in the generated commercial film was hard to understand. Compared to consciously developed commercial films, the generated films had a lesser degree of execution. While these results will require future studies before they can be generalized, the IT type generated a high level of interest through a variety of image shots. However, the willingness to buy was highest for the PT type using image shots focusing on the product's function and production and distribution.

Figure 11 summarizes the results in terms of interest and willingness to buy, or to the films' representation techniques (advertising story, mise-en-scène, editing). The results indicate that mise-en-scène and editing attracts interest, and the advertising story associated with the product function and illustrating production and distribution stimulates willingness to buy.

*Figure 11. Areas of interest and the willingness to buy*

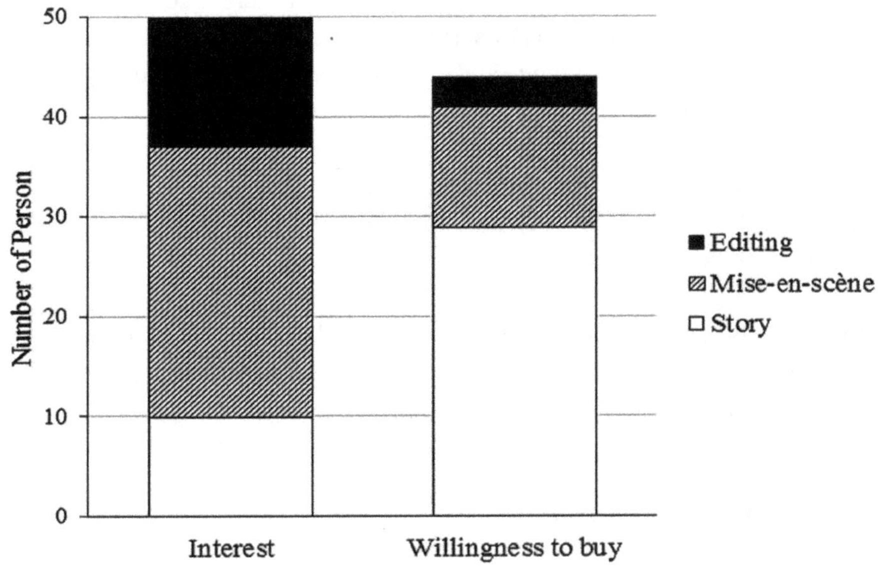


## *Effects of Advertising Expressions*

It is important to evaluate the films developed based on the database output focusing on the advertising image techniques and rhetoric and to investigate and experiment with the viewers' evaluations and feedback. This experiment centered on whether the evaluation and feedback changes by tweaking the advertising story. For interest, 14 people indicated "the scene where it appears that the beer is actually consumed with a gesture, even without a glass," and 6 people indicated "the scene with many people having fun." This indicates that the mise-en-scène for each image shot (scene added: consciously daring to hide the products; buddy added: increasing the number of registered persons) effectively creates interest. Moreover, in terms of willingness to buy, 7 people indicated that they were "deceived by the phrase, all for the customer's 'delight,'" and 7 people indicated "there were many scenes where the products were consumed." This shows that the overall advertising concept of commercial films and the mise-en-scène (copy added: show aimed to portray in writing; acceptance added: increase the number of consumer scenes) effectively stimulates willingness to buy. These results show the effects of advertising expressions and quantitative evaluations.

## *Commercial Film Narratives Catering to Consumers*

Given the effects of commercial films on consumers, companies should employ advertising strategies to attract consumer interests by focusing on the stories showing consumer situations for consumers who are not aware of or do not understand their products or services. For example, the following scenes attracted interest in the experiment:

- A scene showing that the beer is actually consumed with a gesture, even without a glass.
- A scene where many people are having fun.

These are fragments of consumer situation stories in which life scenes are characterized by surprises and things out of the ordinary. On the other hand, companies can target consumers with a certain level of understanding and interest in the products or services and arouse their willingness to buy by focusing on the products and stories of their acceptance and effects. For example, the following scenes stimulated willingness to buy in the experiment:

- Deceived by the phrase "All for the customer's 'delight'!!"
- Many scenes indicating the product consumption.
- The beer was consumed with zest.

These are stories of products with persuasive functions and demonstrate acceptance and effects. This advertising strategy is a type of knowledge that creators of advertisement companies naturally have, which seems to be a rule illustrated by this experiment.

## SOLUTIONS AND RECOMMENDATIONS

### Result of a System Development

Using an advertising story and editing techniques, a system was developed to generate commercial films through an interaction between the users and the system, which was tested with an observational experiment. Since the system easily generates commercial films that comply with a variety of requirements, it can be utilized for various experiments in the future. These types of experiments will clarify and enhance the creative know-how (image techniques and rhetoric) to produce individual advertisements.

### Result of an Experiment

An experiment using commercial films for beer generated the following findings:

- The IT type created the most interest through a variety of image shots.
- The PT type stimulated the highest willingness to buy using a variety of image shots showing the product function and the associated production and distribution.
- Mise-en-scène or editing attracts interest, and the advertising story associated with product function and the supporting production and distribution stimulates willingness to buy.

These findings gradually clarify the relationship between the commercial film techniques and their effects and significantly contribute to the symbolization and systematization of creator's inherent creative know-how.

## FUTURE RESEARCH DIRECTIONS

The experiment in this chapter aimed to show the influence an advertising story has on viewers using beer as the product category. Future researchers could conduct an experiment that utilizes the implemented editing technique or run an experiment with other product categories. The CFPSS used advertising story and editing technique as the basis to generate commercial films. In the future, the system could be evaluated according to the creator and the image techniques and rhetoric menu expanded. Long term research and development of the system will focus on adopting advanced information technologies, such as image processing, preference extraction and information recommendation, and interaction. Furthermore, the researchers plan to develop and experiment with an internet collaboration system.

## CONCLUSION

A commercial film is a complicated body of information and is difficult to encode on levels that make it possible to store the rhetoric in the information system. This chapter has taken the view that the basic structure of the advertising story is the communication structure between businesses and consumers through products and services, and attempted to analyze advertising image techniques and build an information system to generate commercial films. This attempt is a beginning of information system study to support the production of "Individual Advertisements" serving a cultural function. To clarify the creator's inherent creative know-how, many studies from the various points of view are needed.

## ACKNOWLEDGMENT

This work was supported by JSPS KAKENHI Grant Number 22500102.

## REFERENCES

Asanuma, K. (1990). Eizo no tekusuto no giho [Techniques for image text]. Eiga no tameni II [For movie II] (pp. 130-247). Tokyo, Japan: Suiseisha.

Bordwell, D. (1985). *Narration in the fiction film*. Madison, WI: University of Wisconsin Press.

Crask, M. R., & Laskey, H. A. (1990). A positioning-based decision model for selecting advertising messages. *Journal of Advertising Research*, *30*(4), 32–38.

Deleuze, G. (1983). *Image-mouvement.* Paris, France: Les Editions de Minuit.

Huhmann, B. A., & Albinsson, P. A. (2012). Does rhetoric impact advertising effectiveness with liking controlled? *European Journal of Marketing*, *46*(11/12), 1476–1500. doi:10.1108/03090561211259943

Kanai, A. (2001). Cognitive process model toward the rhetoric of the film. *Cognitive Studies*, *8*(2), 139–150.

Kanai, A., & Kato, Y. (2001). Effect of advertising rhetoric on viewer's cognitive process. *Journal of Advertising Science*, *42*, 87–100.

Kawamura, Y. (2003). An analysis of the rhetoric of commercial film: Toward the building of a commercial film production support system based on image rhetoric. In *Proceedings of the 2003 IEEE International Conference on Systems, Man and Cybernetics* (pp.993-1000). Washington, DC. doi:10.1109/ICSMC.2003.1243944

Kawamura, Y. (2004). An analysis of the rhetoric of commercial film: Toward the building of a commercial film production support information system. *Journal of Advertising Science, 45*, 122–139.

Kawamura, Y. (2009). An analysis on the story and editing techniques of commercial film: Toward the building of a commercial film production support information system. *Journal of Advertising Science, 50*, 16–32.

Kobayashi, T., & Shimamura, K. (1997). *Shinban atarashii koukoku* [New advertising: New edition]. Tokyo, Japan: Dentsu.

Laskey, H. A., Day, E., & Crask, M. R. (1989). Typology of main message strategies for television commercial. *Journal of Advertising, 18*(1), 36–41. doi:10.1080/00913367.1989.10673141

Laskey, H. A., Fox, R. J., & Crask, M. R. (1994). Investigation the impact of executional style on television commercial effectiveness. *Journal of Advertising Research, 34*(5), 9–16.

Laskey, H. A., Fox, R. J., & Crask, M. R. (1995). The relationship between advertising message strategy and television commercial effectiveness. *Journal of Advertising Research, 35*(2), 31–39.

Matsumoto, Y., Kitauchi, K., Yamashita, T., Hirano, Y., Matsuda, H., & Asahara, M. (1999). Morphological analysis system ChaSen 2.0 users manual (2nd ed.). Nara Institute of Science and Technology, Matsumoto Labo.

McQuarrie, E. F., & Mick, D. G. (1996). Figures of rhetoric in advertising language. *The Journal of Consumer Research, 22*(4), 424–438. doi:10.1086/209459

McQuarrie, E. F., & Mick, D. G. (1999). Visual rhetoric in advertising: Text-interpretive, experimental, and reader-response analysis. *The Journal of Consumer Research, 26*(1), 37–54. doi:10.1086/209549

McQuarrie, E. F., & Mick, D. G. (2003). Visual and verbal rhetorical figures under directed processing versus incidental exposure to advertising. *The Journal of Consumer Research, 29*(4), 579–587. doi:10.1086/346252

McQuarrie, E. F., & Phillips, B. J. (2005). Indirect persuasion in advertising: How consumers process metaphors presented in picture and words. *Journal of Advertising, 34*(2), 7–19. doi:10.1080/00913367.2005.10639188

Monaco, J. (1977). *How to read a film: the art technology, language, history and theory of film and media*. New York, NY: Oxford University Press.

Mothersbaugh, D. L., Huhmann, B. A., & Franke, G. R. (2002). Combinatory and separative effects of rhetorical figures on consumers' effort and focus in ad processing. *The Journal of Consumer Research, 28*(4), 589–602. doi:10.1086/338211

Ogata, T., Watanabe, K., Hori, K., & Ohsuga, S. (1995). Monogatari seisei shisutemu niyoru koukoku sousaku shien wo mokuteki toshita terebi komahsharu no kouzou bunseki[Structural analysis of television commercials to support advertising creation using a narrative generation system]. *Journal of Advertising Science*, *30*, 1–22.

Phillips, B. J. (1997). Thinking into it: Consumer interpretation of complex advertising images. *Journal of Advertising*, *26*(2), 77–87. doi:10.1080/00913367.1997.10673524

Scott, L. M. (1994). Images in advertising: The need for a theory of visual rhetoric. *The Journal of Consumer Research*, *21*(2), 252–272. doi:10.1086/209396

Shimp, T. A. (1976). Methods of commercial presentation employed by national television advertisers. *Journal of Advertising*, *5*(4), 30–36. doi:10.1080/00913367.1976.10672661

Stathakopoulos, V., Theodorakis, I. G., & Mastoridou, E. (2008). Visual and verbal rhetoric in advertising: The case of 'resonance'. *International Journal of Advertising*, *27*(4), 629–657. doi:10.2501/S0265048708080177

Stewart, D. W., & Furse, D. H. (1986). *Effective television advertising: A study of 1000 commercials*. Lexington, MA: Lexington Books.

Theodorakis, I. G., Koritos, C., & Stathakopoulos, V. (2015). Rhetorical maneuvers in a controversial tide: Assessing the boundaries of advertising rhetoric. *Journal of Advertising*, *44*(1), 14–24. doi:10.1080/00913367.2014.930679

Whitaker, R. (1970). *The language of film*. Englewood Cliffs, NJ: Prentice-Hall, Inc.

## KEY TERMS AND DEFINITIONS

**Advertising Story:** The technique determining the event to focus on to visualize the advertising images. The story is structured by extracting events among the advertising history.

**Editing Technique:** The editing method (structuring) for shots in chronological order to visualize images of events.

**High Involvement Products:** The products that there is a greater degree of enthusiasm and interest in product functions when a consumer purchases a product. Mobile phones, PC, etc.

**Image Rhetoric:** The combination of image techniques such as mise-en-scène (direction) of shots, editing shots, and so on.

**Image Techniques:** The techniques used to express images: advertising story, mise-en-scène technique, editing technique, and sound technique, among others.

**Low Involvement Products:** The products that there is a lesser degree of enthusiasm and interest in product functions when a consumer purchases a product. Coffee, beer, tea, etc.

*Mise-en-Scène* **Technique:** The methodology used to direct and structure shots with components (elements) so as to make images of events.

**Sound Technique:** The methodology related to how to direct and structure shots with sound for characters, the material appearance of shots, and the technique to direct (structure) shot backgrounds and shot-to-shot relationships with specific sound comments.

# Chapter 5
# Applying Digital Storytelling to Business Planning

**Yoko Takeda**
*Yokohama National University, Japan*

## ABSTRACT

*Digital storytelling for business planning has two different modes of perception, thinking, and communication: the narrative and the logical scientific. This chapter pointed out how the structure and the contents of the digital storytelling work influence its effectiveness through examination of works and the audience's evaluation of the works. Critical points regarding the structure of work were the consistency and the balance. The most important link was from a contrast between the initial situation and obstruction in the narrative part, to key success factors deriving in the analytical part. The link represents what is the problem that the storyteller found. Regarding the contents of work, familiarity to the audience—a story of "something like you"—is effective in understanding, persuasiveness and empathy of the story's message.*

## INTRODUCTION

### Digital Storytelling

In this chapter, digital storytelling means a short digital work that combines narration and visual-auditory material, such as photographs, music, and movies, produced by an individual as his or her own story[1]. The origin of digital storytelling was a kind of democratization movement of visual art on the West Coast of the United States in the 1970s–1980s. In the 1990s, the movement developed through the appearance of low-cost and easy-to-use equipment, such as personal computers, digital cameras, and the Internet. In 1994, the San Francisco Center for Digital Media was founded and developed into the Center for Digital Storytelling (CDS) in 1998 (Lambert, 2013). Although a virtual reality game in which players develop their own stories with a character is also called digital storytelling (Murray, 1998), this chapter addresses digital storytelling following the CDS's movement.

DOI: 10.4018/978-1-5225-0432-0.ch005

Copyright © 2016, IGI Global. Copying or distributing in print or electronic forms without written permission of IGI Global is prohibited.

Lambert, one of the founders of the CDS, pointed out that digital storytelling has seven components: self-revelatory, personal or first person voice, scenes of a lived experiences of the storyteller, photos more than moving images, soundtracks, short-length (under five minutes) and simple designs, and the storyteller's ownership of the entire process and distribution (Lambert, 2013). As Lambert (2013) noted, the storyteller's private life need not always be revealed, but telling a storyteller's non-fiction expressed in the first person is recommended because it is the easiest way to deeply reflect himself or herself.

Regardless of whether or not a story is the storyteller's nonfiction, digital storytelling is oriented to be subjective, personal experience-based, emotional, sensory, and self-reflective in general. Through these aspects, digital storytelling contrasts with the ideal of logical scientific presentation in academic society.

Hartley and McWilliam (2009) added the definition of an element: that digital storytelling is a workshop-based practice called a story circle, although the workshop basis is an implicit premise from the beginning of the digital storytelling movement. In a story circle, participants not only learn how to create works but also communicate with each other during the process of developing stories. A story must be told to someone; thus, members of a story circle function as both author of their stories and hearers of other members' stories. In addition, if the workshop has a specific social theme, such as an environmental problem, digital storytelling can assist the social movement by sharing members' consciousness.

Digital storytelling has been applied to a variety of fields, not only visual arts but also a new style of media, education, therapy, and various social movements in public health care, social services, and others. Digital storytelling has spread not only in the United States but also in countries in Europe, Oceania, North America, Asia, Africa, and South America (Hartley & McWilliam, 2009). In Japan, where the workshop for this research was held, workshop-based practices by educational institutes and non-profit organizations have been observed since the 2000 (Nishioka, 2014).

## Digital Storytelling in Business Situation

From the earliest time of the CDS, business use of digital storytelling has been positively attempted. For example, Coca-Cola adopted digital storytelling early in its brand marketing process. The company's brand story appeared on its website and recently has become more interactive with customers on social networking services (SNSs), such as Facebook. Because brand is an identity, a story can be told even for an agent who is not a human being.

The narrative approach did not result directly from the influence of the CDS but has expanded in social sciences from the 1980s and has broadly influenced businesses. A number of narrative approach practices have appeared, such as narrative planning, narrative marketing, storytelling for career development and storytelling in system development. Denning (2007) focused on leadership language; leaders must tell true stories about themselves, think through narratives, and understand the audience's story. Kusunoki (2010) advocated that an excellent corporate competitive strategy is a story. Future scenario planning (Schwartz, 1991; Van der Heijden, 1996; Wade, 2012) is also an example of narrative approach in business. In the early stage of the scenario planning process, one tends to place importance on logical analysis by identifying a focal issue, listing and classifying key factors and driving forces, and selecting scenario logic. In the latter process, the narrative approach becomes more pertinent as it fleshes out, interprets the scenarios and finds indications of the future (Schwartz, 1991). Scenario planning could be regarded as a hybrid version of the narrative approach and logical analysis.

Although a narrative approach in business is not always accompanied by the use of information technology, the usage of digital media is becoming increasingly prevalent these days. The narrative approaches in business have naturally changed to "digital" storytelling.

The focus of this paper is to understand application of digital storytelling to business planning. The differences in digital storytelling for business and non-business, such as art and therapy, are assumed as follows:

- There is a clearer aim of storytelling (i.e., business goal).
- Concrete business methods should be mentioned as conclusions at the end of the storytelling work.
- Evidences for business success are expected.

These traits develop a scientific attitude in storytellers. Thus, we expect that a hybrid style of the narrative and logical analysis would be observed in the digital storytelling for business planning.

## Digital Storytelling as a Narrative

Clearly, digital storytelling is a form of a narrative. A narrative is an organized interpretation of a sequence of events. The function of a narrative is to bring order to disorder and to reflexively provide structure to our very sense of selfhood. The character of the story told depends on to whom the story is being told, the relationship between the narrator and the audience, and the broader social and cultural context (Murray, 2015). The narrative has the power to arouse the imagination, understand circumstances, facilitate communication with other entities, and rebuild the storyteller's own reality.

As compared to a simple narration or text, digital storytelling supposedly strengthens and expands the traits of a narrative. To summarize, the difference between "digital" storytelling and other types of "analogue" narratives, such as a simple narration or text, is assumed as follows:

- Digital storytelling strengthens the sensuous and emotional effect of a narrative in terms of visual images and auditory effects when compared to an analog narrative. The power of making sense of a confused real world might be enhanced using multi-sensory expressions.
- A digital format allows the storyteller to exhibit his reflection to other participants in the workshop. In the editorial process, the authors also tend to become reflective by hearing their own voices.
- Digital storytelling helps broaden social communication in digital form. The storyteller can reach out to a global audience and new narrative possibilities, which go beyond the constraints of time and location, may appear.

## Objectives of This Chapter

The application of digital storytelling to business planning is assumed to be a hybrid version of the narrative approach and logical analysis, which strengthens the sensuous, emotional, reflective and communicative traits compared to an "analog" narrative. It becomes a curious case when one observes how the interaction of narrative and analytical approaches impacts the digital forms in business. This chapter aims to explore the potential of the narrative to create new value and synergy with the traditional analytical approach. This can be achieved by demonstrating a case study of applying digital storytelling to the early stage of business planning. The findings of this research will contribute to business administration because management literature has rarely been exposed to the synergistic effect of the narrative and analytical approaches.

## BACKGROUND

### Narrative Mode and Logical Scientific Mode

Bruner (1996) advocated that human beings have two modes of thinking: the logical scientific mode and the narrative mode. The logical scientific mode is used to explain something causally through a theory that elucidates necessary and/or sufficient conditions. It does not depend on the specific contextual setting. In contrast, the narrative mode is used to understand something through an interpretation process and depends on the specific context and history. A sequence of events is interpreted as having various meanings, and different people can interpret such a sequence in different ways (Bruner, 1996, 2003).

The criteria for the two modes of thinking are different. Logical scientific thinking should verify propositions using context-free logic and evidence. For narrative thinking, the interpretation should not only be rooted in factuality but also be better contextualized and rhetorically fair-minded, and there should be an awareness of the requirements of the narrative, such as a mutual understanding with the audience on how stories are developed and become realistic (Bruner, 1996, 2003). The narrative has a kind of logic regarding consistency and plausibility, but its criteria have very different qualities from that of the logical scientific mode.

In the 1980s, hermeneutics in the literature developed in a variety of social science fields, such as psychology (Murray, 2015). Although the "narrative turn" has appeared in academia in recent years, people in practice have perceived, thought, and communicated with others in the narrative mode from ancient times; the logical scientific mode is rather extraordinary.

However, the logical scientific mode broadly influences ordinary individuals through schools and academic society, whose formal mode is logical scientific. In business administration, although a very punctual logical scientific mode is rarely seen, as it is in academic society, semi-logical scientific thinking is broadly observed. Business administration presentations and reports have a form that is similar to that of academic presentations and papers, although the thoroughness of the literature review and the verification method is weaker than in academia. At least the business planning and assessment process typically require clear logic and some evidence.

On the one hand, a business plan must rigorously solve problems because of the variety of types of stakeholders and required resources, such as money, talent, and facilities. Typically, a business planner puzzles over a number of complicated problems, and the problem solving matches the logical scientific mode that develops propositions logically and verifies them systematically.

On the other hand, a business plan must point out problems that have not yet been solved. Essentially, the purpose of the narrative mode is to find problems (Bruner, 2003). Thus, it could be considered effective, particularly in the early business planning stage. The sensuous and emotional function of the narrative mode is also important to refine thoughts and communicate it to other people (Bower, 1981; Forgas, Bower, & Krantz, 1984). "… emotion powerfully influenced such cognitive processes as free associations, imaginative fantasies, social perceptions, and snap judgments about others' personalities...

when the feeling-tone of a narrative agreed with the reader's emotion, the salience and memorability of events in that narrative were increased (Bower, 1981, p.129).

Although the narrative mode and the logical scientific mode are fundamentally different, explaining and interpreting are linked (Bruner, 1996). Actually, even in a scientific style presentation, presenters frequently insert impressive episodes. The possibility is strong that digital storytelling for business planning includes both narrative and logical scientific modes.

Exploring a form of a link between the narrative and the logical scientific modes is a curious endeavor. When both narrative and logical scientific modes exist in a presentation, what is the structure of the work and how effective is it?

## Structure of Narrative

The narrative in digital storytelling for business planning might have commonalities with folklore, the novel, and other stories. Bruner (1996) defined a (fictional or actual) story of an agent who acts to achieve a goal in a recognizable setting by the use of certain means. Although a number of variations exist, the sequence of events of a story always has a single pattern that begins with an explicit or implicit prorogue representing the ordinariness or legitimacy of its initial circumstances and the hinted evaluation of the end of the story. Next is the most important part: trouble. Trouble means a misfit among agents, acts, goals, settings, and means, and a violation of the initial legitimate expectancy. Then, the agent struggles to recover legitimacy. Finally, restitution of initial legitimacy or a revolutionary change in affairs with a new order of legitimacy is achieved.

Bruner (1996) referred the original concepts of the narratology literature such as Propp (1928). Comparing to the framework of Propp (1928), a prorogue that represents ordinariness corresponds to the initial situation before the functions of a story start. After symptoms of trouble occur, such as absence and interdiction, the main character encounters significant problems. In Propp (1928), the center of trouble is described as villainy or lack. Then, the main character attempts to solve the problem by, for example, departure and struggle. The solution sometimes comes from the power of donors' magical agents (tools). At the end of the story, legitimacy is recovered through, for example, victory, liquidation, or rescue, and revolutionary change comes through, for example, transfiguration, or wedding.

Propp's theory has elaborated on other refined theories such as Greimas (1970). The focus on the forms of narrative as well as its contents have led to the appearance of narrative discourse theories such as Genette (1972). This paper, however, adapts Brunner's theory in the psychology literature concerning the narrative approach based on the simplified framework of the narratology literature such as Propp (1928), and does not aim to conduct a deep analysis of the narrative's contents and structure.

Basically based on Bruner (1996), we suppose that the narrative side of digital storytelling for a business plan has the previously described four units, similar to other types of narratives. We call the four units an old situation (prorogue), obstruction (trouble), the solution (struggle), and a new situation (recovery or change). In our study, the core of the narrative may be considered a unit of obstruction because the workshop in this research was held during an early stage of business planning. Finding a problem is more important in the early stage of business planning than detailed problem solving, and an obstruction is a strong suggestion of where a problem occurs, in contrast to an old situation that represents ordinariness.

This research explores the influences of the structure and contents of digital storytelling on the audience's evaluation of business plans. In particular, we observed a qualitative link between the narrative and the logical scientific modes.

## METHOD

### Digital Storytelling Workshop

During April–July 2014, we held a workshop on business planning using digital storytelling that were instructed by an academic researcher and a business consultant at a Japanese university. Six graduate students participated. Two of them had experience in working with companies and had started a new business in their 40s and 50s. Four of the participants had no work experience and were in their 20s.

Ten sessions on digital storytelling lasting one and one-half hours were conducted. The workshop schedule was as follows:

**Session 1:** Three-minute speech on business plans with an image: What do I want to do and why do I do it?
**Session 2:** My personal history: How is my personal history related to my business plan?
**Session 3:** Presentation of storyboard and discussion.
**Session 4:** Digital storytelling technique and engaging in digital storytelling.
**Session 5:** Presentation of digital storytelling prototype and discussion.
**Sessions 6–8:** Engaging in digital storytelling.
**Sessions 9–10:** Presentation of final digital storytelling work and discussion in front of the audience.

All six participants completed the storytelling work up to session 8. Sessions 9 and 10 were held as an open meeting and six works were presented. Graduate students, staff, and outsiders interested in business planning using digital storytelling participated.

### Data Collected

In the last session held on July 18, 2014, the completed six works were shown to 35 members of the audience and their positive and questionable responses were recorded during the presentation of each work by an audience response system. [2] At the end of each presentation, the audience filled out a questionnaire.

During July–October 2014, the same survey was conducted online. Through the Internet, respondents observed presentations of the digital storytelling works, and during the presentation of each work, their positive and questionable responses were recorded using the online audience response system. At the end of each presentation, they filled out the same questionnaire as the offline one. 39 responses were collected.

A total of 74 members of the offline and online audiences responded to the questionnaire. The audience was 53% male and 47% female, the average score of age was 30.5 years old, and 74% were graduate students and 26% were working. All the participants of the workshop have a basic knowledge of management through university education or through their experience of running a business. A few participants actually have the experience of starting a new business.

The composition of the questionnaire was as follows:

Questions regarding the work after each presentation:

1. Open-ended questions:
    a. Good or interesting points.
    b. Questionable points.
    c. Other points noticed.

2. Prefixed questions:
    a. Overall evaluation of the work (0–10 point scale).
    b. Attribute evaluation of the work.
    c. (1: Unlikely, 2: Rather unlikely, 3: Cannot say, 3: Rather likely, 5: Likely):
        i. I can well understand the contents of the business plan.
        ii. I can understand the business planner's vision and motivation.
        iii. I am interested in the business plan.
        iv. The business plan is persuasive.
        v. I have empathy with the business plan.
        vi. Visual expression is good.
        vii. Narration is good.
        viii. The description of the storyteller's personal experience is good.
        ix. I had a similar experience.
        x. The story is realistic.
        xi. The overall structure is well considered.
        xii. The business plan has a good point of view.
        xiii. The business plan is well considered.
        xiv. I would help if I could.
        xv. I would fund the plan if I were a venture capitalist.

Overall questions at the end of all presentations:

1. The difference between digital storytelling and the traditional presentation style.
2. Compared with the traditional presentation style, digital storytelling is…
3. (5: Effective, 4: Rather effective, 3: Cannot say, 2: Rather ineffective, 1: Ineffective):
    a. Understanding the contents of the business plan.
    b. Understanding the business planner's vision and motivation.
    c. Interest in the business plan.
    d. Persuasiveness of the business plan.
    e. Empathy with the business plan.
4. Open-end questions on overall comments.

The questions pertaining to the evaluation of attributes (1.b.ii.) were selected keeping in mind the types of cognition and behavior. The first type is reasonable, and the objective cognition is mainly affected by the logical scientific mode (No. 1, 11-13). The second type is sensuous, emotional, and its episode memory-related cognition is mainly affected by the narrative mode (No.5-10). The third type is affected by the mixture of both the modes and intention of the final behavior (No. 2-4, 14-15).

## Method of Analysis

Participants of the workshop were instructed to tell a story about what they want to do and why they want do it that reflects their personal history. Instructions were given to keep the total time length to approximately 5 minutes. However, participants were not told the details of the contents and structure of the work. Thus, the contents and structure naturally appeared in the process of developing the work.

Although participants were not told, the work could be divided into two main parts: the narrative part and the analytical part. The researchers identified the parts and units of the works by focusing on the owners of the viewpoint of the story. The part of the story told from the viewpoint of a personal character, including that of the storyteller, was regarded as a narrative. The part of the story viewed and told objectively and scientifically, i.e., from a point of view of God, was regarded as analytical. All storytellers started from the narrative part and ended with the analytical part, except for the beginning of the work (see Figure 3).

The methodology of the analysis, first, is to identify the structure of the parts and units of the works by examining length of time, order, and position throughout the entire work. In addition, we observed qualitative aspects regarding the interaction of each unit.

Second, we observed the audience's response and evaluations that were collected in the workshop and online. The audience's evaluation was measured using data from the audience response system and the questionnaire described in the previous section.

Finally, we qualitatively estimated the influence of the structure and contents of each unit on the audience's evaluation. The first point of view was from the impact of the proportion of the time length of each unit on the evaluation. Second, we observed the contents of the narrative part and focused in particular on the influence of personal experiences in this part. The third point of view was the influence of other factors, such as the quality of the concept, the existence of objective evidence, visual expression, and narration.

## STRUCTURE OF DIGITAL STORYTELLING WORKS

A summary of the digital storytelling works of the workshop participants is provided in Figure 1 and Figure 2. [3]

The structure of the digital storytelling works that the participants developed are indicated in Figure 3. In total, the storytellers' narrative part consumed 53% (average 185 seconds) of the total time and the analytical part consumed 47% (average 167 seconds) of the total time.

The narrative part consisted of four functional units: old situation, obstruction, solution, and new situation. The old situation unit took 51% of the time, the obstruction part took 30%, the solution unit took 14%, and the new situation unit took 4%. Four of the six works had no solution and no new situation unit.

The analytical part consisted of six functional units: factor, resource, evidence, element explanation, method, and expected result. The time length of the analytical part was 29% for the factor, 3% for resources, 11% for evidence, 11% for the element explanation, 43% for the method, and 3% for the expected result.

The participants were not provided instructions regarding the structure of their work during the workshop. Thus, the structure of the work, which is indicated in this section, could be considered as the outcome of the unconscious and spontaneous activities of the participants.

### Structure of the Narrative Part

Two patterns to the composition of the narrative part appeared in the works. The first pattern (Works B, C, E, and F) was that the narrative part includes only the old situation and the obstruction units. In this pattern, the factor unit of the analytical part immediately follows the final obstruction unit of the episode and the solution is never indicated.

*Figure 1. Summary of the digital storytelling works for business planning (Work A, B, C)*

| | |
|---|---|
| **Work A** | **Title: Japanese-style home delivery system in China**<br>**Time Length:** 417 sec, **# of Screens:** 24, **Music:** yes, **Main Character:** Storyteller<br>**Author:** 20s, student with no working experience |
| Narrative part | **Episode 1:** When I was a child in China, I was lonely because my parents lived overseas **(Ob).** One day, my parents gave me a Japanese manga **(So)** and my personality became cheerful, encouraged by Japanese animation **(New).**<br>**Episode 2:** I came to Japan and encountered thoughtful Japanese services **(Old).** I started a small business to export animation character models, but it failed because of the immaturity of the Chinese delivery service **(Ob).** I found a solution for exports to China using the Japanese home delivery service **(So).** |
| Analytical part | **F1:** New style of home delivery service in China<br>**F2:** Customer-oriented service for special needs<br>**E1:** Cases of service for golfers and refrigerated transportation service by Japanese home delivery company<br>**F3:** Marketability of the delivery of fragile goods in Shanghai<br>**E2:** Specific demands for animation character models and level of existing delivery service<br>**M:** Standardization of packet, fee system according to size, human- oriented services, value-added services, staff education, expanding category of fragile goods<br>**ER:** Delivery service that connects human relationships<br> |
| **Work B** | **Title: Recycling system for university insiders**<br>**Time Length:** 307 sec, **# of Screens:** 20, **Music:** yes, **Main Character:** Storyteller<br>**Author:** 20s, student with no working experience |
| Narrative part | **Episode 1:** I moved recently. I wanted to exchange unnecessary and newly required goods and sought people with which to exchange them through SNS **(Old).** I found an appropriate person, but we failed to exchange goods because of a change in the counterpart's situation **(Ob).** |
| Analytical part | **F:** Trusted and easy-to-use recycling system<br>**E:** Problems of existing services<br>**M1:** Use of internal network and system of the university, closed membership only for students and staff of the university, expanding services to other universities<br>**R:** Existing system of my university<br>**M2:** Testing in my university and expanding to other universities<br>**ER:** Service placing value on things and people |
| |  |
| **Work C** | **Title: New style Japanese school for factory workers in China**<br>**Time Length:** 396 sec, **# of Screens:** 14, **Music:** no, **Main Character:** Storyteller<br>**Author:** 20s, student with no working experience |
| Narrative part | **Episode 1:** When I was a college student in China, I was depressed because I failed to enter the expected university **(Ob).** However, I met an excellent and enthusiastic teacher who is handicapped, and I made up my mind to become a teacher **(So).**<br>**Episode 2:** I went to teach Japanese to Chinese factory workers as an intern **(Old)**, and I knew the factory workers faced difficulties learning **(Ob).** |
| Analytical part | **M1:** Japanese school for factory workers of Japanese company in China<br>**F:** Time-saving for busy workers, interactive and practical learning<br>**M2:** Targeting specific industrial area in China where Japanese companies accumulate, small classes at night, practical teaching methods, motivation management, a close relationship with Japanese companies and universities |
| |  |

Narrative Part: Old situation = **Old**, Obstruction = **Ob**, Solution = **So**, New situation = **New**
Analytical Part: Factor = **F**, Resource = **R**, Evidence = **E**, Element Explanation =**EE**, Method = **M**, Expected Result =**ER**

Work B starts from the old situation unit, "I moved recently, and wanted to exchange unnecessary goods," and then the character meets the obstruction, "I failed to exchange the goods because of the change in the counterpart's situation." The potential needs of a trusted and easy-to-use recycling system of the analytical part are indicated.

In episode 1 of Work C, the obstruction unit appears first, "I am depressed because I failed to enter the expected university," followed by the solution, "I met a handicapped teacher, and inspired by her, I made up my mind to become a teacher." As a consequence of episode 1, episode 2 starts from, "I went to teach Japanese to Chinese factory workers when I was an intern," as the old situation, and then the character encounters the obstruction, "I know that the workers faced learning difficulties," is indicated.

*Figure 2. Summary of the digital storytelling works for business planning (Work D, E, F)*

| Work D | **Title: Consulting service supporting the service staff**<br>**Time Length:** 325 sec, **# of Screens:** 9, **Music:** no, **Main Character:** Fictitious character<br>**Author:** 50s, working |
|---|---|
| Narrative part | **Episode 1:** Tama (fictitious character) started a part-time job at a grocery store and loved the job **(Old)**. One day, a customer complained about the quality of the product. Tama apologized, but the customer said that she did not understand the problem. Tama was depressed and quit the job (**Ob**). Later, Tama went to the store and knew that the customer wanted the store to investigate the cause of the accident **(So)**. Tama made up her mind to work at the store again (**New**). |
| Analytical part | **F1 :** Support plan for service staff<br>**F2:** Organizational support for staff, improvement of customer service skill<br>**M:** Visualization and analysis of complaint, consulting to improve customer service skills and motivation of the staff |
| |  |
| Work E | **Title: Promotion of chenpi, the specialty of a hometown**<br>**Time Length:** 328 sec, **# of Screens:** 18, **Music:** no, **Main Character:** Storyteller<br>**Author:** 20s, student with no working experience |
| Narrative part | **Episode 1:** I did not know the goodness of my hometown **(Old1)**.<br>**Episode 1 (continue):** When I was a child, I did not love chenpi (a kind of herb), but I have good memories of eating chenpi with my family **(Old2)**. When I came to Japan to study, I was shocked that dishes tasted strange and noticed that chenpi was good for my health (**Ob**).<br>**Episode 1 (continue):** I also long for a memory of people in my hometown making chenpi **(Old3).** |
| Analytical part | **EE1:** Introduction and effects of chenpi<br>**R:** The hometown is one of the largest producing districts for chenpi<br>**EE2:** Production process of chenpi<br>**EE3:** Application of chenpi<br>**F:** Publicity for Japanese individuals to know about chenpi<br>**M:** Exhibition of chenpi at the school festival |
| |  |
| Work F | **Title: Networking between an illustrator and customers**<br>**Time Length:** 339 sec, **# of Screens:** 12, **Music:** no, **Main Character:** Storyteller<br>**Author:** 40s, working |
| Narrative part | **Episode 1:** I love to collaborate with and support my friends in business. I have a friend, an amateur illustrator who has been engaged in a number of volunteer activities **(Old)**. She is now thinking about working as a professional. I would like to support her (**Ob**). |
| Analytical part | **F1:** Networking between an illustrator and customers<br>**F2:** Networking of existing fans<br>**M:** Communicating with fans on SNS, customer-made illustration service |

Narrative Part: Old situation = **Old**, Obstruction = **Ob,** Solution = **So**, New situation = **New**
Analytical Part: Factor = **F**, Resource = **R**, Evidence = **E,** Element Explanation =**EE**, Method = **M**, Expected Result =**ER**

Following the conclusion of the episodes, the success factors are indicated as analysis, that saves time for busy works, is interactive and facilitates practical learning.

Work E begins with the character's memory as the old situation, "I did not love the specialty of my hometown, chenpi (a kind of herb) when I was a child." Here the obstruction is, "I was shocked that the dishes tasted strange and noticed that chenpi was good for my health after leaving my hometown." The story is linked to the promotion of chenpi in the Japanese market in the analytical part.

Work F starts from the old situation, "I love to collaborate with my friends, and I have a friend, an amateur illustrator," implicitly indicates the obstruction by saying, "My friend is now thinking about working as a professional. I would like to support her." This episode has developed into an idea of networking between an illustrator and customers in the analytical part.

The second pattern of episode composition (Works A and D) was that the episode has a solution and, in one case, also indicates a new situation.

In Work A, the narrative part starts from the obstruction, "As a child, I was lonely in China," and a solution is presented, "My parents gave me a Japanese manga," and a new situation appears, "My personality became cheerful encouraged by Japanese animation." The new situation in episode 1 was con-

*Figure 3. Time length and number of responses of each work*

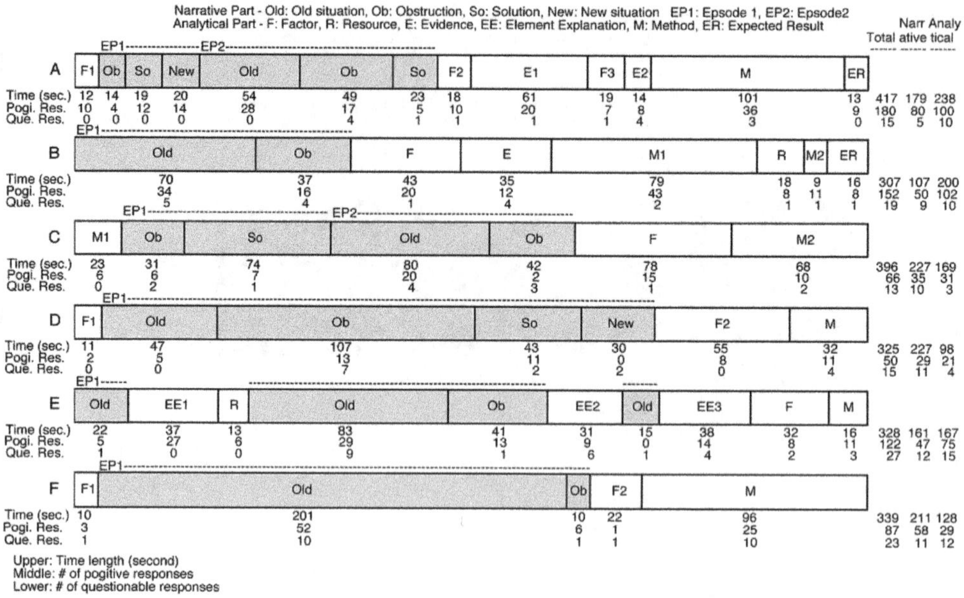

nected to the old situation, "I came to Japan and encountered thoughtful Japanese services." In episode 2, the character again encounters an obstruction, "A small business of exporting animation character models, which I had started, failed because of the immaturity of the Chinese delivery service." This is followed by the solution, "I found a solution from Japanese home delivery service." This finding was linked to the key success factors for a new style of home delivery service in China in the analytical part.

Work D had one episode that starts from the old situation, "Tama (a fictitious character[4]) took up a part-time job at a grocery store and loved the job," followed by the obstruction, "One day, a customer complained about the quality of the product. Tama apologized, but the customer said that she did not understand the problem. Tama was depressed and quit the job." The solution follows, "Later, Tama went to the store and came to know that the customer wanted the store to investigate the cause of the accident," and ends up in the new situation, "Tama made up her mind to work at the store again." (Figure 1 and 2)

## Structure of the Analytical Part

The analytical part represented a very similar style of scientific presentation. The assumption of the key success factors for a business (the factor unit), the concrete methods to satisfy the key success factors (the method unit), the objective evidence for the supporting hypotheses (the evidence unit), the business planner's existing resources (the resource unit), the explanation of business element in detail (the element explanation unit), and the expected result from fulfilling the method (the expected result unit) were observed.

Only the factor and method units that commonly existed in all six works are considered essential for a business plan. In the factor unit, key success factors for a business derived include concepts related to the overall strategy and objective of a business, specialization, targeting of customers, important functions of the business, and important characteristics of a service. Examples of a concept related to the overall strategy and objective of a business include customer orientation, support for the service staff, and support for a friend.

Embodying the concepts of the factor unit drew concrete methods in detail, such as standardization of packet size, usage of closed networks, location of industrial accumulation in a Japanese company, visualization of complaints, exhibition in a school festival, and fans' SNS.

Element explanation units appear only in Work E because the storyteller had to explain the product, chenpi, that is not well known in the Japanese market. The resources that the storyteller (= business planner) already owns appear only in Works B and E. In Work B, the resource is the storyteller belonging to a university and having access to the university's internal network. In Work E, the resource is the storyteller's hometown being one of the largest producing districts of chenpi. In other works, clarification of business elements and resources tends to be weak.

Notably, the evidence and the expected result appear only in Works A and B. The analytical part of Works A and B are said to be, relatively, a scientific presentation style, including theory (= clarifying factor), evidence, and forecast (= expected result). Objective evidence could be considered to reinforce the theory and the consistency with the narrative part in these works. (Figure 3)

## Linkage between the Narrative and the Analytical Part

As mentioned in the section of the structure of the narrative part, we observed that the narrative parts of all works are connected to the logic of the analysis. The narrative part is not isolated from the analytical part in digital storytelling for business planning.

As seen in Figure 4, a typical pattern as observed in Work B, C, E, and F is that the storyteller starts the story to explain the old situation, and then the main character encounters the obstructive situation. The change from the old situation to the obstruction is a clue to derive the key success factors. In the pattern, which contains the solution or a new situation in the narrative part, the consequence of episodes of Work A suggests key success factors. In Work D, the narrative part was presented as if it were a simulation of the analytical part – the proposal of a consulting service, which will support the service staff.

Interestingly, these elements are viewed as similar to the narrative model of leaders' speech in Denning (2007): capture attention with a negative story (Obstruction) >> elicit desire with a positive story to achieve action (Solution) >> reinforce with reason as a neutral story to explain what, how, and why (Analytical part).

Both the logical and emotional linkages were observed between the narrative and the analytical parts. The narratives of all of the works contain an emotional expression. For example, Work A expresses loneliness in childhood and empathy with Japanese cultures, Work B expresses the emotion of avoiding wastefulness, Work C expresses respect for one's teacher and sympathy with learning enthusiasm of factory workers, Work D expresses the service staff's depression, Work E expresses the emotion of longing for one's hometown, and Work F expresses the love of supporting friends in business. These emotional expressions represent the motivations of the storyteller or promote the audience's empathy—although not always successful, as subsequently described.

*Figure 4. Linkage of the narrative part to the analytical part*

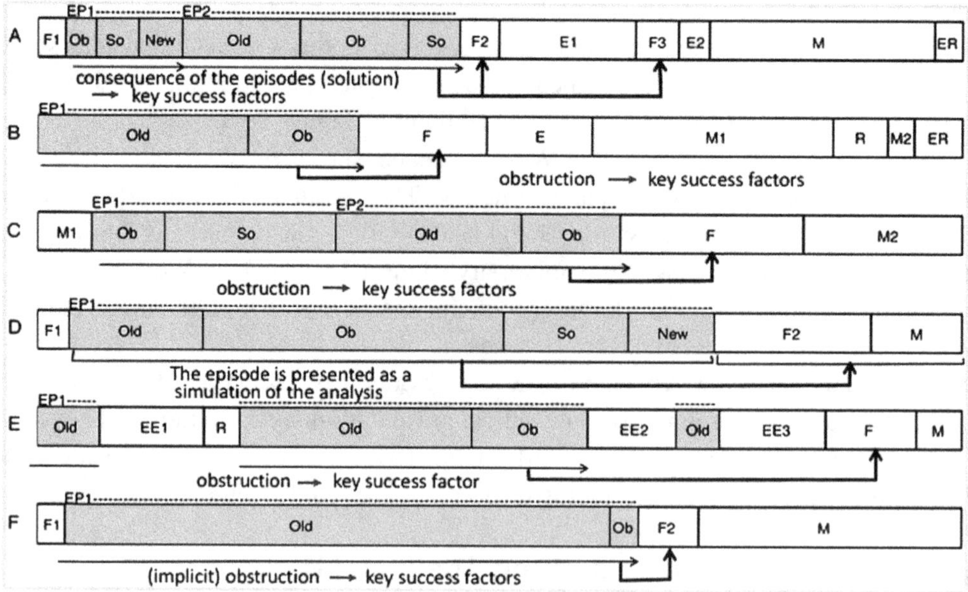


## EVALUATION OF EACH WORK

The audience provided an overall evaluation of each work, an attribute evaluation, and open-end comments using a questionnaire and real-time responses from the audience response system, as previously described.

### Overall and Attribute Evaluation

As Figure 5 indicates, the overall evaluation rank is Works A, B, C, D, E, and F. Works A and B are in the top group and are significantly different from the other works. Work F was evaluated as the lowest among all works, followed by Work E. Works C and D were in the middle. Thus, we consider Works A and B to be in the top group, Works C and D to be in the middle group, and Work E and F to be in the lowest group.

In general, evaluation of the attributes was highly correlated with the overall evaluation (Figure 6).

Seeing the exceptional ranking of attribute evaluation compared to the ranking of overall evaluation, Work E in the lowest group received a relatively high evaluation for understanding the contents of a business plan, vision and motivation, description of personal experience, and point of view, but received a low rating in persuasiveness, similar experience with the audience, and overall structure. Although Work E has a good episode that communicates the storyteller's motivation, it is problematic to the entire structure, as subsequently described.

Work D received a relatively high evaluation in narration, but a low evaluation in the description of personal experience because the storyteller has narration experiences on the job and the main character in the narrative part is fictitious only in Work D.

*Figure 5. Overall evaluation (N=74, 0-10 point)*

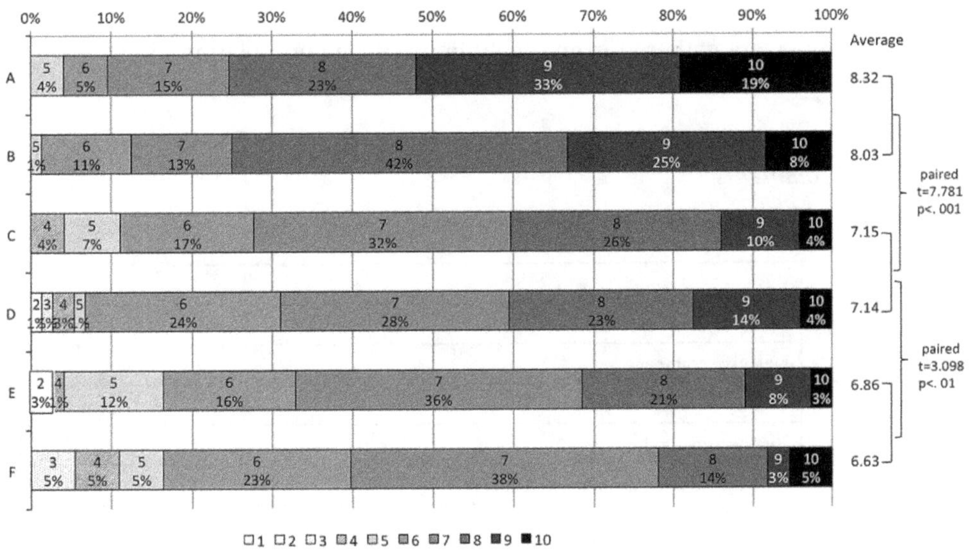


*Figure 6. Average scores of attribute evaluation (N=74, 1-5 point) Real-Time Responses to Each Part of the Story*

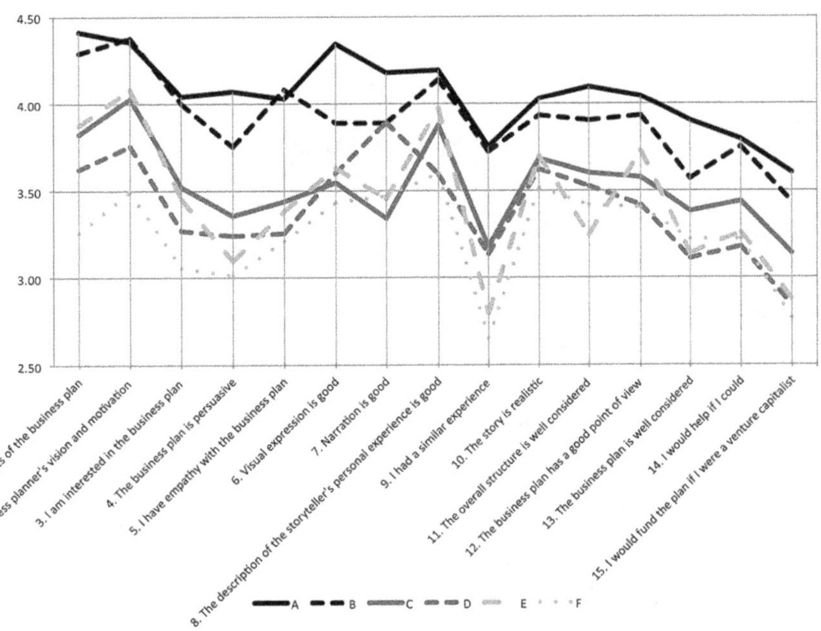


Figure 3 indicates the number of real-time responses during each work presenting. The top group—Works A and B—received the most frequent positive responses. The lowest group, Works E and F, received the most frequent questionable responses. Real-time responses showed the same tendency as those of the overall rating from the questionnaire after the presentation.

## Open-Ended Comments

A total of 691 comments were gathered from the audience. The composition of categories is indicated in Table 1.

*Table 1. Open-ended comments*

| | | Total |
|---|---|---|
| **Positive/Negative** | Base | 691 |
| | Positive comment | 56% |
| | Negative comment | 44% |
| **Category** | Concept of business plan | 31% |
| | Business method | 16% |
| | Linkage between episode and concept | 12% |
| | Shortage of evidence and comparison | 6% |
| | Explanation of element | 2% |
| | New point of view | 2% |
| | Sensory expression | 18% |
| | Motivation | 3% |
| | Sympathy | 3% |
| | Overall impression | 6% |
| | Others | 1% |
| | **Composition of Large Categories** | |
| **Concept of Business Plan (Positive)** | Base | **144** |
| | Mentioning about specific concepts | 62% |
| | Concept is overall good | 38% |
| **Concept of Business Plan (Negative)** | Base | **72** |
| | Concept is unclear/insufficient | 100% |
| **Business Method (Positive)** | Base | **23** |
| | Mentioning about specific methods | 83% |
| | Detailed/concrete description of method is good | 17% |
| **Business Method (Negative)** | Base | **86** |
| | Mentioning about specific methods | 41% |
| | Business method is unclear | 37% |
| | Financial plan is not clear | 20% |
| | Others | 2% |
| **Linkage between Episode and Concept (Positive)** | Base | **53** |
| | Business plan is drawn from the storyteller's personal experience/realistic story | 98% |
| | --> *I also had a same/similar experience* | (35%) |
| | Others | 2% |

*continued on following page*

*Table 1. Continued*

| | | Total |
|---|---|---|
| **Linkage between Episode and Concept (Negative)** | Base | **30** |
| | Shortage/obscurity of linkage between episode and concept | 100% |
| **Sensory Expression (Positive)** | Base | **75** |
| | Photo, drawing | 49% |
| | Narration | 28% |
| | Music | 12% |
| | Others | 11% |
| **Sensory Expression (Negative)** | Base | **48** |
| | Photo, drawing | 38% |
| | Narration | 58% |
| | Music | 4% |

The comments tended to emphasize the rational side of the presentation, including the concepts of the key success factors for businesses, linkages with the episodes and evidence, explanation of business elements, the business method, and new points of view, over the emotional side, including sensory expression, simple empathy, and motivation. A total of 69% of all comments were on the rational side of the presentation. The strength of the rational side of the audiences' evaluation of the digital storytelling work is presumed to be a characteristic of the reaction to the business plan work compared with the work for other application fields, such as artistic expression and therapy.

Considering the characteristics of digital storytelling for a business plan compared with a scientific presentation for a business plan indicates that comments on linkage between episodes and key success factor concepts (12% of all comments) were very important. Interestingly, the positive comments (53 comments) on the linkage between episode and concept were very homogeneous; that is, 98% of the comments were similar to, "It is good because the business plan is drawn from the storyteller's personal experience/realistic story." (Most comments noted the "storyteller's personal experience"; however, for Work D, comments stated "realistic story" because the main character was not a storyteller but a fictitious character.)

Furthermore, among the comments on drawing concepts from personal/realistic experience, 35% stated, "I also had a same/similar experience." The audience found such experiences not only plausible but also familiar. The plausibility and familiarity of the narrative part could become the foundation for the key success factors of business plans, although relatively more subjective than scientific evidence. This finding is critical in considering the function of a story when applied to businesses in general.

Negative comments about the linkage between episode and concept (30 comments) complained about the shortage or obscurity of the linkage (Table 1).

## FACTORS THAT INFLUENCE THE EVALUATION

### Influences of Structure on the Evaluation

The structure of the work is considered to influence the overall evaluation. An attribute evaluation of "Overall structure is well considered" of the top group is superior to that of the middle group (paired t=4.727, p<0.001, df=70), and the rating of the middle group was higher than that of the lowest group (paired t=3.243, p<0.01, df=69) (Figure 6).

As we have already seen in the section on the structure of digital storytelling works and a qualitative analysis of the audience's comments, the narrative part could become the foundation of deriving the key success factors. Typically, the contrast between the old situation and the obstruction units provides a clue to the reasoning for the factor unit in the analytical part.

A comparison among the proportion of the time length of the old situation unit, the obstruction units, and the factor unit of the top group for Work A is 33:38:30 (where the total time of these three parts is 100) and for Work B is 47:25:29. For the middle group, it is 35:32:34 for Work C and 21:49:30 for Work D. In the lowest group, it is 62:21:17 for Work D and is 86:4:9 for Work F (see also Figure 3.)

The proportion of the three units is almost equal in the top and middle groups, although the proportion between the old situation and the obstruction in the narrative part differs slightly for Works B and D. At least the proportion of the factor of the analytical part is typically at approximately 30% in these groups.

Apparently, the balance of these units is incorrect in the lowest group. Work E has a long old situation unit, obstruction is relatively short, and the factor unit is only 17%. Work F has a very long old situation unit that occupies 86%, the obstruction takes a very short time of 4%, and the factor is only 9%. Although identifying exactly the appropriate proportion of units is difficult, if only a long personal story and poor analysis exist, the audience may not find a connection between the story and the business plan.

### Influences of Personal Episodes and the Feeling of "Something Like Me" on Evaluation

As was observed in the section on open-ended comments, 98% of the positive mentions on the linkage between episode and concept were "It is good because the business plan is drawn from the storyteller's personal experience/realistic story." Of these comments, 35% stated, "I also had a same/similar experience."

In the pre-fixed attribute evaluation, "The description of a storyteller's personal experience is good" was rated significantly higher in the top group than in other groups (paired t=4.606, P<0.001, df=70 between top and middle; paired t=4.538, P<0.001, df=68 between top and lowest). "The story has reality" had the same tendency (paired t=3.692, P<0.001, df=70 between top and middle; paired t=4.393, P<0.001, df=68 between top and lowest) (Figure 6). The number of comments that had the same meaning was larger in Work B (21 comments) and Work A (10 comments) than in other groups (average of five comments).

Regarding the attribute evaluation of "I have a similar experience," significant differences existed among the top, middle, and lowest groups (paired t=5.253, P<0.001, df=70 between top and middle; paired t=4.666, P<0.001, df=69 between middle and lowest). The ranking using the average score of this attribute was exactly the same as that of the overall evaluation: Works A, B, C, D, E, and F (Figure 5 and 6).

A relationship exists in which a higher evaluation of personal experience/reality results in a higher overall evaluation. The relationship is much stronger if the experience or realistic story is familiar to the audience. In another words, the feeling of "something like me" positively impacts on the audience.

The top group—Works A and B—well represents the storyteller's personal experience and reality of the story, and the audience perceived that they had a similar experience at the same time. Work C follows the top group in these aspects of evaluation. Regarding Work F, which had the lowest overall evaluation, the audience did not admire the representation of the storyteller's personal experience. Moreover, the reality and familiarity of the story also received a low evaluation, even though Work F presented a long emotional story. Work F's representation of the story was problematic (Figure 6).

Regarding Work D, although the attribute evaluation of personal experience was low because of a fictitious main character, the reality and familiarity of the story were the same as that of Work C, which followed the top group (Figure 6).

In contrast, Work E was rated at the same level as Work C for personal experience and reality, and received the lowest rating—similar to Work F—for familiarity to the audience (Figure 6). Although the storyteller's memory of his or her hometown is well described, the story was about a Chinese student. Therefore, a cultural gap may exist with a Japanese audience, which may have difficulty being empathetic.

These facts might imply that familiarity is more important to the audience than plausibility or reality. Thus, the episode need not necessarily be based on the storyteller's personal experience, but the degree to which the audience has a similar experience to the story is essential. For this reason, Denning (2007) pointed out the story of the audience's problems, the story of who we are, and the common memory story as devices for effective leadership communication.

On the emotional side, plausibility might affect an audience's perception of storyteller motivation but it does not always improve the audience's empathy. Regarding attribute evaluation, in Work E, the storyteller's motivation and vision effectively describes the personal experience and was understood relatively well; however, familiarity, empathy and overall evaluation were low (Figure 5 and 6).

## Influences of Concepts and Evidence on Evaluation

Regardless of the linkage with the narrative part, the quality of the concepts of a business plan is, naturally, essential. The largest share of open-ended comments was on the concept in general. The top group in the overall evaluation—Works A and B—received a larger number of positive comments on the quality of the concept. Moreover, the attribute evaluation of "The business plan has a good point of view" and "The business plan is well considered" was higher in the top group than in the other groups (Figure 6).

The excellence of the concept was considered the basis for the evaluation of the business plan; therefore, if the concept is of very poor quality, the overall evaluation will be low regardless of the quality of the narrative. However, in this research, the average attribute evaluation of the concept rated using these two questions ("a good point view" and "well considered") was higher than at the middle point of the measurement (3.0). The concepts of all of the works are good or average, enabling the narrative part to play the role of enhancing the foundation of the concept.

Regarding the foundation of the concept, only the top group also provided objective evidence in the analytical part. The evidence unit appears twice just after the factor unit in Work A and once in Work B (Figure 3). Objective evidence enhances the accompanying logic deriving factors, in addition to the linkage of the narrative part.

## Influences of Visual and Auditory Expression on Evaluation

Visual and auditory expression techniques are also important for overall evaluations. The number of comments about the techniques of expression was the second largest, following comments on the concept (Table 1). The top group—Works A and B—tended to receive more positive comments than negative comments. The attribute evaluations of "Visual expression is good" and "Narration is good" of the top group were also rated higher than that of the other groups (Figure 6).

The top group used a larger number of screens of pictures compared with the lower group (Figure 1 and 2). As was noted in the section on open-ended comments, in general, the amount of visual expression was positively perceived.

The volume of the narration is important. The recording level of Works C, E, and F was problematic and numerous complaints were received for these works on the level of narration.

Regarding the quality of the narration, the narration of Work D was eminently frequent and some audiences said, "It is professional-like." Actually, the storyteller of Work D has experience with making public announcements for her job. The fluency of the narration tended to be evaluated in a positive manner; however, interestingly, some audiences perceived the narration as somewhat negative, with comments such as "The frequency is too high" The fact that too much frequency of the narration was negative at some point is related to the fact that a familiar experience for the audience affected the overall evaluation. A story told by a professional narrator may be perceived as less familiar than a story told by an amateur.

The impact of music is relatively less compared to the visuals and narration (Table 1). Overall, preference was given to the kind of music that provides a good atmosphere but does not disturb the narration.

# DISCUSSION

## Consistency and Balance of a Story

In the context of application to business planning, digital storytelling has two faces: the narrative and scientific logical analysis. The two faces are not separate, but have a mutual relationship. The works we researched started telling stories from an episode and ended at analysis. The function of the narrative part reinforces the analysis part both rationally and emotionally.

The rational side of the link between the narrative and analysis is that, first, a narrative points to the start of the business. In other words, the narrative represents the problem to solve. The inspiration for the initial concept of a business cannot be deducted from a theory or inducted from objective data. Finding problems is the most appropriate function of the narrative. It means that the business planners not only find problems, but also make other stakeholders understand where the problem lies – in consumer needs or unrevealed market potentials. In particular, obstruction plays a most critical role in finding problems. An incidence of trouble or the lack of something represents problems, and a number of entrepreneurs frequently start a business from an obstruction experience.

Second, a narrative provides rich explicit or implicit hints to derive key success factors, resources, business methods, and expected results. People can guess at the factors from a contrast between the old situation and obstruction, and by following the progress of the episode. Hints of resources are often implicitly indicated in the episode's background. In some cases, the main character gets new devices in an episode, which become hints of the business methods. The scenario is similar to folklore in which magical agents are given by a donor. The end of an episode(s) implies the expected result.

Problem solving and forecasts can be done through analysis; however, new alternatives from new points of view are difficult to find through strict analysis. The narrative is also good at finding new alternatives, similar to finding problems.

The narrative is also good at emotional representation. Although rationality tends to be more important than emotion in the context of business planning, the emotional side functions to enhance the entire consistency of the story.

The emotional side of the link is that, first, a narrative conveys a business planner's motivation and commitment to the business. The motivation and commitment of the entrepreneur are quite important for other people who may cooperate with him or her. A high possibility exists that the business will fail if the entrepreneur is not well motivated and committed.

Second, a part of the audience's empathy for the business plan can be brought from the empathy for the narrative. An audience's empathy is different from the storyteller's motivation. Even the audience sensing the business planner's motivation from the narrative does not always spur their empathy if the narrative is not empathetic enough, such as Work F.

Mixed links exist on both the rational and the emotional sides to form a bridge from the narrative to the analysis: problem finding, alternative finding, conveying the business planner's motivation, and spurring the audience's empathy. Regardless of the quality of the links, every unit should always be linked with other units to make the work effective for the audience. At least one path from one unit to another unit is necessary. The comments show that audiences are very sensitive to how every unit is connected to other units. People do not like inconsistencies in the story (Bruner, 1996).

In addition, the entire structure of a work should be balanced. Too short length of important units, such as obstruction, factor, and method, and too large length of complimentary units, such as element explanation cause an imbalance in the logic of the story, and make the work ineffective.

Consistency[5] and balance of the narrative and analysis represent a kind of logic of digital storytelling for business planning. An audience mentioned the feeling of the logic as follows:

*There is logic in the way of telling a story. When I listen to the story, I felt that my questions were answered one by one (comment for Work C).*

## Power of the Story of "Something Like You"

Another key point in making a narrative effective is familiarity of the episodes to the audience. If the audiences sense, "This story is something like me," the narrative makes the storyteller's message understandable and improves its persuasiveness and empathy. The story need not be exactly same as the audience's experience, and it is adequate if audiences find some essential commonality between episodes and their experience. Although episodes of the personal experiences of the storyteller are generally effective, it is a fact that "Me story" (Lambert, 2013) often has some essential commonality with other people. If the story is heterogeneous to the audience, even a storyteller's experience will not convey the message well.

Conveying the message is more difficult if audiences have divergent experiences. If the characteristics and background of the audience are homogeneous, the storyteller can prepare the story relatively easily. However, in reality, individuals' backgrounds are typically divergent, even if they belong to the same organization or environment.

An excellent presenter is skilled at telling a story that is "something like you," regardless of the audience. Such a presenter might understand the general and essential commonalities among human beings. If a person is skilled at telling a story that is "something like you," telling personal experiences and using the first person is not necessary. Creators such as novelists and filmmakers have made a number of works that enables readers or audiences to sense a commonality with themselves, even when using fictitious characters in a fictitious situation.

Digital storytelling is compatible with broad worldwide social networks. The broadening of the network increases the diversity of the audience and the corroborative team members. Finding commonality among individuals has increased in importance. An education system that teaches the development of a story that is "something like you" is needed, although teaching balance and a mix of links between the narrative and analysis is more difficult. These more general issues face digital storytelling in the era of worldwide networking.

## FUTURE RESEARCH DIRECTIONS

This research is an explorative and qualitative study to find problems rather than to solve problems. A larger amount of data that is objectively measured, and a controlled research design, are necessary to verify the findings of this research.

Furthermore, this chapter does not address certain important points of view, such as the influences of digital storytelling on the storyteller and its influence on the concept of a business plan.

Digital storytelling is broadly known to change the storyteller (Hartley & McWilliam, 2009; Lambert, 2013). Rather, an important objective of digital storytelling is recognition of selfhood and a self-revolution, particularly in the application areas of therapy and education.

Reflection is the critical process of recognition and change of selfhood. Generally, a narrative reflexively provides structure to our very sense of selfhood (Murray, 2015). Seeing personal photographs and listening to the narrations of storytellers through digital storytelling may arouse richer images of selfhood and may induce reflection. Moreover, the workshop system of digital storytelling explicitly enhances the reflection process by enabling discussion with other participants. Observing the reflection process on how stories are developed by participants in the workshop provides clues to the influences of digital storytelling on the storyteller.

In addition, the narrative has the character to bring new points of view to people. Finding problems and alternatives, which was pointed out in this chapter, is the result of the function of expanding viewpoints, and some members of the audience mentioned new ideas for a business plan in the open-ended comments. The business plan itself may have changed because storytellers found new points of view during the process of developing stories. Changing an idea and its factors could be also clarified by observing the process of the workshop.

## CONCLUSION

Digital storytelling for business planning has the unique trait of two different modes of perception, thinking, and communication at the different locations of the work: the narrative and the logical scientific. This chapter pointed out how the structure and contents of the work influence its effectiveness through examination of the works and the audience's evaluation of real-time responses, and prefixed and open-ended questions at the end of each presentation of work.

The consistency and the balance of the narrative and analytical parts were considered to relate to the audience's evaluation. The obstruction unit in the narrative part and the factor and the method units in the analytical part were critical for digital storytelling of business planning. The most important link was from a contrast between the initial situation and obstruction in the narrative part, to key success factors deriving in the analytical part, although all units need at least one connection with other units. Isolated units create a sense of inconsistency for audiences.

Regarding the contents of the narrative, if a narrative is familiar to the audience, and helps them relate to the narrative, i.e., "something like you," it is effective in understanding, persuading and creating an emotional effect on the audience.

The findings of this research show that a narrative creates new value in helping audiences relate to it, "something like you," and has a synergistic effect by creating logical and emotional links between a narrative and traditional analysis.

## REFERENCES


Bower, G. H. (1981). Mood and memory. *The American Psychologist*, *36*(2), 129–148. doi:10.1037/0003-066X.36.2.129 PMID:7224324

Bruner, J. S. (1996). *The culture of education*. Cambridge, MA: Harvard University Press.

Bruner, J. S. (2003). *Making stories: Law, literature, life*. Cambridge, MA: Harvard University Press.

Denning, S. (2007). *The secret language of leadership: How leaders inspire action through narrative*. San Francisco, CA: John Wiley & Sons.

Forgas, J. P., Bower, G. H., & Krantz, S. E. (1984). The influence of mood on perceptions of social interactions. *Journal of Experimental Social Psychology*, *20*(6), 497–513. doi:10.1016/0022-1031(84)90040-4

Genette, G. (1972). *Discours du récit, essai de méthode, Figures III*. Paris, France: Seuil.

Greimas, A. J. (1970). *Du sens: Essais sémiotiques* (Vol. 1). Paris, France: Seuil.

Hartley, J., & McWilliam, K. (Eds.). (2009). *Story circle*. Chichester, UK: Wiley-Blackwell. doi:10.1002/9781444310580

Kanai, A. (2005). Defamiliarization, film cognition and composition. In *Proceedings of the 19th Conference of the Japanese Society for Artificial Intelligence* (3D3-11, pp.1-2). Kitakyushu, Japan: Academic Press.

Kusunoki, K. (2010). *Story toshiteno kyoso senryaku* [Competitive strategy as story]. Tokyo, Japan: Toyo Keizai Shinposha.

Lambert, J. (2013). *Digital storytelling: Capturing lives, creating community* (4th ed.). New York, NY: Routledge.

Murray, J. H. (1998). *Hamlet on the holodeck*. New York, NY: Free Press.

Murray, M. (2015). Narrative psychology. In J. A. Smith (Ed.), *Qualitative Psychology* (3rd ed., pp. 85–106). London, UK: SAGE.

Nishioka, H. (2014). *Kyoiku ni ikasu digital storytelling* [*Digital storytelling on education*]. Tokyo, Japan: Tokyo Tosho Shuppan.

Prince, G. (2003). *A dictionary of narratology* (Revised Ed.). Lincoln, NE: University of Nebraska Press.

Propp, V. (1928). *The morphology of the fairy tale*. Leningrad, USSR: Academia.

Schwartz, P. (1991). *The art of the long view: Scenario planning-protecting your company against an uncertain world*. London, UK: Century Business.

Van der Heijden, K. (1996). *Scenarios*. Chichester, UK: John Wiley & Sons.

Wade, W. (2012). *Scenario planning: A field guide to the future*. Hoboken, NJ: John Wiley & Sons.

## KEY TERMS AND DEFINITIONS

**Analytical Part:** A part of the digital storytelling that was told in the logical scientific mode. In this chapter, the researchers identified the analytical part on whether it was told objectively and scientifically, i.e., from a point of view of God.

**Digital Storytelling:** A short digital work that combines narration and visual-auditory material, such as photographs, music, and movies, produced by an individual as his or her own story.

**Element Explanation Unit:** A unit of the analytical part, in which an unfamiliar or a peculiar business element such as a product, a method, an environmental factor is explained in detail.

**Evidence Unit:** A unit of the analytical part, in which objective evidences for examining the hypotheses in the factor unit are indicated.

**Expected Result Unit:** A unit of the analytical part, in which the expected result from fulfilling the business method in the method unit is forecasted casually.

**Factor Unit:** A unit of the analytical part, in which the key success factors of the business are derived as the hypotheses objectively and analytically.

**Logical Scientific Mode:** A cognition style of human being to explain something causally advocated by Bruner (1996). Interpretation does not depend upon the specific contextual setting.

**Method Unit:** A unit of the analytical part, in which the business methods to satisfy the key success factors are proposed concretely.

**Narrative Mode:** A cognition style of human being to understand something through an interpretation process advocated by Bruner (1996). Interpretation depends upon the specific context and personal and/or communal history.

**Narrative Part:** A part of the digital storytelling that was told in the narrative mode. In this chapter, the researchers identified the narrative part on whether it was told from the viewpoint of a personal character (including the storyteller).

**Narrative:** A sequence of events told by people with oral communication, text, movie, comic, digital presentation, and other devices. A narrative is open to interpretation for the storyteller and the audience.

**New Situation Unit:** A scene(s) of the narrative part, in which a character finds a newly appeared situation after the problems were solved in the solution unit.

**Obstruction Unit:** A scene(s) of the narrative part, in which a character encounters a trouble or shortage of a critical thing.

**Old Situation Unit:** A scene(s) of the narrative part, which represents the initial or the ordinary situation before a character encounters an obstruction.

**Resource Unit:** A unit of the analytical part, in which the business planner's internal resources such as human network, existing facilities, and financial situation are presented.

**Solution Unit:** A scene(s) of the narrative part, in which a character struggles and solves problems that were found in the obstruction unit.

**Story of "Something Like You":** A story making audiences sense some essential commonality with their experience.

## ENDNOTES

1 In this chapter, a "story" denotes a causal sequence of events directly related to a character who is seeking to solve a problem or to achieve a goal. This refers to the fourth definition of "story" of Prince (2003). Then, an "episode" is a series of mutually related events that have distinctive characteristic(s) (Prince, 2003). A story contains one or more episodes.

2 The audience response system used in the offline study was a "clicker" system, which is widely used for teaching assistance. The main function of the clicker is to aggregate the number of clicks by participants, in real time. The audience response system used in the online study was developed as part of the study, and is original. The system adds up the number of clicks in real time while the movie is shown online.

3 The narrative and analysis were determined by whether the point of view is that of the main character (subjective) or God's eye (objective). Events are divided by the appearance of a solution (and result) of an event. The analysis of the structure of a work is based on a discussion by researchers. Thus, a weakness of this study is that the analysis methodology is subjective. An objective methodology should be developed in future research. (The texts shown in Figures 1 and 2 were summarized by the researcher, owing to space restriction in this paper. However, the analyses was conducted on the original movies.)

4 In an interview with the author of Work D, she confirmed that the narrative part of the work is fictitious, based on her experience. In all other works, the authors stated that they were the main characters, and that the contents of the narratives were real-life accounts.

5 The effectiveness of a story does not always improve when the consistency of the story is high. Defamiliarization—a representation that causes feelings of strangeness or a lack of familiarity in the audience—is sometimes used in movies, plays, and novels (Kanai, 2005). Although there is no work that uses defamiliarization in this study, its existence and the mechanism of its effect in the context of business planning should be examined in future research.

# Chapter 6
# Can Computers Create Comics and Animations?

**Miki Ueno**
*Toyohashi University of Technology, Japan*

**Kiyohito Fukuda**
*Osaka Prefecture University, Japan*

**Naoki Mori**
*Osaka Prefecture University, Japan*

## ABSTRACT

*The objective of this chapter is to develop a method for generating and analyzing creative work by using computers. In this chapter, novels, comics, and animations are considered representative creative work because the main method for representing creative work is the use of natural language and pictures. These works focus on interesting issues, which can be explained by computational approaches to narratology. In this chapter, the authors discuss the following three topics. First, a method of semi-automatic story generation by agent-based simulation is presented. Second, methods of generating and analyzing comics on the basis of the features of pictures and stories used are described. Third, the authors introduce a method of estimating the difficulties of translating a storyboard into original pictures in the process of creating animations.*

## INTRODUCTION

How do humans produce creative work? What do individuals imagine, and what do they think of during the creative process? The ultimate purpose of this study is to find an algorithm for the generation of creative, intellectual works, such as novels, comics, and animations, with regard to artificial intelligence. The creative works listed above involve stories and are constructed using sequential components. Further, the popular representation of a narrative utilizes natural language and pictures. For example, novels are constructed using natural language, and this type of language is a very useful means of logically depicting a given situation. However, the number of sentences comprising individual scenes varies considerably,

DOI: 10.4018/978-1-5225-0432-0.ch006

Copyright © 2016, IGI Global. Copying or distributing in print or electronic forms without written permission of IGI Global is prohibited.

and it is therefore difficult for computers to determine scene boundaries. In addition, comics are constructed using both pictures and natural language, and animations are comprised of pictures and sound based on natural language. Note that pictures constitute an effective means of creating stories, because they can convey postures and positions more directly than verbal or written language. This approach allows stories to become comprehensible to a wider audience, regardless of age or nationality.

In Japan, comics and animations are common in popular culture. A key characteristic of these representations are the deformation or exaggeration of characters and other objects in the story. These visual representations contain lyrical and descriptive aspects to depict each situation clearly. Further, these works are often very intellectual, and some popular authors have produced exceptional creative pieces.

Story creation is something of which the vast majority of humans are capable; however, computers can neither create nor understand stories. The authors are very interested in the process of story construction, particularly as regards the development of appropriate models to facilitate computer story creation. Therefore, our goal is to define complete models of story creation for use by computers. However, it is difficult to define models for the entire process and every objective, therefore the authors suggest models for a specific process of creation. Hence, the authors have conducted several studies regarding computational creative stories, focusing on the topics listed below.

- **Story Generation:** Semi-automatic story generation using log data. Continuous transitions are automatically created and are given to writers in order to write unexpected stories that cannot be created by humans only. The aim of this section is to propose a computational method of coherent and unexpected story creation.
- **Comic Generation:** Automatic comic generation focusing on the relationship between transitions of stories and expression of pictures and comic analysis based on two of their features. Continuous transitions expressed by pictures are modeled and the relations between characteristic expressions and the patterns of stories are analyzed. The aim of this section is to suggest computational models for comics focusing on the expressions in pictures.
- **Animation Generation:** Feature vector definition to provide storyboard information and to determine the difficulties involved in scene translation from storyboards to equivalent key animations. The difficulties in transitioning storyboards into original pictures are estimated. The aim of this section is to appropriately assign each scene to each creator of original pictures according to the index of difficulty by a computer functioning like a facilitator.

In this chapter, these studies are introduced using examples, in order to demonstrate the fundamental techniques of computational narratology and the challenges involved in the quantification of story creation.

## BACKGROUND

Recently, automatic story generation and comprehension has attracted considerable interest as a challenging problem in the fields of artificial intelligence. The types of stories are broadly classified into two categories. One is utilizing natural language, the other is utilizing pictures. Novels are written in natural language, while comics and animations are described mainly by pictures. Story information is common, but expression information is specific. Firstly, the background of story generation with natural language is described. With a view towards realizing effective automatic story generation, a number of research papers on automatic story generation based on Case-Based Reasoning (CBR) (Gervás, Diaz-Agudo, Peinado, & Hervás, 2005; Pérez y Pérez & Sharples, 2001; Tuner, 1994) and the problem-solving process (Meehan, 1980), the project on automatic composition of works like Shinichi Hoshi, who was a famous Japanese short story writer (Kouyama & Sumi, 2014; Matsubara et al., 2013; Ogata, Sato, & Komatani, 2014) and some studies on automatic story generation system based on well-known Propp theory (Imabuchi & Ogata, 2012) have been conducted. However, a problem has arisen in that these previous studies have only succeeded in generating lower quality novels rather than original, higher quality ones. The present authors believe that this problem can be attributed to automatic story generation research conducted based on the approach that "a human generates novels via computer"; this means that the computer must reuse original sentences and stories directly.

Secondly, the background of picture stories. Compared with the text stories, there exist only a few studies focused on picture stories such as comics and animation. Pictures are composed of lines and shapes, respectively. Although all of these components are simply collections of dots from a local perspective (Eitz, Hays, & Alexa, 2012), humans perceive them as characters, figures, and symbols based on semantics. However, the semantic comprehension method utilized by humans is unclear. In the field of image processing, the methods of automatically generating in-betweening pictures (Gohara, Sugimoto, & Morishima, 2010) have been proposed. However, limited research has been conducted on computational representations of the process of animation creation.

## STORY GENERATION

In this section, the authors aim to propose a new automatic novel generation technique that does not utilize previously created original novels. This new approach essentially means that "the computer generates novels," that is, the computer can generate coherent and unexpected stories for humans. As a first step towards realizing this goal, the authors have proposed a novel semi-automatic story generation method that utilizes log data of agent-based simulation (ABS) (Fukuda, Mori, & Matsumoto, 2015). Here, ABS is a simulation to investigate the actions and interactions between autonomous agents (Macal & North, 2010). The proposed method is a "middle" approach, where "a human generates novels in cooperation with the computer," i.e., novel generation is conducted via interaction between a human and a computer. In this section, the proposed method is introduced, and its effectiveness and the related difficulties are discussed.

### Proposed Story Generation Method

In this section, the abovementioned semi-automatic story generation method using log data of the ABS is described. This is based on the idea that a human sometimes writes stories and novels based on memories about interactions between humans. To provide a computer with that memory, the authors believe that log data can function as human memory. The proposed method can utilize any log data, such as the results of a numerical simulation or application usage history. However, the log data of the ABS is used here, because of its greater affinity. The proposed method proceeds as follows.

**Step 1:** Setting of the ABS. Some parameters of the ABS are determined by the user.
**Step 2:** Log Data Generation. Two types of log data are generated via the ABS: Status and action logs.

**Step 3:** Event Generation. Events are generated from the action logs. Events are important action logs to generate the story.

**Step 4:** Story Vector Generation. Story vectors are generated from the events and status logs. Story vectors are basic information represented in vector form that is required to generate the story.

**Step 5:** Story Generation. Stories are generated using story vectors through interaction between the user and computer.

Steps 2–4 of the proposed method can be performed automatically. However, steps 1 and 5 cannot be performed by the computer alone. Thus, the former are referred to as the "computer part" and the latter are referred to as the "user part."

## Setting of the ABS (Step 1)

The ABS algorithms are implemented for the proposed method. In this ABS, agents have two internal values (friendship and emotion). In moving toward the sub-goal in the field, agents interact with each other if they are located close to one another. Interactions may change their internal values. The ABS is halted if the friendship value of the agent exceeds a threshold and the agent feels love or affection towards the other agent. The details of the algorithms are as follows. Here, a random number in a normal distribution is represented by $N(\mu,\sigma^2)$, where $\mu$ is the mean and $\sigma^2$ is the variance.

1. The field size is $x_{max} \times y_{max}$, the maximum number of turns is $T_{max}$, the number of player agents is $N_p$, the number of roles is $N_r$, and the action number is $N_a$. Here, turn is a parameter that defines order of each interaction.
2. The environment agent is created, which has scene name $s_{xy}$ at position $(x, y)$ and environment values $b_{xy}$ and $\beta_{xy,t}$. The environment values represent the influence of the environment on the changes of state at each position. Here, $b_{xy}$ is 0 or 1 binary, $\beta_{xy,t}$ is a real number of [-15, 15], and the default of $\beta_{xy,0}$ is defined as [-10, 10].
3. $N_p$ player agents are created. Each player agent has a name, $(x, y)$ point, sex $m$, role in the story $r$, friendship values (f-values) with each player agent $F_t = \left\{f_{1,t}, f_{2,t}, \ldots, f_{N_p,t}\right\}$, love flags with each player agent $L = \left\{\ell_1, \ell_2, \ldots, \ell_{N_p}\right\}$, and an emotion value (e-value) $E_t = \left\{e_{1,t}, e_{2,t}\right\}$. Here, $f \in F$ is a real number of [0, 100], $e \in E$ is a real number of [-100, 100], $m$ and $\ell \in L$ are 0 or 1 binary, and $r$ is a natural number of $(0,N_r]$. In addition, the default of $f_0$ is defined as [25, 75] and the default of $e_0$ is defined as [-25, 25]. Finally, a set of player agents is defined as $P$.
4. Then, the turn $t$ is set to 0. The set of player agents who do not take action is defined as $P_t$ and the set of player agents who have already taken some action is defined as $P_t'$.
5. $P_t$ and $P_t'$ are then updated as $P_t = P, P_t' = \varnothing$.
6. A player agent $i$ is randomly selected from $P_t$. $P_t$ and $P_t'$ are updated as $P_t = P_t / i$, $P_t' = P_t' \cup i$, respectively.
7. $i$ moves to certain Moore neighborhoods as it traverses the distance between the current and target positions. The next target position of $i$ is randomly set when $i$ reaches its existing target.

8. A player agent of non- $i$, labeled $j$, is randomly selected. In addition, the friendship value of $i$ for $j$, represented by $f^i_{j,t}$ and the emotion value of $i$ $e^i_t$ are updated as follows. This update represents psychological influences, such that these values converge on a constant value to indicate that $i$ loses interest in $j$ once a given time has elapsed. Then, $T_{fri}$ and $T_{emo}$ are used to represent the time-elapsed rates of the friendship and emotion values, respectively.

$$f^i_{j,t} = f^i_{j,t} - \frac{\left|N\left(0,1\right)\right| \times b^i_{xy}\left(f^i_{j,t} - 50\right)}{T_{fri}} \tag{1}$$

s.t. $\{j \mid j \neq i, j \in O\}$

$$e^i_t = e^i_t - \frac{\left|N\left(0,1\right)\right| b^i_{xy} e^i_t}{T_{emo}} \tag{2}$$

9. If the other player agents exist in Neumann neighborhoods of $i$, a player agent $k$ is randomly selected from amongst these agents. If no player agents exist, the process moves on to 12.
10. In order to represent the interaction between two player agents, the friendship value of $k$ towards $i$, here labeled $f^k_{i,t}$, and the emotion values of $k$, $e^k_{1,t}$, $e^k_{2,t}$ as follows. The action log for the interaction is saved and $N_a$ is updated to $N_a = N_a + 1$. Now, $I_{fri}$ and $I_{emo}$ represent the friendship and emotion value interaction rates, respectively.

$$f^k_{i,t+1} = f^k_{i,t} + \Delta f^k_{i,t} \tag{3}$$

$$e^k_{1,t+1} = e^k_{1,t} + \Delta e^k_{1,t} \tag{4}$$

$$e^k_{2,t+1} = e^k_{2,t} + \Delta e^k_{2,t} \tag{5}$$

$$\Delta f^k_{i,t} = \left|N\left(0,1\right)\right| \times b^k_{xy} d^k_{i,t} + \beta^k_{xy,t} \tag{6}$$

$$d^k_{i,t} = \frac{2f^k_{i,t} + f^i_{k,t}}{I_{fri}} + \frac{e^k_{1,t}\left(e^k_{2,t} + 100\right)}{I_{emo}} \tag{7}$$

$$\Delta e^k_{1,t} = \left|N\left(0,1.5^2\right)\right| \times \Delta f^k_{i,t} \tag{8}$$

$$\Delta e^k_{2,t} = N\left(0,1.5^2\right) \times \left|\Delta f^k_{i,t}\right| \tag{9}$$

11. If $\Delta f_{i,t}^{k}$ or $\Delta f_{k,t}^{i}$ exceeds a threshold value *h*, the love flag of *k* or *i* for *i* or *k*, which is $\ell_{i}^{k}$ or $\ell_{k}^{i}$, is changed to another binary value.
12. If $P_t \neq \varnothing$, the process returns to 6.
13. A player agent *p* is randomly selected from $P_t'$. If the other player agents exist in Neumann neighborhoods of *p*, a player agent $p'$ is randomly selected from among them. If $\ell_{p'}^{p}$ is 1, *p* confesses his or her love for $p'$ with probability *R*. This confession succeeds with a rate of $R_{suc}$. If *p* confesses, the confession is saved in the action log, regardless of its success or failure. If *p* does not confess, $P_t'$ is updated to $P_t' = P_t' / p$. *R* and $R_{suc}$ are defined as follows.

$$R = \frac{\left| f_{p',t}^{p} - 50 \right|}{100} \tag{10}$$

$$R_{suc} = \begin{cases} \dfrac{0.8 f_{p',t}^{p} + 0.2\alpha}{200} & \left(m^{p} = m^{p'}\right) \\ \dfrac{0.8 f_{p',t}^{p} + 0.2\alpha}{100} & \left(m^{p} \neq m^{p'}\right) \end{cases} \tag{11}$$

$$\alpha = \frac{e_{1,t}^{p'} \times e_{2,t}^{p'}}{100} \tag{12}$$

14. If $P_t' \neq \varnothing$, the process returns to 13.
15. The value of $\beta_{xy,t}$ always varies over time. Hence, $\beta_{xy,t}$ is updated as follows. Here, $a_{env}$ represents the environment variation cycle.

$$\beta_{xy,t+1} = \beta_{xy,0} + 5\sin\left(\frac{2\left(t+1\right)\pi}{a_{env}}\right) \tag{13}$$

16. Finally, *t* is updated to $t=t+1$ and the status log is saved. If $t \geq t_{max}$, the ABS is halted. If $t < t_{max}$, the process returns to 5.

## Log Data Generation (Step 2)

The log data is generated using the ABS, which is implemented for the proposed method, along with the two types of log data mentioned above: Status and action logs. The details of these log types are given below.

- **Action Log:** Action log information is saved if agents perform a specific action in the ABS. The turn, scene name, main agent name, target agent name, action type, action number, the degree of change in the friendship value caused by the action, and the degree of change in the emotion value caused by the action in the action log are saved. Table 1 shows the example of the action logs.

- **Status Log:** The status logs are saved at the end of each turn of the ABS. These comprise the turn information and all the parameters of all the agents. Table 2 shows the example of the status logs.

## Event Generation (Step 3)

In this step, the direct use of action logs to generate story vectors tends to yield an unnatural story. Therefore, events are generated through the compression of action logs. The event generation algorithms are listed below. Table 3 shows the example of the events.

1. The set of action logs obtained via the ABS are defined as *G*.
2. Action logs within *G* that have the same scene names are defined as *G*.

*Table 1. The example of the action logs*

| Turn | Main Agent | Target Agent | Action Type (Action Number) | Position | The Change of F-Value | The Change of E-Value 1 | The Change of E-Value 2 |
|---|---|---|---|---|---|---|---|
| 178 | 0 | 2 | INTERACTION (0) | 7,64,lectureB | -0.6626 | -1.6809 | -0.0026 |
| 179 | 0 | 2 | INTERACTION (1) | 8,64,lectureB | -1.2161 | -0.4531 | 0.6638 |
| 323 | 2 | 1 | INTERACTION (2) | 50,111,lectureA | 1.0534 | 1.3433 | -0.5078 |
| 422 | 1 | 0 | INTERACTION (3) | 49,101,clubroom | 3.0015 | 11.004 | -5.5396 |
| 422 | 0 | 1 | INTERACTION (4) | 48,101,clubroom | 10.663 | 13.993 | -23.709 |
| 431 | 2 | 0 | INTERACTION (5) | 48,109,lectureA | 10.497 | 15.894 | -17.420 |
| 432 | 2 | 0 | INTERACTION (6) | 49,110,lectureA | -6.6434 | -5.2733 | -10.923 |
| 432 | 0 | 2 | INTERACTION (7) | 48,110,lectureA | 3.3707 | 3.5269 | -6.1631 |
| 467 | 1 | 0 | INTERACTION (8) | 46,113,lectureA | 13.929 | 20.447 | 16.303 |
| 484 | 0 | 1 | INTERACTION (9) | 57,112,lectureA | 16.168 | 28.519 | -19.999 |
| 484 | 1 | 0 | INTERACTION (10) | 58,112,lectureA | -26.625 | -47.057 | -55.744 |
| 484 | 1 | 0 | SUCCESS (11) | 58,112,lectureA | 100 | 100 | 100 |

*Table 2. The example of the status logs*

| Turn | Name | Id | Position | Sex | Role | F-Value to 1 | F-Value to 2 | F-Value to 3 | E-Value 1 | E-Value 2 |
|---|---|---|---|---|---|---|---|---|---|---|
| 0 | Hiro | 1 | 90,39,home | 1 | 1 | 72 | 45 | 33 | -5 | -4 |
| 0 | Kana | 2 | 42,44,home | 2 | 2 | 47 | 62 | 50 | 13 | -8 |
| 0 | Yuu | 3 | 67,72,home | 1 | 3 | 37 | 64 | 60 | -13 | 8 |
| 1 | Hiro | 1 | 89,40,way | 1 | 1 | 71.883 | 45.002 | 33.065 | -4.9897 | -3.9986 |
| 1 | Yuu | 3 | 66,73,way | 1 | 3 | 36.955 | 64.053 | 60.009 | -13.053 | 8.0127 |
| 1 | Kana | 2 | 43,44,way | 2 | 2 | 46.985 | 62.027 | 50 | 13.025 | -8.0139 |
| 2 | Yuu | 3 | 65,73,way | 1 | 3 | 36.986 | 64.050 | 59.981 | -13.009 | 7.9878 |
| 2 | Hiro | 1 | 88,41,way | 1 | 1 | 71.845 | 45.018 | 33.145 | -4.9727 | -3.9928 |
| 2 | Kana | 2 | 43,45,way | 2 | 2 | 46.980 | 62.028 | 50 | 13.043 | -8.0200 |

*Table 3. The example of the events*

| Turn | Main Agent | Target Agent | Action Type (Action Number) | Position | The Change of F-Value | The Change of E-Value 1 | The Change of E-Value 2 |
|---|---|---|---|---|---|---|---|
| 178 | 0 | 2 | INTERACTION (0, 1) | lectureB | -0.6626 | -1.6809 | -0.0026 |
| 323 | 2 | 1 | INTERACTION (2) | lectureA | 1.0534 | 1.3433 | -0.5078 |
| 422 | 1 | 0 | INTERACTION (3) | clubroom | 3.0015 | 11.004 | -5.5396 |
| 422 | 0 | 1 | INTERACTION (4) | clubroom | 10.663 | 13.993 | -23.709 |
| 431 | 2 | 0 | INTERACTION (5, 6) | lectureA | 10.497 | 15.894 | -17.420 |
| 432 | 0 | 2 | INTERACTION (7) | lectureA | 3.3707 | 3.5269 | -6.1631 |
| 467 | 1 | 0 | INTERACTION (8) | lectureA | 13.929 | 20.447 | 16.303 |
| 484 | 0 | 1 | INTERACTION (9) | lectureA | 16.168 | 28.519 | -19.999 |
| 484 | 1 | 0 | INTERACTION (10) | lectureA | -26.625 | -47.057 | -55.744 |
| 484 | 1 | 0 | SUCCESS (11) | lectureA | 100 | 100 | 100 |

3. $G$ is divided into sets of action logs with identical main agent names and action types. Furthermore, a new action log is generated from the set of action logs obtained from $G$. The values of $t$, $s_{xy}$, and $N_a$ are defined as those corresponding to the action log with the minimum $t$, and the degree of change in the $F_t$ and $E_t$ values are defined as the sum of all action logs in the set. $G$ is updated as $G = G / G'$.
4. If $G \neq \varnothing$, the method returns to 2.
5. The new action logs generated in 3. are defined as the events.

## Story Vector Generation (Step 4)

Story generation using events directly is difficult. Hence, stories are generated using the story vectors $s$, which are in turn generated by the events. The story vector generation algorithms are the following. Table 4 shows the example of the story vectors.

1. The main agent and the target agent are defined as $i$ and $j$, respectively. The values of the turn $t$, the action number $N_a$, the position of $j$ $(x_{j,t}, y_{j,t})$, the degree of change in the friendship value $\Delta f_t$ and degree of change in the emotion value $\Delta e_t$ are obtained from the event. Furthermore, $m^i$, $m^j$, $r^i$ and $r^j$ are obtained, along with the friendship values of $i$ and $j$ for $j$ and $i$, which are $f^i_{j,t}$ and $f^j_{i,t}$, respectively, and the emotion values of $i$ and $j$, $e^i_t$ and $e^j_t$, respectively, from the status logs.
2. The $s$ is defined as follows.

$$s = \left(t, N_a, m^i, m^j, r^i, r^j, x_{j,t}, y_{j,t}, \Delta f_t, f^i_{j,t}, f^j_{i,t}, e^i_{1,t}, e^i_{2,t}, e^j_{1,t}, e^j_{2,t}, \Delta e_{1,t}, \Delta e_{2,t}\right) \tag{14}$$

*Table 4. The example of the story vectors*

| Turn | Main Agent (*i*) | Target Agent (*j*) | Scene Name | The Change of F-Value | F-Value of *i* | F-Value of *j* | The Change of Emotion of *i* | The Change of Emotion of *j* |
|---|---|---|---|---|---|---|---|---|
| 178 | Hiro, Man, Hero | Yuu, Man, Rival | lectureB | becomes slightly hostile (-1.88) | normal (35.32) | normal (38.74) | sadness → sadness | anger → anger |
| 323 | Yuu, Man, Rival | Kana, Woman, Heroine | lectureA | becomes slightly friendly (1.05) | normal (59.51) | normal (50.0) | anger → anger | fun → fun |
| 422 | Kana, Woman, Heroine | Hiro, Man, Hero | clubroom | becomes slightly friendly (3.0) | normal (48.2) | normal (46.59) | fun → fun | sadness → fun |
| 422 | Hiro, Man, Hero | Kana, Woman, Heroine | clubroom | becomes slightly friendly (10.66) | normal (46.59) | normal (48.2) | sadness → sadness | fun → fun |
| 431 | Yuu, Man, Rival | Hiro, Man, Hero | lectureA | becomes slightly friendly (3.85) | normal (40.17) | normal (38.92) | anger → anger | fun → fun |
| 432 | Hiro, Man, Hero | Yuu, Man, Rival | lectureA | becomes slightly friendly (3.37) | normal (49.43) | normal (40.22) | fun → fun | anger → anger |
| 467 | Kana, Woman, Heroine | Hiro, Man, Hero | lectureA | becomes slightly friendly (13.93) | normal (58.58) | normal (49.61) | fun → fun | fun → fun |
| 484 | Hiro, Man, Hero | Kana, Woman, Heroine | lectureA | becomes slightly friendly (16.17) | normal (63.2) | normal (58.4) | fun → fun | fun → fun |
| 484 | Kana, Woman, Heroine | Hiro, Man, Hero | lectureA | becomes more friendly (-26.62) | normal (58.4) | normal (63.2) | fun → fun | fun → sadness |
| 484 | Kana, Woman, Heroine | Hiro, Man, Hero | lectureA | accepts asking out | normal (58.4) | normal (63.2) | fun → fun | fun → joy |

## Story Generation (Step 5)

In this step, story generation requires six elements: "when," "where," "who (main)," "who (target)," "action," and "result". Five elements are generated using $s$. The "action" element is excluded as it is generated via the interaction between the user and the computer. The story generation algorithms are as follows.

1. "When" is defined as $t$ in $s$.
2. "Who (main)" is defined as the name of main player agent $i$, having $m^i$ and $r^i$ in $s$. "Who (target)" is defined as the name of target player agent $j$, having $m^j$ and $r^j$ in $s$.
3. "Where" is defined as the scene name $s_{x_{j,t}y_{j,t}}$, based on the position $(x_{j,t}, y_{j,t})$ in $s$.
4. The change in the friendship value caused by the action is defined as $w_f$. Note that $w_f$ is defined as follows.

$$w_f = \begin{cases} "\textit{becomes more friendly}" \left(\Delta f_t > 20\right) \\ "\textit{becomes slightly friendly}" \left(0 < \Delta f_t \le 20\right) \\ "\textit{becomes slightly hostile}" \left(-20 \le \Delta f_t < 0\right) \\ "\textit{becomes more hostile}" \left(\Delta f_t < -20\right) \end{cases} \tag{15}$$

5. The friendship values at the action $w^i_{f,t}$ are obtained, along with and the change in the emotion values caused by the action ” $w^i_{e,t}$, ” $w^j_{e,t}$. Here, $w^i_{f,t}$, $w^j_{f,t}$, ” $w^i_{e,t}$, and ” $w^j_{e,t}$ are defined as follows. Now, if the emotion values of *i* and *j* are equal to 0, $w'_{e^k,t}$ is defined as "---" in order to indicate that the player agents have no emotion.

$$w_{f,t} = \begin{cases} "\textit{high}" \left(f_t \ge 70\right) \\ "\textit{normal}" \left(30 < f_t < 70\right) \\ "\textit{low}" \left(f_t \le 30\right) \end{cases} \tag{16}$$

$$\Delta w^i_{e,t} = w_{e^i,t} \rightarrow w_{e^i,t} \tag{17}$$

$$\Delta w^j_{e,t} = w_{e^j,t} \rightarrow w'_{e^j,t} \tag{18}$$

$$w_{e^k,t} = \begin{cases} "\textit{joy}" \left(e^k_{1,t} > 0, e^k_{2,t} > 0\right) \\ "\textit{anger}" \left(e^k_{1,t} < 0, e^k_{2,t} > 0\right) \\ "\textit{sadness}" \left(e^k_{1,t} < 0, e^k_{2,t} < 0\right) \\ "\textit{fun}" \left(e^k_{1,t} > 0, e^k_{2,t} < 0\right) \\ "---" \left(\textit{otherwise}\right) \end{cases} \tag{19}$$

$$w'_{e^k,t} = \begin{cases} "\textit{joy}" \left(e^k_{1,t} + \Delta e_{1,t} > 0, e^k_{2,t} + \Delta e_{2,t} > 0\right) \\ "\textit{anger}" \left(e^k_{1,t} + \Delta e_{1,t} < 0, e^k_{2,t} + \Delta e_{2,t} > 0\right) \\ "\textit{sadness}" \left(e^k_{1,t} + \Delta e_{1,t} < 0, e^k_{2,t} + \Delta e_{2,t} < 0\right) \\ "\textit{fun}" \left(e^k_{1,t} + \Delta e_{1,t} > 0, e^k_{2,t} + \Delta e_{2,t} < 0\right) \\ "---" \left(\textit{otherwise}\right) \end{cases} \tag{20}$$

6. The proposed method provides the user with the five elements defined according to 1. - 4., the friendship values at the action, and the change of emotion values caused by the action. The user then generates an "action" based on this information. The user selects the action from options that have been prepared in advance.

## Story Generation Experiments

To examine the effectiveness of the proposed method and any associated difficulties, user experiments were conducted. Table 5 shows the experimental conditions. In these experiments, five users (Users A–E), all of whom had written novels, made use of the proposed method. These users were aged between 20 and 29. The user-experiment procedure was as follows:

1. The proposed method was used to generate the story vector in the computer part.
2. The users generated stories utilizing the story vector generated in 1. After the story generation stage, the users evaluated the story generation difficulty on a scale of 1 (easy)–5 (difficult). In addition, the users' views on the proposed method were obtained via interview.

## Story Generation Experiment Results

Figure 1 shows the example of the stories generated by the user experiment and Table 6 provides details of the evaluation about the difficulty of story generation evaluation. From Figure 1, Kana asks Hiro out after cutting class taking with him in a part of turn 485. It is difficult for humans to create the story like this. In addition, from Table 6, it is apparent that the mean of the story generation difficulty was 3.6. These results show that the proposed method allows users to create stories that cannot be created by only humans and suggest that the proposed method can create coherent and unexpected stories by automat-

*Table 5. Experimental conditions of generation of story*

| $(x_{max}, y_{max})$ | **(120, 120)** |
|---|---|
| $N_p$ | 3 |
| $N_r$ | 3 |
| Agent Name | Hiro, Kana, Yuu |
| Sex | Man, Woman, Man |
| Role | Hero, Heroine, Rival |
| Parameters | $t_{max}$=6000, $h$=30, $T_{fri}$=200, $T_{emo}$=500, $I_{fri}$=15, $I_{emo}$=500, $a_{env}$=200 |

*Figure 1. Experimental results of generation of story*

Turn179: Hiro ignores Yuu in lecture room B. As a result, Yuu becomes slightly hostile towards Hiro.
Turn323: Yuu shows his textbook to Kana in lecture room A. As a result, Kana becomes slightly friendly towards Yuu.
Turn423: Kana talks with Hiro in Clubroom. As a result, Hiro becomes slightly friendly towards Kana.
Turn423: Hiro helps Kana with her task in Clubroom. As a result, Kana becomes slightly friendly towards Hiro.
Turn432: Yuu gives his loose-leaf paper to Hiro in lecture room A. As a result, Hiro becomes slightly friendly towards Yuu.
Turn433: Hiro falls asleep next to Yuu in lecture room A. As a result, Yuu becomes slightly friendly towards Hiro.
Turn467: Kana studies with Hiro in lecture room A. As a result, Hiro becomes slightly friendly towards Kana.
Turn484: Hiro studies with Kana in lecture room A. As a result, Kana becomes slightly friendly towards Hiro.
Turn485: Kana cuts class taking with Hiro in lecture room A. As a result, Hiro becomes more hostile towards Kana.
Turn485: Kana asks Hiro out in lecture room A. Hiro accepts.

*Table 6. Evaluation about the difficulty of story generation*

| User Name | Difficulty of Story Generation |
|---|---|
| A | 4 |
| B | 4 |
| C | 4 |
| D | 2 |
| E | 4 |
| Mean | 3.6 |

ing the user part. In addition, the users stated that the range of action options was limited. Therefore, a range of actions must be prepared in order to overcome the lack of action versatility and create various stories automatically. Furthermore, the users stated that story planning was easy, because the character settings were unknown. This evaluation shows that it is necessary to provide detailed character settings automatically to realize applications in which "the computer generates novels."

### Story Generation Conclusion

In this section, a proposed semi-automatic story generation method that utilizes log data of the ABS was discussed as a first step towards automatic unexpected story generation for a new automatic novel generation. The algorithms of the proposed method were explained and its efficacy and associated difficulties were discussed. The following future developments are necessary to further refine this method.

- User-selection model construction, which would model users' action choices.
- Development of a control method that would manage the logical coherence and unpredictability of the story.
- Automatic plot generation needed to generate attractive novels. Plots will be generated by rearranging the story.

## AUTOMATIC COMIC GENERATION

In the previous section, the method of automatically generating stories by natural language was discussed. Here, the authors have focused on creative expressions using pictures, which can be understood by humans regardless of their age and nationality. Therefore, the study discussed in this section reports on computer creation and comprehension of comics whose stories are represented by pictures. There have been studies reporting comic creation by combining prepared datasets (Sumi, Sakamoto, Nakao, Mase, & Kunifuji, 2002). Stories represented by pictures involve large numbers of possible transition and expressions of pictures so that it is difficult to define models of pictures for every story. To solve this problem, the authors focused on four-scene comics. It is possible for creators to present any story in four-scene comics. On the other hand, the scene lengths are limited and the stories must be deformed in the interests of simplification. Thus, four-scene comics have clear stories and structures and are therefore suitable for computer engineering-related studies. In this section, research on picture model for automatic comic generation is first introduced (Ueno, Mori, & Matsumoto, 2014). Then, a two-scene comic creation system is constructed. After that, the analysis for comic creation is discussed.

## Comic Generation Picture Model

In order to represent the semantics of pictures to facilitate computer comprehension, each of the elements in a figure, including the background images and balloons, are defined as certain objects. It is difficult to create a reasonable picture model for all pictures. Therefore, two-scene comics are considered here, because two sequential pictures provide sufficient information compared to a single picture, without excessively increasing the problem complexity. In this section, the authors will introduce the method of generating comics and the two-scene generating system. In this method, it is necessary to prepare a dataset comprising images of objects and related object information, area types, drawing operators, and transitions. The picture contains the above information along with a certain history.

The outline of the comic creation method is given below. First, an initial picture $p_0$ is generated by the system. $p_0$ is a blank or a background picture and has several areas determined by the system. The user can utilize $p_0$ as user input. The user operation set in time $t$ is represented by $\boldsymbol{u}_t$, and $\boldsymbol{u}_t$ contains all potential user operations for picture $p_t$, $p_{t+1}$ is created by applying $\boldsymbol{u}_t$ to $p_t$. This is expressed as

$$p_{t+1} = \prod_{u_{i,t} \in \boldsymbol{u}_t} u_{i,t} p_t \, , \tag{21}$$

where $u_i$ represents each user's operations over $t$. The relations between $p_t$, $o_t$, $\boldsymbol{u}_t$, $\{O_t\}$, and $U_t$ are

$$\left\{O_t\right\} = \left\{o_t \in p_t\right\}, \tag{22}$$

$$\left\{U_t\right\} = \left\{\boldsymbol{u}_1, \boldsymbol{u}_2, \ldots, \boldsymbol{u}_t\right\}, \tag{23}$$

$$p_{t+1} = \prod_{u_{i,t} \in \boldsymbol{u}_t} u_{i,t} p_t \cdots = \prod_{u_{i,t} \in \boldsymbol{u}_t} u_{i,t} \prod_{u_{i,t-1} \in \boldsymbol{u}_{t-1}} u_{i,t-1} p_{t-1} = \prod_{j=0}^{t} \prod_{u_{i,j} \in \boldsymbol{u}_j} u_{i,j} p_0 \tag{24}$$

The definite operation of $u_{i,t} \in \boldsymbol{u}_t$ is represented by the drawing operator $\phi$ and the operand object in $p_t$. Each $\phi$ also has specific augments, such as its color, angle, or other objects. Object $o_t$ can represent the object transition. Finally, object $o_n$ in the $n$-th scene adheres to the Markov model, such that

$$o_n = \prod_{i=0}^{N_n^{\max}} \phi_i o_0 \tag{25}$$

where $N^{\max}$ is the total number of $\phi$ to applied to $o$, and $N_n^{\max} \geq n - 1$, because each $u_i$ contains at least one $\phi$.

$\phi$ operates to transform pictures. Further, the product of several $\phi$ is also $\phi$, and the set of base operators is defined as $\{\hat{\phi}\}$. If the number of base operators is increased, the system has greater representative capacity, because it can create a large number of new images utilizing the existing objects. The system described in this section was written using Java and the operator was implemented using a command design pattern (Gamm, Helm, Johnson, & Vlissides, 1995). The base $\phi$ corresponds to the command and the product of $\phi$ corresponds to a macro-command. In Java implementation, an operator product is represented using a queue. For example, $\phi_{crack}$, which represents a cracked transition, is composed of the base drawing operators $\hat{\phi}_{rotate}\hat{\phi}_{divide}$. Thus, two base drawing operators are applied to $o$ in the case of

$$\phi_{crack}o = \hat{\phi}_{rotate}\hat{\phi}_{divide}o \qquad (26)$$

Figure 2 shows the image variation caused by applying the base drawing operators of $\phi_{crack}$.

## Comic Generation System Flow

Based on the picture model, the authors propose the comic generation system. The basic flow of the proposed system is as follows.

1. The base image is set as the background for the initial states. This picture is defined as $p_0$.
2. The system waits for the user input. The user can decide to apply several actions to $p_0$. In this section, the only available user action involves the setting of an object in the object set displayed on the system graphical user interface (GUI). The user can set their chosen object on a specific area of $p_0$ using the $\phi$ and emotion information. Any number of objects can be added to $p_0$, under the condition the only one object is placed in each area. When the user places an object in $p_0'$, new areas are added to the picture in accordance with the set object.
3. After all of the user inputs $u$ are applied to $p_0$, $p_0'$ is obtained, which becomes the 1st scene.
4. The system attempts to change objects in $p_0'$ based on the user-defined drawing operator and the emotion information of the target object. The new image comprising the adjusted objects is obtained via transition DB.
5. After all of the changes have been applied to $p_0'$, $p_1$ is obtained. $p_1$ represents the 2nd scene.
    a. **Two-Scene Comic:** $p_1$ is the final output.
    b. ***n*-Scene Comic:** $p_1'$ becomes $p_2$. The system again waits for user input and repeats the above flow until $p_{n-1}'$ becomes $p_n$.

*Figure 2. Cup (apply $\phi_{crack}$)*

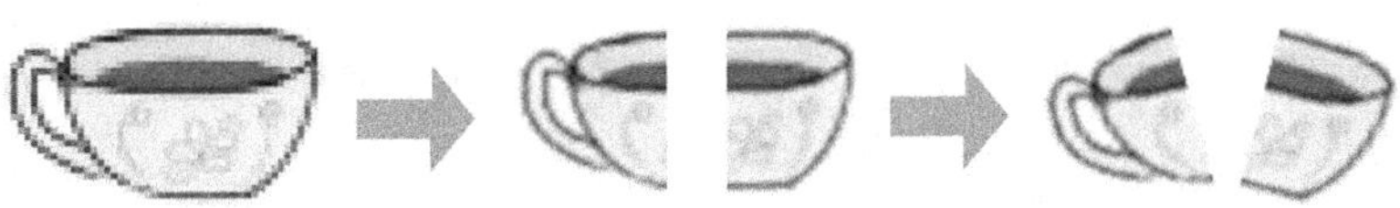

Using this method, two-scene comics can be created via the system. Figure 3 shows the outline of this system procedure.

## Comic Analysis Method

In the previous paragraph, general models of transition of pictures are defined and are applied to the system. Although, several operators are implemented in the system, to depict various scenes, lots of drawing operators should be defined. However, it is difficult to classify and define drawing operator for expressing story transition. Therefore, the relation between object features and story patterns should be analyzed by considering the terms of stories. In comics, there are various kinds of objects and state transitions. The character object usually plays an important role for story transition because characters can act autonomously. The state of character objects are orientations, postures, expressions and so on.

*Figure 3. Outline of two-scene comic creating system*

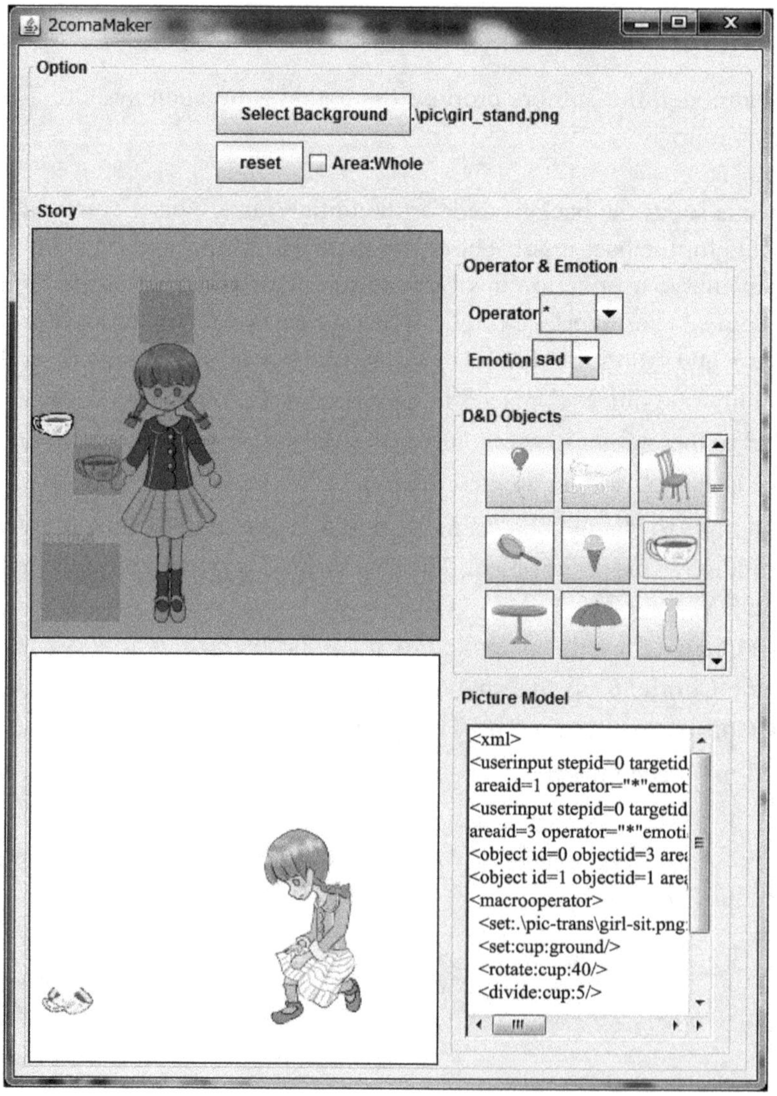

The authors assume that character orientations in an image are strongly related to stories and propose a data format of quantifying these orientations. In order to expand the drawing operator, the relationships between orientation transition patterns, impressions of stories, and balloon shape features are also analyzed utilizing existing comics.

The authors propose a data format in which stories are patterned based on the character orientations in accordance with the following two concepts.

1. Suitable features, for example, automatic modeling based on improved image recognition.
2. Stories have several transitions. Characters are typically the main objects that can transition, so their facial orientation may be strongly related to the content and atmosphere of the stories.

The speech balloon shapes are also used to model the data, in accordance with the following two points.

1. The essential elements of comics are pictures, but natural language such as a character's words are also important. Although analysis of the semantics of words is difficult, the shapes of speech balloons can indicate kinds of character's words such as a whisper or loud voice.
2. Automatic detection of balloon areas and shapes has been reported (Tanaka, Toyama, Miyamichi, & Shoji, 2010).

The proposed data format and each value are as shown in Table 7. The table shows the example of four-scene comic data.

**$n$:** Story number.
**$t$:** Story title.
**$o_j$:** Object $j$ name.
**$d_i^{oj}$:** Facial orientation of object $o_j$ in scene $i$.
**$c_j^k$:** 1 or 0; indicating whether or not type-$k$ balloons appear.

To distinguish between objects of the same type, the object name is added to its number. A lower number is assigned to an object that has appeared previously. In a scene, an object for which the right end is located near the right side of the scene is considered to appear first. This is because scenes in Japanese comics are usually read from top to bottom and from right to left.

Figure 4 shows the example of facial orientations.

The facial orientation of a character is approximately assigned to a single direction based on the following indicators.

**0:** The human object does not appear.
**f:** Front.
**b:** Back.

*Table 7. The example of data of four-scene comics*

| $\#n\ ;\ t\ ;\ o_1{:}d_1o_1d_2o_1d_3o_1d_4o_1, o_2{:}d_1o_2d_2o_2d_3o_2d_4o_2;\ c_1^{\,1}c_1^{\,2}c_1^{\,3}c_1^{\,4}c_1^{\,5},\ c_2^{\,1}c_2^{\,2}c_2^{\,3}c_2^{\,4}c_2^{\,5},\ c_3^{\,1}c_3^{\,2}c_3^{\,3}c_3^{\,4}c_3^{\,5},\ c_4^{\,1}c_4^{\,2}c_4^{\,3}c_4^{\,4}c_4^{\,5}$ |
|---|

*Figure 4. The example of facial orientation*

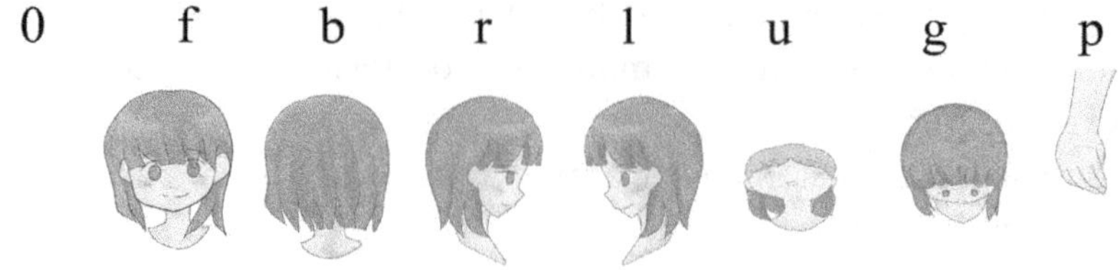


**r:** Right.
**l:** Left.
**u:** Top.
**g:** Bottom.
**p:** Part of the face does not appear.

Figure 5 shows these balloon types.

Further, the balloons are classified into the following five types based on shape, and are assigned corresponding numbers.

1. Oval frame,
2. Zigzag frame,
3. Square frame,
4. Other frame shapes,
5. Printed without frame.

Handwritten balloons are not included in this study. Finally, some cases for which it is difficult to create data are described below.

- **Character Definition:** In some creative works, animals and inanimate objects are personified, so any object that can autonomously act is defined as a character.
- **The Face Does Not Appear:** Only part of a body is drawn in many comic scenes. If the face does not appear, dioj is p.
- **Different Facial and Physical Orientations:** This method focuses on the facial orientation only.
- **It is Difficult to Assign a Single Orientation:** The nearest orientation is assigned.

*Figure 5. The example of balloon types*

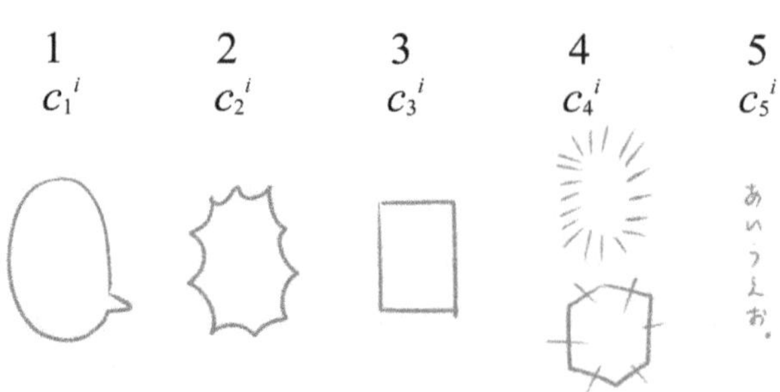

Figure 6 shows four-scene comics and the example data. In this study, the data were created by hand.

## Experiment on Detailed Analysis of One Book

In this experiment, the frequency of object occurrence was investigated and the relationships between expressions and stories are discussed.

- 80 stories from the beginning of "Sketchbook 1" (Kobako, 2003) were used.
- The data were annotated by three graduate students.
- Stories that had two characters or less were used, while stories with more than three characters were omitted. Here, $o_1$ and $o_2$ represent characters 1 and 2 in each story respectively. Based on these conditions, 66 stories were chosen from the original 80.

*Figure 6. The example of four-scene comics*

| $d_i^{o_1}$ | $d_i^{o_2}$ | $c_1^i$ | $c_2^i$ | $c_3^i$ | $c_4^i$ | $c_5^i$ |
|---|---|---|---|---|---|---|
| b | 0 | 0 | 1 | 1 | 0 | 0 |
| f | 0 | 0 | 0 | 0 | 0 | 1 |
| p | 0 | 0 | 0 | 0 | 0 | 0 |
| l | r | 1 | 0 | 0 | 1 | 0 |

The results produced by one of the three annotators are given in this paragraph. Table 8 shows the number of stories per character, Table 9 shows the frequency and order of the $o_1$ and $o_2$ orientations, and Table 10 shows the frequency of the $o_1$ and $o_2$ orientation patterns for the 66 stories. Finally, Table 11 and Table 12 show the balloon pattern frequency. The results of this experiment can be summarized as follows.

- The orientation patterns $d_1^{o_j}$, $d_2^{o_j}$, $d_3^{o_j}$ and $d_4^{o_j}$ can adopt $8^4 = 4096$ potential patterns. A total of 67 orientation patterns were obtained for the 112 characters considered in this study. This constitutes 1.64% of all possible cases. This data number is not sufficient, so the large-scale dataset must be reviewed. Regardless of whether the data is sparse or an increased dataset is used, consideration of these orientations is a highly effective means of estimating story patterns in comics.
- The balloon patterns $c_k^1$, $c_k^2$, $c_k^3$, and $c_k^4$ can be any of $2^{20} = 1048576$ patterns. A total of 61 balloon patterns were obtained for the 80 stories considered in this study. Thus, the number of patterns whose frequency was more than 2 was only 7. This corresponds to $6.68 \times 10^{-4}$% of the potential dataset, so this can be regarded as sparse data.

## Experiment Comparing Three Books

To compare data, the relationships between the stories and balloon patterns for three books were analyzed. The beginnings of each of the 80 stories were used; these stories were contained within two of three books have the same author, and it was therefore assumed that several common patterns would exist between these stories. Table 13 shows the number of variations of two orientation patterns, $d_1^{o_1}$, $d_2^{o_1}$, $d_3^{o_1}$, $d_4^{o_1}$ and $d_1^{o_2}$, $d_2^{o_2}$, $d_3^{o_2}$, $d_4^{o_2}$, and the balloon patterns $c_k^1$, $c_k^2$, $c_k^3$, and $c_k^4$ in the three books. The number of common pattern types are also shown.

*Table 8. Comparison between the number of stories and the number of characters in a story*

| The Num. of Character | The Num. of Stories |
|---|---|
| 0 | 0 |
| 1 | 20 |
| 2 | 46 |
| 3 | 10 |
| 4 | 2 |
| 5 | 0 |
| 6 | 2 |
| Total | 80 |

*Table 9. The frequency of types of direction*

| Direction | Freq. of $d^{o_1}$ (Order) | Freq. of $d^{o_2}$ (Order) |
|---|---|---|
| 0 | 26 (4) | 46 (2) |
| f | 138 (1) | 63 (1) |
| b | 20 (5) | 10 (5) |
| r | 38 (2) | 36 (3) |
| l | 38 (2) | 26 (4) |
| u | 0 (8) | 0 (8) |
| g | 2 (6) | 2 (6) |
| p | 2 (6) | 1 (7) |

*Table 10. The frequency of the orientation pattern in 112 characters of 66 stories*

| $o_1$ | | $o_2$ | | $o_1 \cap o_2$ | |
|---|---|---|---|---|---|
| **Freq.** | **Pattern** | **Freq.** | **Pattern** | **Freq.** | **Pattern** |
| 10 | ffff | 4 | 0fff | 11 | ffff |
| 3 | frrr | 3 | rrrf | 5 | ff0f |
| 3 | ff0f | 2 | rfff | 5 | 0fff |
| 3 | f0ff | 2 | fffr | 4 | f0ff |
| 2 | llll | 2 | ff0f | 3 | rrrf |
| 2 | lllf | 2 | 00rr | 3 | rfff |
| 2 | frfl | 2 | 000f | 3 | lllf |
| 2 | frff | 2 | 000b | 3 | frrr |
| 2 | fflr | | | 2 | llll |
| 2 | fffl | | | 2 | lffl |
| 2 | fffb | | | 2 | frfl |
| 2 | fbbb | | | 2 | frff |
| 2 | f000 | | | 2 | flll |
| | | | | 2 | ffrr |
| | | | | 2 | fflr |
| | | | | 2 | fffr |
| | | | | 2 | fffl |
| | | | | 2 | fffb |
| | | | | 2 | fbbb |
| | | | | 2 | f000 |
| | | | | 2 | 0lff |
| | | | | 2 | 00rr |
| | | | | 2 | 000f |
| | | | | 2 | 000b |
| (The pattern whose frequency lower than 1 is omitted) | | | | | |
| | 42 types | | 35 types | | 67 types |

## Result of Three-Book Comparison

The same balloon patterns were frequently found in the two stories by the same author, while seven balloon patterns were common in all three stories. Table 14 shows the seven types of balloon patterns and their frequencies, while Figure 7 shows four higher-ranking balloon patterns. These seven balloon patterns were found in 81 of 240 stories, and correspond to approximately 30% of all patterns. Therefore, it can be concluded that typical balloon patterns exist. For each of the seven patterns, typical object types and character emotions were drawn in certain scenes. Therefore, balloon patterns can possibly be regarded as a semantic class of stories. In future research, scene and story meanings will be obtained based on training data using automatically extracted balloon patterns.

*Table 11. The frequency of the balloon pattern in 80 stories*

| $c_k^1$ | | $c_k^2$ | | $c_k^3$ | | $c_k^4$ | |
|---|---|---|---|---|---|---|---|
| **Freq.** | **Pattern** | **Freq.** | **Pattern** | **Freq.** | **Pattern** | **Freq.** | **Pattern** |
| 27 | 00000 | 28 | 00000 | 28 | 00000 | 23 | 10000 |
| 27 | 10000 | 26 | 10000 | 28 | 10000 | 17 | 00000 |
| 11 | 00001 | 9 | 00001 | 6 | 00001 | 9 | 00001 |
| 6 | 00010 | 6 | 00010 | 4 | 00100 | 8 | 10010 |
| 4 | 01000 | 5 | 10010 | 3 | 01000 | 7 | 00010 |
| 2 | 10010 | 2 | 00100 | 3 | 10010 | 4 | 01000 |
| 1 | 00100 | 1 | 01000 | 2 | 00010 | 3 | 00100 |
| 1 | 10001 | 1 | 01001 | 1 | 00101 | 2 | 00101 |
| 1 | 11000 | 1 | 10001 | 1 | 00110 | 2 | 01001 |
| | | 1 | 11000 | 1 | 01001 | 2 | 01010 |
| | | | | 1 | 01100 | 2 | 11000 |
| | | | | 1 | 10001 | 1 | 10100 |
| | | | | 1 | 11000 | | |
| 9 types | | 10 types | | 13 types | | 12 types | |

*Table 12. The frequency of the balloon pattern two in 80 stories*

| $c_k^1$~ $c_k^4$ | | $c_k^1 c_k^2 c_k^3 c_k^4$ | |
|---|---|---|---|
| **Freq.** | **Pattern** | **Freq.** | **Pattern** |
| 104 | 10000 | 7 | 10000,10000,10000,10000 |
| 100 | 00000 | 5 | 00001,00001,00001,00001 |
| 35 | 00001 | 5 | 00000,00000,00000,00000 |
| 21 | 00010 | 3 | 00000,00000,10000,10000 |
| 18 | 10010 | 2 | 10000,10000,10000,00000 |
| 12 | 01000 | 2 | 10000,00000,00000,00000 |
| 10 | 00100 | 2 | 00000,00000,00000,00100 |
| 5 | 11000 | | |
| 4 | 01001 | | The pattern whose the frequency |
| 3 | 00101 | | lower than 1 is omitted |
| 3 | 10001 | | |
| 2 | 01010 | | |
| 15 types | | 61 types | |

*Table 13. Comparing the features of three books*

| | Direction $o_1$ | Direction $o_2$ | Balloon |
|---|---|---|---|
| Book 1 | 42 | 35 | 61 |
| Book 2 | 25 | 29 | 42 |
| Book 3 | 20 | 21 | 46 |
| A ∩ B | 3 | 6 | 8 |
| A ∩ C | 4 | 5 | 7 |
| B ∩ C | 4 | 6 | 10 |
| A ∩ B ∩ C | 1 | 3 | 7 |

*Table 14. Common seven balloon patterns among three books*

| Frequency | Balloon Pattern |
|---|---|
| 48 | 10000,10000,10000,10000 |
| 10 | 10000,10000,10000,10010 |
| 6 | 10000,10000,10000,00000 |
| 6 | 10000,10000,00000,10000 |
| 5 | 10000,10000,10000,01000 |
| 3 | 10000,10000,11000,11000 |
| 3 | 10000,10000,10010,10010 |

*Figure 7. Examples of higher-ranking balloon patterns*

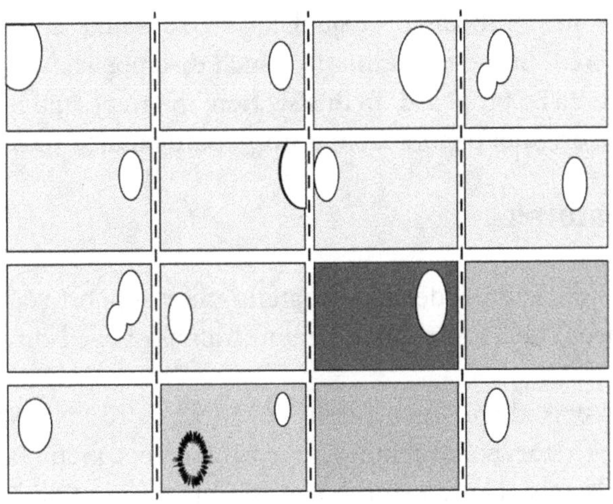

## Comic Analysis Conclusion

In this section, with a view towards realizing story representation for computer operations, a data format through which stories are modeled based on character orientations and balloon types was shown. Using the proposed data format, example data from existing comics can be created and the possibility that their characteristic features are well related to the terms of stories is shown. The following further developments are now required.

- Construction of large-scale data.
- Representation of orientations using angles and vector definitions, in order to realize a class estimation method for application to detailed comic stories based on machine learning.
- Surveying of comic authors to identify the essential elements necessary to create comics.

## ANALYSIS OF ANIMATION STORYBOARD

In the previous section, the authors focused on stories told by pictures. Pictures are the key components not only for comics, but also for animation. The creation of animation has common processes compared to that of comics because one animation is usually a collaborative creation by several animators. In the animation creation process, the storyboard is a very important component as regards story design. Animators draw original pictures in accordance with the storyboard, and these original pictures depict certain events within a very limited timeframe. The directors then connect large numbers of original pictures to create stories. Namely, one story board requires several creators of original pictures. Facilitators should assign the drawing of each scene to the appropriate creator depending on the difficulty in drawing. However, the field of animation is facing labor shortage. Thus, humans strongly hope that computers can play an important role in this process. Here, the process of translating original pictures from storyboards is considered as using computers in one of the important processes of animation. Furthermore, the cost of creating original pictures from storyboards is calculated based on the number of original pictures, but the difficulty is not considered. In order to eliminate such discrepancies, a method for calculating the difficulty of the process should be proposed. In this section, the final goal is to define a difficulty index regarding the creation of an original picture from a storyboard created by an animator.

### Target Works and Features

A method of classifying the difficulty index using a multi-class support vector machine (SVM) (Cortes & Vapnik, 1995) is described. The SVM receives feature values of each cut in a storyboard as input and classifies the output index.

Here, part A of the 10th episode of "Inou Battle Wa Nichijou Kei No Naka De" (Nozomi, 2014) is taken as the dataset. Note that a storyboard contains several elements: pictures, a number of cuts, a number of frames, lines, and cut contents. Thus, a storyboard is a blueprint of an original picture, because the creators create an original picture based on those components. In this section, the following storyboard components are extracted and defined as an SVM input vector.

- **Number of Original Pictures:** The number of original pictures, including the cut.
- **Number of Frames:** The number of frames, including the cut.
- **Cut Content:** The explanations of the cut given in the storyboard.
- **Lines:** The lines (dialogue) of the animated person described in the storyboard.
- **Sound Effects:** Any sound effects or music described in the storyboard.
- **Difficulty Index:** An index representing the difficulty of creating an original picture from the storyboard.

Note that the difficulty index is evaluated from the storyboard and the original picture by the annotators, who produce animation, based on their experience. The lines and cut content are translated into a numerical vector using a bag of words, because they are described in natural language. In addition, the number of original pictures is also used as a vector element.

## Storyboard Analysis Experiment

In order to evaluate the difficulty of translating original pictures into cuts, the index of each cut is evaluated on a five-level scale, where: 1 = easy, 2 = relatively easy, 3 = normal, 4 = slightly difficult, and 5 = difficult. In order to simplify the problem structure and to avoid data bias, indices 1 and 2 are classified as class 1, index 3 is classified as class 3, and indices 4 and 5 are classified as class 5. To evaluate this method, a multi-class SVM was trained using the data set, utilizing a linear kernel and setting the parameter cost to 32. These settings were determined in preliminary experiments. The number of pictures in Part A of the 10th episode of "Inou Battle Wa Nichijou Kei No Naka De" is 130, and Table 15 shows the number of pictures in each class. A five-fold cross-validation identification result of 79.03% was obtained through 100 iterations. As this value is above the 73.08% current baseline, it indicates that the SVM can learn and identify the difficulty index of translating a given storyboard into original pictures.

## Conclusions from Animation Storyboard Analysis

In this section, the authors focus on one of the important processes of animation and a method through which the animation process can be evaluated was shown. The following future developments are required in order to further refine this technique.

- The results of other kernels must be considered.
- Data correlation between multiple evaluators must be considered.
- Cooperation with storyboard creators must be incorporated into the research.

# FUTURE RESEARCH DIRECTIONS

Thus far, the generation of creative work has been mainly discussed in the fields of literature and art; however, recently, it has become a topic of engineering research. Although the authors know very well that a large number of difficult tasks are yet to be achieved for the analysis of creative work by computers, the computational models discussed in this chapter will give readers novel ideas and generate interest on the topic. Some directions for future work are as follows:

- There exists inter-textuality among existing stories. This information is useful for finding common flows in human story comprehension. Some creative work is available on the web under the Creative Commons license. On the other hand, a considerable number of creative works are pro-

*Table 15. Number of pictures per class*

| Class | The Number of Pictures |
|---|---|
| 1 | 28 |
| 3 | 95 |
| 5 | 7 |
| Total | 130 |

tected by copyrights. Copyright is a big problem that prevents the advance of research in this field. In this chapter, the authors prepared the creative work ourselves and will provide these creative products with the related metadata for use in future research work.
- The personality of the characters is the key information of stories because at times, the story patterns are strongly related to the character personalities. Character personality is regarded as a unique distribution of the transition that the character has. Thus, the development of a model of character personality should be focused upon.

## CONCLUSION

In this chapter, the authors introduced several methods and computational models to automatically generate creative work. Novels, comics, and animations were focused upon because they are depicted by pictures and natural languages. Such creative work gives rise to a considerable number of interesting and challenging issues related to computational narratology.

The results of this chapter can be summarized as follows:

1. The authors proposed a method of semi-automatic generation of stories by agent-based simulation (ABS). Compared to the previous method based on existing novels, the proposed method can create flexible transitions for stories. A story is a set of transitions from the current states to the next states; therefore, the definition of appropriate units of transitions and the maintenance of logical coherence and unpredictability are important issues to be tackled in the future.
2. Computational models for generating and analyzing comics are constructed. The authors developed the comic generating system utilizing the prepared object images and the operators that represent image transition. Further, the authors found individual relations between the states of objects in the pictures and the stories.
3. The authors also proposed a method using an SVM to estimate the difficulties of each scene in the storyboard, which is the key process of creating animations. The method encourages human beings to co-create animations with computers by referring to the difficulties of each part.

Computational models for creative work are being developed, and their structure varies according to the aim of the research. If complete models are defined in the future, the authors believe that the computer will be able to create comics and animations along with human beings.

## REFERENCES

Cortes, C., & Vapnik, V. (1995). Support-vector networks. *Machine Learning*, *20*(3), 273–297. doi:10.1007/BF00994018

Eitz, M., Hays, J., & Alexa, M. (2012). How do humans sketch objects? *ACM Trans. Graph.*, *31*(4), 44:1-44:10.

Fukuda, K., Mori, N., & Matsumoto, K. (2015). Analysis of automatic novel generation without existing novels information. In *Proceedings of the 29th Annual Conference of the Japanese Society for Artificial Intelligence (JSAI'15)*. Hakodate, Japan: The Japanese Society for Artificial Intelligence.

Gamma, E., Helm, R., Johnson, R., & Vlissides, J. (1995). *Design patterns: elements of reusable object-oriented software*. Addison-Wesley.

Gervás, P., Diaz-Agudo, B., Peinado, F., & Hervás, R. (2005). Story plot generation based on CBR. *Knowledge-Based Systems Journal, 18*(4-5), 235–242. doi:10.1016/j.knosys.2004.10.011

Gohara, H., Sugimoto, S., & Morishima, S. (2010). Data driven in-betweening for hand drawn rotating face. In *Proceedings of the ACM SIGGRAPH 2010 Posters Article* No. 7. Los Angeles, CA: ACM. doi:10.1145/1836845.1836853

Imabuchi, S., & Ogata, T. (2012). A story generation system based on Propp theory: As a mechanism in an integrated narrative generation system. In H. Isahara & K. Kanazaki (Eds.), *Advances in Natural Language Processing:Proceedings of the 8th International Conference on Natural Language Processing* (Vol. 7614, pp. 312-321). Berlin, Germany: Springer. doi:10.1007/978-3-642-33983-7_31

Kobako, T. (2003). *Sketchbook 1*. Tokyo, Japan: Mag Garden.

Kouyama, S., & Sumi, K. (2014). A discussion of humorous story generation system by using stories of Shinichi Hoshi. In *Proceedings of the 28th Annual Conference of the Japanese Society for Artificial Intelligence (JSAI'14)*. Ehime, Japan: The Japanese Society for Artificial Intelligence.

Macal, C. M., & North, M. J. (2010). Tutorial on agent-based modeling and simulation. *Journal of Simulation, 4*(3), 151–162. doi:10.1057/jos.2010.3

Matsubara, H., Sato, S., Akaishi, M., Sumi, K., Mukaiyama, K., Nakashima, H., & Otsuka, Y. (2013). An attempt at automatic composition of Shin'ichi Hoshi-like short short stories. In *Proceedings of the 27th Annual Conference of the Japanese Society for Artificial Intelligence (JSAI'13)*. Toyama, Japan: The Japanese Society for Artificial Intelligence.

Meehan, J. R. (1980). *The metanovel: writing stories by computer*. New York, NY: Garland Publishing.

Nozomi, K. (2014). *Inou battle wa nichijou kei no naka de* [Battles using special skills in usual scenes]. Tokyo, Japan: SB Creative.

Ogata, K., Sato, S., & Komatani, K. (2014). Automatic generation of very short stories by imitation and substitution. In *Proceedings of the 28th Annual Conference of the Japanese Society for Artificial Intelligence (JSAI'14)*. Ehime, Japan: The Japanese Society for Artificial Intelligence.

Pérez y Pérez, R., & Sharples, M. (2001). MEXICA: A computer model of cognitive account of creative writing. *Journal of Experimental & Theoretical Artificial Intelligence, 13*(2), 119–139. doi:10.1080/09528130010029820

Sumi, Y., Sakamoto, R., Nakao, K., Mase, K., & Kunifuji, S. (2002). Change of individual experiences and interests in comics style. *IPSJ Journal, 43*(12), 3582–3595.

Tanaka, T., Toyama, F., Miyamichi, J., & Shoji, K. (2010). Detection and classification of speech balloons in comic images. *The Journal of The Institute of Image Information and Television Engineers*, *64*(12), 1933–1939. doi:10.3169/itej.64.1933

Turner, S. R. (1994). *The creative process: A computer model of storytelling and creativity*. Oxford, UK: Psychology Press.

Ueno, M., Mori, N., & Matsumoto, K. (2014). *2-scene comic creating system based on the distribution of picture state transition. Advances in Intelligent Systems and Computing* (Vol. 290, pp. 459–467). New York, NY: Springer, International Publishing.

## KEY TERMS AND DEFINITIONS

**Agent-Based Simulation:** Simulation to investigate actions and interactions between autonomous agents.

**Creative Works:** Intellectual products created by humans, such as pictures, novels, and animation.

**Drawing Operator:** The representation of the transition of stories to transform pictures.

**Original Picture:** Key animation which is the start, key, or end scene of motion.

**Plot:** A set of state transitions that are arranged in reading order in narratives.

**Story:** A set of state transitions that are arranged in chronological order in narratives.

**Story Vector:** Information pertaining to the elements of a story that is represented in vector form.

**Storyboard:** Story design that has information required for original picture generation.

# Section 3
# Language and Narrative

# Chapter 7
# Thesaurus with Predicate-Argument Structure to Provide Base Framework to Determine States, Actions, and Change-of-States

**Koichi Takeuchi**
*Okayama University, Japan*

## ABSTRACT

*The goal with this chapter is to discuss the possibility of language resources in determining the states, actions, and change-of-states of characters in narratives. An overview of previous work on linguistic theory and language resources is given then the Predicate-Argument Structure Thesaurus (PT), a Japanese language resource constructed based on the extended framework of the Lexical Conceptual Structure (LCS), is proposed. The PT provides hierarchical clusters of synonyms for 11,900 predicates and 22,000 example sentences annotated with semantic role labels. Each concept has an abstracted LCS, and example sentences are attached to each concept. By virtue of the structure, a correlation of the arguments between other clusters can be determined. The semantic structure of the PT is investigated to enrich generated texts of narratives, and the high possibility of lexical semantics contributing to narrative processing is revealed.*

## INTRODUCTION

In narratives, characters will take actions and cause events, and the results of the events cause other events, so that a sequence of events forms a story. Since events comprise change-of-states, actions, and states that can be expressed using verbs and adjectives, analyses of predicates and their arguments are a key issue for constructing a narrative processing system. In narrative studies, the story structure, e.g., Propp (1968), and discourse structure, e.g., Genette (1972), have been extensively discussed by e.g.,

DOI: 10.4018/978-1-5225-0432-0.ch007

Copyright © 2016, IGI Global. Copying or distributing in print or electronic forms without written permission of IGI Global is prohibited.

Ogata and Kanai (2010); however, lexical semantics, i.e., the semantic structure of predicates and their arguments, has not been thoroughly discussed in narratology. One of the state-of-the art systems of AI-based narrative generation is constructed using a case frame lexicon as a base unit of story grammar. The case frame structure is good for making simple sentences designated by the story grammar; however, the case frame lexicon does not have a mechanism to generate grammatical paraphrases (e.g., causative alternation). The predicate-argument structure in the study of lexical semantics can provide grammatical paraphrases because the goal with lexical semantics is to analyze interactions between grammatical paraphrases and lexical meanings. The predicate-argument structure has also the potential for evaluating the consistency of generated event sequences in accordance with shallow physical constraints of the story world. This function can be effective for *catalyzers*, which are the descriptions of trivial incidents inserted between the core story events for conveying the moods of the scenes (Barthes, 1966). Arai (1985) pointed out the mood as well as the story of the narrative is an essential reason the reader wants to read the narrative more than once. Therefore, the goal with this manuscript is to show the possible contribution of lexical semantics to narratology.

Gruber (1965) proposed describing shared meanings between verbs as a pre-dictionary structure, and this idea is extended as a lexical conceptual structure (LCS) (Jackendoff, 1990; Kageyama, 1996) that can describe the compositional structure of shared meanings of predicates with arguments. The LCS has a transparent structure of not only syntactic derivations, such as the causative, transitive, and intransitive forms of a verb, but also semantic derivations such as between change-of-state and state expressions e.g., *He put the book on the shelf* suggests the book is on the shelf; thus, the LCS is suitable for describing a core conceptual meaning of a predicate, especially for change-of-state.

Large-scale examples are quite useful for constructing language processing systems, e.g., thesauruses of words (i.e., WordNet (WN)), annotation data of predicate-argument relations for texts (e.g., PropBank), and detailed predicate-argument databases (i.e., FrameNet (FN)) that are available in English. These English language resources are used in practical language processing systems (see Background); however, they do not provide decompositional features directly; thus, reconstructing another resource by taking into account the relations between change-of-states and state for predicates is necessary. In addition, Japanese language resources of predicate-arguments are not sufficient compared with English language resources.

Because of such background, a thesaurus of a predicate-argument structure for Japanese is proposed on the basis of an extended framework of the LCS. The thesaurus contains hierarchical concepts of shared meanings for about 11,900 predicates with 22,000 example sentences annotated with semantic role labels. Each of the concepts has an abstracted conceptual structure that enables the description of compositional features of shared meaning. The hierarchical conceptual labels enable users to obtain shallow to detailed concepts, and the upper concepts entails the lower concepts. Thanks to the conceptual structure, our thesaurus can provide flexible modifications to a sentence. For example, if we would like to add a causer to *the door opened*, the thesaurus suggests that it can take a subject-verb-object construction as *a strong wind opened the door*. The modification corresponds with the controlling plot in narratives. The conceptual structure also allows users to obtain semantic relations crossing the hierarchy of concepts. This function can be applied to a consistency evaluation of generated sentences with shallow physical restrictions in the narrated world. For example, the following two sequential sentences *Dr. N made a robot* (*Generate* concept) and *he kept the robot at his side* (*Ongoing* concept) (Hoshi, 1975) are validated with the thesaurus concepts. This is because the existence of the robot is consistent between the two sentences, that is, the *Generate* concept indicates that the robot came into existence, and the

*Ongoing* concept requires that the robot already exists as a precondition. Thus, the proposed thesaurus can provide multi-dimensional relations between predicates with their arguments containing relations between the change-of-state and its goal, which must be the base relations for narrative processing.

## BACKGROUND

The structure of narratives is mainly done in the study of literature. A recent structural analysis of story began with Propp (1968), who revealed functions of actions caused by characters in Russian folktales. As a representative study of the discourse of narratives, Genette (1972) categorized the techniques of how to express a story as a text. Barthes (1966) discussed other types of functions called *catalyzers* and *indices*. The former are trivial actions inserted between consequential actions that compose a plot, and the latter are static descriptions of situations, atmosphere, or nature of characters. The two functions are different from the core actions discussed by Propp but enrich the descriptions of a narrative.

In the study of AI-based narrative generation systems, Lönneker (2005) designed a system architecture that controls the discourse structure and is combined with a traditional natural language generation system. Montfort (2006) proposed an interactive system of narrative variations. These two systems do not generate narratives automatically; therefore, Akimoto and Ogata (2011a, 2011b, 2013) constructed an automatic narrative generation system based on several narrative techniques including story grammar (Propp, 1968) and discourse techniques (Genette, 1972; Jauss, 1970). The system reveals the possibility of automatic generation of text-level narratives but still needs improvement because the system outputs only simple texts of the core events of a story, e.g., *Iwan fights a snake. Iwan was injured in the arm by the snake. Iwan defeated the snake*[1]. Toward more natural narrative generation, two major types of modification are required. The one is to modify these sentences with grammatical variations, e.g., applying cause-effect relations; the other is to insert *catalyzers* and *indices* that describe actions and emotions of characters. The former modification can be done using linguistic knowledge, but the latter is an issue of language generation in computational linguistics.

A successful system in natural language generation is SHRDLU, which is a question-answering system according to the world of toy blocks (Winograd, 1972, 1983). The system was constructed using systemic grammar (Halliday, 1975) and modules of calculating physical restrictions of a block world based on original semantic structure. The keys to success of the system are using detailed linguistic-based knowledge and physical restrictions of the toy world. This indicates that a language generation system can provide consistent texts if it can calculate restrictions and rules of the referred world. In narrative generation, calculation of restrictions and rules of a story world are not possible. Since lexical semantics can provide base conceptual frames shared by predicates, however, these frames can partially support the calculation of physical restrictions. For example, in the catalyzer, *Bond moved towards the desk,* inserted between the core events, *Telephone rang* and *Bond answered* (Barthes, 1966, pp.9-10), the lexical semantic structure can estimate *Bond* is finally located at *the desk* according to the conceptual frame of *Move*. If the locations of Bond, desk, and telephone on which the telephone rang are defined, Bond's moving action can be validated using the conceptual frame and location information. Thus, lexical semantic studies, especially, the study of meaning of predicates, are inevitable for narrative generation.

Many studies have been conducted on the meaning of predicates from the viewpoint of linguistics as well as the construction of natural language resources. In linguistic theory, lexical decomposition has been studied in lexical semantics and syntax. Gruber (1965) proposed an abstracted structure of shared meaning among verbs to determine the synonym expressions in generative grammar. For example, *goes across* and *crossed* in the meaning of *the road goes across the river* and *the road crossed the river* are assumed to have the same structure composed of a combination of features (e.g., *MOTINNAL* and *POSIITIONAL*) and prepositions. This generative semantic approach is extended as LCS (Jackendoff, 1972, 1983, 1990; Kageyama, 1996; Dorr, 1997), which is a framework to clarify the internal semantic structure of words, allows us to explain the meaning of phrases and sentences composed of the conceptual structure of constituents. The LCS was developed by taking into account various kinds of linguistic studies, e.g., syntactic structure, Gruber's theory, argument structure (Grimshaw, 1992), lexical decomposition (McCawley, 1968), and cognitive grammar (Langacker, 1986). The LCS, generative semantics, is mainly applied to analysis of predicates, but, the approach of generative semantics is also adapted to analysis of nominal nouns in the Generative Lexicon by Pustejovsky (1995). Thus, lexical decomposition has been extensively investigated.

The LCS (Jackendoff, 1990) is composed of base types of categories and primitives. The basic categories are *Thing*, *Event*, *State*, *Action*, *Place*, *Path*, *Property*, and *Amount* (Jackendoff, 1972). Since the basic categories are defined as a top level ontology, all the possible primitives and structures are defined under these categories. For example, the conceptual structures for events are defined as

$$[_{\text{Event}}\ \text{GO}\ ([_{\text{Thing}}\ ], [_{\text{Path}}\ ])]$$
$$[_{\text{Event}}\ \text{STAY}\ ([_{\text{Thing}}\ ], [_{\text{Place}}\ ])]$$
$$[_{\text{Event}}\ \text{CAUSE}\ ([\{_{\text{THING} \mid \text{Event}}\}], [_{\text{Event}}\ ])].$$

The subscripts in the brackets denote the ontological categories. The conceptual structure shows that an *Event* can be one of three primitives, *GO*, *STAY*, or *CAUSE*. The primitive *GO* indicates motion along a path; thus, it takes two arguments; one is the *Thing*, which is a moving object, and the other is the *Path* the object goes across. The primitive *STAY* denotes a situation in which the *Thing* is located at the *Place* over a period of time. The primitive *CAUSE* denotes a combinatorial situation in which the *Thing* or *Event* makes the *Event*. The LCS can express a sentential abstracted meaning by using the combinations of the predefined conceptual structures. For example, the conceptual structure of *Ken ran into the house* can be expressed using the Event structure described below.

$$[_{\text{Event}}\ \text{GO}\ ([_{\text{Thing}}\ \text{Ken}], [_{\text{Path}}\ \text{TO}\ ([_{\text{Place}}\ \text{IN}\ ([_{\text{Thing}}\ \text{HOUSE}])])])]$$

In the Event structure, the Path argument takes the conceptual structure of *into* predefined as $[_{\text{Path}}\ \text{TO}\ ([_{\text{Place}}\ \text{IN}\ ([_{\text{Thing}}\ ])])]$, which denotes an end point of the motion. In the Path argument, several types of primitives are predefined, e.g., *FROM*, which denotes a starting point, and *TOWARD*, which denotes a direction; thus, the combination of primitives and structures can describe the conceptual meaning (i.e., moving, change-of-state, and state) of the predicate and semantic relation (i.e., beginning point, direction, and ending point) of its arguments. The LCS is a syntagmatic analysis to clarify a conceptual structure that can explain the syntactic structure of predicates (e.g., variations and alternations); thus, paradigmatic analysis among predicates is not the main issue with the LCS. Examples of paradigmatic issues are how many types of primitives are required, how many types of synonymous groups of predicates exist, and how many types of alternations of verbs exist, which is essential information to construct a practical natural language understanding system.

A paradigmatic study in linguistics was conducted by Levin (1993). Levin investigated large syntactic alternations of English verbs as possible then gathered the types of alternations with example sentences and verb groups into a book. This study can be regarded as that of constructing language resources as well as of linguistics. The study of language resources, which attempts to look over all the types of language expressions, is useful not only for linguistics, but also natural language processing. For example, WN (Fellbaum, 1998) is a large-scale thesaurus of about 150,000 words (i.e., nouns, verbs, adjectives, and adverbs) of English; synonymous words are categorized into a group called synset that denotes a concept of shared-meaning among words; the synsets are organized into a thesaurus, i.e., more generic synsets are assigned to the upper layer and more specific synsets are assigned to the lower layer; a polysemous word is assigned to several synsets. Since the main focus with WN is on the wide coverage of words in English, it does not contain syntactic information; however, it contributes to a practical question answering system called Watson (Baker, 2012) as a database of word senses. This suggests that language resources are helpful in natural language understanding systems.

PropBank (Palmar, Gildea, & Kingsbury, 2005) annotates meanings of verbs and semantic roles of their arguments to syntactic trees in the Penn Treebank (Marcus, Santorini, & Marcinkiewicz, 1993). The meanings of verbs are organized as framesets, which are the categories defined in VerbNet; the categories were originally defined by Levin (1993). In the semantic roles in which various types of theories have been proposed, PropBank provides numbered roles, i.e., Arg0, Arg1, and Arg2, instead of the traditional labels e.g., Agent, Theme and Goal. This approach has advantages of the numbered roles can designate with no ambiguity which semantic role the target verb takes and can be adapted to any theoretical framework by adding notes of corresponding labels to the arguments, e.g., *Arg1: entity going down* in the frameset: *decline.01* (Palmer et al., 2005). The notes of the semantic roles are not consistent labels; thus, it is not easy to find which argument is the ending point of a change-of-state verb in PropBank.

FrameNet (Baker, Fillmore, & Lowe, 1998) is a project for developing consistent semantic frames that denote shared concepts among words and the participants in them by manually analyzing large lexical units and example sentences. Currently, FN provides 170000 annotated example sentences and 10,000 lexical units (i.e., words). The semantic roles of arguments (called frame elements) are defined on a frame-by-frame basis; for example, the frame and frame elements of *John bought a chair from Ken for $50* are

$[_{\text{Buyer}}$ John$]$ $[_{\text{Commerce\_buy}}$ bought$]$ $[_{\text{Goods}}$ a chair$]$ $[_{\text{Seller}}$ from Ken$]$ $[_{\text{Money}}$ for \$50$]$.

The frame name of *buy* is *Commerce_buy*, and the frame elements of the arguments are *Buyer*, *Goods*, *Seller*, and *Money*, which are more frame-dependent detailed role types than the conventional abstracted semantic role crossing verbs first proposed by Fillmore (1968). Since the frame sets and frame elements are organized as ontology, change-of-state and moving can be extracted by manually determining which semantic frames correspond to moving or change-of-state needed for narrative understanding.

WN and FN have systematic semantics and can be extended to linguistic ontology by connecting them with the formal framework (Huang et al., 2010). In another type of ontological study, Dorr (1997) constructed an LCS for Levin's (1993) verb data based on the theory by Jackendoff (1983, 1990); however, Dorr's LCS does not contain any example sentences but only conceptual structures with primitives; thus, it is difficult to use because analyzed example sentences are indispensable to understanding the meaning of structural semantics as well as constructing an automatic analyzing system with machine learning approaches. PropBank has not only annotated example sentences but also has mapping information to

WN (Loper, Yi, & Palmer, 2007) and FN (Palmer, 2009) via SemLink; thus, these English language resources are quite useful for narrative processing systems.

In Japanese language resources, the EDR dictionary (Japan Electronic Dictionary Research Institute [EDR], 1995) contains a lexicon of 270,000 Japanese words, hierarchical concepts of 410,000 types, and a corpus of 200,000 sentences that are fully parsed and their semantic roles are annotated. Since one of the aims with the EDR is to provide corresponding English words, all the concepts are linked to both Japanese and English. The EDR is a large-scale database of Japanese; however, it is difficult to use for Japanese narrative understanding systems because each verb in the lexicon does not contain example sentences; thus, except for the verbs in the corpus, there are no examples annotated with semantic role labels, and the concepts are not designed for decompositional analysis. Therefore, it is not easy to find which concepts correspond to change-of-state or moving.

Japanese WordNet (JWN) was constructed from the translation of English WN, but there are currently no links with other Japanese language resources. Ohara et al. (2003) provide Japanese FN that contains about 100 lexical items[2]. The Information-technology Promotion Agency Lexicon (IPAL) (Kuwahara, Hashimoto, & Murata, 1993) provides systematic semantic roles (with 31 types) of analyzed example sentences with rich grammatical information; however, IPAL is small (i.e., 861 verbs, 136 adjectives, 30 adjectival verbs, and 1081 nouns) and shared-meanings of verbs are on a very abstracted level (on which there are about 40 types).

To summarize the linguistic and language resource studies mentioned above for constructing narrative processing, i.e. validating character change-of-state positions, in particular, we need a language resource that contains systematic conceptual semantics and annotated example sentences; to determine the changing situation of the characters in narratives, semantic relation types between a predicate and its arguments is essential. In the next chapter, the proposed language resource is described.

## PREDICATE THESAURUS

A thesaurus with a predicate-argument structure (PT) is a language resource for providing multi-dimensional relations between predicates and their arguments using the LCS concept. The PT contains nodes that denote concepts of shared meaning, and each node has an abstracted LCS. There are three top-level concepts of the PT, i.e., state, change-of-state, and activity, that come from the aspectual analysis by Vendler (1967). Vendler proposed four types: states, actives, achievements, and accomplishments. Since the difference between achievements and accomplishments is in transitive or intransitive, they are merged into change-of-state. Each meaning of predicates belongs to a node with example sentences. The concept of this structure and perspectives are described below.

### Structure of Thesaurus

As described in the above section, the LCS has several benefits for describing a predicate meaning that is transparent to grammatical derivations and alternations, such as causative, transitive and intransitive expressions. From the viewpoint of using the LCS as a language resource, the structure, i.e., combination of primitives and arguments, are, however, difficult for humans as well as machine learning systems to deal with. This is difficult for the following two reasons.

1. All types of primitives are not revealed in linguistic theory (analysis for all predicates is needed).
2. Semantic relations between words are needed in the beginning before the detailed structure of the meaning for each word embeds several semantic relations between concepts.

Both reasons are related to the total typology of predicates. From the viewpoint of constructing a system for understanding the events and actions of characters in narratives, what types of predicates in terms of change-of-states first need to be determined. A detailed structure of the LCS gives the differences between meanings of predicates using different structures, but comparison of structures is not easy because a structure depends on the argument. In the examples, *X goes to Y* and *X reached Y via Z*, Z denotes a path; thus, the structures are different, but both are the same if we regard them as *Change_of_position_to_goal*. This idea is also looked as the success of WN used in practical natural language systems to which labels not structures are easy to apply. Since a primitive and its structure in the LCS denote a feature of shared meaning among predicates, we map the features to hierarchical concepts, i.e., labels. Figure 1 shows the correspondence between concepts in the PT and decompositional structures on three sentences.

The upper part of the diagram in Figure 1 shows the semantic relations among the LCSs (Kageyama, 1996; Takeuchi, Inui, Takeuchi, & Fujita, 2010) of *oku* (*put*), *idousuru* (*move*), and *aru* (*be*), which are transitive, intransitive and stative verbs, respectively. The conceptual structure of *put* in *Taro puts the book on the shelf*[8] is [CAUSE [ACT [[Taro], ON [book]], BECOME [[book], BE [AT [shelf]]]]], which contains the LCSs of *move* and *be*. Since a component of a structure denotes a feature of a concept, conceptual structures are mapped onto hierarchical conceptual nodes according to the essential feature. The essential feature, meaning, is a type of change-of-state, activity, or stative that will be not related to grammatical modification. For example, in the LCS of *put*, the primitive *CAUSE* can be regarded as

*Figure 1. Mapping partial structures of LCS into hierarchical conceptual nodes in thesaurus*

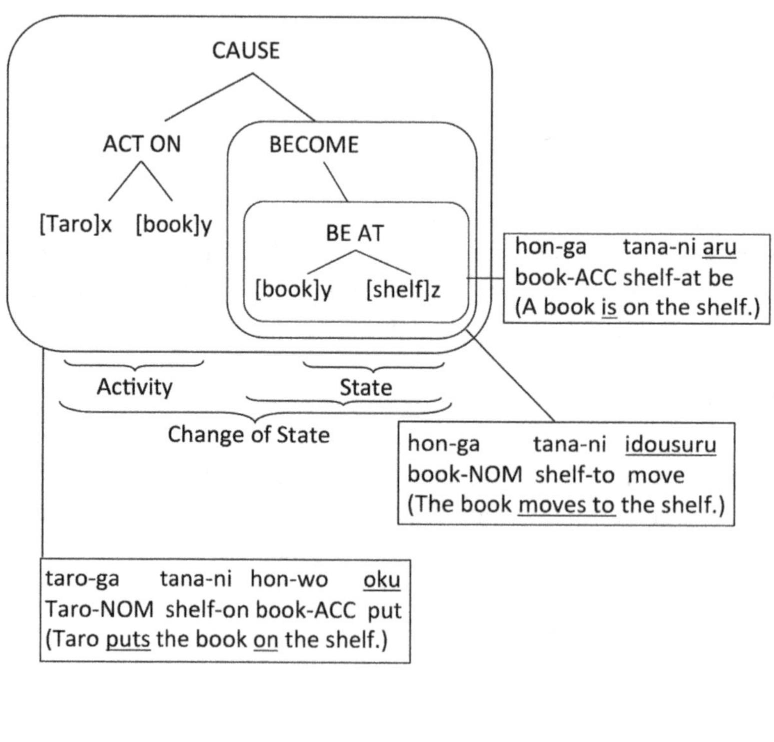

optional; thus, the sub-structure [BECOME [[], BE [AT []]]] is linked to the *Move_to_goal* conceptual node. By means of this link, *put* and *move* are linked to the same conceptual node. This indicates that the primitive *CAUSE* is regarded as optional in the PT, then *put* and *move* have the same LCS structure as

(CAUSE [i]) [BECOME [[j], BE [AT [k]]].

In this description, the structure in parentheses denotes that it is optional, and the description can correspond to intransitive as well as transitive verbs. This description is not the standard LCS, but a specific one for the PT; thus, it is called the thesaurus's LCS (TLCS). The conceptual node *Move_to_goal* is an abbreviated description. The node is located at the 4th layer in the hierarchical structure, then the full description of the concept from the top node is *Change_of_state/Position/Physical/Move_to_goal*. Since the lower concepts inherit the features of the upper concept, this hierarchical concept provides richer information than the TLCS. The node *Move_to_goal*[4] does not only indicate just the *moving something to goal* meaning, but the type of moving is limited to physical positional change. The predicates *inform* and *tell*, for instance, does not denote physical objects but that information moves to someone, so that these predicates are categorized under the other node, i.e., *Change_of_state/Position/Information/Inform_to_others/Inform* in the PT. This hierarchy provides shared/differentiate meaning in an understandable way, i.e., the predicates *put*, *move*, *inform*, and *tell* have change-of-state features; and *put* and *move* are physical position changes, but *inform* and *tell* are changes of positions of information. The description of *inform* and *tell* in the TLCS may not be simple because the argument j must be information to be informed, argument k must be someone, and *BECOME* must be too simple to categorize the special action used in the communication, e.g., the action must be *speak*. Thus, the strict control of the types of primitives has not been maintained, but the base conceptual framework (CAUSE) [BECOME [BE []]] has been. The other additional primitives are incorporated into the TLCS to describe the conceptual meanings. This allows us to expect that the TLCS can be used as base data for determining how many types of primitives would have been needed by organizing the data again.

The predicate *aru (be)* is linked to the *Exist* node, so that the semantic relation between *be* and *move* cannot be linked directly in the hierarchical nodes. Figure 2 shows this situation. Thus, a strategy of using both TLCS descriptions and hierarchical conceptual nodes is taken. The TLCS allows us to obtain semantic relations crossing hierarchical nodes like *be* and *move*; thus, both descriptions of concepts can provide multi-dimensional relations among the predicates.

*Figure 2. Linking between concepts in different leaves with internal structure of TLCS*

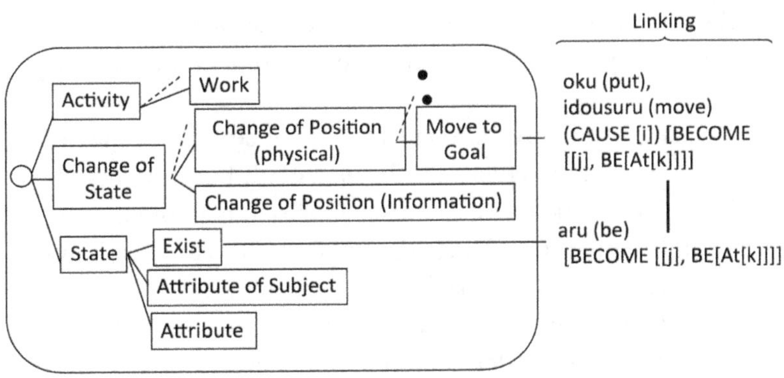

Since most predicates have several meanings, each meaning belongs to a conceptual node. This is a unique point compared with normal dictionaries. In such dictionaries, word meanings are isolated, i.e., there is a more detailed categorization of each word meaning; but in the proposed PT, each meaning of a predicate is categorized into an abstracted concept that denotes a shared meaning among predicates. Thus, a polysemous predicate will belong to several conceptual nodes in the PT. For example, the Japanese predicate *nigiru* has several meanings, e.g., *make (a rice ball)*, *have (someone's secret)*, and *hold (a handrail)*, which are categorized into the concepts *Generate*, *Recognize*, and *Manipulation*, respectively. To designate a meaning of a predicate, its example sentences are attached to it.

## Semantic Relations of Arguments

Each concept node has a TLCS; thus, example sentences are decomposed into arguments, which are linked to the corresponding arguments in the TLCS. For example, the TLCS and example sentences including *oku (put)* and *idousuru (move)* are as follows.

TLCS: (CAUSE [i]) [BECOME [[j], BE [AT [k]]]
[i taro-ga] [k tana-ni] [j hon-wo] oku
Taro-NOM shelf-on book-ACC put
(Taro puts the book on the shelf.)
[j hon-ga] [k tana-ni] idousuru
book-NOM shelf-to move
(The book moves to the shelf.)

The brackets in the sentences denote arguments, and the markers i, j, and k denote links between the TLCS and the sentences in the arguments. In the arguments in Japanese sentences there are Japanese case markers *ga*, *wo*, and *ni*, which are clues to recognize the syntactic position in the sentences. As the sentences including *oku* and *idousuru* show, each argument *ga* is linked to a different argument in the TLCS: the *ga* argument is linked to the *CAUSE* argument in the *oku* case; while the argument linked to the one in *BECOME* in the move case. Thus, the argument links between the TLCS and example sentences provide relations of the corresponding arguments between sentences via the TLCS.

To describe semantic relations between arguments and a predicate in a sentence, we introduce semantic role labels that indicate semantic types between arguments in addition to the TLCS. This is because the TLCS can provide only arguments, i.e., essential factors that complete the meaning of a predicate, and cannot describe adjuncts, e.g., time and location. From the viewpoint of narrative language processing, however, expressions of time and location are essential information of events. Thus, assigning semantic roles to the adjuncts allows us to deal with reason, time, location and condition, which are outside the scope of the lexicon.

As described in the Background section, there have been several studies on semantic role labels, and how to define a set of semantic roles has not been settled; but, roughly speaking, there are three approaches of setting a set of semantic roles. The first approach is to organize consistent semantic role labels crossing predicates (Fillmore, 1968). As a language resource, VerbNet (Kipper, 2005) is constructed with this type of approach. The second approach is that semantic role labels are separately defined on each verb and role labels of arguments are numbered. This approach is applied to PropBank. The third approach is that semantic role labels are defined on each concept, i.e., FN. In the PT we take the first approach because consistent semantic role labels help to improve the performance of automatic semantic role labeling systems (Loper et al., 2007).

Semantic roles were set according to previous English and Japanese linguistics studies (Jackendoff, 1990; Kageyama, 1996; Study Group of Written Japanese Grammar, 2009). In the PT, the basic policies to define semantic role labels are

1. Semantic roles should cover all the factors (i.e., adverbs as well as arguments and adjuncts) that can be dependent on the focusing predicates,
2. Semantic role types should be defined to be as small as possible, and
3. Semantic roles only define an abstracted relation between predicate and argument, and not define the detailed ontological relations.

Policy 3 indicates that semantic roles in the PT do not denote *Buyer* or *Seller* as defined in FN, but denote them in an abstracted level such as *Agent*, *Goal*, and *Source*. The semantic roles are composed of two levels. In the first level, semantic roles denote basic semantic relations, e.g., *Agent*, *Theme*, *Goal*, *Source*, *Reason*, *Condition*, *Time*, and *Location* (31 types); in the second level sub-types of semantic relations and restrictions are described e.g., *Person*, *Time*, *Amount*, *Body_part*, and *Event* (13 types). These sub-types are combined with the semantic roles in the first level, and there are 72 types of second-level semantic roles[5]. The sub-type category is annotated depending on the concept of the predicate. An example of *korashimeru (punish)* as follows.

taro-ga akunin-wo korashime-ta
Taro-Nom evildoers-ACC punish-PAST
Agent Theme (Person)
(Taro punished the evildoers.)

The semantic role *Theme (Person)* denotes that the direct object punishee should have humanity; and this restriction comes from the concept *Dominate* to which the verbs *korashimeru (punish), shihaisuru (dominate)*, and *taihosuru (arrest)* belong. Different from previous work in semantic role labels (e.g., VerbNet), *Source* and *Goal* in the PT denote beginning and ending situations of a change-of-state event, respectively, and the sub-type designates which feature the predicate means. For example, *ageru* (give) takes an indirect object (i.e., *Recipient* in FN), which is regarded as the factor of the ending situation of the event. Thus, the so-called *Recipient* is denoted as *Goal (Person)*, which is decomposed into an ending situation and person as follows.

taro-ga hon-wo hanako-ni age-ta
Taro-NOM book-ACC Hanako-DAT give-PAST
Agent Theme Goal (Person)
(Taro gave the book to Hanako.)

The verb *ageru (give)* belongs to the concept *Give*, which denotes giving something to people. In this concept, the verbs *teikyousuru (supply)*, *ataeru (give)*, and *kubaru (hand out)* are assigned. In the above example, there should be two semantic role of the argument *Taro*, i.e., *Agent* and *Source (Person)*; however, the later label is omitted in the framework of the PT. The reason of this omission is that it is redundant to annotate more than one semantic role label, i.e., in the *Give* concept, the *Agent* argument should be *Source (Person)* if the *Source* argument is omitted in a sentence. Thus, each dependency chunk is annotated with one semantic role label in the example sentences and another possibility of semantic roles is annotated in the concepts. For instance, the cases of arguments being omitted and described are as follows.

taro-ga jitensha-wo kat-ta
Taro-NOM bicycle-ACC buy-PAST
Agent Theme
(Taro bought a bicycle.)
taro-ga jitensha-wo hanako-ni kat-ta
Taro-NOM bicycle-ACC Hanako-DAT buy-PAST
Agent Theme Goal (Person)
(Taro bought a bicycle for Hanako.)

The former example shows that *Taro bought the bicycle*; thus, *Taro* will obtain the *bicycle*, i.e., the semantic roles of *Taro* are *Agent* and *Goal (Person)*, which is omitted in the example. The latter example shows that the dative case is added and the *Goal (Person)* argument occurs in the sentence. As the two examples show, the base argument structure of a concept can be modified by an additional argument (Goldberg, 1995). This indicates that it must be impossible to previously know all the variations of an argument structure, i.e., semantic role label sequences. Thus, as a strategy to collect the variations of the argument structure in a concept, we attempt to collect as many example sentences as possible. This strategy is also the same as with FN. By means of the sub-type structure, the semantic roles can designate the semantic relation of an essential argument with an adjunct feature. For instance, the semantic role labels for the predicate *enkisuru (postpone)* are:

taro-ga kaigi-wo asu-ni enkisi-ta
Taro-NOM meeting-ACC tomorrow-DAT postpone-PAST
Agent Theme Goal (Time)
(Taro postponed the meeting until tomorrow).

The chunk *asu-ni (until tomorrow)* is not an adjunct but an argument of *enkisuru (postpone)*. Thus, the sub-type structure can describe the combination of relation type (*Goal*) and feature (*Time*).

Figure 3 shows an example of a conceptual node, its TLCS, and example sentences with semantic role labels. The conceptual node *Move_one's_possession_from/Buy* has a TLCS and several example sentences of subordinated verbs, and those arguments are linked via semantic role labels and the TLCS. The annotated example sentences allow us to construct automatic semantic role labeling systems (Takeuchi et al., 2010).

## POSSIBILITY OF ENRICHING GENERATED NARRATIVE TEXTS USING PT

Since the PT provides hierarchical concepts, semantic role labels, and semantic structure of predicates, it is possible to improve narrative processing, especially for enriching generated narrative texts. In this

*Figure 3. Example sentences annotated with semantic roles and TLCS at Move_one's_possession_from/ Buy concept*

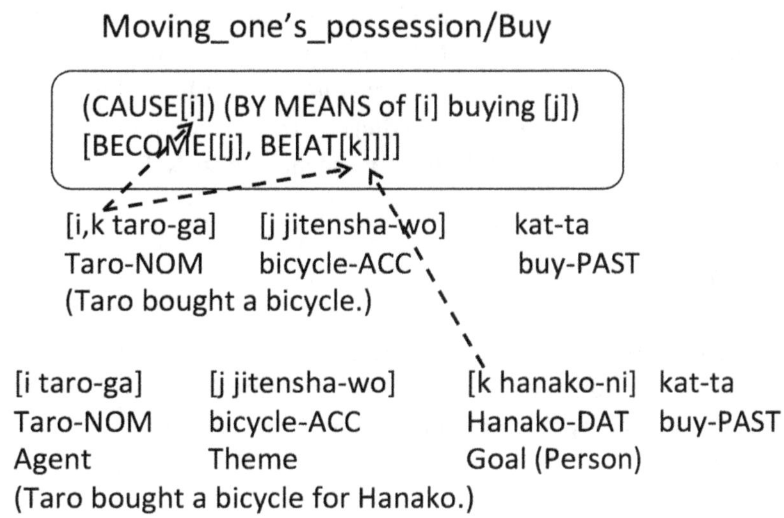


section, we discuss the possibility of the three types of applications, i.e., paraphrasing, connecting sentences, and validating consistency between sentences. The target text of the analyses is output text of the AI-based narrative generation system (Akimoto & Ogata, 2013) and actual text from short stories written by Hoshi (1975).

## Paraphrasing

Making another expression of an input text is a base function to enrich the output texts automatically generated with a narrative generation system or modify surface expressions of existing narratives. The PT provides candidates of paraphrases that cover idiomatic expressions, collocations, other predicates with the same concept, and grammatical paraphrases i.e., transitive, intransitive, and causative alternations. The following example is an output of the AI-based system.

iwan-ga hebinokuni-wo shuppatsu-shita
iwan-Nom the land of snake-ACC depart-PAST
(Iwan departed from the land of snake.)

This sentence can be expressed using other predicates without changing its conceptual meaning using the PT. The paraphrased sentence is

iwan-ga hebinokuni-kara sat-ta
iwan-Nom the land of snake-from leave-PAST
(Iwan left the land of snake.)

The PT can provide the alternative information in which the case marker *wo* can be converted to *kara* in this *Move_from* concept. The PT also provides other predicates with the same concept such as *de-ta* (leave-PAST) and *shukkoku-shita* (leave one's country-PAST); however, incorrect candidates also generated since the PT does not contain detailed selection restrictions of predicates. For example, *shukkou-shita* (depart from a port-PAST) is a predicate categorized in *Move_from* concept, but *iwan-ga hebinokuni-kara shukkou-shita* (Iwan departed from a port of the land of snake) is not a paraphrase of the above sentence because the subject of *shukkou-shita* should be a ship or should be on board a ship. Instead of having selection restrictions of predicates, the PT contains example sentences in each predicate. Thus a paraphrasing system should have a mechanism to select a correct paraphrase from candidates utilizing example sentences.

## Connecting Sentences

Modification of connecting sentences is essential to revise texts of event-based sentence sequences because sentences must not be isolated but have mutual relationships between them. Thus, to clarify the relationships, semantic roles for predicates are used. For example, there are two sentences outputted from the AI-based system.

iwan-ga hebi-to tatakat-ta. iwan-ga ude-wo hebi-de fusyousi-ta.
iwan-NOM snake-with fight-PAST iwan-Nom arm-ACC snake-by wound-PAST
(Iwan fought the snake. Iwan was wounded in his arm by the snake.)

The two sentences should be connected because the cause of the injury described in the second sentence is the *fight* expressed in the first sentence. If the system can recognize a nominative of fight, i.e., *tatakai* (a fight), as the *Reason*, the two sentences can be combined into a sentence using the PT.

iwan-ga hebi-to tatakat-ta-ga, iwan-ga ude-wo
iwan-NOM snake-with fight-PAST-but iwan-Nom arm-ACC
Semantic role: But Experiencer Theme (BodyPart)
hebi-to-no-tatakai-de fusyousi-ta.
snake-with-fight-by was wounded-PAST
Reason
(Iwan fought the snake, but his hand was wounded in the fight with the snake.)

The PT provides the case marker *de* of the noun phrase of *Reason* as well as the base case pattern *ga* and *wo* of *fusyousuru* (be wounded). Since the conjunction *ga* (but) is also defined as the semantic role *But,* the system can output the case marker *ga* if it recognizes that the second sentence is contrasted with the first. The grammatical modification is partially proposed as an interaction narrative generation system (Montfort, 2006) in English; however, automatic modification as a module of a narrative generation system has not been addressed.

## Validation of Consistency between Sentences

The consistency between sentences can be checked using conceptual structure defined in PT. Base policy of the consistency validation is the sentences are inconsistent if and only if the restriction of concepts of the sentences are conflicted. The number of types of concepts is currently about 1080, that is, not so many. Thus, this validation is done on the abstracted level of change-of-state. The following example sentences are come from the short story[6].

N hakase-ha robotto-wo tsukuriageta. sorekara itsumo sobani-oku.
Dr. N-Nom robot-ACC finish to make-PAST after that usually keep at his side
(Dr. N made a robot. After that, he keeps the robot at his side. He always goes together with
dokokae iku-tokimo kanarazu issho-datta.
anywhere when he goes always together-PAST
the robot anywhere he goes.)

In the first sentence, the concept of *X make Y* in PT is *Generate*, which indicates that artifacts exist after they are generated. Thus, after the first sentence, the robot exists and the following two sentences are allowed to mention the robot. From the view of discourse technique of narrative, the second and the third sentences are almost the same meaning, i.e., *Dr. N keeps the robot at his side*. That is, repeating the same meaning with paraphrased sentences; and then the third sentence must be an additional description, i.e., catalyzer. Thus this example text shows that paraphrase and consistency check are the key technologies to make real narrative texts.

The next example text is also come from the short story.
robotto-ha nigedashi-ta. N si-ha oikake-ta-ga tsukamae-rare-nai.
robot-Nom run away -Past Dr. N-Nom chase-PAST-but catch-can-not
(The robot run away. Dr. N chased the robot but he could not catch it.)

The concept of the predicate *nigedasu* (run away) is *Move_from* and the concept of *tsukamaeru* (catch) is *Chase*, however, the predicate of the second sentence is *tsukamae-rare-nai* (cannot catch). Since there is no confliction between two sentences, the text is validated as consistent. As can be seen the example the consistent validation is a moderate check.

## DISCUSSIONS

### Comparing with Other Resources

The PT was manually constructed from the base Japanese dictionary Lexeed (Kasahara et al., 2004), which contains about 11,900 predicates and meanings for each predicate. By categorizing predicates, *CAUSE*, *BECOME*, and *BE* according to the base decompositional framework, we found a wide variety among them. For example, the concept *Move_one's_possession_from*, whose base TLCS is (CAUSE [i]) [BECOME [[j], BE [AT [i]]]], has the following subordinated concepts.

*Buy* whose predicates are *kau (buy)* and *kounyuusuru (purchase)*,
*Borrow_or_rent* whose predicates are *kariru, (borrow/rent)* and *yatou (hire)*,
*Recapture* whose predicates are *dakkaisuru (recapture)* and *torikaesu (get back)*, and
*Plunder* whose predicates are *ubau (rob)*, *nusumu (steal)* and *hittakuru (snatch)*.
The TLCS of each concept is

Buy: (CAUSE [i]) (BY MEANS OF [i] buying [j]) [BECOME [[j], AT[i]]]
Borrow_or_rent: (CAUSE [i]) (BY MEANS OF [i] borrow_or_renting [j])
[BECOME [[j], AT[i]]]
Recapture: (CAUSE [i]) (BY MEANS OF [i] recapturing [j]) [BECOME [[j], AT[i]]]
Plunder: (CAUSE [i]) (BY MEANS OF [i] plundering [j]) [BECOME [[j], AT[i]]].

These TLCSs show that the shared features of these concepts are the *Agent* i obtains the *Theme* j and finally *Theme* j exists on *Agent* i, and the different points among these concepts are the way the *Agent* obtains the *Theme*. Thus, a TLCS points out the abstracted differences between concepts and does not break down the meaning of internal primitives such as *buying* and *borrow_or_renting*. Jackendoff (1990, p. 61) assumed the argument *Money* with his LCS and described exchanging money with buying. From the viewpoint of constructing an ontology, Jackendoff's LCS is interesting; however, the LCS must be very complicated to differentiate the meaning of English *borrow*, *rent*, *recapture*, and *plunder*. Thus, the TLCS can be more suitable for understanding the total types of predicates by maintaining an abstracted level of the conceptual structure.

The hierarchical structure can break down a concept into as many detailed concepts as possible, but currently does not contain overly detailed concepts. For example, *ubau (rob)* and *nusumu (steal)* are categorized into the *Plunder* concept, but the English verbs *rob* and *steal* are different in the manner of affecting other people (Goldberg, 1995, p. 45). Since every verb must have a different meaning, the current thesaurus provides rough categorization from the viewpoint of similar manners and results.

Some verbs have a closed meaning with other verbs in a different viewpoint. A well-known pair is the English verbs *buy* and *sell* in a commerce situation (Fillmore, 1977). The Japanese verbs *kau (buy)* and *uru (sell)* are also the same as in English. Then let us compare the difference in analysis for these verbs with the proposed PT and FN.

taro-ha hanako-kara hon-wo kat-ta
Taro-TOP Hanako-from book-ACC buy-PAST
PT: Agent Source (Person) Theme Buy
FN: Buyer Seller Goods Commerce_buy
(Taro bought the book from Hanako.)
hanako-ha taro-ni hon-wo ut-ta
Hanako-TOP Taro-to book-ACC sell-PAST
PT: Agent Goal (Person) Theme Sell
FN: Seller Buyer Goods Commerce_sell
(Hanako sold the book to Taro.)

The proposed PT differentiates the two concepts *Buy* and *Sell*; thus, it cannot provide the closed relations between the *Agent* of *buy* and the *Goal (Person)* of *sell*. This is because the PT does not take care the predicates from a different viewpoint to maintain semantic role types to a minimum. FrameNet can provide the closed relations between two verbs and the arguments are connected to consistent relation types, i.e., *Seller*, *Buyer* and *Goods*; thus, FN has a more detailed framework that has more semantic role types than the PT. A scene, called a Frame, is assumed with FN, and FN maintains a consistent set of labels of arguments in the Frame. However, it cannot be certain that such a scene has been previously defined, especially from different viewpoints (Takeuchi et al., 2010). In the example assuming a situation in which parents will leave their child in a nursery school, the following two sentences can be closely related from either of two viewpoints, the parents or the school:

The parents viewpoint:
oya-ga kodomo-wo hoikuen-ni azukeru
parent-NOM (their) child-ACC nursery school-to leave someone in the care of
Agent Theme Theme (Person)
(The parents leave their child in the care of a nursery school.)
The school viewpoint:
hoikuen-ga kodomo-wo azukaru
nursery school-NOM (their) child-ACC look after, take someone under one's care
Agent Theme
(The nursery school looks after their child).

Since *azukeru* and *azukaru* are Japanese verbs, Frames that can provide the closed relations between two sentences cannot be found. Related Frames are found, e.g., *Being_obligated* and *Being_obligatory*, but the example sentences do not match the above sentences. Thus, it does not seem to be easy to prepare Frames by taking into account different viewpoints. The Japanese verb *azukaru* is an intransitive form of *azukeru*; therefore, they are the same verb. The two verbs are under the same concept, then in the PT *nursery school* and *their child* are linked to the same argument in the TLCS via a linking marker independent of semantic roles.

## Contribution of Lexical Resource to Narrative Texts

In the previous section, we discussed the possibility of contributing to enriching narrative texts, i.e., paraphrasing, connecting sentences, validating of consistency between sentences. In this section we discuss obstacles to these three contributions.

The paraphrasing function requires a system of semantic roles and predicate concept analyzer. The current accuracy of the analyzer is not high (Takeuchi, Tsuchiyama, Moriya, Moriyasu, & Satoh, 2011); however, the accuracy should be improved by expanding the annotation corpus (Takeuchi, Ueno, & Takeuchi, 2015).

For connecting sentences, the system requires several pieces of information about the sentences and story, i.e., which sentences should be connected semantic relations in the target relations, and appropriate modification rules based on the PT.

For validating consistency, the granularity of the conceptual structure in PT is abstracted; thus, the validation does not work well in some cases. The example text is as follows.

robotto-ga oikaketekuru. N si-ha ki-ni nobot-te
robot-Nom chase Dr. N-Nom tree-Loc clime up-and
(The robot chased Dr. N. He survived by climbing up and hiding in a tree.)
kakureru-koto-de tasukat-ta.
hide-to-by survive-PAST

These sentences contain four predicates, *oikakaru* (chase), *noboru* (clime up), *kakureru* (hide), and *tasukaru* (survive). Simple application of concepts in the PT to the predicates, however, will determine *noboru* (clime up) and *kakureru* (hide) as in conflict because of their different class of concepts. A person can understand *ki-ni noboru* (clime up a tree) is an action to understand *kakureru* (hide). These types of action-cause chains must be an issue of common sense reasoning. We now have many texts such as Wikipedia, as well as language resources; therefore, statistical approaches might be helpful in extracting knowledge of action-event chains.

## FUTURE RESEARCH DIRECTIONS

There are three directions of future work concerning the PT. The first direction is the contribution of natural language processing (NLP) systems, that is, to reveal the effectiveness of the PT for natural language understanding tasks. In the recent research on NLP, abstracted meaning representation (AMR)[7] was proposed and has been applied to improving the question and answering (QA) tasks. Thus, how to apply semantic relations described in the PT to the NLP system must be one of the principal themes. The second direction is to extend the size of the PT, i.e., increase the number of annotated example sentences and lexicons (Takeuchi et al., 2015). As shown in Table 1, the PT is smaller than JWN, which is widely used in the NLP system. Thus, the method for extending the PT by using EDR and JWN should be investigated. The third direction is to extend the framework of the PT. In the textual entailment recognition task, the argument structure of nouns is a key factor (Takeuchi, Ishihara, & Takeuchi, 2014). Thus, how to define consistent argument structures of nouns and incorporate nouns into the PT should be investigated.

## CONCLUSION

In this chapter, the possibility of language resources to determine the states, actions, and change-of-states of characters in narratives was discussed. An overview of previous work of linguistic theory and language resources was given then the PT, a Japanese language resource constructed based on the extended framework of the LCS, was proposed. The PT provides hierarchical clusters of synonyms for

*Table 1. Statistics of PT and comparing it to other Japanese language resources*

| | EDR (Ver 3.0) | JWordNet (Ver 1.1) | IPAL | PT |
|---|---|---|---|---|
| Words | 410000 | 93,834 | 2108 | 11,914 |
| Verbs | 91154 | 15,445 | 861 | 9130 |
| Word meanings | 270000 | 158,058 | 22,370 | 1084 |
| Concepts | 430000 | 57,238 (synsets) | N/A | 1084 |
| Example sentences | 210000 | 48,276 | 22,370 | 23,164 |
| Semantic role types | 28 | N/A | 43 | 72 |
| POS | all | Verb, Noun, Adjective, Adverb | Verb, Noun, Adjective, Adjectival verb | Verb, Adjective, Adjectival verb |

11,900 predicates and 22,000 example sentences annotated with semantic role labels. Each concept has an abstracted LCS, and example sentences are attached to each concept. By virtue of the structure, a correlation of the arguments between other clusters can be determined. The semantic structure of the PT is attempted to enrich generated texts of narratives, and high possibilities of contribution of lexical semantics to narrative processing are revealed.

## REFERENCES

Akimoto, T., & Ogata, T. (2011a). Computational model of narrative discourse theory and reception theory in narratology and its implementation. In *Proceedings of the 13th Annual Conference of the Japanese Society for Language Sciences* (pp. 155-156). Suita, Japan: Academic Press.

Akimoto, T., & Ogata, T. (2011b). A consideration of the elements for narrative generation and a trial of integrated narrative generation system. In *Proceedings of the 7th International Conference on Natural Language Processing and Knowledge Engineering* (pp. 369-377). Tokushima, Japan. doi:10.1109/NLPKE.2011.6138227

Akimoto, T., & Ogata, T. (2013). Towards a discourse mechanism in narrative generation system: Proposal of a system introducing narrative discourse theory and reception theory. *Cognitive Studies*, *20*(4), 396–420.

Arai, H. (1985). *Shinariwo no kiso gijyutsu* [Base techniques for making a scenario]. Tokyo, Japan: Davidsha.

Baker, C., Fillmore, C. J., & Lowe, J. B. (1998). The Berkeley FrameNet project. In *Proceedings of the 36th Annual Meeting of the Association for Computational Linguistics* (pp. 86-90). Montreal, Canada: Association for Computational Linguistics. doi:10.3115/980845.980860

Baker, S. (2012). *Final Jeopardy: The story of Watson, the computer that will transform our world.* Boston, MA: Mariner Book.

Barthes, R. (1966). Introduction à l'analyse structurale des récits. *Communications*, *8*(1), 1–27. doi:10.3406/comm.1966.1113

Dorr, B. J. (1997). Large-scale dictionary construction for foreign language tutoring and inter-lingual machine translation. *Machine Translation*, *12*(4), 271–322. doi:10.1023/A:1007965530302

Fellbaum, C. (1998). *WordNet: an electronic lexical database*. Cambridge, MA: MIT Press.

Fillmore, C. (1968). The case for case. In E. Bach & R. T. Harms (Eds.), *Universals in linguistic theory* (pp. 1–89). New York, NY: Holt, Rinehart, and Winston.

Fillmore, C. (1977). Topics in lexical semantics. In R. W. Cole (Ed.), *Current issues in linguistic theory* (pp. 76–138). Indianapolis, IN: Indiana University Press.

Genette, G. (1972). Discours du récit. essai de méthode, Figures III. Paris, France: Seuil.

Goldberg, A. E. (1995). *Constructions: a construction grammar approach to argument structure*. Chicago, IL: University of Chicago.

Grimshaw, J. (1992). *Argument structure*. Cambridge, MA: MIT Press.

Gruber, J. S. (1965). *Studies in lexical relations*. (Doctoral dissertation). Available from http://hdl.handle.net/1721.1/13010

Halliday, M. A. K. (1975). Language as social semiotic: towards a general sociolinguistic theory. In A. Makkai & V. B. Makkai (Eds.), *The First LACUS Forum*, (pp. 17-46). London: Hornbeam Press.

Hoshi, S. (1975). *Hoshi Shinichi no sakuhin syuu XV* [Anthology of Shinichi Hoshi XV]. Tokyo, Japan: Shinchosha.

Huang, C. R., Calzolari, N., Gangemi, A., Lenci, A., Oltramari, A., & Prevot, L. (2010). *Ontology and the lexicon*. Cambridge, UK: Cambridge University Press. doi:10.1017/CBO9780511676536

Jackendoff, R. S. (1972). *Semantic interpretation in generative grammar*. Cambridge, MA: MIT Press.

Jackendoff, R. S. (1983). *Semantics and cognition*. Cambridge, MA: MIT Press.

Jackendoff, R. S. (1990). *Semantic structures*. Cambridge, MA: MIT Press.

Japan Electronic Dictionary Research Institute. (1995). *EDR: electric dictionary the second edition* [Data file]. Retrieved from https://www2.nict.go.jp/out-promotion/techtransfer/EDR/ index.html

Jauss, H. R. (1970). Literaturgeschichte als provokation. Frankfurt am Main: Suhrkamp Verlag.

Kageyama, T. (1996). *Doushi imiron* [Verb semantics]. Tokyo, Japan: Kurosio Publishers.

Kasahara, K., Sato, H., Bond, F., Tanaka, T., Fujita, S., Kanasugi, T., & Amano, S. (2004). Construction of a Japanese semantic lexicon: Lexeed. In Special Interest Group Technical Reports of Information Processing Society Japan, 2004(1(2003-NL-159)) (pp. 75-82).

Kipper, S. K. (2005). *VerbNet: a broad-coverage, comprehensive verb lexicon* (Doctoral dissertation). Available from ProQuest Dissertations and Theses database. (Paper AAI3179808)

Kuwahara, W., Hasimoto, M., & Murata, K. (1993). Keisankiyou nihongo jishono kaihatsu [On the lexicon of Japanese basic verbs, adjectives, and nouns]. In Special Interest Group Technical Reports of Information Processing Society Japan, 1993(42(1993-CH-018)) (pp. 27-34).

Langacker, R. W. (1986). An introduction to cognitive grammar. *Cognitive Science*, *10*(1), 1–40. doi:10.1207/s15516709cog1001_1

Levin, B. (1993). *English verb classes and alternations*. Chicago, IL: University of Chicago Press.

Lönneker, B. (2005). Narratological knowledge for natural language generation. In *Proceedings of the 10th European Workshop on Natural Language Generation* (pp. 91-100). Aberdeen, UK: Association for Computational Linguistics.

Loper, R., Yi, S., & Palmer, M. (2007). Combining lexical resources: mapping between PropBank and VerbNet. In *Proceedings of the 7th International Workshop on Computational Semantics*. Tilburg, Netherland: Academic Press.

Marcus, M. P., Santorini, B., & Marcinkiewicz, M. A. (1993). Building a large annotated corpus of English: The Penn treebank. *Computational Linguistics, 19*(2), 313–330.

McCawley, J. D. (1968). Lexical insertion in a transformational grammar without deep structure. In *Fourth Regional Meeting of the Chicago Linguistic Society* (pp. 71-80). Chicago: Linguistics Department, University of Chicago.

Montfort, N. (2006). Natural language generation and narrative variation in interactive fiction. In *Proceedings of Computational Aesthetics: Artificial Intelligence Approaches to Beauty and Happiness:Papers from the 2006 AAAI Workshop* (pp. 45-52). Menlo Park, CA: AAAI Press.

Ogata, T., & Kanai, A. (2010). *Monogatariron no jouhougaku jyosetsu* [An introduction of informatics of narratology: on thought and technology of narrative generation 1]. Tokyo, Japan: Gakubunsha.

Ohara, K. H., Fujii, S., Saito, H., Ishizaki, S., Ohori, T., & Suzuki, R. (2003). *The Japanese FrameNet project: a preliminary report*. Poster presented at the Pacific Association for Computational Linguistics, Halifax, Canada.

Palmer, M. (2009). SemLink: linking PropBank, VerbNet and FrameNet. In *Proceedings of the Generative Lexicon Conference*. Pisa, Italy: Academic Press.

Palmer, M., Gildea, D., & Kingsbury, P. (2005). The proposition bank: An annotated corpus of semantic roles. *Computational Linguistics, 31*(1), 71–106. doi:10.1162/0891201053630264

Propp, V. A. (1968). *Morphology of the folktale* (L. Scott, Trans.). Austin, TX: University of Texas.

Study Group of Written Japanese Grammar. (2009). *Contemporary Japanese grammar 2: Syntax and Voice*. Tokyo, Japan: Kurosio Publishers.

Takeuchi, K., Inui, K., Takeuchi, N., & Fujita, A. (2010). A thesaurus of predicate-argument structure for Japanese verbs to deal with granularity of verb meanings. In *Proceedings of the 8th Workshop on Asian Language Resources* (pp. 1-8). Beijing, China: Academic Press.

Takeuchi, K., Ishihara, Y., & Takeuchi, N. (2014). Discussion on semantic structure of nouns from the view of predicate argument structure thesaurus. In *Proceedings of the 28th Annual Conference of the Japanese Society for Artificial Intelligence* (2I5-OS-08b-1). Matsuyama, Japan: Academic Press.

Takeuchi, K., Tsuchiyama, S., Moriya, M., Moriyasu, Y., & Satoh, K. (2011). Verb sense disambiguation based on thesaurus of predicate-argument structure. In *Proceedings of International Conference on Knowledge Engineering and Ontology Development* (pp. 208-213). Setúbal, Portugal: Science and Technology Publications.

Takeuchi, K., Ueno, M., & Takeuchi, N. (2015) Annotating semantic role information to Japanese balanced corpus. In *Proceedings of MAPLEX 2015*. Tendo, Japan: Academic Press.

Vendler, Z. (1967). *Linguistics in philosophy*. Ithaca, NY: Cornell University Press.

Winograd, T. (1972). *Understanding natural language*. New York, NY: Academic Press.

Winograd, T. (1983). *Syntax*. Boston, MA: Addison-Wesley Publishing.

## KEY TERMS AND DEFINITIONS

**Adjunct:** A type of semantic relation between a chunk and a verb. This semantic relation indicates that it is not an essential argument but can occur with any predicate, e.g., time and location.

**Lexical Conceptual Structure:** A framework of describing meaning for predicates. Each structure consists of combinations of a primitive and its arguments. It has a transparent structure for grammatical modifications.

**Lexicon:** An ideal organized word dictionary that would exist in human brain.

**Predicate-Argument Structure:** A method of describing semantic relations between a predicate and its arguments. Each argument normally has different semantic relations; thus, the combinations of semantic relations compose a structure.

**Primitive:** A base semantic factor composed of conceptual structures.

**Semantic Role Label:** A semantic relation type between predicate and its argument.

**Thesaurus:** A framework of organizing hierarchical concepts of nodes.

## ENDNOTES

1 The example text is the output of the narrative generation system (Akimoto & Ogata, 2013). The text is not natural; however, the aim of the system is not to generate natural texts but to generate a correct discourse structure controlled by the discourse theories (Genette, 1972). Thus, natural text generation is the next step of the narrative generation study.

2 We accessed http://jfn.st.hc.keio.ac.jp/ on June 17 2015.

3 Example sentences are described in English in this chapter, however, Japanese predicates and sentences are actually described in the thesaurus.

4 Hereafter conceptual nodes are described in abbreviated form.

5 All types of semantic role are described at http://pth.cl.cs.okayama-u.ac.jp/.

6 Example sentences are partially extracted from the original short story because the original text is long.

7 We accessed http://amr.isi.edu/language.html on June 30 2015.

# Chapter 8
# The Word Order Flexibility in Japanese Novels:
## A Dynamic Syntax Perspective

**Tohru Seraku**
*Hankuk University of Foreign Studies, Korea*

**Akira Ohtani**
*Osaka Gakuin University, Japan*

## ABSTRACT

*In Japanese, whose basic word-order is S(ubject)-O(bject)-V(erb), non-verbal elements may be permuted with the restriction that such elements cannot occur post-verbally. This restriction, however, does not apply to narrative discourse, especially conversations in novels. This discourse phenomenon with post-verbal elements is called "postposing." This chapter reveals several grammatical properties of postposing based on Japanese novels, and present an explicit account in an integrated theory of grammar. More precisely, the narrative data indicate that the syntactic type of postposed element is quite diverse and that, contrary to the prevalent, opposing view, Japanese postposing is not restricted to a matrix clause. These issues are addressed within Dynamic Syntax, a cognitively realistic grammar formalism which specifies a set of constraints on building up a structure online. This architectural design formalises the incremental process of how the reader gradually updates an interpretation by parsing a postposing sentence in narrative discourse.*

## INTRODUCTION

Japanese has been extensively explored from diverse perspectives, ranging from linguistics, literature, psychology, sociology, cognitive science, computer science to brain science (among many other fields). In general, languages exhibit distinct characteristics depending on speech/writing genres. A type of linguistic construction which is typically observed in colloquial dialogue/discourse would be "postposing," where a non-verbal item is positioned post-verbally. This is illustrated in (1)-(3) below, taken from novels, with postposed elements being underlined. (See the Appendix for the method of citation of data and References for the list of novels cited.)

DOI: 10.4018/978-1-5225-0432-0.ch008

Copyright © 2016, IGI Global. Copying or distributing in print or electronic forms without written permission of IGI Global is prohibited.

1. *Holmes tte iu-no, sono-neko*
   H QUOT say-FP that-cat
   'That cat is called Holmes.' (Akagawa, 2015, p. 44)

2. *onaji-kurasu-no-Hiroki-kun-da, bokura-to-wa-bessekai-no*
   the.same-class-GEN-H-N.SU-COP we-and-TOP-another.world-GEN
   'He is Hiroki from our classroom, living in a different world from us.' (Asai, 2012, p. 126, adapted)

3. *'kekkoudesu' jya-nai-ndatte dakara*
   'ok' COP-NEG-FP as.I.said
   'As I said, it's not 'ok'.' (Arikawa, 2010a, p. 71)

The postposed items in these examples are the NP (Noun Phrase) *sono-neko* 'that cat' in (1), the Noun-Modifier (genitive) *boku-to-wa-bessekai-no* 'living in a different world from us' in (2), and finally the Connective *dakara* 'as I said' in (3).

The postposing phenomenon is specific to colloquial dialogue/discourse. To illustrate the point, let us briefly summarise the word order issues in Japanese. Firstly, the basic word order is S(ujbect)-O(bject)-V(erb), as in (4). According to Dryer (2013), the S-O-V order constitutes the largest group, encompassing 565 languages out of the 1377 world languages.

4. *Ken-ga sushi-o tabe-ta*
   K-NOM sushi-ACC eat-PAST
   'Ken ate sushi.'

Secondly, despite the basic order, Japanese allows non-verbal items to be permuted, with the prescriptive restriction that such items cannot be placed after a verb. So, the O-S-V order (5) is possible with the same meaning as expressed by (4). This word-permutation is called "scrambling" in linguistics (Saito, 1985).

5. [different order from (4) but (truth-conditionally) the same meaning as (4)]
   *sushi-o Ken-ga tabe-ta*
   sushi-ACC K-NOM eat-PAST

Thirdly, due to the prescriptive restriction aforementioned, the postposed sentence like (6) is considered to be the "wrong use of language" in formal speech/writing, although it is indeed attested in colloquial form of dialogue/discourse as has been exemplified in (1)-(3) above.

6. [prescriptively incorrect, but attested in narratives]
   *Ken-ga tabe-ta, sushi-o*
   K-NOM eat-PAST sushi-ACC

Compared to other phenomena pertaining to word orders, such as scrambling (see (5)), postposing has received less attention in linguistics and related fields. Against this situation, then, the present chapter first sets out a solid empirical ground of the study on postposing by describing the grammatical properties of the construction in Japanese novels and presenting generalisations based on these data. The chapter then proceeds to develop an explicit account within a formal grammar framework.

More precisely, we have collected naturally-occurring data on postposing from the conversational part of Japanese novels. As will be stated in the "Clarifying the Theme" section, postposing is frequently observed in both colloquial dialogue and discourse, but it is at present difficult to extract relevant data (semi-)automatically from, e.g., dialogue corpora (Guo & Den, 2012; Nomura, 2008). Further, postposing in novels exhibits distinctive discourse properties which are not observed in postposing in dialogue (Seraku, 2015). In particular, the investigation of Japanese novels reveals that a wider array of syntactic element may be postposed than has been assumed in the past literature. This syntactic flexibility poses a challenge for grammar modelling, and we propose a specific solution within Dynamic Syntax (DS) (Cann, Kempson, & Marten, 2005). Further narrative findings will be provided to support this cognitively-oriented grammar account. These data will be useful for research on formal grammar as well as discourse modelling in general. On the other hand, there is an advantage of adopting DS. First, it captures a cognitive feature of language use: the incrementality of comprehending a sentence in speech/writing (Kamide, 2006; Kiaer, 2014). The formal tools defined in this framework are used to provide a cognitively-realistic model of the incremental process of comprehending a postposed string. Second, a growing body of research has been conducted which implements a DS theoretical model for parsing and natural language generation (Eshghi, Purver, & Hough, 2011; Eshghi, Purver, Hough, & Sato, 2013; Purver, Hough, & Gregoromichelaki, 2014). These computational works have primarily targeted English; thus, in order to apply them to Japanese, it is important to first establish an empirical ground and an explicit theoretical model. These are the tasks which the present chapter is concerned with.

## BACKGROUND

### Previous Studies

Japanese postposing, a prescriptively incorrect but well-attested phenomenon where a non-verbal element appears post-verbally, has been hotly debated in language studies from diverse angles: (1) theoretical syntax, (2) functionally-oriented syntax, and (3) dialogue/discourse studies.

In theoretical syntax, the grammatical aspects of postposing have been analysed (Takano, 2014; Takita, 2014; Tanaka, 2001). This research strand is primarily based on data constructed by scholars; in the present chapter, spontaneous data on postposing will be systematically provided, which serve as an empirical basis of our analysis. In all previous studies in this syntactic approach, the core of analysis is "movement" and/or "deletion," syntactic operations posited in what Culicover and Jackendoff (2005) dub "mainstream generative grammar" (Chomsky, 1995). In simple terms, "movement" is an operation to displace a syntactic item at a different site in a syntactic structure; "deletion" is an operation to omit the phonological part of a syntactic item in a structure. For instance, Tanaka (2001) advocates an analysis in virtue of these operations (see, *inter alia*, Abe (1999) and Takita (2014) for similar proposals); a syntactic derivation for the postposed string (7) is shown in (8). Δ designates a position where the postposed item *sushi-o* is located in the basic word order. The co-indexed relation with the subscript $_i$ means that a phonetically null item at the Δ position is co-referent with the postposed item *sushi-o*.

7. *Ken-ga* $\Delta_i$ *tabe-ta,* <u>*sushi-o*</u>$_i$
   K-NOM eat-PAST sushi-ACC
   'Ken ate sushi.'

8. Tanaka's (2001) "movement/deletion" analysis
   1st stage: Juxtaposition of two clause structures
   [*Ken-ga* $\Delta_i$ *tabe-ta*] [*Ken-ga* *sushi-o*$_i$ *tabe-ta*]

   2nd stage: Movement of the postposed item *sushi-o* in the second structure
   [*Ken-ga* $\Delta_i$ *tabe-ta*] [*sushi-o*$_i$ [*Ken-ga* $t_i$ *tabe-ta*]]

   3rd stage: Deletion of everything but the postposed item in the second structure
   [*Ken-ga* $\Delta_i$ *tabe-ta*] [*sushi-o*$_i$ ~~[*Ken-ga* $t_i$ *tabe-ta*]~~]

At the 1st stage in (8), a postposed sentence consists of two parallel structures, the sole difference being that an object position is inhabited by a phonetically null item in the first structure and by the overt form *sushi-o* in the second structure. At the 2nd stage, *sushi-o* is dislocated to the clause-initial position in the second structure. ($t_i$ is a trace of the moved item.) At the 3rd stage, everything but *sushi-o* is phonetically deleted, as visually shown by crossing-out. These processes output the surface string (7). For a critical review of these syntactic approaches, see Takita (2014).

In functionally-oriented syntax, the syntactic/pragmatic aspects of postposing have been handled in "functional" terms (Kuno, 1978; Takami, 1995). A representative example is Kuno's (1978) analysis based on information incompatibility. It is well known that the postposing of a *wh*-phrase is not possible in Japanese. This is exemplified in (9), where * indicates that the sentence is ungrammatical.

9. a. *Ken-ga* *nani-o* *tabe-ta-no*
   K-NOM what-ACC eat-PAST-Q
   'What did Ken eat?'
   b. **Ken-ga* *tabe-ta-no,* <u>*nani-o*</u>
   K-NOM eat-PAST-Q what-ACC

Kuno (1978) contends that the ungrammaticality of (9)b stems from the information incompatibility between the preceding clause and the postposed element. On the one hand, the preceding clause *Ken-ga tabe-ta-no* expresses a meaning relating to a polar question (i.e., *yes-no* question). On the other hand, the postposed element *nani-o* expresses a meaning relating to a *wh*-question. Thus, two distinct, incompatible types of interpretation emerge, and this incompatibility leads to the unacceptability of (9)b. This analysis is concisely displayed in (10).

10. Kuno's (1978) "functional" analysis
    *Ken-ga tabe-ta-no* → polar question: 'Did Ken eat it?'
    *nani-o* → *wh*-question: 'What did Ken eat?'
    mutually incompatible types of question

The data such as (9)b are not found in narratives because they are ungrammatical, in the first place. In our account, however, even such ungrammatical examples can be explained; see the analysis of (42) in the later section "Solutions and Recommendations."

In dialogue/discourse studies, semantic/pragmatic aspects of postposing are studied based on naturally-occurring data (Fujii, 1995; Nakagawa, Asao, & Nagaya, 2008; Nomura, 2008; Ono, 2006). Various discourse/dialogue functions of postposing have been detected. Some of them are not mutually exclusive, and a systematic organisation of these functions is still underway. One of the most comprehensive classifications is offered by Nomura (2008, ch. 2), who divides the postposing functions into three types: afterthought, emphasis, and defoccussing. These functions are important topics in the study of postposing, but the present chapter sets them aside because it concentrates on the grammatical (rather than semantic/pragmatic) facet of the phenomenon. We believe that an adequate account of dialogue/discourse functions should be built upon a solid grammatical foundation. (In this connection, see Purver et al. (2014) for the Dynamic Syntax modelling of the dialogue functions of split utterances in English.)

In these previous studies on Japanese postposing, there are still outstanding issues. First, the process of comprehending a postposed sentence in spontaneous context has been discussed in dialogue/discourse studies, but no formal analysis has been developed. Second, the grammatical aspects of postposing are widely examined in syntax research, but their claims are based on non-spontaneous data. Whilst the native speaker's introspections are useful, such data need to be empirically confirmed. This is where discourse/dialogue studies would come in, but as mentioned above, their main concern is the semantic/pragmatic (but not syntactic) aspects of postposing.

Unlike these past works, the present chapter relies on naturally-occurring materials in order to articulate a grammatical account of how the reader understands a postposed string incrementally in Japanese novels. This will be achieved within Dynamic Syntax, which will be introduced in the next subsection.

## Framework: Dynamic Syntax

This subsection concisely lays out Dynamic Syntax (DS). For a full introduction, see Cann et al. (2005) and Kempson, Meyer-Viol, and Gabbay (2001). For recent developments, see Kempson, Gregoromichelaki, and Howes (2011) and Orwin, Howes, and Kempson (2013). For Japanese applications, see Cann et al. (2005), Kempson and Kiaer (2010), and Seraku (2013).

DS is an explicit model of "knowledge of language" (or "linguistic competence"). In this sense, DS is regarded as "generative" grammar (Chomsky, 1965). Knowledge of language, however, is differently construed within DS; it is a set of constraints on language use, more particularly a set of procedures for building up an interpretation based on linear parsing. In this view of grammar, knowledge of language is a transparent reflection of language use. DS has been employed to model comprehension and production with the same machinery (Purver et al., 2014), but this chapter concentrates on comprehension, especially the incremental parsing process.

Another distinctive feature of DS is that it dispenses with syntactic representations. That is, a string of words is directly mapped onto a semantic structure without any separate level of syntactic representation. DS is a syntactic theory, but the concept of "syntax" here is nothing more than a set of procedures for constructing an interpretation in real time.

The two unique design-properties of DS have so far been set out:

- A structure is progressively updated as a string of words is parsed.
- There is no level of syntactic structure; a string is directly mapped onto a semantic structure.

In what follows, we shall clarify the "format" and "update" of a DS structure in turn.

Let us first delve into the DS format. A DS representation is expressed in a semantic tree. For instance, (11) is mapped onto the semantic tree (12). (The treatment of tense is disregarded; see Cann (2011).)

11. *Ken-ga* *sushi-o* *tabe-ta*
    K-NOM sushi-ACC eat-PAST
    'Ken ate sushi.'

12. Parsing the string (11)

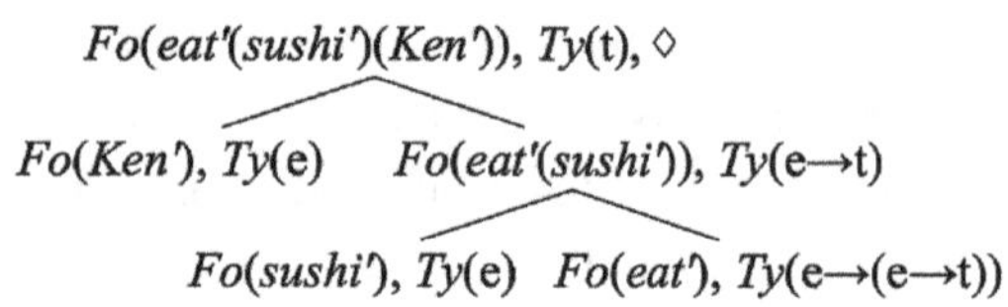


A non-terminal node is binary-branched, with the left daughter being an argument node and the right daughter being a functor node. Each node is decorated with two types of information: content and type. First, the content of *tabe* 'eat' (namely, the denotation of an eating action) is simply notated as *eat'*. This is a two-place predicate, taking *sushi'* as an internal argument and *Ken'* as an external argument. The notation *eat'(sushi')(Ken')* is essentially equivalent to the notation *eat'(Ken', sushi')*. Second, a logical type of content is explicated. The basic types are "type-e" and "type-t." A type-e content denotes an entity, while a type-t content denotes a truth-evaluable statement. Complex typing is based on these basic types; for instance, the type e→t designates a functor which takes a type-e content and returns a type-t content. Content and type information is expressed in statement form, with the use of the following predicates:

- ***Fo*(X):** *Fo* is a "formula" predicate which takes a content X as argument. *Fo(Ken')* declares that the content denoted at this node is *Ken'*.
- ***Ty*(X):** *Ty* is a "type" predicate which takes a type X as argument. *Ty*(e) declares that the content denoted at this node is of type e (denoting an entity).

The top node in (12) is also annotated with ◇, a pointer. The pointer highlights a node under development; there is only a single activated node at a time during DS tree-update.

More decorations on a node are revealed if we see a "partial" tree. For instance, the parse of *Ken-ga* outputs the tree (13).

13. Parsing *Ken-ga* in (11)

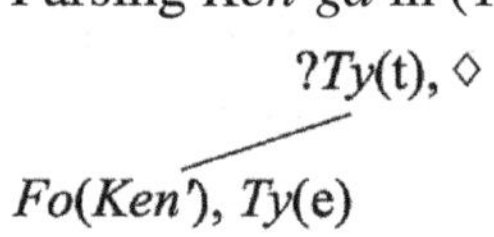

The symbol ? is used to form a requirement. For instance, ?*T*(t) requires that *Ty*(t) will hold at this node. As long as a tree contains outstanding requirements, the tree is incomplete. A DS tree is well-formed iff all requirements are satisfied. The tree (12) is well-formed because no requirements are left in the tree. A string of words is grammatical just in case there exists a parse-route that leads to a well-formed tree.

Now that the format of DS structure has been in place, let us consider how a DS structure is built up in an incremental fashion. The initial state of DS tree-update is defined as the Axiom (14).

14. Axiom (= the initial state)

?*Ty*(t), ◇

The parser progressively updates the initial state until a well-formed tree emerges by running the two types of action: "general" actions and "lexical" actions.

General actions are not lexically triggered and are optionally executed. For example, the general action of Local *Adjunction posits a structurally-unfixed node (i.e., node whose position in a tree is initially uncertain). In the left-hand tree of (15), the unfixed node (shown by a dashed line) may turn out to be a subject node, an object node, etc., at a later stage.

15.

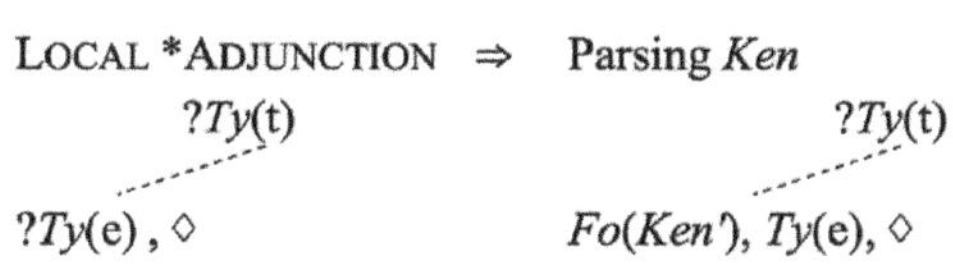


Lexical actions are those encoded in each lexical item. *Ken* encodes the lexical action to annotate a ?*Ty*(e)-node with *Fo*(*Ken'*) and *Ty*(e), as shown in the right-hand tree (15). The nominative case marker *ga* encodes the lexical action to resolve an unfixed node as a subject node, as shown in (16). (A solid line indicates that a structural uncertainty has been resolved.)

16. Parsing *Ken-ga*

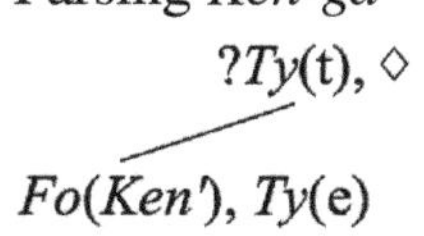


With the sequence of general and lexical actions, a DS tree is progressively updated. The tree (16) is further updated by the general action of Local *Adjunction, the lexical action of *sushi* (decorating the ?*Ty*(e)-node with *Fo*(*sushi'*) and *Ty*(e)), and the lexical action of the accusative case marker *o* (resolving the unfixed node as an object node). These processes are illustrated in (17).

17.

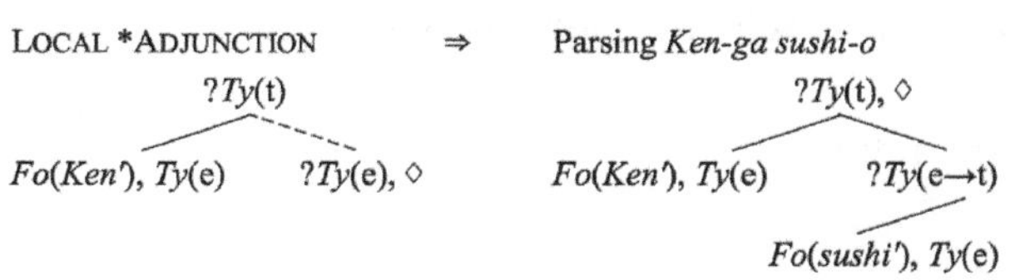

Finally, the parse of *tabe* 'eat' projects a predicate node, and the general action of ELIMINATION (i.e., functional application/type deduction) outputs the final state (18).

18. Parsing *Ken-ga sushi-o table-ta* + ELIMINATION (= the final state)

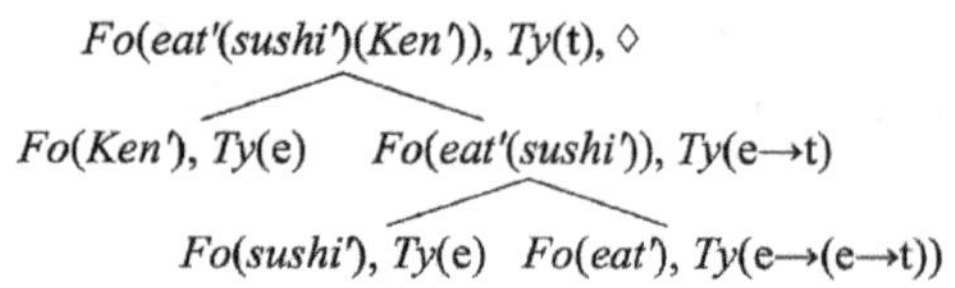


As a DS structure is semantic, it represents the proposition expressed by the string parsed in context. More specifically, the *Fo*-statement at the root node in (18) represents the content of the string parsed: 'Ken ate sushi.'

A DS structure is said to be "well-formed" iff every requirement such as ?*Ty*(t) has been satisfied in the tree. A string parsed is then said to be "grammatical" if there is a parse-route which maps the string onto a well-formed structure.

Exactly the same set of actions used for parsing (11) is run to parse the scrambling analogue (19).

19. *sushi-o* *Ken-ga* *tabe-ta*
sushi-ACC K-NOM eat-PAST
'Ken ate sushi.'

The parse of (19) produces the same tree as (18); what differs is the order in which two unfixed nodes are decorated and resolved. That is, whilst two unfixed nodes are decorated/resolved by *Ken-ga* and *sushi-o* (in this order) in (11), they are decorated/resolved by *sushi-o* and *Ken-ga* (in this order) in (19). For instance, the parse of *sushi-o* leads to the tree (20); the parse of the rest of the string outputs the tree identical to (18).

20. Parsing *sushi-o*

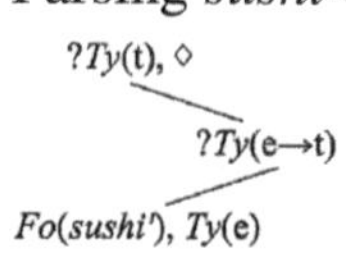


The upshot is that a surface-oriented grammar like DS captures word order variation by reflecting the linear sequence of words parsed.

Crucially for our discussion, LOCAL *ADJUNCTION prohibits the placement of an element at a post-verbal position. In the DS literature (Cann et al., 2005, ch. 6), LOCAL *ADJUNCTION is defined so as to be inapplicable if a current node is decorated with *Ty*(t), as schematically shown in (21).

21. LOCAL*ADJUNCTION (prohibited in the DS literature)

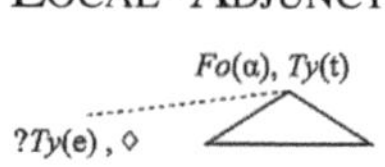

*Ty*(t) declares that a propositional content α is present. This means that LOCAL *ADJUNCTION cannot fire if the parser has processed a verbal item (which projects the core of a propositional structure). Therefore, this action cannot be used to parse a postposed element. For instance, it renders the postposed sentence (22) as ungrammatical because a *Ty*(t)-statement has been present before the parse of *sushi*, even though such examples are attested in colloquial form of language.

22. *Ken-ga* *tabe-ta,* <u>*sushi-o*</u>
K-NOM eat-PAST sushi-ACC
'Ken ate sushi.'

As will be proposed later, this apparent dilemma is solved by relaxing the *Ty*(t)-constraint in colloquial speech/writing. Apart from this proposed relaxing of the constraint, the mechanisms for capturing word order variation in Japanese straightforwardly carry over to the postposing construction.

## ISSUES AND PROBLEMS

### Clarifying the Theme

This chapter is devoted to the grammatical modelling of how the reader processes a postposed sentence incrementally in Japanese novels. In order to explicate the ideas behind this enterprise, let us step back and answer the following fundamental questions:

- Why does this chapter care about postposing (rather than other linguistic constructions)?
- Why does this chapter care about novels (rather than other speech/writing genres)?
- Why does this chapter target Japanese (rather than other languages)?

First, unlike the other word-order phenomena like scrambling, postposing is prescriptively regarded as the "wrong use of language" and is normally not attested in formal speech/writing. Postposing, however, is often found in narratives, and it may be considered to be a factor which characterises narratives. It is thus likely that the detailed examination of postposing will shed light on some grammatical properties specific to the narrative genre. This also raises the question of how to model grammar variations reflected in various speech/writing genres.

Second, postposing is also observed in speech/dialogue materials. Such data, however, often involve multiple sentences simultaneously uttered by distinct speakers, which makes it harder to detect a set of postposed sentences accurately. Consider the example (23) (adapted from Nomura (2008, p. 24)).

23. 1. **A:** *date* *akireteru-mon* <u>*minna*</u>
Because amazed-NML everyone
'Because everyone is simply amazed.'
2. **B:** *soo-na-n*
so-cop-nml
'Is that so?'

3. **A:** *sensee-ga-sa*
   teacher-NOM-FP
   'Teachers'
4. **B:** *aa*
   yeah
   'Yeah.'
5. **A:** *ano, nanika tesuto kubaru-nen-yanka*
   you.know something test distribute-NML-FP
   'You know, they distribute some kind of test, don't they?'

A's utterance in line 1 involves the postposed element *minna* 'everyone.' In addition, a potential case of a postposed element occurs in A's utterance in line 3, namely *sensee-ga-sa* 'teachers.' This may be viewed as a postposed element belonging to A's utterance in line 1, but it could also be thought of as a subject of *kubaru* 'distribute' in A's utterance in line 5. In this way, it is sometimes difficult to accurately identify postposed sentences in spoken materials. Moreover, it is difficult to extract data from dialogue materials which show the "syntactic flexibility" of postposing (see the next section "Data: Syntactic Flexibilities of Postposing"). In fact, Guo and Den (2012) and Nakagawa et al. (2008) collect postposed strings from the "Corpus of Spontaneous Japanese" (National Institute for Japanese Language and Linguistics), but their findings are limited due to collection procedures as well as annotations of the corpus. Guo and Den's (2012) semi-automatic identification detects only 49 instances of postposing out of the 1,610 strings, and their data are limited only to NP-postposing (possibly with a case-marker/postposition).

As another reason for choosing novels as our primary source, it is notable that postposing in novels displays unique discourse properties (Seraku, 2015). In particular, while postposing in dialogue concerns communicative functions such as "clarification" (Nomura, 2008; Ono, 2006), postposing in novels may concern stylistic/rhetoric functions. Consider (24).

24. *fuini Shiori-no-hitomi-wa tsuranukuyouni watashi-o mitsumeru* *fuini* (underlined)
    Suddenly S-GEN-eye-TOP as.if.they.penetrate me-ACC watch suddenly
    'Suddenly, Shiori's eyes watche me as if they penetrate me.'

In (24), *fuini* 'suddenly' has been present in the preceding clause. The duplication of the adverb at the postposed position has a certain stylistic effect. In order to address these issues, however, it is necessary to first provide an explicit analysis of grammatical aspects of postposing and a cognitively-realistic model of how the reader comprehends a postposed string incrementally. This chapter thus targets Japanese novels to offer such a formal foundation for future research.[1]

Third, Japanese is well suited for our enquiry because it exhibits the syntactic flexibility of postposing which is absent from many other languages, as will be illustrated shortly below. In particular, the postposing of noun-modifiers (e.g., genitives, adjectives, relative clauses) is cross-linguistically quite rare (Kuno, 1978), which brings the questions of why Japanese exhibits this unique syntactic characteristic and why such postposing is not possible in a number of other languages such as English. Therefore, in terms of language universals and differences (as well as language-genre variation), Japanese postposing sets a challenge for grammatical analyses.

Having set out the fundamental issues above, let us provide empirical data on Japanese postposing in the next subsection.

## Data: Syntactic Flexibilities of Postposing

We collected postposing data from Japanese novels. While it is possible to (semi-)automatically detect relevant data by using a concordancer or other tools, detections may not be accurate (see the problems mentioned above). In the present chapter, then, the authors manually collect postposing data based on 6 Japanese novels published in 2000's.

Our narrative data indicate that Japanese postposing allows a wider variety of syntactic element to be postposed than many other languages. This syntactic flexibility has been assumed in theoretical/functional linguistic works, but it needs to be empirically confirmed. Although dialogue/discourse studies primarily target semantic/pragmatic issues, a notable exception is Fujii (1995, p. 167), who points out that in Japanese TV programmes, a wide range of syntactic items may occupy a postposed position. As will be reported below, our narrative findings show this syntactic diversity at a discourse level too, and reveal the other syntactic types of postposed element which have been disregarded in Fujii (1995) such as complement clauses and adverbial clauses.

First of all, postposing may be classified in the light of syntactic type of postposed item such as Noun Phrase and Adverb Phrase. Consider the paradigm instances of each syntactic type in (25)-(33).

25. Noun Phrase
*yoku-ga* *nai-na,* *kimi-wa*
greed-NOM absent-FP you-TOP
'You are not greedy.' (Akagawa, 2015, p. 166)

26. Adverb Phrase
*tomari-da-na,* *tabun*
stay-COP-FP probably
'Probably I will stay (in this hotel tonight).' (Akagawa, 2015, p. 194)

27. Postposition Phrase
*mainichi-noyouni* *oaishitemasu-yo,* *40-kai-de*
everyday-like meet.POL-FP 40th-floor-at
'I see you almost everyday at the 40th floor.' (Akagawa, 2015, p. 119)

28. Complement Clause
*tomodachi-kara* *kii-ta-mon,* *[Mei-to-Satsuki-wa* *mou*
friend-from hear-PAST-FP [M-and-S-TOP already
*kono-yo-ni* *inai-nda]-tte*
this-world-in absent-COP]-COMP
'I heard from my friend that Mei and Satsuki were not in this world any longer.' (Asai, 2012, p. 100)

29. Adverbial Clause
*daijoubu,* [*chanto otoko-kotoba-de shabetta-shi* [*asobini kiteiru*
all.right [for.sure male-language-in spoke-and [to.play has.come
*tomodachi-da*]*-tte usotsuiteoita*]*-kara*
friend-COP]-QUOT has.told.a.lie]-because
'It's all right because I spoke in male language for sure and also because I told a lie, pretending I am your friend who has just come to see you.' (Yoshida, 2002, p. 59)

30. Noun-Modifier (relative clause)
*eiga-de kouiu-siin aru-yone, hajimete namae-de yobu*
film-in like.this-scene exist-FP for.the.first.time name-by call
'There is a scene where one calls someone by his/her name for the first time, isn't there?' (Asai, 2012, p. 113, adapted)

31. Noun-Modifier (genitive)
*onaji-kurasu-no-Hiroki-kun-da, bokura-to-wa-bessekai-no*
the.same-class-GEN-H-N.SU-COP we-and-TOP-another.world-GEN
'He is Hiroki from our classroom, living in a different world from us.' (Asai, 2012, p. 126, adapted)

32. Connective
*'kekkoudesu' jya-nai-ndatte dakara*
'ok' COP-NEG-FP as.I.said
'As I said, it's not 'ok'.' (Arikawa, 2010a, p. 71)

33. Interjection
*García-Márquez-goe-da-wa, korya*
G-M-surpassing-COP-FP oh
'Oh, my experience would surpass the world depicted by García Márquez.' (Yamada, 2013, p. 87)

These various syntactic elements may co-occur at the postposed position. This phenomenon is called "multiple postposing" in theoretical linguistics (Abe, 1999), and our narrative materials encompass the attested examples such as (34)-(35).

34. Multiple Postposing: NP + AdvP
*shiawase-souda-ne, Kazumi-chan-wa itsumo*
happy-look-FP K-N.SU-TOP always
'Kazumi always looks happy.' (Ekuni, 2006, p. 351)

35. Multiple Postposing: AdvP + PP + PP
*fuman-tok a aru-wake-nee-daro, yorinimoyotte ore-kara Nozomi-ni*
complaint-like exist-reason-NEG-FP of.all.things I-from N-to
'Of all things, it's never the case that I have a complaint for Nozomi.' (Arikawa, 2010b, p. 172)

In (34), the NP (Noun Phrase) *Kazumi-chan-wa* and the AdvP (Adverb Phrase) *itsumo* 'always' are postposed. In (35), the AdvP *yorinimoyotte* 'of all things,' the PP (Postposition Phrase) *ore-kara* 'from me,' and the PP *Nozomi-ni* 'to Nozomi' are postposed.

As another point of interest, it seems that postposing may take place at an embedded level in Japanese narratives. Consider (36).

| 36. | [*yappari* | *wakatteru* | *kono-hito*]-*to* | *watashi-wa* | *omou* |
|---|---|---|---|---|---|
| | [as.expected | know | this-person]-COMP | I-TOP | think |

'I think this person knows the thing.' (Asai, 2012, p. 74, adapted)

The postposed element *kono-hito* 'this person' serves as a subject of the embedded verb *wakaru* 'know' (< *wakatteru*), rather than the matrix verb *omou* 'think.' Except for Whitman (2000, p. 465), it is widely held in the linguistic literature that Japanese postposing is restricted only to the matrix level, contrary to what example (36) seems to suggest. Japanese postposing may thus occur not only at the matrix level but also at the embedded level.[2]

In sum, the postposing in Japanese displays syntactic flexibilities in terms of both the grammatical type of postposed element and the grammatical level at which postposing occurs. Firstly, the syntactic type of postposed element is quite diverse, as in (25)-(35). Secondly, postposing may take place at an embedded level (contrary to the widespread, contrary view), as suggested in (36). These data will be addressed from a viewpoint of formal grammar in the next section.

## SOLUTIONS AND RECOMMENDATIONS

Couched within Dynamic Syntax (DS), the present section develops an account of Japanese postposing (Seraku, 2015, October; Seraku & Ohtani, 2015, October), broadening empirical coverage of a DS Japanese grammar (see Yamanaka (2008) for a preliminary DS attempt to handle dialogue issues in Japanese). For brevity, the analysis is based on constructed examples which preserve the essence of the narrative data.

Anticipating the conclusion reached in this section, the set of seemingly idiosyncratic data (25)-(35) are analysed in an integrated manner based on the finite set of actions to update a tree-representation (as well as the basic principles of the theory).

- **Noun Phrase (25):** Noun Phrase is arguably the most basic kind of postposing and will be surveyed in detail in this section. Our analysis is formulated with recourse to LOCAL *ADJUNCTION, as has been used in the analysis of Japanese word orders (see "Framework: Dynamic Syntax").
- **Noun-Modifier (30)-(31):** This constitutes a unique property of Japanese postposing and will thus be examined carefully in this section. The analysis relies on the so-called "LINK" device and a variant of LOCAL *ADJUNCTION (called GENERALISED ADJUNCTION).
- **Other Syntactic Types (Except for Connective/Interjection):** The analysis developed for Noun Phrase and Noun-Modifier is easily extendable to other types except for Connective/Interjection. An analysis is thus only briefly provided in this section.
- **Connective/Interjection:** As will be pointed out, these syntactic types affect a non-truth-conditional content. To capture this property, the current formalism needs to be combined with Type Theory with Records (TTR). See "Future Research Directions."

Below, a detailed account will be developed for Noun Phrase and Noun-Modifier in turn. An analysis will then be concisely presented for other syntactic types (except for Connective and Interjection; see "Future Research Directions"). Finally, multiple postposing will be handled as an outcome of the analysis.

## Noun Phrase

The DS framework is used to model postposing in several languages: English (Cann, Kempson, Marten, Otsuka, & Swinburne, 2004), Greek (Chatzikyriakidis, 2011; Gregoromichelaki, 2013), and Mandarin (Wu, 2005). These studies are primarily concerned with NP-postposing, but our narrative data confirm that a much wider range of syntactic items may be postposed in Japanese.

Let us start with the basic example (37), where the postposed element is the NP *sushi-o*.

37. *Ken-ga tabe-ta-yo, sushi-o*
K-NOM eat-PAST-FP sushi-ACC
'Ken ate sushi.'

The parse of the preceding clause *Ken-ga tabe-ta-yo* gives rise to (38), with the gap being notated as x.

38. Parsing *Ken-ga tabe-ta-yo*

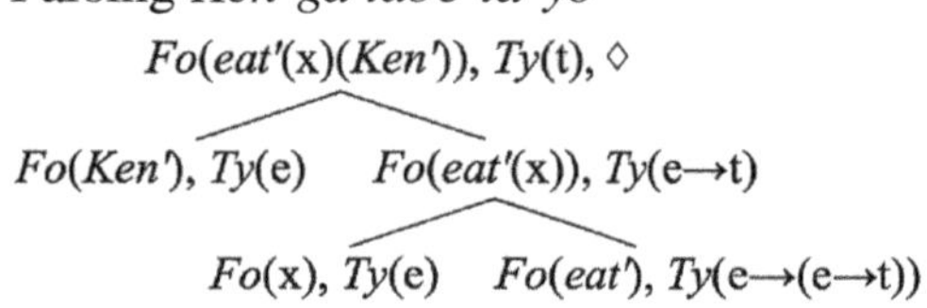


To parse the postposed element *sushi-o*, a ?*Ty*(e)-node must be present.[3] Local *Adjunction, however, cannot be run because it may fire only if a root node is decorated with ?*Ty*(t) (see (15)). This restriction is essential for ensuring the verb-finality of colloquial Japanese. On the other hand, postposing is attested in narrative discourse. To solve this ambivalence, we propose to extend the formalism as in (39).

39. **Proposal**
Local *Adjunction is subject to the ?*Ty*(t)-restriction in formal speech/writing. But this restriction is relaxed in colloquial dialogue/discourse.

The idea behind is that some grammatical rules are "not observed" in casual language, which may be seen prescriptively as the "wrong use of language."

Once Local *Adjunction is allowed to fire at a *Ty*(t)-node, it may induce an unfixed ?*Ty*(e)-node for the postposed item *sushi*. This tree update can be seen in (40).

40. Parsing *Ken-ga tabe-ta-yo, sushi*

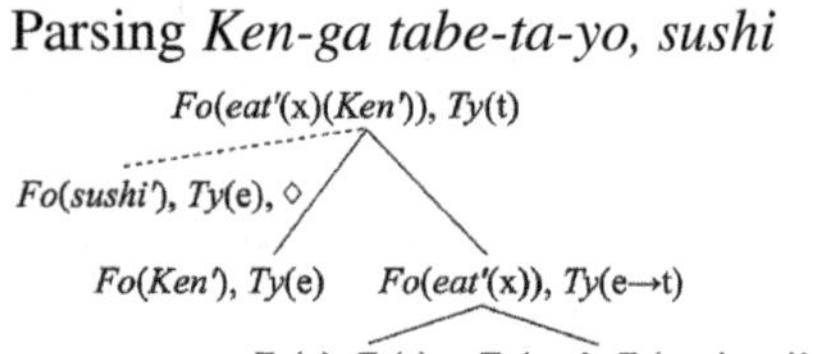

The unfixed node is resolved as an object node by the accusative case marker *o*. Finally, ELIMINATION (i.e., functional application/type deduction) outputs the final state (41).

41. ELIMINATION (executed twice)

*Fo*(*eat′*(*sushi′*)(*Ken′*)), *Ty*(t), ◇

*Fo*(*Ken′*), *Ty*(e)   *Fo*(*eat′*(*sushi′*)), *Ty*(e→t)

*Fo*(*sushi′*), *Ty*(e)   *Fo*(*eat′*), *Ty*(e→(e→t))

The above analysis readily accounts for the occurrences of postposing at an embedded level. With the proposal (39), LOCAL *ADJUNCTION can be performed at a *Ty*(t)-node of any subordinate structure.

Further, not only grammatical examples but ungrammatical examples fall within the analysis. Recall that a *wh*-word cannot be postposed in Japanese. The example (9) is cited here again as (42).

42. a. *Ken-ga nani-o tabe-ta-no*
K-NOM what-ACC eat-PAST-Q
'What did Ken eat?'
b. **Ken-ga tabe-ta-no,* <u>*nani-o*</u>
K-NOM eat-PAST-Q what-ACC

In our DS account, a structure is progressively updated reflecting incremental, left-to-right parsing. This gradual update of a structure explains the ungrammaticality of (42)b. Prior to the parse of the postposed element *nani-o* 'what,' a structure has been built which represents a polar question (i.e., *yes-no* question). In fact, the preceding part, *Ken-ga tabe-ta-no*, if it stands alone, can only express the polar question 'Did Ken eat?' The parse of the postposed item *nani-o*, however, updates the structure so as to represent a *wh*-question. Provided that a DS tree-update is monotonic (i.e., no structural information can be lost), the parse of *nani-o* leads to the failure of tree-update, hence the ungrammaticality of (42)b. Seraku and Ohtani (2015, October) apply this incremental account to other postposing phenomena.

## Noun-Modifier: Relative Clause

In order to handle relative clauses, the DS formalism needs to be enriched with additional mechanisms, which have been independently motivated in the theory (Cann et al., 2005).

Three formal ingredients are introduced here. First, "LINK" enables two distinct trees to be constructed in tandem and paired, as has been demonstrated against various phenomena such as relative clauses, topic constructions, coordinations, and nominalisations. Consider the relative clause example (43).

43. [[*Ken-ga tabe-ta*] *sushi*]-*ga oishii*
[[K-NOM eat-PAST] sushi]-NOM tasty
'Sushi which Ken ate is tasty.'

The relative clause *Ken-ga tabe-ta* projects a propositional tree where an object node is decorated with a variable x (representing a gap). The general action of LINK INTRODUCTION relates this tree to a ?*Ty*(e)-node in a new tree (Kempson & Kurosawa, 2009). A LINK relation is shown by a curved arrow in (44).

44. Parsing *Ken-ga tabe-ta* + LINK INTRODUCTION

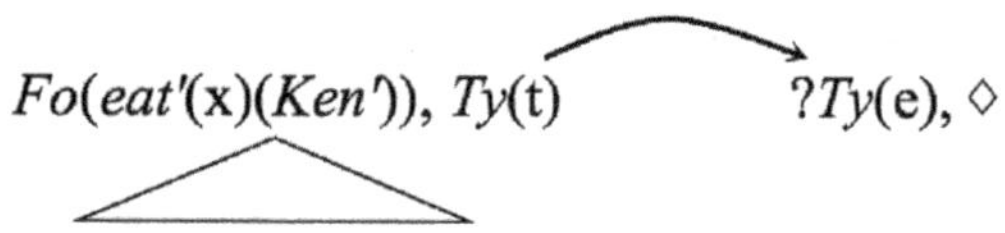


The ?*Ty*(e)-node is decorated by the head noun *sushi*, as in (45).

45. Parsing *Ken-ga tabe-ta sushi*

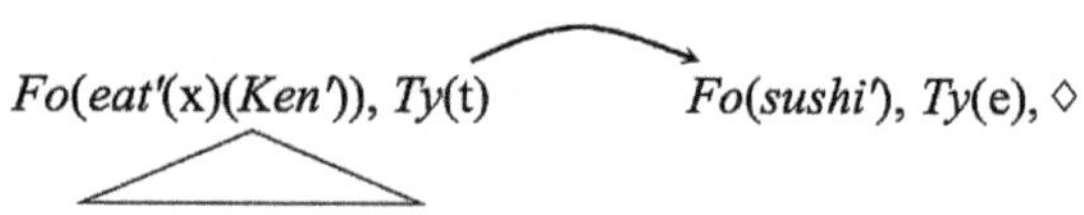


The current node is then identified as a subject node in a new tree by the nominative case marker *ga*, and the tree is fleshed out by the matrix predicate *oishii* 'tasty.'

Second, as a variant of LOCAL *ADJUNCTION, GENERALISED ADJUNCTION is formulated. This general action introduces a globally unfixed ?*Ty*(t)-node which could be resolved anywhere in a tree. An unfixed node introduced by GENERALISED ADJUNCTION is visually shown by a dotted line in (46).

46. GENERALISED ADJUNCTION

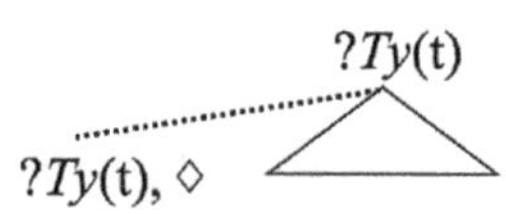


We assume, as with the proposal (39), that GENERALISED ADJUNCTION can also fire at a *Ty*(t)-node in colloquial speech/writing.

Finally, *Tn*-statements indicate node positions in a tree. *Tn*, or a "tree-node" predicate, takes a numeral X assigned to the node as argument. Consider the schematic tree diagram (47).

47. Illustration of *Tn*-statements

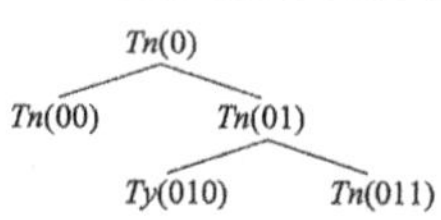


Each node is assigned a numerical value for a node position. The root is assigned "0." If a mother is assigned "α," the left-daughter "α 0" and the right-daughter "α 1."

Employing the theoretical devices introduced above, we now examine (48), where the relative clause *Mari-ga tsuku-tta* at the postposed position modifies the head noun *sushi*.

48. *Ken-ga* *sushi-o* *tabe-ta-yo* [*Mari-ga tsuku-tta*]
K-NOM sushi-ACC eat-PAST-FP [M-NOM make-PAST]
'Ken ate sushi which Mari made.'

After the preceding clause is parsed, Generalised Adjunction introduces a globally unfixed ?*Ty*(t)-node, where the relative clause is parsed. This process can be seen in (49).

49. Parsing the string of (48)

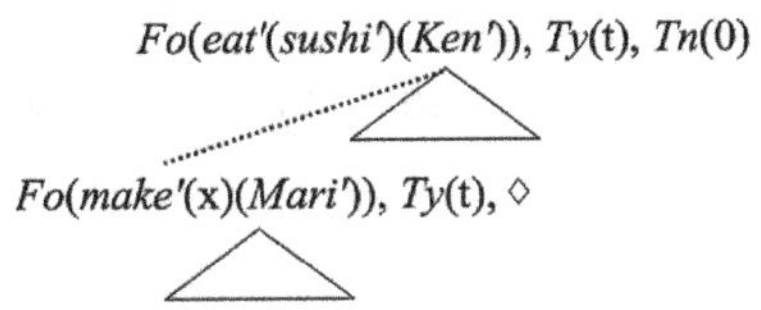


The parser then executes the general action of LINK Introduction, as in (50).

50. LINK Introduction

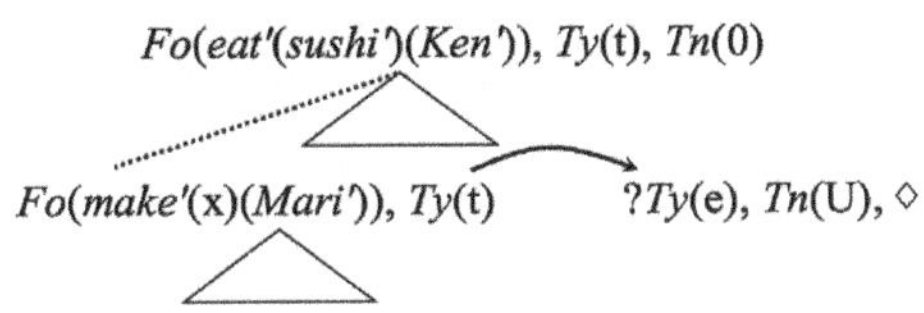


U in *Tn*(U) is a metavariable, a place-holder which is in need of saturation. If the parser identifies the address of the LINKed node with that of the node for *sushi*, *Tn*(U) is updated into *Tn*(010). For the ease of presentation, *Ty*-statements are omitted in (51).

51. Tree-node identification

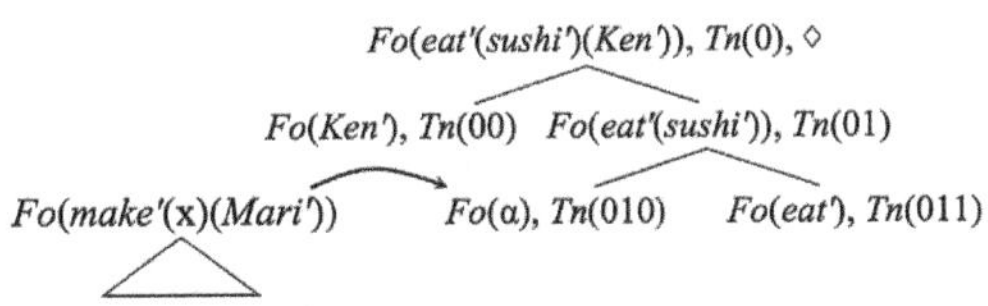


Here, α is a term that denotes sushi which Mary made. (Formally, α is expressed in the epsilon calculus (Cann et al., 2005).) Due to the node-identification process, the node for the relative clause has now been resolved as a node which is LINKed to the node decorated with *Fo*(α).[4]

Within DS, Generalised Adjunction was proposed to treat Japanese relatives (Cann et al., 2005). We speculate that the availability of this action is a necessary (if not sufficient) condition on the post-posing of a noun-modifier. This accounts for why such postposing is impossible in, say, English, where we assume Generalised Adjunction is unavailable. In future work, it must be worked out what other conditions might be, so that the account is extendable to other languages.

## Noun-Modifier: Genitive

Since genitives have not been seriously investigated in DS, we first put forward an account of the genitive *no* in Japanese. An analysis of the genitive-postposing will be proposed subsequently.

The genitive construction in English is noted in passing in Cann et al. (2005), but no detailed account has been developed. This chapter advocates an analysis of genitives in Japanese, claiming that the particle *no* encodes the action to launch a LINK relation with the effect (52). [5]

52. **Proposal:** Parsing the genitive *no*

$$Fo(\alpha), Ty(e) \curvearrowright Fo(U_{R(\alpha,\, U)}), Ty(e), Tn(V), \diamond$$

Two remarks are in order. Firstly, the LINKed node is inhibited by a metavariable U. This is because the genitive *no* may stand alone, as in (53). In such cases, U is pragmatically saturated. If *no* is followed by a noun, U is updated into the content of the noun.

53. *Mari-no*
    M-gen
    'Mari's'

Secondly, $R(\alpha, U)$ is a presupposition for U. $\alpha$ is a content of a pre-*no* NP. $R(\alpha, U)$ declares that $\alpha$ is in relation *R* to U. *R* is saturated pragmatically because the relation in question is vastly context-dependent (Nishiyama, 2003), as shown in (54).

54. *Mari-no-hon*
    M-GEN-book
    'Mari's book' (= 'a book which Mari owns,' 'a book which Mari bought,' 'a book Mari loves,' etc.)

Building on the account of genitives (52), let us turn to the genitive-postposing (55), where we assume that the relation denoted by the genitive *no* is a making relation, though other relations are possible in other contexts.

55. *Ken-ga* *sushi-o* *tabe-ta-yo,* *Mari-no*
    K-NOM sushi-ACC eat-PAST-FP M-GEN
    'Ken ate Mari's sushi.' (Int. 'Ken ate sushi which Mari made.')

The parse of the preceding clause gives rise to a propositional tree. GENERALISED ADJUNCTION induces an unfixed ?*Ty*(e)-node for *Mari*, as shown in (56).

56. Parsing *Ken-ga sushi-o tabe-ta-yo, Mari*

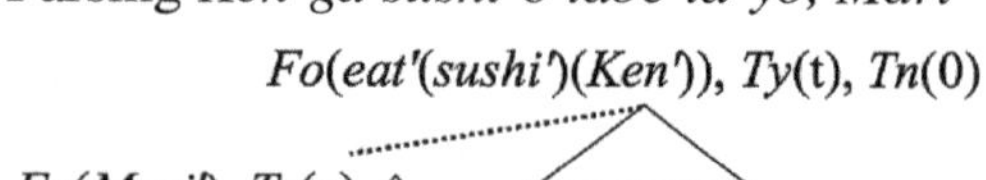


With the proposal (52), the genitive *no* engenders the tree (57). The relation R, provided by the genitive, is contextually saturated as *MAKE*, denoting a making relation. (The issue of how to detect a salient relation in context evokes pragmatic and engineering problems, which are set aside in this chapter.)

57. Parsing *Ken-ga sushi-o tabe-ta-yo, Mari-no*

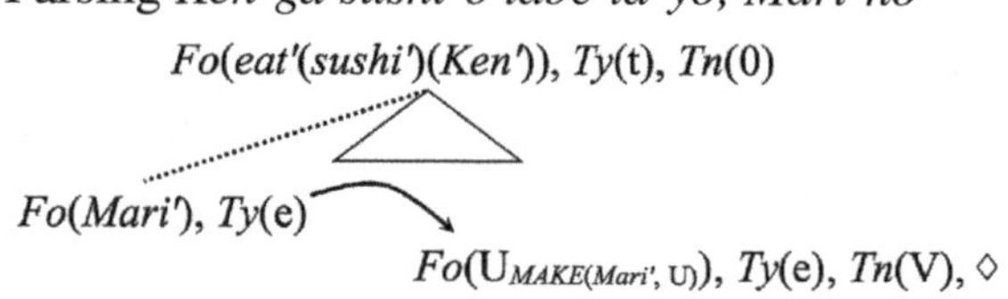

The parser identifies the current node with the node for *sushi* by saturating *Tn*(V) as *Tn*(010). For the sake of simplicity, *Ty*-statements are omitted in (58).

58. Tree-node identification

*Fo*(*eat'*(*sushi'*)(*Ken'*)), *Tn*(0)

*Fo*(*Ken'*), *Tn*(00) *Fo*(*eat'*(*sushi'*)), *Tn*(01)

*Fo*(*Mari'*) → $Fo(sushi'_{MAKE(Mari', sushi')})$, *Tn*(010), ◇ *Fo*(*eat'*), *Tn*(011)

In plain English, $Fo(sushi'_{MAKE(Mari', sushi')})$ declares that the content denoted at this node is sushi which was made by Mari.

As in the case of the postposing of a relative clause, the core machinery underlying the present analysis is GENERALISED ADJUNCTION. It thus follows that the postposing of genitives is not possible in English where we assume this action is unavailable.

Our account makes further predictions. First, a genitive phrase may be multiplied, as in (59).

59. *Ken-ga sushi-o tabe-ta-yo, <u>Mari-no-tomodachi-no-kareshi-no</u>*
K-NOM sushi-ACC eat-PAST-FP M-GEN-friend-GEN-boyfriend-GEN
'Ken ate Mari's friend's boyfriend's sushi.'

In this case, every time *no* is parsed, it induces a LINK relation. The LINKed node induced by the final *no* is identified with the node for *sushi*.

Second, the use of a metavariable in a *Fo*-statement also predicts that (60) is ambiguous.

60. *musuko-ga ka-tta-yo, <u>Ken-no</u>*
son-NOM buy-PAST-FP K-GEN
(i) e.g., 'Ken's son bought something.'
(ii) e.g., 'My son bought Ken's book.'

If the LINKed node induced by *no* is identified with the node for *musuko* 'son,' *Fo*(U) at the LINKed node is saturated as *Fo*(*musuko'*), which yields the interpretation (i). If the LINKed node is identified with the internal-argument node for *kau* 'buy' (< *ka*), *Fo*(U) is pragmatically saturated as, say, *Fo*(*book'*) in context. This process results in the interpretation (ii).

## Other Syntactic Types

The account of Japanese postposing, proposed in the preceding subsections, is applicable to other types of postposing (except for Connective/Interjection), as will be briefly explained below.

- **Adverb/Postposition Phrase.** Consider the postposing of an adverb phrase (61) and the postposing of a postposition phrase (62).

61. *Ken-ga* *hashi-tta-yo* *yukkurito*
K-NOM run-PAST-FP slowly
'Ken ran slowly.'

62. *Ken-ga* *hashi-tta-yo,* *kouen-de*
K-NOM run-PAST-FP park-in
'Ken ran in a park.'

AdvP (Adverb Phrase) and PP (Postposition Phrase) are adjuncts (excluding PPs in ditransitive verbs). In DS, Marten (2002) hypothesises that adjuncts are of type e. Thus, adjunct-postposing can be uniformly handled as with NP-postposing: LOCAL *ADJUNCTION creates an unfixed ?*Ty*(e)-node. To illustrate the point, consider the tree (63) which emerges after parsing (62) prior to the postposition *de* 'in.'

63. Parsing *Ken-ga hashi-tta-yo, kouen*

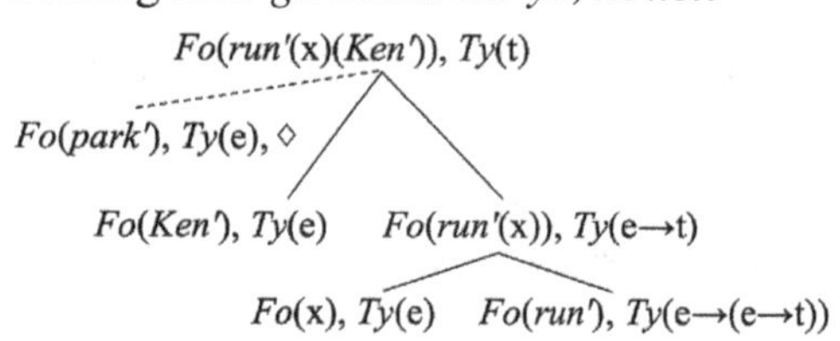


The unfixed node is identified with the *Fo*(x)-node by the parse of the postposition *de*. In the case of AdvP such as (61), it is assumed that an adverb itself encodes an action to resolve an unfixed node.[6]

- **Complement Clause.** Consider the postposing of a complement clause (64).

64. *Mari-wa* *kii-ta-yo,* [*Ken-ga* *sushi-o* *tabe-ta*]*-to*
M-TOP hear-PAST-FP [K-NOM sushi-ACC eat-PAST]-COMP
'Mari heard that Ken ate sushi.'

To analyse a complement clause, DS defines *ADJUNCTION, which induces a ?*Ty*(t)-node.[7] According to Cann et al. (2005), this action cannot fire at a *Ty*(t)-node; we stipulate that in colloquial speech/writing, this restriction is relaxed (cf., (39)). The tree (65) is derived by the parse of *kii-ta-yo* and *ADJUNCTION. An unfixed ?*Ty*(t)-node introduced by *ADJUNCTION is shown by a dashed-dotted line.

65. Parsing *Mari-wa kii-ta-yo* + *ADJUNCTION

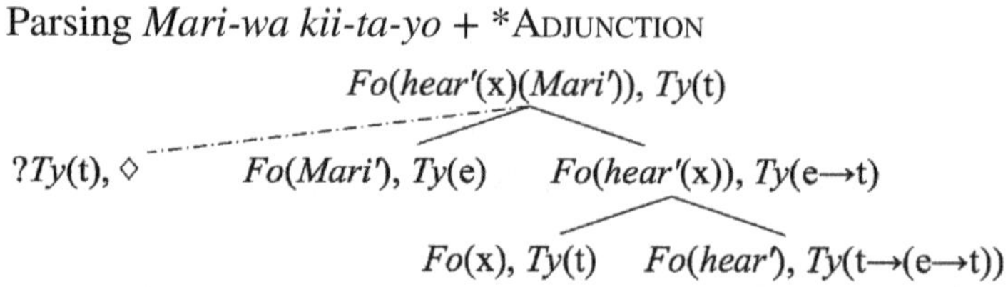


The complement clause is parsed at the unfixed node. This node is then identified with the node decorated with *Fo*(x) by the complementiser *to*.

- **Adverbial Clause.** Consider the postposing of an adverbial clause (66).

66. *Ken-ga* *waratta-yo,* [*Mari-ga* *kita*]-*toki*
    K-NOM smiled-FP [M-NOM came]-when
    'When Mari came, Ken smiled.'

An adverbial clause is analysed by dint of LINK: a LINK relation starts from a *Ty*(t)-node to a ?*Ty*(t)-node, as in (67). The postposed adverbial clause is, then, parsed at the LINKed ?*Ty*(t)-node.

67. Launching a LINK relation

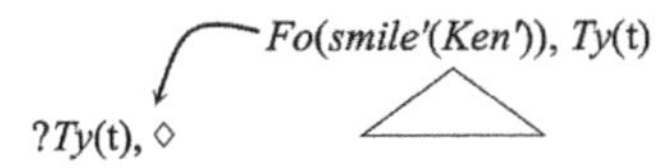


## Summary and Further Consequences

The Dynamic Syntax (DS) account developed thus far formalises the incremental steps of how the reader understands a postposed string in Japanese novels. An apparently heterogeneous set of postposed strings is amenable to this incremental account, as summarised in Table 1.

In winding up the section, it should not go unnoticed that the account also accommodates "multiple postposing" without making any stipulations. Consider (68).

68. *tabe-ta-yo,* *Ken-ga* *sushi-o*
    eat-PAST-FP K-NOM sushi-ACC
    'Ken ate sushi.'

This string instantiates multiple postposing in that two non-verbal elements are positioned post-verbally, the NP *Ken-ga* and another NP *sushi-o*.

To begin with, the tree-logic constraint on unfixed nodes must be clarified: only a single unfixed node can be present at a time (Cann et al., 2005). This is because multiple unfixed nodes of the same locality type collapse and if they are decorated with incommensurate statements, inconsistency arises

*Table 1. The type of postposing and a corresponding set of DS tools for analysis*

| Syntactic Type | Example | Analytical Tool |
|---|---|---|
| Noun Phrase | (25), (37) | Local *Adjunction |
| Adverb Phrase | (26), (61) | Local *Adjunction |
| Postposition Phrase | (27), (62) | Local *Adjunction |
| Complement Clause | (28), (64) | a variant of LOCAL *ADJUNCTION |
| Adverbial Clause | (29), (66) | LINK |
| Noun Modifier (relative clause) | (30), (48) | LINK + a variant of LOCAL *ADJUNCTION |
| Noun Modifier (genitive) | (31), (55) | LINK + a variant of LOCAL *ADJUNCTION |

in the node descriptions. For instance, the tree (69)a appears to involve two unfixed nodes, but they are in fact treated one and the same as in (69)b.[8]

69.

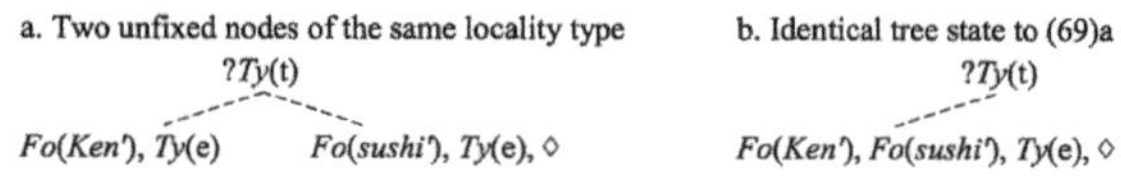


The single unfixed node in (69)b is decorated with incommensurate statements: *Fo*(*Ken'*) and *Fo*(*sushi'*). Thus, the node descriptions are inconsistent, and the tree-update fails.

This constraint is not violated in our account. In (68), an unfixed node is induced for *Ken*, as in (70). This unfixed node is immediately resolved as a subject by the nominative case marker *ga*, as in (71).

70. Parsing *tabe-ta-yo, Ken*

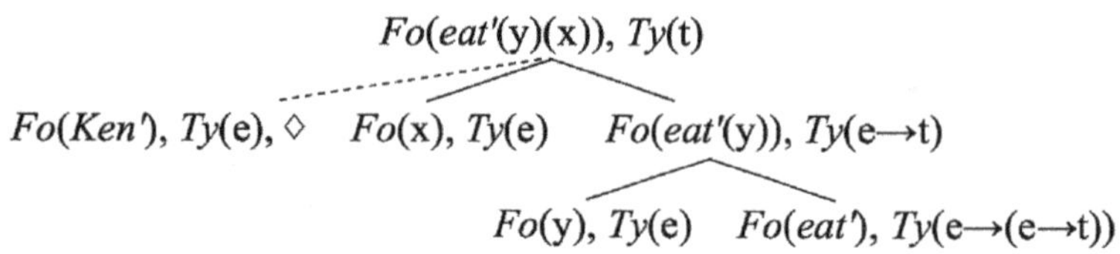


71. Parsing *tabe-ta-yo, Ken-ga*

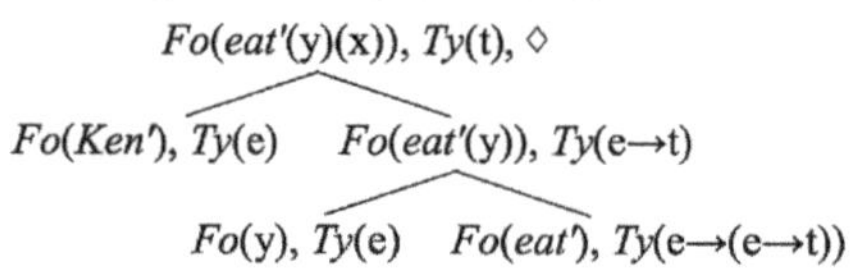


Since no unfixed node remains in the tree, the parser can safely posit an unfixed node, this time for the second postposed item *sushi*. Thus, the parse of the multiple postposed elements is licit.

According to the previous DS analysis of postposing in English, Greek, and Mandarin (see endnote 3), a postposed item is processed at a LINKed node. It is not obvious whether a LINK-strategy can deal with multiple postposing. First, the question remains of how to parse a case particle safely at a LINKed node (see endnote 3). Second, if this issue is solved, multiple LINK relations launched from the same node collapse and inconsistency of descriptions occurs. Consider (72).

72. The LINK-strategy for parsing the multiple postposing (68)

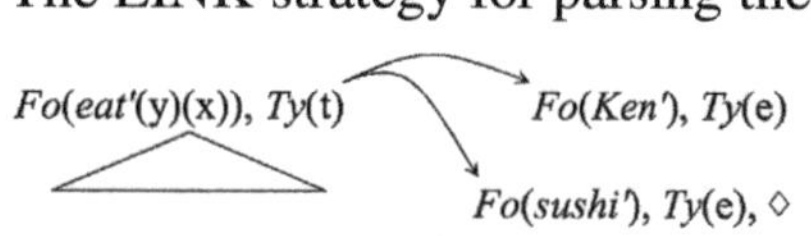


This tree appears to have two LINKed nodes, but these nodes collapse. The collapsed single node is decorated with incompatible statements: *Fo*(*Ken'*) and *Fo*(*sushi'*).[9] By contrast, this problem does not occur in our underspecification-based account.

## FUTURE RESEARCH DIRECTIONS

In the current Dynamic Syntax (DS) setting, a tree expresses a truth-conditional meaning. Yet, to model a full spectrum of meanings requires a tree to represent non-truth-conditional dimensions. Recently, Purver, Gregoromichelaki, Meyer-Viol, and Cann (2010) propose to postulate a "higher-level" structure for this purpose by combining DS with Type Theory with Records (TTR) (Cooper, 2005). The DS-TTR hybrid theory is useful for analysing dialogue issues (Purver et al., 2014). As will be suggested below, it is beneficial for narrative issues too.

### DS-TTR Integration

Purver et al. (2010) suggest that the DS-TTR integration enables a tree to represent the non-truth-conditional part of meaning. In this hybrid approach, a truth-conditional DS tree is LINKed from a higher-level TTR representation which expresses a speech-act (among other things). For example, consider the structure for *Ken runs* (73).

73. Parsing *Ken runs*

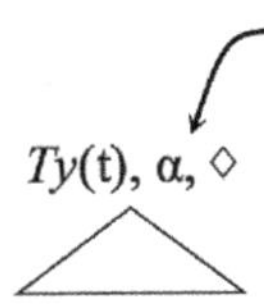


$$\begin{bmatrix} ctxt & \begin{bmatrix} a & : & participantA \\ u_0 & : & utt\text{-}event \\ s_{s0} & : & spkr(u_0, a) \end{bmatrix} \\ cont & \begin{bmatrix} x & : & ken \\ p & : & run(x) \end{bmatrix} \\ inf & \begin{bmatrix} p' & : & assert(u_0, a, p) \end{bmatrix} \end{bmatrix}$$

A *Ty*(t)-node (which denotes a truth-conditional content) is LINKed from the higher-level structure which contains *ctxt*, *cont*, and *inf* fields.[10] The label *ctxt* (context) is assigned the value which specifies utterance participants and an utterance event. The attribute *cont* (content) is assigned as a value the proposition that Ken runs. The attribute *inf* (speech-act info) is assigned the value pertaining to a speech act: the speaker "asserts" the proposition that Ken runs.

### Postposing of Connective/Interjection

An immediate consequence of the DS-TTR integration in the domain of narrative discourse lies in the analysis of the hitherto-neglected kinds of postposing data: the postposing of Connective and Interjection (32)-(33), reproduced here as (74)-(75).

74. Connective

| 'kekkoudesu' | jya-nai-ndatte | dakara |
|---|---|---|
| 'ok' | COP-NEG-FP | as.I.said |

'As I said, it's not 'ok'.' (Arikawa, 2010a, p. 71)

75. Interjection

| García-Márquez-goe-da-wa, | korya |
|---|---|
| G-M-surpassing-COP-FP | oh |

'Oh, my experience would surpass the world depicted by García Márquez.' (Yamada, 2013, p. 87)

The postposed items do not contribute to a truth-conditional content. That is, when *dakara* 'as I said' in (74) and *korya* 'oh' in (75) are taken out, the resulting strings are true in exactly the same set of situations as those for the original sentences (Grice, 1975; Potts, 2005).

We maintain that the postposed connective and interjection in (74)-(75) put their non-truth-conditional meanings at the higher-level structure. As for (75), the higher-level structure in (76) contains $surprised(u_0, a, p)$, declaring that the speaker is surprised by the truth-conditional content of the string, this "surprise" meaning being taken to be a non-truth-conditional meaning contributed by *korya* 'oh.'

76. Parsing the string (75)

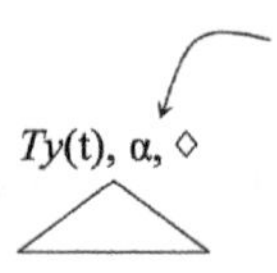


$$\begin{bmatrix} ctxt & \begin{bmatrix} a & : & participantA \\ u_0 & : & utt\text{-}event \\ s_{s0} & : & spkr(u_0, a) \end{bmatrix} \\ cont & \begin{bmatrix} x & : & speaker's\text{-}experience \\ y & : & world\text{-}depicted\text{-}by\text{-}GM \\ p & : & surpass(y)(x) \end{bmatrix} \\ inf & \begin{bmatrix} p' & : & assert(u_0, a, p)\&surprised(u_0, a, p) \end{bmatrix} \end{bmatrix}$$

## LINK at the Speech-Act Dimension

As another potential application of the DS-TTR combination to narrative discourse, the use of LINK at the higher-level, speech-act dimension might be conceivable. First of all, consider the example (77).

77. *tomodachi-kara kii-ta-mon, Mei-to-Satsuki-wa mou kono-yo-ni inai-nda-tte*
friend-from hear-past-FP M-and-S-TOP already this-world-in absent-FP-FP
'I heard that Mei and Satsuki were not in this world any longer.' (Asai, 2012, p. 100)

In "Data: Syntactic Flexibilities of Postposing," (77) was presented as an instance of the postposing of a complement clause. But the string is ambiguous; it has another structure/interpretation illustrated in (78).

78. *tomodachi-kara kii-ta-mon, Mei-to-Satsuki-wa mou kono-yo-ni inai-ndatte*
friend-from hear-past-FP M-and-S-TOP already this-world-in absent-HEAR
'I heard this from my friend; it is said that Mei and Satsuki were not in this world any longer.'

In this second reading, the string is not a case of postposing. The underlined part is not a postposed item but forms a full-fledged sentence. In this reading, *ndatte* serves as a hearsay particle, while in the reading (77), *ndatte* consists of the particle *nda* and the complementiser *tte*. As expected from this decomposition in (77), the hearsay meaning is absent in (77). This decomposition is also syntactically plausible since the complementiser *tte* ensures that the underlined part is a complement clause in (77) but not in (78).

In the "two-sentence" reading (78), the sentences are connected by a comma, rather than a full stop. A comma is generally used to connect two clauses (or phrases), whereas a full stop is used to connect two sentences. We presume that this usage of a comma is a rhetorical technique in narratives whose function may be seen as describing situations denoted by two sentences intimately, vividly, and so on.

Within DS, the LINK device models the association of a phrase to a phrase (e.g., NP coordinations), a phrase to a clause (e.g., topicalisations, relatives), and a clause to a clause (e.g., clausal coordinations). To our knowledge, however, LINK has not been exploited to connect sentences. Our contention is that

LINK can model the association of sentences if LINK is employed at higher-level, speech-act structures. This insight is formulated in (79).

79. **Proposal:**
When sentences are connected by a comma, the speech-act representation of the initial sentence is LINKed from the speech-act representation of the next sentence.

The intuitive idea behind is that each sentence manifests a speech-act (Austin, 1962), and the sequence of sentences are connected via (the representation of) each speech-act.

Let us apply this proposal to (78). After the initial sentence is parsed, a LINK relation holds between two speech-act structures; see the thick arrow in (80).[11] The second sentence is then parsed at the ?*Ty*(t)-node.

80. Launching a LINK relation

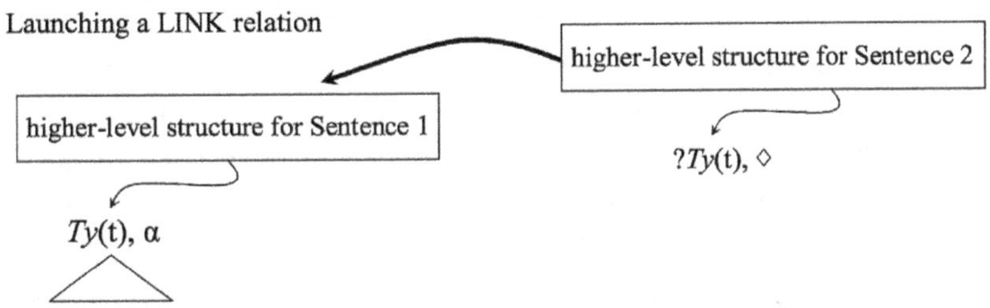


The details of the analysis sketched here need to be worked out, but it nonetheless suggests that a full account of narrative discourse would require non-truth-conditional, "higher-level" representations.

## CONCLUSION

This chapter has been concerned with postposing, a non-prescriptive phenomenon where a non-verbal item appears after a verb. The word-order phenomena have often been explored based on data constructed by scholars, but since postposing is a narrative/dialogue issue, spontaneous data are essential to establish an empirical ground firmly. This chapter collects data from Japanese novels and illuminates the syntactic flexibilities:

- The syntactic type of postposed element in Japanese is more diverse than in many other languages (including Noun-Modifier, Connective, and Interjection).
- Postposing may take place not only at a matrix clause but also at an embedded clause, contrary to what previous studies have generally assumed.

An explicit account of these narrative findings has been put forward within Dynamic Syntax (DS), with the consequence of advancing formal aspects of the framework.

- A seemingly idiosyncratic set of postposing data is explained by a finite set of principles and tree-update actions which are independently motivated and defined in the theory.

- The integration of DS with Type Theory with Records may be fruitful for dealing with non-truth-conditional meanings denoted by connectives and interjections (as well as other narrative data such as the "two-sentence" reading (78)).

As the narrative data reported set an empirical challenge for grammar modelling in general, the adoption of DS as our theoretical background is not a necessary decision. It thus remains to be seen how the data are handled (possibly built upon the DS account) in other formal grammars (e.g., Head-driven Phrase Structure Grammar (Sag, Wasow, & Bender, 2003), Lexical-Functional Grammar (Dalrymple, 2001)). Having said the generality of the problems for grammar analysis, there is still a benefit of adopting DS. The framework enables a cognitively realistic account to be developed, capturing a fundamental property of language use: the incrementality of understanding a sentence in context (Kamide, 2006; Kiaer, 2014).

Finally, it is essential to develop a computationally realistic model. In this respect, too, the adoption of DS would be fruitful. Extensive research has been conducted to implement the DS formalism for developing NLP systems (Eshghi et al., 2011, 2013). This research paradigm includes the development of natural language generation; the core idea is that a generation model employs the same set of DS mechanisms as for parsing except that each generation step is subject to a consistency check with respect to a "goal" structure (Purver et al., 2014). These computational works, however, have so far targeted only English dialogue. In order to extend them to other languages (e.g., Japanese) and other forms of language (e.g., novels, or more generally narratives), what is required is (i) a detailed description of linguistic constructions in some narrative genre and (ii) an explicit model of how such constructions are produced/understood. This chapter has aimed at providing these empirical/theoretical scaffoldings, and our future prospect is to develop an NLP system based on these grounds.

## ACKNOWLEDGMENT

This chapter benefitted from constructive suggestions made by the anonymous reviewers and the editors. All remaining inadequacies are our own. This work was supported by Hankuk University of Foreign Studies Research Fund of 2016, for which the first author is grateful.

## REFERENCES

Abe, J. (1999). *On directionality of movement.* (Unpublished manuscript). Nagoya University, Aichi, Japan.

Akagawa, J. (2015). *Mikeneko Holmes-no-yumekikou* [The dreamy travelogue of Mikeneko Holmes]. Tokyo, Japan: Kobunsha.

Arikawa, H. (2010a). Roru auto. [Roll out] In H. Arikawa (Ed.), *Kujira-no kare* [The man of whale] (pp. 63–111). Tokyo, Japan: Kadokawa Shoten Publishing.

Arikawa, H. (2010b). Yuunouna kanojo. [The able lady] In H. Arikawa (Ed.), *Kujira-no kare* [The man of whale] (pp. 161–213). Tokyo, Japan: Kadokawa Shoten Publishing.

Asai, R. (2012). *Kirishima bukatsu yamerutteyo* [The Kirishima thing]. Tokyo, Japan: Shueisha Publishing.

Austin, J. (1962). *How to do things with words*. Oxford, UK: Clarendon Press.

Blackburn, P., & Meyer-Viol, W. (1994). Linguistics, logic, and finite trees. *Bulletin of Interest Group of Pure and Applied Logics*, *2*, 2–39.

Cann, R. (2011). Towards an account of the auxiliary system in English. In R. Kempson et al. (Eds.), *The Dynamics of Lexical Interfaces* (pp. 279–317). Stanford, CA: Center for the Study of Language and Information.

Cann, R., Kempson, R., & Gregoromichelaki, E. (2008). *Semantics*. Cambridge, UK: Cambridge University Press.

Cann, R., Kempson, R., & Marten, L. (2005). *The dynamics of language*. Oxford, UK: Elsevier.

Cann, R., Kempson, R., Marten, L., Otsuka, M., & Swinburne, D. (2004). On the left and on the right. In D. Adger et al. (Eds.), *Peripheries* (pp. 19–47). Dordrecht, Netherlands: Kluwer. doi:10.1007/1-4020-1910-6_2

Chatzikyriakidis, S. (2011). *Right dislocations in Greek*. (Unpublished manuscript). Centre National de la Recherche Scientifique, Paris, France.

Chomsky, N. (1965). *Aspects of the theory of syntax*. Cambridge, MA: MIT Press.

Chomsky, N. (1995). *The minimalist program*. Cambridge, MA: MIT Press.

Cooper, R. (2005). Records and record types in semantic theory. *Journal of Logic and Computation*, *15*(2), 99–112. doi:10.1093/logcom/exi004

Culicover, P., & Jackendoff, R. (2005). *Simpler syntax*. Oxford, UK: Oxford University Press. doi:10.1093/acprof:oso/9780199271092.001.0001

Dalrymple, M. (2001). *Lexical functional grammar*. New York, NY: Academic Press. doi:10.1163/9781849500104

Davidson, D. (1967). The logical form of action sentences. In N. Rescher (Ed.), *The logic of decision and action* (pp. 81–95). Pittsburgh, PA: University of Pittsburg Press.

Dryer, M. (2013). Order of subject, object and verb. In M. Dryer & M. Haspelmath (Eds.), The world atlas of language structures online. Retrieved from http://wals.info/chapter/81

Eguchi, I. (2000). Nihongo-no kouchibun[Postposed sentences in Japanese] [Study on Language and Culture]. *Gengo Bunka Kenkyu*, *12*, 81–93.

Ekuni, K. (2006). *Tokyo tawa* [Tokyo Tower]. Tokyo, Japan: Shinchosha Publishing.

Eshghi, A., Purver, M., & Hough, J. (2011). *DyLan* (Report No. EECSRR-11-05). London, UK: School of Electronic Engineering and Computer Science, Queen Mary University of London.

Eshghi, A., Purver, M., Hough, J., & Sato, Y. (2013). Probabilistic grammar induction in an incremental semantic framework. In D. Duchier & Y. Parmentier (Eds.), *Constraint solving and language processing* (pp. 92–107). Berlin, Germany: Springer-Verlag. doi:10.1007/978-3-642-41578-4_6

Fujii, Y. (1995). Nihongo-no-gojun-no gyakuten-nitsuite. [On the reversed word orders in Japanese] In K. Takami (Ed.), *Nichieigo-no uhou teni koubun* [Right dislocations in Japanese and English] (pp. 167–198). Tokyo, Japan: Hituzi Publishing.

Gregoromichelaki, E. (2006). *Conditionals in dynamic syntax.* (Unpublished doctoral dissertation). King's College London, London, UK.

Gregoromichelaki, E. (2013). A dynamic perspective on left-right asymmetries. In G. Webelhuth et al. (Eds.), *Rightward movement in a comparative perspective* (pp. 321–368). Amsterdam, Netherlands: John Benjamins. doi:10.1075/la.200.12gre

Grice, P. (1975). In P. Cole & J. Morgan (Eds.), *Logic and conversation* (Vol. 3, pp. 41–58). Syntax and semanticsNew York, NY: Academic Press.

Guo, J., & Den, Y. (2012). Inversion expressions in Japanese conversation. *Koupasu nihongogaku waakushoppu yokoushuu [Proceedings of the workshop on corpus Japanese linguistics]* (pp. 283-288). Tokyo, Japan: National Institute for Japanese Language and Linguistics.

Kamide, Y. (2006). Incrementality in Japanese sentence processing. In M. Nakayama et al. (Eds.), *The handbook of East Asian psycholinguistics* (Vol. 2, pp. 248–256). Cambridge, UK: Cambridge University Press. doi:10.1017/CBO9780511758652.036

Kempson, R., Gregoromichelaki, E., & Howes, C. (2011). *The dynamics of lexical interfaces.* Stanford, CA: Center for the Study of Language and Information.

Kempson, R., & Kiaer, J. (2010). Multiple long-distance scrambling. *Journal of Linguistics, 46*(1), 127–192. doi:10.1017/S0022226709990211

Kempson, R., & Kurosawa, A. (2009). At the syntax-pragmatics interface. In H. Hoshi (Ed.), *The dynamics and mechanism of language* (pp. 47–84). Tokyo, Japan: Kuroshio Publishers.

Kempson, R., Meyer-Viol, W., & Gabbay, D. (2001). *Dynamic syntax.* Oxford, UK: Wiley-Blackwell.

Kiaer, J. (2014). *Pragmatic syntax.* London, UK: Bloomsbury Publishing.

Kuno, S. (1978). *Danwa-no-bunpou* [Grammar of discourse]. Tokyo, Japan: Taishukan.

Marten, L. (2002). *At the syntax-pragmatics interface.* Oxford, UK: Oxford University Press. doi:10.1093/acprof:oso/9780199250639.001.0001

Nakagawa, N., Asao, Y., & Nagaya, N. (2008). Information structure and intonation of right-dislocation sentences in Japanese. Kyoto University Linguistic Research, 27, 1-22.

Nishiyama, Y. (2003). *Nihongo meishiku-no imiron-to-goyouron* [The semantics and pragmatics of noun phrases in Japanese]. Tokyo, Japan: Hituzi Publishing.

Nomura, J. (2008). *Japanese postposing.* (Unpublished doctoral dissertation). University of Hawaii, Manoa, HI.

Ono, T. (2006). Postpredicate-elements in Japanese conversation. In T. Vance & K. Jones (Eds.), *Japanese/Korean Linguistics 14* (pp. 381–391). Stanford, CA: Center for the Study of Language and Information.

Orwin, M., Howes, C., & Kempson, R. (2013). *Language, music and interaction*. London, UK: College Publications.

Potts, C. (2005). *The logic of conventional implicatures*. Oxford, UK: Oxford University Press.

Purver, M., Gregoromichelaki, E., Meyer-Viol, W., & Cann, R. (2010). Splitting the 'I's and crossing the 'you's. In P. Łupkowski & M. Purver (Eds.), *Aspects of semantics and pragmatics of dialogue* (pp. 43–50). Poznań, Poland: Polish Society for Cognitive Science.

Purver, M., Hough, J., & Gregoromichelaki, E. (2014). Dialogue and compound contributions. In A. Stent & S. Bangalore (Eds.), *Natural language generation in interactive systems* (pp. 63–92). Cambridge, UK: Cambridge University Press. doi:10.1017/CBO9780511844492.004

Sag, I., Wasow, T., & Bender, E. (2003). *Syntactic theory* (2nd ed.). Stanford, CA: Center for the Study of Language and Information.

Satio, M. (1985). *Some asymmetries in Japanese and their theoretical implications*. (Unpublished doctoral dissertation). MIT, Cambridge, MA.

Seraku, T. (2013). *Clefts, relatives, and language dynamics*. (Unpublished doctoral dissertation). University of Oxford, Oxford, UK.

Seraku, T. (2015). Nihongo-no kouchibun [Postposed sentences in Japanese]. *Journal of the Society of Japanese Language and Literature. Japanology, 70*, 71–96.

Seraku, T. (2015, October). *A Dynamic Syntax modelling of postposing in Japanese narratives*. Paper presented at the 29th Pacific Asia Conference on Language, Information and Computation, Shanghai, China.

Seraku, T., & Ohtani, A. (2015, October). *The* wh-*licensing in Japanese right dislocations*. Paper presented at Colloque de Syntaxe et Sémantique à Paris 2015, Paris, France.

Takami, K. (1995). *Kinouteki koubunron-niyoru Nichi-Eigo hikaku* [Japanese-English comparisons in functional syntax]. Tokyo, Japan: Kuroshio Publishers.

Takano, Y. (2014). A comparative approach to Japanese postposing. In M. Saito (Ed.), *Japanese syntax in comparative perspective* (pp. 139–180). Oxford, UK: Oxford University Press. doi:10.1093/acprof:oso/9780199945207.003.0006

Takita, K. (2014). Pseudo-right dislocation, the bare-topic construction, and hanging topic constructions. *Lingua, 140*, 137–157. doi:10.1016/j.lingua.2013.12.010

Tanaka, H. (2001). Right-dislocation as scrambling. *Journal of Linguistics, 37*(03), 551–579. doi:10.1017/S0022226701001049

Tanaka, H., & Kizu, M. (2007). Island insensitive constructions in Japanese. *York Papers in Linguistics, 2*, 219–234.

Whitman, J. (2000). Right dislocation in English and Japanese. In K. Takami et al. (Eds.), *Syntactic and functional explorations in honor of Susumu Kuno* (pp. 445–470). Tokyo, Japan: Kuroshio Publishers.

Wu, Y. (2005). *The dynamic syntax of left and right dislocation.* (Unpublished doctoral dissertation). University of Edinburgh, Edinburgh, UK.

Yamada, E. (2013). *Taini sutorizu* [Tiny stories]. Tokyo, Japan: Bungei Shunju.

Yamanaka, A. (2008). *Utterance interpretation, group-defining practices and linguistic meaning*. (Unpublished doctoral dissertation). King's College London, London, UK.

Yoshida, S. (2002). *Saigo-no-musuko* [The last son]. Tokyo, Japan: Bungei Shunju.

## KEY TERMS AND DEFINITIONS

**Dynamic Syntax:** A grammar formalism which specifies a set of procedures for building up a structure (representing a context-dependent interpretation) progressively in real time. See Cann et al. (2005) for a full introduction.

**Incrementality:** The nature of sentence-processing, where a string is processed word-by-word online (and a structure is gradually updated correspondingly).

**LINK:** A device defined in Dynamic Syntax, which allows the parser to construct two distinct tree-structures in tandem and pair them by relating a node in one tree to a node in the other tree.

**Logical Typing:** The combinatorial property of content is designated by logical type. The basic types are type-e ("entity") and type-t ("truth-evaluable statement"). Complex types are defined recursively; if $\alpha$ and $\beta$ are types, so is $\alpha \rightarrow \beta$. An item of type $e \rightarrow t$ may be combined with an item of type e to produce an item of type t.

**Parsing:** The process of analysing a string of words in natural languages based on the principles and rules defined in a particular formal grammar.

**Postposing:** A kind of word-order phenomena, where an element is positioned post-verbally. In Japanese, postposing is prescriptively prohibited but well attested in colloquial register.

**Type Theory with Records:** A variant of constructive type theory enriched with the tools like "record" (mathematical object consisting of sets of label-value pairs) and "record types" (record whose label-value pairs specify typing judgments). See Cooper (2005) for details.

**Unfixed Node:** A type of node in a tree-structure in Dynamic Syntax, whose position in a tree-structure is initially underspecified when it is introduced but will be resolved at a later stage.

## ENDNOTES

1. In the linguistic literature, no due attention has been paid to the non-communicative, stylistic functions of postposing as illustrated in (24) except for Seraku (2015) (see Eguchi (2000) for a related remark). On the other hand, this type of postposing is generally called "Touchihou (inversion)" in literature works without definitions and analyses. This chapter presents a formal preliminary for addressing rhetorical effects of postposing in novels. (See also the "Future Research Directions" section for the data/analysis of the "two-sentence" reading, another case for a distinctive property of postposing in novels.)

2 A possibility still remains that (36) is a case of direct speech. See Whitman (2000, p. 465) for other types of example suggesting that postposing may occur at the embedding level. Whitman (2000), however, does not address the full-spectrum of the data in (25)-(33).

3 In the DS studies on postposing (Cann et al., 2004; Chatzikyriakidis, 2011; Gregoromichelaki, 2013; Wu, 2005), a LINK relation introduces a ?*Ty*(e)-node for a postposed item. Yet, this LINK-strategy cannot be applied to the postposed item *sushio-o* in (37) because (i) the parse of the case marker *o* identifies the node for *sushi* as an object node within a new propositional tree but (ii) the new tree fails to be complete as no elements are subsequently parsed (Seraku, 2013). The LINK-strategy is feasible if a postposed item is not marked by a case particle. Seraku and Ohtani (2015, October) show that the availability of the LINK-strategy predicts the so-called "island-(in)sensitivity" of Japanese postposing (Tanaka & Kizu, 2007).

4 In the present analysis, the relative clause modifies *sushi*. It is also formally allowed to modify *Ken*; in this case, *Tn*(U) is saturated as *Tn*(00), which refers to a subject node in the main tree. This modification possibility, however, is blocked on semantic/pragmatic grounds.

5 Japanese displays other kinds of *no* such as "pronominal nominaliser" and "sentential nominaliser." See Seraku (2013, ch. 4) for various arguments for the view that the genitive *no* constitutes a different lexical item from these kinds of *no*.

6 Marten's (2002) analysis blurs the argument/adjunct divide. If one would like to maintain the divide, we could utilise Davidson's (1967) analysis of adjuncts by using a situation term (Gregoromichelaki, 2006).

7 Cann et al. (2005) define *ADJUNCTION to capture the so-called "long-distance dependency" of a complement clause. This dependency is found in Japanese postposing too (Kuno, 1978, p. 74).

8 If multiple unfixed nodes are of different locality types, they are distinguishable and may thus be present even with incompatible statements. This complication, however, does not affect the present discussion.

9 This is not meant to deny a LINK-strategy for it can be used for Japanese postposing too (see endnote 3). This is in line with the general DS stance that as long as a well-formed tree obtains, there may be multiple parse-strategies licensed by a grammar.

10 In TTR, a record is a finite set of label-value pairs (called "field"), in the form "*l*: *v*" where *l* stands for a label and *v* stands for a value. A record type is a record with fields specifying typing judgments. Purver et al. (2010) replace *Fo*-statements with record types. See Cann, Kempson, and Gregoromichelaki (2008) for a concise introduction to TTR.

11 The tree-operator for a LINK relation connecting two higher-level structures must be distinctly defined from the tree-operator for a usual LINK relation in order to avoid the collapse of LINK relations. Such tree-operators can be formulated in Logic Of Finite Trees (Blackburn & Meyer-Viol, 1994), as has been practiced in the DS literature (Cann et al., 2005; Kempson et al., 2001).

## APPENDIX

Each example cited in this chapter consists of three lines. In the first line, an example sentence is transliterated in the Hepburn romanisation system. The second line specifies grammatical terms with the glosses listed in Table 2, while the third line provides a free translation in English.

*Table 2. Glosses used in the present chapter*

| Abbreviation | Grammatical Term |
|---|---|
| ACC | accusative case |
| COMP | complementiser |
| COP | copula |
| FP | final particle |
| GEN | genitive case |
| HEAR | hearsay particle |
| NEG | negation |
| NML | nominaliser |
| NOM | nominative case |
| N.SU | suffix for a name |
| PAST | past tense |
| POL | polite form |
| Q | question particle |
| QUOT | quotation particle |
| TOP | topic |

# Chapter 9
# The Employment Status and Support Needs of Persons with Disabilities in Japan:
## An Analysis of Narrative using Narratology and Text Mining on a National Survey

**Kai Seino**
*National Institute of Vocational Rehabilitation, Keio Research Institute at SFC, Japan*

**Yuichiro Haruna**
*National Institute of Vocational Rehabilitation, Japan*

**Shun Ishizaki**
*Keio University, Japan*

## ABSTRACT

*This paper has two objectives: (1) to describe the significance and applicability of narratology, which features computational and cognitive approaches, in the field of interpersonal relationship supports for persons with disabilities, and (2) to determine effective work supports by analyzing the narratives of the persons with disabilities. In this chapter, the narratives were operationally defined as free-expression answers obtained from mail-survey questionnaires from people with various disabilities describing their work and work life. The questionnaires were sent to 14,448 people and, of these, 4,546 responded. The survey items included their employment status, problems they encountered before employment, problems in their working life, support required in their working life, and opinions regarding disability employment. The results suggested that employment status and problems at work depended on their disability type and the presence of effective supports.*

DOI: 10.4018/978-1-5225-0432-0.ch009

Copyright © 2016, IGI Global. Copying or distributing in print or electronic forms without written permission of IGI Global is prohibited.

## INTRODUCTION AND PURPOSE

Any effective disability employment support, whether national policy or interpersonal practice, must be based on the reality of the working life of persons with disabilities. However, the national-level surveys (Ministry of Health, Labour and Welfare, 2014a, 2014b) are mainly composed of selective questions for statistical analysis. Although some free-expression questions are usually added, traditional analysis of unstructured descriptions, such as the KJ method or the grounded theory, requires extensive human power for reading, classifying, and compiling the results. This methodological drawback has largely limited our understanding of the quantitative side of the reality. This study attempts to introduce an innovative analysis of the "narrative" of persons with disabilities that is derived from the national big data (National institute of vocational rehabilitation, 2011) in order to determine effective employment supports for persons with disabilities.

In recent years, there has been a growing focus, both internationally and domestically, on promoting the employment of persons with disabilities. In December 2006, the United Nations (2007) adopted the "Convention on the Rights of Persons with Disabilities," which Japan ratified in January 2014. Article 27 of the Treaty prescribes prohibition of discrimination and supports reasonable accommodations for securing the right to work of persons with disabilities. Also, Article 2 of the Japanese "Act for the Promotion of Employment of Persons with Disabilities (Ministry of Health, Labour and Welfare, 2015) " defines vocational rehabilitation as "establishing independence in the career of persons with disabilities by taking measures prescribed in law, including job guidance, vocational training, and job placement." However, several problems persist in the current situation of the employment of persons with disabilities. Although in 2014 the number of persons with disabilities who were employed reached a record high of approximately 430,000 people (the highest for 11 years) (Ministry of Health, Labour and Welfare, 2014a), the practical employment rate is merely 1.82%, which is short of the legal quota of 2.0%. In addition, per company, the ratio of achievement of the legal employment rate is 44.7%, meaning that more than half of all companies do not achieve the minimum legislated employment rate. Furthermore, by law, employers will be obligated to include persons with mental disabilities from 2018 and, as a result, the quota will be raised accordingly. Therefore, the development of effective working support to promote the employment of persons with disabilities is socially expected.

It is important to establish evidence for providing employment supports for persons with disabilities (Yaeda et al., 2012; Yaeda, Ozawa, & Wakabayashi, 2013). The concept of this evidence-based approach originated from 1990s EBM (evidence-based medicine) (Guyatt, 1991; Sackett, Richardson, Straus, Rosenberg, & Haynes, 1997), and evidence in this regard is objectively demonstrated. Sackett et al. (1997) define EBM as the "the conscientious, explicit and judicious use of current best evidence in making decisions about the care of the individual patient." After the introduction of EBM, the concept was extended to other fields, such as nursing, welfare, psychology, and education. In the United States, an Individual Placement and Support (IPS) model was established to provide evidence-based employment support for persons with significant mental illness. However, in Japan, the overall level of evidence acquired regarding the studies of employment support practices was low (Seino & Haruna, 2014). According to the classification of the Agency for Health Care Policy and Research (currently known as the Agency for Healthcare Research and Quality) (Clinton, 1993), meta-analysis is in the highest rank of evidence, followed by randomized controlled trials, whereas practice reports are ranked the lowest. Very few evidence-based clinical programs exist in Japan, such as cognitive rehabilitation programs (Sato et al., 2014), reinstatement support programs (Tashiro, Ito, Yoshida, & Tashiro, 2013;

Kitagawa, Kato, & Koyama, 2011), or group cognitive-behavioral therapy (Tajima et al., 2010). However, evidence for effective employment supports, being important both practically and academically, is still to be determined in Japan.

On the other hand, the idea of "evidence based" has been reasonably criticized. The following criticisms have been made: (1) It downplays qualitative studies on the hierarchy of evidence (Concato, 2004; Manuel, Fang, Bellamy, & Bledsoe, 2008); (2) In the framework of objective fact, it is claimed that it is impossible to acquire the opinions of socially oppressed minorities, therefore, this method fails to capture a pluralistic reality (Gergen, 1994a); and (3) It is also impossible to imitate the medical EBM model in a practice domain based on social sciences because the EBM model assumes only natural sciences as a research background (Yamabe, 2012). Based on the limits of objective facts, social constructivism that provides the relativist conception of reality has come to be recognized (Gergen, 1994b, 1999). Against the backdrop of this social constructivism, a trend that allows a reconsideration of EBM from the perspective of the narrative is NBM (Narrative Based Medicine) (Greenhalgh & Hurwits, 1998). In relation to NBM, it is said that "treating it as the thing which arrests the problem before oneself in a contextual context, and is personal with the characteristic based on the case (that is, based was in narrative), it is difficult to change in the others of the clinical intellect." Saito (2003) features the following five points as elements of the NBM approach: (1) illness as a story; (2) the patient as a storyteller; (3) the allowance of ambiguity of phenomena; (4) the insignificance of linear cause and effect; and (5) dialogue as a treatment. The narrative approach is one that has paid close attention to the narrative understanding of NBM. Since the 1990s, the narrative approach has attracted greater attention in interpersonal help domains, such as medical care, nursing, and psychology. The development of epistemology and the methodology that attached the importance to narrative is known as the "Narrative Turn." (Denzin & Lincoln, 2000). Noguchi defined this narrative approach as "going closer to some reality with the clues in the forms of narratives" (Noguchi, 2005). The narrative approach focuses on the patient or client and emphasizes the integrity and individuality of the person. However, as a result of the case studies' one-sided interest in the narrative approach, there have been almost no statistical or experimental studies that have collected data (Noguchi, 2009).

The integration of quantitative and qualitative analysis is known as the mixed methods approach, and this approach has evolved in recent years (Creswell & Plano Clark, 2007). Integrating evidence and narrative may develop an effective method in employment support areas. Mixed-methods research analyzes the collected data by using both quantitative and qualitative approaches. This approach leads to inferences through integrating the results. When using mixed methods, the validity of the study can be raised (Creswell & Plano Clark, 2007; Hirose, 2012).

Text mining has been examined in recent years in relation to the mixed method approach (Tagaki, 2012; Higuchi, 2014). Text mining is the act of converting text data into quantitative data in order to perform an "interactive analysis of the set of documents" (Feldman & Sanger, 2007). The technique of "data mining, machine learning, natural language processing, information retrieval, and knowledge management" is used in text mining (Feldman & Sanger, 2007). In this paper, the authors have performed a quantitative analysis of the free description statements of persons with disabilities and their supporters (Seino & Haruna, 2015a; Seino, Haruna, & Ishizaki, 2015b).

Therefore, the purpose of this study is (1) to determine the contents of effective employment support from the narrative of persons with disabilities and (2) to evaluate the validity and feasibility of the mixed methods approach using text mining of narratives. The distinct feature of this study is to examine effective employment support by using both narratology and text mining, which has thus far been unexplored in the relevant literature in Japan. By using the integrated method, this study will reveal more effective and more highly relevant employment support that reflects the opinions of persons with disabilities and will help to promote the employment of individuals with disabilities in various kinds of organizations. Also, this research will suggest the possibility that computational narratology data can be analyzed based on narratology and text mining.

## DETAILED BACKGROUND

In addition, the following information concerning the employment situation of persons with disabilities in Japan, narratology, and text mining is preparatory for detailed research questions and methods.

### Narratology

There are a variety of definitions of term "narrative." The novelist Haruki Murakami stated, "narrative exists whether in literary narrative, whether in personal narrative, whether in social narrative." In this study, it is defined as follows: first, literary narrative is the story found in literature, including mythology and folk tales; second, personal narrative is a narrative of an individual and the family; and third, social narrative is a group and social story. Moreover, the term "narrative" has a definition in the wider sense when used as a general term and another definition when used in the narrow sense of the term of "narratology." Narrative in the wider sense is understood as the "act of discussing and being discussed using language of the wide sense" (Yamada, 2007b). On the other hand, narrative in the narrow sense refers to a reproduction of real or fictional events, and it is always accompanied by time restraints (Prince, 2003).

#### Literary Narratology

The narrow sense of narratology is regarded as a literary theory. Narratology is the study of the nature, form, and function of narrative (Prince, 2003). This section gives an overview of the theories of Propp (1968) and Genette (1980). Ogata (2010) organized narratology by using five categories. In the background of narratology, there are (1) "The Poetics" of Aristotle (1997); (2) structuralism, which developed based on the ideas of Saussure; (3) the literary art movement of Russian Formalism (Kuwano & Oishi, 1988); (4) British and American literary theory (Yamoto, 1974); and (5) the literary theory of structuralism (Tsuchida, Aoyagi, & Ito, 1996).

Narrative comprises "story" and "discourse." According to narratology (Prince, 2003), the story concerns the content of the narrative while the discourse concerns the expressive side. Narratology employs both the analysis of story and that of discourse. The relation between the story and discourse has become the main theme of narratology. To illustrate, Russian Formalism regarded the components of narrative as being fabula (corresponding to the story) and sjuzet (corresponding to the discourse). Forster (1927) defined the components of narrative as "story" and "plot" (i.e., discourse). He observed, "Story talks about a case and an event according to progress of time," whereas the plot focuses on the causal relation of incidents and events. Propp (1968) described the fundamental components of any Russian folktale. In particular, he defined the narratological notions of "function" and characters' "roles." "Function" is a character's act defined from the viewpoint of its significance in the story. He described 31 types of "functions" that compose Russian folktales. Characters' "roles" are classified based on the range of performable "functions" by a character and, as a result, he described the following seven "roles:" (1) villain, (2) dispatcher, (3) helper, (4) princess or prize and her father, (5) donor, (6) hero, and (7) false hero. Greimas (1966) classified characters into six actantial models: (1) subject, (2) object, (3) sender, (4) receiver, (5) helper, and (6) opponent. Genette (1980) classified the narrative components into three: story, discourse, and narrating. Furthermore, Genette (1980) divided the discourse categories into three: (1) "tense" (this refers to the temporal relation between discourse and story); (2) "mood" (this refers to the reproduction of the story through the discourse); and (3) "voice" (this refers to the relationship between the narrating and the narrated and the relationship between the narrating and text.) Tense, mood, and voice are further divided into several sub-items. In applied studies of narratology, some researchers analyze and generate stories based on the theories constructed by Propp and Genette (Akimoto & Ogata, 2013; Ogata, 2011; Klein et al, 1974). This approach was exemplified by the study of the narrative generation system of Ogata (2015). In this study, Ogata (2015) devised a conceptual dictionary that can provide the basic components of narrative; specifically, character, objects, and place. Regarding these applied studies, Ogata (1999) suggested a study framework called "computational narratology." This research offered a literary study frame that fused understanding of narratology with the generation of narrative by using artificial intelligence and cognitive science. This study presented the concept of computational narratology in the wider sense.

## Psychological Narratology in the Narrative Approach

This study is considered a psychological narratology, used in the narrative approach. This section gives an overview of the underlying theories associated with psychotherapy. These theories are used to analyze the personal narratives and the social stories in the context of society and culture. Lyotard (1979) described a category of classification of "grand narratives" that can be used to justify various supporting stories that are seen as "little narratives." Also, Foucault (1980) accounted for a classification of "a dominant story," which influences a certain situation, and "an alternative story," which appears when the dominant story is doubted. White and Epston (1990) apply a classification of Foucault to narrative therapy, aiming to excavate the new "alternative story" from the "dominant story" that restricts life. This excavation is conducted by "externalizing" and seeking a "unique resolution" for the problem. Elliott (2005) divided narrative into two classifications: "first order narrative" and "second order narrative." The former focuses on an individual's discussion of their own experience, whereas the latter centers on a researcher's discussion about a personal quest to understand the social world. McAdams and Aubin (1998) analyzed a recited life story and, through the classifications of "a story of recovery" and "a story of the turning point," identified fixed forms, such as "sacred stories."

Moreover, there is a theory, called "literary narratology about story and discourse," which includes psychological narratology. Bruner (1986) classified forms of narrative into (1) "narrative mode," which includes the time-linking information about an event, and (2) "paradigmatic mode," which includes information about the necessary relations between multiple events as well as causal relations. Morgan (2000) views a story (corresponding to the narrative) as "an event connected on temporal axes in succession which becomes a plot (corresponding to the discourse)." Adam (1999) contended that narrative is composed of time, characters, predicates, and events that can change the predicates. Yamada (2007a) distinguished four levels of narrative: (1) real, (2) mutual action, (3) text, and (4) model. In line with Yamada's classification, Shojima (2008) classified narrative into four acts: (1) the side of mutual acts,

(2) the side of the social act, or social historic linkup, (3) something that cannot be discussed because it exists outside of the narrative, and (4) multiple lives or voices surrounding the life of the narrator.

There are some studies of narrative approaches to persons with disabilities. Tagaki's (2008) study examined the speech of persons with disabilities, whereas others have focused on the psychological details of schizophrenia (Komori & Yamada, 2001), narrative approaches to mental disorders (Buchanan-Barker & Barker, 2008; Vuokila-Oikkonen, Janhonen, & Vaisanen, 2004), the speech of aphasic persons (Nouchi, 2008), and the life of a small child undergoing treatment for cancer (Saiki, 2008). Studies of these narrative approaches have thus far used psychological narratology. However, these earlier studies are yet to closely examine the term "narrative" or to adopt a literary narratology method.

### Comparison of Two Narratologies

Literary narratology focuses on a literary narrative while a psychological story centers on social and personal stories. Both literary and psychological narratologies share some characteristics. For example, Russian Formalism, Forster and Bruner, and Morgan all reached the following consensus: narrative can be classified into two elements: (1) those lined up along the event in a time lapse (corresponding to the story) and (2) those lined up along the event in a causal relation (corresponding to the discourse). Also, an interest in the components of story is seen commonly in Propp (1968), Greimas (1966), Ogata (2015), and Adam (1999). The story consists of characters (including their roles and actions), functions, time, objects, places, predicates, and events that can affect the predicates. Additionally, Genette's (1980) classification of "voice" is divided into the time for narrating, a standard, and the persona of the narrator. This level of words and narrative has similar elements as the classification by Elliot (2005), Yamada (2007a) and Shojima (2008). On the other hand, there is a distinct difference between literary and psychological narratologies. Psychological narratology analyzes social and personal narratives, allowing the relationship between individuals, their culture, and society to be clarified.

## Text Mining in the Field of Interpersonal Relationship Support

Along with the development of text mining, natural language processing technology has been developed. From the mid-1990s, some researches, using text mining, have been conducted regarding feelings and evaluations of free descriptive sentences within the domain of natural language processing (Otsuka, Inui, & Okumura, 2007). The studies using free descriptive sentences within free-form answers can solve problems that are inherent in selective answers (Yasuda, 1970) because there is a re-experience-like possibility of consent (Mita, 1965).

However, a problem of analyzing free descriptive sentences is that there is a lack of objectivity in the method of answering, which makes it difficult to analyze the data obtained (Arima & Tsuji, 1987; Tsuzuki, 1975; Hara & Umino, 1984; Asai, 1987). Additionally, the problem of the subjective interpretation of the results has been highlighted by Tsuzuki (1975). In response to these problems, text mining converts qualitative data into quantitative data, which are then classified automatically by a multivariate analysis. This is expected to solve the problems found in the earlier studies. In recent years, text mining has broadly been used in the field of interpersonal support, including studies of employment support for persons with disabilities as well as doctors' explanations for suicide prevention (Kawashima, Koyama, Kawano, & Ito, 2009), needs assessments for persons with disabilities (Tagaki, 2009), support in relation to sexual relationship for those with intellectual disabilities (Kyou, 2012), and employment support for persons with disabilities (Okawa & Honda, 2014; Seino, Haruna, & Ishizaki, 2015b). Text mining has been used alongside the KJ method; however, to date, a study that combines text mining with narratology has not been found.

## The Employment Situation of Persons with Disabilities in Japan

The most current employment situation of persons with disabilities is reported in the 2013 findings of the Ministry of Health, Labour and Welfare, Japan (2014b). Subjects include 8,637 establishments that employ persons with physical, intellectual, or mental disabilities. Within these establishments, there are 7,507 persons employed who have disabilities (66.7% men, 32.3% women). For each occupation, employment status, agreed working hours per week, and obstacles are shown in Table 1. The accommodations provided by the establishments for each obstacle are shown in Table 2.

The study, examining employment status, occupations, and concrete policies used to accommodate persons with disabilities and disorders, has the following four limitations: (1) the study divides disabilities into only three large frames (physical, intellectual, and mental), thereby failing to highlight more detailed characteristics of various disabilities; (2) because of the nature of an establishment, some do

*Table 1. Disability employment status (this table has been created based on the survey results)*

| Disability Type | Working Form | | Working Time | | Job (Top Three) |
|---|---|---|---|---|---|
| | Regular Staff | Non-Regular Staff | Full-Time Employment | Under 20 Hours a Week | |
| Physical Disability | 55.9 | 43.8 | 81.8 | 5.5 | Office work 31.7%<br>Professional and technical work 14.3%<br>Work in retail 13.6% |
| Intellectual Disability | 18.8 | 81.3 | 61.9 | 10.4 | Work in production process 25.8%<br>Work in transportation, cleaning, and packing 21.9%<br>Work in service industry 20.5% |
| Mental Disorder | 40.8 | 58.9 | 68.9 | 4.2 | Office work 32.5%<br>Service work 15.1%<br>Work in service industry 12.9% |

*Table 2. Accommodations at the workplace for persons with disabilities*

| Disability Type | Aspects of the Accommodation (Top Three) |
|---|---|
| Physical Disability | Personnel management, including relocation, etc. 47.9%<br>Employment management, including assistance for attending hospital and taking medicine 41.2%<br>Service for commuting, including providing parking lots and other accommodations 33.8% |
| Intellectual Disability | Job specifications, including the simplification of the process 60.7%<br>Placement of assistance resources 42.8%<br>Personnel management, such as relocation, etc. 38.5% |
| Mental Disorder | Employment management, including assistance for attending hospital and taking medicine 48.0%<br>Personnel management, including relocation, etc. 46.9%<br>Working hours, such as providing flexible working hours, etc. 37.4% |

not understand how to support a person with a disability; (3) the results cannot be determined solely by statistical analysis; and (4) the results cannot be determined only by selective answers because these would not provide a concrete picture of the present situation.

## METHODS: ANALYSIS OF NARRATIVES OF PERSONS WITH DISABILITIES IN RELATION TO WORK

The present study employed the following methods to (1) target a wide range of disability types to refine classifications of disabilities, (2) recognize the work status and needs of persons with disabilities, and (3) integrate a narrative approach based on free-expression answers and quantitative data analysis.

### Survey Method and Participants

#### Survey Method

The secondary analysis was conducted using data collected during the "Examining Workplaces and Communities that Support Independence and Satisfy the Employment needs of Persons with Disabilities and Diseases" survey (National Institute of Vocational Rehabilitation, 2011). The survey period was from July 2008 to December 2009, during which self-administered questionnaires were mailed to participants. A research committee was founded, comprising selected persons from various disability (advocacy) organizations, academic experts, and service providers, to assess the validity of the survey and examine the materials required for the survey. For persons with intellectual and developmental disabilities, clearer explanation was provided about questionnaires, terms were revised, and ruby was added to kanji so that all the participants could comprehend the contents of the survey. Also, the questionnaires were transcribed into braille for visually impaired persons.

This study was approved by the research ethics committee of the National Institute of Vocational Rehabilitation.

#### Participants

The participants were of working age, ranging between 15 and 65 years. They were not asked about previous work experience. A total of 14,448 questionnaires were mailed through disability organizations to their members with the respective disability or disease, and 4,546 valid responses were obtained, providing a recovery rate of 31.5%. The participants consisted of 2,309 males, 2,082 females, and 155 non-gender-identified responses. The mean age was 44.3 years (SD=14.3). The number of participants categorized based on types of disability is shown in Figure 1. Note that diseases other than intractable diseases were classified as "other." In total, 3,956 responses (91.0%) were answered in person by individuals with a disability, 311 responses (7.2%) were answered by deputies on behalf of the participants, and 82 responses (1.9%) were answered by "other." Nonresponses were excluded from this study.

*Figure 1. Disabilities of the participants (multiple answers)*

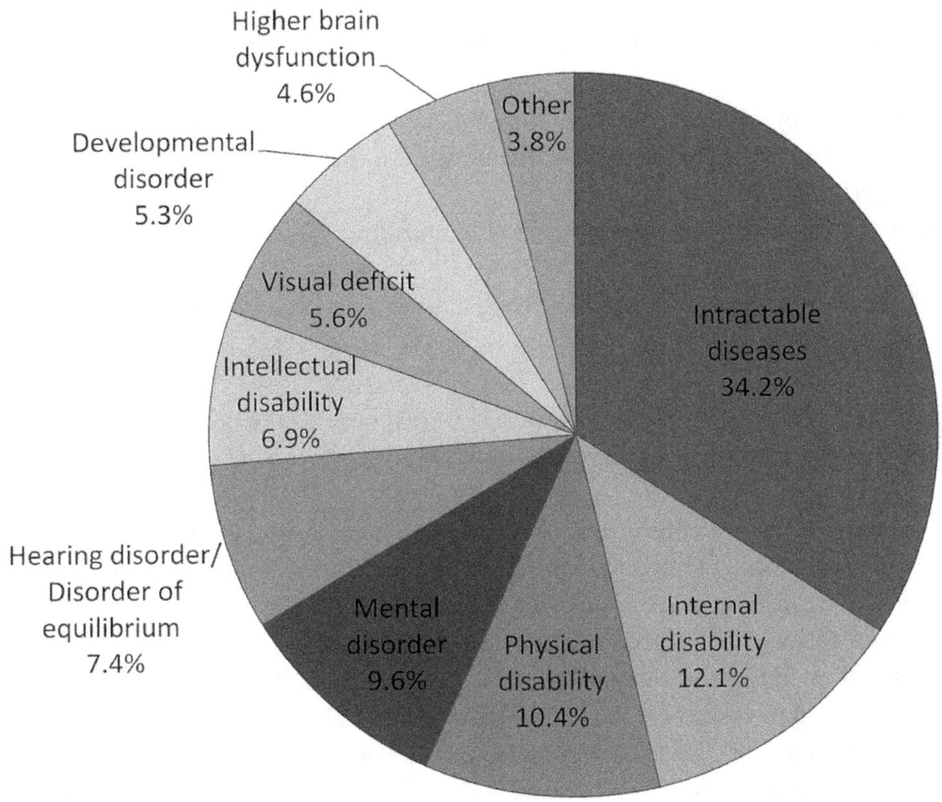


## Analysis Method of Free-Expression Answers

Data analysis of free expression answers was conducted using KH Coder software (Ver2β32). The software was developed for an academic purpose and has the following functions necessary for text mining: the separation of words with a space; morphological analysis; dependency parsing; multivariate analysis, including correspondence and cluster analysis; document retrieval; and coating. KH Coder has been used in over 1000 studies to date (November 1, 2015). In addition, studies on interpersonal assistance using KH Coder have also been conducted (Mihara, 2011; Sakai, Inagaki, Higuchi, & Kato, 2011; Sakuyama, 2012; Yoshihara & Imura, 2008). The analysis consisted of extracting compound words, conducting morphological analysis, listing and searching extracted words, and conducting correspondence and cluster analysis. In particular, the KH Coder's Chasen function was employed in morphological analysis and "Term Extract" in KH Coder was used to extract compound words. Some examples of compound words found as a result of the extraction were "human relationships," "general company/firm," "vocational training," and "disability pension." Then, based on the pre-analysis performed prior to text mining, compound words that had not already been extracted were searched for. Next, terms relevant to a theme and/or question, such as "a job," "work," and "persons with disabilities," were searched for and, finally, associated terms were coded. The unit of analysis was an individual respondent, and the same respondent using the same word multiple times was counted once.

## Definition of "Narrative"

In this study, both the wider and narrow senses of narrative are used depending on the particular contexts of the analysis.

Examples of free expression answers are shown below. (To protect respondents' privacy, some answers are altered, but to the extent that basic meanings are maintained. In what follows, this research conforms to this principle.)

[Concerning work description] In response to the question: "Describe your job in detail."

**Example 1:** Since my legs were injured, I have been assigned paperwork. I am now engaged in computer work. (Physical disability)

[Concerning care and support at the workplace] In response to the question: "Specify the care and support provided in your workplace as a means of assisting your career."

**Example 2:** At my workplace, employees often get acquainted with coworkers at informal meetings, such as drinks parties. I did not attend these parties because of my disease, so I had no opportunity to get to know them. The other day, I took the opportunity of participating in one, and it worked much more effectively than I had expected. (Mental disorder)

**Example 3:** I first wanted to work without mentioning my disease. The other day, a relative of a person who had supported me asked me to work in their office. When I began working there, I soon found that this relative did not care for my condition, so it was a disastrous year. From this experience, I realized that I should conceal my disease because people consider me to be inferior to healthy people. (Intractable disease)

This study analyzes the free descriptive texts that reflect personal stories of persons with disabilities. It clarifies social stories of disability based on the results of multivariate analysis involving text mining. Note that the free descriptive texts treated in this study are partly narrative in the narrow sense while others are narratives in the wider sense.

# RESULTS

The results of the quantitative answers to the multiple-choice questions and the narrative free-expression answers are shown below in terms of employment status and support required in the workplaces of persons with disabilities.

## Employment Status of Persons with Disabilities

### Answers to Multiple-Choice Questions

Table 3 shows the results of multiple-choice answers regarding (1) experience of income-earning work with a disability, (2) employment status, and (3) working hours. Chi-square residual analysis was conducted to determine differences in the percentage of people who "have past and/or present employment experience with a disability," "are (presently) employed," "self-employed workers," "full-time workers," and "part-time workers (i.e., fewer than 20 hours a week)." Regarding employment experience, people who "had and/or currently have paying jobs with a disability" were significantly higher among people with hearing and balance impairments. Regarding the types of employment, a significantly higher percentage of individuals with intractable diseases or with hearing and balance impairments were "(presently) employed," whereas the percentage of "self-employed workers" was significantly higher among visually impaired individuals, physically disabled individuals, and individuals with an internal disability. The percentage of "full-time workers" was significantly higher among individuals with hearing and balance impairments or intractable diseases. The percentage of "part-time workers (e.g., fewer than 20 hours a week)" was significantly higher among individuals with mental disorders, higher brain dysfunction, and visual impairments/disabilities. These results indicate that work experience, type of employment, and working hours differ depending on the type of disability or disease.

## Free-Expression Answers

Free-expression answers were analyzed according to the type of disability or disease, excluding multiple disabilities and diseases. The free-expression question was "Describe your business in detail," resulting in responses from 1,399 participants. A morphological analysis extracted a total of 11,972 words containing 2,632 distinct words. The mean frequency of the extracted words was 2.11 times, with a standard deviation of 5.41 times. As shown in Table 4, the top 10 characteristic words from those extracted were listed for each disability and disease. "Characteristic words" refers to the Jaccard degree of affiliation for each

*Table 3. Employment status of the respondents*

| Disability Type | Employment Experience | Employment Status | | Working Hours | |
|---|---|---|---|---|---|
| | Have Experience of Past and/or Present Employment with a Disability | Employed | Independent Business (Self-Employed) | Full-Time | Fewer than 20 Hours per Week |
| Visual deficit | 84.7% (-0.7) | 77.6% (-2.1)† | 19.0% (11.4) * | 65.0% (1.2) | 22.6% (2.2) * |
| Hearing disorder/ Disorder of equilibrium | 90.2% (2.6) ** | 87.7% (2.7) ** | 6.8% (-4.4)†† | 71.7% (5.0) ** | 12.8% (-6.2)†† |
| Physical disability | 74.9% (-8.3)†† | 77.8% (-2.6)†† | 11.3% (2.7) ** | 61.6% (-0.2) | 19.3% (-0.3) |
| Internal disability | 88.0% (1.7) | 84.3% (1.1) | 10.6% (2.0) * | 61.3% (-0.4) | 17.0% (-3.2)†† |
| Intellectual disability | 81.7% (-2.6)†† | 71.6% (-5.2)†† | 1.5% (-11.1)†† | 48.2% (-6.3)†† | 13.7% (-4.8)†† |
| Mental disorder | 82.7% (-2.4)†† | 77.5% (-2.9)†† | 4.1% (-9.0)†† | 48.9% (-7.2)†† | 32.1% (12.2) ** |
| Developmental disorder | 84.1% (-1.1) | 77.9% (-2.0)† | 3.4% (-7.6)†† | 57.8% (-1.7)† | 18.0% (-1.1) |
| High brain dysfunction | 69.4% (-8.1)†† | 74.3% (-2.9)†† | 4.3% (-5.5)†† | 49.4% (-4.3)†† | 32.8% (8.0) ** |
| Intractable diseases | 86.6% (1.0) | 86.4% (5.0) ** | 9.9% (1.0) | 64.3% (2.9) ** | 20.5% (2.0) |

Adjusted residuals in parentheses $\chi$-square test (compared to other disability types), **Many with $p < 0.01$, *Many with $p < 0.05$, ††Few with $p < 0.01$, †Few with $p < 0.05$.

*Table 4. Top 10 characteristic words relevant to work contents for each disability and disease*

| Visual Deficit | Jaccard Degree | Hearing Disorder/ Disorder of Equilibrium | Jaccard Degree | Physical Disability | Jaccard Degree |
|---|---|---|---|---|---|
| Massage | 0.107 | Office work | 0.049 | Computer | 0.046 |
| Acupuncture massage | 0.05 | Use | 0.019 | Use | 0.024 |
| Physiotherapist | 0.032 | The sense of hearing | 0.01 | System engineer | 0.014 |
| Rehabilitation | 0.024 | Design | 0.01 | Restaurant business | 0.014 |
| Self-employed | 0.022 | Machinery | 0.01 | Assistance | 0.014 |
| General | 0.016 | Assemble | 0.01 | Sales job | 0.011 |
| Work in hospital | 0.016 | Regular employee | 0.01 | Full-time job | 0.007 |
| Teacher | 0.016 | PC operation | 0.01 | Civil servant office work | 0.007 |
| Hospital | 0.014 | Mid-career recruitment | 0.007 | Date base | 0.007 |
| In his or her twenties | 0.008 | System | 0.007 | Return to work | 0.007 |
| **Internal Disability** | **Jaccard Degree** | **Intellectual Disability** | **Jaccard Degree** | **Mental Disability** | **Jaccard Degree** |
| Office work | 0.076 | Cleaning | 0.083 | Cleaning | 0.025 |
| PC | 0.026 | Insert | 0.033 | Part-time job | 0.017 |
| Work | 0.016 | Snacks | 0.020 | Manufacturing industry | 0.014 |
| Manager | 0.016 | Inspection | 0.020 | Factory | 0.014 |
| System engineer | 0.014 | Luggage | 0.020 | Hospital | 0.014 |
| Factory | 0.013 | Dry | 0.013 | Supermarket | 0.014 |
| Desk work | 0.013 | Label | 0.013 | Sales job | 0.013 |
| Dialysis | 0.010 | Board | 0.013 | Current | 0.013 |
| Inspection | 0.010 | Arrange | 0.013 | Confectionery | 0.010 |
| Date input | 0.010 | Pack | 0.013 | Acquaintance | 0.010 |
| **Developmental Disability** | **Jaccard Degree** | **Higher Brain Dysfunction** | **Jaccard Degree** | **Intractable Diseases/ Chronic Disease** | **Jaccard Degree** |
| Cleaning | 0.044 | Rehabilitation | 0.030 | Office work | 0.093 |
| Part-time job | 0.039 | Current | 0.022 | Service work | 0.024 |
| Facility | 0.024 | Agriculture | 0.020 | PC | 0.020 |
| Sort out | 0.023 | PC | 0.019 | Nurse | 0.018 |
| Manufacturing industry | 0.023 | PC operation | 0.018 | Part-time job | 0.016 |
| Company | 0.021 | Company | 0.027 | Current | 0.016 |
| Current | 0.019 | Salad making | 0.010 | Desk work | 0.014 |
| Service work | 0.018 | Transcription from recorded tapes | 0.010 | Sales job | 0.014 |
| Plant | 0.017 | Café | 0.010 | Manager | 0.011 |
| Assistant | 0.017 | Arts and crafts | 0.010 | Cashier | 0.010 |

disability and disease, with a higher number corresponding to a stronger affiliation. More specifically, the Jaccard degree counts the probability of the co-occurrence of particular words along with other particular words in each description, regardless of whether the word has been used once or ten times. The pairs with no comparable words were omitted from the count (Romesburg, 1984). The Jaccard degree ranges from 0 to 1, with higher values signifying higher degrees of frequency.

The characteristic words were interpreted by the analyst, one of the authors, in the context of the original free-expression answers. Examples are as follows:

[Work contents] In response to the question: "Describe your business in detail." (The characteristic words are underlined in the box below.)

**Example 4:** I am working as a *physiotherapist* at a *rehabilitation* center in a *hospital* under private management. (visual deficit)

**Example 5:** I perform *office work* and I am part of the planning section but am not in charge of negotiations with other people. I feel that a person with a *hearing* impairment cannot get promoted in this institution. (hearing/equilibrium disorder)

**Example 6:** Since I *returned to work*, I have been working by *using* a *PC* with my left hand. (physically disabled)

**Example 7:** I am receiving *dialysis*, so I am *inspecting* the quality of products while sitting. It took a long time for me to accept my disease, but I finally did it and found a job for myself. (internal medical condition)

**Example 8:** I am a member of the *cleaning* staff at a welfare institution for elderly people. I am the only employee with a disability. I perform *cleaning* in the order instructed without anyone's help. (intellectual disorder)

**Example 9:** I pack, wrap up, and *arrange* products. I *put* pieces of rice cakes into bags. I make *snacks.* I wash the boxes. (intellectual disorder)

**Example 10:** I have been running my design office for 20 years. I had an epileptic seizure, so I chose to run my own business. I've made an effort to acquire as many certificates as possible. *Currently*, I still experience seizures from time to time. I owe my being able to work to my wife. (mental disorder)

**Example 11:** I am a janitor at a *facility*. I am working comfortably, but the only problem is that I have not been permitted me to work as a full-time employee even though I apply every year. (developmental disorder)

**Example 12:** A civil servant. Although I have a slight disability, I received a retirement recommendation from a *rehabilitation* teacher and retired nine years early. (high brain dysfunction)

**Example 13:** I had a *sales job* with a foreign company for four years. I did *office work* as a contract employee and after that with the same company for one year. The *office work* was work such as calculations, and was performed while sitting down. I then got married and left the job. (intractable disease)

The characteristic words were further classified according to the narrative components of the story (Propp, 1968; Greimas, 1966; Ogata, 2015; Adam, 1999) and were sorted into the story elements: characters, predicates, places, objects, and time (Table 6).

The characters were divided into those representing a specific person or a specific category. Then, the analyst used an idea from Propp's (1968) classification of the role of the character and extracted the role and specific characters from the sentences. The characters were divided into the categories of "a person with no disability," "a person with a disability," and other particular persons. Rehabilitation teachers and acquaintances who introduced the work were considered to be "helpers." The predicate elements were organized into three subclasses: job type, act, and employment status.

These characteristic words could be consistently read as a story with typical job characteristics being found with the selective answer responses: a self-employed person with a visual deficit (impairment), a full-time worker with a hearing disorder or disequilibrium, and a part-time worker with a mental disorder (see Table 5).

Correspondence analysis was conducted to provide more visual results; further, the object of this analysis only concerns nouns with the lowest frequency of 17 (Figure 2).

As shown in Figure 2, words with no particular emergence pattern (commonly seen in the present respondents) are placed closer to the origin. The further a word is placed from the origin and closer to a

*Table 5. Classification of the characteristic words*

| Disability Type | Character | Predicate | Place | Objects | Time |
|---|---|---|---|---|---|
| Visual Deficit (Disability) | A regular person (example: a generally healthy person) | **(Job)** Masseur, Acupuncture Masseur, Physical Therapist, Teacher<br>**(Act)** Rehabilitation (rehabilitation trainer)<br>**(Working status)** Self Employed | Hospital, rehabilitation (rehabilitation facility) | N.A. | 20s (example: "in one's 20s") |
| Hearing Disorder/ Disorder of Equilibrium | Acquired (example: acquired disability), Hearing (example: person(s) with a hearing disorder) | **(Job)** Office work, System (example: system engineer)<br>**(Act)** Design, Assembling, Data Input, Use, Machine, Hearing (example: supporting the life of a child with a hearing disability)<br>**(Working status)** Regular Employee | Hearing (example: special needs schools for those with a hearing disability) | System | N.A. |
| Physical Disability | N.A. | **(Job)** System Engineer, the Restaurant Business, Sales job, Civil Servant office work<br>**(Act)** Use. Providing support (example: supporting office work), Return (example: returning to work)<br>**(Working status)** Full-time business | N.A. | PC, Database | N.A. |
| Internal Medical Condition | N.A. | **(Job)** System Engineer<br>**(Act)** Work, Desk work, Manage (example: managing a facility), Inspection (example: quality inspection), Office work, Dialysis (example: to be on dialysis) | Factory | PC | N.A. |
| Intellectual Disability | N.A. | **(Act)** Cleaning, Inspection, Packing, Arranging, Inserting (example: inserting snacks) | N.A. | Snacks, Label, Baggage, Board, Drying (example: a dry leaf) | N.A. |
| Mental Disorder | Acquaintance | **(Job)** Manufacturing, Sales Job<br>**(Act)** Cleaning, Confectioning<br>**(Working form)** Part-time Job | Factory, Hospital, Supermarket | N.A. | Now |
| Developmental Disorder | N.A. | **(Job)** Manufacturing<br>**(Act)** Cleaning, Sorting, Service Work, Planting (example: planting flowers), Assistant<br>**(Working form)** Part-time job | Facility, company | N.A. | Now |
| Higher Brain Dysfunction | Rehabilitation (Example: A rehabilitation teacher) | **(Job)** Agriculture<br>**(Act)** Data Input, Making Salad, Transcripting Recorded Tapes, Arts and Crafts | Company, Cafe | PC | Now |
| Intractable Diseases | N.A. | **(Job)** Nurse<br>**(Act)** Office work, Service work, Desk Work, Managing<br>**(Working form)** Part-time Job | N.A. | PC, Cash Register | Now |

*Table 6. Support situation in the workplace*

| Accommodations/Adjustments | Necessary but not Equipped in the Workplace |
|---|---|
| Correct understanding of the illness or disability by supervisors and colleagues | 49.8% (24.88)** |
| A human resources policy that allows for promotions regardless of illness or disability | 46.8% (20.64)** |
| Consideration to take time for communication | 43.6% (16.86)** |
| There is support for the acquisition of vocational skills | 41.9% (14.58)** |
| Awareness of management and staff in regard to preventing prejudice and discrimination | 41.1% (13.66)** |
| A full-time counselor is available | 40.7% (13.26)** |
| Efforts are made to listen to the opinions of the person with the disability and improve the (content of) work accordingly | 40.5% (12.89)** |
| Ability is matched with reasonable work | 37.9% (9.76)** |
| I have colleagues, supervisors, and superiors to whom I can turn to for advice | 37.7% (9.63)** |
| The person with the disability is included in group activities in the workplace | 36.8% (8.36)** |
| Skills and job training are provided at the time of employment or during relocation | 36.7% (8.23)** |
| One-on-one individual practice guidance is provided | 36.6% (8.00)** |
| Facilitating taking a break during work | 36.2% (7.61)** |
| Individual adjustments and changes to content and methods of working are made | 35.5% (6.77)** |
| Checking of work content is implemented with an attending physician, specialist, or workplace personnel when necessary | 34.2% (5.09)** |
| Time off is allowed during working hours for medical needs | 32.5% (3.06)** |
| Considerations are given to ambulatory visits | 32.2% (2.66)** |
| Assistance is provided by colleagues and others as needed | 30.9% (1.07) |
| Health management is provided by industrial physicians and/or occupational health nurses in the office | 30.8% (0.92) |
| Places that accommodate rest and health management in the workplace are secured and maintained | 30.3% (0.25) |
| Changes in working hours (e.g., time difference attendance, flexible work) are accommodated | 30.1% (0.06) |
| Shorter working hours are permitted | 28.1% (-2.41)†† |
| Technical support personnel such as a workplace caregivers or sign-language interpreters are available | 27.6% (-3.08)†† |
| Daily health reports are made by the boss or superiors | 24.2% (-7.29)†† |
| Telecommuting is permitted | 23.2% (-8.30)†† |
| Everyone has easy-to-use equipment (i.e., universal design) | 23.1% (-8.57)†† |
| Facilities such as toilets, rest areas, and the cafeteria are user-friendly | 21.5% (-10.64)†† |
| Work manuals and appropriate training are provided | 19.7% (-12.74)†† |
| Equipment and tools used on the job, environment maintenance, and remodeling such as adjustable work desks are provided | 16.9% (-16.34)†† |
| Air conditioning and/or air cleaners are provided | 16.4% (-17.09)†† |
| Facility improvement assists with movement in the workplace (e.g., handrails, passageways, guidance) | 16.4% (-16.85)†† |
| The workplace environment accommodates persons with disabilities (e.g., width of doors, sloped entrances, parking, emergency exits) | 15.6% (-18.00)†† |
| Support equipment for the use of personal computers (including software) is provided | 14.4% (-19.38)†† |
| Medical instruments and support equipment are provided | 11.4% (-23.02)†† |
| Support equipment for individual movement (e.g., electric wheelchairs) is provided | 9.3% (-25.44)†† |

Adjusted residuals of $\chi$-square test are in parentheses (compared to other accommodations), **Many with $p<0.01$, *Many with $p<0.05$, ††Less with $p<0.01$, †Less with $p<0.05$.

*Figure 2. Result of correspondence analysis on work content by disability*

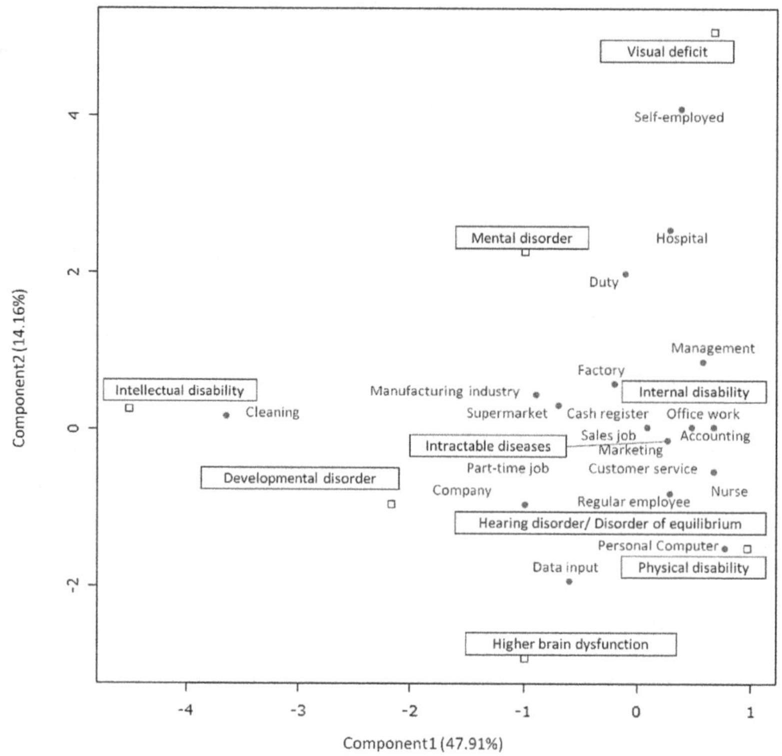


disability characterizes that disability. In addition, words located close together tended to be used concurrently. Therefore, words placed around the origin, such as "cash register," "office work," "accounting," "sales job," and "marketing" were used without particular emergence patterns, but were frequently used in the free expression answer as a whole. These words were also placed near "intractable disease," and "internal disability," which constituted the largest groups of the respondents. "Cleaning" was located near "intellectual disability," "self-employed" was located near "visual deficit," "personal computer" was located near "physical disability," and "company" was located near "developmental disorder;" which was consistent with the typical jobs for each disability.

## Support Required in the Workplace for Persons with Disabilities

### Answers to Multiple-Choice Questions

In this preliminary analysis, all of the respondents with employment experience were included in this analysis regardless of type of disability. Please note that the respondents were so significantly biased that nearly half of them were patients with intractable diseases; not at all representative of the full population of persons with disabilities. The questionnaire enquired about support situations in the workplace, which is important in the working lives of people with illness or disability. Residual analysis of the $\chi$-square test for the answer "Necessary but not equipped in the workplace" was performed (Table 6). As a result, "Necessary but not equipped in the workplace" was significantly chosen over the other choices of "correct understanding of the illness and disability by supervisors and colleagues," "a human resources policy that allows for promotions regardless of illness or disability," and "consideration to take time for communication."

## Free-Expression Answers

The free-expression answers to the question concerning support in the workplace that is necessary for the working lives of those with illness or disability, phrased "Describe the consideration and support situation in the workplace that is important for your working life," were analyzed. The number of people who gave answers to this question was 878. Morphological analysis extracted a total of 27,807 words, containing 2,670 distinct words for analysis. The mean frequency of the extracted word was 4.19 times, with a standard deviation of 20.24 times.

Next, a hierarchical cluster analysis was conducted to obtain an overview of responses. Here, only nouns were included in the analysis (Table 7). In the extracted words, the minimum frequency was 20, and the paragraph was used as the aggregation unit. The distance between the extracted words is expressed using the Jaccard coefficient. The distance between the clusters is set by Ward's method using a sum of squares that is standard for the classification of the cluster (Everitt, 1998).

The assumed stories for each cluster were interpreted by the analyst according to the extracted words in the contexts of the original descriptions, as shown in the following examples:

[Cluster1]

**Example 14 :** I *can* take the day off when my physical condition is bad because I am self-employed and do not work for a company of others. My company understands my disease, and I *can* work at my own pace without *unreasonableness*.

*Table 7. Results of the cluster analysis of extracted words, and assumed stories relating to support needs*

| | Cluster 1 | Cluster 2 | Cluster 3 | Cluster 4 | Cluster 5 | Cluster 6 |
|---|---|---|---|---|---|---|
| Extracted words | Can | Oneself (I) | Hospital | Break | Physical condition | Many |
| | Unreasonableness | Problem | Boss | Duty | Bad | Restroom |
| | Person | Say | Illness | Time | | Go |
| | Now | Necessary | Understanding | | | Hospital |
| | Think | | | | | Now |
| | | | | | | Rest/Break |
| Assumed stories relating to support needs | Accommodation to work without unreasonable difficulty | General need for consideration/ support for the problematic situation experienced by the person with a disability | Understanding afforded by the boss in regard to hospital visits and illness | Consideration for taking breaks during work | Consideration to allow rest at times of aggravation of the physical condition | Consideration for breaks to use the toilet and for hospital visits |

"Can" was used in a variety of meanings such as "I can," "I cannot," and "if I can" in Cluster 1. "Unreasonableness" was used primarily in the following two meanings: "consideration to work without unreasonableness" and "the work is impossible." "Person" was used in the following meanings: "a person in the company," "person with disorder," and "a person without disorder." "Now" was used in the context of "time," and "think" was primarily used to express the subject's thoughts or opinions. Therefore, the contents of Cluster 1 could be interpreted as "it is impossible to work" and "consideration to work without unreasonableness." The analyst therefore named Cluster 1 "Accommodation to work without unreasonable difficulty."

[Cluster2]

**Example 15 :** I have an intractable disease. Therefore I can have symptoms when I am in various locations and must take care of them as soon as possible. I hope the workplace has the understanding to allow me to go to the hospital when *I* want to go.

In Cluster 2, "I" was used to refer to the subjects themselves. "Problem" was used to mean "there is a problem" or "there is no problem." "Say" was used in a variety of meanings such as "it is said," "I said," and "I did not say about the illness," while "necessary" was mainly used in the sense of "such a consideration is necessary;" therefore, the analyst named Cluster 2 "General need for consideration/ support for the problematic situation experienced by the person with a disability."

[Cluster3]

**Example 16:** *Understanding* from colleagues and the *boss*. Their consideration when my condition worsens and/or requires *hospital visits (ambulatory visits).*

"Hospital visits," "illness," and "understanding" were used as necessary considerations and supports in Cluster 3. "Boss" was used to refer to the person the subject wants to understand his/her illness; therefore, the analyst named Cluster 3 "Understanding afforded by the boss in regard to hospital visits and illness." This result aligns with the result of the following multiple-choice answers: "appropriate understanding about illness and/or disability by the boss or colleagues" and "consideration about hospital visits (ambulatory visits)."

[Cluster4]

**Example 17:** Leaving a post temporarily to take *a break* and/or take supplementary food when I have low blood sugar during work, especially during service work.

"A break," "time," and "work" were used in reference to necessary considerations and support mainly in Cluster 4, for example: "the time allowed to take a break during work?" Therefore, the analyst named Cluster 4 "Consideration for taking breaks during work." This result aligns with the result of the following multiple-choice answers: "Making it easier to take a break during work" and "Time off allowed during working hours for medical needs."

[Cluster5]

**Example 18:** I think that you should clearly inform the workplace of your *physical condition* even if it is difficult to talk about it. When your condition is *bad*, you should be honest about it.

"Physical condition" and "bad" were primarily used in reference to consideration and necessary support in Cluster 5, for example: "when I am in bad physical condition," "I am not able to rest," and" I need to rest." Therefore, the analyst named Cluster 5 "Consideration to allow rest at times when the physical condition is aggravated." There were no multiple-choice questions similar to Cluster 5 and, therefore, it was only observed through free expression answers.

[Cluster6]

**Example 19:** My illness causes me to go to the *restroom many* times. I have also been slandered behind my back about this, and this affects my relationships with others.

"Many," "restroom," "go," "hospital," and "rest/break" were used as necessary consideration and support in Cluster 6, for example: "the consideration for needing to go to the restroom many times," and "taking a break to go to the hospital." "Now" was mainly used in reference to time. Therefore, the analyst named Cluster 6 "Consideration for breaks to use the toilet and for hospital visits (ambulatory visits)." There were no multiple-choice questions similar to Cluster 5 and, therefore, it was only observed through free expression answers.

Table 8 shows the characteristic words, including those deleted in the previous process (e.g., "working," "workplace," and "now"), sorted into the elements of the characters, predicates that represent the acts, places, and time. The characters "oneself," "colleague," and "boss" were further interpreted by the analyst according to the classification of Propp's (1968) role of the character: "oneself" was considered as a "main character," while "boss" or "colleague" were considered "helper," "villain," or "persons that are neither helpers nor villains." A villain is a person who behaves without understanding the disability while knowing about the disability. "Persons that are neither helpers nor villains" were those who were not informed of the disability and therefore did not provide special consideration for the person with a disability.

Next, the analyst created a co-occurrence network diagram based on words that are used in conjunction with "boss," "oneself," and "colleagues" and that had been used by more than 15 people to clarify or summarize the act of the character. The higher the frequency of the word, the larger the circle of the word is drawn. The lines connecting the words represent the strength of the co-occurrence (Higuchi, 2014) and, the stronger the co-occurrence, the thicker the line is drawn. The Jaccard degree is represented by the thickness of the edge. The "centrality" is represented by color; dark gray, white, and light gray, with dark gray being most central.

In Figure 3, acts strongly associated with the word "boss" included "understanding," "consideration," and "hospital visits (ambulatory visits)," among others.

In Figure 4, acts strongly associated with the word "oneself" included "understanding" and "consideration," among others.

In Figure 5, acts strongly associated with the word "colleague" included "understanding," "consideration," and "tell," among others.

*Table 8. Classification of the extracted words*

| Character | | Predicate | |
|---|---|---|---|
| **Word Extracted** | **The Number (Frequency) of Occurrences** | **Word Extracted** | **The Number of Occurrences** |
| Boss | 41 | Hospital visits (ambulatory visits) | 87 |
| Oneself | 36 | Work/Duty | 76 |
| Colleague | 17 | Understanding | 69 |
| **Place** | | Day off | 33 |
| Work place/Company | 113 | Say | 27 |
| Restroom | 23 | Go | 26 |
| Hospital | 19 | Break | 25 |
| **Time** | | Tell | 17 |
| Now | 44 | Correspondence | 16 |
| | | Receive | 13 |
| | | Communication | 12 |
| | | Overtime work | 12 |
| | | Know | 12 |
| | | Adjustment | 12 |
| | | Get | 11 |
| | | Aggravation | 10 |
| | | Take | 10 |
| | | Employment | 10 |
| | | Explanation | 10 |
| | | Turn to for advice | 10 |

Using a document search, the relationship between the actions and the characters was interpreted by the analyst from the context of the extracted words in the original descriptions (Table 9). Thus, the word "think," used only in the context involving the responder's thoughts, is not associated with the support. As a result, "understanding and consideration for illness and disability" was denoted as an act performed by superiors and colleague(s), and "going to hospital (hospital visits (ambulatory visits))," "rest," and "break" were denoted as acts performed by the participant themselves. Those stories may relate a typical workplace situation for persons with intractable diseases, who were the largest group of the respondents.

## DISCUSSION

To the best of our knowledge, this study is the first to use a mixed method of narratology and text mining to explore effective employment supports. The narratives of persons with disabilities operated in a complementary manner with quantitative results to afford a better understanding of specific work con-

*Figure 3. Co-occurrence network with strong relation to the word "boss"*

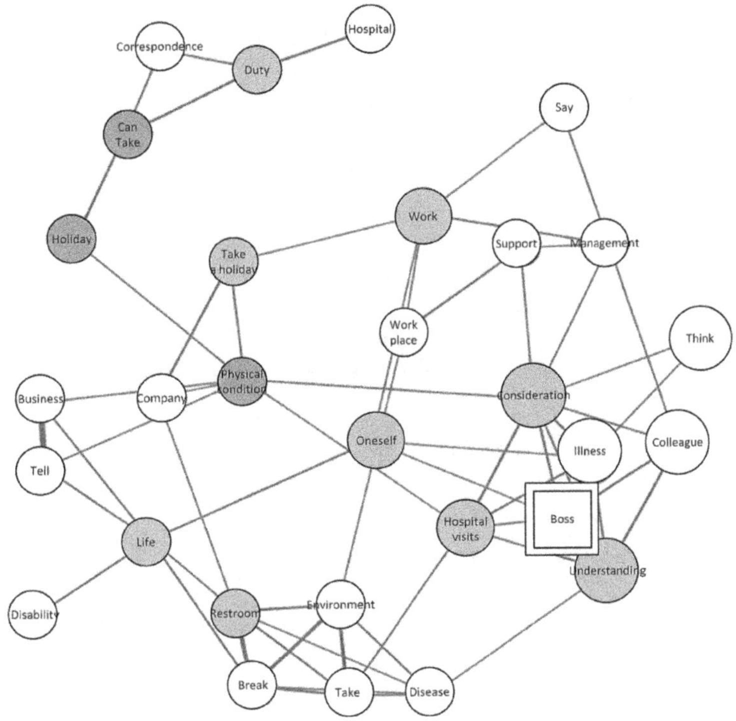


*Figure 4. Co-occurrence network with strong relation to the word "oneself"*

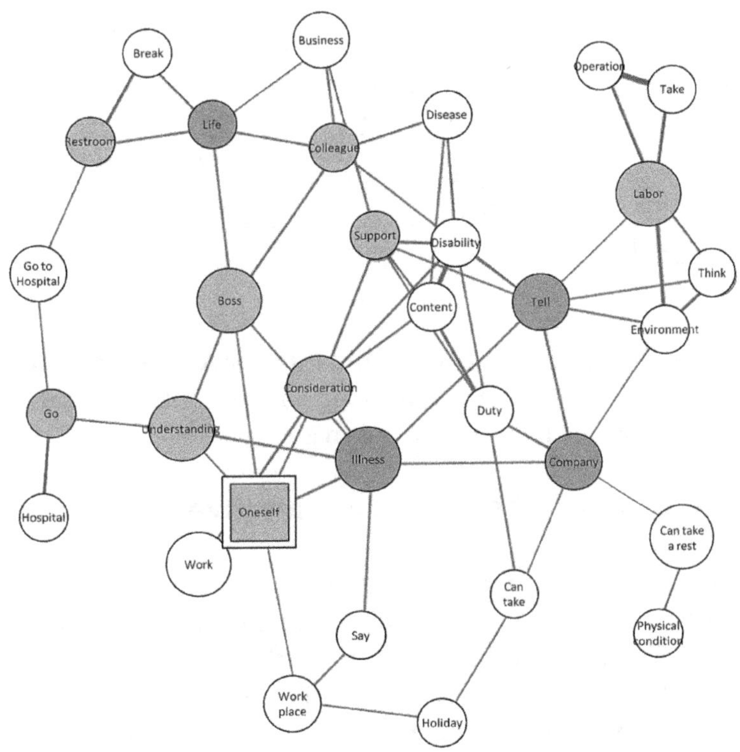

*Figure 5. Co-occurrence network with strong relation to the word "colleague"*

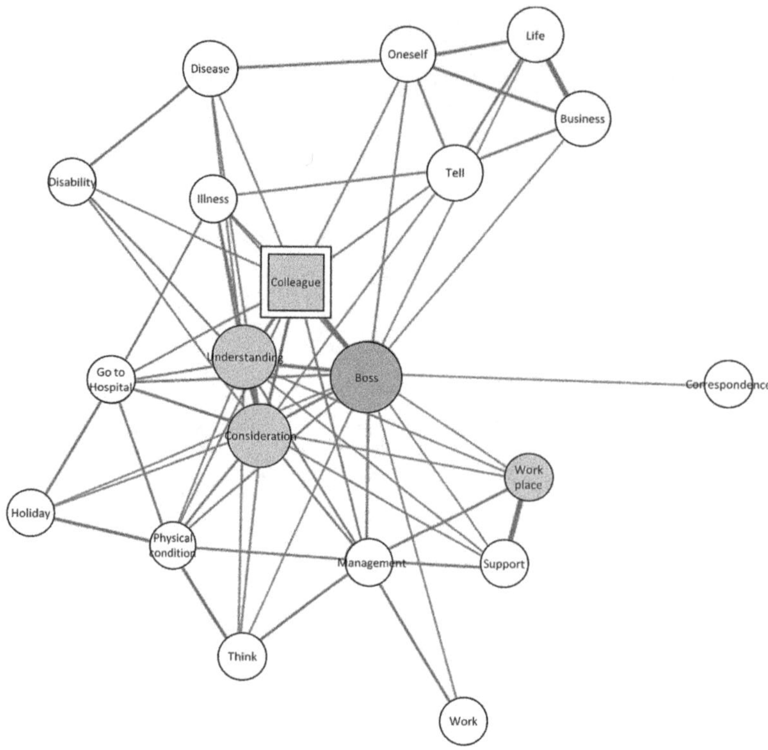


*Table 9. Characters and their acts in terms of support requirements in the workplace*

| Characters | The Main Meaning of the Word That Represents the Act |
|---|---|
| Boss | Understanding, consideration for illness and disability/Consideration regarding hospital visits (ambulatory visits)/Boss knows about the illness/ Boss does not know about the illness/Boss says "health management has failed" |
| Oneself | Going to the hospital/I discuss my illness and have the boss be aware of it/ I did not tell them of my illness/ I can take time off because of my poor physical condition, or for hospital visits (ambulatory visits)/Breaks to use restroom and to recover when in a poor physical condition |
| Colleague | Understanding, consideration for illness and disability |

tents and the concrete forms of support that are required. This study attempted to enhance the usability of text mining by structuring content using narratology and found its efficiency and feasibility in the preparatory process of analysis of a large quantity of free-expression answers.

## Complementary Relationship between the Narrative and Quantitative Results

The present results successfully determined the contents of effective employment support from the narratives of persons with disabilities and found that it was complementary to the quantitative results. In this study, text mining was used to extract elements of the story from the free descriptive answers collected from 4,546 people, as in Tables 4, 5, 7, and 9. The assumed stories from the narratives could enrich the interpretations of the statistical results derived from the chosen answers shown in Tables 3 and 6. The analysis of the narratives of persons with disabilities created a more concrete image of the working status and forms of accommodations present in the workplace for different types of disability, which can be elucidated as follows:

1. Some occupations, or working forms, and work places were strongly associated with some types of disability (Tables 3, 4, and 5). The results indicated the majority still work in typically limited employment status and forms.
2. According to the similarity of employment status, the types of disability were clustered into five groups; (1) intractable diseases, internal disability, hearing disability and physical disability, (2) visual deficits, (3) intellectual disabilities, (4) higher brain dysfunctions, and (5) mental disorders (Figure 2). In relation to employment status, the results indicated that people with a visual deficit are close to self-employment only, those with intellectual disability close only to cleaning jobs, those with mental disorders close to hospital jobs, and those with higher brain dysfunctions do not have any employment characteristics. However, others were characterized of more various and general employment status.
3. The supports and accommodations required for people with a disability were categorized as follows: (1) Accommodation to work without unreasonable difficulty, (2) A general need for consideration/ support for the problematic situation experienced by the person with disability, (3) Understanding afforded by the boss in regard to hospital visits and illness, (4) Consideration for taking breaks during work, (5) Consideration to allow rest at times when the physical condition is aggravated, and (6) Consideration for breaks for to use the toilet and for hospital visits (Table 7). Overall stories were characterized by the relationship in the workplace regarding the treatment and management of disease in the working life (Table 9). As in this preliminary analysis nearly half of the respondents were patients with intractable diseases, the results should be considered to be largely influenced by the needs of those with this condition, masking the needs of other types of disabilities. Similar separate analyses according to the types of disability may identify more specific needs for each type of disability.

Please note some other limitations: (1) our respondents were members of disability organizations, hence, the study does not necessarily consist of a random sample of the disabled population; and (2) the survey was conducted five years ago. Consequently, the relevant policy and practices have progressed and the status or needs may have changed, especially for the persons with intractable diseases, since the new legislation was enforced in 2015.

## Analysis of Narrative Using Text Mining

This study evaluates, for the first time, the validity and feasibility of mixed methods involving text mining of narratives. This was performed in accordance with the framework of computational narratology (Ogata, 1999). The methods may be helpful in the scrutiny of stories involving a larger quantity of textual data. Limitations of text mining for the analysis of narratives may be: (1) text mining concerns only limited information, such as words and their co-occurrence relations; (2) understanding of the result by text mining is not enough and therefore the analyst is necessary to interpret the meaning of words based on their context; and (3) it is not possible to extract causality and time elapsed in regard to the narrow sense of the narrative.

1. The text mining in the present study enhanced the efficiency of the initial preparatory categorizing process. Although text mining would improve the efficiency of the analysis of narratives, the present study found some limitations of text mining in terms of necessity of human involvement, including (1) in naming clusters for the cluster analysis, where the analyst had to read the original free description statement and (2) in assuming stories form separate words according to a context. Intensive involvement of humans may be inevitable in the process of qualitative research, as proposed in the content analysis, the Grounded Theory, and the KJ method. Computational text mining as proposed in the present study should enhance the efficiency of the initial crude categorizing process because much time and human efforts have been consumed in earlier qualitative research.
2. From the perspective of narrative approach, the narratives are considered to be qualitatively important when they reflect (1) specific contents of disabilities, (2) the personal characteristics of persons with disabilities, and (3) causation in personal narrative. In the present study, text mining resolved (1), but not (2) or (3). In text mining, the level of co-occurrence of the words that appeared in the same sentence was evaluated. Characteristics of work contents according to disability types were reasonably well detected by the text mining because a large amount of work content could be characterized by words relating to jobs, tasks, tools, places, etc. Support needs, on the other hand, were more context-dependent. Thus, the individual words should be structured according to the theory of elements of the story, using the classification of stories given from previous studies (Propp, 1968; Greimas, 1966; Ogata, 2015; Adam, 1999). Aside from the story analysis, the discourse analysis that reflects cause-and-effect relationship was not possible because the free-expression answers to particular questions were sometimes only a part of the full narrative.
3. Although the importance of the narratives in the study of supports and interpersonal assistance lies in reflecting the opinions of the participants, the present story analysis does not necessarily obtain the full picture of their difficulties and needs. The conceptual framework of ICF (World Health Organization, 2001), which stands for International Classification of Functioning, Disability and Health and is widely used in the field of interpersonal help, may be an alternative to story analysis in terms of structuring the contents of the narratives of support needs of persons with disabilities.
4. In addition, from the psychological perspective of narratology, this study generates a "second-order narrative" (Elliott, 2005) from the researcher based on the "first-order narrative" (Elliott, 2005) spoken by persons with disabilities.

## FUTURE RESEARCH DIRECTIONS

The present results concerning employment support needs were merely preliminary. They are also significantly biased, with almost half of the respondents being patients with intractable diseases. Similar separate analyses according to types of disability may identify more specific needs for each type of disability. Note that there is no typical or stereotyped "person with disability." It does not make sense to study a random sampled population of persons with disabilities. Rather, it is important to address various situations and needs according to the types of disability.

The future direction of this study of narratology can be the developing of a method by which to unify the two narratologies, performing a more detailed document review of (1) literary story theory and (2) psychological story theory, including computational narratology. As for the direction of research on text mining, use of the conceptual framework of ICF should be studied in terms of structuring the contents of the narratives concerning the support needs of persons with disabilities.

The result of the analysis of narratives is basically a compilation of the opinions of persons with disabilities and, thus, it provides the lowest level of scientific evidence. The present results, suggesting hypothetical effective supports, should be reflected in future quantitative research that pursues stronger evidence. For example, a program evaluation study may be possible where the present results should be implemented in an actual system and support programs with proper implementation manuals, training programs, and fidelity checks, and the outcomes should be evaluated.

## CONCLUSION

This study performed analysis using narratology and qualitative-quantitative mixed method analysis to explore effective employment supports for persons with disabilities using big-data from a national-level survey. Narratology was used for assuming the context of extracted words in text mining. The proposed text-mining method would be efficient and feasible in the preparatory processes of analysis of big-data of free-expression answers. Consequently, this would promote the use of qualitative data, such as narratives of free-expression answers that reflect each person's experience, needs, and thoughts for more effective vocational supports.

## ACKNOWLEDGMENT

The authors would like to thank Ms. Aoi Nomoto (National Institute of Vocational Rehabilitation) and Dr. Kunimasa Sato (National Institute of Vocational Rehabilitation) for their helpful suggestions regarding English structures. We would like to thank Editage (www.editage.jp) for English language editing. This work was supported in part by JSPS KAKENHI Grant Number 26780322.

## REFERENCES

Adam, J. M. (1999). *Le récit.* Paris, France: Presses Universitaires de France.

Akimoto, T., & Ogata, T. (2013). Towards a discourse mechanism in narrative generation system: Proposal of a system introducing narrative discourse theory and reception theory. *Cognitive Studies*, *20*(4), 396–420.

Arima, M., & Tsuji, S. (1987). *Anketochosa no houhou* [Method of questionnaire survey]. Tokyo, Japan: Asakura Publishing.

Aristotle. (1997). Poetics (Matsumoto, N & Oka, M, Trans.). Tokyo, Japan: Iwanami Shoten. (Original work published 335 B.C.).

Asai, A. (1987). *Chosa no gijutsu* [The technique of investigation]. Tokyo, Japan: JUSE Press.

Becker, D. R., & Bond, G. R. (Eds.). (2002). *Supported employment implementation resource kit*. Rockville, MD: Center for Mental Health Services, Substance Abuse and Mental Health Services Administration.

Bruner, J. (1986). *Actual minds, possible worlds*. Cambridge, MA: Harvard University Press.

Buchanan-Barker, P., & Barker, P. J. (2008). The Tidal commitments: Extending the value base of mental health recovery. *Journal of Psychiatric and Mental Health Nursing*, *15*(2), 93–100. doi:10.1111/j.1365-2850.2007.01209.x PMID:18211556

Clinton, J. J. (1993). Agency for health care policy and research: Improving health care through guidelines and outcomes research. *Hospital Formulary*, *28*(11), 933–942. PMID:10130235

Concato, J. (2004). Observational versus experimental studies: What's the evidence for hierarchy? *Journal of the American Society for Experimental Neuro-therapeutics*, *1*(3), 341–347. doi:10.1602/neurorx.1.3.341 PMID:15717036

Creswell, J. W., & Plano Clark, V. L. (2007). *Designing and conducting mixed methods research*. London, UK: Sage Publications.

Denzin, N. K., & Lincoln, Y. S. (Eds.). (2000). *Handbook of qualitative research*. London, UK: Sage Publications.

Elliott, J. (2005). *Using narrative in social research*. London, UK: Sage Publications.

Everitt, B. S. (1998). *The Cambridge dictionary of statistics*. Cambridge, UK: Cambridge University Press.

Feldman, R., & Sanger, J. (2007). *The text mining handbook: Advanced approaches in analyzing unstructured data*. Cambridge, UK: Cambridge University Press.

Forster, E. M. (1927). *Aspects of the novel*. London, UK: Edward Arnold.

Foucault, M. (1980). Power/knowledge. (C. Gordon., L. Marchall., J. Mepham, & K. Soper, Trans.). New York, NY: Pantheon Books. (Original work published 1972, 1975, 1976, 1977).

Genette, G. (1980). *Narrative discourse: An essay in method* (J. E. Lewin, Trans.). Ithaca, NY: Cornell University Press. (Original work published 1972)

Gergen, K. J. (1994a). *Toward transformation in social knowledge*. London, UK: Sage Publications.

Gergen, K. J. (1994b). *Realities and relationships*. Cambridge, MA: Harvard University Press.

Gergen, K. J. (1999). *An invitation to social construction*. London, UK: Sage Publications.

Greenhalgh, T., & Hurwitz, B. (Eds.). (1998). *Narrative based medicine*. London, UK: BMJ Books.

Greimas, A. J. (1966). *Sémantique structurale*. Paris, France: Larousse.

Guyatt, G. H. (1991). Evidence-based medicine. *American College of Physicians Journal Club*, *114*, A16.

Hara, J., & Umino, M. (1984). *Shakaichosaenshu* [Social investigation practice]. Tokyo, Japan: University of Tokyo Press.

Higuchi, K. (2014). *Quantitative text analysis for social researchers: A contribution to content anayisis*. Kyoto, Japan: Nakanishiya Press.

Hirose, S. (2012). The present and future of the mixed methods research. *Yamaguchi Medicine, 61*(1-2), 11-16.

Kawashima, D., Koyama, T., Kawano, K., & Ito, H. (2009). Physicians' explanatory model for suicide prevention: Text-mining analysis of physicians' statements to suicidal patients. *The Japanese Journal of Personality, 17*(2), 121–132. doi:10.2132/personality.17.121

Kitagawa, N., Kato, C., & Koyama, T. (2011). Clinical issues and additional strategies of the return-to-work program for depression. *Japanese Journal of Psychiatric Treatment, 26*(2), 149–156.

Klein, S., Aeschlimann, J. F., Appelbaum, M. A., Balsiger, D. F., Curtis, E. J., Foster, M.,... Salsieder, D. F. (1974). *Modeling Propp and Levi-Strauss in a meta-symbolic simulation system*. Computer Sciences Technical Report 226. Computer Sciences Department, the University of Wisconsin.

Komori, Y., & Yamada, M. (2001). Seishinbunretsubyou no kazokushinrikyouiku niokeru naratibu apurochi[Narrative approach in family psychology education of schizophrenia]. *Family Therapy Research, 18*(2), 143–150.

Kuwano, T., & Oishi, M. (Eds.). (1988). *Forumarizumu: Shitekigengoron* [Formalism: Poetic language theory]. Tokyo, Japan: Kokushokankoukai.

Kyou, S. (2012). Hogosha to shisetsushokuin no "chitekishougaisha no sei" nitaisuru ishiki: Tekisutomainingu niyoru bunseki[Consciousness for "the sex of person with intellectual disability" of a protector and the staff of facilities: Analysis by the text mining]. *Shimane University Social Welfare Journal, 4*, 1–16.

Lyotard, J. F. (1979). *La condition postmoderne*. Paris, France: Minuit.

Manuel, J., Fang, L., Bellamy, J. L., & Bledsoe, S. E. (2008). Evaluating evidence. In R. M. Grinnell & Y. A. Unrau (Eds.), *Social work research and evaluation: Foundation of evidence-based practice* (8th ed., pp. 482–495). New York, NY: Oxford University Press.

McAdams, D. P., & St. Aubin, E. (Eds.). (1998). Generativity and adult development. Washington, DC: American Psychological Association.

Mihara, H. (2011). Volunteer activity support by students for the leisure activity of handicapped people and their families: Participating in beach volleyball and cooking with the handicapped people in the university. *Japanese Journal of Social Welfare, 51*(4), 153–162.

Ministry of Health. Labour and Welfare. (2014a). *Heisei25nen shougaishakoyoujokyo no shuukeikekka* [Aggregate results of the 2013 disability employment situation]. Retrieved from http://www.mhlw.go.jp/stf/houdou/0000029691.html

Ministry of Health. Labour and Welfare. (2014b). *Heisei25nendo shougaishakoyoujittaichosakekka* [(Actual) Conditions of employment of persons with disabilities survey result in fiscal year 2013]. Retrieved from http://www.mhlw.go.jp/stf/houdou/0000068921.html

Ministry of Health. Labour and Welfare. (2015). *Shougaisha no koyo no sokushintou nikansuru horitsu* [Act for the promotion of employment of persons with disabilities]. Retrieved from http://law.e-gov.go.jp/htmldata/S35/S35HO123.html

Mita, M. (1965). *Gendainihon no seishinkouzou* [Mental structure of Japan]. Tokyo, Japan: Koubundo.

Morgan, A. (2000). *What is narrative therapy?* Adelaire, Australia: Dulwich Center Publication.

National institute of vocational rehabilitation. (2011). *Empirical Research for Effective Cooperation of Supports for Independent Life and Work of Persons with disabilities*. Chiba, Japan: National Institute of Vocational Rehabilitation.

Noguchi, Y. (Ed.). (2005). Naratibu no rinshoshakaigaku [Clinical sociology of narrative]. Tokyo, Japan: Keiso shobo.

Noguchi, Y. (Ed.). (2009). Naratibu apurochi [Narrative approach]. Tokyo, Japan: Keiso shobo.

Nouchi, M. (2008). Shitsudokushou no "katari" o kikukoto. [Listening to the "talk" of dyslexia] In Y. Yamada (Ed.), *Jinsei to yamai no katari* [Narrative of the life and the illness] (pp. 51–78). Tokyo, Japan: University of Tokyo Press.

Ogata, T. (1999). Proposal of computational narratology. In *Proceedings of IPSJ SIG Computers and the Humanities* (pp. 53-60). Academic Press.

Ogata, T. (2010). "Monogatari seisei sisutemu" no haikei oyobi monogatari to bungaku no aida. [Backgrounds of the "narrative generation system" and "relations between narrative and literature"] In T. Ogata & A. Kanai (Eds.), *Monogatariron no jouhougaku josetsu: monogatari seisei no shisou to gijutsu wo megutte* [An introduction to the informatics of narratology: about the thought and technologies of narrative generation] (pp. 186–258). Tokyo, Japan: Gakubunsha.

Ogata, T. (2011). Narrative generation system as the practice of "informatics of narratology.". *Journal of Japan Society for Fuzzy Theory and Intelligent Informatics*, *23*(5), 676–685.

Ogata, T. (2015). Building conceptual dictionaries for an integrated narrative generation system. *Journal of Robotics. Networking and Artificial Life*, *1*(4), 270–284. doi:10.2991/jrnal.2015.1.4.6

Okawa, H., & Honda, T. (2014). Shuroushienryouiki no esuesutiunei ni hituyonagijutsu: tekisutomaininguhou o mochiite [Techniques necessary for the SST administration in employment support domain: Using the text mining method]. In *Proceedings of SST Promotion Association 19th Annual Scientific Meeting* (p.62). Sendai, Japan: Academic Press.

Otsuka, H., Inui, T., & Okumura, M. (2007). *Opinion mining engine*. Tokyo, Japan: Corona Publishing.

Prince, G. (2003). *A dictionary of narratology* (Revised edition). Lincoln, NE: University of Nebraska Press.

Propp, V. Y. (1968). *Morphology of the folktale* (L. Scott, Trans.). Austin, TX: University of Texas Press. (Original work published 1928)

Romesburg, H. C. (1984). *Cluster analysis for researchers*. Belmont, CA: Lifetime Learning Publications.

Sackett, D. L., Richardson, W. S., Straus, S. E., Rosenberg, W., & Haynes, R. B. (1997). *Evidence-based MEDICINE: how to practice and teach EBM*. London, UK: Churchill Livingstone.

Saiki, S. (2008). Shounigan no kodomo no toubyoutaiken. [Narrative based medicine and clinical intellect? Narrative of a pediatric cancer patient] In Y. Yamada (Ed.), *Jinsei to yamai no katari* [Narrative of life and illness]. (pp. 103–132). Tokyo, Japan: University of Tokyo Press.

Saito, S. (2003). Naratibubeisudomedisun to rinshochi. [Narrative based medicine and clinical intellect] In Y. Yamada (Ed.), *Jinsei to yamai no katari* [Narrative of the life and the illness] (pp. 133–163). Tokyo, Japan: University of Tokyo Press.

Sakai, S., Inagaki, Y., Higuchi, K., & Kato, H. (2011). Jidouyougoshisetunai niokeru kodomokanbouryoku no naiyou no bunseki[Analysis of contents and correspondence of violence among children in a child nursing home]. *Child Abuse & Neglect*, *13*, 115–124.

Sakuyama, F. (2012). Hito, kankyo, kankei oyobi joukyou otoushitekangaeru sosharuwaku no shouten[The focus of social work from a person, environment, relationships, and situation perspective]. *Japanese Journal of Social Welfare*, *53*(1), 79–90.

Sato, S., Iwata, K., Furukawa, S., Matsuda, Y., Hatsuse, N., & Ikebuchi, E. (2014). The effects of the combination of cognitive training and supported employment on improving clinical and working outcomes for people with schizophrenia in Japan. *Clinical Practice and Epidemiology in Mental Health*, *10*(1), 18–27. doi:10.2174/1745017901410010018 PMID:24600481

Seino, K., & Haruna, Y. (2014). Hokeniryo, fukushi, kyouikubunya niokeru shougaisha no shuuroushien no genjo [The current state of employment support of disabled persons in the field of education and medicine and welfare]. In *Proceedings of Vocational Rehabilitation Society 42rd Annual Meeting*. Iwate, Japan.

Seino, K., & Haruna, Y. (2015a). Chiiki niokeru kenriyougo toshiteno shuroushien noarikatanikansuru kenkyuu [The study on employment support as advocacy in the region]. In *Proceedings of Kanto Branch, Japanese Society for the Study of Social Welfare 2014 Annual Meeting*. Tokyo, Japan: Academic Press.

Seino, K., Haruna, Y., & Ishizaki, S. (2015b). Analysis using text mining for the narrative told about work of persons with disabilities. In *Proceedings of the Japanese Cognitive Science Society 32rd Annual Meeting*. Chiba, Japan: Academic Press.

Shojima, S. (2008). Multilayered contexts in which narrative is generated and interpreted: Toward the next narrative based inquiry. *Kyoto University Research Studies in Education*, *54*, 138–151.

Tagaki, M. (2008). Experiences of people with acquired long-term physical disability: Life stories of persons with spinal cord injuries in japan. *Qualitative Psychology Nexus*, *7*, 51–79.

Tagaki, M. (2009). A mixed method of qualitative analysis and text mining of qualitative data in a municipal action plan for a disabled policy. *Journal of Social Problems*, *58*, 71–86.

Tagaki, M. (2012). Sosharuwaku niokeru ebidensu toha nanika [What is the evidence in the social work?]. In Japanese Society for the Study of Social Welfare (Ed.), Taironshakaifukushigaku [Discussion social welfare studies] (pp. 124-144). Tokyo, Japan: Chuohoki Publishing.

Tajima, M., Okada, Y., Nakamura, S., Otowa, K., Numa, H., Ono, H., & Akiyama, T. (2010). Effect examination of group cognitive-behavioral therapy for people taking a leave of absence due to depression. *Japanese Journal of Psychiatric Treatment*, *25*(10), 1374–1378.

Tashiro, T., Ito, T., Yoshida, S., & Tashiro, K. (2013). Trial of the integrated reinstatement support program on residual symptoms in remitted depression patients: To deal with pathologic variety. *Japanese Journal of Psychiatric Treatment*, *28*(6), 805–814.

Tsuchida, T., Aoyagi, E., & Ito, N. (1996). *Gendaibungakuriron* [Contemporary literature theory]. Tokyo, Japan: Shinyosha.

Tsuzuki, A. (1975). Shitsumonshicyosa no igi. [The significance of the questionnaire] In M. Arima & E. Murakami (Eds.), *Shinrigakukenkyuhou 9* [Psychology Research Methods 9]. Tokyo, Japan: University of Tokyo Press.

United Nations Enable. (2007). *Convention on the rights of persons with disabilities*. Retrieved from http://www.un.org/esa/socdev/enable/rights/convtexte.htm

Vuokila-Oikkonen, P., Janhonen, S., & Vaisanen, L. (2004). "Shared-rhythm cooperation" in cooperative team meetings in acute psychiatric inpatient care. *Journal of Psychiatric and Mental Health Nursing*, *11*(2), 129–140. doi:10.1111/j.1365-2850.2003.00679.x PMID:15009487

White, M., & Epston, D. (1990). *Narrative means to therapeutic ends*. New York, NY: W. W. Norton & Company.

World Health Organization. (2001). International classification of functioning, disability and health: ICF. Geneva, Swiss Confederation: World Health Organization.

Yaeda, J., Fujikawa, M., Wakabayashi, I., Ozawa, A., Ishihara, M., Nishimura, S., & Iwanaga, K. (2012). Shokugyourihabiriteshon no ebidensu towa nanika?[What is the evidence of vocational rehabilitation?]. *Japanese Journal of Vocational Rehabilitation*, *25*(1), 24–26.

Yaeda, J., Ozawa, A., & Wakabayashi, I. (2013). Shokugyourihabiritesyhon to shougaishakoyoubunya niokeru kenkyuudoukou[Research trends in vocational rehabilitation and employment of persons with disabilities policy]. *Japanese Journal of Rehabilitation*, *156*, 22–33.

Yamabe, S. (2012). Sosharuwaku niokeru ebidensu tohananika: Purorogu [What is the evidence in the social work?: Prologue]. In Japanese Society for the Study of Social Welfare (Ed.), Taironshakaihukushigaku [Discussion social welfare studies] (pp. 85-87). Tokyo, Japan: Chuohoki Publishing.

Yamada, Y. (2007a). Shitsutekikenkyuu niokeru taiwatekimoderukouseihou[Interactive model construction method in qualitative research]. *Japanese Journal of Qualitative Psychology*, *6*, 174–194.

Yamada, Y. (2007b). *Shitsutekishinrigaku no houhou: Katari o kiku* [Method of qualitative psychology: Listening to narrative]. Tokyo, Japan: Shinyousha.

Yamoto, T. (1974). *Bungakugijyuturon* [Literature technique theory]. Tokyo, Japan: Kenkyusha.

Yasuda, S. (1970). *Shakaichousa no keikaku to kaiseki* [Planning and analysis of social research]. Tokyo, Japan: University of Tokyo Press.

Yoshihara, M., & Imura, O. (2008). Psychological aspects in parents of muscular dystrophy patients: Based on analysis of the free description in questionnaires. *The Japanese Journal of Rehabilitation Psychology*, *35*(1), 49–60.

## KEY TERMS AND DEFINITIONS

**Employment:** Being employed in public organizations, private firms, or administrative agencies with decent payment and contracts on either a full-time or part-time basis, or being self-employed, excluding welfare-based work or volunteer work with subminimum wages.

**Employment Support:** A support for employment preparation, job hunting, vocational life, etc.

**Literary Narrative:** A narrative found in literature, including mythology and folktales.

**Personal Narrative:** A narrative concerning an individual and the family.

**Social Narrative:** A narrative of a group and the society. This is contrasted with personal narrative.

**Narrative in the Wider Sense:** The individual's act to narrate using his or her own language.

**Narrative in the Narrow Sense:** A reproduction of a real or fictional event and is always accompanied by time restraints.

# Chapter 10
# Quantitative Research into Narrative:
## Statistical Analysis of "The Tale of Genji"

**Gen Tsuchiyama**
*Doshisha University, Japan*

## ABSTRACT

*Stylometry is the application of quantitative analysis, primarily to written language, to identify variations in style. Statistical analysis of linguistic characteristics is applied to identify authorship, creation period, and creation order. This study involves stylometric research into "The Tale of Genji," which is a Japanese classical literary work. "The Tale of Genji" is a long story consisting of 54 volumes. However, in the last 13 volumes, the content is different from that in the other volumes, and the writing quality differs from that of the previous 41 volumes; thus, it has long been theorized that the 13 volumes was written by a different author. The result of an analysis using the word frequency for auxiliary verbs found no evidence that positively support the theory of separate authorship. Therefore, the results indicate that the possibility that there are multiple authors of "The Tale of Genji" is low.*

## INTRODUCTION

This study involves quantitative research into the formation process of "The Tale of Genji," which is a Japanese classical literary work, using a stylometric method. The stylometry is the application of quantitative analysis, primarily to written language, to identify variations in style. Statistical analysis of linguistic characteristics is applied to identify authorship, creation period, and creation order. Using different approaches, many studies have discussed authorship or the creation periods of historical manuscripts, such as classical literature, by focusing on descriptive content or investigating historical facts. In contrast, stylometry collects quantitative data obtained from sentences, analyzes the data to understand the literary styles, and draws conclusions.

In stylometry, it is assumed that an author's personality is reflected in his or her writing style and that this relationship can be determined empirically. This assumption is echoed in the French maxim

DOI: 10.4018/978-1-5225-0432-0.ch010

Copyright © 2016, IGI Global. Copying or distributing in print or electronic forms without written permission of IGI Global is prohibited.

"Le style c'est l'homme." The maxim is said to be derived from "Le style c'est l'homme même," a line from a speech delivered by Georges-Louis Leclerc, Comte de Buffon (1707-1788), on his admission to the French Academy of Sciences. Leclerc was a naturalist and scientist famous for "Buffon's needle problem." In P. Guiraud (1954), Leclerc's maxim was construed to mean "A style reveals a human's true self," and it is understood that readers form impressions of author based on their styles. However, there are various and diverse concepts of style, depending on the field of study.

In stylometry, a style is a countable and descriptive form that considers quantitative elements in sentences, such as the frequencies of letters and words and the average lengths of words and sentences. The personality of an author or a literary work is considered to be reflected in these formal elements. Word meaning and descriptive content are not considered. In this respect, stylometry differs from humanistic literature studies. Stylometry uses statistically analyzed quantitative data to explain differences between the styles of different authors, a specific author's stylistic changes over time, and other matters.

## BACKGROUND

This study involves quantitative research into the formation process of "The Tale of Genji" using a stylometric method, which involves multivariate analysis. We clarified the quantitative characteristics and trends in the main text using a statistical method. In this study, we present the analysis results with a level of transparency capable of withstanding quantitative debate. Based on these results, the first objective was to quantitatively investigate the different author theory and then to investigate the formation process.

In addition, although, as mentioned previously, there have been quantitative investigations into the research of multivariate analysis, which has not commonly been used to study "The Tale of Genji." In particular, to the best of our knowledge, no study has investigated author identification using multivariate analysis. Therefore, the originality of this study is that it is based on the quantitative method.

"The Tale of Genji" is a classic work from the Heian period, which has been widely read throughout the ages. The work describes the customs and culture of the aristocratic society of the era. It is one of the oldest known long stories thought to be penned by Murasaki Shikibu—a prominent female author in the Heian period. At that time, the ability to write using Chinese logograms was considered an important cultural accomplishment. However, the tale was probably written entirely in Japanese *kana* (phonograms) because it was written for female readers. In this respect, it is a significant work in the history of Japanese literature.

The main theme in the first part of the story is the romantic life of the main character, Hikaru Genji, who is the son of an ancient Japanese emperor. Hikaru's mother dies when he is an infant, and he is brought up in the imperial court by his young stepmother. When he grows older, Hikaru and his stepmother fall in love. However, Hikaru recognizes that their love is forbidden and he tries to forget this love affair.

When he visits a rural town, he encounters his "ideal" girl. Although he has already married for political reasons, the girl (Murasaki no Ue), eventually becomes his beloved partner.

His legitimate wife gives birth to a son; unfortunately, the child dies in infancy. Then, because of his scandalous relationship with Murasaki no Ue, the Emperor forces Hikaru to move to a distant land.

In the capital, the Emperor is troubled by bad dreams, and he believes that he is having these bad dreams because he has banished Hikaru Genji. Therefore, the Emperor orders Hikaru Genji to return to the capital and transfers the purple, the color traditionally associated with the Emperor, to the new Emperor—the son born to Hikaru Genji and his stepmother. The new Emperor knows about their love affair and confers supreme power on Hikaru Genji. When Hikaru Genji is 40 years old, his other wife becomes romantically involved with another man, and Murasaki no Ue dies. These events mark the end of the first part of the tale. As the story concludes, Hikaru looks back over his life.

"The Tale of Genji" is a long story consisting of 54 volumes. Hikaru Genji is the main character in the first 41 volumes. However, in the last 13 volumes, the story shifts to the time after Hikaru Genji's death. In general, these 13 volumes are referred to as the third part. The content and the writing quality in this part differ from that in the other volumes. Thus, it has long been theorized that the third part was written by a different author. In the third part, the first three volumes, "Nioumiya," Volume 43, "Kobai," and Volume 44, "Takekawa" are referred to as "Nioumiya Sanjo," and the last 10 volumes, beginning with Volume 45, "Hashihime," are referred to as "Uji Jujo." It has also been suggested that "Nioumiya Sanjo" and "Uji Jujo" were written by different authors, in part because Uji is some distance away from the capital.

In developing a theory for the formation process of "The Tale of Genji," the focus was on the 33 volumes of the first part. Based on objective data derived from surveying the situations wherein the main characters appear, it has been generally accepted that the first part consists of two series. The first, the "Murasaki no Ue" series, consists of 17 volumes and the second, the "Tamakazura" series, consists of 16 volumes. This conclusion is based on the finding that the main characters that first appear in the "Murasaki no Ue" series also appear in the "Tamakazura" series, whereas characters that first appear in the "Tamakazura" series do not appear in the "Murasaki no Ue" series.

In addition, in the second part, the characters from the "Tamakazura series" only appear in Volumes 34–37, "Wakana Jo," "Wakana Ge," and "Kashiwagi." Based on an investigation of the content, it has been theorized that Volume 38, "Suzumushi," and Volume 39, "Yugiri," are additional volumes.

In the third part, Volume 45, "Hashihime," Volume 49, "Yadorigi," and Volume 53, "Tenarai," all begin with the phrase "In those days." Although the possibility that the third part can be divided into four blocks has been suggested, research into the formation process was not developed as completely as the research into the first part and second part.

In this study, we investigated the formation process of the 13 volumes that comprise the third part quantitatively using statistical methods to find calculable elements related to the expression formats in the text, such as parts-of-speech distribution ratios, word frequencies, and word lengths.

## STYLOMETRY METHODS

### Author Identification

Although statistical techniques have become more sophisticated, stylometry studies date back to the 19th century. Quantitative analysis of sentences was suggested by Augustus De Morgan (1806-1871), a well-known English mathematician. De Morgan is quoted in a book written by his wife, S. E. De Morgan (1882), as saying, "I should expect to find that one man writing on two different subjects agrees more nearly with himself than two different men writing on the same subject." De Morgan suggested a simple statistical approach: "Count a large number of words in Herodotus—say all the first book—and count all the letters; divide the second numbers by the first, giving the average number of letters to word in that book. Do the same with the second book. I should expect a very close approximation." (p. 216).

Inspired by De Morgan, in 1887, T.C. Mendenhall, an American physicist and meteorologist, proposed that authors could be identified through quantitative analysis. Mendenhall (1887) examined the literary works of three representative English writers, Charles Dickens (1812-1870), William Makepeace Thackeray (1811-1863), and John Stuart Mill (1806-1873). Differing from De Morgan, who suggested using the average number of letters in a word, Mendenhall (1887) used frequency distributions, which aggregate the appearance frequencies of words by the number of letters they contain. Mendenhall (1887) referred to this technique as a "word spectrum," in analogy to a spectrogram that explains the composition of an inorganic substance in metal engineering. In recent stylometric studies, the phrase "word-length distribution" has replaced "word spectrum."

Mendenhall (1901) also used the word spectrum method to analyze the poetic dramas of William Shakespeare (1564-1616). It has long been speculated that some of the plays attributed to Shakespeare were not in fact written by Shakespeare. It has been suggested that the philosopher Francis Bacon (1561-1626) wrote a number of satirical dramas to protest tyranny, a common theme in his philosophical writings. Bacon's social position prevented him from writing this type of work under his own name, and thus his plays were publicly attributed to Shakespeare. Mendenhall (1901) analyzed the respective word spectra of Shakespeare and Bacon's literary works. As a result, Mendenhall (1901) clarified the differences in their habitual stylistic characteristics. He determined that Shakespeare primarily used four-letter words while Bacon primarily used three-letter words and concluded that Shakespeare and Bacon were not the same person. Mendenhall's quantitative study was cited in literature published in Japan, which reflects the magnitude of the impact of his work.

## Prediction of Creation Order

In 1867, prior to Mendenhall's use of word spectra to analyze Shakespeare's poetic dramas, L. Campbell undertook a quantitative analysis using the appearance frequencies of words to predict the writing period of Plato's dialogues.

Although Plato's writing period is thought to be as many as 50 to 60 years, the writing order of the dialogues is largely unknown. However, it is known that Aristotle mentioned that "Laws" was Plato's last literary work. Plato's thinking obviously developed over time; therefore, it was important to determine the writing order in order to understand Plato's thoughts systematically. Campbell (1867) used the lexicon to examine vocabularies that are commonly used in "Timaeus," "Critias," and "Laws," which are later dialogues, but are rarely used in other dialogues. By examining the occurrences of these vocabularies, Campbell concluded that "Sophist," "Statesman," and "Philebus" were also later dialogues. This accomplishment positioned Campbell as a pioneer in stylometry studies. It should be noted that prior to Campbell's work, W. Dittenberger studied the writing order of the dialogues in 1881 by focusing on the appearance ratio of synonymous word pairs and obtained almost the same result as that of Campbell.

Although Mendenhall's word spectrum method is known in Japan as an early technique that lead to the development of stylometry, Campbell (1867) and Dittenberger's (1881) earlier investigations are significant as pioneering quantitative studies.

## CASE STUDIES

As described previously, quantitative analysis of a sentence involves its length and the frequencies of the words it contains. Similar to word length, sentence length is also used as an analytical item. Cases studies that use these analysis items are reviewed in the following.

### Word Length

A 1963 investigation by Brinegar is a representative study that used word lengths to identify an author. Brinegar investigated 10 letters written by Quintus Curtius Snodgrass. The letters, known as the QCS letters, were published in the New Orleans Daily Crescent in 1861. They criticized the Civil War. There was speculation that the actual writer was Mark Twain (1835-1910), the well-known author of "The Adventures of Tom Sawyer." Brinegar (1963) collected sentences written by Twain before the QCS Letters were published, sentences written during the same period, and sentences written after publication. He added up the word-length, performed a chi-square test and a t-test respectively, and concluded that the letters had not been written by Mark Twain.

O'Donnell (1966) analyzed "The O'Ruddy" (1903), a novel consisting of 33 chapters authored by Stephen Crane (1871-1900) and Robert Barr (1849-1912). Crane died before the work was completed, and the point at which Barr took over was not known. The result of a two-group discrimination analysis of 18 items, including their word-length distributions, concluded that Chapters 1 through 24 were written by Crane and Chapters 26 through 33 were written by Barr. A similar problem, i.e., identifying multiple authors, occurs with regard to "Uji Jujo," the last ten volumes of "The Tale of Genji," a Japanese classical literary work. This problem will be described below in detail.

The word-length-distribution analysis technique developed De Morgan and later used by Mendenhall has been used till recent years as an analysis method that is effective for author identification.

### Word Frequency

Mosteller and Wallace (1963) analyzed articles among a collection of 85 articles that have come to be known as "The Federalist Papers." Seventy-seven articles were originally published serially in New York newspapers from October 1787 through August 1788 to promote ratification of the Constitution of the United States of America. An additional eight articles, along with the original 77, were published in book form by J. and A. McLean in 1788. Although all 85 articles were known to be written by James Madison (1751-1836), John Jay (1745-1829), and Alexander Hamilton (1755-1804), definitive authorship could not be assigned to 12 articles. Thirty words, such as on, upon, while, and whilst, which occurred irrespective of content, were selected from sentences for which the author was known. These words were studied using discrimination analysis and Bayes' theorem. The results showed that Hamilton often used "while" and that Madison used "whilst." Since many of the above vocabularies were function words expressing grammatical functions, the analytical results showed that function words were effective for author identification.

In a recent study, Binongo (2003) identified the author of the final volume (Volume 15) of a series of American fantasy novels known as the "Oz" books. Lyman Frank Baum (1856-1919) is usually cited as the author; however, Baum died in 1919, and the final volume in the series was not published until 1921. Consequently, it has been suggested that Volume 15 was not a posthumous publication of a Baum manuscript, but rather was written by Ruth Plumly Thompson (1891-1976), an author of children's literature. Binongo (2003) used function words to analyze the principal components and concluded that Thompson was the author.

As well as word length, word frequency is a common factor used in quantitative sentence analysis. It has been shown empirically that function words, such as prepositions, conjunctions, auxiliary verbs, and articles, are effective for author identification in analyses of Western languages.

### Other Analysis Items

In addition to the distributions of word and sentence lengths, word frequency, which is an index of vocabulary richness, and part-of-speech distributions are often used for analysis. Antosch (1969) obtained a ratio of verbs to adjectives and indicated that the ratio depended on the category of sentences. Antosch also reported that this ratio was high in folk tales and low in scientific articles.

Punctuation frequency has also been studied. In his work on "The O'Ruddy," O'Donnell (1966) analyzed the punctuation frequency as well as the word lengths. Chaski (2001) calculated the punctuation frequencies in sentences written by five women and performed a chi-square test. The results showed that the punctuation frequencies effectively identified the authors.

## JAPANESE LITERATURE STUDIES USING STYLOMETRIC METHODS

An early study on quantitative analysis of a sentence in Japanese was "Bunsho Sinrigaku," written by Kanji Hatano in 1935. Since the psychology of writing described by Hatano considers relationships between the characteristics of a sentence and the character of a writer, it is different in nature from stylometry in a narrow sense; however, many of the involved analytical methods are similar. Hatano (1935) analyzed "Kin to Gin" ("Gold and Silver"), written by Junichiro Tanizaki, and "Amagaeru" ("Tree Frog"), written by Naoya Shiga, and showed that the ratio of verbs was high in the former, while the ratio of nouns was high in the latter. He also measured the average sentence lengths to show that the styles differed for the two authors, the average sentence lengths were 49.2 letters for the former author and 32.1 letters for the latter. Hideo Kobayashi, a well-known Japanese author who developed literary criticism as an independent art form in Japan, acknowledged that he had been influenced by Hatano (1935).

Yasumoto (1957) conducted an early study on quantitative analysis of word frequencies in Japanese sentences. Similar to Mendenhall's author identification study on Shakespeare and Bacon, Yasumoto (1957) analyzed "The Tale of Genji," which is thought to have been written by Murasaki Shikibu (973-1014) in the Heian Period. Yasumoto divided "The Tale of Genji" into "Uji Jujo" and the other 44 volumes to perform a statistical hypothesis test. Twelve items, including the frequencies of nouns, declinable words, postpositional particles, and auxiliary verbs, were used for the test. One hundred words were extracted randomly from each volume, and the frequency of each item was obtained from these words. Here, it should be noted that not all of the sentences in "The Tale of Genji" were analyzed.

Yasumoto (1957) also performed a study based on the psychology of writing. From the results, he considered that the styles found in "Uji Jujo" were characterized by detailed descriptions through fictional, declinable, close, and continuous concepts and that the styles of the other 44 volumes were characterized by intuitive descriptions through melodramatic, indeclinable, dramatic, and intermittent configurations. Therefore, he concluded that the author of "Uji Jujo" was not the author of the other volumes.

In addition, Yasumoto (1977) used 12 variables obtained from a sampling similar to that used in Yasumoto (1957) to perform factor analysis and reexamine "Uji Jujo" from the perspective of multiple authors. As a result, he confirmed his previous conclusion, i.e., that the styles found in "Uji Jujo" differed from those of the other volumes; however, based on this analysis, he did not conclude that the authors were different.

Arai (1997) extracted samples from the central part of each volume of the Uji Juro, whose locations depended on the lengths of the volumes, to perform a statistical test on the frequencies of syllable onset strings and vowel strings in the kana syllabary table. As a result, he concluded that the author of "Uji Jujo" was not different from the author of the other volumes.

All of these quantitative studies on "The Tale of Genji" have provided meaningful results; however, the analyses were not performed on the entire work. Murakami and Imanishi (1999) used multi-variate analysis techniques to perform a quantitative study of all of the sentences in "The Tale of Genji." In this study, the appearance ratios of specific functions words, i.e., auxiliary verbs, were used to predict the creation order of the volumes that comprise "The Tale of Genji" by quantification the third part. Tsuchiyama and Murakami (2014) performed multivariate analysis, such as principal component analysis, of "The Tale of Genji" and used the appearance ratios of auxiliary verbs and postpositional particles and the word-length distributions to perform author identification for "Uji Jujo" and the preceding "Nioumiya Sanjo." As a result, they concluded that "Nioumiya Sanjo" and "Uji Jujo" were likely written by the same author as we will describe later.

Jin and Murakami (1993) focused on contemporary Japanese writing. Rather than using conventional analysis items, Jin and Murakami (1993) examined the states of words appearing before punctuation marks in the literary works of Yasushi Inoue, Yukio Mishima, and Atsushi Nakajima. The study showed that characteristics of these authors could be identified by analyzing their use of punctuation marks.

Jin (2002) performed discrimination analysis of diaries and compositions of ordinary people, instead of sentences of professional writers studied so far, to identify writers. As a result of the analysis, he showed that characteristics of writers appeared in bigram of postpositional particles for diaries and in trigram for compositions. Bigram of postpositional particles means a pattern in which postpositional particles appear in succession when parts of speech other than postpositional particles in a sentence are neglected. In the same manner, trigram means a pattern of three in succession.

## ANALYTICAL METHODOLOGY

In this analysis, we primarily used principal-component analysis based on correlation coefficient matrices, which is a method of dimension reduction that can be applied to multi-dimensional data. Information is reduced by seeking new composite variables within the original data variables. The results are expressed as a distribution diagram of principal-component scores for first and second principal components. In the distribution diagram, the first principal components are represented on the horizontal axis, and the second principal components are represented on the vertical axis. The amount of information contained in each principal component is evaluated according to its contribution rate. The first and second principal component contribution rates are also shown in the distribution diagram.

The primary analysis item used in this study is the frequency with which each word appeared in the target text. Word counts were divided on the basis of their parts of speech. In stylometry, the frequency of content words, such as nouns, verbs, adjectives, and adverbs, is not considered an effective metric for authorship attribution as the frequency of these content words is mainly determined by the nature of the text. In contrast, the frequency of function words, including postpositional particles and auxiliary verbs, is less affected by the text. Therefore, they are useful for the identification of authorship; in this study we focused our analysis mainly on the frequency of function words.

## ANALYSIS OF AUTHORSHIP OF "THE TALE OF GENJI"

### Postpositional Particles

In the word-frequency analysis, we investigated two types of functional words, postpositional particles and auxiliary verbs, which have been determined to be effective for quantitatively identifying authors.

The total number of postpositional particles was 119694, consisting of 56 different words. PCA was performed on the top 15 postpositional particles with appearance frequencies greater than 1000. The top 15 consisted of vocabulary with appearance frequencies of 1346 or more. The accumulated frequency was 110566, making up 92.3% of the total number. Figure 1 shows the results of the PCA. Although Volume 42, "Nioumiya," of "Nioumiya Sanjo" is positioned outside of the 95% confidence ellipse of the other 41 volumes, the 95% confidence ellipses of "Nioumiya Sanjo" and "Uji Jujo" overlap that of the other 41 volumes.

*Figure 1. Principal component analysis appearance frequency results for top 15 postpositional particles*

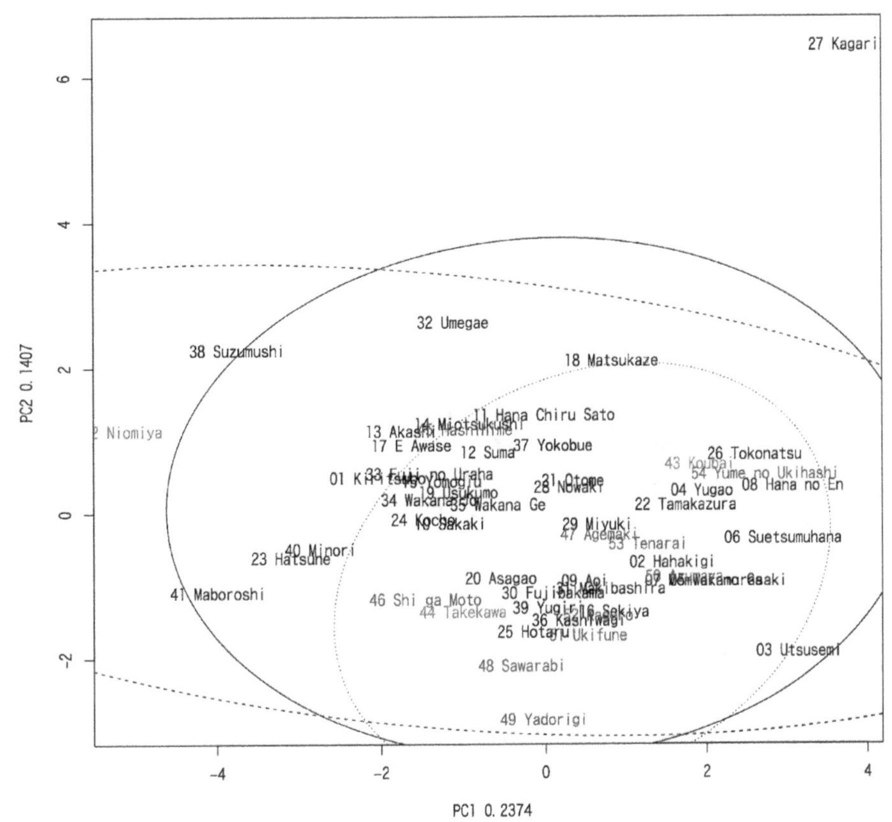

Volumes 11, 16, and 27, "Hanchirusato," "Sekiya," and "Kagaribi," respectively, contain less than 1000 words. Consequently, it was analyzed again after these volumes were excluded from the analysis. The top 15 postpositional particles were taken from words with appearance frequencies greater than 1000. These words had appearance frequencies of 1341 or more, with an accumulated frequency of 109864, making up 92.4% of the total number. The analysis results reveal that the 95% confidence ellipses of "Nioumiya Sanjo" and "Uji Jujo" overlap the 95% confidence ellipse of the other 41 volumes. Furthermore, the results did not change significantly by increasing or decreasing the number of variables.

These results reveal no significant discrepancy between the appearances of postpositional particles in "Nioumiya Sanjo" and "Uji Jujo" and in the other 41 volumes.

## Auxiliary Verbs

The total number of auxiliary verbs was 43624, consisting of 26 different words. Component analysis was performed on the top 12 words with appearance frequencies greater than 1000. The top 12 auxiliary verbs had appearance frequencies of 1267 or more. The cumulative frequency was 38523, making up an 88.3% of the total number of words. The principal component analysis results are shown in Figure 2. The 95% confidence ellipses for "Nioumiya Sanjo" and "Uji Jujo" overlap with the 95% confidence ellipse for the other 41 volumes. Furthermore, although the 95% confidence ellipses of "Nioumiya

*Figure 2. Principal component analysis appearance frequency results for top 12 auxiliary verbs*

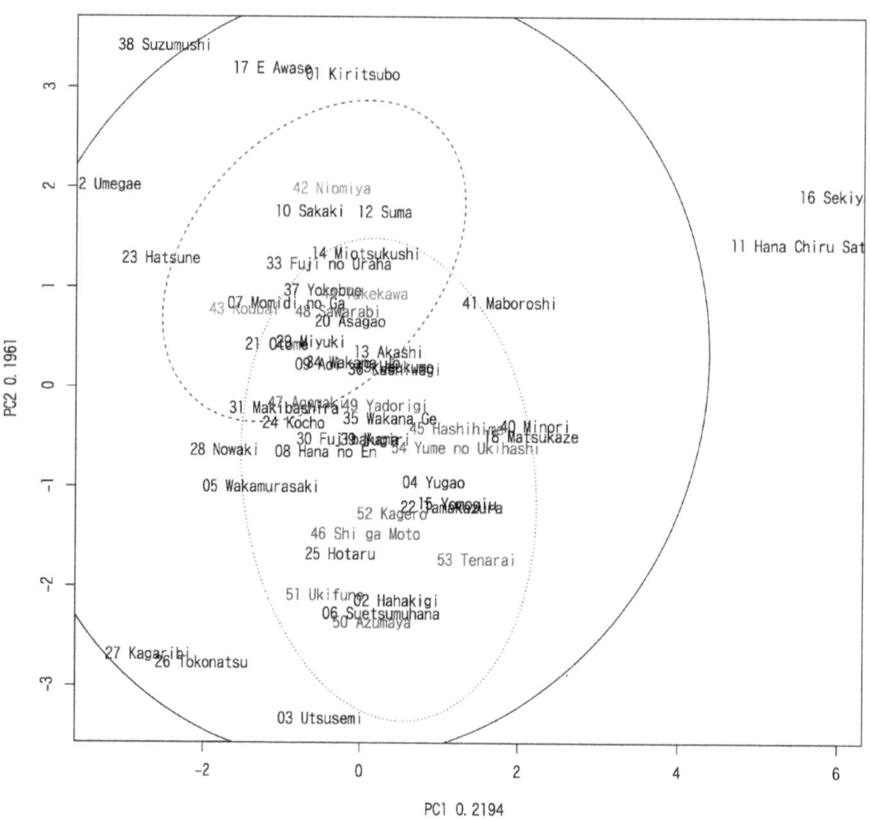

Sanjo" and "Uji Jujo" overlap, it is surmised that the various volumes for each group have appearance trends for different auxiliary verbs.

As in the postpositional particle analysis, the three volumes with less than 1000 words were excluded from the analysis, and the analysis was performed again. Principal component analysis was performed on the top 12 auxiliary verbs with appearance frequencies greater than 1000. The accumulated frequency was 38287, making up 88.3% of the total number. "Nioumiya Sanjo," "Uji Jujo," and the other 41 volumes exist together, and no significant difference between the appearance frequencies of auxiliary verbs is evident. Furthermore, "Nioumiya Sanjo" and "Uji Jujo" volumes do not exist together, and it is possible that their respective appearance trends are related to different auxiliary verbs. This result did not change significantly even if the number of variables was increased or decreased.

In terms of the appearance frequencies of nouns, no significant differences between "Nioumiya Sanjo" and "Uji Jujo" and the other 42 volumes were evident.

## Analysis Results

An analysis to test the theory of separate authorship of "Nioumiya Sanjo" and "Uji Jujo" was performed based on a quantitative analysis of the appearance ratios of postpositional particles and auxiliary verbs, which are considered effective analysis terms to identify authors. However, no significant differences were found between the trends in "Nioumiya Sanjo" and "Uji Jujo" and that in the 41 volumes remain-

*Figure 3. Principal component analysis appearance-frequency results for top 102 nouns*

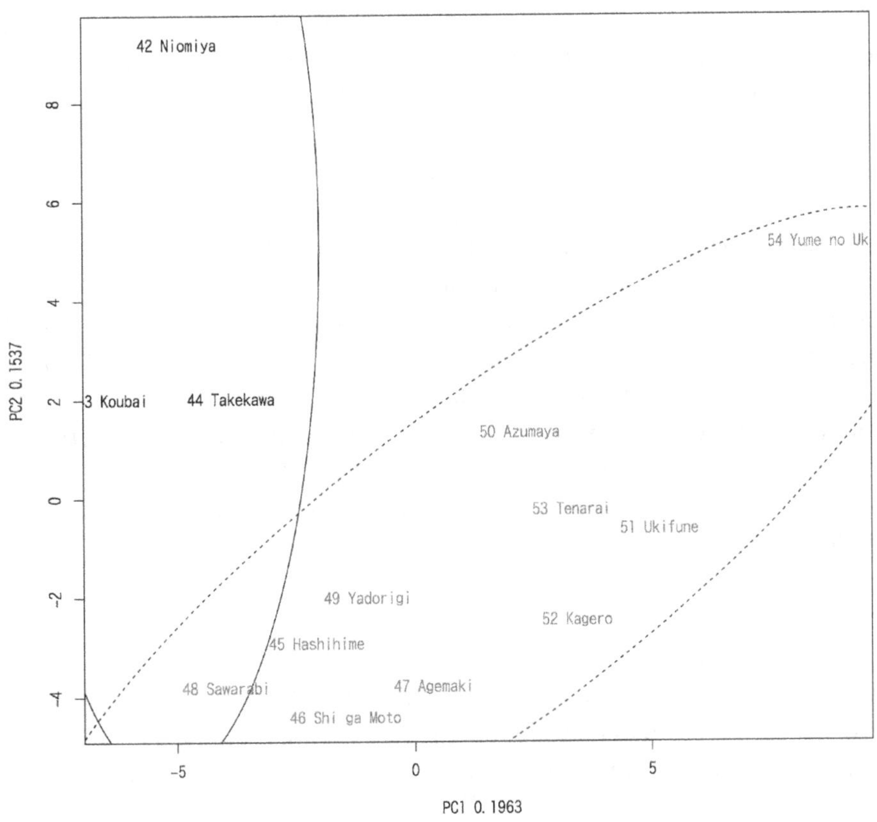

ing after excluding these 13 volumes. In other words, the word-frequency analysis results do not support the theory of separate authorship of "Nioumiya Sanjo" or "Uji Jujo" as we have previously described.

The result of an analysis using the word frequency for auxiliary verbs found no evidence that positively support the theory of separate authorship of "Nioumiya Sanjo" or "Uji Jujo." Therefore, the results indicate that the possibility that there are multiple authors of "The Tale of Genji" is low.

## ANALYSIS ON THE FORMATION PROCESS OF THE THIRD PART OF "THE TALE OF GENJI"

To discern the formation process, we performed a quantitative investigation in which the analysis target was limited to the third part of "The Tale of Genji," i.e., the 13 volumes of "Nioumiya Sanjo" and "Uji Jujo." This analysis clarified the quantifiable trends and characteristics in these 13 volumes.

In word-frequency analysis, the objective is not to identify the author. Thus, is it appropriate to include parts of speech other than postpositional particles and auxiliary verbs. In this analysis, the top 10 nouns, pronouns, verbs, auxiliary verbs, adjectives, adjective verb, adverbs, adnominal adjectives, postpositional particles, and auxiliary verbs with the highest word totals were analyzed.

### Nouns

The total number of nouns was 20687, consisting of 2798 different nouns. As the number of different nouns exceeded 100, PCA was performed on approximately the top 100 words in terms of appearance frequency. Therefore, analysis was performed on 102 words with appearance frequencies of 31 or more. The accumulated frequency of the top 102 words was 11397, making up 55.1% of the total number of nouns. The PCA analysis results are shown in Figure 3. Although the 95% confidence ellipses overlap, significant differences are evident in the word frequencies in "Nioumiya Sanjo" and "Uji Jujo." Furthermore, there are different word-appearance-frequency trends between the first five volumes and the later five volumes of "Uji Jujo."

An investigation in which the analysis target was limited to "Uji Jujo" was performed. The total number of nouns in "Uji Jujo" is 18186, and the number of different words is 2541. As above, PCA was performed on approximately the top 100 in terms of appearance frequency. Words in the top 99 were those with appearance frequencies of 28 or more. The accumulated appearance frequency was 10211, making up 56.1% of the total number of nouns. The results of the PCA, as shown in Figure 4, were that the first five volumes and the latter five volumes of "Uji Jujo" did not exist together, and differences were recognized between the word-appearance-frequency trends. Therefore, we found that there are differences between the appearance frequencies of nouns in the first five volumes and in the latter five volumes of "Uji Jujo."

### Pronouns

An analysis was also performed on pronouns. As the number of different pronouns was less than 100, PCA was performed on words with frequencies of two or more, which equates to the appearance frequencies of the top 28 words. The accumulated frequency of these 28 words was 835, making up 99.2% of

*Figure 4. Principal component analysis appearance-frequency results for top 99 nouns in "Uji Jujo"*

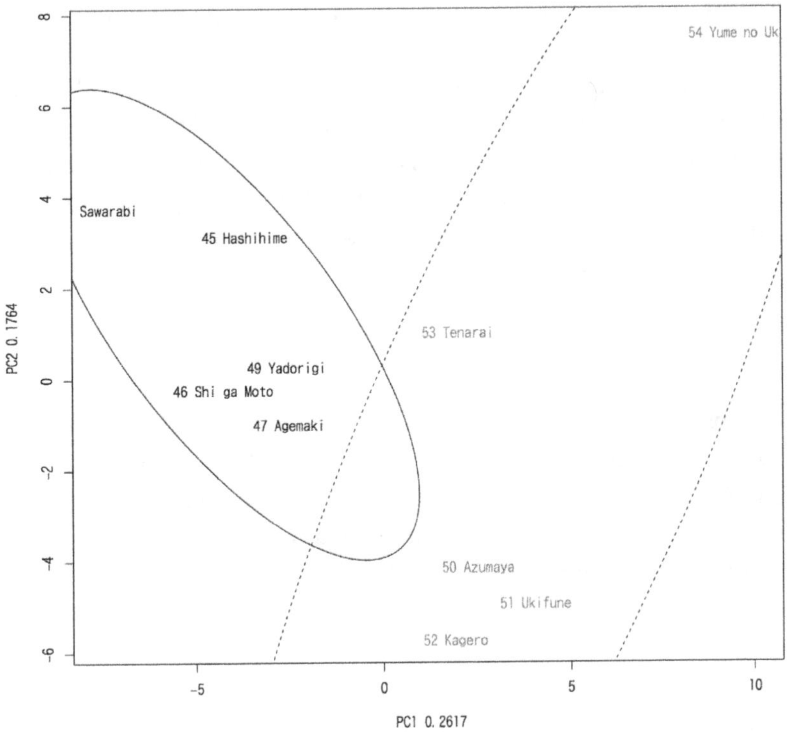


*Figure 5. Principal component analysis appearance-frequency results for top 28 pronouns*

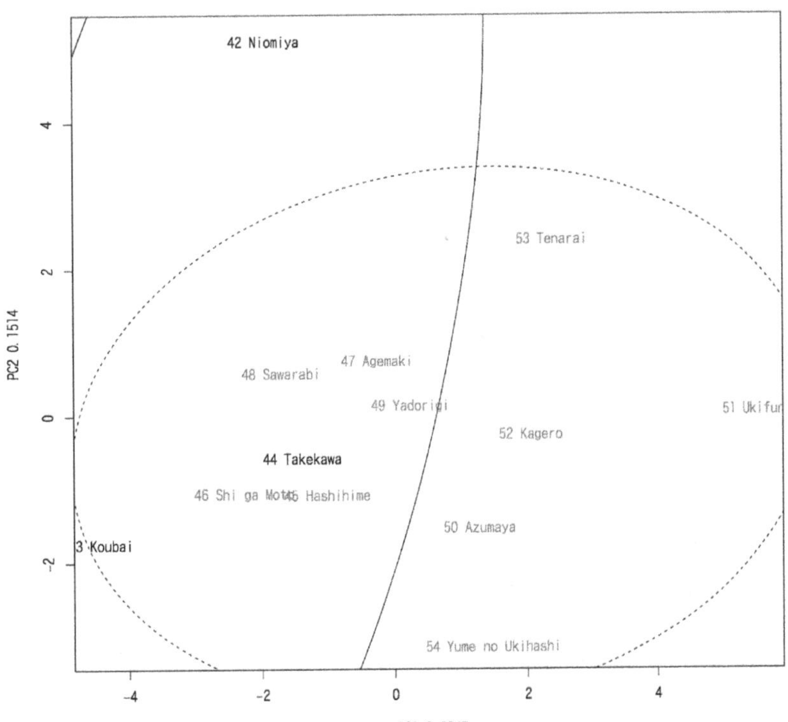

the total number of words. The analysis results obtained from the PCA are shown in Figure 5. No differences are evident between the appearance frequencies of words in "Nioumiya Sanjo" and "Uji Jujo."

The total number of words in "Uji Jujo" is 764, and the number of different words is 34. PCA was performed on words with frequencies of two or more, limiting the target to "Uji Jujo" and equating to the top 28 words in terms of appearance frequency. The accumulated frequency of the top 28 words was 758, a 99.2% share of the total number of words. The analysis results obtained from the PCA are shown in Figure 6. While the 95% confidence ellipses for both groups overlap, the target of both groups do not exist together, and differences between the word-appearance-frequency trends of the first five volumes and latter five volumes of "Uji Jujo" are evident.

## Verbs

The total number of verbs is 20932, and the number of different words is 2835. The top 101 verbs in terms of appearance frequency equated to those with frequencies of 28 or more. The accumulated frequency was 11969, representing 57.2% of the total number of verbs. The results are shown in Figure 7. Similar to the results for nouns, a difference between the appearance-frequency trends of the first principal components is observed for "Nioumiya Sanjo" and "Uji Jujo." In addition, with regard to the second

*Figure 6. Principal component analysis appearance-frequency results for top 28 pronouns in "Uji Jujo"*

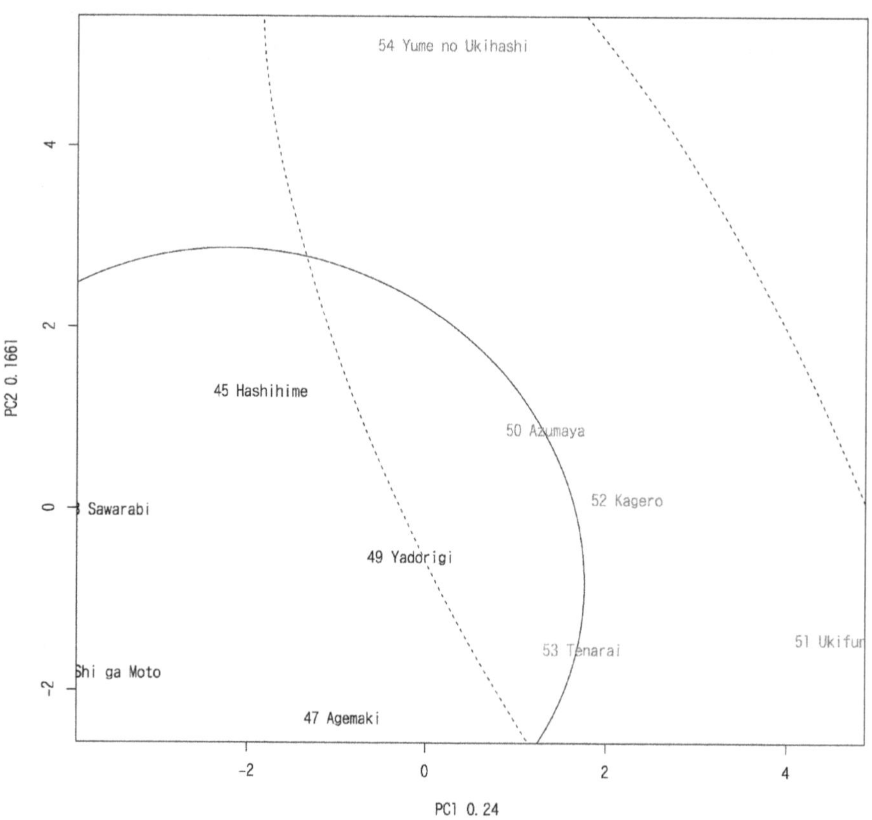

*Figure 7. Principal component analysis appearance frequency results for top 101 verbs*

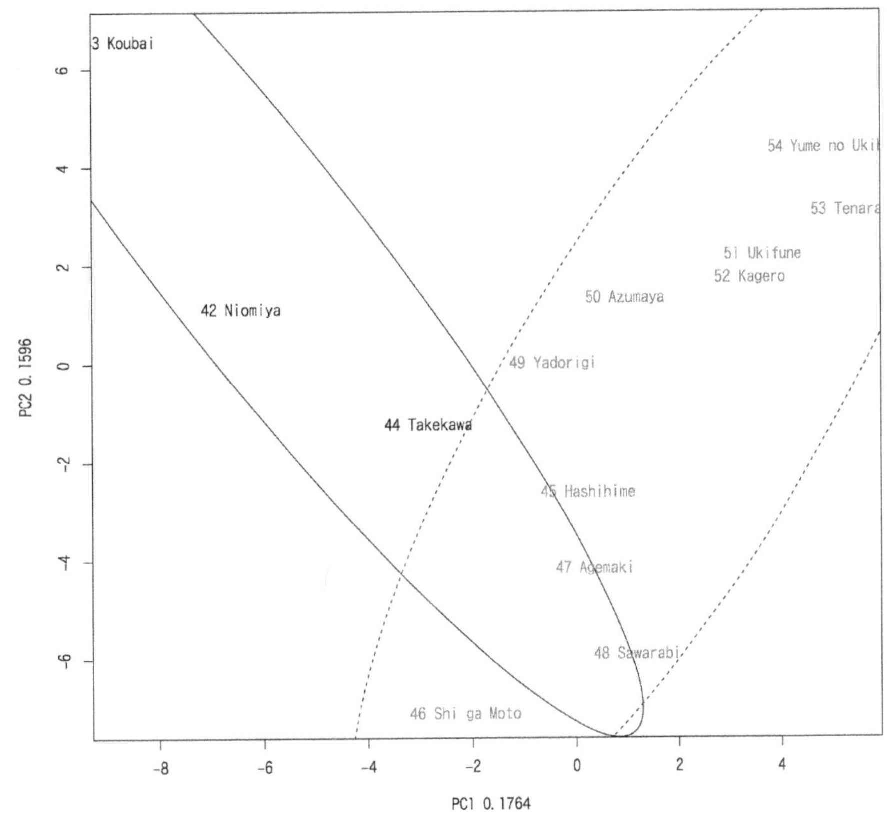


principal components, it is surmised that there are differences between the word-appearance-frequency trends of the first five volumes and of the latter five volumes of "Uji Jujo."

The total number of verbs in "Uji Jujo" is 18767, and the number of different words is 2660. The top 99 verbs in terms of appearance frequency equate to words with appearance frequencies of 25 or more. The accumulated frequency of the top 99 words was 10735, representing 57.2% of the total number of verbs. The analysis results are shown in Figure 8. Differences between the appearance-frequency trends of the first principal components are evident for the first five volumes and latter five volumes of "Uji Jujo."

## Subsidiary Verbs

The total number of subsidiary verbs is 6206, with seven different words. PCA was performed on words with appearance frequencies of two or more. The top six words had appearance frequencies of two or more. The analysis results are shown in Figure 9. Since Volume 44, "Takekawa" of "Nioumiya Sanjo," and Volume 46, "Shiimoto" of "Uji Jujo," are located approximately in the same place, no differences between their word-appearance frequencies can be recognized for "Nioumiya Sanjo" and "Uji Jujo."

The total number of subsidiary verbs in "Uji Jujo" is 5480, including seven different words. PCA was performed on words with appearance frequencies of two or more, which corresponded to the top six in terms of appearance frequency. The analysis results obtained from the PCA are shown in Figure 10. In

*Figure 8. Principal component analysis appearance frequency results for top 99 verbs in "Uji Jujo"*

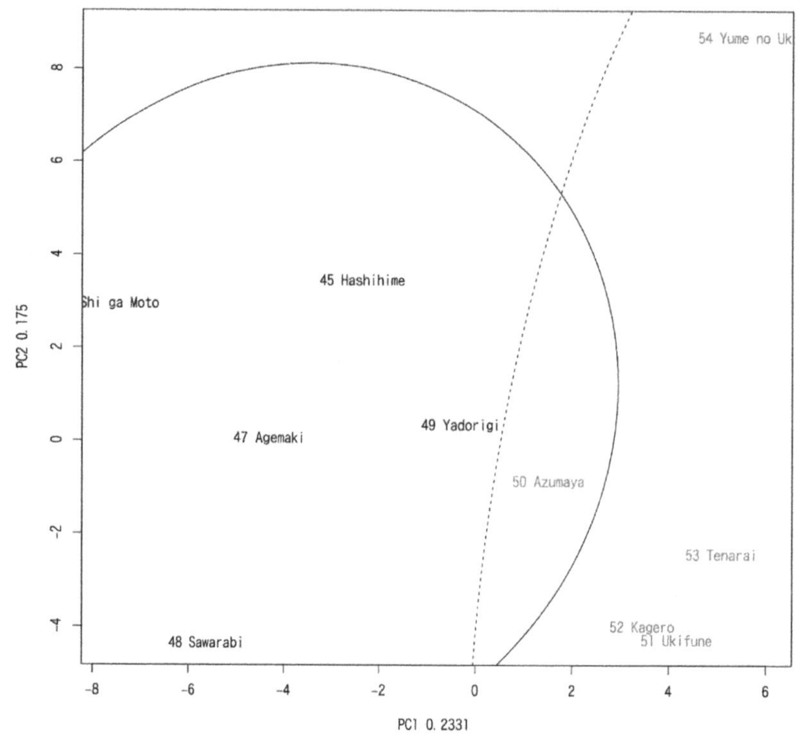


*Figure 9. Principal component analysis results for total number of subsidiary verbs*

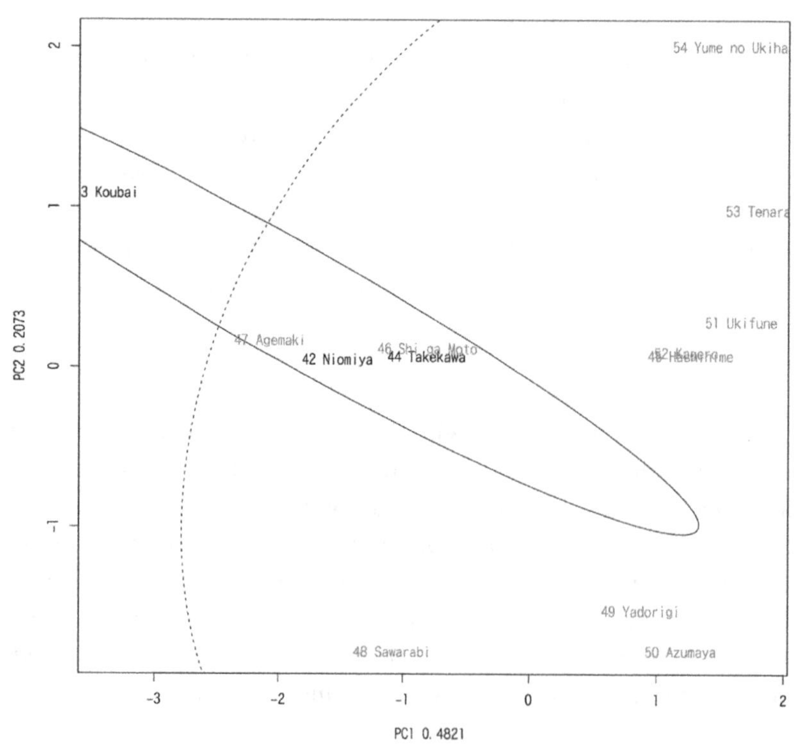

Figure 10, Volume 45, "Hashihime," and Volume 49, "Yadorigi," which belong to the first five volumes, are located proximate to the later five volumes. No significant differences are observable between the first five and latter five volumes of "Uji Jujo."

## Adjectives

The total number of adjectives is 7111, with 544 different words. The top 99 in terms of appearance frequency correspond to those with appearance frequencies of 16 or more. The accumulated frequency was 5329, comprising 74.9% of the total number of adjectives. The results are shown in Figure 11. Significant differences are observed between "Nioumiya Sanjo" and "Uji Jujo." In addition, there are differences between the appearance frequencies for the first five and latter five volumes of "Uji Jujo."

The total number of adjectives in "Uji Jujo" is 6386, with 517 different words. The top 99 words in terms of appearance frequency have appearance frequencies of 14 or more. The accumulated frequency was 4807, comprising 75.3% of the total number of adjectives. The results are shown in Figure 12. While Volume 48, "Sawarabi," which belongs to the first five volumes, and Volume 54, "Yume no Ukihashi," which belongs to the latter five volumes, are positioned separately from the other volumes, the 95% confidence ellipses of the first five and latter five volumes overlap, and no significant differences are

*Figure 10. Principal component analysis appearance frequency results for top six subsidiary verbs in "Uji Jujo"*

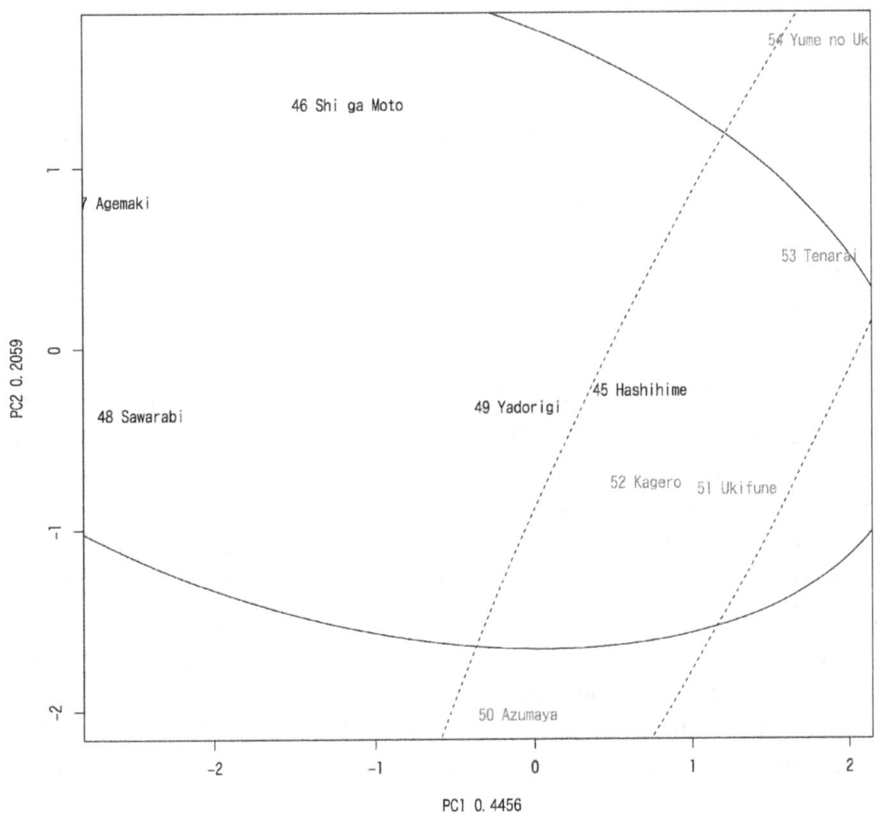

*Figure 11. Principal component analysis appearance frequency results for top 99 adjectives*

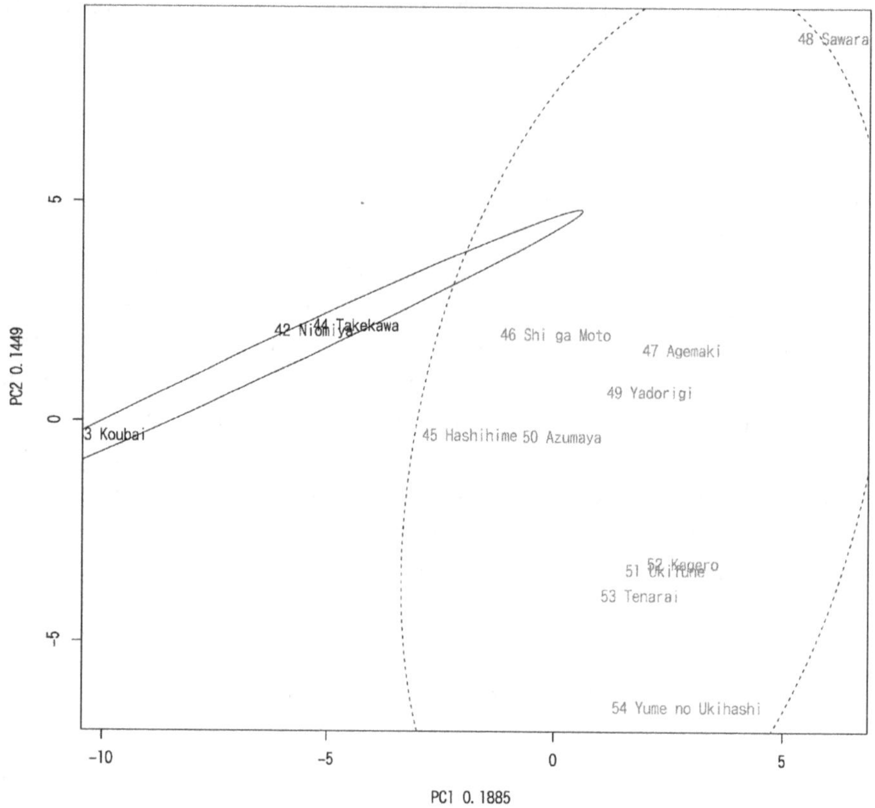


observed between the word appearance frequencies of the two groups. However, in terms of first principal components, as the targets of the two groups are somewhat divided in terms of positive and negative, it is thought that they exhibit different trends.

## Adjective Verbs

The total number of adjective verb is 3037, with 425 different words. The top 99 words in terms of appearance frequency correspond to those with frequencies of seven or more. The accumulated frequency was 2368, comprising 78.0% of the total number of adjective verb. From the results obtained through principal component analysis (Figure 13), significant differences can be recognized between the appearance frequencies of these words in "Nioumiya Sanjo" and "Uji Jujo."

The total number of adjective verb in "Uji Jujo" is 2734, with 404 different words. The top 103 words in terms of appearance frequency appeared six or more times. The accumulated frequency was 2154, comprising 78.8% of the total number of adjective verb. The results obtained from the PCA are shown in Figure 14, and it is considered that there are significant differences between the appearance frequencies of these words in the first five and latter five of "Uji Jujo." Although significant differences are also recognized between the adjectival noun frequencies in "Nioumiya Sanjo" and "Uji Jujo," although no significant differences were recognized between the first five and latter five volumes of "Uji Jujo."

*Figure 12. Principal component analysis appearance frequency results for top 99 adjectives in "Uji Jujo"*

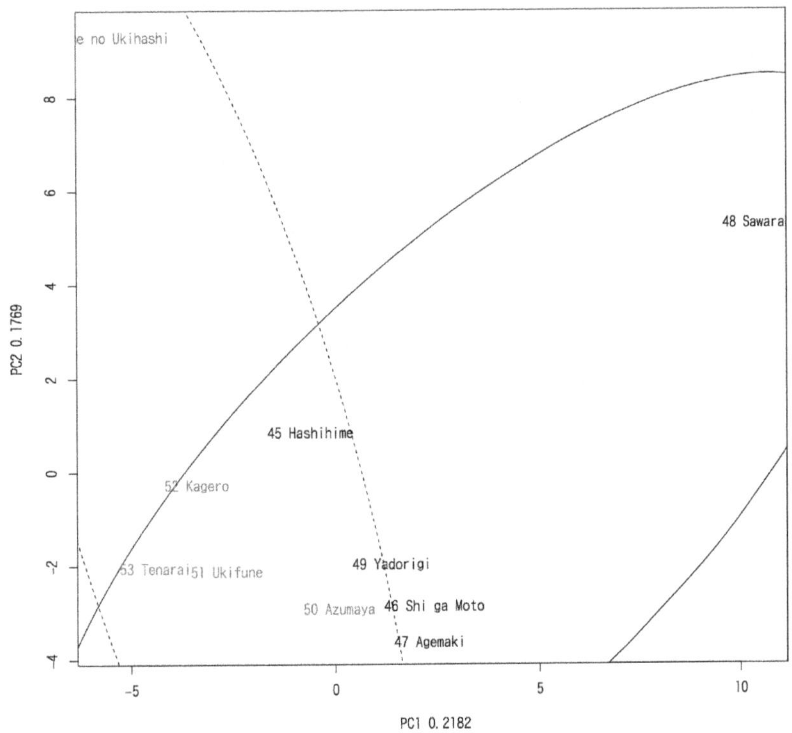


*Figure 13. Principal component analysis appearance frequency results for top 99 adjective verb*

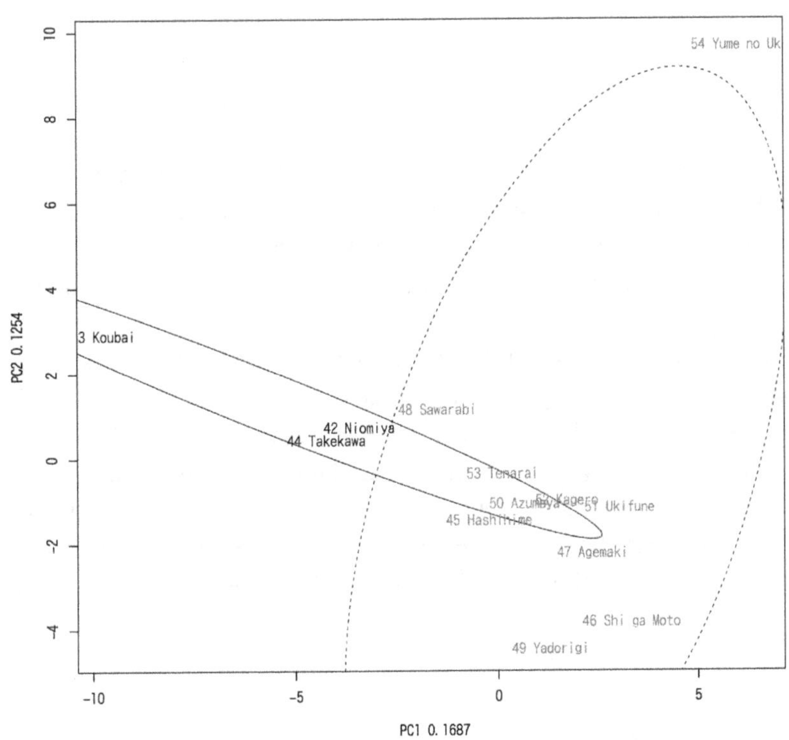

*Figure 14. Principal component analysis appearance frequency results for top 103 adjective verb in "Uji Jujo"*

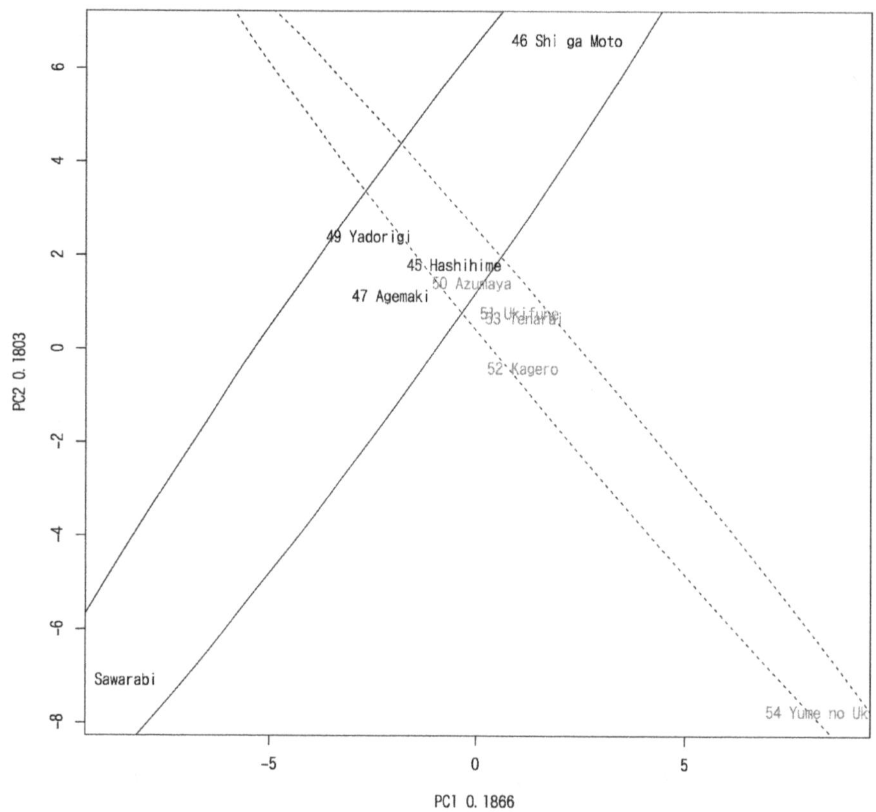


## Adverbs

The total number of adverbs is 5191, with 186 different words. In the PCA, the top 94 words appeared with frequencies of four or more. The accumulated frequency was 5057, comprising 97.4% of the total number of words. The results are shown in Figure 15. Whereas Volume 42, "Nioumiya," is positioned outside, no significant differences are observed between the appearance frequencies of words in "Nioumiya Sanjo" and "Uji Jujo."

The total number of adverbs in "Uji Jujo" is 4686, with 179 different words. In the PCA, the top 102 words in terms of appearance frequency appeared three or more times. The accumulated frequency was 4591, making up 98.0% of the total. The results obtained from the PCA are shown in Figure 16. Whereas Volume 54, "Yume no Ukihashi," which belongs to the latter five volumes, is positioned separately in relation to the other four volumes, the various volumes of the two groups exist together. Thus, no significant differences are recognized between the appearance frequencies of adverbs in "Nioumiya Sanjo" and "Uji Jujo" or between those in the first five and latter five volumes of "Uji Jujo."

*Figure 15. Principal component analysis appearance frequency results for top 94 adverbs*

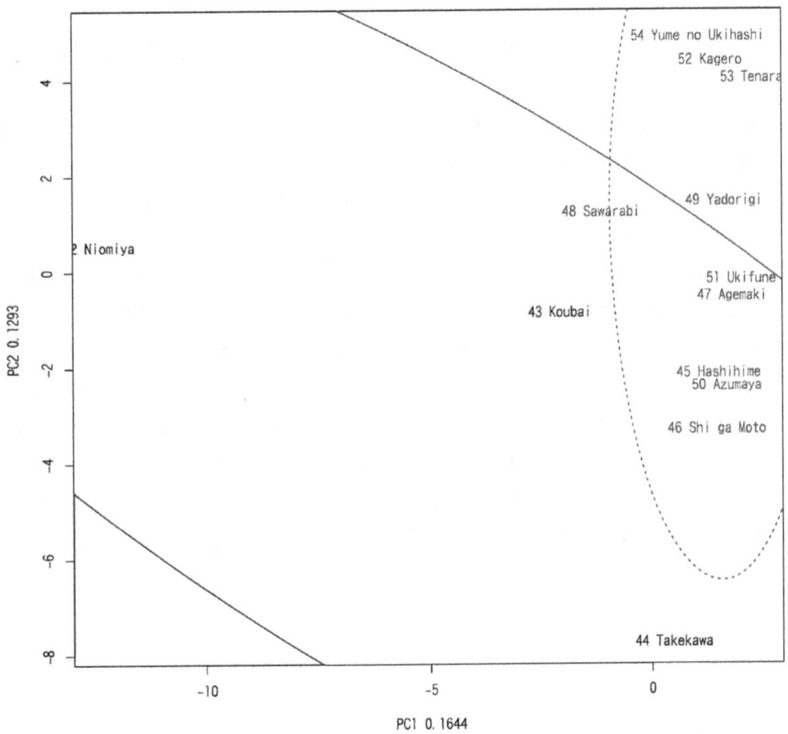


*Figure 16. Principal component analysis appearance frequency results for top 102 adverbs in "Uji Jujo"*

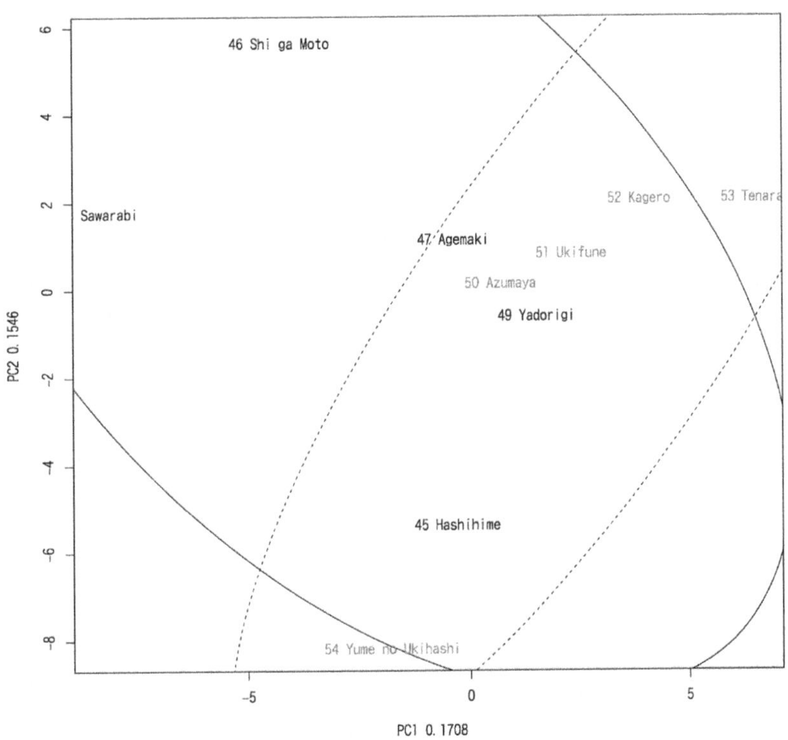

## Postpositional Particles

The total number of postpositional particles is 40075, with 54 different words. In the PCA, the top nine words with appearance frequencies of 1000 or more were used. The top nine words had frequencies of 1368 or more. The accumulated frequency was 33126 words, comprising 82.7% of the total number of words. The results obtained from the PCA are shown in Figure 17. Since Volume 44, "Takekawa," exists with "Uji Jujo," no significant differences are recognized between the appearance frequencies of these words in "Nioumiya Sanjo" and "Uji Jujo."

The total number of postpositional particles in "Uji Jujo" is 35785, with 54 different words. In the PCA, the top nine words with frequencies of 1000 or more were used. The top nine words had frequencies of 1218 or more. The accumulated frequency was 29493, comprising 82.4% of the total. The PCA results are shown in Figure 18. With regard to the positive and negative elements of the first components, it is evident that the first five and latter five volumes exist separately. Thus, differences between the quantitative trends of the two groups can be recognized. Although no significant differences are recognized between the appearance frequencies of postpositional particles in "Nioumiya Sanjo" and "Uji Jujo," significant differences are recognized between their appearance frequencies in the first five and latter five volumes of "Uji Jujo."

*Figure 17. Principal component analysis appearance frequency results for top 9 postpositional particles*

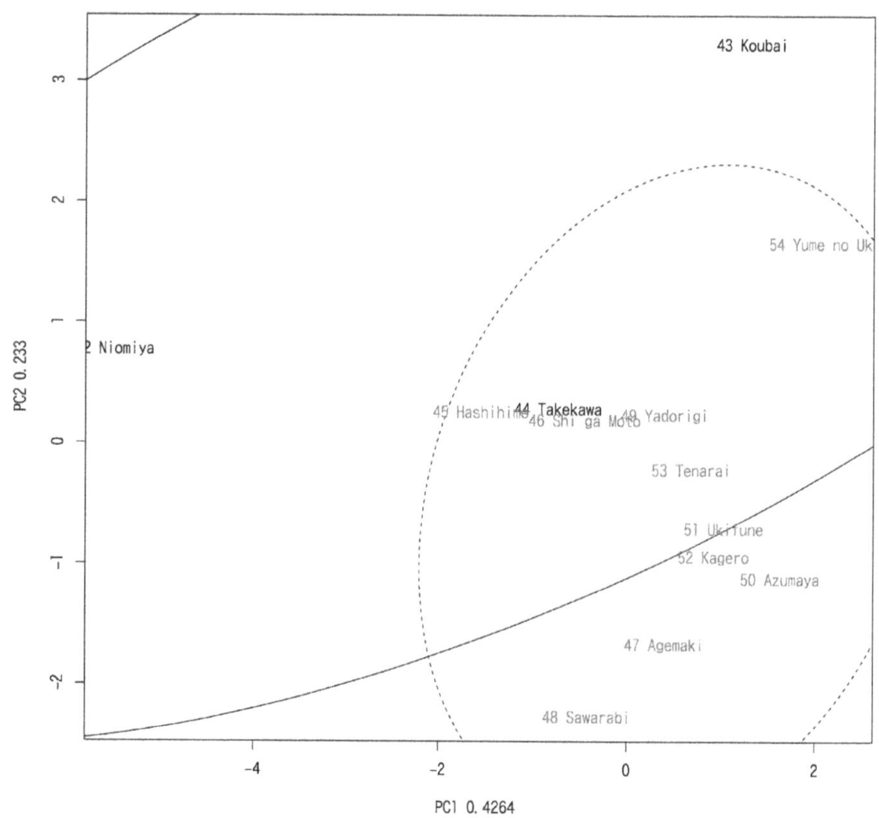

*Figure 18. Principal component analysis appearance frequency results for top 9 postpositional particles in "Uji Jujo"*

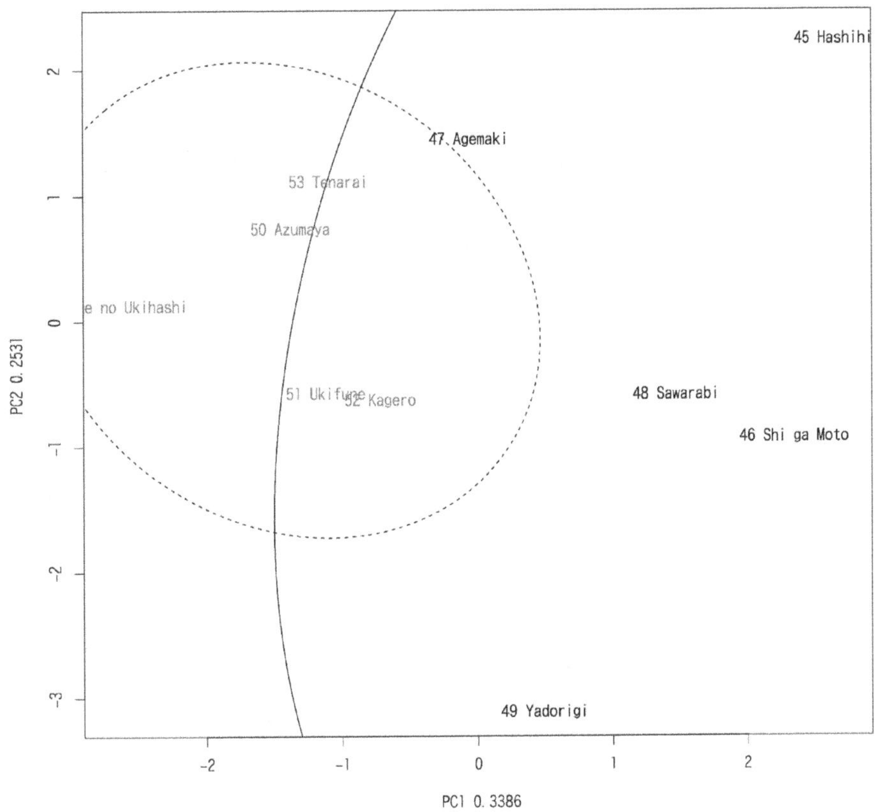


## Auxiliary Verbs

The total number of auxiliary verbs is 15188, with 25 different words. PCA was performed on the top eight auxiliary verbs in terms of appearance frequency, whose frequencies exceeded 1000. The top eight auxiliary verbs corresponded to those with appearance frequencies of 1007 or more. The accumulated frequency was 10800, comprising 71.1% of the total number of auxiliary verbs. No significant differences between the word frequency trends in "Nioumiya Sanjo" and "Uji Jujo" are observed.

PCA that included words with low frequencies of three or more was performed. These included the top 23 words in terms of appearance frequency. Significant differences were found between "Nioumiya Sanjo" and "Uji Jujo" in terms of appearance frequency. The accumulated frequency of the top 23 words was 15186, which was 100% of the total number of words. The analysis results are shown in Figure 19. Volume 48, "Sawarabi," of "Uji Jujo" and Volume 23, "Kobai," of "Nioumiya Sanjo" are located in the same vicinity. Thus, differences between the appearance frequencies of words in "Nioumiya Sanjo" and "Uji Jujo" are observed.

The total number of auxiliary verbs is 13733, with 25 different auxiliary verbs. PCA was performed on the top five words, whose appearance frequencies exceeded 1000. The top five words had appearance frequencies of 1083 or more. The accumulated frequency was 6291 words, comprising 50.4% of the total

*Figure 19. Principal component analysis appearance frequency results for top 23 auxiliary verbs*

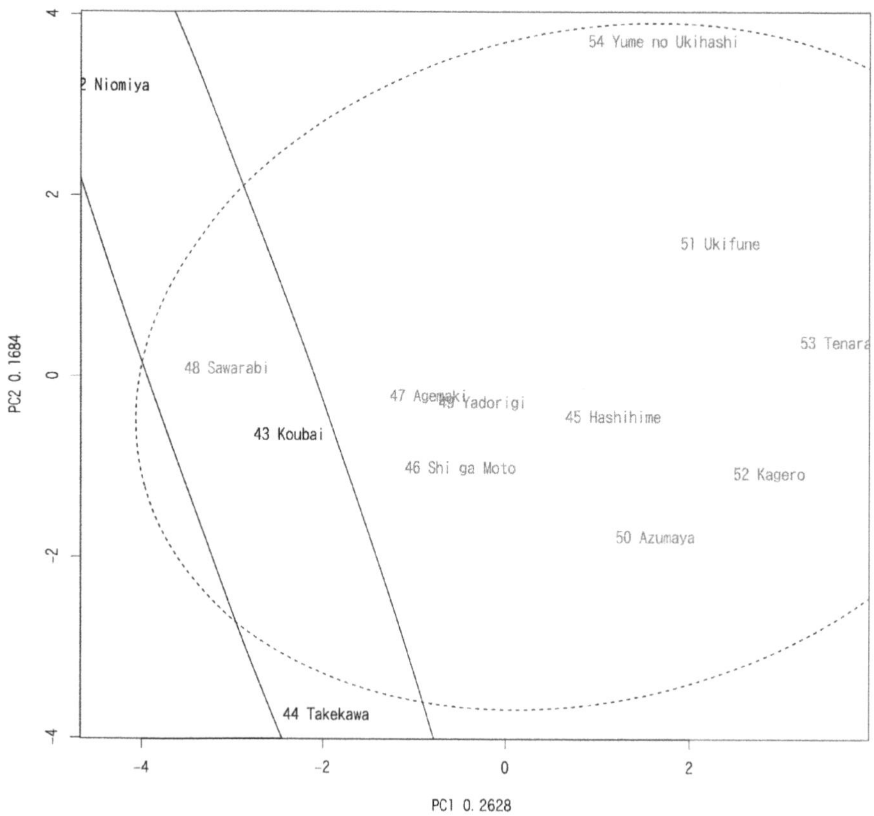


number of words. Comparing the first five and latter five volumes of "Uji Jujo," Volume 46, "Shiimoto," which belongs to the first five volumes, is separated from the other four volumes, and general differences between the appearance frequency trends are recognized.

PCA was performed on the top 23 words with appearance frequencies of three or more. The accumulated frequency was 13731, which is 100% of the total. Figure 20 shows the analysis results. Significant differences can be seen between the appearance frequencies of the first components in the first five and latter five volumes.

The results of the PCA revealed differences between the trends of auxiliary verbs in "Nioumiya Sanjo" and "Uji Jujo" and between those in the first five and latter five volumes of "Uji Jujo."

## Analysis Results

The analysis target was limited to the 13 volumes of "Nioumiya Sanjo" and "Uji Jujo," and their word frequencies were analyzed. The results show that the trends for nouns, verbs, adjectives, and adjective verb differed in "Nioumiya Sanjo" and "Uji Jujo."

Next, the analysis target was limited to "Uji Jujo." When the appearance frequencies of words were analyzed, differences between the appearance trends for nouns, pronouns, verbs, adjectives, adjective verb, postpositional particles, and auxiliaries in the first five and latter five volumes of "Uji Jujo" were

*Figure 20. Principal component analysis appearance frequency results for the top 23 auxiliary verbs in "Uji Jujo"*

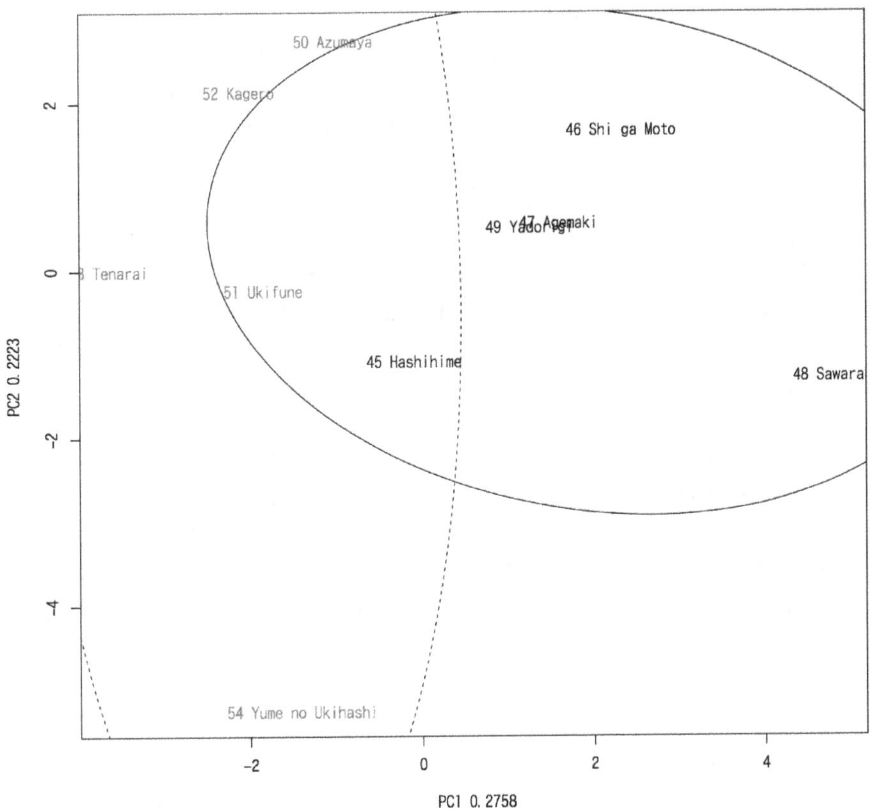


recognized. From quantitative analysis of the other 41 volumes and "Uji Jujo," there is little evidence to support the theory of separate authorship of "Uji Jujo." However, significant quantitative differences exist between the first five and latter five volumes of "Uji Jujo."

## FUTURE RESEARCH DIRECTIONS

This study quantitatively analyzed "The Tale of Genji" by using stylometry. In addition to "The Tale of Genji," determining authorship and chronology is problematic for many classical Japanese literary works. We believe that it is possible to apply this analysis method to various Japanese literary works. As stylometry has become increasingly accurate and popular, quantitative analyses of such literature have increased. Although the main purpose of stylometric investigations is to identify authorship and predict the chronology, there has not been sufficient recent research of the latter. Therefore, we expect that the number of such studies will increase and advance with the advent and growth of stylometric methods.

## CONCLUSION

This study involved a quantitative analysis of "The Tale of Genji" using stylometry. We have presented the results sufficiently detailed to encourage quantitative debate. We considered two possibilities. One is that "The Tale of Genji" had multiple authors. The other is that there are two separate groups of text within "Uji Jujo." Our findings suggest that the latter is more plausible.

In the quantitative analysis of the frequencies of nouns, verbs, adjectival nouns, and adjective verbs in the 13 volumes that comprise the third part of "The Tale of Genji," different quantitative trends were observed in "Nioumiya Sanjo" and "Uji Jujo."

In addition, Ukifune first appears as the main heroine in Volume 49 "Yadorigi," which is the fifth volume of "Uji Jujo." Thus, the first four and the last six volumes of "Uji Jujo" appear to be separate in terms of their plot. Alternatively, as Volume 45, "Hashihime," Volume 49, "Yadorigi," and Volume 53, "Tenarai" all begin with the phrase "In those days," it is possible to consider dividing the third part into four separate sections. However, the word frequency analysis clearly suggests different stylistic characteristics in the first five and last five volumes of "Uji Jujo."

From the results given above, it is suggested that the 13 volumes that comprise the third part of "The Tale of Genji" be classified into three groups: "Nioumiya Sanjo," the first five volumes of "Uji Jujo," and the later volumes of "Uji Jujo." We conclude that the analysis presented in this study provides evidence of the existence of two groups with different quantitative characteristics in the first five and last five volumes of "Uji Jujo."

We have presented some quantitative features of "The Tale of Genji" derived from statistical analysis. We hope that these findings will contribute to literary research. However, the stylometric approach requires inspiration from the humanities to interpret the analytical results, and we hope that further discussion among scholars from both backgrounds will advance the discipline of literary studies and deepen our understanding of "The Tale of Genji."

## REFERENCES


Antosch, F. (1969). The diagnosis of literary style with the verb-adjective ratio. In L. Doleszel & R. Bailey (Eds.), *Statistics and style*. New York, NY: Elsevier.

Arai, H. (1997). Genji monogatari/Uji Jujo no sakusha mondai: Hitotsu no keiryou gengogakuteki approach[The Tale of Genji/Uji Jujo authorship problem: one quantitative linguistic approach] [Hitotsubashi Treatise]. *Hitotsubashi Ronshu*, *117*(3), 397–413.

Binongo, J. N. G. (2003). Who wrote the 15th book of Oz? An application of multivariate analysis to authorship attribution. *Chance*, *16*(4), 375–388.

Brinegar, C. S. (1963). Mark Twain and the Quintus Curtius Snodgrass letters: A statistical test of authorship. *Journal of the American Statistical Association*, *58*(301), 85–96. doi:10.1080/01621459.1963.10500834

Campbell, L. (1867). *The Sophistes and Politicus of Plato*. London, UK: Clarendon Press.

Chaski, C. E. (2001). Empirical evaluations of language-based author identification techniques. *Forensic Linguistics*, *8*, 1–65.

De Morgan, S. E. (1882). *Memoir of Augustus de Morgan*. London, UK: Longmans, Green, and Company.

Dittenberger, W. (1881). Sprachliche Kriterien für die Chronologie der Platonischen Dialoge. *Hermes*, *16*(3), 321–345.

Guiraud, P. (1954). *La stylistique*. Paris, France: Presses universitaires de France.

Hatano, K. (1935). *Bunsho sinrigaku* [Psychology of writing]. Tokyo, Japan: Sanseido.

Jin, M. (2002). Authorship attribution based on n-gram models in postpositional particle of Japanese. *Mathematical Linguistics*, *23*(5), 225–240.

Jin, M., & Murakami, M. (1993). Authors' characteristic writing style as seen through their use of commas. *Behaviormetrika*, *20*(1), 63–76. doi:10.2333/bhmk.20.63

Mendenhall, T. C. (1887). The characteristic curves of composition. *Science*, *ns-9*(214S), 237–246. doi:10.1126/science.ns-9.214S.237 PMID:17736020

Mendenhall, T. C. (1901). A mechanical solution of a literary problem. *Popular Science Monthly*, *60*(2), 97–105.

Mosteller, F., & Wallace, D. L. (1963). Inference in an authorship problem: A comparative study of discrimination methods applied to the authorship of the disputed Federalist Papers. *Journal of the American Statistical Association*, *58*(302), 275–309.

Murakami, M., & Imanishi, Y. (1999). Quatitative analysis of auxiliary verb of The Tale of Genji. *Journal of Information Processing*, *40*(3), 774–782.

O'Donnell, B. (1966). Stephen Crane's the O'Ruddy: A problem in authorship discrimination. In Leed (Ed.), The Computer and Literary Style (pp. 107-115). Kent, OH: Kent State University Press.

Tsuchiyama, G., & Murakami, M. (2014). A quantitative analysis on the formation of the third part of "The Tale of Genji", *Computer and Humanities Symposium Essays*, 2014(3), 213-220.

Yasumoto, B. (1957). Uji Jujo no sakusha: Bunsho sinrigaku ni yoru sakusya suitei[The author of Uji Jujo: Inferring the author through stylometry]. *Japanese Psychological Review*, *2*(1), 147–156.

Yasumoto, B. (1977). Gendai no buntai kenkyu[Stylometric research in recent years] [the Japanese language]. *Nihongo*, *10*, 395–423.

## KEY TERMS AND DEFINITIONS

**Adjective Verb:** A specific part of speech that functions as an adjective in Japanese, also known as adjectival noun.

**Heian Period:** The period between 794 and 1185. This period is named after the capital city of Heian-Kyo, now known as Kyoto.

**Nioumiya Sanjo:** The first three volumes (Volume 42-44) in the third part of "The Tale of Genji," are named after the main character, Nioumiya. After the volumes, the story shifts to the time after Hikaru Genji's death.

**Postpositional Particles:** A particle that accompanies other words, such as nouns, verbs, and adjectives, to indicate the relation between words in a sentence.

**Principal Component Analysis:** A statistical method to reduce multi-dimensional data by converting a set of correlated variables into principal components, which are a set of uncorrelated variables.

**Subsidiary Verb:** A verb that accompanies a regular verb to express tense, aspect, voice, or mood.

**Uji Jujo:** The last ten volumes (Volume 45-54) in "The Tale of Genji," which is named after the main plot of the story in these volumes. It has long been considered the volumes were written by different authors.

# Section 4
# Cognition, Culture, and Narrative

# Chapter 11
# Assessing the Appeal Power of Narrative Performance by using Eyeblink Synchronization among Audience

**Ryota Nomura**
*The University of Tokyo, Japan*

**Takeshi Okada**
*The University of Tokyo, Japan*

## ABSTRACT

*In this chapter, the authors showed that eyeblink synchronization enables researchers to investigate the appeal power of narrative performance empirically. The proposed method relies on the ability of audience members as epistemic agents to recognize and understand the performance. As spontaneous eyeblinks loosely co-vary with individual's allocation and release of attentions, the timings of eyeblinks could be entrained by the details of narrative performances as the common inputs. Thus, the standard basis accumulated by the collective eyeblink responses enables experimenter to judge whether or not a particular performance contains universal appeal to sense-making. Here, the authors introduced that the empirical studies to assess the appeal power of Rakugo (a traditional narrative performance). An expert artist, compared to a novice performer, created implicit breakpoints on participants' attentional process. It were discussed that the applicable scopes of the eyeblink relevant indices, upcoming research on eyeblink synchronization, and new research on human collective behaviors.*

## INTRODUCTION

In the context of research on narrative performance[1], evaluation of the performance is a difficult problem. In this chapter, the authors propose universal quantitative methods to examine the appeal power of particular narrative performances. The assumption of these methods is quite simple: the appeal power of a performance can be defined as the forces that significantly provoke coherent responses among au-

DOI: 10.4018/978-1-5225-0432-0.ch011

Copyright © 2016, IGI Global. Copying or distributing in print or electronic forms without written permission of IGI Global is prohibited.

dience members. Therefore, synchronous patterns of unintentional reactions among an audience could be measured as indices of the appeal power of narrative performances. The authors specifically utilize eyeblinks as responses for this purpose.

## BACKGROUND: THE UNIVERSAL STRUCTURE OF NARRATIVE PERFORMANCE

### The Common Elements of Narrative Performance

Narrative performance contains three elements as its essential nature: performer, script[2], and audience. Grotowski (1968) speculated of the role of the theater audience: "Can theatre exist without audience? At least one spectator is needed to make it a performance" (p. 32). Also, Goodwin (1986) noted that "The meaning of the story will be found to have thus emerges not from the actions of the speaker alone, but rather as the product of a collaborative process of interaction in which the audience plays a very active role" (p.283) in a special issue of the journal Text titled "The Audience as Co-Author." A script expressed by a performer becomes a performance thanks to their audience. A narrative performance is created as time elapses. A performer generates their performance through interactions between their own conditions and the atmosphere of the audience on that day. Therefore, no two performances are exactly the same, even if a storyline is prepared beforehand. Thus, every performance is created in improvised way to some extent. In order to investigate narrative performances empirically, researchers have to evaluate the performances in an objective way.

### Methodological Difficulties of Studying Live Narrative Performances

A live narrative performance always exists only one time. Although live performance of such a nature moves people, it contains too many complicated elements to explore its generative rule in detail. Given these circumstances, the appeal power of performance is very difficult to be evaluated adequately. Many researchers have attempted to explore this dynamic nature of creation by identifying and categorizing the components of performance. The criteria and the procedure of this kind of analysis have usually been ad-hoc. At the same time, owing to the lack of definite criteria, scores or objective evaluations were seldom given unlike in the research fields of e.g. sports or games. These situations have often prevented researchers from comparing and discussing the results obtained from investigations of narrative arts from a common perspective.

Epistemological change is needed in order to create methods to assess the appeal power of narrative performance. Previous methods such as categorizing of components depended on the epistemic ability of researchers. Contrary to this, the authors propose an alternative method that depends on the epistemic ability of audience members. Eyeblink synchronization could be used as an index to assess the appeal power of performance. The appeal power of the performance is often attributed to the performer(s) per se. More precisely, however, the appeal power of the performance is never defined by only the component of performer, but also by that of audience participations. The appeal power of a particular performance, which is actualized as scripts embodied by the performer(s), is the probability to provoke certain cognitive and emotional responses from audience members. In this meaning, this appeal power of performances is determined by the audience as well as the performer(s). Thus, it is very natural to assume that the appeal power of performance, or at least a large part of its nature, could be assessed by focusing on the coherency of an audience's reactions, relying on the epistemic ability of audience members.

A performer and audience are constantly open to possibility of future interactions. Hence, a performance can vary moment to moment based on embodied interactions between the performer and the audience. Primarily, the term 'audience' here refers the audience members who are sharing time and space with the performer. Secondarily, however, the audience could be any audience members elsewhere in the world who would be fascinated by the performance. This is possible only if the performance possesses a certain potential to facilitate sense-making (De Jaegher & Di Paolo, 2007) in a universal way. This potential could be released through audiences actively interpreting the meaning of the performance. In this second relationship, even though a given audience's response does not affect the performance, the audience members could be indeed coordinated by the performance along with the process of sense-making. The basic idea of the new technique, focusing on this universal potential of sense-making, is to accumulate the responses of each audience member. Obviously, these responses reflect subjective experiences of each audience. However, the accumulation of these responses as a collective behavior must exhibit distinctive patterns in accordance with the potential of sense-making. This would provide an objective standard basis for assessment of the performance—at least in the sense of commensurability among people.

As an objectively observable response, the authors focus on an audience's eyeblinks while they appreciate narrative performances. As described below, human eyeblinks play a role as a mirror that unintentionally reflects mental states. Therefore, eyeblink synchronization could serve as an index of the appeal power of narrative performance.

## MEASURES OF THE APPEAL POWER OF PERFORMANCE FOCUSING ON EYEBLINK FEATURES

People are seldom aware that the visual world is intermittently interrupted by their own eyeblinks. Thus, people are usually able to believe that the world is continuous. However, the visual world is constructed in each moment by using fragments of obtained visual information. As a result, the perceived visual world depends on the timing of eyeblinks, which is influenced by people's cognitive and emotional states. Famous film editor Walter Murch (2001) pointed out the following:

*So it seems to me that our rate of blinking is somehow geared more to our emotional state and to the nature and frequency of our thought than to the atmospheric environment we happened to find ourselves. Even if there is no head movement ..., the blink is either something that helps an internal separation of thought to take place, or it is an involuntary reflex accompanying the mental separation that is taking place anyway (p. 62).*

It has been suggested that this unintentional separation of thought helps individuals to select important information (Nakano, Yamamoto, Kitajo, Takahashi, & Kitazawa, 2009) and to integrate perceived information and pre-existing knowledge within one's internal processing (Nakano, Kato, Morito, Itoi, & Kitazawa, 2013).

## Definition and Types of Eyeblinks

A blink is defined as 'a temporary closure of both eyes, involving movements of the upper and lower eyelids' (Blount, 1927). Human eyeblinks are classified into three types. Voluntary blinks refer to the eyeblinks that obviously involve an individual's intentional control (Stern, Walrath, & Goldstein, 1984). Reflective blinks mean eyeblinks that are induced by some external eliciting stimulus such as a flashing light or a sudden loud sound (Stern et al., 1984). Since reflective eyeblinks are elicited approximately 10 msec after the presentation of the external stimulus, this eyeblink type is not considered delayed. Spontaneous blinks are another type of eyeblinks that are not classified as voluntary or reflective blinks. Spontaneous blinks occur unconsciously but periodically (Kwon et al., 2013). One study has reported that blink rates correlate with the number of member of a social group present in primates (Tada, Omori, Hirokawa, Ohira, & Tomonaga, 2013). This result suggests that eyeblinks co-opted social functions in group communication, although they originally had physiological functions.

## Functions of Spontaneous Blinks in Human

People blink 20 or 30 times per minute in natural settings (Doughty, 2001). The visual world is lost for 400 msec each blink (van der Werf, Brassinga, Reits, Aramideh, & Ongerboer de Visser, 2003). Thus, individuals lose approximately 10 percent (i.e., 6 sec) of visual information in a minute (Nakano et al., 2009). However, individuals subjectively experience the world is continuous. This indicates that individuals' spontaneous blinks selectively process important information for us.

Attention allocation and release makes us possible to look at targets of their interest selectively. Previous studies have reported that timings of spontaneous blink events are related to explicit attentional breaks (Hall, 1945; Drew, 1951; Stern et al., 1984). In addition, a more recent neurological study (Nakano et al., 2013) has demonstrated that spontaneous eyeblinks are actively involved in the release of attention. As spontaneous blinks are loosely tied to attentional processes, the intervals between eyeblinks (i.e., IBI, inter-blink intervals) vary with relatively large variances both within individuals and between individuals. In summary, the blink rate systematically varies in accordance with task type and mental state.

## Appeal Power of Narrative Performance and Eyeblink Synchronization

Individuals selectively look at targets of their interest rather than objectively viewing the world. In this sense, 'people see only what they want to see.' This is a very subjective process. However, this does not mean that the eyeblinks occur at random or independent from external stimulus. The timings of an audience's eyeblinks change in accordance with the interpreted meaning of narrative performance. Thus, the timing of an audience's eyeblinks would be rather simultaneous due to stimulation by common inputs if the sense-making potential of the narrative performance exerts a significant influence on the cognitive processes of all audience members. As the result, the timing of eyeblinks between audience members could become very similar. Of course, narrative performances that have low appeal power to audience members would not be able to guide the eyeblinks of audience members to have closer timings, and each individual's eyeblink intervals would be independently maintained. Thus, eyeblink synchronization could serve as an index of appeal power as an objective standard basis of cognitive commensurability among audience members. Eyeblink synchronization could indicate how a narrative performance commonly diverts and attracts audience members' attentions over time. Therefore, eyeblink synchronization make researchers to investigate the influence of the appeal power of narrative performances, which is individual's subjective and usually invisible inner process, based on the objectively observable behavior. Because eyeblinks rates change in each few seconds, eyeblink synchronization is good to examine its correspondence relationships to audio-visual information of external stimuli.

## Advantages of Eyeblink Synchronization as an Index

In recent years, many physiological measurements have been proposed as indices of the emotional effects of audio-visual stimulus including narrative performance. Compared to other kinds of proposed measurements, eyeblink synchronization is more advantageous when measuring the appeal power of narrative performance.

First, researchers can interpret the meaning of results more straightforwardly by using eyeblink synchronization. Researchers can judge that participants do not perceive visual information with certainty when they are blinking. Moreover, occurrence timings of eyeblinks can be understood in terms of attention allocation and release cycle. Thus, occurrence timings of eyeblink synchronization, where participants' attention is collectively allocated or released, can be easily tagged with respect to the time stamps of audio-visual stimulus. When using e.g. participants' body movements or heart-rate variability, in contrast, researchers may interpret results in an arbitrary way if constraints are not posed by experiment procedures and stimuli. For example, although elicitation of an emotion can influence heart-rate variability, researchers cannot judge whether or not these effects are contributing to the response to stimuli even when other factors, such as remembering of past experiences, are fully eliminated.

Second, eyeblink-based indices are sensitive enough to capture participants' internal changes in accordance with time-varying stimuli on the order of seconds. Usually, eyeblinks occur approximately 20 or 30 times per minute (Doughty, 2001). Therefore, eyeblink synchronization would be a useful index for various narrative performances.

Finally, eyeblinks are able to be observed externally and their data are easy to handle. Thus, unlike MRI, EEG, or electrodermal activity monitoring, neither the use of specialized and expensive machines nor pretreatment of data to remove artifacts is necessary.

## Methodological Consideration

To synchronize eyeblinks between audiences, it is necessary that eyeblink timing is reliable both within audiences and between audiences as time-varying information. Intra-person reliability of eyeblink timing is supported by findings that spontaneous blinks were synchronized within participants over several sessions when they viewed the same short video (Nakano et al., 2009). In contrast, inter-person reliability depends on the time-varying nature of stimulus. For instance, spontaneous eyeblinks are likely to occur at punctuation marks when people read a text (Hall, 1945). Because reading speed is different with each reader, eyeblinks would only co-occur here by coincidence. In the same way, spontaneous eyeblinks would not synchronize more strongly than by chance when people appreciate non-time-varying visual arts such as paintings or photos. Also, a previous study has reported that eyeblink synchronization among participants was not observed both when an audience viewed a video without audio information and when the audience was presented with only a voice while viewing a static image taken from the video clip (Nakano & Kitazawa, 2010). Therefore, eyeblink synchronization occurs based on an integration of multimodal information, with visual information being a dominant trigger. Hence, the applicable scope of eyeblink synchronization would be limited to assessing time-varying performances in which visual information is dominant.

Eyeblink synchronization seems to depend on characteristics of audience members as well as the quality of performances. For instance, audience members who have viewing experience are more likely to synchronize their eyeblinks in a laboratory experiment setting (Nomura, Hino, Shimazu, Liang, & Okada, 2015a). In contrast, non-experienced audience members increase synchronization of their eyeblinks as a story develops. Thus, researchers can use this method to compare the appeal power of a narrative performance by keeping the characteristics of audience members constant. More properly, researchers must assure the representativeness of samples in line with the aim of their particular study. Eyeblink synchronization is sensitive enough to prove differences between two performances of the same story acted by the same artist, in front of different types of audience (Nomura et al., 2015a). Thus, this measurement is especially useful for intra-individual comparisons of performances in studies on the role of expertise.

## A Practical Guide for Analysis

### Surrogate Data Analysis

The first one is called surrogate data analysis. This analysis has been developed for measuring the degree of synchronization among many firing neurons by focusing on inter-spike intervals (i.e. ISI: Ikegaya et al., 2004). As an analogy to firing neurons, inter-blink interval (i.e., IBI) was defined as the duration between the onset of eyeblink response and the onset of the next eyeblink response in a time series. Total audience eyeblinks are counted within a particular time window and their proportion of all audience members who blinked is calculated. The time window is usually set to 0.25 sec, a duration over which individuals cannot repeat eyeblink responses.

To test whether or not mean frequency of eyeblinks at each time point is statistically significant, a null hypothesis is formed. The null hypothesis is that there is no difference between the frequency of original data and the average of randomized frequency data created from the original data. The procedure to make randomized data is to shuffle the order of IBIs in the original data within each participant. Although the randomized data maintain the mean and S.D. of the IBIs of the original data, they lose the information about eyeblink timings. This procedure is applied to all time trains of eyeblink responses gained from each participant, forming a random dataset.

In a study that used this analysis (Nomura & Okada, 2014), 1000 random datasets were prepared for comparison with original data. The first (the last) 2.5% of the histogram depicted by using the 1000 random datasets was set as the higher (lower) criteria for rejection (Figure 1). The null hypothesis was rejected at each time point if the mean frequency of eyeblinks of the original data within each group exceeded the higher criteria or lower criteria. In other words, at such time points, there were statistically significant differences between the mean frequency of eyeblinks within an observed group and the mean frequency when eyeblinks occurred randomly. The analyzer could identify the time points where the higher (lower) criteria were exceeded as time points at which the number of eyeblinks is increasing (decreasing).

*Figure 1. Eyeblink synchronization during viewing Rakugo performance (cited from Figure 4 – 5 in Nomura & Okada, 2014)*

*Note. The X-axis shows time (data points at 5–second intervals) and the y-axis shows frequency of eyeblink occurrence averaged within the experimental group. (A) –(C) were observed immediately after the plot keywords "sake", "Do you like aona (greens)? [Master → Gardener]", and "Kuramakara Ushiwakamaruga [abbr.]", respectively (D) – (E) were observed at the utterances of "Do you like aona (greens)? [Gardener → Joiner]" and "Aona? I hate it", respectively. (F) – (G) were not related to keywords nor scene changes.*

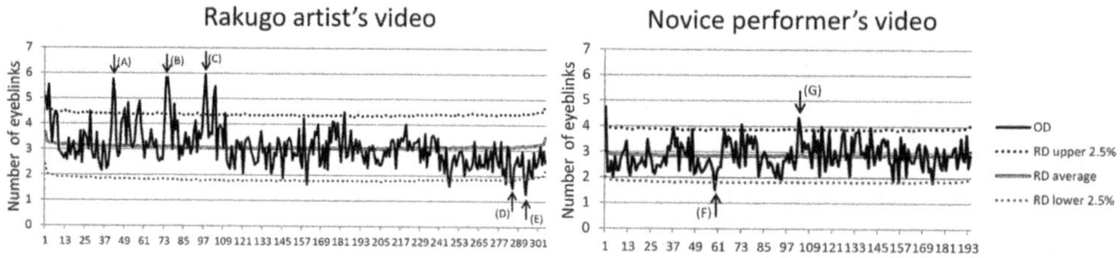


## Distance-Based Analysis of Blink Trains: $D^{spike}$ and $D^{interval}$

The second analysis uses an index of asynchrony. Regarding synchronization of firing neurons, a considerable number of indices have been proposed. $D^{spike}$ and $D^{interval}$ (Victor & Purpura, 1997) are two such indices. Both $D^{spike}$ and $D^{interval}$ evaluate the distances of two different spike trains. The advantage of distance-based indices for applying to eyeblink data is these indices do not assume any interactions within a group or any stochastic distribution.

The distance between two spike trains is defined as the minimum cost of transforming one spike train into the another by following three procedures: spike insertion (cost 1), spike deletion (cost 1) and shifting a spike by some interval $\Delta t$ (cost q$|\Delta t|$). If q = 0, the distance just means the difference in spike counts (Figure 2). If q becomes larger, the distance approaches the number of co-occurred spikes. In this case, the cost is kept low by means of deleting and reinserting co-occurred spikes rather than shifting them. Note that parameter q should be determined with consideration to the nature of spike trains (i.e. a time scale of interested phenomena) rather than in an arbitrary manner.

If two time trains of spikes share similar patterns, the distance is lower. Thus, the distance-based index indicates asynchrony. While $D^{spike}$ calculates the distance at each time point of the spikes, $D^{interval}$ uses spike-by-spike intervals for cost evaluation. In one study of eyeblink synchronization (Nomura et al., 2015a), $\Delta t$ was set at 0.25 sec and the cost per time unit q was set at 1 in accordance with the time

*Figure 2. Schematic illustrations of calculation method for (A) Dspike and (B) Dinterval (cited from Figure 1 in Nomura et al., 2015a)*

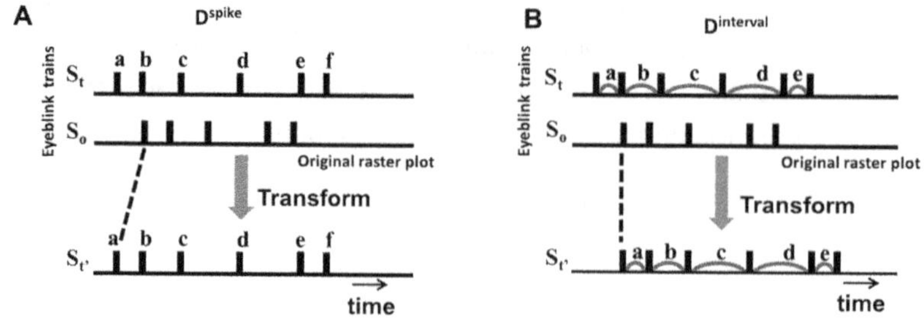

scale of analysis. It is better for researchers to confirm that the global behaviors seen in results are observed regardless of the specification of this parameter by, for instance, conducting simulations while systematically changing this parameter.

## THE EMPIRICAL STUDIES USING EYEBLINK SYNCHRONIZATION

### Measuring Expertise of Narrative Artists by Using Eyeblink Synchronization

In this section, the authors describe empirical studies using eyeblink synchronization in detail as examples of studies that used this measure. Especially, eyeblink synchronization among spectators of Rakugo[3], a traditional Japanese story-telling performance, was examined (Nomura & Okada, 2014). During and after the *Meiji* (1868——1912) era, performances emphasizing simplicity with limited stage production were inherited by the Rakugo practice community in Tokyo. In this cultural tradition, performances done in a legitimate way are called *honzunpo*, meaning orthodox and valid. Eyeblink synchronization is an index that can be used to measure the expertise of Rakugo artists in this tradition. If eyeblink synchronization is able to assess the appeal power of performances, it could be predicted that a performance of an expert Rakugo artist synchronizes the eyeblinks of his audience more than that of a novice performer does.

#### The Features of Rakugo as a Narrative Performance

Rakugo artists learn and develop their expertise through a traditional apprenticeship. In the legitimate practice of Rakugo theatre, *yose*, different artists act the same story during different performances. Thus, the repertories of the stories are shared by the community of professional Rakugo artists. A large part of repertories have been inherited from senior artists to junior artists. Junior performers are prohibited to act any stories before receiving permission by the senior artist who taught the story, in some cases, or by his/her master.

In the theatre, theme music played with traditional instruments, *shamisen*, is the sign for starting the performance. A Rakugo artist, wearing traditional Japanese clothes, *kimono*, comes up from stage right and walks to the center of the stage. The artist sits down on a square-cushion, *zabuton*, and starts to talk. In the Rakugo practice, artists uses only a Japanese hand towel, *tenugui*, and a Japanese fan, *sensu*, as stage properties. They use these properties to resemble a variety of things. For example, *tenugui* is used like a wallet and a letter. *Sensu* is used as if it were a Japanese sword, *katana*, chopsticks, and so on. In order to understand and enjoy the performance, spectators have to imagine the situations and to interpret what represented by the properties. In this sense, Rakugo is a kind of narrative performance that is constructed with the support of the audience.

Story-telling artists start their talk with a daily small talk called *makura*, 'pillow' in literal translation. In *makura* talk, Rakugo artists test the atmosphere of the audience by acting short jokes or gags and, if needed, implicitly explaining story-relevant knowledge by touching on some components of a story for first-time viewers in advance. Rakugo artists decide what story they will perform just before appearing on the stage or even during the *makura* talk, taking into account the story season, program flow, audience sensitivity, and so on.

Once a story is started, a Rakugo artist acts many characters while giving his head a shake in each turn of the conversation. The story mainly develops through conversation that explicitly and implicitly explains the situation, too. Sensory information such as texture, shape, and weight of things is expressed by the artists' line of sight or gestures. These details of expressions enrich the world of the story and facilitate the imagination of audience.

## Performance of Rakugo as an Improvised Act

Most Rakugo stories are comedies that depict the daily lives of ordinary people in the Edo era (1603–1867) of Japan (Yamamoto, 2006; Maeda, 1958). As stories of Rakugo have been orally inherited, there are no fixed texts, except for some literature created for live performances as well as for written books in the *Meiji* era. Although the rough story-line for each story is widely known in terms of its typical text, what utterances and gestures are done is not exactly determined in advance.

Rather, in Rakugo performance, scripts are acted by an artist through the negotiation between the artist and the spectators facing him/her. In this practice, improvisational performance emerges in each moment through a process whereby a script is embodied by the performer's voices and actions. Similar to improvisational compositions in jazz sessions, the performer can change the acted text by adding or subtracting utterances of characters and even scenes. Thus, the acted performance is just an instance that is selected from a numerous set of potential acts that could come to constitute the performance. Hence, similar to the other kinds of narrative performance, a Rakugo performance always exists only one time. As Hanks (1995, p. 190) noted, "artistic discourse is viewed as emergent in the event … No longer defined by a canonical written text, it is a kind of practice". The script of a Rakugo performance should be viewed as emergent in this practice, not as a static text.

We are thus naturally able to apply eyeblink synchronization methods to assess the appeal power of Rakugo performance. We start by demonstrating the results of observations of audiences' eyeblink responses in a quasi-theater setting and go on to more-rigorous experiments. In the experimental settings, however, recorded videos were used in order to maintain the equality of stimuli to participants. Finally, the authors return to the systematic observation of the eyeblinks of audience members as a group in which spectators interact with each other.

## Eyeblink Synchronization and the Appeal Power of Narrative Performance

In an observational study (Nomura & Okada, 2014, Study1), the authors reported that audience eyeblinks could synchronize among members through appreciation of a story-telling performance in Rakugo settings. Significant increases in eyeblinks detected by surrogate data analysis were related to the change of scenes and conversational turns. On the other hand, significant decreases in eyeblinks were found in accordance with acts where the performer placed emphasis on his gestures and facial expressions. These results suggests that narrative performance can guide timings of attention allocation and release, resulting in the time points of eyeblink occurrences becoming close together between audience members in such a theatre setting.

However, there exists another possibility: that the significant increase and decrease of eyeblinks are mainly due to interactions among audience members. In addition to this, it is possible that the domain knowledge of audience members gained through their viewing experience, regardless of the details of the performance, lets them fully predict the next twists of the performance. In order to show that details of narrative performance guide timings of attentional processes, it is necessary to demonstrate that the degree of synchronization varies according to the appeal power of the performance. Thus, it was hypothesized that a performance acted by an expert Rakugo artist, compared to that acted by a novice performer, would synchronize eyeblinks to a greater extent among audience members. The hypothesis would be supported if the differences are found in a laboratory experiment with individual subject in which all participants were first-time viewers. As an expert artist and a novice performer would act the same story (i.e., the story-line and punch-line are shared), the degree of eyeblink synchronization among audience members would be attributable to the differences in the details of expressions of these two performances.

Nomura and Okada (2014, Study2) reported that with the videotaped performance of the expert performer, compared to that of the novice performer, participants synchronized their eyeblinks more frequently and intensely. The deviations from mean frequency of each instance of increased eyeblink frequency detected were approximately 1.8 times larger than the higher criteria. Moreover, the eyeblinks synchronized between audience members were not tied to explicit attentional breaks (e.g., a theatrical blackout). Rather, eyeblink synchronization occurred at implicit semantic segmentations embodied as expressions by the expert artist (Nomura & Okada, 2014). Previous studies (Nakano & Kitazawa, 2010; Nakano, Kato, & Kitazawa, 2011) have pointed out that eyeblinks of a speaker entrain eyeblinks of a listener[4]. In the current study, although this possibility was examined, this proposition was not supported. This contrasting result likely arose because videotaped Rakugo performances used in this experiment contained richer audio-visual information than the video used in the previous studies. These results suggest that expert artists create implicit breakpoints in audience members' attentional processes.

## Story and Detail of Expressions

To clarify the relationships between significant increases and decreases in eyeblinks and the contents of performances, the sequences of linguistic, non-linguistic, and para-linguistic features of a performance were analyzed (Nomura & Okada, 2014). The performed story was called *Aona*, meaning literally 'greens' (Figure 3).

Note. Each pair of arrows (↓↑) shows interactions between characters in the story. Large double arrows depict incongruence between original and mimicked interactions.

*Figure 3. Outline of Aona (translated and cited from Figure 3 in Nomura & Okada, 2014)*

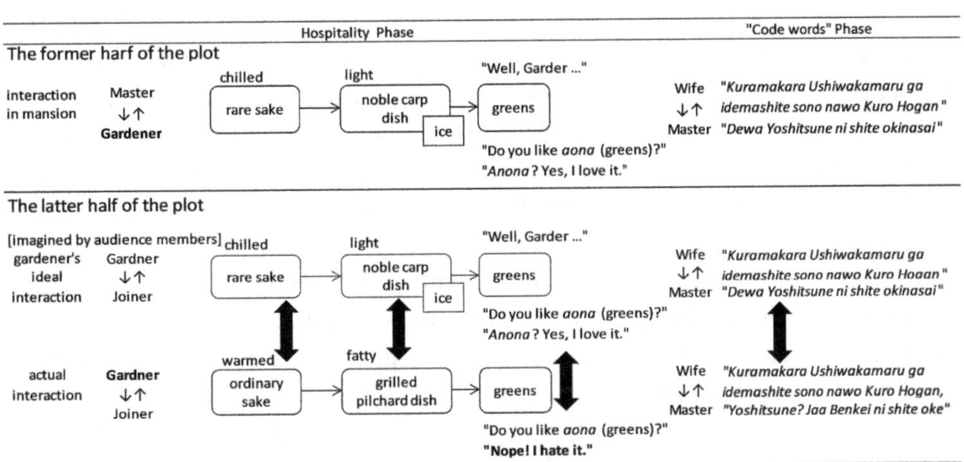

In this story, a gardener is incidentally invited to eat fish and to drink sake at a large mansion, and the gardener delightfully enjoys them. The master of the house asks the gardener whether he likes boiled *aona* (greens) or not. The gardener replies that he likes *aona* very much. When the master calls his wife to ask her to bring a dish of boiled greens, the wife improvisationally paraphrases her answer into a secret code language meaning that there are no greens left. As soon as the master listens to the code words, he apologizes to the gardener for failing to provide a dish of boiled greens. Because the gardener feels embarrassment and asks the master what is going on, the master explains the meanings of the code words.

The code words uttered by the wife are a kind of word play based on the phonological similarity between "*(aona wo) Kurau*" (people in the mansion have eaten all the greens) and "Kuro Hogan." Because Kuro Hogan is an alias of Minamoto-no Yoshitsune, the master replies "Yoshitsune" in order to convey the meaning of "*Yoshitoke*" (stop providing the dish) by using the same sound of "Yoshi-." The choice of the name "benkei" is just tangential: Benkei was a vassal of Yoshitsune. The last nonsense word highlights the fact that this narrative is just a comic story. The gardener is deeply moved by the considerateness of the master's wife to use the code words in order not to experience a feeling of shame in front of the guest, and decides to mimic the conversation in his own house with his wife.

Soon after arriving at his house, the gardener explains the code language to his wife. To their good fortune, their construction joiner friend visits them. However, the gardener fails at every recommendation of greens in the course of the visit because he tries to imitate his experience at the master's house exactly. The gardener asks the joiner whether he likes boiled greens or not in the hope that he would have the chance to say the code words, but the joiner replies that he does not like them. The gardener is astonished and again tries to make the joiner say that he likes greens. The joiner looks at the gardener in disbelief, but finally cooperates with the prompt. Then, the wife of the gardener falls out and shouts the code words.

Significant increases in eyeblinks were found at changes of scenes in the anterior half of the story. Interestingly, an increase in eyeblinks also emerged at the end of explanations of the 'code words' by the master of the mansion. Since all of the participants were first-time viewers, they did not know how the story would develop. Increases in eyeblinks seemed to indicate that participants actively anticipated the next twists of the story, and released their attention at the end of the explanation of the code words that was previously hidden for both the audience members and the gardener.

Significant decreases in eyeblinks were found in the posterior half of the story. In particular, the degree of decrease was strong at the scene where the gardener was astonished at the reply of his construction joiner friend. In this scene, the Rakugo artist, acting as the gardener in that story, expressed a variety of non-linguistic detailed expressions during a 10-sec lasting pause. Soon after he changed characters, the artist stopped moving his Japanese fan and slightly directed his line of sight to stage right. He looked down and rapidly looked up towards the face of the (imagined) joiner. He smiled a bit but his left cheek was stiff, and he wiggled the fan in his hand. He blinked very rapidly, sniffed, and almost cried. He rubbed the tail of his left eye.

In this scene, almost no participants blinked. This indicates that they were allocating their attentions to the artist's series of actions. The eyes of the audience were attracted by his facial expressions and body movements, and their attention allocation was strongly guided by the performance. Indeed, the performance of a novice performer did not elicit a significant decrease of eyeblinks at the same scene. It would be reasonable to assume that the appeal power of Rakugo performance was quantified by the extent of eyeblink synchronization in this study.

## What Does Eyeblink Synchronization Measure?

One of the essential conditions of 'good' narrative performances is to provide audience an engrossing experience that can be described as 'being carried away by the story.' The authors acknowledge that the idea of quantifying this condition seems controversial in the context of the longstanding research history of narratology. However, different from written narratives, a live narrative performance always exists only one time. Particularly in the situation of live performance, nothing is left if the audience members do not view it or allocate their attentions to it. Eyeblink synchronization measures universal potential of appeal to sense-making, which is the foundation of an engrossing audience experience. Eyeblink timing sensitively varies with visual attention by reflecting a performance's sense-making potential. If the performance has only local appeal to or limited potential for appeal to an audiences' sense-making, eyeblinks occur independently of it, in the audiences' own pace. Consequently, the probability of eyeblink occurrence in this case approaches chance over a given period (i.e., the time-mean throughout the performance). Thus, by evaluating the frequency and intensity of the deviations from chance at every time point, a researcher can explore the sense-making potential of a narrative performance.

Because eyeblink synchronization is an attention-sensitive measurement, it could be induced by stimuli irrelevant to the sense-making potential of a narrative performance, such as flashing lights or loud sounds (Kwon et al., 2013). However, if one controls the measurement environment so that spontaneous eyeblinks naturally occur (i.e., create a stationary or at least quasi-stationary state), eyeblink synchronization will correspond to the appeal of a narrative performance.

## APPLICABLE SCOPE OF EYEBLINK SYNCHRONIZATION

Good narrative performances provide an audience with an engrossing experience. Eyeblink synchronization is a good tool to capture the universal potential of appeal in terms of sense-making of the wider narrative performance. Eyeblink synchronization could be applied to a variety of situations beyond the setting of a comedy theatre. From the viewpoint of rhetoric, the index of eyeblink synchronization can be applied to quantify the appeal power of many kinds of speeches. For instance, researchers could study the relationships between the appeal powers of speeches by presidential contenders and the following election results. Based on the same reasoning, the index of eyeblink synchronization could reveal the appeal power of lectures in a university class. The difference between fascinating lecturers and ordinary ones may be explained by the appeal powers of their performance in the classes.

Focusing on the nature of eyeblinks that relates attention allocation and release with external audio-visual information, this component is widely applicable to the appreciation of visual products, such as movie and commercial messages. Previous research (Nakano et al., 2009; Nakano & Kitazawa, 2010) indeed demonstrated that eyeblink synchronization occurred during watching short movies. Paralleling with the methods based on brain science (e.g., Dmochowski et al., 2014) and eye-tracking studies (e.g., Christoforou, Christou-Champi, Constantinidou, & Theodorou, 2015), eyeblink synchronization could be utilized to predict viewers' decision making and behaviors.

## FUTURE RESEARCH DIRECTIONS

### Future Research in Eyeblink Synchronization

Blinking is a very common behavior in human beings. However, this fact makes people forget the important role of the eyeblink in social communication, beyond its physiological role. Research on both eyeblink response and its synchronization would provide further implications for understanding the nature of human communication.

### Eyeblink Synchronization and Variability of Eyeblink Rate within Individuals

One possible research direction would be to explore individuals' interest regarding audio-visual information based on variability of IBI distribution. One of the author's studies (Nomura et al., 2015a) has reported that individuals' logarithmic standard deviations of IBIs predict transportive experience (see van Laer, De Ruyter, Visconti, & Wetzels, 2014) during watching videos of Rakugo performance. This suggests that individuals who show high IBI variability feel more transportive experiences. In other words, transportive experience seems to be induced through a way of viewing in which durations of attention allocation and release vary moment to moment, rather than eyeblink frequency being maintained at a constant rate. This result implies that rest points as well as a climax are necessary for enjoyment of a total transportive experience. Further research is needed to explore the relationship between eyeblink-related statistics such as S.D. within individuals and viewer interest.

### The Effect of Interaction among Audience Members on Eyeblink Synchronization

An explorative study that we conducted (Nomura, Liang, & Okada, 2015b) demonstrated a new paradigm to estimate interactions among audience members focusing on eyeblink synchronization. To estimate the effect of interactions among audience members, the degree of eyeblink synchronization of audience members in actual theatre settings was compared to that collected in a solitary experiment (Nomura et al., 2015a) as the control condition. The results demonstrated that asynchrony $D^{interval}$ in situations where the audience members interact with each other were much lower than that of the control condition for approximately 30 – 60%. This suggests that interactions among audience members facilitate eyeblink synchronization. Moreover, the effect of interaction was stronger for first-time viewers than for frequent viewers. The authors of this chapter termed this attractive effect 'inter-spectator forces' as an analogy to inter-molecular forces. In future research, the nature of inter-spectator forces, such as crowdedness of audience and air of excitement analogous to density and kinetic potentials would be issues to explore.

### Measuring Device and Automated Measuring

On the issue of wider applications of eyeblinks synchronization, it is necessary to discuss usability of measurements and measuring devises. Several kinds of methods have been developed for observations of eyeblinks using equipment such as VTR (video tape record), EOG (electro-oculography), EMG (electromyography) of the orbicularis oculi muscle, magnetic sensors, or optical sensors. In recent years, instruments have become more compact and portable. Moreover, devices aimed to be run on a general-purpose PC have been developed. One such device, THE EYE TRIBE, is an eye tracker down-sized to the small size of 20 x 1.9 x 1.9 cm. The maker distributes software development kits for C#, C++, and Java. High usability would make it easier for researchers to conduct experiments. The authors of this chapter have developed a system to measure and analyze eyeblink synchronization in experimental settings (Shimazu & Nomura, 2015)[5].

Collective measurement by multichannel observations is a promising approach in this field. For instance, JINS MEME is a glasses-shaped device that captures eyeblinks using EOG. Wearable eyeblink sensors would widen the applicability of eyeblink measurements in actual theater, classroom, art museum, or street settings. In future applications, a speaker could gain rapid and precise feedback of his/her appeal power as perceived by the audience based on real-time recording and processing. It would truly be the future when feedback loop devices actualized by information technology make narrative practitioners, such as teachers and instructors, 'feel' the atmosphere of an audience in a physical sense.

## DEVELOPMENT OF NEW RESEARCH FIELDS

### Eyeblink Synchronization as Human Collective Behaviors

Eyeblink synchronization, as a collective behavior, will serve as a clue to shed light on the nature of human group dynamics. Human behaviors sometimes synchronize with each other. The sounds of many hands clapping in the theatre self-organize, leading to synchronization (Néda, Ravasz, Brechet, Vicsek, & Barabási, 2000). On the Millennium Bridge in London, the walking rhythms of many people synchronize (Strogatz, Abrams, McRobie, Eckhardt, & Ott, 2005). Unlike these cases, the eyeblink response of an audience member per se does not influence on the other audience member, because they are not facing each other. Additionally, eyeblink response is unintentional, at least in most settings of narrative performance. Alternative mechanisms have to be considered.

### Mechanisms of Eyeblink Synchronization

Previous studies have reported that spontaneous blinks were synchronized between participants when they viewed the same video of a 25-minute narrative story (Nomura & Okada, 2014) as well as short scenes of a movie (Nakano et al., 2009). These results suggest that synchronization of eyeblinks occurs due to coordination of eyeblink timings triggered by external stimulus. In other words, the timings of eyeblinks are entrained by common inputs ('forced-entrainment'; see Childs & Strogatz, 2008). At the same time, in other studies, eyeblink synchronization was better facilitated when audience members could interact with each other in an actual vaudeville setting than when audience members viewed the video separately (Nomura et al., 2015a). Thus, it also seems that eyeblink synchronization occurs due to 'mutual entrainment' (Childs & Strogatz, 2008) within an audience.

### Potentials of Narrative Performance Study: Perspective of Complex System

Eyeblink synchronization is a phenomenon that arises in systems with intermediate degrees of freedom. At this level of degrees of freedom, analytical techniques are not applicable directly due to complex interactions, while theories of mean field based on the law of great numbers approximate this phenomenon too loosely. One possible way to study it is to test global features while ignoring local changes. With this approach, researchers have to gain numerous cases using automated measurement devices. Another possible way is to simulate the collective behaviors of audience members in the theatre. Variables that organize global patterns must be selected as the parameters. Such simulations would provide insights for modeling inter-spectator forces and their relations to eyeblink synchronization. The results of these simulations could be used for designing physical environments (i.e., layout of audience seat), theatre programs, and coordinating spectators' atmospheres, leading to engrossing narrative performance.

## CONCLUSION

In this chapter, the authors showed that eyeblink synchronization enables us to investigate narrative performance empirically. An epistemological turn accompanies the adoption of the alternative methods proposed. Most previous studies used subjective judgments or categorization by a few (usually two or three) researchers or experienced viewers. In contrast, the proposed method relies on the ability of audience members as epistemic agents to recognize and understand the performance. The standard basis, defined in terms of the collective responses accumulated, enables us to judge whether or not a particular performance contains universal appeal to sense-making.

## REFERENCES

Blount, W. P. (1927). Studies of the movements of the eyelids of animals: Blinking. *Quarterly Journal of Experimental Physiology (Cambridge, England)*, *18*(2), 111–125. doi:10.1113/expphysiol.1927.sp000426

Childs, L. M., & Strogatz, S. H. (2008). Stability diagram for the forced Kuramoto model. *Chaos: An Interdisciplinary Journal of Nonlinear Science*, *18*(4), 043128. doi:10.1063/1.3049136 PMID:19123638

Christoforou, C., Christou-Champi, S., Constantinidou, F., & Theodorou, M. (2015). From the eyes and the heart: A novel eye-gaze metric that predicts video preferences of a large audience. *Frontiers in Psychology*, 6. PMID:26029135

De Jaegher, H., & Di Paolo, E. (2007). Participatory sense-making. *Phenomenology and the Cognitive Sciences*, *6*(4), 485–507. doi:10.1007/s11097-007-9076-9

Dmochowski, J. P., Bezdek, M. A., Abelson, B. P., Johnson, J. S., Schumacher, E. H., & Parra, L. C. (2014). Audience preferences are predicted by temporal reliability of neural processing. *Nature Communications*, 5. PMID:25072833

Doughty, M. J. (2001). Consideration of three types of spontaneous eyeblink activity in normal humans: During reading and video display terminal use, in primary gaze, and while in conversation. *Optometry and Vision Science*, *78*(10), 712–725. doi:10.1097/00006324-200110000-00011 PMID:11700965

Drew, G. (1951). Variations in reflex blink-rate during visual-motor tasks. *The Quarterly Journal of Experimental Psychology*, *3*(2), 73–88. doi:10.1080/17470215108416776

Goodwin, C. (1986). Audience diversity, participation and interpretation. *Text*, *6*(3), 283–316. doi:10.1515/text.1.1986.6.3.283

Grotowski, J. (1968). *Towards a poor theatre*. New York, NY: Simon and Schuster.

Hall, A. (1945). The origin and purposes of blinking. *The British Journal of Ophthalmology*, *29*(9), 445–467. doi:10.1136/bjo.29.9.445 PMID:18170143

Hanks, W. F. (1995). Language and communicative practices. In M. Bloch, P. Bourdieu, & J. L. Comaroff (Eds.), *Series critical essays in anthropology*. Boulder, CO: Westview Press.

Ikegaya, Y., Aaron, G., Cossart, R., Aronov, D., Lampl, I., Ferster, D., & Yuste, R. (2004). Synfire chains and cortical songs: Temporal modules of cortical activity. *Science*, *304*(5670), 559–564. doi:10.1126/science.1093173 PMID:15105494

Kwon, K. A., Shipley, R. J., Edirisinghe, M., Ezra, D. G., Rose, G., Best, S. M., & Cameron, R. E. (2013). High-speed camera characterization of voluntary eye blinking kinematics. *Journal of the Royal Society, Interface*, *10*(85), 20130227. PMID:23760297

Maeda, I. (1958). *Kamigata Rakugo-no rekishi* [The history of Kamigata Rakugo]. Osaka, Japan: Sugimoto Shoten.

Murch, W. (2001). *In the blink of an eye: A perspective on film editing* (2nd ed.). Los Angeles, CA: Silman-James Press.

Nakano, T., Kato, M., Morito, Y., Itoi, S., & Kitazawa, S. (2013). Blink-related momentary activation of the default mode network while viewing videos. *Proceedings of the National Academy of Sciences of the United States of America*, *110*(2), 702–706. doi:10.1073/pnas.1214804110 PMID:23267078

Nakano, T., Kato, N., & Kitazawa, S. (2011). Lack of eyeblink entrainments in autism spectrum disorders. *Neuropsychologia*, *49*(9), 2784–2790. doi:10.1016/j.neuropsychologia.2011.06.007 PMID:21699907

Nakano, T., & Kitazawa, S. (2010). Eyeblink entrainment at breakpoints of speech. *Experimental Brain Research*, *205*(4), 577–581. doi:10.1007/s00221-010-2387-z PMID:20700731

Nakano, T., Yamamoto, Y., Kitajo, K., Takahashi, T., & Kitazawa, S. (2009). Synchronization of spontaneous eyeblinks while viewing video stories. In *Proceedings of the Royal Society of London B: Biological Sciences*. doi:10.1098/rspb.2009.0828

Néda, Z., Ravasz, E., Brechet, Y., Vicsek, T., & Barabási, A. L. (2000). Self-organizing processes: The sound of many hands clapping. *Nature*, *403*(6772), 849–850. doi:10.1038/35002660 PMID:10706271

Nomura, R. (2012). The Rakugo-learning environment: An alternative epistemology. In *Proceedings of The Macrotheme Conference on Education and Training 2012, 44*. Espace Vocation Paris Haussaman Saint-Lazare, Paris, France.

Nomura, R., Hino, K., Shimazu, M., Liang, Y., & Okada, T. (2015a). Emotionally excited eyeblink-rate variability predicts an experience of transportation into the narrative world. *Frontiers in Psychology*, *6*(477). doi:10.3389/fpsyg.2015.00447 PMID:26029123

Nomura, R., Liang, Y., & Okada, T. (2015b). Interaction among audience facilitate eyeblink synchronization. *PLoS ONE, 10*(10), e0140774. doi:10.1371/journal.pone.0140774 PMID:26479405

Nomura, R., & Okada, T. (2014). Spontaneous synchronization of eyeblinks during story-telling performance. *Cognitive Studies: Bulletin of the Japanese Cognitive Science Society, 21*(2), 226–244.

Schank, R., & Abelson, R. (1977). *Scripts, plans, goals, and understanding. Erlbaum.* Hillsdale, NJ: Psychology Press.

Shimazu, M., & Nomura, R. (2015). *Development of automated measuring and analyzing system for eyeblinks of viewing audience.* Oral presented and communicative demonstrated at Interaction 2015 the 19th symposium of Information Processing Society of Japan.

Stern, J. A., Walrath, L. C., & Goldstein, R. (1984). The endogenous eyeblink. *Psychophysiology, 21*(1), 22–33. doi:10.1111/j.1469-8986.1984.tb02312.x PMID:6701241

Strogatz, S., Abrams, D., McRobie, A., Eckhardt, B., & Ott, E. (2005). Theoretical mechanics: Crowd synchrony on the millennium bridge. *Nature, 438*(7064), 43–44. doi:10.1038/438043a PMID:16267545

Tada, H., Omori, Y., Hirokawa, K., Ohira, H., & Tomonaga, M. (2013). Eye-blink behaviors in 71 species of primates. *PLoS ONE, 8*(5), e66018. doi:10.1371/journal.pone.0066018 PMID:23741522

van der Werf, F., Brassinga, P., Reits, D., Aramideh, M., & Ongerboer de Visser, B. (2003). Eyelid movements: Behavioral studies of blinking in humans under different stimulus conditions. *Journal of Neurophysiology, 89*(5), 2784–2796. doi:10.1152/jn.00557.2002 PMID:12612018

van Laer, T., De Ruyter, K., Visconti, L. M., & Wetzels, M. (2014). The extended transportation-imagery model: A meta-analysis of the antecedents and consequences of consumers' narrative transportation. *The Journal of Consumer Research, 40*(5), 797–817. doi:10.1086/673383

Victor, J. D., & Purpura, K. P. (1997). Metric-space analysis of spike trains: Theory, algorithms and application. *Network (Bristol, England), 8*(2), 127–164. doi:10.1088/0954-898X_8_2_003

Yamamoto, S. (2006). *Zusetsu Rakugo-no rekishi* [The history Rakugo with illustrations]. Tokyo, Japan: Kawade Shobo Shinsha.

## KEY TERMS AND DEFINITIONS

**Audience:** Firstly, collected spectators at a (usually theatre) performance. Secondly, potential spectators who would encounter the performance via a medium.

**Entrainment:** A phenomena that two distinct components with different oscillatory rhythms become to show a common rhythm through interactions.

**Expert:** Trained practitioners who have elaborated skills and knowledge of a particular domain. It is classified as routine expert and adaptive expert.

**Eyeblink:** A temporary closure of both eyes, involving movements of the upper and lower eyelids. It is classified as voluntary, reflective, and spontaneous eyeblinks.

**Eyeblink Synchronization:** A phenomena that eyeblinks of more than one person coincide. It could be induced by common external inputs, such as a narrative performance or a movie.

**Narrative Performance:** Performances that are mainly embodied by an individual's voice. Usually, non-linguistic and para-linguistic strategies are also used for these acts.

**Rakugo:** One of the Japanese traditional narrative performances. Most of the stories are comedy that depicts daily lives of ordinary people in *Edo* era of Japan.

## ENDNOTES

1 Narrative performance, in this chapter, refers to a performance that is acted towards an audience, including its story and discourse (i.e., content and expression) relating to events and situations. A narrative performance is actualized by performer(s) interacting with the audience member(s).

2 Here, "script" means the script for a given performance in a theater. For discussion regarding the usage of the term "script" in cognitive science, see Schank and Abelson (1977).

3 Movies of Rakugo performances are available on YouTube, uploaded by the official account of the Rakugo Association (https://www.youtube.com/user/rakugodcc).

4 This result implies that speaker's eyeblinks would be also entrained by the listener's eyeblinks in situations of natural compensation. However, professional Rakugo artists may not be entrained by an audience's eyeblinks because they usually 'feel' the internal states of audience members rather than 'see' it (Nomura, 2012).

5 The software is distributed freely for academic and non-commercial use only. Please contact the first author if interested in this software.

# Chapter 12
# The Dilemma of Suspense: Neuronarratology, Cognitive Neurosciences, and Computer Technology

**Sara Uboldi**
*University of Modena and Reggio Emilia, Italy*

**Stefano Calabrese**
*University of Modena e Reggio Emilia, Italy*

## ABSTRACT

*The new generation Narratology shows a renewed heuristic scenario, involving an intense dialogue among Humanities, Cognitive Neuroscience and Computer Technology. The case of suspense is emblematic: the pleasure that suspense exercises on the human mind can be precisely explained by identifying the mechanisms of reward provided by neurological and imaging studies. At the same time, patterns of automatic generation of narrations highlight the profound implications of a heated debate between Narratology and Computer Technology, in order to understand the processes of reception and inference during the narrative immersion in storyworlds. At the end of their overview on of a cross-disciplinary approach to suspense analysis, the authors report a case study considered of interest, by a group of researched, called Liquid Narrative Group, of North Caroline State University.*

## INTRODUCTION

Todorov called *narratology* or *science of narrative* a new type of theory that could be applied to all domains of narrative (Todorov, 2001). The neologism alludes to social and natural sciences, such as sociology and biology. In the contemporary "narrative turn", the application of narratological tools to extra-narratological research problems has become more and more common, resulting in a multitude of compound or subdomains. The post-structuralism approaches include methodological variations: Natural Narratology, Critical Narratology, Cognitive Narratology, etc, but also the discipline of Cognitive Poetics. Others approaches focus on thematic and ideology-critical concerns, as Post-Colonial Narratology or Feminist Narratology

DOI: 10.4018/978-1-5225-0432-0.ch012

Copyright © 2016, IGI Global. Copying or distributing in print or electronic forms without written permission of IGI Global is prohibited.

In particular, Cognitive Narratology focuses on the intellectual and emotional processing of narratives as carried out by humans. This approach is not restricted to literary narratives: everyday "natural" and oral narratives are considered to represent an underlying anthropological competence in its original form (Fludernik, 2009). Cognitive approaches also play a crucial role in Artificial Intelligence (AI) research, which aims to model or simulate human narrative intelligence. Cognitive Narratology focuses on the mental states, personal skills, and dispositions that provide grounds for narrative experiences. Research on the link between mind-narrative contains multiple methods of analysis and different corpora, such as textual, fictional and nonfictional, computer-mediated narratives including interactive fictions, games and blogs, comics and graphic novels; cinematic narratives, but also storytelling in face-to-face interaction. Similarly, theorists who have been working in this area have adapted descriptive and explanatory tools from a variety of fields, in part because of the cross-disciplinary nature of research on the mind-brain itself. Source disciplines include linguistics, semiotics, computer science, philosophy, psychology, and other domains, in addition to narratology.

Approaches to narrative and mind continue to emerge, evolve, and cross-pollinate. The latest frontier of post-classical narratology (a subdomain of Cognitive Narratology) is Neuronarratology. Neuronarratology is an emergent perspective which includes the linguistic and cognitive contributions to the Cognitive Poetics and the neurological studies of human mind structure and function. This new approach – recognized and theorized by Stefano Calabrese (2009) – makes use of Neuron mirror theory (Rizzolatti, Fogassi, & Gallese, 2001), thus of biological bases formed by mirror neurons in order to understand the empathic effects deriving from the interaction between author, reader and literary text.

The contribute of Neurosciences is relevant for this new concept of narrativity as anthropological competence and problem solving practice. Neuro-imaging studies point out the principal cerebral areas involved in story production and fruition, such as the medial and prefrontal cortex (m-PFC) where the working memory is sited, and the cingulate cortex, which is implied in connecting the stories to spatial dimensions and in creating mental images. Thanks to these areas it is possible to image the development of the stories in time and space. Moreover the m-PFC is also involved in to TOM jointly with the temporal junction (TPJ) and part of temporal lobe. These areas are activated during social interaction of everyday life, as like in the narratives and in the fruition of narratives, where fictional characters are met. For all this reason, the stories supply tools for social acting, through increasing the empathic and social abilities. For examples, Neurobiology applied to narrative studies reveals as the high emotional stories improve the production of cortisol and oxytocin, hormones that are involved in the social attention and affectionate relations.

Therefore Neuroscience and the new-generation narratology prove that narration is an embodied experience able to involve the deepest dimension of body. The Feeling of Body Theory (FOB) allows the perception of actions, states and emotions of fictional characters recording them in the body of stories' users. The research on human attention and perception provide relevant indications about what is perceived as salient and attractive by the human brain. Recently, suspense seems to have considerably attracted the scientists' effort.

During fMRI studies, areas associated with TOM and predictive inference are activated in the reception of a literary text. In particular, the frontal-medial cortex, the bilateral frontal regions, the premotor lateral cortex and the temporal parietal and posterior temporal areas are activated when the subjects adopt the perspective of the protagonist and influence his mental state (Lehne & Koelsch, 2014, pp. 118 ss.).

In other words, it seems that suspense is generated and proliferates by the discrepancy between the protagonist's awareness and knowledge of a forced reader to resort to a Theory of Mind or Mind Reading and to complex game of predictions and anticipations (Jin et al., 2009, pp. 142 ss.).

Now days, the neuroscientists have switched to a redefinition of the phenomenon of suspense as: i) an affective state associated with the conflict, dissonance, instability and uncertainty, selected to ii) create resolution and homeostasis, iii) grant an emotional meaning to events, iiii) direct anticipation and prediction of events.

Against this background, chapter will examine the most recent data on the use of suspense produced by cognitive and neuroscientific studies, making reference to the relationship between this rhetorical device, music, cinema and the generation of stories through computational systems and new technologies (Story-based Systems or Technologies).

In particular, the results of research conducted by the researchers of Liquid Narrative Group, at North Carolina State University (Bae & Young, 2008), will be taken into consideration.

The software development for the generation of flashback and foreshadowing (Minstrel and Suspenser) provides data and models of interest for the new frontier of narratology, identifying significant aspects of the mechanism of story fruition and users' cognitive responses, in terms of suspense and surprise.

## BACKGROUND

### Homeostatic Theory

If we imagine every narrative as a succession of questions and answers, more or less manipulated by a narrator, we could say that the suspense persists until when there are neither questions nor answers, and narrative tension goes out in the silence of a certainty (Rabkin, 1973).

Xavier Pérez wrote that the story ends when the question "and what happens next?" no longer has meaning, when the full potential of exposed meanings from "once upon the time" was resolved with the successful closures, "and they lived happily and contented" (Pérez, 2001).

Until this moment, the reader/spectator does not stop feeling a relentless desire to know which coincides with suspense.

On the basis of the open or closed definition of a fictional world, also because a certain refractory to final closure in the the twentieth century novels, the role and diffusion of suspense issues, in the globalized contemporary, has been addressed by major studies of neuro-cognitive and neuro-linguistics fields.

Since the early twentieth century, in the scientific community the idea was widespread idea that narrative suspense and dynamic stress phenomena could play a primary role in the definition of a person' emotional dimension. According the psychologist Wilhelm Wundt, tension (*Spannung*) and resolution (*Lösung*) are the two poles of the emotional constituent. Talking about emotions and literary texts, however, it is necessary to distinguish between emotions evoked by events (special topics such as murder, kidnapping, etc…) or plot structure at deep level (background) and the emotions aroused from less structural aspects of the text on the surface (foreground). In this latter case, the reference is to the words, the grammatical structure, the rhetorical effects (e.g. anacoluthon), and all the narratological devices able to perceive the phonetic, syntactic or semantic structures as familiar, thus capturing the cognitive attention.

Now, the distinction between foreground and background has recently been taken up by Jacob's Poetic Neurocognitive Model, which recognized two different neuronal circuits specialized on background and foreground text analysis (Jacobs, 2013).

In particular, a deep circuit is solicited by so-called subliminal suspense – the state of hope and uncertainty induced by macro-structural levels of the text – as resulted from a series of fMRI tests. These studies have evidenced that the literary and musical suspense activate similar responses in the brain involving the limbic and paralimbic systems. Music is able to generate sequences of expectations causing a state of tension similar to the one triggered by the skilful narrative plot manipulation and script activations in daily life (Koelsch, 2012). In evolutionary terms, the dynamic tension of suspense corresponds to the need for psychological homeostasis, or to the innate human tendency toward resolution of dissonance, interpretative conflicts and cognitive uncertainty, in order to restore a state of brain neurochemical balance.

Hence, the pleasure generated by suspense therefore acts as a reward and incentive during the exercise of the essential function of anticipation and generation of expectations.

The predictive activities stimulate the dopamine production, while the degree of uncertainty is strongly related to the pleasure generated by the resolution; this makes the effects of suspense similar to the biochemical condition that characterize the extreme sports.

Suspense is therefore a homeostatic tool that intervenes in a process described by different models, also based on the fact that many people are permeable to suspense even in the case of repeated exposure. For example, the philosopher Nöel Carroll (1996) has subjected to fifty visions of *King Kong* noting every time a strong and repeated increasing in suspense, thereby giving rise to different hypotheses about the possible manipulation of memories during the tension states.

More specifically, fMRI investigations revealed that brain regions activated by suspense are associated with mind reading or TOM, and predictive behaviour. In fact, the prefrontal cortex, the bilateral frontal regions, the lateral premotor cortex and temporal-parietal areas were activated when subjects are engaged in reading stories with suspense and they were brought to adopt the protagonist' perspective and infer his mental state.

So, suspense plays a role in relation to the discrepancy between the protagonist and the reader, using the instrument of Mind Reading.

Suspense carries a cognitive functioning and intelligence.

Recently, Lisa Zunshine (2014) spoke of this issue as a pedagogical tool to be introduced in the programs of primary and secondary education, capable to improve the predictive ability of children and adolescents.

The tensional devices of detective stories (novel or film, both modes were tested) have proven to be able to intervene directly in the language areas (in particular, the posterior temporal areas interfering with specialized circuits in acustic-phonetic processing, orthographic mapping and semantic integration of information), one more time with a marked involvement of suspense in the neuronal processes of prediction and anticipation (Fitch, von Graevenitz, & Nicolas, 2009).

## CINEMA AND NEURONAL CONTROL

Based on reviewed results, it is possible to redefine the value of suspense itself, as an affective state associated with the conflict, dissonance, instability and uncertainty selected in human evolution:

**Step 1:** Create homeostasis after event resolution.
**Step 2:** Give to the event a potential emotional meaning.
**Step 3:** Direct the anticipation processes.

In this regard, the experiments conducted between 2004 and 2008 by a group of cinema researchers and neuroscientists are crucial. In these tests, participants were subjected to fmRI while viewing of various types of film sequences: frames from Hitchcock's movie (*Bang You're Dead*), Sergio Leone's *The Good and the Bad*, TV frames and, finally, filmed scenes of a city park (Hassan et al., 2008).

The brain activities of each subject was monitored and the correlated results showed highly surprising activation in the area of vision and in the time and sequences of activation. The results show that the cognitive and emotional responses of users are, to some extent, predictable. Tests have shown that the subjects react before highly structured texts, such as the films of Hitchcock, while the simple exposure to filmed images of real life events sequences were not sufficient to obtain verifiable responses of activation of the same neuronal areas; test results in Collective Engagement Power of the images orienting the reactions of the viewers indicate that in Hitchcock's case over 65% of the cortex reacted in the same way, 45% in Leone's case, 18% for the TV serial, and less than 5% for the real life film (Hassan, Yang, Vallines, David, & Rubin, 2008).

In fact, Hitchcock works are able to guide the neuronal responses of the audience; they provide crucial neuroscientific evidence to explain the success and the emotionally manipulative power exercised by suspense, in which Hitchcock was a master.

According to André Bazin's famous formulation (Bazin, 1967, p. 24), most art films are direct to realism and choose to allow the viewer more freedom, refusing to orient her attention. The directors employ instruments as like the sequence plan, the range focalization, the multi-spatial composition, or other conventions in order to guarantee the viewer as a space of distance/judgment and flexible interpretations.

The Hitchcock Hollywood style, on the contrary, aimed to getting the highest possible control of the viewer through the use of such filmic conventions as suspense, a trap to capture the audience's cognitive and emotional response.

Psychologists believe that they obtained the test results permit the formulation of a taxonomy of the control operated by narrative on the mind, where finally we find the vision of real life sequences. At the end, these sequences are unconnected, un-semantic and inconsistent. At the other end a strict control so that if it is not accompanied by a tense performance, implied an over-simplification is implied.

The film directors add that different styles and genres (drama, thriller, comedy) can activate different areas of the brain even in presence of suspense mechanisms. This difference may be observed in relation to different segments of the same movie, or even for individual scenes without mounting, or sintax. In Hitchcock's film, for example, two-minute sequences show an increased level on neuronal correlation in subjects toward 2/3 of segment, namely at the climax of the episode; in particular, by activating the dorso-lateral prefrontal cortex (dorso-lateral PFC), the area destined to higher cognitive functions.

## SUSPENSE, PLEASURE, AND STRESS: IMMUNE-PHYLAXIS

Recently, suspense seems to have attracted even greater attention from neuroscientists, who in the course of fMRI investigations revealed that the reception of a literary text with suspenseful structure areas associated with Theory of Mind and inference are activated. In particular, the medial frontal cortex (m-PFC), the bilateral frontal regions, the lateral premotor cortex, the temporal-parietal and posterior temporal areas are activated, especially when the subjects adopted the perspective of the protagonist and infer details of its mental state (Lehne & Koelsch, 2014).

Now, neuroscientists have formed a new definition of the phenomenon as an affective state associated with the conflict, the dissonance, the instability and uncertainty activated by the need to create resolution and homeostasis, grant an emotional meaning to events, direct the processes of anticipation and prediction.

In order to understand the suspense homeostatic power, scientists refer to anxiety as a kind of a surrogate primary emotion of fear, which we feel when facing a dangerous situation during which the brain receives information from external stimuli necessary for an emergency (Koelsch et al., 2013).

The amygdala collects data directly from eyes, mouth, thermal and pressure receptors and compares their inputs with information already stored in memory or coming from the automatic nervous system. Note that this type of feedback is also active in the states of mental simulation, or memory, imagination or immersion in fictional worlds with risk representations.

The difference between fear and anxiety lies on the value or potential of a hazardous event, in the sense that the first takes over when the danger is imminent, the second when the risk is potential.

During states of uncertainty and tension, the central nervous system reacts by releasing hormones that mediate both the immediate response (such as adrenaline and noradrenaline), and hormones that take the medium term responses (corticotropin, adreno-cortico-trope and cortisol).

While the first group of substance acts at the level of the muscles, through the reaction (fight or flight) or immobilization (freezing), the second act on the energy reserves, the balance of body fluids and the transformation of complete proteins into simple sugars.

These changes create stress which, as we well know, can lead to a progressive weakening of the immune system, cognitive and neuro-vegetative activities, and frequent mood change; but it must be remembered that stress is also a tool aimed at the restoration of adaptive balance, or rather the establishment of a new corporal and cognitive asset.

Since the term stress indicates a factor that disturbs an initial balance, we might consider any positive or negative event that comes unexpected or new as stress.

It is interesting to note that in scientific language and in the standard language, indicates whether the event that produces the answered in the same sequences, so things could be as follows:

**Step 1:** The predictive orientation of an individual should be considered as a baseline disturbed by an event aimed at generating the orientation uncertainty and anxiety.
**Step 2:** The disturbing element is definable "strain", a term borrowed from physics that indicates the degree of deformation of a plane.
**Step 3:** The strain causes stress in the plane.
**Step 4:** The plane/person tries to resist deformation.
**Step 5:** The stress produced resistance however, it tends to re-establish a balance.

If this model has the advantage of showing stress (Macri, Capogrossi Colognesi, 2011) – in our case, then suspense – as a factor that helps to restore a reassuring balance for the person, it can also provides us with an explanation of its genesis. This kind of stress, indeed, is capable of enhancing our cognitive competences and our abilities to adapt to situations, promoting alternative life history strategies and therefore making humans the most creature "plastic and flexible" of the creatures of the organic world.

In conclusion, suspense gives us a coefficient of lower middle stress that improves the memory processes, makes us more alert, creates new categorical connections, enables us to deal promptly with potentially dangerous stimuli and, finally, helps to protect us from massive doses of stress.

The individual adapts quickly to minor exposure to stress developing a strong reliance, just as an exposure to minor stressful events of acts as a vaccine against actual stress.

In this sense, the pleasure given by the immersion in detective stories, thrillers or other narratives with suspended structure seems to be justified by the value of the adaptive stress, as our brains exploit stories to stimulate the tools of Theory of Mind and arouse anxiety, only for the purpose of training simulative scenarios and stimulate immune-phylaxis.

## Info-Generation of Suspense: The Aid of Neuronarratology

In 2008, researchers of North Caroline State University, the founders of Liquid Narrative Group, examined the possibility of providing effects of retrospections, also called *prolepsis* or *flashforward*, through devices of Artificial Intelligence (AI), on the assumption that such effects are instrumental to obtaining emotions such as excitement, curiosity and surprise (Bae & Young, 2008).

Researches began from the canonical distinction including story time (fable) and discourse time (plot), but oppose the distinction between a flashback and foreshadowing. While the latter implicitly alludes to a future event in such manner which does not allow the reader to know what will happen to the end, the *flashforward* is explicit presents a future event in such a way to tell the reader what will happen in details.

In short, the *foreshadowing* is an example of mention in advance in an explicit form, the *flashforward* is an example of advance information in explicit form, whereby in a movie if the flashback usually lighting a backstage or a subplot to support to the main narrative line, the *foreshawing* provides incomplete or implied.

In the case of incompleteness, it can be understood only retrospectively (this entails a double movement forward and backward). In the case of partial incompleteness, the attention of the reader viewer tends to be focused on a certain event in order to make him wish that the interactive virtual environments focused on narratives. The interaction with a virtual character activities multiple forms of foreshadowing, that *foreshawing* of possible outcomes of current actions.

When we read a story, we want not only to gather information but also being rewarded whith some type or stimulate an emotional interest. The psychologist Keith Oatley (1994) has identifies internal or external effects generated by the reading of a narrative.

The internal effects are produced through the reader's empathy with the characters in a story and are always of an emotional type.

The external effects are produced thanks to the readers' consideration of the text's enunciation and are always of the cognitive type, such as curiosity and surprise.

On one side, we have therefore the emotional interest generated by highly structured organization patterns, but it may also be useful to examine the notion of *postdictability,* which contributes the value of the cognitive interest, with no regard for the type of story told.

Postdictability is a form of systemic understanding and closing of a story when multiple threads are knotted resulting in a compact, uniform "well-warp-tissue": we could then translate the word by "macro-structural decoding" (Oatley, 1994).

Now, as the cognitive interest is defined as surprise or curiosity in relation to totally unexpected events but without any relation to postdictability, cognitive interest cannot take place, as it would fail to build a logical-sequential structure. The Liquide Narrative Group scholars discuss of postdictable surprise (which is unexpected form of decoding) as the same condition for a virtuous use of the transgression of the reader' expectation.

In conclusion, considering the perception of surprise evoked by reading suspenseful narratives, the authors attach great importance to the cognitive relevant role which postdictability assumes in our retroactive building of the story.

In fact, the Liquid Narrative Group intend to develop an integrated system for the generation of stories, namely software capable of "creating a sense of inevitability and unity in history anticipation unexpected events" on the system does not have memory (Bae & Young, 2008, p. 159).

At this point, the scholars automatically entered moments of flashback and foreshadowing of the stories intended to cause cognitive surprise perceptions in the reader.

It is interesting to note that, for these researches, the software is based on a player model that simulated the reasoning of a 'model-reader' of the story. In fact, because the human skills of planning depends on a set of preferences, constraints on basic and textual knowledge already acquired, and memories of memories, software will take all of this into rigorous account in order to simulate reader inferences.

It should be remembered that the purpose of the Liquid Narrative Group is the computer generation of suspense by using gaming or designing narrative itineraries that can improve cognitive anxiety of users and their 'waiting emotions'.

The system evaluates its effectiveness in producing effects of surprise through the manipulation of event expectations and postdictability by flashback and foreshadowing.

In particular, for these scholars the surprise is characterized by the sudden occurrence of an unexpected turn, when events are presented after the fact, or even omitted – and thus resemble curiosity, with the difference that in this last case the reader is aware of how the initiating events (IE) are absent or not fully described.

As regards the flashback, the software connects a series of crucial events (Significant Event SE) to the purposes of the fable and identifies the set of initiators events for determining their separation, in order to find the possibility to omit them without creating misunderstandings relatively the crucial events (SE) indicated previously.

Next, the software selects the initiating events (IE) which are potentially more effective and have lower impact on the narrative rhythm delaying the event time after the appearance of initiating events (IE).

A model of "surprising" story building by software consist of a story in which a criminal named Jack is developing biological weapons and he decided to kidnap the famous scientist Cohen imprisoning him in the fortress of Skeleton Island (Bae & Young, 2008, pp. 163-164).

**Story Background:** The criminal known as Jack has been developing biological weapons of devastating proportions. To accomplish the final stages of weapon development, he kidnapped the famous scientist, Dr. Cohen, and brought him to his private fortress on Skeleton Island. Jack expected that the FBI would soon send Smith, their top agent, to rescue Dr. Cohen. To keep the troublesome Smith out of his hair, Jack ordered his own agent, Erica, to monitor Smith and capture him if he is assigned to Dr. Cohen's rescue operation.

**Story Structure:**

**Step 1:** Erica installs a wiretap in Smith's home while he is away.

**Step 2:** Erica eavesdrops on the phone conversation in which Smith is given the order to rescue Dr. Cohen.
**Step 3:** Erica meets with Smith.
**Step 4:** Erica tells Smith that her father was kidnapped by Jack and taken to Skeleton Island, and she asks Smith to save her father.
**Step 5:** Erica gives Smith the blueprints of Jack's fortress, with her father's cell marked.
**Step 6:** Erica provides Smith with a boat for transportation to Skeleton Island.
**Step 7:** Before going to the island, Smith hides a diamond in his shoe.
**Step 8:** Smith goes to the port containing Erica's boat.
**Step 9:** Smith rides the boat to Skeleton Island.
**Step 10:** Smith sneaks into the cell marked on the map containing Erica's father.
**Step 11:** Jack and his guard capture Smith as he enters the cell.
**Step 12:** The guard disarms Smith.
**Step 13:** The guard locks Smith into the cell.
**Step 14:** Smith bribes the guard with the diamond in his shoe.
**Step 15:** The guard unlocks the door.
**Step 16:** Smith leaves the cell.
**Step 17:** Smith sneaks to the lab where Dr. Cohen is captured.
**Step 18:** Smith fights the guards in the lab.
**Step 19:** Smith takes Dr. Cohen from the lab.
**Step 20:** Smith and Dr. Cohen ride the boat to shore.

The researchers say such that the steps 7 and 14 are caused (IE) separable from the event crucial 15 (SE), so their omission does not affect any event to precede the step 15.

The reader is, in fact, unaware of the absence of 7 and 14 before15 is executed, so the software confirms their postdicibility checking that the reader cannot infer 15 before seeing 7 and 14. Only then will a preview partially showing step 7 (minimum allusion, farthest from 15) be implemented, for example, showing only the diamonds or shoes or someone who hides something.

In virtual environments characteristic of interactive videogames, retrospection and anticipation are normally associated with the knowledge of a person moved by the user, who can decide to degree of explicitness fully satisfying their curiosity and their surprise: exactly what reader of a detective stories have tried to do and appreciated since by the editorial release of the Edgar Allan Poe' tales.

## FUTURE RESEARCH DIRECTIONS

The main goal of this chapter is bring the focus of attention on potential of a multidisciplinary approach among narratology, cognitive neuroscience and applied computing. The paradigm that identifies the suspense as evolutionary device will be supported by new evidence thanks to a renewed heuristic approach, opens to disciplinary contaminations.

## CONCLUSION

Creating suspense involves more, necessary and optional, conditions; the optional conditions mainly serve to intensify the feeling of suspense during reader experience. Suspense can be considered as a progressive emotion. Suspense is mostly experienced during reading and involves the reader into story by driving him/her to reassess stories, events and characters in the new light.

New research in the field of cognitive neuroscience field find empirical evidence of the experience of literary reading and, ultimately, on itsevolutionary implications.

In addition and in parallel with these developments, a 'Cognitive Poetics' is now flourishing in the Anglo-Saxon contest and in Italy, where it assumes the name of Neuronarratology. The Neuronarratology appears as a research perspective able to offer a genuine dialogue and exchange across disciplinary fields: Humanities, Cognitive Neuroscience and Computer Science.

## REFERENCES

Bae, B.-C., & Young, R. M. (2008). A use of flashback and foreshadowing for surprise arousal in narrative using a plan-based approach. In *Proceeding of the International Conference on Interactive Digital Storytelling (ICIDS08)* (pp. 156-167). Erfurt, Germany. doi:10.1007/978-3-540-89454-4_22

Bazin, A. (1967). *Che cos'è il cinema*. Milano: Garzanti.

Calabrese, S. (2009). *Neuronarratologia*. Bologna: Archetipolibri.

Carroll, N. (1996). The paradox of suspense. In P. Vorderer, H. J. Wulff, & M. Friedrichsen (Eds.), *Suspense: Conceptualizations, theoretical analyses, and empirical explorations* (pp. 71–91). Mahwah, NJ: Lawrence Erlbaum Associates.

Fitch, W. T., Von Graevenitz, A., & Nicolas, E. (2009). Bio-aesthetic, dinamics and aesthetic trajectory: A cognitive and cultural perspective. In M. Snov & O. Varatarian (Eds.), *Neuroaesthetic* (pp. 59–102). Amityville, NY: Baywood Publishing Company.

Fludernik, M. (2009). *An introduction to narratology*. London: Routledge.

Hassan, U. A., Yang, E., Vallines, I., David, H. J., & Rubin, N. (2008). A hierarchy of temporal receptive windows in human cortex. *The Journal of Neuroscience, 28*(10), 2539–2550. doi:10.1523/JNEUROSCI.5487-07.2008 PMID:18322098

Jacobs, A. M. (2013). *Neurocognitive models of literary reading*. Retrieved October 13, 2001, from https://www.researchgate.net/publication/235952745_Neurocognitive_Model_of_Litera

Jin, H., Liu, H. L., Mo, L., Fang, S. Y., Zhang, J. X., & Lin, C. D. (2009). Involvement of the left inferior frontal gyrus in predictive inference making. *International Journal of Psychophysiology, 71*(3), 142–148. doi:10.1016/j.ijpsycho.2008.08.009 PMID:18822322

Koelsch, S. (2012). *Brain and music*. West Sussex, UK: John Wiley & Sons.

Koelsch, S., Skouras, S., Fritz, T., Herrera, P., Bonhage, C., Küssner, M. B., & Jacobs, A. M. (2013). The roles of superficial amygdala and auditory cortex in music-evoked fear and joy. *NeuroImage*, *81*, 49–60. doi:10.1016/j.neuroimage.2013.05.008 PMID:23684870

Lehne, M., & Koelsch, S. M. (2014). Tension resolution patterns as a key element of aesthetic experience: Psychological principles and underlying brain mechanism. In J. P. Huston (Ed.), *Art, aesthetic and the brain* (pp. 122–138). New York: Oxford University Press.

Macrì, S., & Capogrossi Colognesi, S. (2011). *Che cos'è lo stress*. Roma: Carocci.

Oatley, K. (1994). A taxonomy of the emotions of the literary response and a theory of identification in fictional narrative. *Poetics*, *9*(23), 53–74.

Pérez, X. (2001). *La suspense cinematografica*. Roma: Editori Riuniti.

Rabkin, E. S. (1973). Narrative suspense: "When Slim Turned Sideways". New York: Ann Arbor.

Rizzolatti, G., Fogassi, L., & Gallese, V. (2001). Neurophysiological mechanism underlying the understanding and imitation of action. *Nature Reviews. Neuroscience*, *2*(9), 661–669. doi:10.1038/35090060 PMID:11533734

Todorov, T. (2001). Structural analysis of narrative. In V. B. Leich (Ed.), The Norton anthology of theory and criticism (pp. 2099-2016). Norton.

Zunshine, L. (2014). Theory of mind as a pedagogical tool. *Interdisciplinary Literary Studies*, *16*(1), 89–105. doi:10.5325/intelitestud.16.1.0089

## KEY TERMS AND DEFINITIONS

**Analepsis:** Analepsis or flashback is the narration of an event at a point later than its chronological place in a story.

**Feeling of Body:** The term Feeling of Body (FOB) is introduced by Vittorio Gallese and Hannah Wojciehowsk, respectively a neuroscientist at the University of Parma (Italy) and a narratologist of University of Texas (Austin, USA) in a Contribute of 2011, with the title How Stories Make Us Feel: Toward an Embodied Narratology, dedicated to a literary narratology based on perception embodied. More specifically, the two scholars explain how the functional mechanism of liberated embodied simulation enables the FOB and characterizing one important level of our relationships with namely our empathic co-feeling with other activated by writing and registered within our own bodies.

**Mirror Neurons:** The mirror neurons are a set of neurons situated in the premotor cortex, discovered by neuroscientists Vittorio Gallese and Giacomo Rizzolatti. The mirror neurons system responds when we perform an action and also when we see someone else perform that action or living an emotion.

**Prolepsis:** Prolepsis or flashforward is a figurative device in narrative in which a future event is prefigurated.

# Chapter 13
# Fact, Narrative, Visualization as Fiction, and Love:
## Analysis of the Japanese Film *The Land of Hope*

**Yukiko Ogawa**
*Hosei University, Japan*

## ABSTRACT

*This chapter's subject matter is "The Land of Hope", a Japanese film inspired by facts. The primary aim is to apply structural analysis of narrative, a method commonly used for natural language text, to film, which is an audiovisual text. This research will adopt methods for decomposing the film into component units and rules for linking them that are appropriate to the physical/representational characteristics of the medium, and propose a procedure for visualizing the narrative structure using a single diagram. The second aim is to sketch the aspects of narrative content that structural analyses – which only regard its formal aspects – overlook, supporting the argument with knowledge from film cognition research and by focusing on particular themes. This chapter's research deals with a practical simulation that analyzes a film's form and content with an integrated approach, and advocates the methodology that is applicable to any film in principle.*

## INTRODUCTION

What cognitive effect do a film's story and rhetorical devices have on the viewer? The key interest and mission of film cognition research – this author's field – are to elucidate the particular nature of the cognition that they trigger in a viewer, and the strength of their effects. This research requires that a preliminary analysis be conducted for each film that is to be studied in order to understand the essential substance of its form and content. The reason is that without analytically ascertaining the various particular qualities of a film's style of expression, one cannot even hypothesize about what cognitive effects require experiment. This is where a specific methodology for film analysis is called for, which can be carried out in advance to support the film cognition research. In principle, one can describe the

DOI: 10.4018/978-1-5225-0432-0.ch013

Copyright © 2016, IGI Global. Copying or distributing in print or electronic forms without written permission of IGI Global is prohibited.

formal narrative structure of any narrative text, regardless of medium; however, most of the texts that have been treated thus far have been natural language text, and texts which are essentially audiovisual have been neglected.

So the primary objective of this chapter is to carry out structural analysis of narrative of a particular Japanese film, and describe its narrative structure, which is part of the film's formal aspects. How should one divide a long text like a film, which is composed of many symbol elements? And how should one link them together systematically, in order to create a comprehensive visual diagram of its structure? A simulation analysis method will be proposed that will extend the frontiers of methodology for analyzing an audiovisual text, which is unpopular material for structural analysis of narrative. *The Land of Hope* (2012), directed by Sion Sono is used as material of this simulation analysis. This is a fictional film which is however based on an actual event, the Great East Japan Earthquake, which will go down in history as a major disaster of the early twenty-first century. The film is a fictional depiction of various issues arising from the disaster, interwoven with the universal human theme of love.

A narrative with a meaning is a comprehensive theme, i.e. it has a semantic massive structure, consisting of components where localized smaller themes are embedded to hierarchical sub-episodes. On the point that a narrative is a coherence of physically decomposable parts, and since an audiovisual material is the same as a written material, the same analytical methodology of natural language text can be appropriately applied to films. However needless to mention the difficulty of such a research, to exhaustively extract all symbols that constitute the film expressions after mechanically decomposing it, the fact that it is fundamentally impossible to systematically express the narrative content is the point which must be challenged. In case of a film, analysts can introduce some perspectives, the significance of local symbols constituting the massive structure, namely, besides discussing on the predictive analysis of cognitive effects, it is thought that no other method to narrow the content exists. Therefore, in this chapter as a secondary method, while incorporating the knowledge already obtained in film cognition research by the author, two of the expressive creativity in *The Land of Hope* – fusion of fact and fiction, form of love and its sublimation – the author extract the essence of the content through the predictive analysis of cognitive effects.

## BACKGROUND

### Academic Circumstances over Structural Analysis of Narrative

In this section, after having followed the origin of structural analysis of the narrative and its academic process, related research in cognitive science affected by narratology or narratological approach were applied to give the outline.

#### The Origin of Structural Analysis of Narrative

First of all, as the methodology to analyze the narrative structure which serves as the formal aspects of a film, the academic process and outline of structural analysis of narrative will be introduced in the following. This methodology is a linguistic theory of Ferdinand de Saussure (1857–1913) proposed in early 20th century that fundamentally overturned the classic sign theory. Affected by his theory, several Russian formalists left behind some predominant poetic and philosophical studies (e.g., Shklovsky, 1971; Bakhtin, 1989), and as one from them, Vladimir Propp (1895–1970) published "Morphology of the Folktale" (Propp, 1987) after extracting the common structure of about 350 pieces called Russian fairy tales. His study clarified the certain arrangement, or the universal narrative structure by extracting 31 functions to calculate roles of the characters in narratives, but its publication didn't arouse any response at that time. However, it was translated to English in 1958 when researchers were increasingly interested in the potential structure of narratives along with the study of myth of Claude Lévi-Strauss (1908–2009), and "Morphology of the Folktale" finally came into the spotlight as a structuralism approach practiced 30 years ago. This study became the direct prototype of structural analysis of narrative. Due to the excellent work of C. Bremon, A. J. Greimas, T. Todorov, R. Barthes, and G. Genette after Lévi-Strauss (e.g., Barthes, 1979; Genette, 1985), the structuralism approach helped the completion of narratology, and on the same time narratology has also been actively utilized as the basic idea to support the fundamentals, for example, it is used to assume and organize the mental activities such as memory, comprehension, inference, and knowledge representations in the form of narratives in cognitive science and ultimately used in artificial intelligence (AI) approach studies aiming to narrative generation by computers (e.g., Ogata, Hori, & Ohsuga, 1996; Ogata, 2007).

## Theoretical Applications from Narratology to Cognitive Science

In the 1970s, the early period of AI and the mature period of narratology, the concept of schema or script that means knowledge representation was proposed from AI by Rumelhurt (1975) and Thorndyke (1977) as "story grammar." It was used as a cognitive framework for processing popular stories, as well as a concept of cognitive science to explain narrative structures. Then after the 1980s, the relationship between the narrative and the reader's cognition became a popular topic in cognitive science. The studies explored which narrative structures can be easily recalled from short-term memory, what kind of mental representations of story can be transferred to narrative comprehension, and which narrative elements were inferred online or offline (Kintsch, 1992; Zwaan & Radvansky, 1998; Sundermeier, Van den Broek, & Zwaan, 2005). During this period, cognitive science intended to clarify the fundamental properties of cognition such as memory, comprehension, and inference. As this was applicable to the framework of story grammar, structural analysis of narrative was also conducted in such studies. These studies analyzed the functions of each narrative element from the viewpoint of causality. Specifically, they examined the relationship between attempt and outcome, or goal and plans of actions, then demonstrated the use of causal chain diagrams or tree diagrams that presented the entire narrative structure (Fletcher & Bloom, 1988; Tapiero, van den Broek, & Quintana, 2002; Trabasso & Wiley, 2005).

The popularity of such analytical research in the 1980s, and in the early 1990s when the research was most en vogue, is owed to two facts: first, that short texts were well-suited to research aimed at elucidating the basic properties of human cognitive processes, such as memory, comprehension and inference; and second, that there was high academic interest at the time in the concept of 'interestingness' (Schank, 1979), particularly in that of stories. The compound sensation of cognitive and emotional interestingness that a reader finds in a story was explained by various studies during this period from various cognitive angles, such as the reader's memory, comprehension and inference (Kintsch, 1980). However, the once-popular research of cognitive interestingness began to die out in the 1990s, when cognitive science began to engage properly with the emotional facet of human beings. The 1990s, when the faculty of emotion, which until then had received little serious attention, came to be recognized as one of the two internal systems comprising a human being and as valid an object of scientific research as cognition, may be said to be one of the transition periods of cognitive science. It was this climate that gave rise to the trend of researchers attempting to explain the interestingness of stories from an emotional angle (Iran-Nejad, 1987), which eventually overshadowed research that sought to do so from the cognitive angle. As a result, structural analysis of narrative fell out of favor without ever having been applied to a wider range of texts.

## Film Cognition Research in Cognitive Science

In this section, after having followed the trend of the research around enjoyment as the paradigm of cognition toward media, hypotheses and models evaluated in author's film cognition research concerned with that paradigm or knowledge obtained from there are given as the outline.

### Enjoyment as the Paradigm of Cognition toward Media

The debate on interestingness curtailed after the above paradigm shift in cognitive science, and instead 'enjoyment' took its place as a major topic. Interestingness is a concept that handles the relationship between pre-existing knowledge structures and input; in contrast, the concept of enjoyment encompassed various aspects – namely the physiological, cognitive and emotive aspects – of the response structure's reaction to media as a complex whole (Vorderer, Klimmt, & Ritterfeld, 2004). Rather than being limited to text, the framework of the concept of enjoyment accommodates works of audio/visual art, such as music and video. Furthermore, it includes not only the test subject's cognitive and emotional aspects, but also the physiological aspect, over which he/she cannot exercise complete control. The wide scope of its applications and the breadth of its range are advantages that the concept of enjoyment offers over previous concepts.

Originally, enjoyment is a concept rooted in mood management theory explaining that the emotion of exposing yourself to the contents selected from certain media is based on the hedonistic needs and motivation, but the knowledge that high-level negative emotions can bring about high-level enjoyment to the contrary of the hedonistic theory has been proposed by multiple studies based on this concept (Appel, 2008; de Wied, Zillmann, & Ordman, 1994; Green, Brock & Kaufman, 2004; Green et al., 2008; Maio & Esses, 2001; Oliver, 1993, 2007, 2008; Oliver, Weaver, & Sargent, 2000; Raney, 2002, 2004, 2005; Raney & Bryant, 2002; Zillmann, 1998). Refer to Ogawa (2011) for them in detail. Instead of avoiding negative emotions, the receiver expects stronger taste of them, and that experience can lead to mental reward from someone else – if this is true, the nature of enjoyment should be something generated from a mental state in direct opposition to hedonism based on the mood management theory and the basic definition should also be adapted. What is the specific phase consisting the cognition toward enjoyment and what kind of visual representation can induce enjoyment (or cannot induce enjoyment)? It is hard to say that there are enough case studies and research carried out about the causality of these cognitive and expressive characteristics.

### Role of "Story" and "Rhetoric" in Film Cognition

In order to reveal the mechanism underlying cognition of images, this author has been running experiments to test her own model of the above concept of enjoyment. The study, detailed in Ogawa (2011), chose as its material the television drama series *Chura-san* (2001, NHK). It set up a hypothesis that enjoyment is composed of three elements: a positive system and a negative system, which are the internal systems that mediate the viewer's cognition and emotion, and a message evaluation phase. This model was proved by the tests to be a model that adequately explains the composite mechanism of the cognitive and affective responses to narrative moving images with a strong sense of storyline. In the subsequent study, Ogawa and Kanai (2013) hypothesized the model depicted in Figure 1. 'Irrational cutting' refers to a visual rhetoric that cuts the continuity between shots of an image, and 'Cognition Induced by Irrational Cutting' to the cognitive effect engendered by a narrative moving image that prioritizes rhetoric over plot. Experiments were conducted, using as materials *Tower of TARO* (2011, NHK), a television drama series with a strong sense of storyline, and *Yumeji* (1991) directed by Seijun Suzuki, a Japanese film teeming with visual rhetoric, in order to test whether conceptual thought (concept reflection) was stimulated more by cognition toward enjoyment or cognition induced by irrational cutting.

The key results are as follows. (1) In the storyline-driven *Tower of TARO*, cognition toward enjoyment was the only determinant of concept reflection, and cognition induced by irrational cutting, i.e. comprehension of the image itself, was not required. (2) On the other hand, in the highly rhetorical *Yumeji*, both cognition toward enjoyment and cognition induced by irrational cutting were determinants of concept reflection. *Yumeji*, therefore, prompted the viewer to activate in parallel both cognition toward enjoyment, and cognition induced by irrational cutting, and then to engage in concept reflection. This was achieved by its representational style with its narrative fragments that do not exhibit a clear progression, but are interlaced with enjoyable elements; and the image itself is guaranteed to trigger thought, as images do by nature. The study of Ogawa and Kanai (2013) suggested at the versatility of the model in Figure 1, which can accommodate and accurately explicate the composite mechanism of cognitive and affective response to diverse films; and in doing so, the model is also able to account for the films' representational originality, which tends to lie in the balance between story and rhetoric, as variance in the coefficients between each construct.

*Figure 1. Cognitive structured model for film cognition composed of enjoyment and irrational cutting*

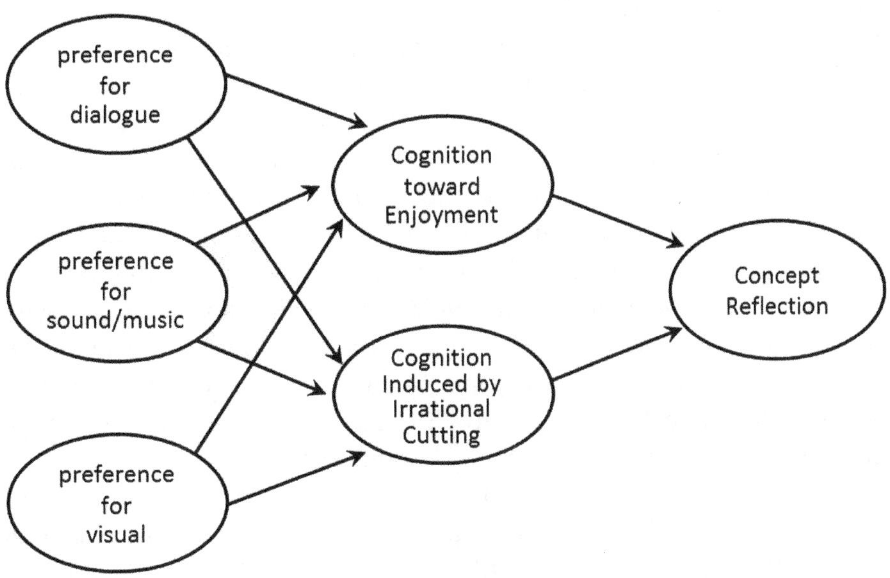

## Necessity of Comprehensive Film Analysis

As cited among the aforementioned prior studies in film cognition research engaged by the author, a concrete narrative moving image is surely selected, only after assessing its expressive individuality from the story and the rhetoric point of view, the shot, scene or sequence to be used for the experiment are determined. Initially, the narrative moving image that became a candidate of the experiment material at this stage should be subjected to a structural analysis of narrative. Whereby the entire narrative structure, as well as, once the hierarchy and functions of each unit in the whole have been identified, the shot, scene or sequence suited to the purpose of each film cognition research should be appropriately selected on such grounds. At the same time, for the specific shot, scene or sequence that is selected at that point, in order to make a reasonable hypothesis about the cognition to be verified, there is a need to perform in advance a predictive analysis on the cognitive effects of any representation that is brought to the viewer. This is the structure's so called formal aspects analysis that extracts the essence of content, it is a part of the entire analysis that should be applied as a prerequisite for film cognition research. From the standing point of the author such as the above, and based on the awareness of the challenges, we perform, from the next section in this chapter, a simulation as a comprehensive analysis to capture both the whole and its parts, form and content, structure and predictive cognitive effect, using the Japanese film *The Land of Hope* as material.

# ANALYSIS

## Material of the Present Analysis

### *About Sion Sono* [1]

Sion Sono who directed the film *The Land of Hope*, was born in Aichi prefecture in Japan in 1961. He was a cinephile from an early age and also a dedicated fan of the surreal manga of Fujio Akatsuka. He held doubts in so-called "common sense" and as a youth, he expressed these doubts in his thinking and actions. He tells the story of how he wondered why people need to wear clothes, and on one occasion he went to school completely naked, whereupon he was reprimanded by the teacher. When he was a high school student, he hoped to be a singer songwriter, and would write lyrics during school classes. He says that, as he had ample time, he honed his skills such as in embellishing his language, whereby his lyrics transformed into modern poetry. This was the starting point for a desire for self-expression that welled up within him and of self-realization. Eventually, he decided to try his hand behind the camera, making his directing debut with *I Am Sion Sono!!*, a film he devised and directed, in 1985. During the 1990s, he shot independent films with strong underground tendencies. He described how he led the performance collective *Tokyo Gagaga*, which staged a performance through the streets of Shibuya, waving banners of his poetry and shouting out nonsensical slogans. At night, they placed a replica of the statue of the dog Hachiko alongside the original outside Shibuya Station, observing the reactions of people using the location as a rendezvous point (the above refers to Hayami (2013)).

From 2001, he signed a contract with a major film production company and began to shoot full-scale dramas on a commercial basis. His works began to attract a cult status in Japan. Later, he received formal approval to show his films in overseas film festivals, where he earned high appraisal and won many prestigious awards. His key achievements are: the Caligari Film Award and the FIPRESCI Prize at the 59th Berlin International Film Festival for *Love Exposure* (2008), formal acceptance in the Orizzonti and competition sections at the 67th Venice International Film Festival for *Cold Fish* (2010), and formal acceptance for the 64th annual Cannes Film Festival Directors' Fortnight for *Guilty of Romance* (2011). In addition, the two leading actors of his film *Himizu* (2011) received the Marcello Mastroianni Award at the 68th Venice International Film Festival. Many of "A SONO SION'S FILM"s tackle heavy human and social themes such as suicide, abuse, unauthorized photography, sex, violence, brain-washing by new religions, family breakdown, and murder. His cinematic depictions are at times gut-wrenching for the viewer – so violent and repulsive that one cannot bear to watch. He, however, has said that he "doesn't want to simply be branded as a person who films such things." Although less prominent in his oeuvre, there are a number of his films filled with his unique sense of image that shed light on the essence of human life and issues that touch on social reasoning, depicting a representation that is not at all eccentric, for example, it is *The Land of Hope*. His representations span an extraordinary breadth (Sono & Oshima, 2015).

### About "The Land of Hope"

The follow up to *Himizu* which is his first work to tackle the Great East Japan Earthquake occurred on March 11, 2011, *The Land of Hope* is a fictional story set in Japan following the Great East Japan Earthquake and consequent nuclear disaster where, sometime later, another major earthquake occurs, causing a tsunami and nuclear disaster in the same manner as at Fukushima. The locations are fictional – a town called Oba in a prefecture known as Nagashima. The Ono household, comprising four members – Yasuhiko (*Isao Natsuyagi*) and his wife Chieko (*Naoko Otani*) along with their son Yoichi (*Jun Murakami*) and his wife Izumi (*Megumi Kagurazaka*) – are dairy farmers. Their neighbors, the Suzukis, are a farming couple – Ken (*Denden*) and Meiko (*Mariko Tsutsui*) who cultivate vegetables, whose son Mitsuru (*Yutaka Shimizu*) is still not ready to settle down, although his girlfriend Yoko (*Hikari Kajiwara*) is practically a member of the family. The film narrates the intertwining stories of two families, Ono and Suzuki, neighbors living about 20 kilometers radius from the Nagashima No. 1 Reactor, with the main focus being the Ono family.

## Structural Analysis of Narrative of "The Land of Hope"

### Procedure

#### *Step 1: Decomposition to Units and Identification of Functions in Episode*

First of all, the entire film *The Land of Hope* is decomposed into shots. A shot is a fragment of a film taken through a single continuous exposure without stopping the camera, and is the minimum unit of a footage that constitutes a scene or sequence. A scene is a unit of the upper shot in the narrative moving image, it refers to the coherence of a series of actions and events that occurred in continuous time and space. In general, it consists either of a number of shots, or time and space, otherwise it ends with the variations of both and proceeds to the next scene. A sequence is a unit of an upper scene, and constitutes a distinct coherence of the overall narrative moving image. Although a series of scenes or shots, or 1 scene or shot can be a sequence, generally it often consist of a series of scenes. A series of scenes that constitutes the sequence, need not to necessarily depict actions and events that occur in the same continuous time and space. If we replace the units that constitute these 3 images to natural language text units, a shot as word, a scene as phrase or sentence, a sequence would then corresponds to a coherence, such as a paragraph. The Land of Hope is 2 hours 10 minutes and 21 seconds long, comprising 972 shots, 122 scenes and 22 sequences.

A shot is a cut of camera exposure; a scene is an extract of time and space switching created mechanically, and as per defining a sequence, in other words, defining how the sequence interprets the coherence in the film, the point of view of analysts is required. Therefore, in the present analysis disruptive points on the plot appear, so we introduce the concept of "episode" first to show the coherence of story continuity depicted in scenes where events and states occur. The plot development of *The Land of Hope* is made up in style of 4 episodes turnover, so it is appropriate to determine that the first sequence is setup when the depiction switches from one episode to another. As the concept of "episode" is introduced, in Table 1 show the hierarchal relationship of the units and which functions are realized in elements of each sequence in different episodes.

*Table 1. Distribution to episode and identification of functions in episode of each sequence constituting "The Land of Hope"*

| Seq. No. | Scene No. | Shot No. | Distribution to Episode | Sequence Summary |
|---|---|---|---|---|
| | from ⇒ to | from ⇒ to | Functions in Episode | |
| 1 | 1 ⇒ 16 | 1 ⇒ 31 | (Setting of entire narrative) | Each character's daily life |
| | (16 scenes) | (31 shots) | - | |
| 2 | 17 ⇒ 33 | 32 ⇒ 57 | (Theme of entire narrative) | Nagashima great earthquake occurs, causing a tsunami and nuclear disaster in the same manner as at Fukushima |
| | (17 scenes) | (26 shots) | - | |
| 3 | 34 ⇒ 46 | 58 ⇒ 122 | Upper Episode | All residents within a 20 kilometer radius of the nuclear reactor are compulsorily evacuated |
| | (13 scenes) | (65 shots) | Outcome | |
| 4 | 47 ⇒ 52 | 123 ⇒ 171 | Upper Episode | Yoichi and Izumi move voluntarily to a locality away from Oba |
| | (6 scenes) | (49 shots) | Outcome | |
| 5 | 53 ⇒ 52 | 172 ⇒ 184 | Episode No.1 | The situation of the Suzuki household who has compulsorily evacuated to the gymnasium |
| | (1 scene) | (13 shots) | Setting | |
| 6 | 54 ⇒ 58 | 185 ⇒ 214 | Episode No.2 | Yasuhiko and Chieko's daily life after the Nagashima great earthquake and tsunami, and nuclear disaster |
| | (5 scenes) | (30 shots) | Setting | |
| 7 | 59 ⇒ 61 | 215 ⇒ 244 | Episode No.1 | The situation of the Suzuki household who has compulsorily evacuated to the gymnasium |
| | (3 scenes) | (30 shots) | Setting | |
| 8 | 62 ⇒ 76 | 245 ⇒ 411 | Episode No.3 | The situation of Yoichi and Izumi who has voluntarily moved to a locality away from Oba |
| | (15 scenes) | (167 shots) | Setting | |
| 9 | 77 ⇒ 52 | 412 ⇒ 434 | Episode No.1 | The situation of Mitsuru and Yoko in the stricken area seeking Yoko's parents |
| | (1 scene) | (23 shots) | Attempt | |
| 10 | 78 ⇒ 79 | 435 ⇒ 477 | Episode No.4 | Yoichi calls on Yasuhiko, and Yasuhiko persuades Yoichi to take refuge in the distance |
| | (2 scenes) | (43 shots) | Attempt | |

*continued on following page*

*Table 1. Continued*

| Seq. No. | Scene No. from ⇒ to | Shot No. from ⇒ to | Distribution to Episode / Functions in Episode | Sequence Summary |
|---|---|---|---|---|
| 11 | 80 ⇒ 86 (7 scenes) | 478 ⇒ 528 (51 shots) | Episode No.3 / State | The situation of Yoichi and Izumi who has voluntarily moved to a locality away from Oba |
| 12 | 87 ⇒ 88 (2 scenes) | 529 ⇒ 540 (12 shots) | Episode No.1 / State | The situation of the Suzuki household who has compulsorily evacuated to the gymnasium |
| 13 | 89 ⇒ 91 (3 scenes) | 541 ⇒ 598 (58 shots) | Episode No.2 / Event | The situation of Yasuhiko and Chieko who receive a call from the staff of the government office |
| 14 | 92 ⇒ 52 (1 scene) | 599 ⇒ 601 (3 shots) | Episode No.1 / Event | The situation of Mitsuru and Yoko who are going to enter the "Entry Prohibited" zone |
| 15 | 93 ⇒ 98 (6 scenes) | 602 ⇒ 689 (88 shots) | Episode No.4 / Event | The situation of Yasuhiko and Chieko who receive a second call from the staff of the government office with Yoichi |
| 16 | 99 ⇒ 101 (3 scenes) | 690 ⇒ 755 (66 shots) | Episode No.2 / Event | From Yasuhiko and Chieko's daily life to the disappearance of Chieko |
| 17 | 102 ⇒ 103 (2 scenes) | 756 ⇒ 770 (15 shots) | Episode No.1 / State | The situation of Mitsuru and Yoko in the stricken area seeking Yoko's parents |
| 18 | 104 ⇒ 108 (5 scenes) | 771 ⇒ 801 (31 shots) | Episode No.3 / State | The situation of Yoichi and Izumi who has voluntarily moved to a locality away from Oba |
| 19 | 109 ⇒ 113 (5 scenes) | 802 ⇒ 870 (69 shots) | Episode No.4 / Event | The situation of Yasuhiko and Chieko who receive a final call from Yoichi and Izumi |
| 20 | 114 ⇒ 119 (6 scenes) | 871 ⇒ 924 (54 shots) | Episode No.2 / Outcome / Resolution | The shooting of cattle by Yasuhiko, and the double suicide of Yasuhiko and Chieko |
| 21 | 120 ⇒ 121 (2 scenes) | 925 ⇒ 966 (42 shots) | Episode No.3 / Outcome / Desired State | The situation of Yoichi and Izumi who are taking taking refuge in the distance from Oba |
| 22 | 122 ⇒ 522 (1 scenes) | 967 ⇒ 972 (6 shots) | Episode No.1 / Outcome / Subgoal | The situation of Mitsuru and Yoko in the stricken area seeking Yoko's parents |

Since sequences No. 1 and 2 correspond to the setting of entire narrative, they do not belong to any episode. Sequences No.3 and 4 are upper moments occurred before branching of episodes No.1–4, they are responsible for small consequences and new events occurred in the theme of the film. Then, sequences No.5–22 belong to one of the 4 episodes. They are elements which play any functions in sequences of different episodes as described in "Function in episode" column, so the 4 episodes are considered the elements of entire plot of narrative. Also, each sequence were named the functions with reference to the terms used in story grammar of Thorndyke (1977).[23]

### *Step 2: Description of the Diagram*

Subsequently, the 22 units that were identified as a sequence in Step 1 will be linked from the point of view of causality, then the procedure that draws the diagram for overviewing the entire narrative structure is shown. As shown in Table 1, the sequence of *The Land of Hope* interchanges characters with the variations in time and space, is split at the switching point of the multiple episodes constituting the film.

In order to draw a diagram, sequences are conveniently utile. Basically, the sequences are arranged from the top downwards and linked in numerical order. In response to the event that the earthquake occurred in sequence No.2, after the outcome of "seek refuge" is drawn in sequence No.3 and sequence No.4, since each pair is branched to the lower episode that narrate the arduous situation that was faced, it is judged by the character that appears and place each sequence in the corresponding episode chain (Figure 2).

This procedure is repeated until all the sequences have been arranged on the diagram, then the sequences are connected with arrows to indicate their relationships. Refer to the Symbol Legend in Figure 2. First, the arrow labeled "sequential chain," which connect the 22 sequences in ascending order, indicate the actual progression of the visual images (order in which the events are presented). The arrows "each pair's episode," which connects the sequences along each chain, indicate the flow of the episodes comprising *The Land of Hope*. However, the three sequences on the episode of Ono household chain have a strong causal relationship with the sequences on the episode of Yasuhiko & Chieko chain and the episode of Yoichi & Izumi chain. As such, they have been linked to other sequences with "causal chain" arrows or with "sequential chain" arrows, but not with the "each pair's episode" arrows. The numbers above each sequence denote the starting point of the sequence within the film's running time. The circle for each sequence come in nine sizes that correspond with the length of the sequence: the larger the circle, the longer the sequence.

## Interpretation of the Narrative Structure of "The Land of Hope"

The Setting and Theme from the opening to be presented until sequence No.4 are the introductory part of the entire film. Here the presented theme with the plot until greeting the resolution after sequence No.20, is composed of 4 episodes that run in parallel and proceed in interlaced manner after sequence No.5. The episode of Yasuhiko & Chieko (sequence No.6–) is the main episode of *The Land of Hope*, the episode of Yoichi & Izumi, son of Yasuhiko (sequence No.8–), is a sub-episode that is told in density, second only to the main episode. Including the episode of Ono household (sequence No.10–) that plays a role in connecting the prior two episodes, for the Ono household side episode branched into 3, the episode of Mitsuru & Yoko (sequence No.5–) that forced the saved Suzuki household side is relatively short and is inserted contrastingly, thus the plot progresses in such a rhythm. *The Land of Hope* is a film where it is possible to extract very clearly the structural description that comprise the entire narrative.

## Significance and Merit of the Present Analysis

Through a two-step procedure, structural analysis of narrative of the film *The Land of Hope* was shown. The significance of showing this on one film is that, if a methodology that draws a diagram for overviewing the entire structure of the long text can be established for a film consisting of a plurality of symbol elements, films with a variety of narrative and visual representation with ingenious formats can also be analyzed with the same procedures, putting such film in the context of narratology and film cognition research would be opened. In the case of long audiovisual text, a shot is obviously used as a unit to draw a diagram, as a scene is cumbersome and too granulated, the point is to use a sequence, yet unlike a shot or scene, a sequence differs in that the switching point cannot be determined physically. What becomes necessary is, the procedure to identify each sequence's functional element in the narrative structure shown in Step 1. In the present analysis, splitting the sequence at the switching point of the episode was

*Figure 2. Diagram of the narrative structure of "The Land of Hope"*

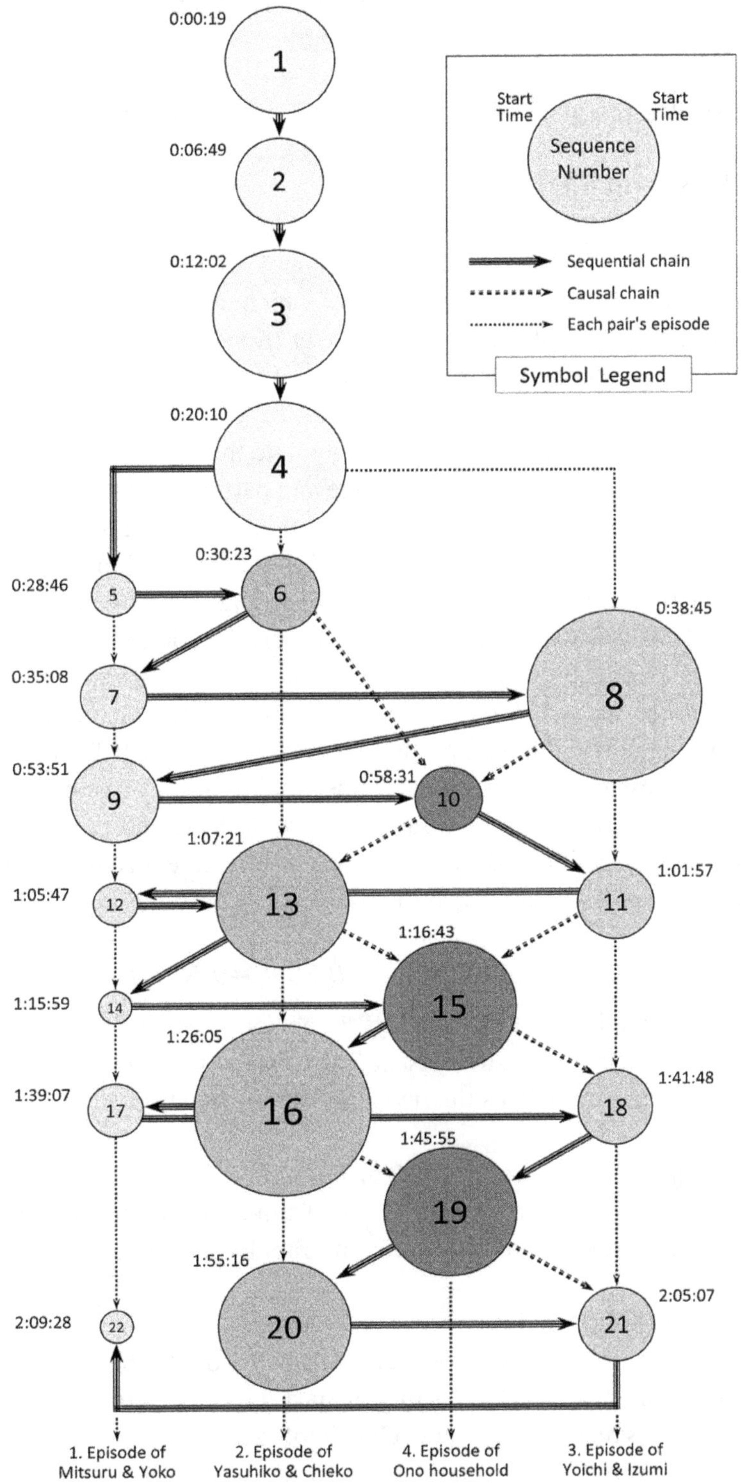

successful. There is a necessity to flexibly arrange decomposition rules of sequences depending on the film, however the merit of the methodology is that it can ensure a reference for extracting the abstract unity which is a sequence simulated by the present analysis.

## Analysis of Predictive Cognitive Effects of "The Land of Hope"

### Rhetoric to Fuse Fact and Fiction

Although *The Land of Hope* is a fictional film, Sono has made it clear through his own words that it is a film with a strong non-fictional color, the groundwork of which was laid through frequent personal visits to Fukushima in the wake of the disaster of March 11, 2011 (Sono, 2012a). The setting and details of the film abundantly reflect the people Sono met on his visits to Fukushima, and the sights he saw there: a house that is divided half way down its garden into the part inside the 20km evacuation area and the part outside it; the dairy farmer who killed himself, leaving a note that said 'If only the nuclear plant didn't exist'; a family whose members had to leave their home and part with one another (Sono, 2012b). Paradoxically, the information and insights gleaned in Fukushima, which heighten the realism of *The Land of Hope*, allow the film to transcend the local plight, and to set the mind of any Japanese viewer astir.

With such thorough preliminary interviews and investigation, it would have been possible to create a documentary. The reason that Sono chose to insist on fiction was to preserve the ethical standpoint granted to the creator by maintaining a certain distance with the real-life Fukushima, and to attempt to express things that were only achievable through fiction. Sono has stated that films should not be made by imagination alone and that he prevented himself from taking artistic leaps of imagination in this film by assimilating stories and lines told to him by his interviewees; and he chose fiction because if he were to document the disaster, he would have had to leave out too much (Sono & Sato, 2012). The following section examines the shots of effective visually in two specific scenes in order to explore how such thoughts manifested themselves in representation.

#### *Visualization of the Invisible: In Sequence No.8 (0:38:45–0:53:50)*

Sequence No.8 is a corresponding part of "Setting" in episode No.3 which expands sequence No.22 to the Desired State. It is becomes the strongest factor to start the so-called voluntary evacuation to far-away of Yoichi and Izumi, it visualizes the invisible fear of radiation.

- **Plot toward the Applicable Scene (Scene No. 71–):**
  In the hospital waiting room, Izumi hears a story from another expectant mother, whose breast milk was found to contain traces of cesium. Izumi rapidly develops a terror of internal exposure to radiation.
- **Rhetoric of the Shot (Shot No. 322):**
  As she returns home, radioactive particles, usually not visible to the naked eye, are seen through Izumi's eyes, shown as white specks floating against a red background. This sight, shown from Izumi's perspective, was realized through CG technology (Figure 3).

*Figure 3. Screen capture (0:47:11) (© "Kibô-no Kuni" Production Partnership, 2012). Radioactive particles which are seen through Izumi's eyes, shown as white specks floating against a red background.*

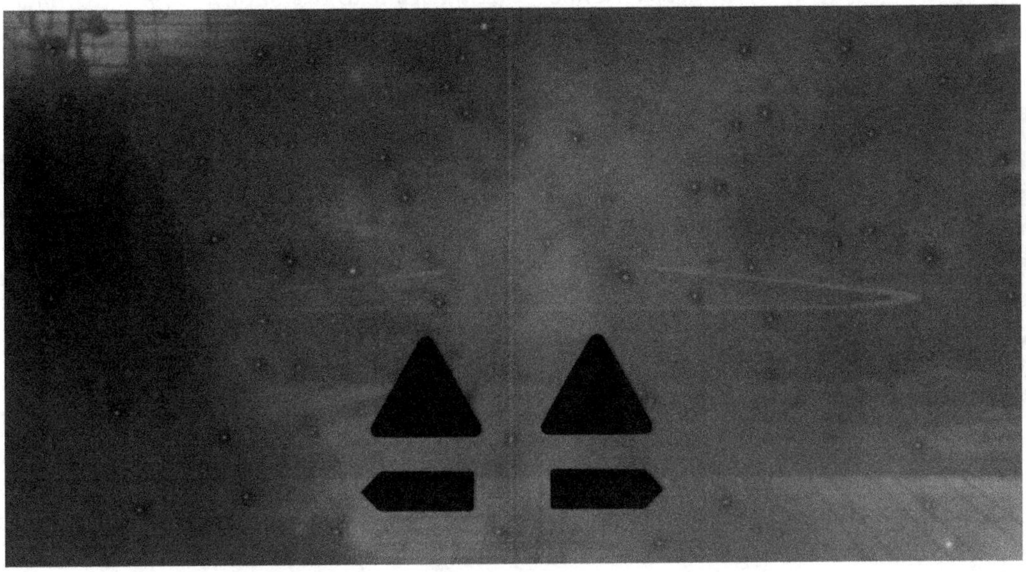

### *Visualization of Radioactivity Metaphor: In Sequence No. 10 (0:58:31–1:01:56)*

Sequence No.10 is a corresponding part of "Attempt" in episode No.4 with entanglement Yasuhiko & Chieko and Yoichi & Izumi. In order to enhance the persuasiveness of strongly encouraging words of Yasuhiko to Yoichi about the evacuation, the metaphor of unavoidable fact that is not to be able to escape from radioactivity is visualized.

- **Plot toward the Applicable Scene (Scene No. 78–):**
  Yoichi comes to tell Yasuhiko that he has decided to take his pregnant wife Izumi from their temporary shelter to resettle somewhere further away.
- **Rhetoric of the Shot (Shot No. 475):**
  Yasuhiko and his wife sit facing Yoichi, separated by a fence approximately 1.0 meters tall with stakes at 30 centimeter intervals that have been hammered down. This is an image shot combined with dialogue (Figure 4).
- **Dialogue:**
  **Yasuhiko:** *Life hammers many stakes into our lives. This time, radioactivity was that stake. [...] Stakes are a terrible enemy. Perhaps we can't avoid the stakes altogether. But there are stakes that we can run away from. So run. Running away is a sign of strength. Run away, because you're strong.*

The shots in Figures 4 and 5, which achieve visual representations that are inconceivable in reality, serve as perfect examples of the visualization technique that is only possible with fictional films. Visualization of invisible things and metaphors are a form of the aforementioned rhetoric that involves irrational cutting. If the knowledge that Ogawa and Kanai (2013) suggested is proper, then the shots in Figures 4 and 5 will stimulate viewers' conceptual thought (concept reflection). But with the film such

*Figure 4. Screen capture (1:01:39) (© "Kibô-no Kuni" Production Partnership, 2012). Yasuhiko and his wife sit facing Yoichi, separated by a fence with stakes that have been hammered down.*

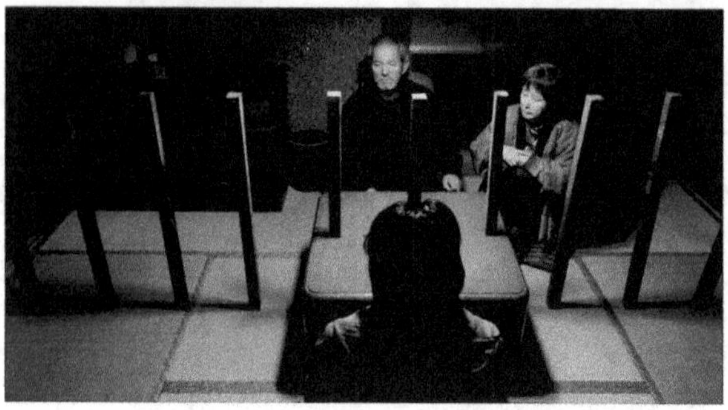

*Figure 5. Screen capture (1:37:44) (© "Kibô-no Kuni" Production Partnership, 2012). Yasuhiko and Chieko are shown from a distance, singing the folk song and dancing together.*

as *The Land of Hope*, in which the story and rhetoric are well-balanced and not necessarily in a trade-off relationship, how in fact will cognition toward enjoyment and cognition induced by irrational cutting be related? This is an issue that requires investigation, applicable as it is to other films of a similar characteristics. If, hypothetically, we postulate that storyline is rooted in facts, and that rhetoric is rooted in fiction, and viewers of *The Land of Hope* exhibit no clear trend with regard to either type of cognition, it may prove the effectiveness of the rhetoric of this film, which merges fact with fiction.

## Enjoyment Caused by Love and Death

Besides rhetoric that melds fact and fiction, there is another angle that should be analyzed, and that is the pervasive theme of love – a prevalent theme in Sono's oeuvre. It has been portrayed in all its aberrations with an utterly abnormal directorial touch, in works such as *Love Exposure*, *Cold Fish* and *Guilty of Romance* that were awarded at film festivals. The love depicted in *The Land of Hope*, however, is an orthodox love without a hint of deviancy, and the Sono hallmarks seem atypically absent. But perhaps this is a somewhat shortsighted view. According to Sono, his intention in *The Land of Hope* was to demonstrate how defiance may be shown at the individual level (Sono, 2012b). The film's ending of love to the death is a symbol of individual resistance to the status quo, individuals baring fangs against the multitudes.

If Sono's typical eccentric depiction of sex is a representation of ultimate love as seen from an *erotic* perspective – then the relationship between Yasuhiko and Chieko and its fate could be said to be a representation of its diametric opposite, *the other* ultimate love. This love, then, that is represented with a serene touch that is 'unlike Sono' at first glance, is in fact very much 'like Sono' – like the man whose motto is to go off far in an extreme direction (Matsue & Yoshida, 2012). The shots in two specific scenes will be examined here as well.

### *Bon Festival Dance and Walking toward the Sunset: in Sequence No.16 (1:26:05–1:45:54)*

Sequence No.16 in episode No.2 corresponds to sequence No.20 for Yasuhiko and Chieko inserted as an opposite "Event" before greeting the outcome of the tragic love. Sunset ahead of two loved characters walking is a metaphorical representation of hope; this shot symbolizes the title of this film.

- **Plot toward the Applicable Scene (Scene No. 100–):**
  One day, drawn by the sound of festive music, Chieko goes missing. When Yasuhiko calls her and receives no response, he realizes she is missing and races about searching, but to no avail. Finally he takes the car and drives through town for searching her.
- **Rhetoric toward the Applicable Shot (Shot No. 754–755):**
  The dramatic music fades out and is replaced by a traditional folk song. Chieko, wearing yukata, is shown center screen, dancing a festive dance, which leads into a full screen view from a side angle. Yasuhiko is seen to alight. The scene cuts to Yasuhiko's perspective, where he can see Chieko dancing. They are shown from a distance, singing the folk song and dancing together, for around 30 seconds (Figure 5).
- **Dialogue:**
  **Yasuhiko:** *Hey Chieko!! Hey…!!"*
  **Chieko:** *Oh, dad!!*
  **Yasuhiko:** *Chieko, you have come very in the distance!! Let's go home.*
  **Chieko:** *Let's dance a little more!! Ready? cha-chan-ga-chan….* (Figure 5).
  After they are shown embracing, Chieko pesters Yasuhiko into piggybacking her, and they walk towards the sunset, with Yasuhiko saying,
  **Yasuhiko:** *Oh, you got heavy….* (Figure 6).

### *Love and Death: In Sequence No. 20 (1:55:16–2:05:06)*

Sequence No.20 corresponds to "Outcome" of the episode of Yasuhiko & Chieko and "Resolution" of the entire narrative at the same time. It contrasts the depiction of hope in sequence No.16, and represents the feeling of hopelessness of two characters who love each other but are forced to choose death.

*Figure 6. Screen capture (1:38:47) (© "Kibô-no Kuni" Production Partnership, 2012). Chieko pesters Yasuhiko into piggybacking her, and they are walking towards the sunset.*

- **Plot toward the Applicable Scene (Scene No. 119–):**
  Chieko is shown from behind, stooped by the flowerbed, digging the ground. Yasuhiko walking towards her from behind the no-entry fence. The only sound is of Chieko digging, as he approaches silently from behind, stopping at her rear and staring at her back. Then he turns the pistol on Chieko, ready to fire (Figure7).
- **Rhetoric toward the Applicable Shot (Shot No. 896–912):**
  The colorful flower bed which always does frame in. A camera is sometimes replaced by bird's eye view. The contrast between Chieko's innocent manner and Yasuhiko's tragical appearance is effective acting direction. Music is not inserted.
- **Dialogue:**
  **Yasuhiko:** *Chieko, always together..., let's be together forever, OK?*
  **Chieko:** *What do you say?, Always together, together forever, Of course*
  **Yasuhiko:** *All right. ...I love you.*
  **Chieko:** *Gee..., what do you say...?*
  They embrace again although their eyes do not meet.
  **Yasuhiko:** *Shall we die?*
  **Chieko:** *OK. If with dad, I can die. I am all right anytime....*
  **Yasuhiko:** *I'm sorry..."*
  **Chieko:** *Don't say sorry.... At any time, don't say sorry. Always we are together.*
  **Yasuhiko:** *Shall we die?*
  **Chieko:** *We shall die?*
  **Yasuhiko:** *...Yes...*
  **Chieko:** *OK. We shall die....* (Figure 8).

The theme of love is woven into each of the episodes in Figure 3, along with their respective dire straits; but it is only the "episode of Yasuhiko & Chieko" (Sequence No.6–) in which ultimate love is consummated in death. Yoichi and Izumi are last seen smiling and saying, "It's fine as long as there's love" (Sequence No.21, Scene No.121, Shot No.964); Mitsuru and Yoko on the land in the final scene of the film, repeating the words "One step, one step..." like an incantation (Sequence No.22, Scene

*Figure 7. Screen capture (2:01:16) (© "Kibô-no Kuni" Production Partnership, 2012). Chieko who has not noticed Yasuhiko aiming the pistol at her.*

*Figure 8. Screen capture (2:03:30) (© "Kibô-no Kuni" Production Partnership, 2012). Yasuhiko proposes death "Shall we die?" Chieko assents readily, though with a sad expression "OK."*

No.122, Shot No.971). According to Sono, it is up to the viewer to decide whether this ending, in which hope and despair intermingle, is an ending of hope (Sono, 2012b).

From around Sequence No.16 when the prelude, which leads to the climax at Sequence No. 20, begins to play, the viewer's cognition toward enjoyment will likely start to rise willy-nilly, as he/she empathize with each pair and await the denouement with bated breath. It is also clear that the aforementioned sequences containing rhetoric based on effective irrational cutting, and these sequences devoted to enjoyment were placed away from each other within the narrative structure. However, what if we look at cognition of *The Land of Hope* as an entire film, rather than its distinctive sequences and scenes? The technique of juxtaposing the elderly couple; Yasuhiko and Chieko compelled by their mutual love to take their own lives, and the young couples; Yoichi and Izumi, Mitsuru and Yoko deciding to live after confirming their love – or the rhetoric triggered by irrational cutting that was employed to make the feelings of each pair more convincing – can they be said to have served enjoyment? Or did they leave an impact that is not picked up by enjoyment? It is the task of film cognition research to assess such matters.

## FUTURE RESEARCH DIRECTIONS

The procedures of structural analysis of narrative, shown through simulation analysis in the first half of this chapter, will be applied to some other films, in order to verify the usability and versatility of the methodology. Once a number of patterns in the decomposition criteria of sequences by this process is found, the systematical analysis utility of this methodology will be further ensured. Moreover, the analysis of the film's entire structure and, with respect to the hypothesis of the film cognition research that is posited by fusing a predictive analysis of the cognitive effects of localized representation shown in the second half of this chapter will be done, then carry out the actual verification experiment, the author intend to complete this series of research process.

Cognition toward narrative moving image can always shed light on visual representation itself; visual representation is always created with a view to the cognitive effect it will trigger. They are two sides of the same coin, and so film analysis should always precede film cognition research in order to provide an angle to examine; and the knowledge and models obtained in film cognition research should always be utilized as perspectives in film analysis. Film analysis carried out from such perspectives can then contribute in return to constructing hypotheses for modifying and enhancing new models in film cognition research. If film analysis and film cognition research build a complementary relationship, it can reveal new knowledge and understanding that close in on the essence of film-viewing. Then, perhaps by applying that knowledge in actual film making, it might advance production of more essential and creative films. This is the direction that research should aim for in the future.

## CONCLUSION

In the first place, this chapter has attempted to describe the narrative structure by implementing a structural analysis of narrative of the Japanese film *The Land of Hope*, which serves as the formal aspect of the audiovisual long text consisting of multiple symbols. In the second place, for the narrative content that cannot be fully explained by the structural analysis of narrative, this chapter has attempted to make a film analyzing description while quoting the knowledge already suggested from film cognition research by the author. Through the practical simulation of applying structural analysis of narrative on films, it has suggested that this methodology that originally used only on natural language texts also had the possibility of applying on audiovisual text. Moreover, through the restoration of existing knowledge gained from film cognition research on the sketch of the content deployed while referring to the diagram based on the structural analysis of narrative, a part of the research via cognitive science approach on narratology and film studies has been specifically suggested. This chapter shows a precious example for studies of the necessity of comprehensive film analysis both from the formal aspects and content.

## REFERENCES

Appel, M. (2008). Manche mögen's heiß. Ergebnisse der deutschsprachigen Version eines Instruments zur Erfassung des Emotionsmotivs[Some like it hot. Results of the German language version of an instrument for the assessment of the need for affect]. *Diagnostica*, *54*(1), 2–15. doi:10.1026/0012-1924.54.1.2

Bakhtin, M. M. (1989). *Marxism and the philosophy of language* (T. Kuwano, Trans.). Tokyo, Japan: Miraisha. (Original work published 1929)

Barthes, R. (1979). *Introduction à l'analyse structurale des récits* (H. Hanawa, Trans.). Tokyo, Japan: Misuzu Shobo. (Original work published 1966)

de Wied, M., Zillmann, D., & Ordman, V. (1994). The role of empathic distress in the enjoyment of cinematic tragedy. *Poetics*, *23*(1-2), 91–106. doi:10.1016/0304-422X(94)00010-4

Fletcher, C. R., & Bloom, C. P. (1988). Causal reasoning in the comprehension of simple narrative texts. *Journal of Memory and Language*, *27*(3), 235–244. doi:10.1016/0749-596X(88)90052-6

Genette, G. (1985). *Narrative discourse* (H. Hanawa & R. Izumi, Trans.). Tokyo, Japan: Suiseisha. (Original work published 1972)

Green, M. C., Brock, T. C., & Kaufman, G. E. (2004). Understanding media enjoyment: The role of transportation into narrative worlds. *Communication Theory*, *14*(4), 311–327. doi:10.1111/j.1468-2885.2004.tb00317.x

Green, M. C., Kass, S., Carrey, J., Herzig, B., Feeney, R., & Sabini, J. (2008). Transportation across media: Repeated exposure to print and film. *Media Psychology*, *11*(4), 512–539. doi:10.1080/15213260802492000

Hayami, Y. (2013). *Akuma no DNA - Sono Sion* [Devil's DNA - Sion Sono]. Tokyo, Japan: Shodensha Publishing.

Iran-Nejad, A. (1987). Cognitive and affective causes of interest and liking. *Journal of Educational Psychology*, *79*(2), 120–130. doi:10.1037/0022-0663.79.2.120

Kintsch, W. (1980). Learning from text, levels of comprehension, or - Why anyone would read a story anyway. *Poetics*, *9*(1-3), 87–98. doi:10.1016/0304-422X(80)90013-3

Kintsch, W. (1992). How readers construct situation models for stories: The role of syntactic cues and causal inferences. In A. F. Healy, S. M. Kosslyn, & R. M. Shiffrin (Eds.), *Essays in honor of William K. Estes* (pp. 261–278). Hillsdale, NJ: Lawrence Erlbaum Associates, Inc.

Maio, G. R., & Esses, V. M. (2001). The need for affect: Individual differences in the motivation to approach or avoid emotions. *Journal of Personality*, *69*(4), 583–615. doi:10.1111/1467-6494.694156 PMID:11497031

Matsue, T., & Yoshida, M. (2012). *Sono Sion eiga zenkenkyu 1985-2012* [Study of all "A SONO SION'S FILM"s 1985-2012]. Tokyo, Japan: Yosensha.

Ogata, T. (2007). To the rhetoric of story from Propp: Centering around the rhetoric of de-composition and recomposition. *Cognitive Studies*, *14*(4), 532–558.

Ogata, T., Hori, K., & Ohsuga, S. (1996). An analysis of narrative structure and generation process for narrative generation system. *Cognitive Studies*, *3*(1), 72–109.

Ogawa, Y. (2011). A cognitive-affective mechanism concerning enjoyment of a television drama: Verification and consideration of paradoxical enjoyment by empathy for the characters. *Cognitive Studies*, *18*(1), 79–99.

Ogawa, Y., & Kanai, A. (2013). Rhetoric of biopic and viewer's reconsideration: A verification that how TARO's enjoyment and YUMEJI's irrational cutting cause an effect in concept reconsideration. *Cognitive Studies*, *20*(2), 224–248.

Oliver, M. B. (1993). Exploring the paradox of the enjoyment of sad films. *Human Communication Research*, *19*(3), 315–342. doi:10.1111/j.1468-2958.1993.tb00304.x

Oliver, M. B. (2007). Appreciation as audience response: The case of tragic, poignant, and touching entertainment. In A. Bartsch, J. Eder, & K. Fahlenbrach (Eds.), *Audiovisuelle Emotionen* (pp. 207–219). Köln, Germany: Halem.

Oliver, M. B. (2008). Tender affective states as predictors of entertainment preference. *Journal of Communication*, *58*(1), 40–U14. doi:10.1111/j.1460-2466.2007.00373.x

Oliver, M. B., Weaver, J. B. III, & Sargent, S. L. (2000). An examination of factors related to sex differences in enjoyment of sad films. *Journal of Broadcasting & Electronic Media*, *44*(2), 282–300. doi:10.1207/s15506878jobem4402_8

Propp, V. (1987). *Morphology of the folktale* (S. Kitaoka & M. Fukuda, Trans.). Tokyo, Japan: Suiseisha. (Original work published 1928)

Raney, A. A. (2002). Moral judgment as a predictor of enjoyment of crime drama. *Media Psychology*, *4*(4), 305–322. doi:10.1207/S1532785XMEP0404_01

Raney, A. A. (2004). Expanding disposition theory: Reconsidering character liking, moral evaluations, and enjoyment. *Communication Theory*, *14*(4), 348–369. doi:10.1111/j.1468-2885.2004.tb00319.x

Raney, A. A. (2005). Punishing media criminals and moral judgment: The impact on enjoyment. *Media Psychology*, *7*(2), 145–163. doi:10.1207/S1532785XMEP0702_2

Raney, A. A., & Bryant, J. (2002). Moral judgment and crime drama: An integrated theory of enjoyment. *Journal of Communication*, *52*(2), 402–415. doi:10.1111/j.1460-2466.2002.tb02552.x

Rumelhart, D. E. (1975). Notes on a schema for stories. In D. G. Bobrow & A. Collins (Eds.), *Representation and understanding: Studies in cognitive science* (pp. 211–236). New York, NY: Academic Press.

Schank, R. C. (1979). Interestingness: Controlling inferences. *Artificial Intelligence*, *12*(3), 273–297. doi:10.1016/0004-3702(79)90009-2

Shklovsky, V. (1971). *Theory of prose* (T. Mizuno, Trans.). Tokyo, Japan: Serica Shobo. (Original work published 1925)

Sono, S. (2012a). *Kibô no Kuni* [The Land of Hope]. Tokyo, Japan: Little More.

Sono, S. (2012b). Kibô no Kuni - Mada owatteinai genpatsu no mondai[The Land of Hope -Problem of the nuclear disaster which has not been yet over]. *Tsukuru*, *42*(8), 128–133.

Sono, S., & Oshima, A. (2015). Interview: Ore ha itan jya-nai[Interview: I am not a heretic]. *Bungakukai*, *69*(11), 26–41.

Sono, S., & Sato, Y. (2012, October). Kibô no Kuni long interview - Sono Sion, genpatsu wo egaku[The Land of Hope long interview - Sion Sono depict a nuclear disaster]. *Kinema Junpo*, *1622*, 87–91.

Sundermeier, B. A., Van den Broek, P., & Zwaan, R. A. (2005). Causal coherence and the availability of locations and objects during narrative comprehension. *Memory & Cognition*, *33*(3), 462–470. doi:10.3758/BF03193063 PMID:16156181

Tapiero, I., van den Broek, P., & Quintana, M. P. (2002). The mental representation of narrative texts as networks: The role of necessity and sufficiency in the detection of different types of causal relations. *Discourse Processes*, *34*(3), 237–258. doi:10.1207/S15326950DP3403_1

Thorndyke, P. W. (1977). Cognitive structures in comprehension and memory of narrative discourse. *Cognitive Psychology*, *9*(1), 77–110. doi:10.1016/0010-0285(77)90005-6

Trabasso, T., & Wiley, J. (2005). Goal plans of action and inferences during comprehension of narratives. *Discourse Processes*, *39*(2&3), 129–164. doi:10.1080/0163853X.2005.9651677

Vorderer, P., Klimmt, C., & Ritterfeld, U. (2004). Enjoyment: At the heart of media entertainment. *Communication Theory*, *14*(4), 388–408. doi:10.1111/j.1468-2885.2004.tb00321.x

Zillmann, D. (1998). Does tragic drama have redeeming value? *Siegener Periodikum für Internationale Literaturwissenschaft*, *16*, 1–11.

Zwaan, R. A., & Radvansky, G. A. (1998). Situation models in language comprehension and memory. *Psychological Bulletin*, *123*(2), 162–185. doi:10.1037/0033-2909.123.2.162 PMID:9522683

## KEY TERMS AND DEFINITIONS

**Enjoyment:** One of the cognitive effects which viewers receive from any narrative with a clear storyline. The main component of this cognitive effect is empathy.

**Fact:** Any actual event itself which has really occurred, and has not been edited or processed for representation through the media.

**Fiction:** Any story which has not really occurred, or any fact that is dramatized for representation through the media.

**Love:** Both a passive emotion that seeks to accept the object of affection in its entirety and an active emotion that vigorously pursues the object of affection.

**Narrative:** One whole entailing structure composed of a number of small elements which are not necessarily events. They are connected by some kind of criteria, for example in a temporal chain, a causal chain, and so on. Narrative is a broader concept of story.

**Sion Sono:** A director, scriptwriter, poet, and performer who was born in Aichi prefecture in Japan in 1961.

**Story:** A sequential chain composed of multiple events according to the order in which they occurred.

**Structural Analysis of Narrative:** A method of analysis which seeks to systematically schematize the functional linkage relationships between each element constituting a narrative.

**Visualization:** To make a visual representation of something such as by photography, imaging or painting.

## ENDNOTES

1 This section is described in reference to what Sion Sono talked about in "Hello from Studio Park" that was broadcasted on December 20, 2011 by NHK (Japan Broadcasting Corporation) General TV. This program cannot be shown in NHK archives as of July, 2015.

2 Story grammar is a theory which expressed rule changes in narrative structure, for example it created the following formula: "Setting → Characters + Location + Time" (Phase 2), "Episode → Subgoal + Attempt + Outcome" (Phase 5). This formula is read as "left side components make the right side components." Since the elements of upper phase are shifted to the left in the bottom phase, if we look at the right composition we will understand the terms in the left.

3 "Plot" means the chain of events and the state of characters who were projected on the screen. In contrast, it is generally called "story" refers to the chain of events that is assumed to have occurred to the characters including the time that is not projected on the screen. It should be noted that the word "story" in "story grammar" means "narrative" in this chapter.

# Chapter 14
# You Tell Me in Emojis

**Tüge T. Gülşen**
*Istanbul Bilgi University, Turkey*

## ABSTRACT

*As communication is predominantly realized on digital platforms, both the language used and the way actors of communicative events create and perceive messages have changed and taken new forms and functions. Emoticons, which have been transformed into emojis, have become a new language phenomenon that promise new research areas in various fields from linguistics to media studies, cognitive science to narrative studies. This chapter aims at exploring how computer users have integrated emojis in their daily narrative practices not only as emotive devices but also as conceptual tools and create a new mode of language to communicate their stories on digital platforms.*

## INTRODUCTION

The growing interest in communication brought the query about how messages are constructed and people interpret and make meaning out of messages. Towards the second half of the 20th century, scholars with the interest to understand how the process of communication between different agents is realized proposed communication models. They in fact aim at "identifying the elements of a process and then suggesting how, through connection, they work in a generalized way" (Hill, 2007, p.6). In the course of time, as new paradigms in communication practices emerged, these models evolved, and the language constructed and reconstructed by the participants of communicative processes has gone through major transformations in the course of time. With the emergence of digital technologies both the communication models together with the participants and the language and certainly the discursive features of communicative events that they utilize have taken new forms and meanings. In daily communicative practices, people started constructing and comprehending messages in different forms on different digital platforms. With the spread of digital messaging platforms that enable users to send synchronous and asynchronous messages, users have transformed their everyday literacy practices and adapted their multimodal literacy experiences to messaging systems. Today, it is certainly common that users construct linguistic texts that are accompanied by visual or rather iconic and even pictorial texts to communicate both emotive

DOI: 10.4018/978-1-5225-0432-0.ch014

Copyright © 2016, IGI Global. Copying or distributing in print or electronic forms without written permission of IGI Global is prohibited.

and conceptual messages. It is evident that in majority of digital communities, emojis have become an indispensable language unit utilized to communicate meanings.

This paper is going to focus on the language or coding system utilized in messaging systems that has evolved into multi-modal systems and the participants' attachment to such systems, one of which is the emojis that almost every user spontaneously and voluntarily use while messaging during their encounters through digital media. Today, emojis, the new icons that refer to various meanings in the digital context, have become one of the means of digital narratives, and emojis have gone further than being merely emotive elements in the construction of digital narrative and started function as semantic units in the language evolving on digital platforms.

# BACKGROUND

## Language and Reality

Ludwig Wittgenstein uses a fascinating metaphor for language, *an ancient city*. He describes language as "a maze of little streets and squares, of old and new houses, and of houses with additions from various periods; and this surrounded by a multitude of new boroughs with straight regular streets and uniform houses" (Wittgenstein, 1986, p.8). This metaphor manifests his conception of language as a logically ordered system that functions as "a form of life", an organic entity. As Litwack (2009) argues, people experience various practices within forms of life, and "they are capable of a very wide range of expression and perception" (p.21). Then, it can be concluded that people have the potential to have different experiences of language use and communication while they are integrated in this organic entity. The term *language-game* used by Wittgenstein refers to "the fact that the *speaking* of language is part of an activity, or of a form of life" (Wittgenstein, 1986, p.11). The language-games are the socially integrated linguistic activities that people are involved in and through which they construct and reconstruct meaning depending upon not only linguistic knowledge (vocabulary, grammar) but also knowledge of socially constructed discursive features of the language. Litwack (2009) refers to the act of 'knowing' as this type of capacity that is demonstrated through actions like answering a question correctly or making a correct description of something. Then, meaning in language is socially constructed, and it is something that is negotiated in the community since "without the possibility of public agreement or correction, it makes no sense to speak of truthful or false assertions of any kind" (p. 17). Wittgenstein in *Tractatus* makes "a distinction between that which can be *said* in language and that which can only be *shown*" (p. 60). Bertrand Russell, in his *Introduction* to *Tractatus* asserts that Wittgenstein is concerned with that "the whole function of language is to have meaning," and "in order that a certain sentence should assert a certain fact there must, however the language may be constructed, be something in common between the structure of the sentence and the structure of the fact" (p. 8).

Wittgenstein was influenced by Schopenhauer during his early years. His use of the term "field of vision" reminds us of Schopenhauer's famous quote "every man takes the limits of his own field of vision for the limits of the world," which reflects the idea that knowledge is limited to human experience, and Wittgenstein brings the use of language in this world of reality. Language whose whole function must be to have and also to convey meaning consists of signs (not necessarily a word) that are attributed meaning within social environment. How do we come to learn the meanings of words like car, building, red (Wittgenstein's example)? It is through being a participant in a social community of language users of the same kind. For example, when a signifier (say the word car) is used to signify an object (signified) is commonly used and agreed upon, language users internalize the sign made up of the word and the object together and learn a piece of knowledge. In the field of vision, whenever a subject sees the same object, s/he knows that it is a car. As Wittgenstein (1986) also states, "the ostensive definition explains the use – the meaning – of the word when the overall role of the word in language is clear" and poses the question if one could define the word *red* by pointing to an object that was not red (p.14). Further, to him, "only someone who already knows how to do something with it can significantly ask a name" (p.15). Thus, one should already have developed the conceptual framework of colours for example in order to understand the ostensive definition of the word *red* and use the word meaningfully. On the other hand, how do we come to learn the meanings of words like sad, difficult, or pain (Wittgenstein's example)? In defining such words, the meaning that the language user intends to convey is a subjective matter, or an object of the sensual world of the subject, "this is not a matter of knowledge, but of the expression of an experience through language, which is a public activity" (Litwack, 2009, p.16). To make it clearer, if someone has pain, s/he groans, makes certain gestures and physical movements, which are also considered as the nonverbal or paralinguistic form of language. Others' understanding of pain would be limited to the physical responses that they can observe on the person with pain because these responses are all part of the language shared in the community. Nevertheless, the one observing another in pain cannot come to *know* what pain that is experienced is; on the contrary, what s/he does could be limited to her/his association of that pain (other's sensual experience) with her/his previous experience of pain, which could naturally be completely different; "I can only *believe* that someone else is in pain, but I *know* it if I am" (Wittgenstein, 1986, p.102). Thus, "I tell someone I am in pain. His attitude to me will then be that of belief; disbelief; suspicion; and so on" (p.103), which sounds Cartesian.

Wittgenstein (1986) states, "when I think in language, there aren't 'meanings' going through my mind in addition to the verbal expression: the language is itself the vehicle of thought" (p.107). It is the verbal language through which we label the nonverbal expressions like gestures, sounds and physical reactions and this is the way we construct thoughts regarding real life. That is, the pain can still be expressed with sounds or physical reactions, but then such sounds or physical reactions would not be a form of language on their own if there were no linguistic language to be used in developing the conceptual framework of *pain* that people could develop on the basis of the comparisons that they can make between their subjective experiences and others'. Then, memory is where people could store those reactions in cases of pain, for example, and language without memory does not exist or vice versa. How about other thoughts? How do we construct images in our minds and then transfer these images into words either in oral, written, and visual forms? How do we come to learn the order of the words and the function words that help us make grammatical connections between words? Man, similar to other creatures, can in a way express say pain, but language is more than this ability; man can construct a socially acceptable and negotiated set of meanings and syntactic rules that are recognised, internalised and actively used to make meaningful utterances. And yes, not all grammatically correct sentences make sense like "I am in Paris and Istanbul now," which does not match with our conception of truth since you cannot be in two different places at the same time. As long as the words selected are connected to each other in the expected order and the set of these words constitutes a truth, it is meaningful. When we go back to our assumption of absence of a verbal language, we should say that thinking without language is impossible. As Wittgenstein (1986) states, the statement that "I believe I can think without words" leads to nothing, and "the analysis oscillates between natural science and grammar" (p.119). The world of truth for man is far more complex to imagine, the subjectivity of man, the self, logic, morality, perception are all components of the human world that constructs its own means of expression which is the language. As Bertrand Russell states, "what we cannot think we cannot think, therefore we also cannot say what we cannot think" (Wittgenstein, 1921, p.16). Thus, human language is not merely a system of codes but a complex logically ordered functioning system.

Human language in physical world is the mode of communication merely between human perception of the physical reality and this complex logically ordered functioning system. While an individual's perception of physical reality constitutes to the language code attributed to that object of meaning, the meaning is conveyed. However, when it comes to emotions, verbal language is inadequate in communicating an emotion, which is nonverbal (Nikolejeva, 2012, p.277). Then, people perceive emotions as represented meanings that trigger related memories stored in memories of previous experiences and they communicate the emotive meanings that they label through verbal language. To illustrate, they label the physical reactions, sounds and gestures as "pain" and the verbal unit "pain" communicates participants' emotive messages. However, this is the meaning-making process in face-to-face encounters. What happens if communication takes place through written language? A writer has to find elaborated verbal expressions to explain the "pain" in the narrative and describe even the nonverbal language elements to convey the meaning. When it comes to children readers, comprehension is easier when the linguistic language is accompanied with visual texts to communicate the emotive messages. "In multimedial texts, embedded mind-reading is in addition conveyed through the interplay of verbal and visual information" (Nikolejeva, 2012, p. 285). Thus, in storybooks, emotions are conveyed through multimodal texts where meanings are constructed through both linguistic and visual texts where both modes of representations contribute to each other rather to create the perception of nonverbal meanings. Today, multimodality is not limited to children's storybooks. The digital platforms make use of multimodal texts, and actors of the contemporary communicative events are both the creators and the readers of such texts and thus meanings.

## Narratives of the Digital World

Narratives can be in very simple terms defined as storytelling. In a narrative situation the primary means is speech at personal level, and in different communities it is the cultural means of storytelling that constitute to the oral tradition of peoples of such communities. When transferred to the written mode, the linguistic coding system is the means through which the narrator tells a story. The stories that derive from the oral traditions display certain discursive features that make up the narratives in that particular culture, and the stories recorded in the written mode manifest different discursive features specific to that language, culture, literary period, and also the writer. The discursive features that construct the narrative in *Beawolf* are evidently different from that of *Tales from the Thousand and One Nights*.

Narratives are actualized not only through spoken and written modes of language but also images and icons. Multimodal texts where both linguistic and visual representations collide form narratives. The combination of linguistic texts and visual texts that form narratives in stories or novels is not a new thing that we discuss though. As Hallet (2009) argues "narrative meaning can, therefore, no longer be regarded as a result of language-in-writing but of the combination and integration of different modes and media that contribute to and participate in the process of narration as a whole" (p.140). Initially, the narratives of children stories or novels whose stories transmitted merely through linguistic texts are supplemented by visual texts such as photos from historical archives, maps, graphs, etc. Wolf (2011) maintains that narratology is no longer a discipline limited to the verbal narratives and argues that it is expanded to inter-disciplinary research rather than being limited to literary research only. Wolf analyzes the narrative potential in sculpture, and outlines how narratology could function through different media like music and film.

With the rise of digital technology new narratives emerged, and contrary to the linear nature of verbal narratives in classical narratology, the digital narratives emerge in multi-dimensional forms. The interactive nature of digital texts bring a new dimension to narratives, and contrary to print texts, digital texts are realized through "a program that reacts to the actions of the user by executing certain modules of code" (Ryan, 2011, p. 35). This expands the theory of narratology to the area of cybertexts and hypertexts. Narratives, which are the bodies where signs, discourse and story are combined, are distinguished from other text types in the digital area. Game designs, transmedia storytelling and ergodic literature have been within the interest of this new theory of narratology (Aarseth, 1997, 2012; Black, 2012; Jenkins, n.d.; Eskelinen, n.d.). The user in this way is one of the actors of the story told rather than being the passive listener/reader of the story told. In digital cases like alternate reality games, masses of users take part in the story as the problem solvers and contribute to the flow of the narrative that is embedded behind the code.

The digital technology brought also new media that users utilize to construct their narratives at personal levels. In a way, the spoken narratives of daily life are very much replaced with written or rather multimodal digital texts in digital platforms. Beside the narratives in digital games and stories, new narratives emerge in social media platforms and messaging systems. These new narratives eventually brought in their distinguishing signs, discourses and stories in new communicative events.

## The Transformation in Communication Models

The communication models evolved from linear structures to circular ones that also take the response of the receiver into account, which consequently created a special focus on the perception and interpretation of the message. The social context and the motivations of the participants that resulted in the production and reproduction of the discourses have also gained importance. The theory of sign that Saussure developed established the basis of modern linguistics, which also created alternative ways of interpreting the act of meaning making between the sender and the receiver in the field of communication. As the communication models evolved from a linear structure to circular ones, the theory of sign (the *signifier* and the *signified*) became more significant due to the fact that there appeared an intention to interpret what the sender constructs and how the receiver perceives it in distinct social context. As Halliday (1996) states, "a social reality (or a 'culture') is itself an edifice of meanings – a semiotic construct," from which it can be concluded, "language is one of the semiotic systems that constitute a culture" (p.89). Thus, understanding a language constitutes to interpretation of semiotic signs within a socio-cultural context. This perception of language shapes how scholars perceive literacy practices today. Literacy today is the competency in interpreting various signs (both written and visual) in specific social contexts where language is produced as a social practice. This perception of literacy competence also discourse competencies that require knowledge and ability to produce language within the boundaries of the social contexts. The participants of digital communities, e-mail or messaging groups experience and practice different modes of literacy practices from the past literacy experiences. Language utilized in digital spaces manifests itself in multi-modal semiotic systems that users construct or make meaning out of. The visual and written texts are generally interwoven and they complete one another to construct meaning. Thus, it is a diverse "social reality" that we have been actors of.

The perception of language as a social practice both in oral and written modes consequently leads to language shaped within the boundaries of the social context where language is produced. As Kress (1997) asserts, written language is the "visual medium" and carries the "features of spatial design" whose manipulation refers to the "productive aspects of writing/print" (p.120). The same applies to the manipulation of written language in computer-mediated communication, which requires not only the written but also the visual mode of language. It is the age of multi-modal texts, and participants of any discourse community are required to master the necessary skills to interpret signs produced in the digital social spaces just as Kress (1997) estimated towards the end of the nineties; "the technologies of communication just as much as the information-based economies of the day after tomorrow will actually need, demand, visual modes of representation and communication" (p.99). Today in every sphere of daily life, individuals make use of multimodal literacy skills to make meaning out of their world, construct, reconstruct, convey and circulate their multi-modal texts. Communication through digital tools eventually created new modes of language, both verbal and visual. The digital spaces where users, who are in fact the participants of multi-modal discourses, produce language in social contexts. They at the same time offer new ways of manipulating language in mediated discourses.

Consequently, according to Communication Accommodation Theory, people in the communication processes alter the way they interact with others in order to show their similarities with the other participants, which in fact contributes to the construction of discourses and discourse communities. We may define the language utilized in digital spaces as sets of signs, texts or rather discourses, manipulated by the participants of digital discourse communities who continuously negotiate meanings over the texts produced and share the common features and conventions of digital discourses. The digital communities then create their own language that function within the boundaries of the negotiated conventions that they use to interact with each other. While the visual texts master the language of the digital world in general, the written language has also transformed. Users started finding tactics that enable them to respond to messages quickly and spontaneously. One of such tactics is using abbreviations the meaning of which is negotiated and agreed upon in the digital communities. Users, for instance, prefer typing "pls" instead of "please," or "4U" instead of "for you." When one user types "LOL" in a chat room, all other receivers understand that the sender "laughs out loud" which means s/he has found the previously sent message funny. The transformation in language has not been limited to such abbreviations due to time constraint in messaging, and the users managed to invent a new language consisting of both written words and icons for a different reason other than time concerns. When verbal language is inadequate in explaining reality that requires paralinguistic elements to be expressed, users replaced such elements of language systems with digital iconic or pictorial elements in order to construct meaning.

## Communication on the Digital Platforms

Communication in social encounters has taken new forms and functions with the computer technology. Today when it is the social interaction that is central to the discussion, usually it is the social media use that is analyzed. In fact, even before the launch of social media, in business electronic mails (emails) became the main means of communication that brought new perspectives and varying debates about interpersonal communication specifically in workplaces. Emails enabled individuals to communicate with both single individuals and groups. It became practical to discuss with a group of people without being obliged to set a meeting time and discuss. Moreover, written language made the discussed points concrete, and it was an advantage to go back to the previous emails and come to solid conclusions about the discussion points. What remained problematic was the communication of emotions that people could express through the use of nonverbal cues in face-to-face interactions. Kato, Kato, and Akahori (2007) concluded that in communication via emails, low emotional cue transmissions lead to frustration, anger and anxiety among the participants of the communication group. One might argue that in business emails it may not be necessary to communicate emotions; however, it is suggested that the problems in accurately communicating emotions is significant in building a sound relationship among employees and their customers and making informed decisions (Byron, 2008). Byron (2008) argues "verbalization of emotion and the presence of nonverbal emotional cues may moderate the relationship between sender and receiver characteristics and the likelihood that receivers will inaccurately interpret senders' emotion" (p.320). The spreading digital technologies eventually showed that emails could only be one of the media that people use for fast and easy communication that they intend to substitute oral language in face-to-face communication with written language. Social media users 'like' the posts of their 'friends' with a simple click to state their opinions, but while commenting on such posts or posting any text themselves they used verbal written language still devoid of emotional cues. Instant messaging and cell phone based messaging services technologies brought talk-like written texts, whose language, or rather the evolution of language, is also studied by linguists. Users evolved into language users who write like they talk. They have started producing their daily narratives on digital platforms and sharing not only incidents but also emotions and attitudes through synchronous and asynchronous messages. Nevertheless, the problem that linguistic language does not provide users the necessary linguistic resources, the nonverbal cues, which they can utilize to communicate their emotions and attitudes, required a different tactic from using abbreviations.

Due to the fact that "nonverbal communication is indispensable for many communicative functions" (Burgoon & Walther, 2013, p.737), studies in the field of computer–mediated communication (CMC) and management reserve a considerable place for the issue of communication of emotions. Compared to face-to-face communication, CMC concentrates on "how the social meaning of interactions is affected by the absence of nonverbal cues when communicators substitute text-based electronic messaging for face-to-face (FTF) encounters" and offers two positions; one that addresses to the absence of nonverbal vocal and physical cues that lead the participants of the social interaction to miss the other parties' personal characters, feelings, and attitudes and thus a less effective communication, and the other position that refers to the potential of the participants to adapt to the new medium and find their paths into more effective communication despite the absence of such verbal and physical cues (Walther, Loh, & Granka, 2005). Nonverbal vs. face-to-face communication research is connected to different communication theories and paradigms some of which are social presence theory, media richness theory and adaptation theories, and the use of emoticons and emojis can be explained through these theories.

Burgoon & Walther (2013) define social presence as "salience of one's partner(s) in a conversation, or the sense that others are participating", and state that while face-to-face communication enables a high level of social presence, CMC that equip the users with no nonverbal cues conveys very little social presence. They explain the media richness theory, on the other hand, focuses on the communication system's potential to convey nonverbal messages as well as verbal messages, immediacy of feedback from the participants engaged in the communicative act, their potential to personalize messages and use a natural language, which addresses to an overall potential of language used in CMC that enabled the alternatives to communicate nonverbal messages. Finally, Burgoon & Walther (2013) explain that as adaptation theories focused on CMC users' ability to adapt to the absence of nonverbal cues and how they manage alternative coding systems to communicate their social beings, the social information processing proposes that CMC users, who are "interpersonally oriented" and "adapt the communication cues that are available to them in order to exchange social information," have the potential to "substitute verbal and textual content and style variations to transact information about themselves, their emotions, attitudes, and interpersonal orientations" (p.740). All in all, while considering the absence and the consequent need for nonverbal cues in CMC, it is clear that the users have the potential and the ability to adapt, produce, reproduce and establish new coding systems to feed their desire to realize their social beings. As in all social contexts, a new form of social interaction inevitably brings its own discourses that are constructed and reconstructed by the participants of the new discourse community. Referring back to the communication models and the theories of language as social semiotics and computer-mediated communication, we need to revisit the communication patterns and language use in the current interpersonal communication realized through text messaging.

Digital technology transformed not only the way we communicate with others but also the language we use in different settings. Digital communication has primarily brought instant communication that covers a vast number of people and area. Among different tools, messaging systems have long been a favorite means of communication. The smart phone technology has provided people with communication opportunities online, and customers are attracted by the fast and easy access to the Internet. In return, the GSM operators have developed new packages for users that would attract the smart phone users with cheaper Internet connection. Nowadays, the GSM operators are offering promotions primarily in the Internet packages, and customers, especially young people, are more interested in them. With the rise in the smart phones, millions of people are reachable online and they would rather use instant messaging in different social settings where they cannot make phone calls for different reasons. People send each other mobile phone based messages (SMS), communicate through Facebook messenger, Whatsapp, Line, Instagram, etc. In the meantime, there has been a decline in the number of people using SMS and a considerable rise in the use of Internet-based messaging systems like Whatsapp that requires only an Internet connection. As a great number of public places like cafes, hotels, universities, and so on offer free Wi-Fi, messaging with others using Whatsapp is totally free, and even if users use their Internet packages, it is still more reasonable for customers to communicate with people via such messaging systems.

Beside the economic aspect of the increasing demand in Whatsapp, users prefer this application for its practicality. Initially, this application provides fast messaging among other users; users can chat fast and easily. Secondly, users not only send text messages but also share photographs, videos and even web links with others very easily. All they need is the Whatsapp application downloaded on their smart phones and an Internet connection. Last but not the least, users can create Whatsapp groups and communicate with not only individuals but also groups of people. Today, it is very common that students taking the same courses, for example, create their Whatsapp groups since it is an effective and fast way of communication with different people interacting with each other simultaneously, or people invite groups of people to certain social occasions. People who are continuously online share their daily narratives and instances of certain emotions and attitudes. The growing trend especially youngsters is to instantly share what they do, how they feel, what they think, how they treat someone, etc. There is an enormous network among people sharing every experience in real life with people who belong to the same digital community with. Who would not like to know about others and be known by others at almost no cost?

Whatsapp has become one of the most popular means of interpersonal and group communication that has brought different digital skills to people. Skilled Whatsapp users type texts extremely fast and they message each other as if they were talking to the others. It also created a different cognitive processing in the users since now they must read, understand and evaluate so fast that they could compose a reply to the others. The new generation in a way voluntarily use written codes more than spoken codes in their daily narrative practices. In the meantime, users also realize that the interpersonal interaction that they experience in face-to-face communication is not the same as the relationship that they build through their smart phones. While both face-to-face and digital communication have their own pro's and con's, users eventually develop new tactics to compensate both the time they need to respond to the other user(s) and the absence of nonverbal cues that they seek to manifest their social presence.

## MAIN FOCUS OF THE CHAPTER

Under the light of theories of media studies, narratology, semiotics, and CMC reviewed above, the main focus of this chapter is to explore how emojis have become the new medium in digital platforms to share daily narratives, emotions and attitudes with other users. Emojis, offered as digital applications, have become an indispensable element in the language we use in messages. The exploration of emojis from this perspective will allow researchers construct a view of looking at emojis that may shape future studies, which could further extend the research areas which have mostly concentrated on gender differences and motivation mostly in professional environment so far. Looking at how emojis are used in everyday narratives, it may be useful to redefine certain characteristics of emojis, which could bring new insights to future research.

### Emojis are Conventional

As it is explained on the website emojipedia.org, emojis which originated from Japan mean *picture letters* in Japanese. Emoticons are user-generated signs created to convey messages referring to the emotional state of the participants in the communicative process. Users extend the use of punctuation marks and create face-like icons with emotional expressions that are agreed upon and circulated. Emojis, on the other hand, are a set of standardized icons that have certain meanings. The linguistic and communicative potential of emoticons have resulted in the evolution of emoticons into *emoji* applications mobile technology in creating a new language, or a new sign system that is widely used in creating daily narratives, and recently they are attributed a significant importance in the new iOS and Android developments, which makes them one of the essentials of the mobile technology market. The way that users choose emoticons to express certain emotions and attitudes has brought the conventional forms of using these icons. Users started using punctuations symbols to convey messages that also involve signs for emotions. When they were happy, they *typed the* sign:-), or when they were upset they *typed*:-(. When they were sad, they cried in their messages:'-(, and they also cried when they were very happy:'). Sometimes they did not know what to do:/, sometimes they were surprised:-o, or sometimes they were winky ;-). The developmental process of emojis makes these icons standardized, and as users make use of the same icons to convey the same or similar meanings, the sets of these icons become conventional. Today, there seems to be an agreement upon the usage of certain icons for certain emotions and attitudes, which makes the icons semantic units.

Comesaña et al. (2013) refer to computers users' preference of using emoticons "an automatic processing of valance" and state that "this preferential and enhanced processing can have a positive effect on the communication mediated by computers by allowing faster and more stable access to affective processing" (p.594). Emojis influence both the way the actors of communicative events construct messages and the way the messages are perceived. Studies show that these iconic nonverbal units that represent positive, negative and neutral emotions affect the interpretation and perception of messages, and they also affect the mood of the receivers of messages and how the commitment of the person who generates the message is perceived in different social environments (Huang, Yen, & Zhang, 2008; Luor, Wu, Lu, & Tao, 2010; Ganster, Eimler, & Krämer, 2012). Thus, the affective automatic processing of emoticons, which is preferential and enhanced, positively influence CMC as it enables faster access to the evaluation process (Comesaña et al., 2013). Research shows that emotions, attitudes and attention are not correctly perceived by Internet users if they are exposed to linguistics texts without emoticons, and when emoticons contribute to the linguistic texts as emotive elements in the same contexts, the perception of users change to a great extent (Lo, 2008). Since emoticons serve the communication processes as verbal tools that function as nonverbal cues, they are termed as quasi-nonverbal cues. Garrison, Remley, Thomas, and Wierszewski (2011) study emoticons as "a conventionalized linguistic feature" in the instant messaging discourse, thus a semiotic and rhetorical element which makes it far more than a paralinguistic feature while they also allow users to be inventive despite the conventions and have the control of their rhetorical use of emoticons. In fact, emojis are visual and spatial representations similar to linguistic features of language systems, which enhance the conceptual framework of paralinguistic features of language in CMC. Hence, rather than treating emoticons or emojis merely paralinguistic or quasi-nonverbal elements in CMC, it would be more meaningful to treat them also as semiotic elements, units or constructs that contribute to the meaning-making processes in digital platforms. While emojis today are embedded in linguistic texts generally as verbal emotive devices, they also constitute to meaningful linguistic chunks and convey messages that require both affective and cognitive processing, and they have become a conventional form of language that is contributory to the verbal language.

## Emojis are Conceptual

While emoticons merely translate the emotions and attitudes of the users, emoji icons offer a wider range of icons also including emotions but not limited to them though. Today the vast menu of mobile emoji applications contains numerous conceptual emojis, too. The emojis not only compensate the absence of nonverbal cues but also replaces the verbal expressions with small icons to convey messages fast and easily. There are certain icons that refer to occasions like Christmas, birthdays, Halloween, weddings or celebrations in general. Also, there are certain icons that refer to common signs like +18, no smoking, parking lot, no mobile phones allowed, WC etc. And there are many more icons like various animals, architectural designs, buildings, vehicles, weather signs, plants and even the zodiac signs.

Today users can create endless combinations of emojis to tell their experiences, thoughts, emotions, etc. In other words, users construct messages using both emotive cues and conceptual cues to communicate their narratives. If emojis were to serve the users to compensate the absence of nonverbal cues addressing to the emotional states of users only, why would the software designers and producers create that vast collection of icons? This is because the language in messaging in digital communities has reached a level beyond the emoticons and emojis that express emotions and has become a new form of *picture language*. As Griffith (2014) states, there is "a return to hieroglyphics," which has significant implications in interpersonal communication in different social encounters. Similar to the Egyptian hieroglyphics that bring ancient narratives to our time, today the emoji texts tell the stories of users on digital platforms. Steinmetz (2014) argues that the use of emojis has transformed our way of communication and adds that they "have become such a critical part of our hyperconnected exchanges that they are emerging as a dialect all their own" (p.52). As Steinmetz (2014) depicts, humans' journey into visual literacy started from prehistoric cave drawings and evolved into pictographs in Sumerian tablets, then into hieroglyphics, "coat of arms" that communicate kinship, brand logos, cartoons and comics, computer icons, and finally emoticons and emojis. In 2007, the Unicode Consortium was agreed to expand the scope of symbols to encompass emoji, and Apple's new Swift programming language "will allow programmers whose native languages don't use the Roman alphabet to write code that makes more sense to them" (Devilla, 2014). This is also considered to be important in teaching youngsters coding, which is one of the most significant skills of the new generation.

People in daily life communication practices use emoji actively when they are engaged in messaging. Anyone using Whatsapp can show you own or others' messages where you can see the use of emojis. Users can easily interpret messages like U or a response to a message that states coffee is ready could be something like . Most of us must have typed a birthday message similar to or express that we are so sorry for a friend's loss . Recently I have encountered a Facebook post shared by a former student of mine, and here it is (Figure 1).

She says "Aaaaannnnd the last 9…" and uses those emojis. Can you guess what she means? She was expecting a baby and those were the last 9 days before the delivery, and she could perfectly communicate her excitement and narrates her experience as a prospective mother, which I 'liked.' Or before someone in Istanbul leaves the office, he may send a message to his spouse like . What does this message mean? It actually means that he is leaving the office at 6 o'clock and going home taking the bus, boat and the tube, which is a common experience for many residents of Istanbul. The user here uses the emoji icons as semantic units and narrates a fragment of time in his life free from the need for linguistic words or grammar.

Examples can be varied, but we all see that using emojis either as a visual support to scripts or without any scripts is getting more and more common among users and they function as a new language and discourse that enable them to construct new pictorial narratives. The users perceive the representations of everyday life within the limits of their experiences and the mind replaces the similar representations with the standard icons, and neither the comprehension nor the construction of such texts seems complicated to the Internet users today.

*Figure 1.*

## Emojis are Cross-Cultural

Today, even the Microsoft Word software programs that we use all over the world is adapted to the use of emoticons, and when we type a colon and a hyphen with a closing parenthesis, it automatically changes them into the icon ☺, for instance. This is between the emoticons and emoji application that involves mostly elaborated icons. Users in digital messaging go beyond creating their signals of emotions through the use of commas, colons, semi-colons, hyphens, etc. since the mobile technology offers alternative keyboards that enable users to make use of a vast variety of emojis. Thus, one of the first things that a person does when they buy a new mobile phone, laptop, or tablet is to download an emoji keyboard application, which has become as essential as the alphabetical keyboard for users. They offer sets of different menus[1] for a great variety of emojis that do not convey emotional cues but even ideas or concepts themselves, which are available in different countries for users from different cultural and linguistic backgrounds. The mobile applications for emojis offer signs that are beyond the expression of merely emotions and even further they carry meanings across cultures. Users from different countries, culture and linguistic backgrounds share the same icons to communicate similar emotions, attitudes and concepts while constructing their daily narratives. Thus, emojis have become a sort of universal language for users.

Nevertheless, as in all language phenomena, there occurs the need for cultural expressions to express culture-specific narratives. Emojis have become so common among users that there appeared the need for icons that refer to certain cultural signs. The Turkish GSM operator Turkcell, for example, offered their customers a new messaging application BIP where users can use culture-specific icons like *simit* (a popular pastry with sesame that Turkish people often eat as snacks), tea (the traditional Turkish drink which people drink in traditional small glasses). The users communicate their everyday experiences using the culture-specific icons. These icons are not limited to food though. The icon for seagulls is significant since it is a common daily practice that people share their *simit* with the seagulls following the boats they take from one side of the city of Istanbul to the other side. These users communicate their experiences using both linguistic and visual codes. The meanings in verbal exclamations like "aaa" that explains surprise and "haha" that refers to laughter are completed with smilies but this message shows how conceptual emojis are used to build a daily narrative in a cultural context. Besides, the Turkcell BIP application offers users a famous Turkish cartoonist's cartoon characters. Users who do not prefer using smiling faces of emojis can use one of these characters to say hi, agree, or show any other emotions. This indicates that using a pictorial iconic language on digital platforms has become an important voluntary mode of language for users, and as all languages this new digital hieroglyphics requires cultural signs through which culture-specific discourses are constructed (Figure 2).

## Emojis are Creative

Beside the messaging applications, how far can users go with emojis? Well, quite far. Users can use their creativity to construct a variety of messages. They started with the titles of literary works represented in emojis. Here are some examples (Figures 3-5).

Can you recognize the title? "Lord of the Rings" of course. How about this?

It is "Grapes of Wrath" indeed. Would you like to see a more challenging one?

It is not easy, is it? This is "1984." There are many more examples like these, and some are really pushing the readers' limits of emoji-literacy. One can also find a large collection of TV-series or movie

*Figure 2.*

*Figure 3.*

*Figure 4.*

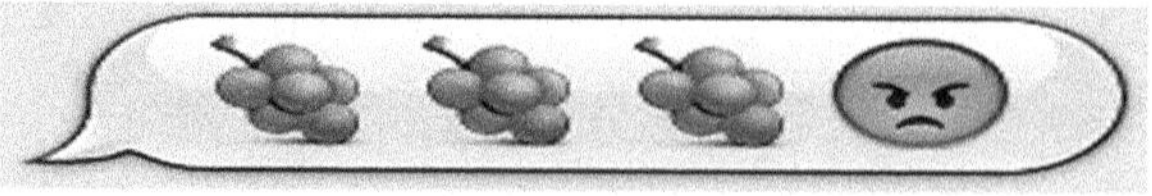

*Figure 5.*

titles in emojis on the Internet. Such creations of emoji texts have become like a digital game among users. They push the limits of their digital creativity, and in the meantime they contribute to the construction of a new language code. However, it is not surprising that Generation Y'ers who were born into the digital world and competent in reading multimodal texts are quite competent in understanding the pictorial meanings. It seems that Generation Z will be even more competent in constructing and comprehending texts in emojis.

The emojis have evidently become the means of narratives and it went even further than simply emoji-translating the titles. Fred Benenson's 2009 Kickstarter-funded emoji-translation of *Moby Dick* titled *Emoji Dick*, which retells Herman Melville's story in emojis, is in Library of Congress Catalog (Hoffberger, 2013). Although it could have been quite difficult to understand the novel in solely emojis because some might be unclear in meaning or there could be multi-meanings in the emoji combinations. Thus, it would require the reader to read or know the story beforehand. However, the emoji narrative text accompanied with linguistic narrative text is an interesting reading experience for readers. This example may not mean that in future novels will be written in emojis or there would be emoji versions of linguistic novels; however, it is a significant indicator that shows how much our language and certainly culture are influenced by digital literacy practices, and also how common digital practices could evolve into institutionally approved sign systems.

## Emojis are Socially Constructed

Another indicator that makes us see the emoji-based texts as a different mediated language and discourse is that it is treated as a socially constructed phenomenon like any other language. Similar to the actors using linguistic language to express themselves and reveal their social identities, the actors using emojis need a wide range of resources to define themselves while constructing their language, discourse and signs. Thus, similar to the verbal language that is used in communication, the emoji icons are criticized for being both sexist, homophobic and not offering racial diversity. The angel is a boy , the dancing ones are female  as males are too cool to dance. Families are depicted as heterosexual nucleus families  who preferably have a male child, and love is between a man and a woman . Recently, an Apple spokesperson declared, "Apple supports and cares deeply about diversity, and is working with The Unicode Consortium to update the standard so that it better represents diversity for all of us" (Mlot, 2015). For the new version of Apple operating systems, Apple decided to add new icons, which will allow users to select one of six color options, from yellow to dark brown and the  is there in different skin colors (Figure 6).

*Figure 6.*

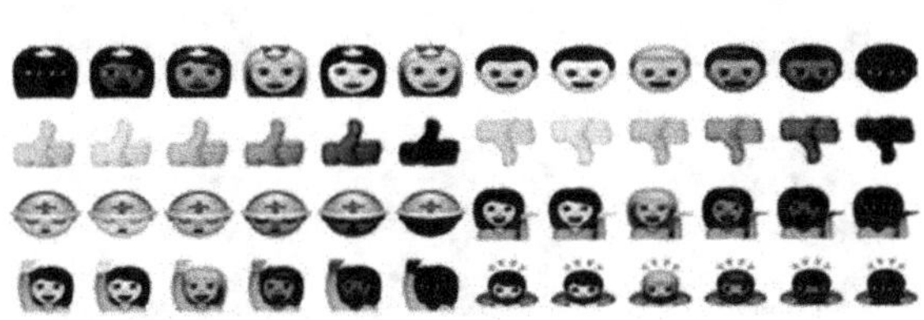

Moreover, the new emoji icons cover new sets of families with same-sex parents, different combinations of siblings (Figure 7).

The emojis are adapted to be a politically correct coding system, which shows that the mobile technology treats emojis as a distinct language and a socially constructed discourse. It is a language that is promoted. This means the adaptability of the emoji icons into the society's social values and norms is as significant as the availability of the local language in a country where the mobile technology is marketed. Similar to the culture-specific icons mentioned before, new emoji items will enable users reveal their identities and construct their narratives distinct to their social, cultural, political, racial, sexual identities.

## Emojis are Innovative

Mobile technology has already integrated emojis into their systems as one of the indispensable characteristics and developed new applications to attract the customers. The iOS technology team developed the "Keymoji" which is a special keyboard that translates your texts into a series of emoji icons; while users type their script, the Keymoji will predict what is intended to be said and translate the message into emojis in a comprehensible way. As Beasley (2014) explains, this new *keymoji* makes use of "a crowdsourced database of emoji combinations that can then be substituted for words in your text messages, emails, tweets, and other communications (via Re/code)" (para.2). Also, today users can choose among ready-made emoji combinations from the emoji application menus. Users can both create their own narratives and make use of emoji chunks to construct their texts, which is also part of their process of learning a new digital language (Figure 8).

*Figure 7.*

*Figure 8.*

Moreover, "users can use the included Keymoji application to upload their own emoji translations for any phrase at all and it will be added to the global database, enabling others across the globe to use them on their own phones" (Beasley, 2014, para.3), which might in future result in a digital universal coding system that makes communication across borders easier. The Google Handwriting Input on Android is one of such developments which more recent. This application is designed for print and cursive writing in 82 languages and 20 different scripts including hand-drawn emoji support. Although Lopez (n.d.) questions whether emojis could be one of the languages included, it is evident that the market of digital technology considers emojis as one of the parameters when they launch a new application or manufacture a product. For now, one can see the word "emoji" underlined red in Word, which means it is not in the dictionary of Microsoft Word; however, it is already in the dictionary. Moreover, "the Face with Tears of Joy emoji" has recently been chosen as the 2015 Word of the Year by Oxford Dictionaries (Figure 9).

The Word program will recognize the word "emoji" soon, I believe. The digital communication devices integrated into every sphere of social life enrich the vocabulary of grammatical languages. Authors try and adapt new collocations in their use of words like "emoji" and in time they will be adapted and widely used. For example, I used the word "translation" with emoji because a literary book was rewritten with emojis, and this indicates the legitimization of emojis as a language, or I named texts written in emojis "emoji-based texts," which manifests an approach towards texts constructed using emojis that

*Figure 9.*

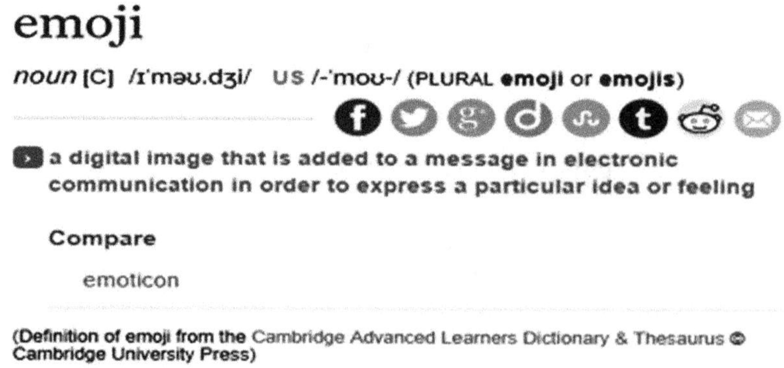

**emoji**

*noun* [C] /ɪˈməʊ.dʒi/ US /-ˈmoʊ-/ (PLURAL **emoji** or **emojis**)

a digital image that is added to a message in electronic communication in order to express a particular idea or feeling

**Compare**

emoticon

(Definition of emoji from the Cambridge Advanced Learners Dictionary & Thesaurus © Cambridge University Press)

they represent a new discursive field with its own texts. Even now while trying to explain this linguistic adaptation, I use words and phrases that are not traditionally used in a similar text about a grammatical language. A new language is emerging eventually, and future practices and technological developments will continue to transform users' communication and language experiences. Today, people have their digital tablets (and it is interesting that the term tablet is a common digital term today) that they carve touching the screens and construct their narratives.

## FUTURE RESEARCH DIRECTIONS

One of the questions is whether emojis have become a global language that people can make meaning of around the world. As emotions are universal, emotive cues are certainly meaningful for all; however, the conceptual cues may have different meanings that people from different cultures attribute varied meanings to. There is a gap in the research field that explores emojis across cultures. Also, as explained above, in Turkey, Turkish users are offered culture-specific icons, and further research could investigate to what extent users use culture-specific and global icons to construct their daily narratives.

## CONCLUSION

Innovations in digital technology have been causing major differences and offering various alternatives in people's communication processes. Users are engaged in communicative events in different ways, and the digital devices are already embedded into their daily literacy practices. The digital spaces where users interact with each other certainly have their own features, restrictions, flexibilities and resources that require users to adapt, construct, reconstruct and also create tactics for. Language as a social phenomenon can never be considered isolated from social practices; thus, as communication patterns vary, language takes new forms to meet the needs of users to effectively communicate and make meaning out of their social environment. Emoticons that evolved into emojis and brought new mobile applications thereby emerge as a new system of codes that users voluntarily use while messaging. As the use of emoji applications spread, the mobile technology project development teams, marketing professionals and manufacturers develop a growing interest in this new phenomenon because it has economic potential. New applications are developed, promoted and marketed to the mobile technology users. It might be a bit early to estimate how far the use of emojis and the applications developed will go for now. However, we should admit that we could never estimate that one day we could be offered a *Keymoji* when we were typing:-) to show that we are happy to our digital encounters whose faces and consequently gestures and mimics were invisible to us, nor could we foresee the hot debates revolving around the sexist, homophobic and racist elements of a set of icons. And one day we might be proficient emoji readers who can interpret emoji narratives. One thing for sure is that almost all users use emojis at different levels for different purposes, but they use them and they want emoji applications be downloadable on their mobile devices. It is like customers' demand for Bluetooth years ago, which is quite outdated today. It is likely that the communicative and also the linguistic potential of emojis will certainly lead to new product designs, marketing strategies and new consumer preferences.

As these icons emerged as an alternative to compensate the absence of nonverbal cues in digital communication, today they refer to not only emotional states but also concepts, situations, experiences and ideas. Users not only express their emotions but also convey concrete messages like  to mean that she is at the hairdressers' and will be ready at 10 o'clock, for example. During holiday time, users may encounter a lot of emoji-texts telling people's holiday experiences on digital platforms. Instead of writing down what people experience on holiday, they simply construct their pictorial narratives like . The message is quite expressive. The users who are exposed to such texts cognitively construct mental images of experiences told in emojis, which is better remembered better than linguistic texts. The age of digital technology is the age of visual representations; thus, users are more likely to actively participate in the construction of such visual narratives. Moreover, it is also more practical for the users to construct their narratives than creating linguistic texts. Similar to the alternative ways of constructing or rather coding stories in digital games and transmedia storytelling, emojis offer a new media to construct users' stories. What new functions and forms emojis will have in future may not be so clear, but it cannot be denied that this new digital hieroglyphics will continue to be in the center of our daily lives and academic research.

## REFERENCES


Aaeseth, E. (2012). A narrative theory of games. In *Proceedings of the International Conference on the Foundations of Digital Games*. Copenhagen, Denmark: Academic Press.

Aarseth, E. (1997). *Cybertext: Perspectives on ergodic literature*. The Johns Hopkins University Press.

Beasley, M. (2014, September 17). *Keymoji keyboard for iOS 8 translates everything you type into emoji*. Retrieved from http://9to5mac.com/2014/09/17/keymoji-keyboard-for-ios-8-translates-everything-you-type-into-emoji/#

Black, M. L. (2012). Narrative and spatial form in digital media: A platform study of the SCUMM engine and Ron Gilbert's the Secret of Monkey Island. *Games and Culture*, *7*(3), 209–237. doi:10.1177/1555412012440317

Burgoon, J. K., & Walther, J. B. (2013). Media and computer mediation. In M. L. Knapp & J. A. Hall (Eds.), *Nonverbal communication* (pp. 731–770). doi:10.1515/9783110238150.731

Byron, K. (2008). Carrying too heavy a load? The communication and miscommunication of emotion by email. *Academy of Management Review*, *33*(2), 309–327. doi:10.5465/AMR.2008.31193163

Comesaña, M., Soares, A. P., Perea, M., Piñeiro, A. P., Fraga, I., & Pinheiro, A. (2013). ERP correlates of masked affective priming with emoticons. *Computers in Human Behavior*, *29*(3), 588–595. doi:10.1016/j.chb.2012.10.020

Devilla, J. (2014). *Swift fun fact #1: You can use emoji characters in variable, constant, function, and class names*. Retrieved from http://www.globalnerdy.com/2014/06/03/swift-fun-fact-1-you-can-use-emoji-characters-in-variable-constant-function-and-class-names/

Eskelinen, M. (n.d.). *(Introduction to) cybertext narratology*. Retrieved from http://cybertext.hum.jyu.fi/articles/123.pdf

Ganster, T., Eimler, S. C., & Krämer, N. C. (2012). Same same but different? The differential influence of smilies and emoticons on person perception. *Cyberpsychology, Behavior, and Social Networking*, *15*(4), 226–230. doi:10.1089/cyber.2011.0179 PMID:22394421

Garrison, A., Remley, D., Thomas, P., & Wierszewski, E. (2011). Conventional faces: Emoticons in instant messaging discourse. *Computers and Composition*, *28*(2), 112–125. doi:10.1016/j.compcom.2011.04.001

Griffith, E. (2014, July 21). A return to hieroglyphics. *Fortune*.

Hallet, W. (2009). The multimodal novel: The integration of modes and media in novelistic narration. In R. Sommer & S. Heinen (Eds.), Narratology in the age of cross-disciplinary narrative research [e-book]. (pp. 129–153). Retrieved from http://0-eds.b.ebscohost.com.opac.bilgi.edu.tr/eds/ebookviewer/ebook/bmxlYmtfXzMwMjg3N19fQU41?sid=6d15df8c-9514-48a8-afbd-b5665e8c6089@sessionmgr112&vid=24&format=EB&rid=15

Halliday, M. A. K. (1996). 'Introduction', language as a social semiotic: The social interpretation of language and meaning. In P. Cobley (Ed.), *The communication reader*. London, UK: Routledge.

Hill, A. (2007). *Key themes in interpersonal communication: Culture, identities and performance*. Retrieved from http://0-eds.b.ebscohost.com.opac.bilgi.edu.tr/eds/ebookviewer/ebook/bmxlYmtfXzIzNDMwMl9fQU41?sid=1b1de240-d673-4e1f-b2a2-21c8b83cd32e@sessionmgr115&vid=2&format=EB&rid=1

Hoffberger, C. (2013, February 19). *Library of Congress accepts first emoji novel*. Retrieved from http://www.dailydot.com/culture/library-congress-emoji-moby-dick/

Huang, A. H., Yen, D. C., & Zhang, X. (2008). Exploring the potential effects of emoticons. *Information & Management*, *45*(7), 466–473. doi:10.1016/j.im.2008.07.001

Jenkins, H. (n.d.). *Game design as narrative architecture*. Retrieved from http://interactive.usc.edu/blog-old/wp-content/uploads/2011/01/Jenkins_Narrative_Architecture.pdf

Kato, Y., Kato, S., & Akahori, K. (2007). Effects of emotional cues transmitted in e-mail communication on the emotions experienced by senders and receivers. *Computers in Human Behavior*, *23*(4), 1894–1905. doi:10.1016/j.chb.2005.11.005

Kress, G. (1997). *Before writing: Rethinking the paths into literacy*. New York, US: Routledge.

Litwack, E. B. (2009). *Wittgenstein and value: The quest for meaning*. Retrieved from http://ehis.ebscohost.com/eds/ebookviewer/ebook/bmxlYmtfXzM0NDUyMF9fQU41?sid=3eb83088-fb29-4181-99ff-771539f7990e@sessionmgr4005&vid=1&format=EB&lpid=lp_12&rid=0

Lo, S. K. (2008). The non-verbal communication functions of emoticons in computer-mediated communication. *Cyberpsychology & Behavior, 11*(5), 595–597. doi:10.1089/cpb.2007.0132 PMID:18817486

Lopez, N. (n.d.). *Google's new keyboard app lets you handwrite messages to your friends, emoji included.* Retrieved from http://thenextweb.com/insider/2015/04/15/googles-new-handwriting-input-keyboard-lets-you-sketch-messages-to-your-friends-emoji-included/

Luor, T., Wu, L., Lu, H.P., & Tao, Y.H. (2010). The effect of emoticons in simplex and complex task-oriented communication: An empirical study of instant messaging. *Computers in Human Behavior, 26*, 889–895. doi:10.1016/j.chb.2010.02.003

Mlot, S. (2015). *Apple adds diverse emojis to OS X, iOS Betas*. Retrieved from http://www.pcmag.com/article2/0,2817,2477318,00.asp

Nikolejeva, M. (2012). Reading other people's minds through word. *Children's Literature in Education, 43*(3), 273–291. doi:10.1007/s10583-012-9163-6

Ryan, M. L. (2011). The interactive onion: layers of user participation in digital narrative texts. In B. Thomas & R. E. Page (Eds.). *New narratives: Stories and storytelling in the digital age*. Retrieved from http://0-eds.a.ebscohost.com.opac.bilgi.edu.tr/eds/ebookviewer/ebook/bmxlYmtfXzQ3NzE2NF9fQU41?sid=f26ccbf4-cbc8-4e3f-8bf9-227e9654122b@sessionmgr4002&vid=3&format=EB&rid=3

Steinmetz, K. (2014, July28). Not just a smiley face. The emoji boom is changing the way we communicate. *Time*.

Walther, J. B., Loh, T., & Granka, L. (2005). Let me count the ways: The interchange of verbal and nonverbal cues in computer-mediated and face-to-face affinity. *Journal of Language and Social Psychology, 24*(1), 36–65. doi:10.1177/0261927X04273036

Wittgenstein, L. (1921). *Tractatus Logico-Philosophicus*. Retrieved from http://www.gutenberg.org/files/5740/5740-pdf.pdf

Wittgenstein, L. (1986). *Philosophical investigations*. Oxford, UK: Blackwell Publishing.

Wolf, W. (2011). Narratology and media(lity): The transmedial expansion of a literary discipline and possible consequences. In G. Olson (Ed.), *Current trends in narratology* (pp. 145–180). doi:10.1515/9783110255003.145

## KEY TERMS AND DEFINITIONS

**Computer-Mediated Communication (CMC):** The communicative process where synchronous or asynchronous human interaction is realized through the use of electronic devices.

**Discourse:** The socially constructed conventional forms of representations and codes, and of language in both written and spoken modes that construct cultural and social meanings.

**Emoji:** A small digital image or icon that represents facial expressions, common objects, places and types of weather, animals, people, etc. used to express an idea or emotion in digital communication.

**Emoticon:** A set of printable characters which functions as meta-communicative representation of emotions that is used to represent a human facial expression and convey an emotion in digital communication.

**Narratology:** The theory and study of knowledge or criticism that concentrates on the structure and function of narratives and its themes, conventions, codes and symbols.

**Nonverbal Communication:** The form of communication that does not make use of linguistic language but utilizes body language (gestures, facial expressions, posture and body stance), volume and tone of voice, speed, etc. to exchange meaning in communication processes.

**Semantic Unit:** The set of semantic elements or structures that conveys the meaning of linguistic signs.

**Semantics:** The study of the meaning of linguistic expressions.

## ENDNOTE

1 See the appendix for the menu.

## APPENDIX

*Figure 10.*

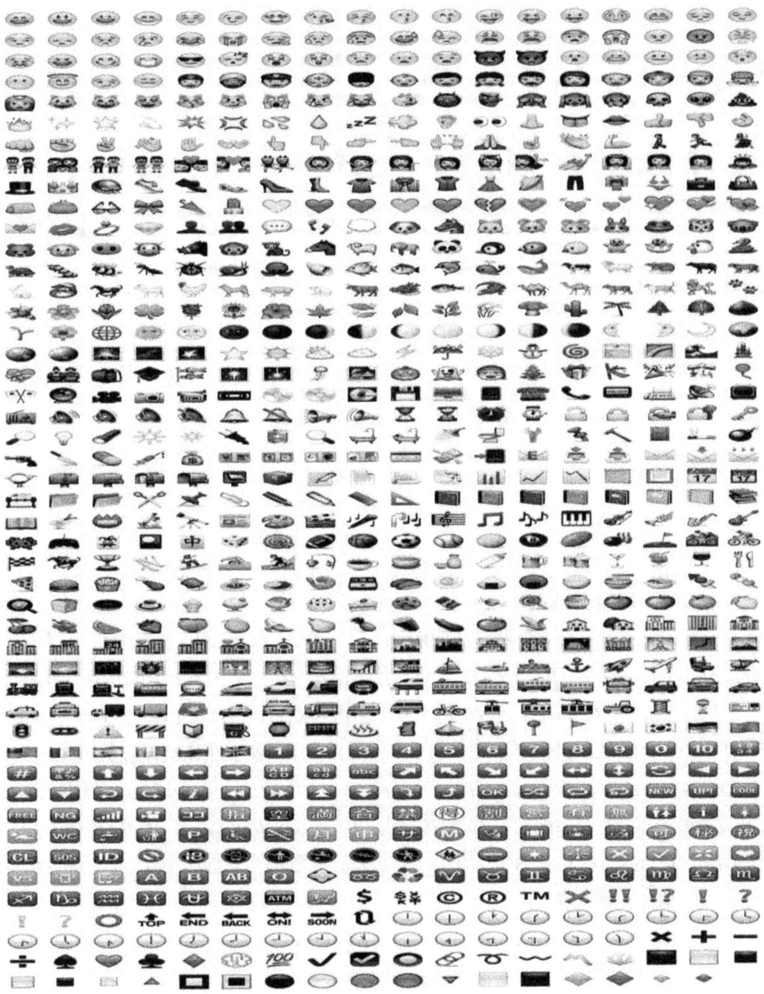

# Chapter 15
# Non-Story, Nostalgia, and Film Cognition:
## Nostalgia-Based Narrative Rhetoric Composition

**Akihito Kanai**
*Hosei University, Japan*

## ABSTRACT

*In addition to the stories' or characters' goal-directed actions, the non-story narrative and nostalgia aspects are important issues for narrative cognitions such as film cognition. In this chapter, the film cognitive effects related to re-defining nostalgia through cutting techniques and defamiliarization of narrative rhetoric are particularly analyzed. Using a cognitive and computational model, the rhetoric of the film is classified into four kinds of nostalgia including non-nostalgia, and analyzed in particular from the cognitive process perspective as it related to non-story and nostalgia. Next, a computerized classification is used to compose rhetoric and generate films for various kinds of nostalgia. The generated films revealed both the narrow story and broad non-story aspects of the rhetoric, narrative, and cognition of the past and the film.*

## INTRODUCTION

Narrative cognition is accomplished through the simultaneous processing of many factors. Generally, a story and its cognition are important factors to narrative cognition. Consequently, research on story grammar has been the primary computational and cognitive approach to narratives (e.g., Rumelhart, 1975; Thorndyke, 1977). Although these previous approaches primarily focused on the characters' goal-directed actions, recent focus has turned to the visual narrative structure (e.g., Cohn, 2013, 2014). In addition to the stories' or characters' goal-directed actions, the non-story narrative and nostalgia aspects are important issues for narrative cognitions such as film cognition. Generally, a film consists of several

DOI: 10.4018/978-1-5225-0432-0.ch015

Copyright © 2016, IGI Global. Copying or distributing in print or electronic forms without written permission of IGI Global is prohibited.

past images, which are viewed during certain period of time after being filmed. Therefore, even one past image in a film without a specific story, words, or an event, also known as a non-story narrative, can evoke various forms of nostalgia based on the viewer's cognition. Non-story visual narrative and nostalgia effects should be the focus of research on narrative film cognition.

Nostalgia does not always follow comfortable cognition. Some nostalgia is evoked from a lost good past. Other nostalgia is evoked from an unforgettable bad past. Both types of nostalgia must be considered. Furthermore, nostalgia may emerge suddenly with a non-story. For these reasons, to compose various kinds of narrative film rhetoric, both kinds of nostalgia found in non-story narratives must be examined. In this chapter, the focus is on the computational and cognitive approach to non-story visual narrative and nostalgia in order to discuss and explore the entire narrative concept.

Theories on narratives in literature make a strong distinction between story (fabula) and discourse (syuzhet) (Genette, 1980). In the study of film cognition and creation, an equivalent distinction is made between the story and film itself. A story can be defined in a narrative as all implicit or explicit events. Nevertheless, a film not only has a story structure, but also visual and audio structures. In this chapter, the focus is on the film structure, in particular from the perspective of "the rhetoric of the film." Kanai (2001b, 2002) defined the rhetoric of the film, based on Chatman (1990), as a combination of the film techniques based on the sender's purpose. Some rhetoric enables a viewer to watch a film and to relate to its story. The process of the viewer coming to understand the past story may lead to some nostalgia effects. Conversely, many films have a primary purpose other than to tell a story. This happens when the purpose of the director is the film rhetoric itself, or the non-story rhetorical aspects rather than the story. In addition, nostalgia effects can emerge from emphasized details of the past, which are the non-story and cutting aspects of the film. When the above issues are considered, a system for computational narrative film generation must include story and non-story rhetorical aspects.

Computational film creation can be argued as the choice of rhetoric type used as a strategy in order for the viewers' cognitive processes to relate to various kinds of nostalgia. In this chapter, using a cognitive and computational model, the rhetoric of the film was classified into four kinds of nostalgia including non-nostalgia. The rhetoric of the film was analyzed in particular from the cognitive process perspective as it related to non-story and nostalgia. Next, a computerized classification is used to compose rhetoric and generate films for various kinds of nostalgia. The generated films revealed both the narrow story and broad non-story aspects of the rhetoric, narrative, and cognition of the past and the film. Without using story structures and goal-oriented characters, nostalgia-based visual narrative rhetoric could be composed.

Many cognitive effects from narrative films are created through the interaction between cognitive process, story, discourse, and rhetoric. For example, irrational rhetoric cutting techniques for narrative space and time in the film can change the viewer's cognitive transition from story-driven to rhetoric-driven processing. Based on cognitive transition due to narrative processing from story-based to non-story based, cognitive effects such as intensive nostalgia effects can emerge.

In this chapter, the film cognitive effects related to re-defining nostalgia through cutting (coupure) techniques and defamiliarization of narrative rhetoric are particularly analyzed. Deleuze (1985) argued irrational cuts in the film related to the time image. For example, the sudden appearance of a past image in the present image is an irrational cut. The authors define the cutting technique as a technique to create irrational cuts in a film. Cutting techniques are used to generate an irrational relationship or an unfamiliar situation in the film and to create an alienation effect (Brecht & Willett, 1964).

To discuss re-defined nostalgia, the chapter focuses on three kinds of nostalgias suggested by Davis (1979): "simple nostalgia" "reflexive nostalgia" and "interpreted nostalgia." Simple nostalgia emerges from an affection for the past without cognitive transition and defamiliarization. On the contrary, reflexive and interpreted nostalgia emerge from the reality and the uncertainty about the past as related to unfamiliar situations, with cognitive transition and defamiliarization based on the cutting techniques.

The authors had proposed the film rhetoric composition system especially for non-story (NS) type narratives. The authors improved the system by using the theories of nostalgia and film cognition to compose various strategic narratives through the system. To implement the system, they focused on the relationship between narrative rhetoric such as cutting techniques, viewer's cognition including cognitive transition, and nostalgia effects.

# BACKGROUND

## Nostalgia and Rhetoric

For a narrative film generation system that includes past images, various nostalgia with story and non-story narratives can be used as part of the rhetoric composition strategy.

In general, nostalgia refers to a longing for the past. Holbrook and Schindler (1991) defined it as a preference toward objects (people, places, or things) that were more common when one was younger.

Nostalgia has mainly been argued as a lost good personal and historical past by researchers like Stern (1992). In contrast, Davis (1979) argued that there were three kinds of nostalgia: simple nostalgia, reflexive nostalgia, and interpreted nostalgia. Simple nostalgia emerges from the good past. Reflexive nostalgia can emerge from both the good and bad past. Interpreted nostalgia can emerge from the reality or the uncertainty about the past. The places of the past include not only the good aspects, but also the bad aspects such as the ruins or the scars of wars, massacres, or disasters. Therefore, simple nostalgia for past glory is only one aspect of nostalgia. For example, Boym (2001) discussed the ruins of post-communist cities and their reflective nostalgia. In addition, with regard to cognitive processes, reflexive (reflective) and interpreted nostalgia are more closely related to the narratives' non-story elements. As another example, *Nostalgia for the Light* (2010), directed by Chilean director Patricio Guzmán, was a film that used the non-story narrative and illustrated bad aspects of the past, such as the Pinochet dictatorship, and uncertain aspects of the past, such as astronomy and remains. The diversity and complexity of nostalgia could be observed in *Nostalgia for the Light*.

Higson (2014) discussed post-modern nostalgia as a celebration of styles, images, and consumer items associated with the past, or with a particular past. These objects, styles, images, and items can be elements of non-story type rhetoric. Moreover, the traces of the past that suddenly appear in present time originally had non-story narrative aspects.

## Narrative Film Rhetoric and Cognition

Nostalgia can emerge from various different types of film rhetoric. There are two different purposes related to the rhetoric of the film (Kanai, 2001b, 2002). This difference is very important to the study of rhetoric cognition and generation because viewers' cognitive processes and effects can change according to these two types. For example, intensity and quality of viewers' cognitive effects such as nostalgia effects differ based on the rhetoric types.

The first purpose is to tell a consistent story. In this case, the totality of the film is important. Therefore, the rhetoric of film itself is subordinated to the totality. The viewers of this type of rhetoric can comprehend the totality and the story-based on the discourse about events (Avrahami & Kareev, 1994). In addition, some nostalgia effects emerge from the totality of the past.

Dialectic continuity is used in story-type rhetoric (Eisenstein, 1942; Kanai & Kodama, 2010). For example, spatial continuity ensures that the viewers can understand the characters' relative locations, even when they are not in the same frame. Moreover, continuity editing allows for temporal manipulation (Bordwell, 1985). Continuity can be created by placing identical elements in continuous shots. A viewer tends to recognize the rhetoric of the moving image as a visual narrative to understand the story (Cutting, Brunick, & Canden, 2012; Cutting & Iricinschi, 2014). There is a tendency is to interact with the montage, a dialectic aspect of film editing. When the rhetoric is structured to tell a consistent story, the viewers' constraint regarding the desire to understand the consistent story fits the rhetoric of the film; in other words, the viewers' relate to this film within this constraint. One kind of nostalgia effect based on the constraint emerges from S-type rhetoric. The specified period of the story can evoke thinking and feelings about the good past.

However, "rhetoric of a film with a purpose of telling a consistent story" (S-type rhetoric) is only one visual narrative possibility. "Rhetoric of a film with a purpose other than telling a consistent story" (NS-type rhetoric) also exists. In NS-type rhetoric, the purpose of rhetoric is to create a pure audiovisual situation or to make the story contents or the totality appear unclear. This type emphasizes subtle elements, such as individual shots or details. NS-type rhetoric is used in many artistic films, documentary films, music videos, and advertisements. For example, films directed by American documentary director Frederick Wiseman have no one consistent story, but do have a consistent narrative (Benson & Anderson, 1989). The focus of NS-type rhetoric is based on the film's associations between the objects and moods, rather than on the events of a story. Such associations create cognitive effects that do not arise in the process of comprehending a story.

In contrast to S-type rhetoric, discontinuity must be emphasized in order to create NS-type rhetoric. In this context, based on the destabilization created by discontinuity, the viewer sometimes cannot infer a consistent story from the images. Consequently, attention to the rhetoric itself is enhanced once the constraint is relaxed. Discontinuities can be created by placing different elements in continuous shots. The other kinds of nostalgia, such the reality of the past, emerge from the NS-type rhetoric as a constraint relaxation occurs that diminishes the desire to understand a consistent story.

Based on the cutting techniques used to make generate irrational relationships with time or characters in continuous shots, a viewer or a reader can feel less constrained with regard to story comprehension and reset the viewpoint to subtle elements, such as individual shots. Nostalgia effects from S-type rhetoric are generated by setting the story in the past, such as the events or the characters. On the contrary, nostalgia effects from NS-type rhetoric are created by the rhetoric alone and unfamiliar situations in the past.

In addition, there are two different cognitive process types for the rhetoric of film. Cognitive effects from certain rhetoric, such as S-type rhetoric, are primarily generated by the story or consistent narrative (cognitive process type-1). Conversely, the cognitive effects from the other rhetoric, such as NS-type rhetoric, are caused by the rhetoric of films, in particular the cutting techniques (cognitive process type-2). Many films combine both type of rhetoric. Therefore, the viewers transfer cognitive processes from type-1 to type-2 while viewing the same film.

Unfamiliar situations can emerge through the sudden appearance of a segment of NS-type rhetoric (Kanai, 2006). In this case, viewers sometimes cannot follow a consistent story. Therefore, attention to the situation itself is enhanced through cognitive process type-2.

When the rhetoric of a film is structured to tell a consistent story, the viewers' constraint with regard to the desire to understand a consistent story is in accordance with the film rhetoric. The viewers relate to this film within this constraint. This means that most viewers more readily relate to S-type versus NS-type rhetoric. Conversely, in order to appropriately relate to NS-type rhetoric, viewers must relax their constraints in terms of the need to understand a consistent story.

The authors used a thirteen minute section from Godard's *First Name Carmen* as an example of NS-type rhetoric, and investigated the tendencies of the story as a constraint on the viewers' film cognition (Kanai, 2001a). In the investigation, forty-six subjects (undergraduate students) were tested. Afterwards the authors investigated the viewers' cognition of the film using an investigation table. Kanai (2001a) paid extra attention to the subjects' seven-level evaluations based on their levels of interest in order to determine the film's cognitive effects. The authors examined the relationships between these evaluations, the recognition of the film's rhetoric, and the story by using the investigation table. This table included several open questions, such as "the reason for his/her evaluation," "what were the intentions of the director," "what were the characteristic techniques?" There were also questions regarding interest levels.

In the investigation, the viewer's internal constraint relaxation with regard to the need for a story was defined as he/she did not refers to the understanding of the story when determining the level of interest.

The investigation suggested the following points. First, people who relaxed this constraint rated the level of interest significantly higher than those who did not. Second, when the internal constraint with regard to the story was not relaxed, the level of interest was rated higher by those who could see purposes in the film's rhetoric other than the story. Third, when this internal constraint was not relaxed, even when the viewer could see purposes for the rhetoric other than the story, the evaluated level of interest remained low.

The investigation and the later experiments of Kanai (2001b, 2003) revealed that viewers could relate to NS-type rhetoric when the internal constraint with regard to the story was relaxed. Both relaxing the internal constraint and realizing the purpose in the rhetoric (the associated logic of the shots) may be effective in order to relate to rhetoric elements other than a consistent story.

## NON-STORY NARRATIVE

As previously discussed above, in order to relate to a film with NS-type rhetoric, many viewers must first relax their constraints in terms of the need to comprehend a story and to shift their viewpoints so that they have some associative logic and non-story narrative with regard the film shots that are independent of the story.

Cognitive process type-1, the process in which the viewers understand the story, has some cognitive effects. In this process, the "experience" of the film's goal-directed characters and consistent narrative may lead to some affective response. However, the cognitive effects such as nostalgia effects may arise from other sources, as well as cognitive process type-2.

When the constraint is relaxed, an irrational cut of NS-type rhetoric may cause a "resetting of viewpoint" and "affect, which does not arise through comprehending a story, but through the audiovisual situations" (Kanai, 2001b). A resetting of viewpoint indicates that the viewer's viewpoint shifts from the need to be told a story to a grasp of the non-story narrative. This reflects the object associations within the moving image and the "mood" or the details of the moving image. "Affect, which does not arise through comprehending a story, but through the audiovisual situation" is caused by the audiovisual situation that emerges from the film's mood and object associations. Nostalgia effects may also arise from the unfamiliar audiovisual situation.

In NS-type rhetoric, the editing, recording, and photography are not always subordinate to the overall story. As stated above, the focus is on non-story narrative, the film's mood and object associations or the reality related to the unfamiliar situations rather than on the events in the story. Such associations and situations cause cognitive effects that do not arise in the process of comprehending a story. Kanai (2001a) indicated that when a viewer is able to relax his or her constraint with regard to the need to comprehend a story, this strengthens those cognitive effects including nostalgia effects, which do not arise in the process of comprehending the story. On the contrary, with S-type rhetoric, the cognitive effects including nostalgia effects are those generated by the overall story. The nostalgia effects that emerge from NS-type rhetoric and those that emerge from S-type rhetoric may be different.

The reality related to the unfamiliar situations was argued by the Russian Formalists (Shklovsky, 1965). Previous studies on film cognition primarily discussed the reality effects related to the condition of being natural and less deviated with regard to movements (Visch & Tan, 2009; Rooney, Benson, & Hennessy, 2012). Nevertheless, the unfamiliar situations derived from non-story rhetorical elements create new realities; nostalgia effects and meaning relate to unknown memories and affects that do not arise through story comprehension alone. Unfamiliar situations can emerge through the sudden appearance of a section of NS-type rhetoric. In this case, a viewer sometimes cannot understand the consistent story. Therefore, attention to the situation itself is enhanced. Because the unfamiliar situations generate new cognitive effects related to unknown memories and affects that do not arise through story comprehension, the appearance can shift the transition in viewers' cognitive processes from type-1 to type-2.

NS-type rhetoric is created through cutting techniques used to make irrational relationships between 1) the rhetorical elements of two shots; 2) events and images; or 3) sounds and images (Kanai & Ogata, 2004). The irrational relationships through the cutting techniques are used in many artistic films and music videos in order to generate situations unfamiliar to the viewers and to create new realities.

For example, the British band New Order's music video, *Bizarre Love Triangle* (1986), directed by Robert Longo, used various cutting techniques. Some continuous shots of the video had no event relationship. This created irrational relationships between two shots (approach 1). However, there was a relationship between the music and images, as the rhythm of the music and the speed of the shot transitions were coordinated. However, in middle sections of the music video, there were shots without music used to generate the irrational relationships between images and sound (approach 3). At conclusion of the *Bizarre Love Triangle* video, the same shots were repeated in the upper side of the frame, which created a discontinuity regarding the events and images (approach 2). Our psychological experiment results indicated that viewers rated the scene without music higher for reality and strangeness (Kanai, 2003).

Although *Bizarre Love Triangle* was not connected to a nostalgia narrative, the three approaches used to create irrational relationships within the elements of rhetoric based on Chatman (1990) could be applied to computational narrative film composition for nostalgia and cognitive transition.

## NON-STORY AND NOSTALGIA EFFECTS

To manage various kinds of nostalgia, Naito and Kanai (2012a, 2012b) re-defined the nostalgia as emotions arising from the rise and fall in other times in the place. In this chapter, based on the re-defined nostalgia, Davis's three kinds of nostalgia, simple, reflexive, and interpreted, are especially re-analyzed based on cognitive processes and the rhetoric of the film for non-story narratives. Because the connections to the past, the memories, and the present always involve discontinuity, non-story narratives and nostalgia effects are more closely related to each other.

Past images of specific places can evoke simple, reflexive, and interpreted nostalgia from cognitive processes type-1 and type-2. A diversity in nostalgia and narrative is actualized through a strategic approach to the non-story and cognitive processes. Simple nostalgia is related to the story. Simple nostalgia from the film mainly emerges from the interaction between the narrative's story aspect and cognitive process type-1. On the contrary, reflexive nostalgia from the film emerges from the interaction between both the narratives' story and non-story aspects and cognitive processes type-1 and type-2. Interpreted nostalgia from the film emerges from the interaction between the narrative's non-story aspect and cognitive process type-2.

For example, three kinds of nostalgia can emerge from past images of Kamakura, which was the capital city of Japan between 1192 and 1333 (Kamakura shogunate). Kamakura is a city particularly used in Japanese films. Many leading Japanese film directors, such as Yasujiro Ozu, Mikio Naruse, Seijyun Suzuki, Shinichiro Sawai, and Hirokazu Koreeda have shot films there. In addition, between 1936 and 2001, Shochiku, a Japanese major film company, located their Ofuna film studio in Kamakura city. This city is not only favored by Japanese directors. German director Wim Wenders shot *Tokyo-Ga* (1985) in Kamakura in order to visit and explore the land of Ozu's films. *Zigeunerweisn* (1980), a film directed by Seijyun Suzuki that was set in the Taisho period (1912-1926), was shot in Kamakura during the late 1970s. The story and the rhetoric of the film evoked simple nostalgia, a good past, for not only the Taisho period but also for late 1970s film rhetoric. However, the rhetoric of *Zigeunerweisn* was the mix of S-type and NS-type rhetoric. In this film, viewers gradually realized the destabilization created through the discontinuity of the time and the space and the sudden appearance of the unfamiliar situations. The NS-type rhetoric aspect and the cognitive transition used to process type-2 can evoke reflexive and interpreted nostalgia. *Zigeunerweisn* viewers first experienced a good past from cognitive process type-1, a good and bad past from cognitive processes type-1 and type 2, and finally the reality of the past from cognitive process type-2.

*Correspondencia Jonas Mekas - J.L. Guerin* (2011), directed by Spanish film director José Luis Guerín, included a scene filmed at the Ozu's grave in Kamakura. This scene consisted not only of the grave, but also of the ants on the grave. As the viewers could not help watching the ants wandering, simple nostalgia for Ozu or Kamakura did not emerge alone from the scene. The film's viewers could experience cognitive transition through the irrational cutting to the ants.

Three kinds of nostalgia also emerge from past images of Tokyo, Japan's capital city. After the destruction caused by World War II, Tokyo circa the 1950s was a rebuilding era. This has been the target for nostalgia narratives. For example, *Always:Sunset on Third Street* (2005), directed by Takashi Yamazaki, evoked viewers' simple nostalgia for Tokyo in 1958 by using a good past story without cognitive transition. On the contrary, *Glory to the Filmmaker!* (2007), directed by Takeshi Kitano, in part imitated *Always: Sunset on Third Street.* However, as other parts emphasized the reality of the bad and poor side of 1950s Tokyo and represented one of many false imagined images of the director who appeared in the film, the viewers could not evoke a story-based simple nostalgia. Instead they evoked reflexive or interpreted nostalgia with cognitive transition.

Three kinds of nostalgia easily emerge from the films that include war narratives. *Tokyo-Ga* could be first observed with simple nostalgic view for the film world of Yasujiro Ozu. Generally, the films of Ozu have been connected to the lost beautiful past of Japan and cinema. Nevertheless, the films of Ozu, especially those shot after the World War II, slightly illustrated the shadows of the war. The films of Ozu did not alone evoke simple nostalgia. For example, *Tokyo Story* (1953) included the dialogue between a father who lost his son in the battlefield and the son' wife. This scene was the climax of *Tokyo Story* and evoked not only simple nostalgia but also reflexive or interpreted nostalgia for World War II. On the contrary, *Tokyo-Ga* quoted the crying wife scene from *Tokyo Story* so that original story and context was modified and the property of the cognitive constraint was lessened. In *Tokyo-Ga*, the film rhetoric of *Tokyo Story* became apparent. Film rhetoric alone can evoke all kinds of nostalgia.

## NOSTALGIA-BASED NARRATIVE RHETORIC COMPOSITION SYSTEM

The three kinds of nostalgia and non-nostalgia can be used for various rhetoric composition. Nostalgia-based narrative rhetoric generation can include both a story approach and non-story narrative approach.

The interaction between story understanding and constraint relaxation is one of the most important aspects of films. The authors proposed a film rhetoric composition system (FRCS) that can approach this interaction (Kanai & Ogata, 2004).

In general, film creation requires choosing and mixing rhetoric types, S-type or NS-type, according to a director's strategy based on the constraints of story comprehension. FRCS can generate different types of rhetoric from the same visual elements according to a strategy to intensify cognitive effects.

FRCS focused on the continuity and discontinuity, or the rational and irrational relationships, in the rhetoric of the film. Continuity is used in much S-type rhetoric. In contrast, discontinuity must be emphasized to create NS-type rhetoric. In this context, the viewer sometimes cannot comprehend a consistent story from the film. Consequently, attention to the rhetoric itself or cognitive process type-2 is enhanced. Discontinuities can be created using cutting techniques: placing different elements in continuous shots or irrational elements in the same shot. Different or irrational elements are emphasized through FRCS as based on these three irrational relationships in the rhetoric of the film:

**Approach 1:** Relationship between rhetorical elements of two shots
**Approach 2:** Relationship between one event and image
**Approach 3:** Relationship between sound and image

NS-type rhetoric may also have different kinds of continuity, such as actors, objects, sounds, or photographic tones. The interplay between continuity and discontinuity is important in order for the system to compose the rhetoric of the film. In NS-type rhetoric, one or more of the above discontinuity approaches may be used to generate cognitive effects through the audiovisual context. On the contrary, in S-type rhetoric, rational relationships regarding these three approaches are important.

The authors revised the system, which can compose nostalgia-based narrative rhetoric to generate three kinds of intense nostalgia effects in viewers (Naito & Kanai, 2012b). FRCS includes three parts: 1) the mechanism for retrieval of shots from rhetorical techniques; 2) the shot database based on rhetorical elements such as event, time, space, and sound; 3) the mechanism for a combination of shots. The user can decide which approaches to use to create discontinuities. FRCS then retrieves the shots from the database that fits the strategy chosen for the approaches. The shots are edited as a sequence of shots and outputted. Our system in particular uses the nostalgia effects from the story or cutting aspects of the film. By using the computational and cognitive approaches, many different films can be made from the same photos, shots, or stories in order to study the nature of nostalgia and narrative.

To develop the system, the focus was placed on continuity and discontinuity in the rhetoric of the film. In particular, focus was place on the property of the past so that the system could control the three kinds of nostalgia. The nostalgia-based FRCS can create films by using one or more S-type and NS-type rhetoric approaches through which the user can observe all possibilities of nostalgia cognition.

The revised system uses approaches 1 and 2 to enhance cognitive process type-2 as it relates to nostalgia. In addition, the system for nostalgia reuses three kinds of nostalgia from Davis (1979) as based on the two types of cognition processes.

The present version of the system uses a database of visual materials and captions from places such as Tokyo, Kamakura, and Hashima Island from 1950s time era to the present time. Tokyo and Kamakura were discussed in the previous section. Hashima Island, commonly known as Gunkanjima (Battleship Island) in Japan, was approved as a UNESCO World Heritage site in 2015 as a part of "Site of Japan's Meiji Industrial Revolution: Iron and Steel, Shipbuilding and Coal Mining"; this created controversy between Japan and the Republic of Korea. Although the island's population was over 5000 in the 1950s, the island has been abandoned since the mine closed in 1974. Because of the island's complex history, visual images of Hashima Island can generate various nostalgia effects not only stemming from the good lost past, but also the negative aspects or the reality of the past.

After users select the place and the types of nostalgia, the system can output strategic narrative rhetoric for nostalgia by controlling the past and the present images of the places and the explanatory captions based on the place and time.

First, simple nostalgia rhetoric can be composed by presenting consistent narratives such as images of the place's past and its present based on continuity editing using explanatory captions in order to secure the viewers' story comprehension (Figure 1). Based on story-based narrative processing (cognitive process type-1) simple nostalgia for good lost past images emerges.

Second, reflexive nostalgia rhetoric with regards to the timeline of the narrative can be composed using cutting techniques (Figure 2). In this case, the timeline of a composed visual narrative is not generated through a real time series. The cutting techniques used with place images creates a comparison between the past and the present and can cause the viewer to engage in both story and non-story processing (cognitive process type-1 and type-2).

*Figure 1. Simple nostalgia*

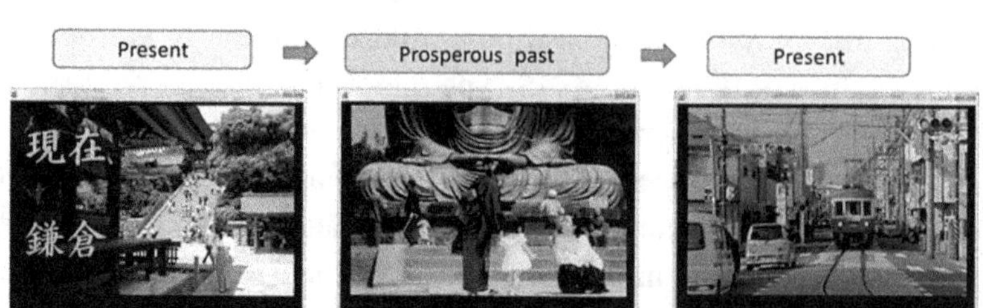

*Figure 2. Reflexive nostalgia*

Third, interpreted nostalgia rhetoric can be composed by presenting other present period pictures as an irrational cutting after presenting an image of the place's past and the present (Figure 3). The irrational cutting techniques can produce the viewers' cognitive transition and generate interpreted nostalgia for the reality of the past images based on non-story processing (cognitive process type-2). In addition, explanatory captions are infrequently used to compose interpreted nostalgia rhetoric. Repetition cutting techniques are used to make the irrational cuts.

Fourth, by accepting three kinds of nostalgia, the system can generate non-nostalgia rhetoric for the places. Non-nostalgia rhetoric can be created by presenting images without explanatory captions for which there is no specifiable information regarding the places and the time.

For example, if the user's chosen place is Kamakura, our system can compose simple nostalgia rhetoric for Kamakura by first presenting a consistent narrative without the cutting techniques. In this case, the first scene is the present image of Kamakura and the next scene is an image of Kamakura's prosperous past, with captions for every era. With regard to story grammar, simple nostalgia rhetoric provides a certain setting, time, and space for the viewer. Second, the system can compose reflexive nostalgia rhetoric for Kamakura by presenting several comparisons of present images and the mixed-ordered past images of Kamakura, with captions for every era. In this case, the period of first past scene is unspecified. With regard to story grammar, reflexive nostalgia rhetoric provides an uncertain setting for the viewers. Third, the system can compose reflexive nostalgia rhetoric for Kamakura by not only showing the present and the past images of Kamakura, but also inserting other unspecified images as irrational cuts in order to generate unfamiliar situations without captions. With regard to story grammar, the reflexive nostalgia provides no certain setting for the viewers.

*Figure 3. Interpreted nostalgia*

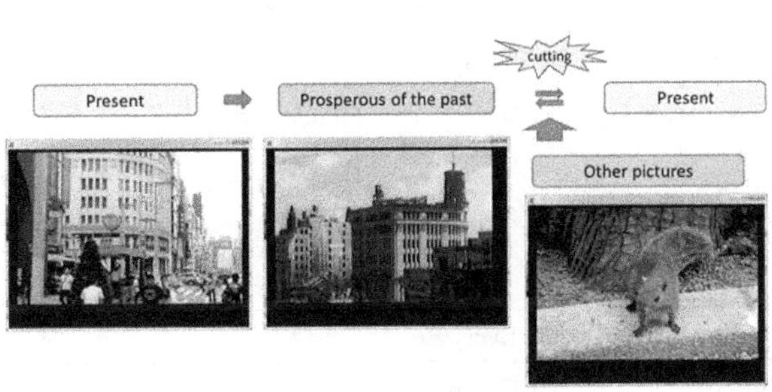

Table 1. illustrates the time structure examples and the property of three kinds of narrative rhetoric composed for nostalgia. Non-nostalgia rhetoric can be composed with no specific information on the times and the places of the continuous images (Figures 1-3).

## DISCUSSION AND FUTURE RESEARCH DIRECTIONS

Nostalgia effects are essential for cognition about the past. Film has a closer relationship with the past. Nostalgia-based film rhetoric composition can broaden the potential for narrative generation, especially from the perspective of non-story narratives, without using the story grammar and characters' goal-directed actions that were the central focus in previous studies. For example, Jhale and Young (2010) argued that visual discourse generation formed story events. Although story-based plots and characters' goal-directed actions are essential for visual narrative cognition and generation, stories can also constrain this (Ogata & Kanai, 2010). Past images in a film not associated with a specific story, words, or an event can evoke many kinds of nostalgia based on the viewers' cognition. The past images and the cutting techniques, which can relax constraint with regard to the story, can be the main components of visual narrative generation system.

Furthermore, the nature of NS-type film rhetoric can be analyzed whether or not nostalgia effects emerge. As previously discussed, NS-type film rhetoric can be composed through the discontinuity of the events or the settings. The type of nostalgia is determined by the types of the cognitive processes generated through the reliability of the rhetorical elements with regard to the time and place.

The topic of non-nostalgia NS-type rhetoric is also an important issue in film rhetoric composition. Nostalgia can emerge from every film. Nonetheless, some film directors, whose purpose is to create timeless films located in unknown places, do not want to generate nostalgia effects with viewers. Non-nostalgia based narratives can be composed using the strategy for the nostalgia effects. Moreover, every film not only has past aspects but also present aspects, as the film may be viewed in the present time. To emphasize the present aspects of films, the strategy for the non-nostalgia cognitive effects must be involved. With cutting the cognition related to the past, non-nostalgia cognitive effects are generated.

It is also important to note that some nostalgia may relate to social memory. For example, a beautiful and successful past can be fixed in the social memory as simple nostalgia. In Japan, this is reflected in

*Table 1. Time structure examples and property of three kinds of narrative rhetoric composed for nostalgia*

| | Simple Nostalgia | | Reflexive Nostalgia | | Interpreted Nostalgia | |
|---|---|---|---|---|---|---|
| Time Structure | Time (s) | Visual | Time (s) | Visual | Time (s) | Visual |
| | 0~24<br>25~48<br>49~72<br>73~96 | Present time<br>1960s<br>1970s<br>Present time | 0~16<br>17~36<br>37~52<br>53~72<br>73~96 | Present time<br>1970s<br>Present time<br>1960s<br>Present time | 0~10<br>17~36<br>37~52<br>53~72<br>73~84<br>84~96 | Present time<br>1950s<br>Other Places<br>Present Time<br>1970s<br>1950s |
| Caption | Every Era | | Every Era | | 1/3 Era | |
| Property | Good Lost Past Images | | Comparative of Past Images | | Reality of Past Images | |
| Story | Certain Setting | | Uncertain Setting | | No Certain Setting | |

the Japanese Showa era 30s (A.D. 1955-1964), which is the background for *Always: Sunset on Third Street*. On the contrary, the past can be viewed from the other viewpoints such as the dark view in *Glory to the Filmmaker!*, from which other kinds of nostalgia may emerge. The system presented in the chapter can create such viewpoints and may splinter fixed memories in order to create the other histories. The social memory should not be one fixed on beautiful stories alone.

The present version of the system is only a prototype. More detailed research on the visual images for nostalgia, the system's database, and other techniques for non-story narrative film rhetoric such as editing and cinematography are needed.

Simple nostalgia emerges from the good lost aspects of the past. Other nostalgia emerges from the negative aspects of the past. However, it is difficult to accomplish the narratology of positive and negative narratives. The present version of the system uses only narratology of non-story visual narratives. In addition, the relationship between nostalgia and the other cognitive effects such as various emotions are still being questioned. Simple nostalgia, reflexive nostalgia, and interpreted nostalgia can emerge simultaneously. The manner in which these three kinds of nostalgia overlap is also an important issues for nostalgia research.

In addition, the Portuguese and Galician word saudade has a similar meaning to other nostalgia (Lévi-Strauss, 1996). As it includes the more downfall aspects than simple nostalgia, saudade is familiar to pathos narrative. Saudade-based narrative film rhetoric composition can expand the system's potency.

## CONCLUSION

The nostalgia effects are created by interaction between cognitive processes and story and non-story rhetorical aspects of the narrative. If the viewers' cognitive processes are transited by defamiliarization from unfamiliar situations, both simple nostalgia for the good past as well as nostalgia for the bad past are enhanced by the rhetoric of the film.

Situations that are unfamiliar to the viewer can be generated through a non-centric computer program for NS-type rhetoric. Because the focus of composed NS-type rhetoric is on the relationships between rhetorical elements rather than on the events of a past story, the identical elements in the individual shots can generate reality effects used for reflexive or interpreted nostalgia.

The author re-developed a film rhetoric composition system (FRCS) that can emphasize various rhetorical aspects of moving images using a strategy to create nostalgia. The FRCS can generate various kinds of NS- and S-type rhetoric for nostalgia effects by using cutting techniques to create irrational or rational relationships between 1) two shots; 2) events and images; and 3) images and sounds. The intensities of viewer's nostalgia effects differed according to the strategy used for the relationships.

Our system can use four kinds of narrative rhetoric related to non-story, nostalgia, and cognition. The user can decide which strategic narrative approaches to use for nostalgia by establishing either discontinuity or continuity in the rhetoric of the film.

In summary, the nostalgia effects can be enhanced or reduced by controlling the interaction between the narrative's cognitive processes, the story consistencies, and non-story rhetorical aspects. If the viewers' cognitive processes are transited based on non-story narrative using the cutting techniques, reflexive and interpreted nostalgia effects from non-story type rhetoric of the film will emerge. By using the computational approach with the cutting techniques, the system can generate many different films from the same shots or stories, and thus study the nature of nostalgia and NS- and S-type rhetoric.

Finally, for computational narrative film generation, in particular about the specific place, many kinds of nostalgia can be actualized using a strategy that employs story and non-story cognitive and rhetorical aspects.

## REFERENCES

Avrahami, J., & Kareev, Y. (1994). The emergence of events. *Cognition*, *53*(3), 239–261. doi:10.1016/0010-0277(94)90050-7 PMID:7842635

Benson, T. W., & Anderson, C. (1989). *Reality fictions: The films of Frederick Wiseman*. Southern Illinois University Press.

Bordwell, D. (1985). *Narration in the fiction film*. Madison, WI: University of Wisconsin Press.

Boym, S. (2001). *The future of nostalgia*. New York, NY: Basic Books.

Brecht, B., & Willett, J. (1964). *Brecht on theatre: The development of an aesthetic*. New York, NY: Hill and Wang.

Chatman, S. (1990). *Coming to terms: The rhetoric of narrative in fiction and film*. Ithaca, NY: Cornell University Press.

Cohn, N. (2013). Visual narrative structure. *Cognitive Science*, *34*(3), 413–452. doi:10.1111/cogs.12016 PMID:23163777

Cohn, N. (2014). You're a good structure, Charlie Brown: The distribution of narrative categories in comic strips. *Cognitive Science*, *38*(7), 1317–1359. doi:10.1111/cogs.12116 PMID:24646175

Cutting, J. E., Brunick, K. L., & Canden, A. (2012). Perceiving event dynamics and parsing Hollywood films. *Journal of Experimental Psychology*, *38*(6), 1476–1490. PMID:22449126

Cutting, J. E., & Iricinschi, C. (2014). Re-presentations of space in Hollywood movies: An event-indexing analysis. *Cognitive Science*, *35*, 1–23. PMID:25087776

Davis, F. (1979). *Yearning for yesterday: a sociology of nostalgia*. New York: Free Press.

Deleuze, G. (1985). *L' Image-temps*. Paris, France: Les Editions de Minuit.

Eisenstein, S. M. (1942). *The film sense* (J. Leyda, Trans.). New York, NY: Harcourt Brace.

Genette, G. (1980). *Narrative discourse: An essay in method* (J. E. Lewin, Trans.). Ithaca, NY: Cornell University Press.

Higson, A. (2014). Nostalgia is not what it used to be: Heritage films, nostalgia websites and contemporary consumers. *Consumption Markets & Culture*, *17*(2), 120–142. doi:10.1080/10253866.2013.776305

Holbrook, M. B., & Schindler, R. M. (1991). Echoes of the dear departed past: Some work in progress on nostalgia. In R. H. Holman & M. R. Solomon (Eds.), *Advances in Consumer Research, 18* (pp. 330–333). Provo, UT: Association for Consumer Research.

Jhale, A., & Young, M. R. (2010). Cinematic visual discourse: Representation, generation, and evaluation. *IEEE Transactions on Computational Intelligence and AI in Games*, *2*(2), 69–81. doi:10.1109/TCIAIG.2010.2046486

Kanai, A. (2001a). The story as a constraint on film. In *Proceedings of the Third International Conference on Cognitive Science* (pp. 503-506). Beijing, China: Academic Press.

Kanai, A. (2001b). Cognitive process model toward the rhetoric of the film. *Cognitive Studies*, *8*(2), 139–150.

Kanai, A. (2002). Film rhetoric and cognition. In *Proceedings of 17th Congress of the International Association of Empirical Aesthetics* (pp. 209-212). Takarazuka, Japan: Academic Press.

Kanai, A. (2003). Non-story type film rhetoric and cognitive effects. In *Proceedings of the Fourth International Conference on Cognitive Science* (pp. 259-264). Sydney, Australia: Academic Press.

Kanai, A. (2006). Reality of unfamiliar situations on moving image. In *Proceedings of 19th Congress of the International Association of Empirical Aesthetics* (pp. 800-803). Avignon, France: Academic Press.

Kanai, A., & Kodama, K. (2010). Film edit design: Story and irrational cutting. *Cognitive Studies*, *17*(3), 444–458.

Kanai, A., & Ogata, T. (2004). Non-story processing on the film rhetoric composition system. In *Proceedings of 18th Congress of the International Association of Empirical Aesthetics* (pp. 433-436). Lisbon, Portugal: Academic Press.

Lévi-Strauss, C. (1996). *Saudades de São Paulo*. São Paulo, Brasil: Companhia das letras.

Naito, Y., & Kanai, A. (2012a). The narrative structure of nostalgia cognition and film. In *Proceedings of the International Conference on Cognitive Science'12*. Sapporo, Japan: Academic Press.

Naito, Y., & Kanai, A. (2012b). Nostalgia and film creation. In *Proceeding of the 26th Annual Conference of the Japanese Society for Artificial Intelligence, 2012*, (1N1-OS-1a-2). Yamaguchi, Japan: Academic Press.

Ogata, T., & Kanai, A. (2010). *Monogatariron no jyohogaku jyosetsu: Monogatariseisei no shiso to gijyutsu wo megutte* [An introduction to informatics of narratology: Towards the thoughts and technologies of narrative generation]. Tokyo, Japan: Gakubun-sha.

Rooney, R., Benson, C., & Hennessy, E. (2012). The apparent reality of movies and emotional arousal: A study using physiological and self-report measures. *Poetics*, *40*(5), 405–422. doi:10.1016/j.poetic.2012.07.004

Rumelhart, D. E. (1975). Notes on a schema for stories. In D. G. Bobrow & A. Collins (Eds.), *Representation and understanding: Studies in cognitive science* (pp. 211–236). New York, NY: Academic Press.

Shklovsky, V. (1965). Art as technique. In *Russian formalist criticism: Four essays* (L. T. Lemon & M. J. Reis, Trans. & Eds.). Lincoln, NE: University of Nebraska Press. (Original work published 1917)

Stern, B. B. (1992). Historical and personal nostalgia in advertising text: The fin de siècle effect. *Journal of Advertising*, *21*(4), 11–22. doi:10.1080/00913367.1992.10673382

Thorndyke, P. W. (1977). Cognitive structures in comprehension and memory of narrative discourse. *Cognitive Psychology*, *9*(1), 77–110. doi:10.1016/0010-0285(77)90005-6

Visch, V. T., & Tan, E. S. (2009). Categorizing moving objects into film genres: The effect of animacy attribution, emotional response, and the deviation from non-fiction. *Cognition*, *110*(2), 265–272. doi:10.1016/j.cognition.2008.10.018 PMID:19118823

## KEY TERMS AND DEFINITIONS

**Cognitive Transition:** The transition in cognitive narrative processing, especially from story-based to non-story based.

**Cutting Technique:** A technique used to irrationally cut film to create an irrational relationship.

**Interpreted Nostalgia:** Nostalgia that emerges from the reality or the uncertainty of the past with cognitive transition and defamiliarization.

**Non-Story Narrative:** A collection of elements including images or texts, without a consistent story or specific event.

**Nostalgia:** The emotions that arise from the rise and fall of other times in the place.

**Reflexive Nostalgia:** Nostalgia that emerges from both the good and bad past with cognitive transition and defamiliarization.

**Simple Nostalgia:** Nostalgia that emerges from the good past without cognitive transition and defamiliarization.

# Chapter 16
# *Kabuki* as Multiple Narrative Structures

**Takashi Ogata**
*Iwate Prefectural University, Japan*

## ABSTRACT

*This chapter seeks to undertake a comprehensive survey and analysis of "kabuki" to aim to explore a narrative generation-reception and narrative production-consumption model of "kabuki" from the viewpoint of an information system, and in particular, a narrative generation system. A fundamental concept of the modeling is "multiplicity," or multiple narrative structures. In addition, the author associates the model to the concept of the "Geino Information System: GIS," representing a system model in which multiple narrative generation and production mechanisms or processes are included. This chapter also presents introductory knowledge on "kabuki", including the history and basic terms, as background for the discussion.*

## INTRODUCTION

This chapter aims to survey and analyze *kabuki* in order to explore and create a "narrative generation-reception model" or a "narrative production-consumption model" of *kabuki* from the viewpoint of an information system or, in particular, a narrative generation system. A fundamental concept applied to this task is that of "multiplicity" or "multiple narrative structures" in *kabuki*. In addition, this chapter seeks to bridge a comprehensive survey and analysis of *kabuki* based on the concept of multiplicity or multiple narrative structures with a more generalized conceptual model, including both narrative generation-reception and production-consumption processes.

The synthesized narrative generation architecture that the author has been designing and developing, i.e., the "Integrated Narrative Generation System: INGS" (Ogata, 2010; Akimoto & Ogata, 2014), forms the background of this study. Moreover, it represents an objective into which the results of this study can be fed. The INGS has been explained in detail in the introductory chapter of this book. It is a basic or fundamental system that has a narrative generation process by a single subject operating on a basis similar to that of an individual human being. However, the ultimate goal of the author's narra-

DOI: 10.4018/978-1-5225-0432-0.ch016

Copyright © 2016, IGI Global. Copying or distributing in print or electronic forms without written permission of IGI Global is prohibited.

tive generation project, including the development of INGS, is to involve one or more INGSs to realize various narrative generation application systems and social distribution mechanisms using automatic narrative generation functions, etc. By social distribution, the author means mechanisms to be linked to a new type of business model for social applications using the WWW for the narrative generation system itself, a content business mechanism using narrative generation functions, etc. This chapter anticipates the relevant concepts and directions for the future social distribution of INGS through exploring and constituting a narrative generation model of *kabuki*.

In particular, the conceptual model referred to as the "*Geino* Information System: GIS" (Amino, Kawamura, & Ogata, 2002; Kawamura & Ogata, 1997, 2000, 2002) is associated to INGS in this plan. Although the Japanese word *geino* carries the meaning of entertainment and amusement, it simultaneously has complex and historical signification that includes elements from Shinto shrine rituals and magical tradition. The GIS is designed to be a system model in which multiple narrative generation and production mechanisms or processes perform a social level task using one or more INGSs. It is a framework in which various levels of narrative generation processes can be driven by the authors, receivers, characters, actors, and actresses included in the system. In short, INGS and GIS are designed, respectively, to correspond to narrative generation-reception and narrative production-consumption as an entire system. A *kabuki* play is a collection of multiple narratives built around original scenarios, authentic and related histories, and the actors' private scenes. It is intended for the construction to be connected with plans for a future narrative generation system comprising several other narrative generation systems. This chapter will explore the conceptual design of the "GIS including INGS" by surveying and analyzing *kabuki* according to the concept of multiplicity and multiple narrative structures.

This study is also related to the "Expanded Literary Theory: ELT" (Ogata, 2002, 2014) that was described in the introductory chapter to this book, which provides some of the background for the author's research and development project, insofar as this intends to study *kabuki* as a literary and artistic genre using a computational approach. Although narrative generation studies have generally focused on formal mechanisms, it is anticipated that the contents to be represented or used by such formal mechanism are an important factor of narrative generation research in the future. Additionally, tackling Japan's unique art genre of *kabuki* represents a step in a new direction in cultural approaches to narrative generation. Cultural elements will be used to form a characteristic for each narrative generation system. The *geino* in GIS is strongly associated with a historical flow of artistic tradition in Japanese culture, in which *kabuki* is rooted as a representative genre.

## BACKGROUND

This section introduces the following two background models relating to GIS and INGS, respectively: multiple narrative structures and narrative generation.

### The Model of Multiple Narrative Structures and GIS

Multiple narrative structures refer to a conceptual model by which a narrative text is multiply constituted; at the same time, the narrative generation process is also multiply executed. For example, a narrative text involves several subjects, such as a narrator inside the narrative and an author outside of the text, and also contains an independent world that differs from the real world. The constituents including characters, objects, spaces, etc., show both internal signs, such as a character's emotion and the semantics of space and objects, and external signs, such as the outward appearances of a person and an object. Additionally, a narrative generation mechanism, or a narrative production mechanism to be exact, can be divided into a part that corresponds to the process of generating a narrative text at a single (similar to the individual) level of generation and a part equivalent to the process of conducting more complicated or circulative production at the collective level. The former is the process through which only a single narrative text, including multiple processing that corresponds to the elements inside the narrative text, is incrementally generated, while the latter indicates social multiple narrative contents containing a variety of single generation processes to be linked to social production organizations, such as the production companies for television, newspapers, movies, publishing, computer games, and so on.

From the point of view of the ELT, this model is partially related to the theory of polyphonic voices by Bakhtin (1963) and that of intertextuality by Kristeva (1980), as these theories also consider multiple relationships inside a narrative or with other narratives. However, the model of multiple narrative structures is more inclusive because it is also associated with multiplicity through social organizations as part of the narrative production-consumption system. A social organization that conducts narrative creation is also a subject or agent of narrative generation at a collective or macro level.

The model of multiple narrative structures is a system model to be finally realized technologically, if only partially, as a narrative generation program, though it still remains a theoretical model. In particular, the model is intended to be designed and implemented as a GIS system that includes or uses one or more INGS systems. The GIS that plays narrative production and consumption as a multiple narrative structures' model is equivalent to a kind of meta-mechanism for INGS as a narrative generation and reception mechanism. GIS was originally based on the survey and analysis of Japanese folklore, performing arts, including *kabuki*, and angles of the modern entertainment business. A *geino* organization such as an entertainment agency or promoter is a synthetic narrative production-consumption system that aggregates a variety of narrative generation-reception processes of scenarios as well as the lives of actors or actresses, etc. GIS is a comprehensive and multiple framework in which various narrative generation processes are driven by authors, receivers, characters, actors and actresses, directors, and producers, etc. It is therefore one of the systems of multiple narrative structures. *Kabuki* as viewed in a *geino* system can be regarded through a concrete appearance of GIS including INGS. This chapter corresponds to the first report that directs the design and implementation of GIS through the survey and analysis of *kabuki*.

Figure 1 shows an original conceptual version of GIS. In this figure, a GIS system is divided into the "*geino* producer mechanism" and "receiver mechanism." The "geino history" is not a concrete mechanism but represents the resulted contents and a circular historical collection. The *Geino* producer mechanism continuously creates "*geino* works," "life works," and "*geinojins* (geino performers)," using each of the resources. "*Geino* event" and "*life* event" under the "*geino* history" mean individual social events constituted by *geino* works, life works, and *geinojins*; and "*geino* event sequence" and "life event sequence" are events that are sequentially produced by the *geino* producer mechanism. On the other hand, the receiver mechanism is a framework that includes a narrative receiver as an individual person or as a collective of people. For instance, an audience member of a *kabuki* play forms an image from the *kabuki* experience, talks about the impression to her husband, and writes an essay on her personal blog. The speech and essay correspond to the "trail information." The *geino* producer mechanism produces

*Figure 1. The original GIS model*

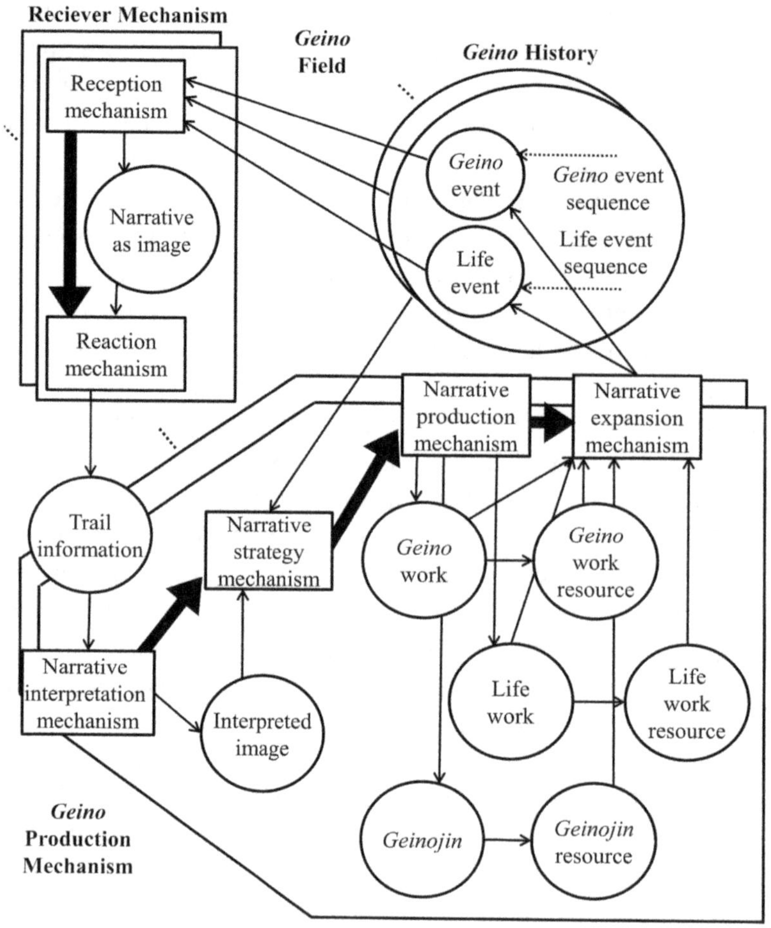


the next and new events according to such trail information and other types of information. The main work here, on the part of the author, is to transform and extend this original GIS model based on the INGS and the *kabuki* investigation.

## Narrative Generation and INGS

The next background of relevance is that of INGS. Although this has been developing incrementally, it is already functional. INGS is an organized collection of computer programs that synthesizes the previous design and development of narrative generation mechanisms by the author. The system also aims to form a foundation of future research by the author, including various application systems and experimental studies. In addition, it will continue to be implemented incrementally to meet the following needs, among others: requirements from the application systems, expanding dictionaries for semantic concepts and words, etc., various types of knowledge bases, and the necessary improvement and deepening of the system design. In the context of this study, INGS will be contained in GIS as a single narrative generation function at a macro level for circulative narrative generation and socially distributed narrative production.

Before a simple overview of INGS, reference will be made to the current situation of the narrative generation system. At present, the development of narrative generation systems has been a practical and technical subject. As a guideline, the majority of past narrative generation systems is divided into two groups of approaches based on artificial intelligence (AI) techniques that support their development: a problem-solving approach and a structural approach. Moreover, as a third approach, an integral or synthesized approach is also coming into force.

A chief strategy for the former is planning, or having a goal-plan strategy (Schank & Abelson, 1977). For example, TALE-SPIN (Meehan, 1980) applied the method to a system that automatically generated different stories from a story world based on characters' actions to achieve specific goals. Although more comprehensive and complicated, DAYDREAMER (Mueller, 1990) and MINSTREL (Turner, 1994) are also classified into this group. The system based on the Aesop World (Okada & Endo, 1992) utilizes large-scale conceptual dictionaries that employ goal-plan mechanisms of characters as the basic method for story generation.

By contrast, the structural approach involves a narrative generation process based on narrative structural formalizations, such as story grammar and story schema. GESTER (Pemberton, 1989) and JOSEPH (Lang, 1999) are both narrative generation systems consisting of an interpreter with both a story grammar and a world model. The story grammar in each system defines the abstract structure of stories, and the world model contains elements embodied within the story structure: actors or characters, objects, and causal relations between events. BRUTUS (Bringsjord & Ferrucci, 1999) employs a blended approach using various methods related to problem solving and planning as well as structural techniques such as story grammar and theme structure.

Synthesized systems, such as the above-mentioned DAYDREAMER, MINSTREL, and BRUTUS, may be grouped into the third approach.

Moreover, there are differences between "story" and "narrative" generation. A story generally means a sequential flow of events and an element in a narrative. A narrative is a more comprehensive concept that includes a story as well as the discourse: namely, the structure of how to narrate the story and the narration itself. The main theme of previous research has been the "story." In this sense, many narrative generation systems should be called story generation systems.

Although INGS adopts the story-grammar approach as a basic method, it pragmatically uses both of the methods in an organized mechanism. In overview, the former method is mainly used for the modeling of characters, and the latter one is mainly used to make storylines. However, INGS provides a new synthetic architecture including a variety of components that are not contained in the frameworks. INGS uses the organic combination in a consistent architecture of previously independent mechanisms or programs. The system organically collects various elements in narrative generation relating to story generation, discourse or plot generation, and surface expression generation, such as language, pictures, and music.

On the other side, a recent tendency in the design and development of narrative generation systems has been to adopt contemporary literary theories such as narratology. One of the essential characteristics of narrative generation research into INGS is also to introduce narratology and literary theories as the ELT to be concretely used in the mechanisms of the system.

Figure 2 presents an outline of INGS as a collective attempt in which various narrative techniques and knowledge are organized in a synthetic system associated with certain literary theories to realize ELT. See the introductory chapter in this book for further details on INGS.

*Figure 2. An overall architecture of INGS*

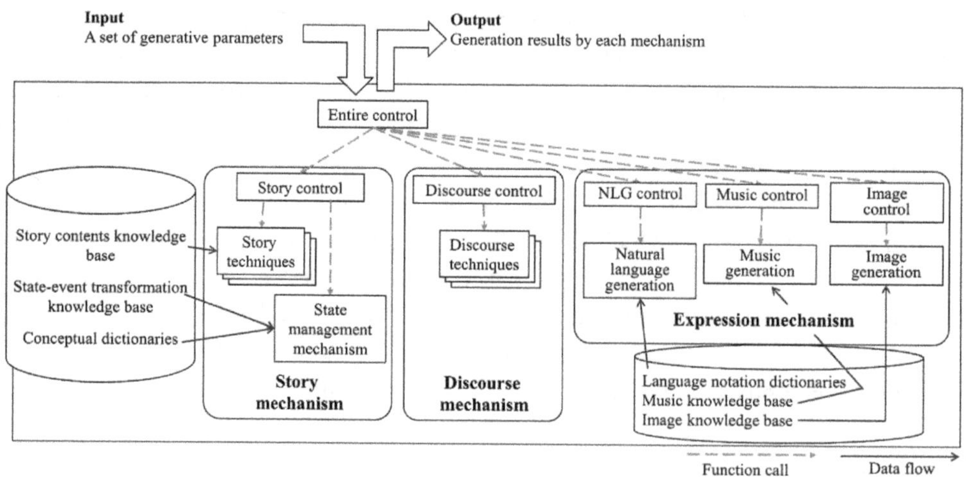


This chapter seeks to undertake a comprehensive survey and analysis of *kabuki* to introducing the acquired methods and techniques into GIS, including INGS, according to the design image based on both the system architectures of GIS and INGS. Overview, the parts of "narrative production mechanism" and "narrative expansion mechanism" in the system model of GIS are corresponded to INGS.

## WHAT IS *KABUKI*? A SHORT OVERVIEW

The Japanese for *kabuki* (歌舞伎) consists of the three Chinese characters: "song" (*ka*, 歌), "dance" (*bu*, 舞), and "acting" (*ki*, 伎). At the same time, the term originated from the verb *kabuku* (かぶく, 傾く), meaning "to incline" and "lean away." The word generally implies strange, unusual, or unconventional styles; and it has shaped the mental image of the tradition of *kabuki*.

A *kabuki* play is a collection of a variety of narratives: namely, it has the appearance of a multiple narrative structure in the sense that its whole is a multiple structure; therefore, its narrative generation should comprise a combination of several narrative generation processes. At the same time, a *kabuki* play forms multiple narrative structures in the sense that it contains narrative structures in various levels. Kawatake (2003) maintains that *kabuki* has a chimeral nature because of its amalgamation of diverse elements in a wide variety of aspects. This chapter will approach the elements from the viewpoint of a system that integrates various mechanisms or processes.

Before the multiple narrative structure(s) are discussed, an overview of the history and characteristics of *kabuki* is first provided as relevant background knowledge for the reader in the section that follows. Although Kawatake (2003) presents a comprehensive description of *kabuki*, this is summarized and edited to include the author's own opinions on the basis of the content of the book and a small pamphlet by Kawatake (1992) to give a compact overview of the main concepts and terms of *kabuki*.

## A History of *Kabuki*

In its pioneering days (the early seventeenth century), *kabuki* was performed by women. Most of the first *kabuki* plays were called *yujo* ("prostitutes") *kabuki*; but later, the performers changed to "boys" (*wakashu kabuki*), and then to "adult men" (*yaro kabuki*). According to Kawatake (1992), a direct reason for these changes was the suppression of the Tokugawa shogunate government. However, Imao (1979) asserts that the mixing of men and women was not necessarily a rare phenomenon in the traditional flow of Japanese folkloric *geino* performing arts, and the change from the *yujo kabuki* to the *yaro kabuki* was hence potentially based on the flexible social system of *geino*. In the *yaro kabuki*, *kabuki* acquired the basic styles and forms that have continued up until now. Over about the following 360 years (and about 400 years if its beginnings are taken as *yujo kabuki*), *kabuki* has held on to its tradition, experiencing many changes and innovations.

*Kabuki* originated in "the review-like-entertainment, consisting of medleys of songs and dances" (Kawatake, 1992) of O-Kuni of Izumo (1572–?) and her troupe of itinerant female performers. It is a historically important fact that the first form of *kabuki* was established by female performers. From 1603, when she was known to have arrived in Kyoto, O-Kuni set up a stage similar to that of *Noh* drama at the Kitano Shrine or Shijo Gawara on the banks of the River Kamo. The genre performed by O-Kuni and her troupe was originally that of *nembutsu odori* ("dance chanting the name of Buddha") that inherited the tradition of the dance of *furyu* ("elegance") as a folk theatrical art. The genre consisted of elements of dramatic interludes, short scenes with a simple narrative structure, and accompanying music played on the *shamisen*. The style created by O-Kuni, *O-Kuni odori*, was the origin of *O-Kuni kabuki* as a genre of drama. After *O-Kuni kabuki*, there was a proliferation of female troupes called *yujo kabuki*. However, in 1629, the Tokugawa government prohibited the *yujo kabuki* for corrupt public morals. Since this prohibition, with very few exceptions, women or actresses have not been permitted to appear at any licensed theatres for *kabuki* up until the present age. Through this historical process, all of the players of *kabuki* changed from women or actresses to men or actors. In particular, the dramatic characters of women have been performed by men as the *onnagata*—an actor playing a female role. The *onnagata* has been inherited until now as one of the most important elements related to magical power in *kabuki*.

In 1651, the *wakashu kabuki* was also prohibited for having the same corrupt morals by the government. It was the next form, *yaro kabuki*, which established the fundamental style of classical *kabuki* that has been inherited by modern *kabuki*, as performed today. At this new stage of its development, luckily or unluckily, *kabuki* had opportunities for qualitative evolution as a genre in dramatic arts in the wider sense. In addition to simple singing and dancing styles that centered on a scene, *kabuki* began to have longer stories, more logical plots, and more realistic performing styles. These were some of the most essential elements for the subsequent expansion of *kabuki*.

The first artistically important age was the Genroku era (1688–1704). Chikamatsu Monzaemon (1653–1724), who was one of the greatest authors during this period, wrote a variety of plays, including *kabuki* and *ningyo-joruri*, with excellent stories and plots, beautiful words and representation, and tense theatrical effects. Sakata Tojuro (1647–1709), who was a pioneering actor, created the soft and romantic playing style (*wagoto*), and Yoshizawa Ayame (1673–1729) created the foundation of the art of the *onnagata*.

In its early days, the central area for *kabuki* was the *Kamigata* (Kyoto and Osaka), which was where the performers worked. But Edo (current Tokyo) also became a central place of performance from this age. One of the representative actors in Edo of the Genroku era was Ichikawa Danjuro I (1660–1704), who created the *aragoto* (vigorous) style as opposed to the above *wagoto*.

From the viewpoint of genre, *kabuki* was a kind of organic collection of previously diverse *geino* genres. *Kabuki* originally inherited various classical performing arts, including mainly *bugaku* (ancient court dances), the above *furyu* and *nembutsu odori*, and *Noh* and *kyogen* (masked dance-drama and its attendant farces). The biggest innovation regarding the scenarios through all of the history of *kabuki* was the introduction of the scenarios of *ningyo-joruri*, which is a kind of puppet theatre. In a *ningyo-joruri* play, narrators (*tayu*) narrate a written scenario (*joruri*) with accompanying *shamisen* music by the players, and some *ningyo-tsukai* precisely manipulate the puppet dolls in time with the narration and music. Many popular classical *kabuki* works have *ningyo-joruri* scenarios as their origin. Although Chikamatsu Monzaemon wrote many *kabuki* scenarios, he was at the same time an author of *ningyo-joruri*, and many of his works have been adapted to *kabuki* to be played by human actors. In the adaptation, words narrated by *tayu* in *ningyo-joruri* are divided into the parts of the narration by *takemoto* (narrators) and the speech and action of actors. The greatest works that follow were also originally written for *ningyo-joruri*: *Kanadehon Chushingura*,[1] *Sugawara Denju Tenarai Kagami*,[2] and *Yoshitsune Sembon Zakura*.[3] (For each *kabuki* work with a superscript (number), the English title and other information are shown in the Appendix.)

Although *ningyo-joruri* itself diminished in the second half of the eighteenth century, *kabuki* plays originating from *ningyo-joruri*, called *joruri kyogen*, *gidayu kyogen*, or *maruhon kabuki*, formed the main group of *kabuki* works, producing many great authors, such as Kino Kaion (1663–1742), Takeda Izumu I (?–1747) and II (1691–1756), Namiki Sousuke (1695–1751), and Chikamatsu Hanji (1725–1783), among others. On the other hand, pure *kabuki*, which was a sub-genre originally written as *kabuki*, also had many great authors, such as Namiki Shoza (1730–1773), Nagawa Kamesuke (1771–1785, historical records), Namiki Gohei (1748–1808), Tsuuchi Jihei II (1679–1760), and Sakurada Jisuke (1734–1806), among others. In their age, Nakamura Nakazo I (1736–1790), Ichikawa Danjuro V (1741–1804), and Nakamura Utaemon I (1714–1791) were also known as excellent actors.

In the early years of the nineteenth century, at the end of the Edo era, a variety of *kabuki* styles or sub-genres were created: In *ki-zawamono* that were changed from *sewamono*, thieves and murderers became the heroes in plays in which cruelty and eroticism abounded, and in *henge-mono*, a "transformation dance," a single performer displayed his skill in a medley of contrasting roles. "Transformation" of characters is one of the important features of *kabuki* drama and narrative. The following are known as outstanding *kabuki* writers and works: Tsuruya Namboku IV (1755–1829) (*Yotsuya Kaidan*,[4] *O-Some no Schichiyaku*[5]); Segawa Joko III (1806–1881) (*Kirare Yosa [Yo ha Naake Ukina no Yokogushi]*,[6] *Sakura Giminden*[7]), and Kawatake Mokuami (1816–1893) (*Sannin Kichisa Kuruwa no Hatsugai*,[8] *Aoto Zoushi Hana no Nishiki-e*[9]). Celebrated actors of this era were Matsumoto Koshiro V (1764–1838), Ichikawa Danjuro VII (1791–1859), and Ichikawa Kodanji IV (1812–1866), among others.

The Emperor Meiji restored imperial rule in 1868 and the Edo era ended. Under the considerable influence of western culture and knowledge, *kabuki* also encountered a crisis. A variety of play schools appeared, such as *shinpa* ("New School") and *shingeki* ("New Theatre"), i.e., western plays in Japanese translation. Moreover, with the development of technologies in modern society, new media for entertainment, including cinema and television, also appeared. However, in this drastically changing historical landscape, *kabuki* has continued to evolve as a mixed and active genre of art and entertainment, integrating both longstanding classical traditions and novel experimental trials. The history of *kabuki* is divided into the age of classical tradition of the Edo era, spanning about 260 years, and the age of new *kabuki* since the Meiji era, lasting for 150 or more years. *Kabuki* plays were always contemporary works through the Edo era. In contrast, since the Meiji era, the main staging style has repetitively used classical repertories. However, also based on the circumstances of the time, the world of *kabuki* has created many plays with new forms and styles that clearly differ from the classical works. The history of *kabuki* is formed by the synthesis of these two periods.

Symbolic and creative actors in the new age were Ichikawa Danjuro IX (1838–1903), Onoe Kikugoro V (1844–1903), Ichikawa Sadanji I (1842–1904), Ichikawa Danzo VII (1836–1911), and Nakamura Utaemon V (1865–1940). New generations of writers, such as Tsubouchi Shoyo (1859–1935), Fukuchi Ochi (1841–1906), Okamoto Kido (1872–1939), Mayama Seika (1878–1948), Uno Nobuo (1904–1991), Hojo Hideji (1902–1996), and Mishima Yukio (1925–1970) provided many new *kabuki* scenarios (Nakamura, 2006).

## Characteristics of *Kabuki*

*Kabuki* has a variety of characteristics as a complicated *geino* genre based on the historical accumulation of tradition. This section provides a simple overview of the background knowledge needed to consider the multiple narrative structures of *kabuki*, based on the summarized explanation by Kawatake (1992, 2003) mainly. First, several elements of the stage and audience are shown in Table 1.

Next, the *kabuki* repertoire is divided into the two broad categories of drama and dance. The first drama can be considered dependent upon the following two categories: "pure *kabuki*" and *Gidayu-kyogen* (Table 2) and "history plays" and "contemporary plays" (Table 3). The second major genre is dance (Table 4).

Next, in *shamisen* music, there are various schools and styles as far as *kabuki* is concerned, such as "singing style" (including *Nagauta* ("long song")) and "narrative style" including *Kiyomoto*, *Tokiwazu*, and *Gidayu*.

*Table 1. Several elements of the stage and audience*

| Element | Overview |
|---|---|
| Hanamichi | This is used as one of the entrances and exits for the actors. At the same time, it is also a part of the stage as an acting area. For instance, when a leading actor is entering or acting in the position of *shichisan* ("seven-three"), which is a particular position between the curtained room at the back of the theatre and the main stage, some of the audience members often do *kakegoe* by the actor's *yago* (house name). The *suppon*, situated in the seven-three special position in the *hanamichi*, is the position through which supernatural characters appear and hide. |
| Revolving Stage | One role of the revolving stage in the middle of the main stage is to reduce the intermission time. Another important role is visual, as the audience is able to appreciate "any contrast in lighting" and the "appearance or atmosphere between different sets." |
| Official Curtain | *Kabuki* uses two types of curtain (*maku*). *Joshiki-maku* ("formal" or "official" curtain), which is used for plays from the traditional repertoire, is the horizontally pulled curtain with three colors. The "drop" curtain (*doncho*) is mainly used for dances, dance-dramas, and modern *kabuki* plays. |
| Other Stage Mechanisms | In the *geza* ("lower seat") or *o-hayashi-beya* ("musicians' room"), which is a hidden room to the far left of the stage, musicians play the background music with instruments such as *shamisen*, flute, and many types of drums. On the other hand, in the *yuka* ("floor"), to the far right of the stage, a narrator or *tayu* provides the narration, accompanied by a *shamisen* musician. This form was adapted for *kabuki* from the style of *ningyo-joruri*. |

*Table 2. Pure kabuki and Gidayu-kyogen*

| Genre | Overview | Examples |
|---|---|---|
| Pure *Kabuki* | This term refers to original *kabuki* plays that were written specifically for performance by *kabuki* actors. | *Sukeroku*;[10]*Soga no Taimen*;[11]*Benten Kozo*;[12]*Yotsuya Kaidan* |
| Gidayu Kyogen | This refers to the most popular *kabuki* repertoire that is adapted from *ningyo-joruri*. "*Gidayu*" is a great artist (*tayu*) in the Genroku era who created a new style of *ningyo-joruri*, and "*kyogen*" means story drama. As the plots of *ningyo-joruri* scenarios are generally very tense and complicated, the introduction contributes to *kabuki* plays to increase the quality of the scenarios. | *Sugawara Denju Tenarai Kagami*; *Yoshitsune Sembon Zakura*; *Kanadehon Chushingura* |

*Table 3. History plays (jidai-mono) and contemporary plays (sewa-mono)*

| Genre | Overview | Sub-genre | Overview | Examples |
|---|---|---|---|---|
| History Plays (or Period Plays) (*Jidai-mono*) | These deal with events relating to the nobility or the warrior class and are set in the distant past for the audience. Solemn scenes appear in many *jidai-mono*. There are the three types, as displayed by sub-genre. | Court Drama (*O-cho-mono*) | This type is set in the Heian era (794–1185 or 1192) and the principal characters are imperial or aristocratic figures from that period. | *Sugawara Denju Tenarai Kagami*; *Imoseyama Onna Teikin*[13] |
| | | *Jidai-mono* in its narrow meaning | This is set approximately 450 years from the Genji and Heike clan wars of the twelfth century to the "Warring States" period of the sixteenth century. | *Yoshitsune Sembon Zakura*; *Ichi-no-Tani Futaba Gunki*;[14]*Kumagai Jinya*;[15]*Honcho Nijushiko*;[16]*Ehon Taikoki*;[17]*Soga no Taimen* |
| | | *O-ie-mono* ("Great House" play) | This dramatizes a political incident in which a politician in feudal Japan plots to usurp the family's power. | *Meiboku Sendai Hagi*;[18]*Kagamiyama*;[19]*Kanadehon Chushingura* |
| Contemporary Plays (*Sewa-mono*) | These are dramas that are played in the present for pre-modern audiences, and ordinary events and scenes appear in many cases. | Ordinary | The theme of love and death is frequently dealt with. | *Sonezaki Shinju*;[20]*Shinju Ten no Amijima*;[21]*Godairiki Koi no Fujime*;[22]*Shimpan Utazaimon*[23] |
| | | A special type is *Ki-zewamono* ("raw" *sewa-mono*) | It gives "a racy portrayal of raw life in Edo, at that time, with thieves, criminal-priests and prostitutes figuring prominently." | *Sannin Kichisa*; *Shiranami Gonin Otoko*[24]; *Kirare Yosa* |

For the music and sound effects, *hyoshigi* and *geza* music are impressive elements. *Hyoshigi* is a sound effect for creating a unique atmosphere for every scene (particularly, the ending and climax of each scene), played by an expert performer (*kyogen-sakusha*) on the right-hand side of the *kabuki* stage. On the other hand, *geza* music, as stated in the history of *kabuki*, is played as background music and a variety of sound effects to create a unique auditory atmosphere.

Next, *mie* is one of the visual effects for creating "stylized acting and pictorial beauty" (Kawatake, 1992), which is a formal method of *kabuki* to stop the body actions of actors and temporal progression

*Table 4. Dance-dramas from Noh, dance of comic pieces, and pure kabuki dance*

| Genre | Overview | Examples |
|---|---|---|
| Dance-Dramas deriving from *Noh* | These were transformed from particular *Noh* plays. This type forms a relatively big group called "*matsubame-mono*." | *Musume Dojoji;*[25]*Momiji-gari.*[26] "Other dance-dramas" closely follow the *Noh* originals. There are famous works such as: *Kanjincho;*[27]*Tsuchigumo;*[28]*Funa Benkei*[29] |
| Dance of Comic Pieces | These are adaptations of *kyogen* farces similar to the above group formally. However, in the quality of the scenarios, many stories of *Noh* are serious and solemn, while stories of *kyogen* are funny and humorous. | *Migawari Zazen;*[30]*Bo Shibari*[31] |
| Pure *Kabuki* Dances | These were originally intended for *kabuki*. For instance, a group of pure *kabuki* is made to draw festivals and street scenes in daily life in the Edo era with delightful and colorful techniques. | *Seki no To;*[32]*Echigo-jishi;*[33]*Noriai-bune;*[34]*Sanja Matsuri;*[35]*Mizu-uri*[36] |

to make a picture on the stage beyond a realistic style of performance (further, photographs record the figures (Ohkura, 2001)). In this way, *kabuki* depicts a posed picture in the temporal flow of a story and the actions of the performers. This pictorial effect has two directions according to the type of the performance by an actor or the quality of the *kabuki* plays: *aragoto* and *wagoto* (Table 5).

Kawatake (1992) concludes that *kabuki* is "a world of stylized beauty" and "the staging, costumes and stylization of music, movement and speech, combine to raise even the ordinary and mundane to an altogether different dimension." This opinion is certainly a fair representation of one of the important features of *kabuki*. But, on the other hand, in the author's opinion, *kabuki* has further had the quality of portraying excellently realistic and humane narratives that draw on human emotion and behavior, and has dealt with important, essential, and symbolic issues in each age.

From a theoretical viewpoint, the author considers *kabuki* to have had many characteristics that differ from the basic concept of Western drama since Aristotle (1895). Aristotle aimed at constituting a general theory of drama through the analysis of a tragedy. A drama for him is a systematic artificial object that has a tense structure for representing a story or a plot placed in the central position. In overview, for Aristotle, a drama was a system in which a variety of different elements, such as language rhetoric

*Table 5. Aragoto and wagoto*

| Style | Overview | Example |
|---|---|---|
| Aragoto ("wild" or "rough" style) | *Aragoto* is a typical style of Edo *kabuki* that represents the great power of a superhuman hero using exaggerated and symbolic actions, poses, speeches, and makeup (*kumadori,* "drawing shadows"). In many cases, *kabuki* plays for the *aragoto* are simple or extremely dramatic in their stories and *aragoto*-like scenes frequently appear in ordinary *kabuki* plays. | Ichikawa Danjuro I was famous as a creator of the *aragoto* style.The art of *aragoto* was inherited from the Danjuro line until the current Ichikawa Ebizo XI (1977–). Ichikawa Danjuro VII selected the eighteen *aragoto* plays as his family repertoire called *kabuki juhachiban* ("The *kabuki* Best Eighteen"). The *kabuki juhachiban* includes *Shibarak u;*[37]*Kenuki;*[38]*Narukami;*[39]*Kanjincho*, etc. |
| Wagoto ("gentle" style) | *Wagoto* was created at *Kamigata* (Kyoto and Osaka) with contrasting features to *aragoto*. The *wagoto* is a style representing the events in the daily life of ordinary humans (men and women). In many cases, the stories are realistic and psychological. The *wagoto*-like scenes and styles frequently appear in rather *aragoto*-like plays, such as *jidai-mono*. | Sakata Tojuro in *Kamigata* was the first great creator of *wagoto*. In particular, he established a play style for the *shinju-mono* by Chikamatsu Monzaemon. |

and the performer's acting, were organized according to a plot that was a central element in the drama. *Kabuki* is not a drama in this Western sense.

*Kabuki* was not originally a genre of drama, but a *geino* genre, which centered on extempore impression and dance for a short scene. The original method for using *kabuki* scenarios by the early authors was to structurally place scenes and dances into a consistent but simple story or plot to create a scenario to which other episodes were added. In other words, a story or a plot for a *kabuki* play was only a kind of convenient tool to connect the originally fragmental scenes and dances. In this sense, stories or plots in *kabuki* scenarios were not, so to speak, a primary norm in the meaning of Aristotle. Of course, the historical development and improvement of *kabuki* produced a new idea that emphasized the scenarios as structured and complicated stories or plots, especially through the introduction of *ningyo-joruri*. However, the fact that, in the production process of a *kabuki* play, a stage director traditionally does not exist and the actors produce the *kabuki* play through collaborative activity shows that creating a *kabuki* play is not necessarily effected in line with the ordinary drama production process, in which a story or a plot in a scenario hierarchically governs the entire structure, such as staging, acting performance, and theatrical representation, etc. Actually, *kabuki* sometimes emphasizes an actor's performance and actions themselves more than the story, as one of the many characteristics of the scenario. For instance, the "transformation" of a character has been a popular motif in appraisal of the effectiveness of an actor's actual performance on the stage. In many cases, the motif deals with the transformation from a human to a specter or monster and is relevant to the basic story structure of the round trip between an ordinary world and an extraordinary one. This partial story structure transcends the logic of the entire story.

*Kabuki* studies have a very long history with a correspondingly huge accumulation of writings in Japan. These originated in the huge quantities of books called *kabuki-hyoban-ki* that were published through the Edo era. The main content is the reporting and criticizing by audience members of the actors and the staging of *kabuki*. This tradition led to the modern form of *kabuki* criticism after the Meiji era. Folkloric, historical, and sociological studies have also continued to relate to *kabuki*. However, there have been few narratological studies that have analyzed the various levels of narrative structures and forms in *kabuki*. Further, although model/system-oriented approaches to *kabuki* (the broad category of classification to which this chapter also belongs) are still an uncultivated field of research, some studies have appeared relating *kabuki* and *ningyo-joruri* to cognitive science (Ebihara, Kurumisawa, Iwasawa, & Ohya, 1997; Shibuya, Morita, Fukuda, Ueda, & Sasaki, 2012).

Finally, in this section, "what is *kabuki*?" is an issue that needs to be clarified, though it may have been indicated in the above description. In particular, what in *kabuki* should be introduced into INGS, and further, GIS including INGS? The following three points are considered here in relation to this. The first is fundamental: *kabuki* is an actual example by which to consider the model of multiple narrative structures and GIS. Second, as stated above, the origin of *kabuki* studies was the report of an actor and the stage performance, while the mainstream was traditionally a kind of interpretive criticism. In contrast, there have been few modeling or systemic approaches. This author's approach will be able to open a new possibility in *kabuki* and the application of its studies. Third, *kabuki* has been developed and continued as a nongovernmental business since the Edo era. The study of *kabuki* as narrative generation by the author intends to provide a clue as to how to aim at distributing GIS and INGS socially in the future.

## MULTIPLICITIES OF *KABUKI* TO DESIGN GIS

*Kabuki*, which is considered a synthetic and comprehensive narrative generation and production framework that includes multiple elements, processes, and mechanisms, can be an important real narrative object for designing and developing GIS, including INGS in the future. The main part of this section views elements of *kabuki* from 15 topics to survey and analyze the narrative's multiple characteristics. The following short sub-section will attempt to bridge the above survey and analysis results with designing a more concretized and precise version of GIS including INGS.

### Multiplicities of *Kabuki*

*Kabuki* is a comprehensive system or "process" that combines both a simple and monolithic narrative generation-reception mechanism and a more complicated, inclusive, and circulative narrative production-consumption mechanism. Simply speaking, in the former, one or more authors as the senders create narrative content or scenarios for a work of *kabuki*, and many other persons, such as actors and stage artists, produce a real stage play. By contrast, the recipients receive the play on the stage of a theater. On the other hand, the latter cyclically reiterates a monolithic narrative generation and reception process to organically integrate each of the created contents into a sequence or story for the production of narratives at a larger and more comprehensive level, namely, a narrative production-consumption level. At both of the levels, the system of *kabuki* is not a monolithic system differing from the model of Aristotle, but a pluralistic system in which various elements other than a story or plot may be the central seeds for the creation of a play or sequence.

The idea of narrative generation by the author derives from the above process by using agents. An "agent" corresponds to a person relevant to the generation-reception mechanism, who is further part of the organization relevant to the production-consumption mechanism of a *kabuki* play. Many agents are shown in the following list: (1) individuals and groups on the sender side, including actors, author(s), stage artists and technicians, and director(s), etc.; (2) organizations of entertainment agencies as narrative production agents, including producer(s) and promoters, etc.; (3) contact personnel in *kabuki* theaters, audiences, and reviewers. These consist of both agents for the narrative generation-reception process and for the narrative production-consumption process.

In addition to the above elements, "content" means a level or aspect of *kabuki* that is created through the process of generation and reception and of production and consumption. Content as a monolithic work or play is created through the generation and reception process, while an iterative creation process makes a series of *kabuki* plays into an organized story that is more than merely a collection of each work through the level of production and consumption.

Basically, process, agent, and content are three criteria for the survey and analysis of *kabuki*. However, the following description does not necessarily follow these criteria in a strict sense. The next fifteen elements have been preliminarily or tentatively considered: (1) real incident, (2) work, (3) genre, (4) material or topic, (5) person, (6) story and plot, (7) actor and place, (8) time (era or age), (9) style (form or pattern), (10) theatre (stage and seating), (11) audience, (12) text, (13) production of scenario (*daicho*), (14) direction, and (15) stage performance.

## Real Incident

Stories or plots in *kabuki* are very often constructed based on actual or real incidents, for instance, historically famous events and facts for *jidai-mono*. On the other hand, *sewa-mono* frequently uses contemporary events in the daily life of ordinary people. Typically used historical sets of events have been repeatedly introduced and arranged in many *kabuki* works. The relationships between a real incident and its fictionalization were diverse and complex. The fictional parts of a real incident, such as a character's formation, have sometimes had a large influence on making people's imaginings. Aristotle (1895) and the chapter of *Hotaru* ("firefly") in *Genji monogatari* ("The tale of Genji") by Murasaki Shikibu (the middle age of the Heian era) commonly and independently discussed that fictions are better than historical facts in respect of the latter merely representing individual events, while the former are abstractly and precisely constituted through a selection of idealized events and their intended formation. In such sense, the formation of fictional narratives in *kabuki* through the iterative precision of real incidents may indicate the generation of ideal narratives dependent upon the gradual relationships between real historical or contemporary facts and fictional events.

One of the most famous examples that illustrates a mutual relationship between social fact and fictional arrangement is a work based on the so-called social incident of *the forty-seven samurais of Ako* or *Chushingura. Kanadehon Chushingura* was the greatest work of a variety of similar works written by gathering materials regarding this historical event by many authors. Many works of *shinju-mono* by Chikamatsu Monzaemon, such as *Sonezaki Shinju*, were also created on the basis of actual stories that men and women really experienced and people had heard of in the same age. *Adauchi-mono* by the Soga brother (*Kotobuki Soga no Taimen*) and Araki Mataemon (1599-1638) (*Iga-goe Dochu Sugoroku* and *Iga-goe Norikake Gappa*) were also such examples.

## Work

Through the historical development process of *kabuki*, a work was often adapted to other works using various types of methods for editing and revision. Although influential relationships among works are also ordinary phenomena in the current artistic environment, very quick and active transformational phenomena, especially in the Edo era, would have partially relied on the lack of awareness of copywriting. However, a more essential and practical reason for such an outstanding production style was that the revision of a work was easy to adapt to the unique characteristics of author, theatre, actor, and troupe. In particular, the systematic property of *kabuki* whereby various elements in a work organically relate to each other enables a work to flexibly transform into other works through various key points of change. Further, such revision and transformation often cross over to the next "genre."

The fictional dramatization of a historical event by *Ako samurais* can also be considered from the viewpoint of the problem of influence and inheritance from a work to another work. Until *Kanadehon Chushingura* was completed, a series of works, including *Onikage Musashi Abumi*[40] by Azuma Sampachi and *Goban Taiheiki*[41] by Chikamatsu Monzaemon, were continuously being created. Even after *Kanadehon Chushingura*, many related works, including a famous work of the Meiji era, *Genroku Chuushingura*[42] by Mayama Seika (1878-1948), have been written until now.

## Genre

Creating a new work based on one or more past works in the same or another genre was a commonly used method in Japanese dramatic or *geino* genres such as *Noh* and *ningyo-joruri*. This method of creation reached a unique and extreme level in *kabuki*. *Kabuki* can be considered a synthetic collection of diverse previous *geino* genres, including *Noh*, *kyogen*, and *ningyo-joruri* as dramatic *geino* genres; *katarimono* (narration) such as *sekkyo-bushi* in the middle ages and a variety of novels in the Edo era; and the music of *Noh* and *kyogen*, *shamisen* in the Edo era, and *katarimono* such as Gidayu by Takemoto Gidayu (1651–1714). This has never been an extreme discourse. The fact that *kabuki* was almost the sole popular contemporary dramatic genre in the Edo era may perhaps be explained by its synthesized features.

As mentioned in the previous part, introducing *ningyo-joruri* into *kabuki*, of which the adaptation called *Gidayu-kyogen* was the lower genre, was the most innovative factor in the evolution of *kabuki*. In particular, blending with scenarios of *ningyo-joruri* contributed to introducing strong narrativity into the dramas of *kabuki*, which had previously been very arbitrary in their points of narrative, as originally constructed to be centered upon characteristics of dance and as a kind of entertainment. Table 2 in the previous section provided a simple explanation and some examples. On the other hand, the *kabuki* works based on the form of *Noh* are called *matsubame-mono*, as seen in Table 4. As a general tendency, according to the properties of the original genres, many scenarios of *Gidayu-kyogen* have very long and complicated stories compared to *matsubame-mono* works, which are formed by short and clear stories.

## Material or Topic

Materials or topics commonly used in many *kabuki* works already exist, which have been categorized under many groups. The explanation by the author will seek to address this characteristic of *kabuki* in the framework of the circulative evolution process of *kabuki*. For instance, when a *kabuki* work is created using certain existing material, and subsequent work is produced based on such editing of a previous work, the latter work forms a variation of the former while using the same material or topic as the original work. This continuous flow has produced many groups of *kabuki* works according to the same respective materials. Although this may be similar to the theme of "real incident," the material or topic referred to here is not necessarily a "real" incident. Fictional events were also utilized. Further, "real" and "fictional" can be changed through a *kabuki* generation sequence or the circulative evolution process. A *kabuki* work that is created from a real incident or event serving as material can change or transform the event to the level of an event as fictional narrative. In the age of the Edo *kabuki*, selecting specific material for a *kabuki* play was not necessarily a free or arbitrary act based on the likelihood and hobby of the author. Each organized collection of materials prepared for *kabuki* works was called *sekai* ("world"), which was prioritized as an important task in the first stage of the production process of a *kabuki* play. A *sekai* means organized and systematized topical information for a *kabuki* play and the background narrative world upon which the work is placed. In general, relationships between freedom and constraint are not simple in traditional Japanese arts such as *kabuki*, *ningyo-joruri*, and *Noh*. Particular "forms (*kata*)" that constraint and limit free creative acts can sometimes be strong productive and innovative media. The *sekai* also has a productive design that amplifies creativity by constraint and limitation and holds practical importance for the production of each *kabuki* work.

A variety of *sekai* were prepared in Edo *kabuki*, and each of them was used to produce a series of works. For instance, *adauchi-mono* based on the material, topic, or theme of *adauchi*, meaning a kind of revenge story, has a popular *sekai* in classical *kabuki* and *ningyo-joruri*. In addition, the *sekai* of *adauchi-mono* hierarchically contains various specific lower-genres according to the characteristics of the corresponding materials, such as *Soga-kyodai-mono*, *Chushingura-mono*, and *Igagoe-mono*. These form each *sekai*. Different works based on the same *sekai* have been written by different authors. For example, by adopting the same *sekai* of *Igagoe-mono*, Chikamatsu Hanji and Nagawa Kamesuke, who were known as genius writers, respectively wrote *Igagoe Dochu Sugoroku*[43] as a *ningyo-joruri* work and *Igagoe Norikake Gappa*[44] as a *kabuki* work. These two works are similar in their macro level plots, though there are also many remarkable differences. By contrast, other authors wrote quite different works from the original story for a *sekai*. For instance, *Tokaido Yotsuya Kaidan* by Tsuruya Namboku VI developed a surprising novel narrative using the *sekai* of *Chushingura-mono*, whose typical use is seen in *Kanadehon-Chushingura*. In addition to materials at the level of event, many popular historical characters, such as Minamoto Yoshitsune (1159–1189) and Akechi Mitsuhide (1528–1582), also appear as universal materials as part of a *sekai* for producing and imagining the works of *kabuki*.

## Person

"Person" in *kabuki* is mainly divided into the level of an "actor" who plays on the stage and that of a "(dramatic) character" in the narrative of the work. The two types of persons form multiple relationships on the temporal and spatial levels. First, a person plays a dramatic character in a *kabuki* play; at the same time, the existence accompanying the real name also has essential meaning. In *kabuki*, the aspect of "an actor plays" frequently has a more important meaning than representing a universal drama or story. A *kabuki* scenario in the Edo era was not originally written with the names of characters in the story, but with the names of the actors who really played the drama. In other words, in classical *kabuki* works, a scenario was ordinarily written according to the characteristics of the actors; therefore, the actors were not selected on the basis of any artistic viewpoints based on a preliminarily written scenario. There were many critics of the weak points of such kind of star system. And after the Meiji era, scenario-centered drama production also became a popular method. However, the tradition of the star system emphasizing the actors has also remained in contemporary *kabuki*.

Although the person as an actor is certainly a human who has an actual body in the real world, he also, in many cases, has the following two parts: (1) an actual existence as an actor who is represented by *gei-mei* (a stage name); and (2) an actual existence as a human who is shown by the *hon-myo* (a real name). This duplicate appearance of an actor is, so to speak, a spatial property that is common among many *geino-jins* (entertainers) and actors. At the same time, another significant fact is that each *geimei* accompanies a temporal property that has been inherited from age to age, in other word, respective unique stories or histories. This means that two or more actors with the same *geimei* exist in historical continuity, forming a story, though they have different bodies in their real lives. Each actor with the same *geimei* is plotted in a temporally continuous flow.

On the other hand, the person as a character involved in the *kabuki* play as a narrative work is, in many cases, not merely a character who exists within the limited drama world, but also a character who appears in other *kabuki* works, other works in other genres, and historical and non-fictional descriptions, for example. A character in a *kabuki* work who overlaps with other characters in other works and genres is an existence that creates each scenario through various relationships with other characters on the spatial and temporal levels. This feature of the person is, therefore, related to the above "real incident," "work," "genre," and "material or topic." Various elements in the person form multiple relationships on both temporal and spatial levels. The existence of actors themselves and their faces are not hidden, in the figurative meaning, through dramatic performance, unlike realistic dramas. A phenomenon to show the fact is that a group of audiences plays the *kakegoe* to an actor on the stage by "the name of the house" during the *kabuki* performance, referring to the actor's actual existence and not the name of the character. By contrast, actors sometimes show their real faces on the stage, and not the role of each character.

There are various multiple persons and narratives, such as the actor as a character who appears in a drama and narrative; present and near past events and the narratives performed by the actor; the present and near past narrative or story performed by the actor as a real human; and actors and the narratives of the past ages until that of the present actor. The multiplicity of Bando Tamasaburo V (1950–), who is one of the most excellent *onnagata* in contemporary *kabuki*, can be considered partially as follows: Bando Tamasaburo is the stage name of the actor, whose real name is Shinichi Morita. The name of Bando Tamasaburo has a history and accompanying narratives, for instance, as a female dancer who also existed in the Meiji era. Morita Kanya XII (1846–1897), who is a great-grandfather of Tamasaburo (although Tamasaburo was really an adopted son in the Morita family), was one of the greatest theatrical promoters. Tamasaburo as an actor also has various narratives and stories. Of course, he is a *kabuki* actor, at the same time, he is also a movie director, a performer of various genres, a creator or director of new *kabuki* plays (a famous attempt is the adaptation of some literary works by Izumi Kyoka (1873–1939) for *kabuki*), and recently an educator of young *kabuki* players.

## Story and Plot

In *kabuki* narratives, in the wider sense used by the author, difficulty in perception may be caused by the multiplicity derived from the various complicated levels. The author sometimes thinks that mechanisms or methods for editing various elements of the levels in *kabuki* may be associated with a kind of "arbitrariness," so to speak. However, the multiplicity of *kabuki*, in which various acts of editing overlap in complicated ways, gains new and unique characteristics beyond the respective original editing acts. Finally, the arbitrariness will change to a kind of "inevitability" or "necessity" through the multiple editing processes. Such characteristics in *kabuki* often appear in a single element too, e.g., at the level of scenarios, plots, or stories. The "closeness" of the kind of "retribution" stories was a feature in the whole of the Edo literature that differs from modern and contemporary literature. *Kabuki* amplified the feature through the dramatic bodies of the actors.

In addition, story and plot are, strictly speaking, different concepts in narratology. A plot means the structure of narrative flow as represented in a written or played work (e.g., a scenario in drama and a performance on the stage), while a story is a structure of an event sequence that our brain imagines and reconstitutes from a narrative work, especially on the basis of the plot. In *kabuki*, the progression of a plot corresponds to the progression of a story. Both concepts are closely connected in a real work, and they are integrally treated in this chapter.

In the typical flow of a *kabuki* play, at first, the individual parts in the plot may seem to be arbitrary and monotonic for many audiences in the theatre. However, when these originally fragmentary parts are organically connected, for instance, by special elements such as a character and an object, suddenly, a highly inevitable aspect appears, such that the audiences cannot imagine any possibilities. In such situation, the audiences often encounter a narrative development constituted by strange and extraordinary story logics, which are based on the intellectual backgrounds of the era and therefore differ from the ordinary logics of the current society. The characters frequently select very strange actions. At the same time, the impression is too strong to consider and imagine other possibilities of action or story, despite being certainly very strange. Many audiences experience a heaviness of feeling, as if all other action selections were essentially impossible.

Sometimes, in a long *kabuki* play, as typically seen in *Gidayu-kyogen*, the plot progresses with the feeling of "enervation (or listlessness)" from the beginning to the middle. In contrast, after these parts, in many cases unanticipated by the audience, the plot rises to a rapid and sudden climax, e.g., to the point of transformation or metamorphoses of a main character (Imao, 1970). An essential significance of viewing a *kabuki* play is to experience that, at the level of plot, a typical world setting is gradually transformed qualitatively to an inevitable narrative in a unique temporal sense on the stage.

In *Daimotsu no Ura* in *Yoshitsne Sembon Zakura*, when a ferryman transforms to Taira no Tomomori (1152–1185), who is really a great head of a distinguished family, "Heike," the narrative rapidly develops to a battle with Minamoto no Yoshitsune, who is the head of another distinguished family, "Genji." The clear contrast of a peaceful, *wagoto-* and *sewa-mono*-like scene in the first half with that of the furious, dramatic, *aragoto-* and *jidaimono*-like scene make a very strong impression on the audiences. For example, *Sukeroku Yukari no Edo Zakura* produces a sharp and surprising impression on the audiences. Hanakawado Sukeroku appears on the stage as a beautiful young man and comical scenes continue. Then, Sukeroku shows his true character as Soga no Goro, who is the main character of a classical *sekai* in an *adauchi-mono*, in the final part. The multiplicity of the levels of story and plot represented by both works simultaneously shows the multiplicity of historical ages or worlds.

## Actor and Place

Watanabe (1989) states that a limited number of actors in a theatre troupe have been able to play many repertories of *kabuki* by performing a variety of dramatic characters. To realize this, a theatre troupe needed to make preliminary preparations and necessary arrangements to construct a variety of places on the stage: stage settings for various fictional places and characters' costumes for various roles of characters. Both characters and costumes in *kabuki* are categorized as a patterned system, and the combinations are limited. This mechanism enables an actor to be able to play many different character roles using a limited number of costumes (and the closely related maquillage) and combinatorial processing. Similarly, places on the stages in *kabuki* can also be constructed by using a limited number of stage settings and combinations. *Kabuki* plays, as theatrical arts with real constraints of each stage, have manifold combinations of limited stage settings, characters, and costumes. Further, the same book asserts that the number of components for combinatorial construction is actually rather small. *Kabuki* as a system has the possibility to produce many thinkable plays according to the combinations of the preliminarily prepared stage settings, costumes, and maquillage for characters and actors as real humans. Such features show that *kabuki* is more of a symbolical art than a realistic one. As described above, as various *kabuki* plays on one stage can be constructed by utilizing typical components, including stage settings, character types with costumes and maquillage, and actors, the written works are also highly colorful in relating to symbolic combinations of components. Critical views concerning such quality of *kabuki* have, however, been voiced. For example, Takechi Tetsuji (1912–1988), who was a critic and producer of Japanese *geino* (Mori, 2010), including *kabuki*, proposed the idea that *kabuki* plays, especially those originating from *ningyo-joruri*, should be produced according to the original texts that had highly realistic features before they were drastically changed by the individual techniques of *kabuki* actors and various forms or patterns. He practiced the idea through producing and creating new *kabuki* plays.

*Date no Juyaku* [45] is the most extreme example in which only one main actor plays ten or more characters' roles by changing costumes and maquillages on a stage that continues to alter to different stage settings. The true title indicates not the narrative content but the difficulty for the chief actor. Concerning place, for instance, the same stage setting at the entrance space of Yoshiwara Nakano-cho, one of the most luxuriant places in Edo, has commonly been used for many different *kabuki* plays, such as *Kagotsurube Sato no Eizame*[46] and *Yoshiwara Suzume.*[47] Audiences who have seen many *kabuki* plays would encounter a same stage setting for different ones.

## Time (Era or Age)

Different historical times are frequently mixed or overlapping in a *kabuki* play. Such temporal multiplicity has also been related to the censoring system by the Edo government, in addition to artistic requirements. The direct representation of contemporary events of the same age could not be permitted under the political situation. A work based on a contemporary, real incident repeatedly changed the temporal setting to a past age and was expressed under a different temporal setting, using a *sekai* of a different age. The change and movement of time and era was simultaneously connected to the change of spatial elements—the components for space and place. An interesting phenomenon regarding temporal and spatial change is that it creates an overlapping of spaces and characters from different historical times. For example, various types of costumes and places simultaneously appear in one historical setting. In contrast with the above description, this temporal and spatial multiplicity may not necessarily have been a simple result of the political censoring system. Aesthetic and artistic strategies may have played a hand in these techniques.

Although the material of *Kana Dehon Chushin-gura* was a real incident that occurred in the Genroku era, the temporal positioning of the story was in the Muromachi era (1338–1573). However, the characters' styles and the stage settings in these different times were mixed and overlapping in the play. Although the temporal setting of a story was in the Ashikaga era, for example, the standard for the stage space was clearly the Genroku era. As another example, *Sugawara Denju Tenarai Kagami* set the story time in the age of Sugawara Michizane (845–903), who was the actual model, in the Heian era. However, there existed various historical contradictions. For instance, while Sugawara Michizane and Fujiwara Shihei, who was a villain hero, wore the costumes of the Heian era, Takebe Genzo, who was a teacher of a *terakoya* (the Edo-style school) as a fictional character, wore the costume of *samurai* in the Edo era. Various costumes in different eras were mixed in all scenes of this work.

## Style (Form or Pattern)

"Style" is here used to mean "performing style," in which various styles appeared to be adopted on the actual stages in *kabuki* plays, such as for dance, music, narration, and action forms or patterns by actors. There were a variety of multiplicities and possibilities dependent upon the constraint of prepared elements and combinations. The music accompanying the actors' actions has included many genres, such as *nagauta*, *kiyomoto*, *tokiwazu*, and *o-zatsuma,* etc. The narration by a *takemoto*, corresponding to a *tayu* in *ningyo-joruri*, has been transformed for a playing style for human actors instead of one for artificial puppets. While all parts of the scenario of a work are narrated by several *tayu* in *ningyo-joruri*, the scenario of a *kabuki* work is divided into the parts of *katari* (narration) by *takemoto* and *serihu* (speech) by human actors. The artistic blending of *kabuki* and *ningyo-joruri* has given birth to another aesthetic technique called *ningyo-buri* in *kabuki*, which is a unique performing style in which a human actor imitates or simulates the action of the puppet in *ningyo-joruri*. This represents one of the interesting and complicated multiple structures in *kabuki*.

The most significant method to actually control a performing style of an actor is, perhaps, "form (*kata*)." Each form is a kind of pattern or norm for actors regarding body actions and the corresponding sets of costumes and maquillage, etc. There are many forms that have been historically inherited by many actors. For an actor, to select a particular form means determining various elements for constructing the stage of a *kabuki* play, such as costume, music, narration, and stage setting, as well as their combination. Therefore, a form is not only an element that constraints an actor, but also an actual framework determining the entire style of a stage or play. The main part of training actors in *kabuki* is for them to learn and know various forms inherited from its past history. At the same time, the creativity of *kabuki* has been engendered by maintaining form or partially or entirely destroying it.

There have been different types of forms for Sato Tadanobu as a fox in *Yoshitsune Sembon Zakura*. For instance, Ichikawa Ennosuke III (1939–) created a bold form to represent a fox's actions with magical powers. By contrast, the form of Onoe Kikugoro VI (1885–1949) was more humble and realistic. On the other hand, the audiences get to see *ningyo-buri* especially in *Gidayu-kyogen*. In the last half of the scene of *Domyoji* in *Sugawara Denju Tenarai Kagami* (*Domyoji* is one of the most famous and excellent *ningyo-joruri* scenarios written by Miyoshi Shoraku), a wooden statue appears and walks over to help the main character, Sugawara Michizane, as a "scapegoat." In *ningyo-joruri*, a puppet operated by three *ningyo-tsukai* plays a wooden statue that is an acting entity in this scene. In a more complicated *kabuki* version of the play, a real actor plays a wooden statue, like a puppet. This is also a kind of *ningyo-buri*. Kataoka Nizaemon XV (1945–) in contemporary *kabuki* is also known for excellent plays of *Domyoji* in addition to other works. He represents multiple bodies with his real body through the circulative transformation of wooden statue to puppet, then to man, and then back to puppet and wooden statue again on an impressive stage.

## Theatre (Stage and Seating)

The *hanamichi*, described in the previous section, is a mechanism on the *kabuki* stage that has multiple usages. Many academic studies have endeavored to determine the origin and meaning of the *hanamichi* (Suwa, 1991; Kurata, 2013). A narratological feature originating from the *hanamichi*, or a narratological concept that is symbolic of it, is "fluidity" (Ogata, 2014) in the relationship of the stage and seating in a theatre. Without an actor entering through the seats directly, by utilizing the *hanamichi*, *kabuki* can symbolically represent a situation of multiplicity in which the stage and seats are complicatedly blended in an integral space. Main actors or characters in a *kabuki* play appear and disappear through the *hanamichi*. In the seats of *kabuki* theatre, though these are also related to the next topic of "audience," there are special seats, such as *sajiki* ("grand tier") and *tachimiseki* ("standing room"), and various related customs, such as *kakegoe* from the upper gallery including the *tachimiseki*.

The *hanamichi* primarily and pragmatically functions as the entrance and exit for the stage and backstage. However, the *hanamichi* is also a place for dance and narration, especially narrations of reminiscence and self-introduction. In *Sukeroku Yukari no Edo-zakura*, the chief character, Sukeroku, performs a very long, stylistic, and impressive dance on the *hanamichi* in the first appearance. Moreover, the *hanamichi* can also be a passage to strange worlds through which ghosts and monsters appear and disappear. In *Meiboku Sendai Hagi*, Nikki Danjo, who is a strange entity hatching a bad political plan to destroy his lord's house and usurp it, appears from the *hanamichi* in a cloud of white smoke. Originally, the *hanamichi* was a place where an actor would receive flowers from the audience (Suwa, 1991). The current *hanamichi* still retains the function of the platform on which a character greets the audience as an actor. Although the greeting on the *hanamichi* is sometimes criticized in the point that the smooth flow of a *kabuki* play is obstructed, for the audience, the friendship with actors (and not characters) is also an attractive element that is part of the pleasure of *kabuki* plays. An example in which the whole of a theatre containing the stage and seats becomes a large and inclusive stage is the scene of *Numazu* in *Igagoro Dochu Sugoroku*. Two unique characters go down to the seats from the stage and walk around them while in conversation with each other. Further, they sometimes talk to the audience. In such situation, the *kakegoe* from the seats will also blossom. At such times, the fictional space and real space are multiply blended within the same theatre.

## Audience

*Kabuki* is primarily an object to be viewed in the theatre by the audience. Of course, this does not necessarily mean that only the phenomenon of viewing in the physical space of the theatre can be an absolute experience for the audience. However, it is also certain that *kabuki* is closely, essentially, and mutually bound with the existence of the theatre. As seen in the examples of the *hanamichi* and *kakegoe* in the previous section, the audience also plays a part in the multiple editing of *kabuki*. The difference between seeing a *kabuki* play as a movie and in the theatre is considered to be greater than the difference between seeing a movie on television and at the cinema. The viewpoint in a movie has already been prepared based on the creator's intention and technique. Rather, when an audience views a movie at the cinema, the viewpoint in the work does not change according to the place in which the audience views it. On the other hand, in the case of *kabuki*, there are various different viewpoints according to the place in the theatre. Unlike the movie film, a *kabuki* play on the stage does not have any fixed viewpoints which correspond to the camera work in the movie. Therefore, the action of an audience viewing the stage itself plays a role in the viewpoint as one of the narratological techniques. Certainly, the above description may be a common feature for all theatrical dramas, but the stage of *kabuki* containing the *hanamichi*, *seriagari*, and music players, etc., is more complicated than the stage styles of other many genres of drama. This fact brings a variety of influences to the action of viewing by the audience.

In particular, in the previous *kabuki-za*, the audience could not see the *hanamichi* from the back of the second, third, and fourth floors. The audience in these seats guessed and imagined an actor's actions on the *hanamichi* based on the voice and situational atmosphere. In the above *Sukeroku Yukari no Edo-zakura*, a very long and flowery dance played by Sukeroku on the *hanamichi* creates a very fast climax. During this time, the audience gazes at invisible things using only their imagination. Also, in several seats at the back side of the first floor by the *hanamichi* of the previous *kabuki-za*, the audience could not see a part of the stage due to a large and red hole. Although the above problems were solved in the currently used new style of *kabuki-za*, the large difference in viewing *kabuki* by the location of the seats is still an interesting property of this theatre. On the third or fourth floor, when a person closest to an audience plays the *kakegoe*, the feeling of excitement and pleasure also increases for the audience. By contrast, when the sound of plastic bags and voices of speech create a terrible atmosphere, the multiplicity of the play on the stage and the strange play by the seats remains in the audiences' mind as a harsh but impressive memory. As a recent memorable example, in March 2015, the author viewed the scene of *Domyoji* in *Sugawara Denju Tenarai Kagami* with a historical performance by Kataoka Nizaemon

XV at the forward side of the second floor in the *kabuki-za*. The sound of plastic bags by an audience member nearby was overlapping with the narration by Kan-shojo (Nizaemon), who was playing the climax scene on the stage. This was certainly an impressive phenomenon in the traditional theatre, though an unpleasant experience. Including the possibility of such bad experiences, the audience in the actual theatre is an important factor of viewing a *kabuki* play.

## Text

Reading or receiving a novel or a poem is an experience involving a person reading words that are physically represented on the paper, and the text in such case means the enumeration of the words themselves. In contrast, receiving a drama on the stage is, in the primary sense, to perceive humans' physical actions around the stage settings and decors. Unlike a book, a drama on the stage is not a representation solely based on the enumeration of words, but is also a collection of body actions and sometimes the stage itself accompanying these actions. *Kabuki* has a tradition of essays and criticisms originating from the *Yakusha Hyoban-ki* in the Edo era (Taguchi, 2003), which was a series of books that commented on the *kabuki* actors. The style has been persistently dependent upon the fact that an audience really views a *kabuki* play on the stage in a theatre. This fact indicates that the text in *kabuki* has been the individual stage performance as a collection of body actions by actors and stage settings. This tradition has not yet been corrupted on the present *kabuki* scene. For example, the works of critique, which are theoretical or academic texts, by Watanabe (2012), a famous researcher and critic of *kabuki* and the other *geino*, are based on his viewpoint and experience as an audience member of *kabuki*. However, as he also says in his book, it is a fact that *kabuki* works have another level of text similar to a scenario that differs from the text as a stage performance by actors. Although the rise of scenarios as reading material is a relatively new phenomenon, it is currently possible for people to read and appreciate the scenarios of classical *kabuki* works in the form of books. In short, the text of *kabuki* has a multiplicity consisting of the "first (level) text" as a stage performance by actors performing on the stage and the "second (level) text" as the scenario of words written by authors. Further, as an additional feature to the above multiplicity of texts, there have been multiple relationships among different genres, such as the multiplicity and transformational relationships between *Noh* and *kabuki*, *kyogen* and *kabuki*, and *ningyo-joruri* and *kabuki*, etc. In the case that a scenario of *ningyo-joruri* has been adapted to *kabuki* according to its narratological or dramatic structure, the resulting *kabuki* scenario is equivalent to a multiple text that retains elements of the original *ningyo-joruri*.

The scenario of a *kabuki* work, e.g., *Kagotsurube Sato no Eizame*, can be considered the first text(s), though, strictly speaking, differences exist according to the version. By contrast, in the second texts that are really performed, the forms of Sano Jirozaemon, who is the hero in the work, have been played still recently by various *kabuki* actors, such as Nakamura Kanzaburo XVIII (1955–2012), Nakamura Kichiemon II (1944–), and Onoe Kikugoro VII (1942–), who have given different renditions and impressions to the audiences. A reason why people repeatedly view *kabuki* plays of the same title is related to the level of the second text. For instance, a group of people wants to see or confirm how a current actor plays the second text depending upon the form created by a past actor, which has been historically inherited by his successors. Moreover, people hope to encounter the present scene or place in which a new second text comes into being through the excellent rendition of an actor or actors. Next, there are many differences between a scenario of *ningyo-joruri* and the version that is adapted to *kabuki*. All parts of a scenario in the former are written for the narration by narrators (*tayu*). In the real play, *tayu* precisely narrate all of the descriptions and *serihu* (speech or words), while its adaptation to the stage of a *kabuki* play requires varied edits and revisions from the *ningyo-joruri* scenario, such as the parts of the narration by a *take-moto* corresponding to the *tayu* in *ningyo-joruri*; the parts of body actions by human actors; the parts of speech or *serihu* by actors; and music in the *kabuki* style. Imao (2010) presents a precise analysis of transformational methods between respective scenarios of *ningyo-joruri* and *kabuki*.

## Production of Scenario ("Daicho")

The production of actual performance scenarios, which in the book of a scenario is called *daicho*, was very simple in the initial days of *kabuki* because the typical works, which had only a single structure containing but a few scenes, were not completed dramas but an assortment of entertainments and dances. However, *kabuki* works gradually came to have large-scale and complicated structures. The production mechanisms also developed to become more systematic, thanks to excellent authors, especially from *ningyo-joruri*, such as Chikamatsu Monzaemon and Kino Kaion. As a result, a new type of scenario production style was invented through which several authors created a scenario working collaboratively. According to Imao (2009), a hierarchy existed among a group of authors in a theatre. The top level was occupied by the *tate-sakusha*, who planned the entire structure of a work and wrote the most important parts. This collaborative production style continued until the Meiji era, when the system of *tate-sakusha* ended.

In a *ningyo-joruri* work, *Sugawara Denju Tenarai Kagami*, a common theme through the famous three *dans* (parts) (*Domyoji*, *Igami no Gonta*, and *Terakoya*) was "separation." According to Watatabe (2009), another common theme, "scapegoat," was also added to the first theme. Each *dan* was written by three different great authors, respectively: Miyoshi Shoraku, Namiki Sosuke, and Takeda Izumu I. Although there has been some discussion over who the *tate-sakusha* was in case of this miracle work, the difference among the *tate-sakusha* and other level of authors was usually clear. For each author, there was a history of rising from the lower to the higher level of the hierarchy and finally to reaching the utmost rank of the *tate-sakusha*, at least in the happy cases. It is a famous case that Tsuruya Namboku IV, who was known as one of the greatest and most famous *kabuki* authors, rose to become a *tate-sakusha* in his forties, but continued to be active as the first author in the *kabuki* world for over 25 years until his death.

## Direction

The property of *kabuki* plays whereby various different historical ages and places of a narrative are mixed rather than representing a realistic standard influences the production of each actual stage. Various styles of blending or overlapping of costumes, language of speech, music, etc., sometimes exceed ordinary situations. Maquillage or the make-up and costumes of characters are designed according to the form or kind of traditional norm to be used for each typical character. Such very symbolic and formal features frequently ignore the realistic consistency and naturalness of the entire staging. One of the reasons may certainly be the disordered confusion of forms through historical accumulation. Innovative plans to return realistic styles of play to *kabuki* have actually been proposed by some actors, such as Ichikawa Danjuro IX in the Meiji era. However, since over-realistic and symbolic styles form a tense tradition and also a unique beauty involving the audience, *kabuki* grew into a more heterogeneous and synthesized dramatic genre than one of pure realism. Another topic that differs from the issue of stage representation in the above sense is that *kabuki* has not traditionally had a person playing a managerial and integrating role similar to that of a director on the stage. The role of a director of a *kabuki* play was conducted according to the naturally collaborative work of the actors who really performed the play. This making style is partially relevant to the symbolic features of *kabuki*, which arose from the characteristic of materials of various levels held by the system being freely combined and edited to complete a work. In addition, a traditional training style of *kabuki*, in which the actors accumulated the knowledge of diverse playing forms over a long time, was also one factor in enabling collaborative work among actors to direct an actual stage performance.

As mentioned with regard to the topic of time (era or age), for *Sugawara Denju Tenarai Kagami*, the historical setting is the Heian era. The hero, Kan Shojo, modeling Sugawara Michizane, and the anti-hero, Fujiwara Shihei, modeling Fujiwara Tokihira (871–909), appear on the stage wearing the costumes of the Heian era, and one of the major characters, Takebe Genzo, appears in the garb of a *samurai* in the Edo era, while the main setting is a *terakoya* (school) in the mountains of Kyoto in the Edo style. Further, the makeup of the face of Fujiwara Shihei does not represent a human but undoubtedly that of a monster. The characteristic of having no director has also been inherited by the modern form of *kabuki*. When Mishima Yukio produced the last *kabuki* play, *Chinzei Yumihari Zuki*,[48] in the National Theatre of Japan in 1969, in his final days, he came to despair of the selfishness of the actors who ignored direction and wanted to make the stage and play by their own self-direction.

## Stage Performance

*Kabuki* in the Edo era was a contemporary drama of that age. Therefore, each *kabuki* play was basically performed in the style of *toshi-joen*, which means that all of the parts are played continuously, in one or two days. However, in truth, the actual form was not necessarily simple as there were complex rules or performing systems. A basic pattern was that two types of newly created works of *jidai-mono* and *sewa-mono* were mutually played in the program for a series of *kabuki* performances. By contrast, after the Meiji era, the *midori-joen*—a new performing style in which mainly the classical works of Edo *kabuki* were repeatedly performed—gradually spread and became popular, though many new works (scenarios), including the sub-genre of *shin-kabuki* ("new *kabuki*"), were also written by many modern authors. The *midori-joen* is a stage performance style consisting of different works through which a *kabuki* program is constituted. The works include, for instance, the following types of play: *dan* (a part cut by the *joshiki-maku* [curtain]) and a scene in a *dan* in long, classical, pure *kabuki* or *Gidayu-kyogen* works, a part or a scene in *shin-kabuki*, a *kabuki* dance, and a *Noh* and *kyogen*-based play, etc. These more or less fragmental works were collected to form a program. The audience who is interested in the entire story in a play contained in a *midori-joen* cannot comprehend it adequately only on the basis of the part that they are really viewing on the stage. Many audience members try to understand the part that they are viewing through a preliminary and parallel reading of the explanation in which the entire story is described. On the other hand, other audience members may also abandon an understanding of the story to experience an ecstasy of happiness by enveloping themselves in the formal beauty of the stage. Also, certain audience members will repeatedly view the same *kabuki* play performed by different actors to gradually and naturally come to understand and learn a story. For good or ill, as *midori-joen* is at present usually structured as a well-known play, the audience frequently encounters the same plays in their continuing experience of *kabuki* viewing. However, editing and alteration at the level of a scenario is sometimes undertaken in preparation of its performance as contemporary *kabuki*. Since it is difficult to directly aim at actually realizing the original scenarios of classical *kabuki* plays on the stage in contemporary performances, the temporal, spatial, and thematic conditions or constraints of the scenarios are in many cases adapted for current society. Finally, one of the characteristics of *kabuki* related to the topic of stage performance, as described by Watanabe (2012) and other critics, is that it has been a kind of star system or actor-centric system with one or more central actors often writing, revising, or editing a scenario. Producing and directing have also in many cases been conducted by the actors.

There is an interesting example concerning the *midori-joen*, which is partially the practice in which a book was edited according to the form of *midori-joen* (Yuda, 1965). Similar to real stage performances by a *midori-joen*, this book collected only the parts of some long scenarios. Reading this book is therefore similar to the experience of viewing a *kabuki* program on stage. As an example of editing *kabuki* scenarios, in the National Theatre in Japan, an organization or a group called *bungei-ka* ("creative section") edits scenarios for stage performance. This indicates an approach to "production by editing a work itself." An example is seen in Chikamatsu Monzaemon (*Chikamatsu Zenshuu* ("The complete works of Chikamatsu",) 1985–1994, Tokyo: Iwanami-shoten), in the form of a part of a scenario sometimes being used for part of another work with another title. There are various examples of such type of adaptation or editing in Chikamatsu. It corresponds to an editing style of *kabuki* according to which there is gradual development through incremental changes among works.

## Toward Introducing *Kabuki* Knowledge into GIS Including INGS

Based on the above preliminary survey and analysis of *kabuki*, this subsection briefly looks at a macro level design plan toward GIS including INGS in a conceptual level. As described repeatedly in this chapter, INGS is a simple narrative generation system that corresponds to the first mechanism in the modeling of the author's comprehensive narrative generation research, though the current version of INGS does not have the ability to generate synthetic narratives using knowledge acquired through the survey of *kabuki* from the angle of a narrative generation system. For the second mechanism, it is necessary to concentrate on the meta-level mechanism that controls the use of one or more INGS(s), namely, GIS. This is the meaning of the term, "GIS including INGS." The above survey results will be able to contribute to any part of INGS and GIS. However, it is too difficult to simply divide them, for instance, by simply thinking that the "character" and the "actor" in the "person" can, respectively, be associated with INGS and GIS. However, a character is partially a narrative element to be stored into a portion of GIS in its connection with the narrative world (*sekai*).

On the other hand, Figure 3 tentatively plots the knowledge of *kabuki* that has been dealt with in the above description to give direction for the extension of GIS including INGS. A variety of knowledge elements concerns in the generation of a *kabuki* play on the stage, in a theatre that has the seating and the audiences. This kabuki *play* is produced a comprehensive narrative generation and production mechanism, the GIS including INGS in the author's model, using various types of *kabuki* knowledge as stated above. These knowledge elements are corresponded to each knowledge base, storing historical, cultural, and other information regarding *kabuki*. *Kabuki*-related domain specific knowledge bases are aimed to be included in GIS, while more general and domain dependent knowledge bases are intended to be developed in INGS. Moreover, this single generation and reception of a *kabuki* play is repeatedly for extending to the production and consumption at the social level.

*Figure 3. Overview of kabuki production using multiple knowledge structures*

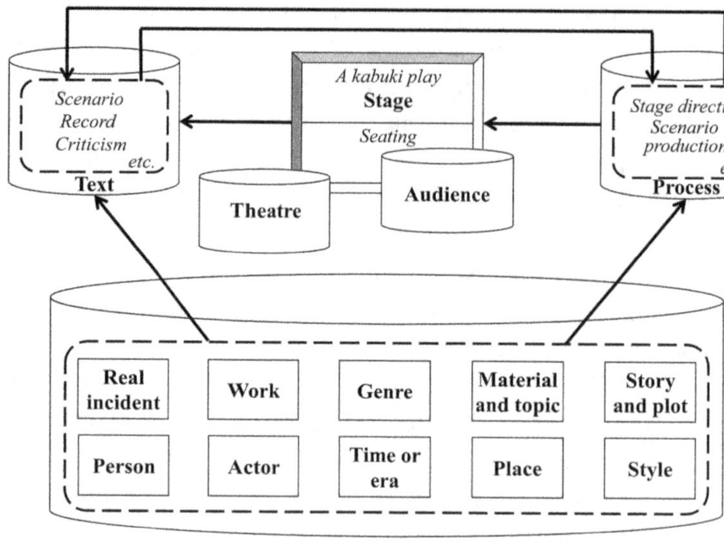


## FUTURE RESEARCH DIRECTIONS

The main short term plans concerning *kabuki*'s survey and analysis are presented.

- The modeling and design of GIS including INGS based on the introduction of elements and knowledge of *kabuki*: The first objective, followed by a preliminary attempt, is to design a more detailed GIS including INGS model, extended by the survey of *kabuki*. It also draws on the next theme, namely deepening the survey and analysis of *kabuki* itself. In particular, based on Figure 3, knowledge of multiplicity will be analyzed and classified in detail in order to stage the design for experimental implementation.
- Deepening the survey and analysis of *kabuki* itself as an information system: The survey and analysis of this chapter is still a preliminary version of the analysis of *kabuki* itself. This *kabuki* analysis, along with the following system design and implementation, form a mutual process in that the *kabuki* analysis is progressed towards the systematization of GIS including INGS or directed by it, and the system design and implementation require more detailed, precise, and systematic *kabuki* analysis. On the other hand, as the author cannot cover all of the large worlds of *kabuki*, it is also necessary to limit the necessary range for the research objective at the current stage.
- An experimental implementation and the verification of GIS including INGS: Although this topic accompanies the expansion and precision of INGS that is placed in GIS as the chief part(s), it is possible to use the current, tentative version in the GIS experiment system because it can act as an entire system. One of the future issues is to develop a meta-level mechanism to control the mutual relationship between the two mechanisms to make a sequential story of narrative works from the narrative content. In addition, multiple narrative structures can be seen in each constituent element in the narrative generation-reception and production-consumption mechanisms. INGS will be able to tackle this issue by enhancing knowledge bases for elements including persons and other features.

- The applicable system design and implementation, including the social distribution experiments: A current ambitious goal of GIS including INGS is to perform experiments at the social level, such as the distribution through the Web of the generated narratives or the generation mechanism itself. To carry out such socially open experiments, application systems of GIS including INGS need to be developed by limiting and constraining direct objectives. Further, as stated in the introductory chapter to this book, a narratological concept in this respect represents "fluidity and fixation" in the ELT (Ogata, 2014). For the social distribution of GIS including INGS, the fluid aspect of narrative generation is connected to the generation and distribution on the online system, and the fixed aspect is associated with publishing in the form of a book the processes and results of the narrative generation. Moreover, by social distribution, the author also means a new type of business model for social applications using the Web, etc., for the narrative generation system itself, or for a content system including narrative generation systems. The author anticipates directions for future research on social distribution of the GIS including INGS through a greater understanding of *kabuki* and its multiple narrative structures model.

## CONCLUSION

The model of multiple narrative structures of *kabuki* is related to the following two levels: narrative generation-reception and narrative production-consumption. In the author's narrative generation research, these correspond, respectively, to a mechanism as a simple system, INGS, and a meta-level mechanism containing one or more simple narrative generation system(s), GIS. This chapter, at first, introduced the two frameworks as background content, the goal being to survey and analyze the multiple narrative knowledge structures of *kabuki* for the first macro-level design plan of GIS including INGS. The final part of this chapter presented a rough GIS model that extended the original GIS model on the basis of the multiple narrative knowledge structures surveyed. The model discussed here will contribute to actually developing an experimental and practical system with INGS, in particular, with social distribution mechanisms of narrative generation, using the Web, etc.

This is an incomplete and preliminary attempt at developing an implemented GIS in the future. Therefore, it is anticipated that future research will contain: (1) the modeling and design of GIS including INGS based on the introduction of various elements or knowledge of *kabuki*; (2) the deepening of the survey and analysis of *kabuki* itself as an information system; (3) the experimental implementation and verification of GIS including INGS; and (4) applicable system design and implementation including social distribution experiments through the Web, etc.

## ACKNOWLEDGMENT

This work was supported by JSPS KAKENHI Grant Number 26330258.

## REFERENCES


Akimoto, T., & Ogata, T. (2014). An information design of narratology: The use of three literary theories in a narrative generation system. *The International Journal of Visual Design*, *7*(3), 31–61.

Amino, T., Kawamura, Y., & Ogata, T. (2002). Hierarchical generation of *geino*-idol stories: Toward *geino* information system and narrative marketing. In *Proceedings of 17th Congress of the International Association of Empirical Aesthetics* (pp. 549-552). Academic Press.

Aristotle. (1895). The poetics of Aristotle (S. H. Butcher, Trans.). London, UK: Macmillan. Retrieved from https://archive.org/details/poeticstranslate00arisuoft

Bakhtin, M. (1984). *Problems of Dostoevsky's poetics* (C. Emerson, Trans.). University of Minnesota Press. (Original work published 1963)

Bringsjord, S., & Ferrucci, D. A. (1999). *Artificial intelligence and literary creativity: Inside the mind of BRUTUS, a storytelling machine*. Mehwah, NJ: Lawrence Erlbaum.

Ebihara, K., Kurumisawa, J., Iwasawa, S., & Ohya, J. (1997). Virtual KABUKI system. *IEICE technical report (Image engineering), 96*(507), 61-67.

Imao, T. (1970). *Henshin no shisou* [The theory of metamorphosis]. Tokyo, Japan: Hosei University Press.

Imao, T. (1979). *Kabuki wo miru hito no tameni* [For people viewing kabuki]. Tokyo, Japan: Tamagawa University Press.

Imao, T. (2009). *Kawatake Mokuami* [Kawatake Mokuami]. Kyoto, Japan: Minerva Shobo.

Imao, T. (2010). *Kabuki–<Tsuusetsu> no kenshou* [Kabuki: The verification of 'common views']. Tokyo, Japan: Hosei University Press.

Kawamura, Y., & Ogata, T. (1997). The generation process of entertainment character image. In *Proceedings of the International Conference on Cognitive Science 1997* (pp. 293-294). Academic Press.

Kawamura, Y., & Ogata, T. (2000). A conceptual framework on geino organization model for artificial geino performers with lives. In *Proceedings of the Fifth International Symposium on Artificial Life and Robotics* (pp. 793-796). Academic Press.

Kawamura, Y., & Ogata, T. (2002). A trial on narrative interpretation of *geino* information system. In *Proceedings of IEEE, International Conference on Systems, Man and Cybernetics (CD-ROM)*. doi:10.1109/ICSMC.2002.1175727

Kawatake, T. (1992). *Kabuki: its beauty and tradition* (C. Holmes, Trans.). Tokyo, Japan: Japan Arts Council.

Kawatake, T. (2003). *Kabuki: Baroque fusion of the arts*. Tokyo, Japan: The International House of Japan.

Kristeva, J. (1980). *Desire in language: A semiotic approach to literature and art*. New York, NY: Columbia University Press.

Kurata, Y. (2013). *Bunraku no rekishi* [A history of bunraku]. Tokyo, Japan: Iwanami Shoten.

Lang, R. R. (1999). A declarative model for simple narratives. In *Narrative intelligence: Papers from the 1999 AAAI fall symposium, Technical Report (FS-99-01)* (pp. 134-141). North Falmouth, MA: Academic Press.

Meehan, J. R. (1980). *The metanovel: Writing stories by computer*. New York, NY: Garland Publishing.

Mori, A. (2010). *Takechi Tetsuji toiu geijutsu–Amarini kontenporarii na* [Arts of Takechi Tetsuji: Very contemporary]. Tokyo, Japan: Shinyosha.

Mueller, E. T. (1990). *Daydreaming in humans and machines*. Ablex.

Nakamura, T. (2006). *Kabuki no kindai-Sakka to sakuhin* [The modern age of kabuki: authors and works]. Tokyo, Japan: Iwanami Shoten.

Ogata, T. (2002). Expanded literary theory: Cognitive/computational expansion of literary theories and narratology. In *Proceedings of 17th Congress of the International Association of Empirical Aesthetics* (pp. 163-166). Takarazuka, Japan: Academic Press.

Ogata, T. (2010). Monogatari seisei sisutemu no taikyoku-teki kekkou-Monogatari no gijutsu to keiei heno jo. [The macro architecture of a narrative generation system: An introduction to narrative technology and management] In T. Ogata & A. Kanai (Eds.), *Monogatariron no johogaku josetsu-Monogatari seisei no shiso to gijutsu wo megutte* [An introduction to the informatics of narratology: About the thoughts and technologies of narrative generation] (pp. 259–340). Tokyo, Japan: Gakubunsha.

Ogata, T. (2014). Expanded literary theory for automatic narrative generation. In *Proceedings of Joint 7th International Conference on Soft Computing and Intelligent Systems and 15th International Symposium on Advanced Intelligent Systems* (pp. 1558-1563). Kitakyushu, Japan: Academic Press.

Ohkura, S. (Photographs) (2001). Kabuki today: the art and tradition. Tokyo, Japan: Kodansha International.

Okada, N., & Endo, T. (1992). Story generation based on dynamics of the mind. *Computational Intelligence*, *8*(1), 123–160. doi:10.1111/j.1467-8640.1992.tb00341.x

Pemberton, L. (1989). A modular approach to story generation. In *Proceedings of the Fourth Conference on European Chapter of the Association for Computational Linguistics* (pp. 217-224). doi:10.3115/976815.976845

Schank, R. C., & Abelson, R. P. (1977). *Scripts, plans, goals, and understanding: An inquiry into human knowledge structures*. Mahwah, NJ: Lawrence Erlbaum.

Shibuya, Y., Morita, Y., Fukuda, H., Ueda, K., & Sasaki, M. (2012). Asynchronous relation between body action and breathing in bunraku: Uniqueness of manner of breathing in Japanese traditional performing arts. *Cognitive Studies*, *19*(3), 337–364.

Suwa, H. (1991). *Kabuki no houhou* [Methods of kabuki]. Tokyo, Japan: Bensei Shuppan.

Taguchi, A. (2003). *Kabuki to ningyou joururi* [Kabuki and ningyo-joruri]. Tokyo, Japan: Yoshikawa-kobunkan.

Turner, S. R. (1994). *The creative process: A computer model of storytelling and creativity*. Mahwah, NJ: Lawrence Erlbaum.

Watanabe, T. (1989). *Kabuki–Kajo naru kigo no mori* [Kabuki: The forest of excessive signs]. Tokyo, Japan: Shinyosha.

Watanabe, T. (2009). *Kabuki no mikata* [Kabuki's viewpoints]. Tokyo, Japan: Kadokawa Gakugei Shuppan.

Watanabe, T. (2012). *Watashi no kabuki henreki–Aru gekihyo-ka no kokuhaku* [My kabuki wandering: A confession by a drama critic]. Tokyo, Japan: Engeki Shuppansha.

Yuda, Y. (Ed.) (1965). Bunraku joruri shuu [A selection of bunraku and joruri works]. Tokyo, Japan: Iwanami Shoten.

## KEY TERMS AND DEFINITIONS

**Expanded Literary Theory (ELT):** A concept for a research field in which narratology and literary theories are organically introduced into computational and cognitive approaches.

**Geino Information System (GIS):** A system model of *geino* production and consumption. GIS has been considered a framework in which various levels of narrative generation processes were driven by authors, receivers, characters, actors, and actresses.

**Integrated Narrative Generation System (INGS):** A synthetic narrative generation system architecture integrating the previous studies by the author.

**Multiple Narrative Structures (Model):** A conceptual model by which a narrative text is multiply constituted and the narrative generation process is also multiply executed.

# APPENDIX

*Table 6.*

| | English Title | First Performance | | Notes |
|---|---|---|---|---|
| | | Year | Theatre (City) | |
| 1 | The Treasury of Loyal Retainers | 1748 | *Takemoto-za* (Osaka) | Originally, *ningyo- joruri* |
| 2 | Sugawara's Secrets of Calligraphy | 1746 | *Takemoto -za* (Osaka) | Originally, *ningyo-joruri* |
| 3 | Yoshitsune and Thousand Cherry Trees | 1747 | *Takemoto -za* (Osaka) | Originally, *ningyo-joruri* |
| 4 | Ghost story of Yotsuya | 1825 | *Nakamura-za* (Edo) | |
| 5 | Osome and Hisamatsu | 1813 | *Morita-za* (Edo) | |
| 6 | Scarred Yosaburo | 1853 | *Nakamura-za* (Edo) | |
| 7 | Mount Higashi Flower Book | 1851 | *Nakamura-za* (Edo) | |
| 8 | Three Thieves Called Kichisa | 1860 | *Ichimura-za* (Edo) | |
| 9 | The Glorious Picture Book of Aoto's Exploits | 1862 | *Ichimura-za* (Edo) | |
| 10 | Sukeroku Flower of Edo | 1811 | *Ichimura-za* (Edo) | Formal name: *Sukeroku Yukari no Edo-zakura* |
| 11 | The Soga Brothers' Confrontation | 1676 | *Nakamura-za* (Edo) | Formal name: *Kotobuki Soga no Taimen* |
| 12 | Benten the Thief | | | In *Aoto Zoshi Hana no Nishiki-e* |
| 13 | An Example of Noble Womanhood | 1771 | *Takemoto-za* (Osaka) | Originally, *ningyo-joruri* |
| 14 | Chronicle of the Battle of Ichi-no-Tani | 1751 | *Toyotake-za* (Osaka) | Originally, *ningyo-joruri* |
| 15 | Kumagai's Field Headquarters | | | In *Ichi-no-Tani Futaba Gunki* |
| 16 | Twenty-Four Examples of Filial Piety | 1766 | *Takemoto-za* (Osaka) | Originally, *ningyo-joruri* |
| 17 | Picture Book Taikoki | 1799 | *Toyotake-za* (Osaka) | Originally, *ningyo-joruri* |
| 18 | The Famous Trees of Sendai | 1777 | *Naka-no-shibai* (Osaka) | |
| 19 | Mt. Kagami | 1782 | *Geki-za* (Edo) | Formal name: *Kagamiyama Kokyo no Nishikie*, Originally, *ningyo-joruri* |
| 20 | Lovers' Suicide at Sonezaki | 1703 | *Takemoto-za* (Osaka) | Originally, *ningyo-joruri* |
| 21 | Lovers' Suicide at Amijima | 1720 | *Takemoto-za* (Osaka) | Originally, *ningyo-joruri* |
| 22 | The Pledge of Love | 1794 | *Nishi-no-shibai* (Kyoto) | |
| 23 | O-some and Hisamatsu | 1780 | *Takemoto -za* (Osaka) | Originally, *ningyo-joruri* |
| 24 | The White Wave Five | | | Formal name: *Aoto Zoshi Hana no Nishiki-e* |
| 25 | The Maiden at Dojoji Temple | 1753 | *Nakamura-za* (Edo) | |
| 26 | Maple Viewing | 1887 | *Shintomi-za* (Tokyo) | Originally, *Noh* (by Kanze Kojiro Nobumitsu (1435-1516)) |
| 27 | The Subscription Scroll | 1840 | *Kawarazaki-za* (Edo) | Originally, *Noh* (*Ataka*) |
| 28 | Earth Spider | 1881 | *Shintomi-za* (Tokyo) | |
| 29 | Benkei in the Boat | 1885 | *Shintomi-za* (Tokyo) | |
| 30 | A Substitute for Meditation | 1910 | *Ichimura-za* (Tokyo) | Originally, Kyogen (*Hanako*) |
| 31 | Tied to a Pole | 1916 | *Ichimura-za* (Tokyo) | |

*continued on following page*

*Table 6. Continued*

| | English Title | First Performance | | Notes |
|---|---|---|---|---|
| | | Year | Theatre (City) | |
| 32 | Love at the Osaka Barrier | 1784 | *Kiri-za* (Edo) | Formal name: *Tsumoru Koi Yuki no Seki-no-to* |
| 33 | Echigo Lion | 1811 | *Nakamura-za* (Edo) | |
| 34 | Ferry-Boat | 1843 | *Ichimura-za* (Edo). | |
| 35 | Sanja Festival | 1832 | *Nakamura-za* (Edo) | Formal name: *Yayoi no Hana Asakusa Matsuri* |
| 36 | Water-Seller | 1813 | *Morita-za* (Edo) | |
| 37 | Wait! | 1697 | *Nakamura-za* (Edo) | |
| 38 | The Tweezers | | | In *Narukami Fudo Kitayama Zakura* |
| 39 | The Thunder God | 1742 | *Sadoshima-Chogoro-za* (Osaka) | Formal name: *Narukami Fudo Kitayama Zakura* |
| 40 | Onikage Musashi Stirrup | 1710 | *Sasazuka-za* (Osaka) | |
| 41 | Go Board Taiheiki | 1710 | *Takemoto -za* (Osaka) | Originally, *ningyo-joruri* |
| 42 | Genroku Chushingura | 1934 | *Kabuki-za* (Tokyo) | |
| 43 | Through Iga Pass with Tokaido Board Game | 1783 | *Takemoto -za* (Osaka) | Originally, *ningyo-joruri* |
| 44 | Through Iga Pass with Riding Kappa | 1776 | *Arashi-za* (Osaka) | |
| 45 | Ten Characters' Roles of Date | 1815 | *Kawarazaki-za* (Edo) | |
| 46 | Kagotsurube: The Bewitching Sword | 1888 | *Chitose-za* (Tokyo) | |
| 47 | Yoshiwara Sparrow | 1768 | *Ichimura-za* (Edo) | |
| 48 | The Crescent Moon | 1969 | *Kokuritsu-gekijo* (Tokyo) | |

# Compilation of References

Aaeseth, E. (2012). A narrative theory of games. In *Proceedings of the International Conference on the Foundations of Digital Games*. Copenhagen, Denmark: Academic Press.

Aarseth, E. (1997). *Cybertext: Perspectives on ergodic literature*. The Johns Hopkins University Press.

Abe, A. (1998). Applications of abduction. In *Proceedings of the ECAI98 Workshop on Abduction and Induction in AI* (pp. 12-19). Academic Press.

Abe, A. (2002). Computational generation of affective phrase. In *Proceedings of SCI2002*, (vol. 16, pp. 261-266). Academic Press.

Abe, H., Ogata, T., & Onodera, K. (2009). An analysis of products introducing rhetoric in advertising and the prototype system implementation. In *Proceedings of the 23rd Annual Conference of the Japanese Society for Artificial Intelligence* (1J1-OS2-4). Takamatsu, Japan: Academic Press.

Abe, J. (1999). *On directionality of movement*. (Unpublished manuscript). Nagoya University, Aichi, Japan.

Adam, J. M. (1999). *Le récit*. Paris, France: Presses Universitaires de France.

Akagawa, J. (2015). *Mikeneko Holmes-no-yumekikou* [The dreamy travelogue of Mikeneko Holmes]. Tokyo, Japan: Kobunsha.

Akaishi, M. (2006). A dynamic de-composition/re-composition framework for documents based on narrative structure model. *Transactions of the Japanese Society for Artificial Intelligence*, *21*(5), 428–438. doi:10.1527/tjsai.21.428

Akimoto, T., & Ogata, T. (2010). Implementing a narrative discourse system as a mechanism in narrative generation: A hybrid approach of AI and narratology. In *Proceedings of the 7th International Conference on Cognitive Science* (pp. 359-360). Beijing, China: Academic Press.

Akimoto, T., & Ogata, T. (2011a). Computational model of narrative discourse theory and reception theory in narratology and its implementation. In *Proceedings of the 13th Annual Conference of the Japanese Society for Language Sciences* (pp. 155-156). Suita, Japan: Academic Press.

Akimoto, T., & Ogata, T. (2012). A narratological approach for narrative discourse: Implementation and evaluation of the system based on Genette and Jauss. In *Proceedings of the 34th Annual Conference of the Cognitive Science Society* (pp. 1272-1277). Sapporo, Japan: Academic Press.

Akimoto, T., & Ogata, T. (2015b). An investigation of effects of computer-generated narratives on humans' narrative creations. In *Proceedings of 32nd Annual Meeting of the Japanese Cognitive Science Society* (pp. 462-471). Chiba, Japan: Academic Press.

Akimoto, T., Kurisawa, Y., & Ogata, T. (2013c). A mechanism for managing the progression of events by states in integrated narrative generation system. In *Proceedings of the 2nd International Conference on Engineering and Applied Science* (pp. 1605-1614). Tokyo, Japan: Academic Press.

Akimoto, T., Ono, J., & Ogata, T. (2013). Designing information contents with automatic narrative generation system. In *Proceedings of the 5th International Conference of International Association of Societies of Design Research* (pp. 5424-5435). Tokyo, Japan: Academic Press.

Akimoto, T., Endo, J., & Ogata, T. (2013a). The expansion of paths in the mutual transformation mechanism of music and narrative. *International Journal of Cognitive Informatics and Natural Intelligence*, *7*(4), 44–63. doi:10.4018/ijcini.2013100103

Akimoto, T., Imabuchi, S., Endo, J., Ono, J., Kurisawa, Y., Kamada, M., & Ogata, T. (2013b). Development of a generation/expression system of narratives in the style of a folk tale, KOSERUBE Version 1. *Transactions of the Japanese Society for Artificial Intelligence*, *28*(5), 442–456. doi:10.1527/tjsai.28.442

Akimoto, T., & Ogata, T. (2011b). A consideration of the elements for narrative generation and a trial of integrated narrative generation system. In *Proceedings of the 7th International Conference on Natural Language Processing and Knowledge Engineering* (pp. 369-377). Tokushima, Japan. doi:10.1109/NLPKE.2011.6138227

Akimoto, T., & Ogata, T. (2012). A narratological approach for narrative discourse: Implementation and evaluation of the system based on Genette and Jauss. In *Proceedings of the 34th Annual Conference of the Cognitive Science Society* (pp. 1272-1277), Austin, TX: Cognitive Science Society.

Akimoto, T., & Ogata, T. (2013). Towards a discourse mechanism in narrative generation system: Proposal of a system introducing narrative discourse theory and reception theory. *Cognitive Studies*, *20*(4), 396–420.

Akimoto, T., & Ogata, T. (2014a). An information design of narratology: The use of three literary theories in a narrative generation system. *The International Journal of Visual Design*, *7*(3), 31–61.

Akimoto, T., & Ogata, T. (2014b). Circulative narrative generation based on the mutual transformation between narrative conceptual structures and music in the integrated narrative generation system. *Journal of Robotics. Networking and Artificial Life*, *1*(3), 198–202. doi:10.2991/jrnal.2014.1.3.6

Akimoto, T., & Ogata, T. (2015a). A visual interface for a collection of computer-generated narratives. *Information Engineering Express*, *1*(4), 43–52.

Akimoto, T., & Ogata, T. (2015a). Evaluation of a narrative discourse generation system based on the concept of "norm and deviation". *Journal of Robotics. Networking and Artificial Life*, *2*(1), 50–53. doi:10.2991/jrnal.2015.2.1.12

Akimoto, T., & Ogata, T. (2015b). Experimental development of a focalization mechanism in an integrated narrative generation system. *Journal of Artificial Intelligence and Soft Computing Research*, *5*(3), 177–188. doi:10.1515/jaiscr-2015-0027

Akimoto, T., Ono, J., & Ogata, T. (2012). Narrative Forest: An automatic narrative generation system with a visual narrative operation mechanism. In *Proceedings of the 6th International Conference on Soft Computing and Intelligent Systems & the 13th International Symposium on Advanced Intelligent Systems* (pp. 2164-2167). Kobe, Japan. doi:10.1109/SCIS-ISIS.2012.6505319

Alani, H., Kim, S., Millard, D. E., & Weal, M. J. (2003). Automatic ontology-based knowledge extraction and tailored biography generation from the Web. *IIIE Intelligent Systems,* 14-21.

Amino, T., Kawamura, Y., & Ogata, T. (2002). Hierarchical generation of *geino*-idol stories: Toward *geino* information system and narrative marketing. In *Proceedings of 17th Congress of the International Association of Empirical Aesthetics* (pp. 549-552). Academic Press.

Amino, T., Kawamura, Y., & Ogata, T. (2002). Hierarchical generation of *geino*-idol stories: Toward *geino* information system and narrative marketing. In *Proceedings of 17th Congress of the International Association of Empirical Aesthetics* (pp. 549-552). Takarazuka, Japan: Academic Press.

Anderson, T. S. (2015). From episodic memory to narrative in a cognitive architecture. In *Proceedings of 6th Workshop on Computational Models of Narrative* (pp. 2-11). Atlanta, GA: Academic Press.

Antosch, F. (1969). The diagnosis of literary style with the verb-adjective ratio. In L. Doleszel & R. Bailey (Eds.), *Statistics and style*. New York, NY: Elsevier.

Appel, M. (2008). Manche mögen's heiß. Ergebnisse der deutschsprachigen Version eines Instruments zur Erfassung des Emotionsmotivs[Some like it hot. Results of the German language version of an instrument for the assessment of the need for affect]. *Diagnostica*, *54*(1), 2–15. doi:10.1026/0012-1924.54.1.2

Arai, H. (1985). *Shinariwo no kiso gijyutsu* [Base techniques for making a scenario]. Tokyo, Japan: Davidsha.

Arai, H. (1997). Genji monogatari/Uji Jujo no sakusha mondai: Hitotsu no keiryou gengogakuteki approach[The Tale of Genji/Uji Jujo authorship problem: one quantitative linguistic approach] [Hitotsubashi Treatise]. *Hitotsubashi Ronshu*, *117*(3), 397–413.

Arikawa, H. (2010a). Roru auto. [Roll out] In H. Arikawa (Ed.), *Kujira-no kare* [The man of whale] (pp. 63–111). Tokyo, Japan: Kadokawa Shoten Publishing.

Arikawa, H. (2010b). Yuunouna kanojo. [The able lady] In H. Arikawa (Ed.), *Kujira-no kare* [The man of whale] (pp. 161–213). Tokyo, Japan: Kadokawa Shoten Publishing.

Arima, M., & Tsuji, S. (1987). *Anketochosa no houhou* [Method of questionnaire survey]. Tokyo, Japan: Asakura Publishing.

Aristotle. (1895). The poetics of Aristotle (S. H. Butcher, Trans.). London, UK: Macmillan. Retrieved from https://archive.org/details/poeticstranslate00arisuoft

Aristotle. (1895). The poetics of Aristotle (S. H. Butcher, Trans.). London, UK: Macmillan; Retrieved from https://archive.org/details/poeticstranslate00arisuoft

Aristotle. (1997). Poetics (Matsumoto, N & Oka, M, Trans.). Tokyo, Japan: Iwanami Shoten. (Original work published 335 B.C.).

Aruga, H., & Ogata, T. (1998). Structural analysis of tragic story and formalization of general rules. In *Proceedings of the 12rd Annual Conference of the Japanese Society for Artificial Intelligence* (pp. 697-700). Tokyo, Japan: Academic Press.

Asai, A. (1987). *Chosa no gijutsu* [The technique of investigation]. Tokyo, Japan: JUSE Press.

Asai, R. (2012). *Kirishima bukatsu yamerutteyo* [The Kirishima thing]. Tokyo, Japan: Shueisha Publishing.

Asanuma, K. (1990). Eizo no tekusuto no giho [Techniques for image text]. Eiga no tameni II [For movie II] (pp. 130-247). Tokyo, Japan: Suiseisha.

Austin, J. (1962). *How to do things with words*. Oxford, UK: Clarendon Press.

Avrahami, J., & Kareev, Y. (1994). The emergence of events. *Cognition*, *53*(3), 239–261. doi:10.1016/0010-0277(94)90050-7 PMID:7842635

Bae, B. C., Cheong, Y. G., & Young, M. R. (2011). Automated story generation with multiple internal focalization. In *Proceedings of 2011 IEEE Conference on Computational Intelligence and Games* (pp. 211-218). Seoul, South Korea. doi:10.1109/CIG.2011.6032009

Bae, B.-C., & Young, R. M. (2008). A use of flashback and foreshadowing for surprise arousal in narrative using a plan-based approach. In *Proceeding of the International Conference on Interactive Digital Storytelling (ICIDS08)* (pp. 156-167). Erfurt, Germany. doi:10.1007/978-3-540-89454-4_22

Baker, C., Fillmore, C. J., & Lowe, J. B. (1998). The Berkeley FrameNet project. In *Proceedings of the 36th Annual Meeting of the Association for Computational Linguistics* (pp. 86-90). Montreal, Canada: Association for Computational Linguistics. doi:10.3115/980845.980860

Baker, S. (2012). *Final Jeopardy: The story of Watson, the computer that will transform our world.* Boston, MA: Mariner Book.

Bakhtin, M. (1984). *Problems of Dostoevsky's poetics* (C. Emerson, Trans.). MN: University of Minnesota Press. (Original work published 1963)

Bakhtin, M. M. (1989). *Marxism and the philosophy of language* (T. Kuwano, Trans.). Tokyo, Japan: Miraisha. (Original work published 1929)

Bal, M. (2004). *Narrative theory: Critical concepts in literary and cultural studies* (Vol. I-IV). Routledge.

Barber, H. (2008). *Generator of adaptive dilemma-based interactive narratives* (Thesis). Department of Computer Science. The University of York, York, UK.

Barry, P. (2009). *Beginning theory: An introduction to literary and cultural theory* (3rd ed.). Manchester, UK: Manchester University Press.

Barthes, R. (1966). Introduction à l'analyse structurale des récits. *Communications*, *8*(1), 1–27. doi:10.3406/comm.1966.1113

Barthes, R. (1979). *Introduction à l'analyse structurale des récits* (H. Hanawa, Trans.). Tokyo, Japan: Misuzu Shobo. (Original work published 1966)

Barthes, R., & Duisit, L. (1975). An introduction to the structural analysis of narrative (L. Duisit, Trans.). *New Literary History*, *6*(2), 237–272. doi:10.2307/468419

Bartlett, F. C. (1923). *Psychology and primitive culture.* London: Cambridge University Press.

Bazin, A. (1967). *Che cos'è il cinema.* Milano: Garzanti.

Beasley, M. (2014, September 17). *Keymoji keyboard for iOS 8 translates everything you type into emoji.* Retrieved from http://9to5mac.com/2014/09/17/keymoji-keyboard-for-ios-8-translates-everything-you-type-into-emoji/#

Becker, D. R., & Bond, G. R. (Eds.). (2002). *Supported employment implementation resource kit.* Rockville, MD: Center for Mental Health Services, Substance Abuse and Mental Health Services Administration.

Benson, T. W., & Anderson, C. (1989). *Reality fictions: The films of Frederick Wiseman.* Southern Illinois University Press.

Bers, M. U. (1999). Narrative construction kit: "Who am I? Who are you? What are you?". *Narrative Intelligence: Papers from the 1999 AAAI Fall Symposium, Technical Report* (FS-99-01, pp. 44-52), North Falmouth, Massachusetts.

Binongo, J. N. G. (2003). Who wrote the 15th book of Oz? An application of multivariate analysis to authorship attribution. *Chance*, *16*(4), 375–388.

Binsted, K. (1996). *Machine humour: An implemented model of puns.* (Ph. D. Thesis). University of Edinburgh.

Binsted, K., & Ritchie, G. (1994). An implemented model of punning riddles. *Proceedings of, AAAI94*, 633–638.

Binsted, K., & Takizawa, O. (1998). BOKE: A Japanese punning riddle generator. *Journal of the Japanese Society for Artificial Intelligence*, *13*(6), 920–927.

Blackburn, P., & Meyer-Viol, W. (1994). Linguistics, logic, and finite trees. *Bulletin of Interest Group of Pure and Applied Logics*, *2*, 2–39.

Black, M. L. (2012). Narrative and spatial form in digital media: A platform study of the SCUMM engine and Ron Gilbert's the Secret of Monkey Island. *Games and Culture*, *7*(3), 209–237. doi:10.1177/1555412012440317

Blount, W. P. (1927). Studies of the movements of the eyelids of animals: Blinking. *Quarterly Journal of Experimental Physiology (Cambridge, England)*, *18*(2), 111–125. doi:10.1113/expphysiol.1927.sp000426

Bolter, J. D. (1991). *Writing space: The computer, hypertext and the history of writing*. Lawrence Erlbaum.

Booth, W. C. (1983). *The rhetoric of fiction*. Chicago: University of Chicago Press. doi:10.7208/chicago/9780226065595.001.0001

Bordwell, D. (1985). *Narration in the fiction film*. Madison, WI: University of Wisconsin Press.

Bower, G. H. (1981). Mood and memory. *The American Psychologist*, *36*(2), 129–148. doi:10.1037/0003-066X.36.2.129 PMID:7224324

Boym, S. (2001). *The future of nostalgia*. New York, NY: Basic Books.

Brecht, B. (1964). *Brecht on theatre: The development of an aesthetics* (J. Willett, Trans. & Ed.). London: Methuen. (Original work published 1950)

Brecht, B., & Willett, J. (1964). *Brecht on theatre: The development of an aesthetic*. New York, NY: Hill and Wang.

Breton, A. (1969). *Manifestoes of surrealism*. Ann Arbor, MI: University of Michigan Press. (Original work published 1924)

Brinegar, C. S. (1963). Mark Twain and the Quintus Curtius Snodgrass letters: A statistical test of authorship. *Journal of the American Statistical Association*, *58*(301), 85–96. doi:10.1080/01621459.1963.10500834

Bringsjord, S., & Ferrucci, D. A. (1999). *Artificial intelligence and literary creativity: Inside the mind of BRUTUS, a storytelling machine*. Lawrence Erlbaum.

Bruner, J. (1986). *Actual minds, possible worlds*. Cambridge, MA: Harvard University Press.

Bruner, J. (1991). The narrative construction of reality. *Critical Inquiry*, *18*(1), 1–21. doi:10.1086/448619

Bruner, J. (2003). *Making stories: Law, literature, life*. Cambridge, MA: Harvard University Press.

Bruner, J. S. (1996). *The culture of education*. Cambridge, MA: Harvard University Press.

Buchanan-Barker, P., & Barker, P. J. (2008). The Tidal commitments: Extending the value base of mental health recovery. *Journal of Psychiatric and Mental Health Nursing*, *15*(2), 93–100. doi:10.1111/j.1365-2850.2007.01209.x PMID:18211556

Burgoon, J. K., & Walther, J. B. (2013). Media and computer mediation. In M. L. Knapp & J. A. Hall (Eds.), *Nonverbal communication* (pp. 731–770). doi:10.1515/9783110238150.731

Byron, K. (2008). Carrying too heavy a load? The communication and miscommunication of emotion by email. *Academy of Management Review*, *33*(2), 309–327. doi:10.5465/AMR.2008.31193163

Calabrese, S. (2009). *Neuronarratologia*. Bologna: Archetipolibri.

Callaway, C. B., & Lester, J. C. (2002). Narrative prose generation. *Artificial Intelligence*, *139*(2), 213–252. doi:10.1016/S0004-3702(02)00230-8

Campbell, L. (1867). *The Sophistes and Politicus of Plato*. London, UK: Clarendon Press.

Cann, R. (2011). Towards an account of the auxiliary system in English. In R. Kempson et al. (Eds.), *The Dynamics of Lexical Interfaces* (pp. 279–317). Stanford, CA: Center for the Study of Language and Information.

Cann, R., Kempson, R., & Gregoromichelaki, E. (2008). *Semantics*. Cambridge, UK: Cambridge University Press.

Cann, R., Kempson, R., & Marten, L. (2005). *The dynamics of language*. Oxford, UK: Elsevier.

Cann, R., Kempson, R., Marten, L., Otsuka, M., & Swinburne, D. (2004). On the left and on the right. In D. Adger et al. (Eds.), *Peripheries* (pp. 19–47). Dordrecht, Netherlands: Kluwer. doi:10.1007/1-4020-1910-6_2

Carroll, N. (1996). The paradox of suspense. In P. Vorderer, H. J. Wulff, & M. Friedrichsen (Eds.), *Suspense: Conceptualizations, theoretical analyses, and empirical explorations* (pp. 71–91). Mahwah, NJ: Lawrence Erlbaum Associates.

Chambers, N., & Jurafsky, D. (2008). Unsupervised learning of narrative event chains. In *Proceedings of 46th Annual Meeting of the Association for Computational Linguistics: Human Language Technologies* (pp. 789-797). Columbus, OH: Academic Press.

Chambers, N., & Jurafsky, D. (2010). A database of narrative schemas. In *Proceedings of Seventh International Conference on Language Resources and Evaluation* (pp. 1614-1618). Malta: Academic Press.

Chambers, N., & Jurafsky, D. (2009). Unsupervised learning of narrative schemas and their participants. In *Proceedings of Joint Conference of the 47th Annual Meeting of the Association for Computational Linguistics and the 4th International Joint Conference on Natural Language Processing of the Asian Federation of Natural Language Processing* (pp. 602-610). Suntec, Singapore. doi:10.3115/1690219.1690231

Chambers, N., Wang, S., & Jurafsky, D. (2007). Classifying temporal relations between events. In *Proceedings of the 45th Annual Meeting of the ACL on Interactive Poster and Demonstration Sessions* (pp. 173-176). doi:10.3115/1557769.1557820

Chaski, C. E. (2001). Empirical evaluations of language-based author identification techniques. *Forensic Linguistics*, *8*, 1–65.

Chatman, S. (1980). *Story and discourse: Narrative structure in fiction and film*. Cornell University Press.

Chatman, S. (1990). *Coming to terms: The rhetoric of narrative in fiction and film*. Ithaca, NY: Cornell University Press.

Chatzikyriakidis, S. (2011). *Right dislocations in Greek*. (Unpublished manuscript). Centre National de la Recherche Scientifique, Paris, France.

Cheong, Y. G., & Young, R. M. (2015). Suspenser: A story generation system for suspense. *IEEE Transactions on Computational Intelligence and AI in Games*, *7*(1), 39–52. doi:10.1109/TCIAIG.2014.2323894

Childs, L. M., & Strogatz, S. H. (2008). Stability diagram for the forced Kuramoto model. *Chaos: An Interdisciplinary Journal of Nonlinear Science*, *18*(4), 043128. doi:10.1063/1.3049136 PMID:19123638

Chomsky, N. (1965). *Aspects of the theory of syntax*. Cambridge, MA: MIT Press.

Chomsky, N. (1995). *The minimalist program*. Cambridge, MA: MIT Press.

Christoforou, C., Christou-Champi, S., Constantinidou, F., & Theodorou, M. (2015). From the eyes and the heart: A novel eye-gaze metric that predicts video preferences of a large audience. *Frontiers in Psychology*, 6. PMID:26029135

Clinton, J. J. (1993). Agency for health care policy and research: Improving health care through guidelines and outcomes research. *Hospital Formulary*, *28*(11), 933–942. PMID:10130235

Cohn, N. (2013). Visual narrative structure. *Cognitive Science*, *34*(3), 413–452. doi:10.1111/cogs.12016 PMID:23163777

Cohn, N. (2014). You're a good structure, Charlie Brown: The distribution of narrative categories in comic strips. *Cognitive Science*, *38*(7), 1317–1359. doi:10.1111/cogs.12116 PMID:24646175

Comesaña, M., Soares, A. P., Perea, M., Piñeiro, A. P., Fraga, I., & Pinheiro, A. (2013). ERP correlates of masked affective priming with emoticons. *Computers in Human Behavior*, *29*(3), 588–595. doi:10.1016/j.chb.2012.10.020

Compagnon, A. (1998). *Le demon de la theorie: Litterature et sens commun*. Paris: Seul.

Concato, J. (2004). Observational versus experimental studies: What's the evidence for hierarchy? *Journal of the American Society for Experimental Neuro-therapeutics*, *1*(3), 341–347. doi:10.1602/neurorx.1.3.341 PMID:15717036

Cooper, R. (2005). Records and record types in semantic theory. *Journal of Logic and Computation*, *15*(2), 99–112. doi:10.1093/logcom/exi004

Cortes, C., & Vapnik, V. (1995). Support-vector networks. *Machine Learning*, *20*(3), 273–297. doi:10.1007/BF00994018

Crask, M. R., & Laskey, H. A. (1990). A positioning-based decision model for selecting advertising messages. *Journal of Advertising Research*, *30*(4), 32–38.

Creswell, J. W., & Plano Clark, V. L. (2007). *Designing and conducting mixed methods research*. London, UK: Sage Publications.

Culicover, P., & Jackendoff, R. (2005). *Simpler syntax*. Oxford, UK: Oxford University Press. doi:10.1093/acprof:oso/9780199271092.001.0001

Cutting, J. E., Brunick, K. L., & Canden, A. (2012). Perceiving event dynamics and parsing Hollywood films. *Journal of Experimental Psychology*, *38*(6), 1476–1490. PMID:22449126

Cutting, J. E., & Iricinschi, C. (2014). Re-presentations of space in Hollywood movies: An event-indexing analysis. *Cognitive Science*, *35*, 1–23. PMID:25087776

Dalrymple, M. (2001). *Lexical functional grammar*. New York, NY: Academic Press. doi:10.1163/9781849500104

Danto, A. C. (1965). *Analytical philosophy of history*. London: Cambridge University Press.

Davidson, D. (1967). The logical form of action sentences. In N. Rescher (Ed.), *The logic of decision and action* (pp. 81–95). Pittsburgh, PA: University of Pittsburg Press.

Davis, F. (1979). *Yearning for yesterday: a sociology of nostalgia*. New York: Free Press.

Davis, R., & Lenat, D. B. (1982). *Knowledge-based systems in artificial intelligence*. New York, NY: MkGraw-Hill.

De Jaegher, H., & Di Paolo, E. (2007). Participatory sense-making. *Phenomenology and the Cognitive Sciences*, *6*(4), 485–507. doi:10.1007/s11097-007-9076-9

De Morgan, S. E. (1882). *Memoir of Augustus de Morgan*. London, UK: Longmans, Green, and Company.

de Wied, M., Zillmann, D., & Ordman, V. (1994). The role of empathic distress in the enjoyment of cinematic tragedy. *Poetics*, *23*(1-2), 91–106. doi:10.1016/0304-422X(94)00010-4

Deleuze, G. (1983). *Image-mouvement*. Paris, France: Les Editions de Minuit.

Deleuze, G. (1985). *L' Image-temps*. Paris, France: Les Editions de Minuit.

Denning, S. (2007). *The secret language of leadership: How leaders inspire action through narrative*. San Francisco, CA: John Wiley & Sons.

Denzin, N. K., & Lincoln, Y. S. (Eds.). (2000). *Handbook of qualitative research*. London, UK: Sage Publications.

Devilla, J. (2014). *Swift fun fact #1: You can use emoji characters in variable, constant, function, and class names*. Retrieved from http://www.globalnerdy.com/2014/06/03/swift-fun-fact-1-you-can-use-emoji-characters-in-variable-constant-function-and-class-names/

Dittenberger, W. (1881). Sprachliche Kriterien für die Chronologie der Platonischen Dialoge. *Hermes*, *16*(3), 321–345.

Dmochowski, J. P., Bezdek, M. A., Abelson, B. P., Johnson, J. S., Schumacher, E. H., & Parra, L. C. (2014). Audience preferences are predicted by temporal reliability of neural processing. *Nature Communications*, 5. PMID:25072833

Dorr, B. J. (1997). Large-scale dictionary construction for foreign language tutoring and inter-lingual machine translation. *Machine Translation*, *12*(4), 271–322. doi:10.1023/A:1007965530302

Doughty, M. J. (2001). Consideration of three types of spontaneous eyeblink activity in normal humans: During reading and video display terminal use, in primary gaze, and while in conversation. *Optometry and Vision Science*, *78*(10), 712–725. doi:10.1097/00006324-200110000-00011 PMID:11700965

Drew, G. (1951). Variations in reflex blink-rate during visual-motor tasks. *The Quarterly Journal of Experimental Psychology*, *3*(2), 73–88. doi:10.1080/17470215108416776

Dryer, M. (2013). Order of subject, object and verb. In M. Dryer & M. Haspelmath (Eds.), The world atlas of language structures online. Retrieved from http://wals.info/chapter/81

Dundes, A. (1965). *The study of folklore*. Prentice Hall.

Dyer, M. G. (1983). *In-depth understanding: A computer model of integrated processing for narrative comprehension*. Cambridge, MA: MIT Press.

Ebihara, K., Kurumisawa, J., Iwasawa, S., & Ohya, J. (1997). Virtual KABUKI system. *IEICE technical report (Image engineering)*, *96*(507), 61-67.

Eguchi, I. (2000). Nihongo-no kouchibun[Postposed sentences in Japanese] [Study on Language and Culture]. *Gengo Bunka Kenkyu*, *12*, 81–93.

Eisenstein, S. M. (1942). *The film sense* (J. Leyda, Trans.). New York, NY: Harcourt Brace.

Eitz, M., Hays, J., & Alexa, M. (2012). How do humans sketch objects? *ACM Trans. Graph.*, *31*(4), 44:1-44:10.

Ekuni, K. (2006). *Tokyo tawa* [Tokyo Tower]. Tokyo, Japan: Shinchosha Publishing.

Elliott, J. (2005). *Using narrative in social research*. London, UK: Sage Publications.

Elson, D. K., & McKeown, K. R. (2007). A platform for symbolically encoding human narratives. In *Intelligent Narrative Technologies: Papers from the 2007 AAAI Fall Symposium, Technical Report* (FS-07-05).

Endo, Y., & Ogata, T. (2002). Hyper-comic system as representation field of narrative discourse. In *Proceedings of 17th Congress of the International Association of Empirical Aesthetics* (pp. 555-558). Takarazuka, Japan: Academic Press.

Endo, Y., & Ogata, T. (2003). Hyper-comic system as consideration of rhetoric. In *Proceedings of The 4th International Conference on Cognitive Science* (pp. 111-116). Sydney, Australia: Academic Press.

Endo, Y., & Ogata, T. (2004a). A rhetorical analysis of a Japanese comic for hyper-comic system. In *Proceedings of 18th Congress of the International Association of Empirical Aesthetics* (pp. 502-508). Lisbon, Portugal: Academic Press.

Endo, Y., & Ogata, T. (2004b). Multilayered discourse in hyper-comic. In *Proceedings of the Ninth International Symposium on Artificial Life and Robotics* (*Vol.1*, pp. 49-52). Beppu, Japan: Academic Press.

Eshghi, A., Purver, M., & Hough, J. (2011). *DyLan* (Report No. EECSRR-11-05). London, UK: School of Electronic Engineering and Computer Science, Queen Mary University of London.

Eshghi, A., Purver, M., Hough, J., & Sato, Y. (2013). Probabilistic grammar induction in an incremental semantic framework. In D. Duchier & Y. Parmentier (Eds.), *Constraint solving and language processing* (pp. 92–107). Berlin, Germany: Springer-Verlag. doi:10.1007/978-3-642-41578-4_6

Eskelinen, M. (n.d.). *(Introduction to) cybertext narratology*. Retrieved from http://cybertext.hum.jyu.fi/articles/123.pdf

Everitt, B. S. (1998). *The Cambridge dictionary of statistics*. Cambridge, UK: Cambridge University Press.

Feldman, R., & Sanger, J. (2007). *The text mining handbook: Advanced approaches in analyzing unstructured data*. Cambridge, UK: Cambridge University Press.

Fellbaum, C. (1998). *WordNet: an electronic lexical database*. Cambridge, MA: MIT Press.

Fendt, M. W., & Young, R. M. (2014). Adapting IRIS, a non-interactive narrative generation system, to an interactive text adventure game. In *Proceedings of the 27th International Florida Artificial Intelligence Research Society Conference* (pp. 244-249). Pensacola Beach, CA: Academic Press.

Fillmore, C. (1968). The case for case. In E. Bach & R. T. Harms (Eds.), *Universals in linguistic theory* (pp. 1–89). New York, NY: Holt, Rinehart, and Winston.

Fillmore, C. (1977). Topics in lexical semantics. In R. W. Cole (Ed.), *Current issues in linguistic theory* (pp. 76–138). Indianapolis, IN: Indiana University Press.

Fitch, W. T., Von Graevenitz, A., & Nicolas, E. (2009). Bio-aesthetic, dinamics and aesthetic trajectory: A cognitive and cultural perspective. In M. Snov & O. Varatarian (Eds.), *Neuroaesthetic* (pp. 59–102). Amityville, NY: Baywood Publishing Company.

Fletcher, C. R., & Bloom, C. P. (1988). Causal reasoning in the comprehension of simple narrative texts. *Journal of Memory and Language*, *27*(3), 235–244. doi:10.1016/0749-596X(88)90052-6

Fludernik, M. (2009). *An introduction to narratology*. London: Routledge.

Forgas, J. P., Bower, G. H., & Krantz, S. E. (1984). The influence of mood on perceptions of social interactions. *Journal of Experimental Social Psychology*, *20*(6), 497–513. doi:10.1016/0022-1031(84)90040-4

Forster, E. M. (1927). *Aspects of the novel*. London, UK: Edward Arnold.

Foucault, M. (1980). Power/knowledge. (C. Gordon., L. Marchall., J. Mepham, & K. Soper, Trans.). New York, NY: Pantheon Books. (Original work published 1972, 1975, 1976, 1977).

Freedman, J., & Comb, G. (1996). *Narrative therapy: The social construction of preferred realities*. Haddon Craftsmen.

Freud, S. (1900). *Die traumdeutung*. Leipzig, Wien: Franz Deuticke.

Fujii, Y. (1995). Nihongo-no-gojun-no gyakuten-nitsuite. [On the reversed word orders in Japanese] In K. Takami (Ed.), *Nichieigo-no uhou teni koubun* [Right dislocations in Japanese and English] (pp. 167–198). Tokyo, Japan: Hituzi Publishing.

Fujita, T., & Ota, J. (2015). *Jinkoubutsu kougaku nyuumon* [Introduction to artifact engineering]. Tokyo, Japan: University of Tokyo Press.

Fukuda, K., Mori, N., & Matsumoto, K. (2015). Analysis of automatic novel generation without existing novels information. In *Proceedings of the 29th Annual Conference of the Japanese Society for Artificial Intelligence (JSAI'15)*. Hakodate, Japan: The Japanese Society for Artificial Intelligence.

Gamma, E., Helm, R., Johnson, R., & Vlissides, J. (1995). *Design patterns: elements of reusable object-oriented software*. Addison-Wesley.

Ganster, T., Eimler, S. C., & Krämer, N. C. (2012). Same same but different? The differential influence of smilies and emoticons on person perception. *Cyberpsychology, Behavior, and Social Networking*, *15*(4), 226–230. doi:10.1089/cyber.2011.0179 PMID:22394421

Garrison, A., Remley, D., Thomas, P., & Wierszewski, E. (2011). Conventional faces: Emoticons in instant messaging discourse. *Computers and Composition*, *28*(2), 112–125. doi:10.1016/j.compcom.2011.04.001

Gavins, J., & Steen, G. (Eds.). (2003). *Cognitive poetics in practice*. Routledge. doi:10.4324/9780203417737

Genette, G. (1972). Discours du récit. essai de méthode, Figures III. Paris, France: Seuil.

Genette, G. (1972). Narrative discourse: An essay in method (J. E. Lewin, Trans.). Cornell University Press.

Genette, G. (1972). *Discours du récit, essai de méthode, Figures III*. Paris, France: Seuil.

Genette, G. (1972). *Discours du récit, essai de methode, Figures III*. Paris: Seuil.

Genette, G. (1980). *Narrative discourse: An essay in method* (J. E. Lewin, Trans.). Ithaca, NY: Cornell University Press. (Original work published 1972)

Genette, G. (1982). *Palimpsestes: la littérature au second degré*. Paris: Seuil.

Genette, G. (1985). *Narrative discourse* (H. Hanawa & R. Izumi, Trans.). Tokyo, Japan: Suiseisha. (Original work published 1972)

Gergen, K. J. (1994a). *Toward transformation in social knowledge*. London, UK: Sage Publications.

Gergen, K. J. (1994b). *Realities and relationships*. Cambridge, MA: Harvard University Press.

Gergen, K. J. (1999). *An invitation to social construction*. London, UK: Sage Publications.

Gervás, P. (2013a). Stories from games: Content and focalization selection in narrative composition. In *Proceedings of I Spanish Symposium on Entertainment Computing*. Madrid, Spain: Academic Press.

Gervás, P. (2013b). Propp's morphology of the folk tale as a grammar for generation. In *Proceedings of 2013 Workshop on Computational Models of Narrative* (pp. 106-122). Hamburg, Germany: Academic Press.

Gervás, P., Lönneker-Rodman, B., Meister, J. C., & Peinado, F. (2006). Narrative models: Narratology meets Artificial Intelligence. In *Proceedings of International Conference on Language Resources and Evaluation* (pp. 44-51). Academic Press.

Gervás, P., Lönneker-Rodman, B., Meister, J. C., & Peinado, F. (2006). Narrative models: Narratology meets artificial intelligence. In *Proceedings of Satellite Workshop: Toward Computational Models of Literary Analysis, 5th International Conference on Language Resources and Evaluation* (pp. 44-51). Genoa, Italy: Academic Press.

Gervás, P. (2009). Computational approaches to storytelling and creativity. *AI Magazine*, *30*(3), 49–62.

Gervás, P. (2015). *Computational drafting of plot structures for Russian folk tales*. Cognitive Computation;

Gervás, P., Diaz-Agudo, B., Peinado, F., & Hervás, R. (2005). Story plot generation based on CBR. *Knowledge-Based Systems Journal*, *18*(4-5), 235–242. doi:10.1016/j.knosys.2004.10.011

Gohara, H., Sugimoto, S., & Morishima, S. (2010). Data driven in-betweening for hand drawn rotating face. In *Proceedings of the ACM SIGGRAPH 2010 Posters Article* No. 7. Los Angeles, CA: ACM. doi:10.1145/1836845.1836853

Goldberg, A. E. (1995). *Constructions: a construction grammar approach to argument structure*. Chicago, IL: University of Chicago.

Goodwin, C. (1986). Audience diversity, participation and interpretation. *Text*, *6*(3), 283–316. doi:10.1515/text.1.1986.6.3.283

Grasbon, D., & Braun, N. (2001). A morphological approach to interactive storytelling. In *Proceedings of CAST 2001, Living in Mixed Realities: Conference on Artistic, Cultural and Scientific Aspects of Experimental Media Spaces* (pp. 337-340). Sankt Augustin, Germany: Academic Press.

Greenhalgh, T., & Hurwitz, B. (Eds.). (1998). *Narrative based medicine*. London, UK: BMJ Books.

Green, M. C., Brock, T. C., & Kaufman, G. E. (2004). Understanding media enjoyment: The role of transportation into narrative worlds. *Communication Theory*, *14*(4), 311–327. doi:10.1111/j.1468-2885.2004.tb00317.x

Green, M. C., Kass, S., Carrey, J., Herzig, B., Feeney, R., & Sabini, J. (2008). Transportation across media: Repeated exposure to print and film. *Media Psychology*, *11*(4), 512–539. doi:10.1080/15213260802492000

Gregoromichelaki, E. (2006). *Conditionals in dynamic syntax*. (Unpublished doctoral dissertation). King's College London, London, UK.

Gregoromichelaki, E. (2013). A dynamic perspective on left-right asymmetries. In G. Webelhuth et al. (Eds.), *Rightward movement in a comparative perspective* (pp. 321–368). Amsterdam, Netherlands: John Benjamins. doi:10.1075/la.200.12gre

Greimas, A. J. (1966). Sémantique structurrale: recherché de method. Paris: Larousse.

Greimas, A. J. (1966). *Sémantique structurale*. Paris, France: Larousse.

Greimas, A. J. (1970). *Du sens: Essais sémiotiques* (Vol. 1). Paris, France: Seuil.

Grice, H. P. (1957). Meaning. *The Philosophical Review*, *66*(3), 377–388. doi:10.2307/2182440

Grice, P. (1975). In P. Cole & J. Morgan (Eds.), *Logic and conversation* (Vol. 3, pp. 41–58). Syntax and semanticsNew York, NY: Academic Press.

Griffith, E. (2014, July 21). A return to hieroglyphics. *Fortune*.

Grimshaw, J. (1992). *Argument structure*. Cambridge, MA: MIT Press.

Grotowski, J. (1968). *Towards a poor theatre*. New York, NY: Simon and Schuster.

Gruber, J. S. (1965). *Studies in lexical relations*. (Doctoral dissertation). Available from http://hdl.handle.net/1721.1/13010

Guiraud, P. (1954). *La stylistique*. Paris, France: Presses universitaires de France.

Guo, J., & Den, Y. (2012). Inversion expressions in Japanese conversation. *Koupasu nihongogaku waakushoppu yokoushuu* [*Proceedings of the workshop on corpus Japanese linguistics*] (pp. 283-288). Tokyo, Japan: National Institute for Japanese Language and Linguistics.

Guyatt, G. H. (1991). Evidence-based medicine. *American College of Physicians Journal Club, 114,* A16.

Hall, A. (1945). The origin and purposes of blinking. *The British Journal of Ophthalmology, 29*(9), 445–467. doi:10.1136/bjo.29.9.445 PMID:18170143

Hallet, W. (2009). The multimodal novel: The integration of modes and media in novelistic narration. In R. Sommer & S. Heinen (Eds.), Narratology in the age of cross-disciplinary narrative research [e-book]. (pp. 129–153). Retrieved from http://0-eds.b.ebscohost.com.opac.bilgi.edu.tr/eds/ebookviewer/ebook/bmxlYmtfXzMwMjg3N19fQU41?sid=6d15df8c-9514-48a8-afbd-b5665e8c6089@sessionmgr112&vid=24&format=EB&rid=15

Halliday, M. A. K. (1975). Language as social semiotic: towards a general sociolinguistic theory. In A. Makkai & V. B. Makkai (Eds.), *The First LACUS Forum,* (pp. 17-46). London: Hornbeam Press.

Halliday, M. A. K. (1996). 'Introduction', language as a social semiotic: The social interpretation of language and meaning. In P. Cobley (Ed.), *The communication reader.* London, UK: Routledge.

Hamano, S. (2008). *A-kitekucha no seitaikei* [Ecosystem of architecture]. Tokyo, Japan: NTT Publishing.

Hanks, W. F. (1995). Language and communicative practices. In M. Bloch, P. Bourdieu, & J. L. Comaroff (Eds.), *Series critical essays in anthropology.* Boulder, CO: Westview Press.

Hara, J., & Umino, M. (1984). *Shakaichosaenshu* [Social investigation practice]. Tokyo, Japan: University of Tokyo Press.

Hartley, J., & McWilliam, K. (Eds.). (2009). *Story circle.* Chichester, UK: Wiley-Blackwell. doi:10.1002/9781444310580

Hartsook, K., Zook, A., Das, S., & Riedl, M. O. (2011). Toward supporting stories with procedurally generated game worlds. In *Proceedings of 2011 IEEE Conference on Computational Intelligence and Games* (pp. 297-304). Seoul, South Korea. doi:10.1109/CIG.2011.6032020

Hassan, U. A., Yang, E., Vallines, I., David, H. J., & Rubin, N. (2008). A hierarchy of temporal receptive windows in human cortex. *The Journal of Neuroscience, 28*(10), 2539–2550. doi:10.1523/JNEUROSCI.5487-07.2008 PMID:18322098

Hasumi, S. (1985). *Monogatari hihan josetsu* [An introduction to narrative criticism]. Tokyo: Chuokoronsha.

Hatano, K. (1935). *Bunsho sinrigaku* [Psychology of writing]. Tokyo, Japan: Sanseido.

Hayami, Y. (2013). *Akuma no DNA - Sono Sion* [Devil's DNA - Sion Sono]. Tokyo, Japan: Shodensha Publishing.

Hecht, B., Starosielski, N., & Dora-Abrams, D. (2007). Generating educational tourism narratives from Wikipedia. In *Intelligent Narrative Technologies: Papers from the 2007 AAAI Fall Symposium, Technical Report* (FS-07-05, pp. 37-44), Arlington, Virginia.

Herman, D. (2000). Narratology as a cognitive science. *Image and Narrative, 1*(1).

Herman, D. (2003). *Narrative theory and the cognitive sciences.* CSLI.

Higson, A. (2014). Nostalgia is not what it used to be: Heritage films, nostalgia websites and contemporary consumers. *Consumption Markets & Culture, 17*(2), 120–142. doi:10.1080/10253866.2013.776305

Higuchi, K. (2014). *Quantitative text analysis for social researchers: A contribution to content anayisis.* Kyoto, Japan: Nakanishiya Press.

Hill, A. (2007). *Key themes in interpersonal communication: Culture, identities and performance.* Retrieved from http://0-eds.b.ebscohost.com.opac.bilgi.edu.tr/eds/ebookviewer/ebook/bmxlYmtfXzIzNDMwMl9fQU41?sid=1b1de240-d673-4e1f-b2a2-21c8b83cd32e@sessionmgr115&vid=2&format=EB&rid=1

Hirose, S. (2012). The present and future of the mixed methods research. *Yamaguchi Medicine, 61*(1-2), 11-16.

Hobbs, J. R. (1990). *Literature and cognition*. CSLI.

Hoffberger, C. (2013, February 19). *Library of Congress accepts first emoji novel*. Retrieved from http://www.dailydot.com/culture/library-congress-emoji-moby-dick/

Holbrook, M. B., & Schindler, R. M. (1991). Echoes of the dear departed past: Some work in progress on nostalgia. In R. H. Holman & M. R. Solomon (Eds.), *Advances in Consumer Research, 18* (pp. 330–333). Provo, UT: Association for Consumer Research.

Hori, K. (2005). Do knowledge assets really exist in the world and can we access such knowledge?: Knowledge evolves through a cycle of knowledge liquidization and crystallization. *Lecture Notes in Computer Science, 3359*, 1–13. doi:10.1007/978-3-540-32279-5_1

Hori, K. (2007). *Sozo katsudo shien no riron to oyo* [Theories and applications of creativity support]. Tokyo: Ohmsha.

Hosaka, Y., & Ogata, T. (2002). Story generation based on narratology and representation with CG animation. In *Proceedings of 17th Congress of the International Association of Empirical Aesthetics* (pp. 561-564). Takarazuka, Japan: Academic Press.

Hoshino, J. (2004). Storytelling and AI. *Transactions of the Japanese Society for Artificial Intelligence, 19*(1), 29–34.

Hoshi, S. (1975). *Hoshi Shinichi no sakuhin syuu XV* [Anthology of Shinichi Hoshi XV]. Tokyo, Japan: Shinchosha.

Hovy, E. H. (1993). Automated discourse generation using discourse structure relations. *Artificial Intelligence, 63*(1-2), 341–386. doi:10.1016/0004-3702(93)90021-3

Huang, A. H., Yen, D. C., & Zhang, X. (2008). Exploring the potential effects of emoticons. *Information & Management, 45*(7), 466–473. doi:10.1016/j.im.2008.07.001

Huang, C. R., Calzolari, N., Gangemi, A., Lenci, A., Oltramari, A., & Prevot, L. (2010). *Ontology and the lexicon*. Cambridge, UK: Cambridge University Press. doi:10.1017/CBO9780511676536

Huhmann, B. A., & Albinsson, P. A. (2012). Does rhetoric impact advertising effectiveness with liking controlled? *European Journal of Marketing, 46*(11/12), 1476–1500. doi:10.1108/03090561211259943

Ikegaya, Y., Aaron, G., Cossart, R., Aronov, D., Lampl, I., Ferster, D., & Yuste, R. (2004). Synfire chains and cortical songs: Temporal modules of cortical activity. *Science, 304*(5670), 559–564. doi:10.1126/science.1093173 PMID:15105494

Imabuchi, S., & Ogata, T. (2012). A story generation system based on Propp theory: As a mechanism in an integrated narrative generation system. In H. Isahara & K. Kanazaki (Eds.), *Advances in Natural Language Processing: Proceedings of the 8th International Conference on Natural Language Processing* (Vol. 7614, pp. 312-321). Berlin, Germany: Springer. doi:10.1007/978-3-642-33983-7_31

Imabuchi, S., & Ogata, T. (2012). A story generation system based on Propp theory: As a mechanism in an integrated narrative generation system. In H. Isahara & K. Kanzaki (Eds.), *Advances in Natural Language Processing: Proceedings of the 8th International Conference on Natural Language Processing (LNAI)* (*vol. 7614*, pp. 312-321). Berlin, Germany: Springer. doi:doi:10.1007/978-3-642-33983-7_31 doi:10.1007/978-3-642-33983-7_31

Imabuchi, S., Akimoto, T., Ono, J., & Ogata, T. (2012). KOSERUBE: An application system with a Propp-based story grammar and other narrative generation techniques. In *Proceedings of the 6th International Conference on Soft Computing and Intelligent Systems & the 13th International Symposium on Advanced Intelligent Systems* (pp. 248-253). Kyoto, Japan. doi:10.1109/SCIS-ISIS.2012.6505320

Imabuchi, S., & Ogata, T. (2012). *A story generation system based on Propp theory: As a mechanism in an integrated narrative generation system. Lecture Notes in Artificial Intelligence* (Vol. 7614, pp. 312–321). Berlin, Germany: Springer.

Imabuchi, S., & Ogata, T. (2013). Lecture Notes in Computer Science: Vol. 8210. *Methods for generalizing the Propp-based story generation mechanism* (pp. 333–344). Berlin, Germany: Springer. doi:10.1007/978-3-319-02750-0_36

Imabuchi, S., & Ogata, T. (2014). Integrating the event generation mechanism in the Propp-based story generation mechanism into the integrated narrative generation system. *Journal of Robotics. Networking and Artificial Life*, *1*(2), 164–168. doi:10.2991/jrnal.2014.1.2.14

Imao, T. (1970). *Henshin no shisou* [The theory of metamorphosis]. Tokyo, Japan: Hosei University Press.

Imao, T. (1979). *Kabuki wo miru hito no tameni* [For people viewing kabuki]. Tokyo, Japan: Tamagawa University Press.

Imao, T. (2009). *Kawatake Mokuami* [Kawatake Mokuami]. Kyoto, Japan: Minerva Shobo.

Imao, T. (2010). *Kabuki–<Tsuusetsu> no kenshou* [Kabuki: The verification of 'common views']. Tokyo, Japan: Hosei University Press.

Iran-Nejad, A. (1987). Cognitive and affective causes of interest and liking. *Journal of Educational Psychology*, *79*(2), 120–130. doi:10.1037/0022-0663.79.2.120

Ishii, K., & Ogata, T. (1998). A study on the methodology of hypertext novels based on a prototyping. In *Proceedings of the 12th Annual Conference of the Japanese Society for Artificial Intelligence* (pp.701-702). Tokyo, Japan: Academic Press.

Ishizaki, S. (1988). Generating Japanese text from conceptual representation. In D. D. McDonald & L. Bole (Eds.), *Natural language generation system* (pp. 256–279). Springer-Verlag. doi:10.1007/978-1-4612-3846-1_7

Ito, M. (1999). Sakushi Android Yuming [Poem making Android Yuming]. *JSAI SIG Report, SIG-LSE-9903-S2*.

Jackendoff, R. S. (1972). *Semantic interpretation in generative grammar*. Cambridge, MA: MIT Press.

Jackendoff, R. S. (1983). *Semantics and cognition*. Cambridge, MA: MIT Press.

Jackendoff, R. S. (1990). *Semantic structures*. Cambridge, MA: MIT Press.

Jacobs, A. M. (2013). *Neurocognitive models of literary reading*. Retrieved October 13, 2001, from https://www.researchgate.net/publication/235952745_Neurocognitive_Model_of_Litera

Japan Electronic Dictionary Research Institute. (1995). *EDR: electric dictionary the second edition* [Data file]. Retrieved from https://www2.nict.go.jp/out-promotion/techtransfer/EDR/ index.html

Jauss, H. R. (1970). Literaturgeschichte als provokation. Frankfurt am Main: Suhrkamp Verlag.

Jauss, H. R. (1982). *Toward an aesthetic of reception* (T. Bahti, Trans.). Minneapolis, MN: University of Minnesota Press. (Original work published 1970)

Jenkins, H. (n.d.). *Game design as narrative architecture*. Retrieved from http://interactive.usc.edu/blog-old/wp-content/uploads/2011/01/Jenkins_Narrative_Architecture.pdf

Jhale, A., & Young, M. R. (2010). Cinematic visual discourse: Representation, generation, and evaluation. *IEEE Transactions on Computational Intelligence and A.I. in Games, 2*(2), 69-81.

Jhale, A., & Young, M. R. (2010). Cinematic visual discourse: Representation, generation, and evaluation. *IEEE Transactions on Computational Intelligence and AI in Games*, *2*(2), 69–81. doi:10.1109/TCIAIG.2010.2046486

Jin, H., Liu, H. L., Mo, L., Fang, S. Y., Zhang, J. X., & Lin, C. D. (2009). Involvement of the left inferior frontal gyrus in predictive inference making. *International Journal of Psychophysiology*, *71*(3), 142–148. doi:10.1016/j.ijpsycho.2008.08.009 PMID:18822322

Jin, M. (2002). Authorship attribution based on n-gram models in postpositional particle of Japanese. *Mathematical Linguistics*, *23*(5), 225–240.

Jin, M., & Murakami, M. (1993). Authors' characteristic writing style as seen through their use of commas. *Behaviormetrika*, *20*(1), 63–76. doi:10.2333/bhmk.20.63

Kageyama, T. (1996). *Doushi imiron* [Verb semantics]. Tokyo, Japan: Kurosio Publishers.

Kamide, Y. (2006). Incrementality in Japanese sentence processing. In M. Nakayama et al. (Eds.), *The handbook of East Asian psycholinguistics* (Vol. 2, pp. 248–256). Cambridge, UK: Cambridge University Press. doi:10.1017/CBO9780511758652.036

Kanai, A. (2001a). The story as a constraint on film. In *Proceedings of the Third International Conference on Cognitive Science* (pp. 503-506). Beijing, China: Academic Press.

Kanai, A. (2002). Film rhetoric and cognition. In *Proceedings of 17th Congress of the International Association of Empirical Aesthetics* (pp. 209-212). Takarazuka, Japan: Academic Press.

Kanai, A. (2003). Non-story type film rhetoric and cognitive effects. In *Proceedings of the Fourth International Conference on Cognitive Science* (pp. 259-264). Sydney, Australia: Academic Press.

Kanai, A. (2005). Defamiliarization, film cognition and composition. In *Proceedings of the 19th Conference of the Japanese Society for Artificial Intelligence* (3D3-11, pp.1-2). Kitakyushu, Japan: Academic Press.

Kanai, A. (2006). Reality of unfamiliar situations on moving image. In *Proceedings of 19th Congress of the International Association of Empirical Aesthetics* (pp. 800-803). Avignon, France: Academic Press.

Kanai, A., & Ogata, T. (2004). Non-story processing on the film rhetoric composition system. In *Proceedings of 18th Congress of the International Association of Empirical Aesthetics* (pp. 433-436). Lisbon, Portugal: Academic Press.

Kanai, A., & Ogata, T. (2004a). Aspect of non-story processing and film rhetoric composition in the narrative generation mechanism. In *Proceedings of the Ninth International Symposium on Artificial Life and Robotics* (pp. 162-165). Beppu, Japan: Academic Press.

Kanai, A., & Ogata, T. (2004b). Non-story processing on the film rhetoric composition system. In *Proceedings of 18th Congress of the International Association of Empirical Aesthetics* (pp. 433-436). Lisbon, Portugal: Academic Press.

Kanai, A. (2001). Cognitive process model toward the rhetoric of the film. *Cognitive Studies*, *8*(2), 139–150.

Kanai, A., & Kato, Y. (2001). Effect of advertising rhetoric on viewer's cognitive process. *Journal of Advertising Science*, *42*, 87–100.

Kanai, A., & Kodama, K. (2010). Film edit design: Story and irrational cutting. *Cognitive Studies*, *17*(3), 444–458.

Kanai, A., Ogata, T., & Shinohara, K. (2002). Film rhetoric generation system for intensive cognitive system. In *Proceedings of IEEE International Conference on Systems, Man and Cybernetics (CD-ROM)*. Yasmine Hammamet, Tunisia: IEEE.

Kanasugi, T., Matsuzawa, K., & Kasahara, K. (1996). ABOUT suiron no "kotoba asobi" heno tekiyou [Application of ABOUT Reasoning to solving Wordplays]. *Technical Report of IEICE, NLC96-31.*

Karatani, K. (1993). *Origins of modern Japanese literature*. Durham, UK: Duke University Press. (Original work published 1980)

Kasahara, K., Sato, H., Bond, F., Tanaka, T., Fujita, S., Kanasugi, T., & Amano, S. (2004). Construction of a Japanese semantic lexicon: Lexeed. In Special Interest Group Technical Reports of Information Processing Society Japan, 2004(1(2003-NL-159)) (pp. 75-82).

Kasahara, K., Matsuzawa, K., Ishikawa, T., & Kawaoka, T. (1996). Viewpoint-based measurement of semantic similarity between words. In *Proceedings of the 5th International Workshop on Artificial Intelligence and Statistics (LNS112)* (pp. 433-442). doi:10.1007/978-1-4612-2404-4_41

Kato, Y., Kato, S., & Akahori, K. (2007). Effects of emotional cues transmitted in e-mail communication on the emotions experienced by senders and receivers. *Computers in Human Behavior*, *23*(4), 1894–1905. doi:10.1016/j.chb.2005.11.005

Kawamura, Y., & Ogata, T. (1997). The generation process of entertainment character image. In *Proceedings of the International Conference on Cognitive Science* (pp. 293-294). Seoul, South Korea: Academic Press.

Kawamura, Y., & Ogata, T. (1997). The generation process of entertainment character image. In *Proceedings of the International Conference on Cognitive Science 1997* (pp. 293-294). Academic Press.

Kawamura, Y., & Ogata, T. (2000). A conceptual framework on geino organization model for artificial geino performers with lives. In *Proceedings of the Fifth International Symposium on Artificial Life and Robotics* (pp. 793-796). Academic Press.

Kawamura, Y., & Ogata, T. (2000). A conceptual framework on *geino* organization model for artificial *geino* performers with lives. In *Proceedings of the Fifth International Symposium on Artificial Life and Robotics* (pp. 793-796). Oita, Japan: Academic Press.

Kawamura, Y. (2003). An analysis of the rhetoric of commercial film: Toward the building of a commercial film production support system based on image rhetoric. In *Proceedings of the 2003 IEEE International Conference on Systems, Man and Cybernetics* (pp.993-1000). Washington, DC. doi:10.1109/ICSMC.2003.1243944

Kawamura, Y. (2004). An analysis of the rhetoric of commercial film: Toward the building of a commercial film production support information system. *Journal of Advertising Science*, *45*, 122–139.

Kawamura, Y. (2009). An analysis on the story and editing techniques of commercial film: Toward the building of a commercial film production support information system. *Journal of Advertising Science*, *50*, 16–32.

Kawamura, Y., & Ogata, T. (2002). A Trial on Narrative Interpretation of Geino Information System. In *Proceedings of IEEE, International Conference on Systems, Man and Cybernetics (CD-ROM)*. Yasmine Hammamet, Tunisia. doi:10.1109/ICSMC.2002.1175727

Kawashima, D., Koyama, T., Kawano, K., & Ito, H. (2009). Physicians' explanatory model for suicide prevention: Text-mining analysis of physicians' statements to suicidal patients. *The Japanese Journal of Personality*, *17*(2), 121–132. doi:10.2132/personality.17.121

Kawatake, T. (1992). *Kabuki: its beauty and tradition* (C. Holmes, Trans.). Tokyo, Japan: Japan Arts Council.

Kawatake, T. (2003). *Kabuki: Baroque fusion of the arts (F. & J., Connel Hoff, Trans.)*. Tokyo, Japan: The International House of Japan.

Kawatake, T. (2003). *Kabuki: Baroque fusion of the arts*. Tokyo, Japan: The International House of Japan.

Kayamori, O., & Ogata, T. (2003). Analysis and scenario generation of TVCFs based on the relations between story and brand. In *Proceedings of the 17th Annual Conference of the Japanese Society for Artificial Intelligence* (2G2-06). Niigata, Japan: Academic Press.

Kempson, R., Gregoromichelaki, E., & Howes, C. (2011). *The dynamics of lexical interfaces*. Stanford, CA: Center for the Study of Language and Information.

Kempson, R., & Kiaer, J. (2010). Multiple long-distance scrambling. *Journal of Linguistics*, *46*(1), 127–192. doi:10.1017/S0022226709990211

Kempson, R., & Kurosawa, A. (2009). At the syntax-pragmatics interface. In H. Hoshi (Ed.), *The dynamics and mechanism of language* (pp. 47–84). Tokyo, Japan: Kuroshio Publishers.

Kempson, R., Meyer-Viol, W., & Gabbay, D. (2001). *Dynamic syntax*. Oxford, UK: Wiley-Blackwell.

Kiaer, J. (2014). *Pragmatic syntax*. London, UK: Bloomsbury Publishing.

Kintsch, W. (1980). Learning from text, levels of comprehension, or - Why anyone would read a story anyway. *Poetics*, *9*(1-3), 87–98. doi:10.1016/0304-422X(80)90013-3

Kintsch, W. (1992). How readers construct situation models for stories: The role of syntactic cues and causal inferences. In A. F. Healy, S. M. Kosslyn, & R. M. Shiffrin (Eds.), *Essays in honor of William K. Estes* (pp. 261–278). Hillsdale, NJ: Lawrence Erlbaum Associates, Inc.

Kipper, S. K. (2005). *VerbNet: a broad-coverage, comprehensive verb lexicon* (Doctoral dissertation). Available from ProQuest Dissertations and Theses database. (Paper AAI3179808)

Kitagawa, N., Kato, C., & Koyama, T. (2011). Clinical issues and additional strategies of the return-to-work program for depression. *Japanese Journal of Psychiatric Treatment*, *26*(2), 149–156.

Klein, S., Aeschlimann, J. F., Appelbaum, M. A., Balsiger, D. F., Curtis, E. J., Foster, M., . . . Salsieder, D. F. (1974). *Modeling Propp and Levi-Strauss in a meta-symbolic simulation system*. Computer Sciences Technical Report 226. Computer Sciences Department, the University of Wisconsin.

Klein, S., Aeschlimann, J. F., Appelbaum, M. A., Balsiger, D. F., Curtis, E. J., Foster, M., & Salsieder, D. F. et al. (1974). *Modeling Propp and Levi-Strauss in a meta-symbolic simulation system. Computer Sciences Technical Report, 226*. Madison, WI: University of Wisconsin.

Kobako, T. (2003). *Sketchbook 1*. Tokyo, Japan: Mag Garden.

Kobayashi, F., & Ogata, T. (2004a). Narrative and music as variation: Transformation of musical structure based on narrative discourse theory. In *Proceedings of the Ninth International Symposium on Artificial Life and Robotics* (*Vol.1*, pp. 170-173). Beppu, Japan: Academic Press.

Kobayashi, F., & Ogata, T. (2004b). A musical variation system by the structural correspondence between music and narrative. In *Proceedings of 18th Congress of the International Association of Empirical Aesthetics* (pp. 555-559). Takarazuka, Japan: Academic Press.

Kobayashi, T., & Shimamura, K. (1997). *Shinban atarashii koukoku* [New advertising: New edition]. Tokyo, Japan: Dentsu.

Koelsch, S. (2012). *Brain and music*. West Sussex, UK: John Wiley & Sons.

Koelsch, S., Skouras, S., Fritz, T., Herrera, P., Bonhage, C., Küssner, M. B., & Jacobs, A. M. (2013). The roles of superficial amygdala and auditory cortex in music-evoked fear and joy. *NeuroImage*, *81*, 49–60. doi:10.1016/j.neuroimage.2013.05.008 PMID:23684870

Komori, Y., & Yamada, M. (2001). Seishinbunretsubyou no kazokushinrikyouiku niokeru naratibu apurochi[Narrative approach in family psychology education of schizophrenia]. *Family Therapy Research, 18*(2), 143–150.

Kouyama, S., & Sumi, K. (2014). A discussion of humorous story generation system by using stories of Shinichi Hoshi. In *Proceedings of the 28th Annual Conference of the Japanese Society for Artificial Intelligence (JSAI'14)*. Ehime, Japan: The Japanese Society for Artificial Intelligence.

Koyama, Y. (2009). Futatsu no kontentsu sangyou sisutemu [Two content industrial systems]. In H. Deguchi, H. Tanaka & Y. Koyama (Eds.), Kontentsu sangyou ron: Konkou to denpa no Nippon gata moderu [Studies of content industries: Mixture and diffusion of Japanese content] (pp. 61-90). Tokyo, Japan: University of Tokyo Press.

Kress, G. (1997). *Before writing: Rethinking the paths into literacy*. New York, US: Routledge.

Kristeva, J. (1980). *Desire in language: A semiotic approach to literary work and art*. Columbia University Press.

Kristeva, J. (1980). *Desire in language: A semiotic approach to literature and art*. NY: Columbia University Press. (Original work published 1969)

Kumagai, S., Funakoshi, S., Akimoto, T., & Ogata, T. (2012). Development of a language dictionary and a simple narrative sentence generation mechanism. In *Proceedings of the 26th Annual Conference of the Japanese Society for Artificial Intelligence* (1N1-OS-1a-3). Yamaguchi, Japan: Academic Press.

Kuno, S. (1978). *Danwa-no-bunpou* [Grammar of discourse]. Tokyo, Japan: Taishukan.

Kurata, Y. (2013). *Bunraku no rekishi* [A history of bunraku]. Tokyo, Japan: Iwanami Shoten.

Kurisawa, Y., & Ogata, T. (2013). A consideration of a norm-deviation mechanism in the integrated narrative generation system. *Proceedings of Language Sense Engineering Research Group in Japanese Artificial Intelligence Society, 44*, 25–35.

Kusunoki, K. (2010). *Story toshiteno kyoso senryaku* [Competitive strategy as story]. Tokyo, Japan: Toyo Keizai Shinposha.

Kuwahara, W., Hasimoto, M., & Murata, K. (1993). Keisankiyou nihongo jishono kaihatsu [On the lexicon of Japanese basic verbs, adjectives, and nouns]. In Special Interest Group Technical Reports of Information Processing Society Japan, 1993(42(1993-CH-018)) (pp. 27-34).

Kuwano, T., & Oishi, M. (Eds.). (1988). *Forumarizumu: Shitekigengoron* [Formalism: Poetic language theory]. Tokyo, Japan: Kokushokankoukai.

Kwon, K. A., Shipley, R. J., Edirisinghe, M., Ezra, D. G., Rose, G., Best, S. M., & Cameron, R. E. (2013). High-speed camera characterization of voluntary eye blinking kinematics. *Journal of the Royal Society, Interface, 10*(85), 20130227. PMID:23760297

Kyou, S. (2012). Hogosha to shisetsushokuin no "chitekishougaisha no sei" nitaisuru ishiki: Tekisutomainingu niyoru bunseki[Consciousness for "the sex of person with intellectual disability" of a protector and the staff of facilities: Analysis by the text mining]. *Shimane University Social Welfare Journal, 4*, 1–16.

Lakoff, G. P. (1972). Structural complexity in fairy tales. *The Study of Man, 1*, 124.

Lambert, J. (2013). *Digital storytelling: Capturing lives, creating community* (4th ed.). New York, NY: Routledge.

Lang, R. R. (1999). A declarative model for simple narratives. In *Narrative Intelligence: Papers from the 1999 AAAI Fall Symposium* (Technical Report FS-99-01, pp. 134-141), North Falmouth, MA.

Lang, R. R. (1999). A declarative model for simple narratives. In *Narrative intelligence: Papers from the 1999 AAAI fall symposium, Technical Report (FS-99-01)* (pp. 134-141). North Falmouth, MA: Academic Press.

Lang, R. R. (1999). A declarative model for simple narratives. In *Narrative intelligence: Papers from the 1999 AAAI fall symposium, Technical Report* (FS-99-01, pp. 134-141), North Falmouth, Massachusetts.

Langacker, R. W. (1986). An introduction to cognitive grammar. *Cognitive Science*, *10*(1), 1–40. doi:10.1207/s15516709cog1001_1

Laskey, H. A., Day, E., & Crask, M. R. (1989). Typology of main message strategies for television commercial. *Journal of Advertising*, *18*(1), 36–41. doi:10.1080/00913367.1989.10673141

Laskey, H. A., Fox, R. J., & Crask, M. R. (1994). Investigation the impact of executional style on television commercial effectiveness. *Journal of Advertising Research*, *34*(5), 9–16.

Laskey, H. A., Fox, R. J., & Crask, M. R. (1995). The relationship between advertising message strategy and television commercial effectiveness. *Journal of Advertising Research*, *35*(2), 31–39.

Laurel, B. (2013). *Computers as theatre* (2nd ed.). Boston: Addison-Wesley Professional.

Lebowitz, M. (1985). Story-telling as planning and learning. *Poetics*, *14*(6), 483–502. doi:10.1016/0304-422X(85)90015-4

Lehne, M., & Koelsch, S. M. (2014). Tension resolution patterns as a key element of aesthetic experience: Psychological principles and underlying brain mechanism. In J. P. Huston (Ed.), *Art, aesthetic and the brain* (pp. 122–138). New York: Oxford University Press.

Lerdahl, F., & Jackendoff, R. (1983). *A generative theory of tonal music*. Cambridge, MA: MIT Press.

Levin, B. (1993). *English verb classes and alternations*. Chicago, IL: University of Chicago Press.

Lévi-Strauss, C. (1996). *Saudades de São Paulo*. São Paulo, Brasil: Companhia das letras.

Lévi-Strauss, C. (1964). *Mythologiques 1: Le cru et le cuit*. Paris: PLON.

Li, B., & Riedl, M. O. (2010). An offline planning approach to game plotline adaptation. In *6th Conference on Artificial Intelligence for Interactive Digital Entertainment* (pp. 45-50). Stanford, CA: Academic Press.

Li, B., & Riedl, M. O. (2015). Scheherazade: Crowd-powered interactive narrative generation. In *Proceedings of the 29th AAAI conference on artificial intelligence* (pp. 4305-4306). Austin, TX: Academic Press.

Li, B., Lee-Urban, S., Appling, D. S., & Riedl, M. O. (2012). Automatically learning to tell stories about social situations from the crowd. In *Proceedings of the Third Workshop on Computational Models of Narrative* (pp. 142-151). Istanbul, Turkey: Academic Press.

Litwack, E. B. (2009). *Wittgenstein and value: The quest for meaning*. Retrieved from http://ehis.ebscohost.com/eds/ebookviewer/ebook/bmxlYmtfXzM0NDUyMF9fQU41?sid=3eb83088-fb29-4181-99ff-771539f7990e@sessionmgr4005&vid=1&format=EB&lpid=lp_12&rid=0

Lönneker, B. (2005). Narratological knowledge for natural language generation. In *Proceedings of the 10th European Workshop on Natural Language Generation* (pp. 91-100). Aberdeen, UK: Association for Computational Linguistics.

Lönneker-Rodman, B. (2005). Narratological knowledge for natural language generation. In *Proceedings of the 10th European Workshop on Natural Language Generation* (pp. 91-100). Aberdeen, Scotland: Academic Press.

Loper, R., Yi, S., & Palmer, M. (2007). Combining lexical resources: mapping between PropBank and VerbNet. In *Proceedings of the 7th International Workshop on Computational Semantics*. Tilburg, Netherland: Academic Press.

Lopez, N. (n.d.). *Google's new keyboard app lets you handwrite messages to your friends, emoji included.* Retrieved from http://thenextweb.com/insider/2015/04/15/googles-new-handwriting-input-keyboard-lets-you-sketch-messages-to-your-friends-emoji-included/

Lo, S. K. (2008). The non-verbal communication functions of emoticons in computer-mediated communication. *Cyberpsychology & Behavior, 11*(5), 595–597. doi:10.1089/cpb.2007.0132 PMID:18817486

Luor, T., Wu, L., Lu, H.P., & Tao, Y.H. (2010). The effect of emoticons in simplex and complex task-oriented communication: An empirical study of instant messaging. *Computers in Human Behavior, 26*, 889–895. doi:10.1016/j.chb.2010.02.003

Lyotard, J-F. (1979). *La condition post moderne*. Paris: Les edition de Minuit.

Lyotard, J. F. (1979). *La condition postmoderne*. Paris, France: Minuit.

Macal, C. M., & North, M. J. (2010). Tutorial on agent-based modeling and simulation. *Journal of Simulation, 4*(3), 151–162. doi:10.1057/jos.2010.3

Macrì, S., & Capogrossi Colognesi, S. (2011). *Che cos'è lo stress*. Roma: Carocci.

Maeda, I. (1958). *Kamigata Rakugo-no rekishi* [The history of Kamigata Rakugo]. Osaka, Japan: Sugimoto Shoten.

Magerko, B. S. (2006). *Player modeling in the interactive drama architecture.* (Ph.D. thesis). University of Michigan, Ann Arbor, MI.

Maio, G. R., & Esses, V. M. (2001). The need for affect: Individual differences in the motivation to approach or avoid emotions. *Journal of Personality, 69*(4), 583–615. doi:10.1111/1467-6494.694156 PMID:11497031

Manuel, J., Fang, L., Bellamy, J. L., & Bledsoe, S. E. (2008). Evaluating evidence. In R. M. Grinnell & Y. A. Unrau (Eds.), *Social work research and evaluation: Foundation of evidence-based practice* (8th ed., pp. 482–495). New York, NY: Oxford University Press.

Manurung, R., Ritchie, G., Pain, H., Waller, A., O'Mara, D., & Black, R. (2008). The construction of a pun generator for language skills development. *Applied Artificial Intelligence, 22*(9), 841–869. doi:10.1080/08839510802295962

Marcus, M. P., Santorini, B., & Marcinkiewicz, M. A. (1993). Building a large annotated corpus of English: The Penn treebank. *Computational Linguistics, 19*(2), 313–330.

Marten, L. (2002). *At the syntax-pragmatics interface*. Oxford, UK: Oxford University Press. doi:10.1093/acprof:oso/9780199250639.001.0001

Mateas, M., & Sengers, P. (Eds.). (2003). *Narrative intelligence*. Amsterdam: John Benjamins Publishing. doi:10.1075/aicr.46

Matsubara, H., Sato, S., Akaishi, M., Sumi, K., Mukaiyama, K., Nakashima, H., & Otsuka, Y. (2013). An attempt at automatic composition of Shin'ichi Hoshi-like short short stories. In *Proceedings of the 27th Annual Conference of the Japanese Society for Artificial Intelligence (JSAI'13)*. Toyama, Japan: The Japanese Society for Artificial Intelligence.

Matsue, T., & Yoshida, M. (2012). *Sono Sion eiga zenkenkyu 1985-2012* [Study of all "A SONO SION'S FILM"s 1985-2012]. Tokyo, Japan: Yosensha.

Matsumoto, Y., Kitauchi, K., Yamashita, T., Hirano, Y., Matsuda, H., & Asahara, M. (1999). Morphological analysis system ChaSen 2.0 users manual (2nd ed.). Nara Institute of Science and Technology, Matsumoto Labo.

Matsuoka, S. (1992). Narrative archetypes and media. In *Proceedings of Interactive AI Symposium 92 Nagoya: New Paradigm for Artificial Intelligence-AI in Media Space-* (pp. 61-66). Nagoya, Japan: Academic Press.

Matsuzawa, K., Abe, A., Kanasugi, T., & Nagamori, C. (1997). Gainen-base wo mochita network-kata "kotoba asobi" no teian [Proposal of wordplays on the network using the conceptual base]. In *Proceedings of the 3rd Annual Meeting of the ANLP*, E5-4 (pp. 577-580).

Matsuzawa, K., Kanasugi, T., & Abe, A. (1998). Computer jou no gengo kankaku jitsugen ni mukete: B-kyu machine [Computational language sense: Perpetual word-playing machine]. In *Proceedings of the JSAI Annual Meeting*, 37-11 (pp. 685-686).

McAdams, D. P., & St. Aubin, E. (Eds.). (1998). Generativity and adult development. Washington, DC: American Psychological Association.

McCawley, J. D. (1968). Lexical insertion in a transformational grammar without deep structure. In *Fourth Regional Meeting of the Chicago Linguistic Society* (pp. 71-80). Chicago: Linguistics Department, University of Chicago.

McIntyre, N., & Lapata, M. (2009). Learning to tell tales: A data-driven approach to story generation. In *Proceedings of Joint Conference of the 47th Annual Meeting of the Association for Computational Linguistics and the 4th International Joint Conference on Natural Language Processing of the Asian Federation of Natural Language Processing* (pp. 217-225). Suntec, Singapore. doi:10.3115/1687878.1687910

McQuarrie, E. F., & Mick, D. G. (1996). Figures of rhetoric in advertising language. *The Journal of Consumer Research, 22*(4), 424–438. doi:10.1086/209459

McQuarrie, E. F., & Mick, D. G. (1999). Visual rhetoric in advertising: Text-interpretive, experimental, and reader-response analysis. *The Journal of Consumer Research, 26*(1), 37–54. doi:10.1086/209549

McQuarrie, E. F., & Mick, D. G. (2003). Visual and verbal rhetorical figures under directed processing versus incidental exposure to advertising. *The Journal of Consumer Research, 29*(4), 579–587. doi:10.1086/346252

McQuarrie, E. F., & Phillips, B. J. (2005). Indirect persuasion in advertising: How consumers process metaphors presented in picture and words. *Journal of Advertising, 34*(2), 7–19. doi:10.1080/00913367.2005.10639188

Meehan, J. R. (1980). *The metanovel: Writing stories by computer*. Garland Publishing.

Meehan, J. R. (1980). *The metanovel: writing stories by computer*. New York, NY: Garland Publishing.

Meister, J. C. (2003). *Computing action: A narratological approach*. Walter de Gruyter.

Mendenhall, T. C. (1887). The characteristic curves of composition. *Science, ns-9*(214S), 237–246. doi:10.1126/science.ns-9.214S.237 PMID:17736020

Mendenhall, T. C. (1901). A mechanical solution of a literary problem. *Popular Science Monthly, 60*(2), 97–105.

Mihara, H. (2011). Volunteer activity support by students for the leisure activity of handicapped people and their families: Participating in beach volleyball and cooking with the handicapped people in the university. *Japanese Journal of Social Welfare, 51*(4), 153–162.

Min, W., Ha, E. Y., Rowe, J., Mott, B., & Lester, J. (2014). Deep learning-based goal recognition in open-ended digital games. In *Proceedings on 10th Annual Conference of Artificial Intelligence and Interactive Digital Entertainment* (pp. 27-43). Santa Cruz, CA: Academic Press.

Ministry of Economy, Trade, and Industry. (Eds.). (2007, May). "KANSEI" Initiative—Suggestion of the Fourth Value Axis. *Ministry of Economy, Trade, and Industry Press Release*. Retriever from http://www.meti.go.jp/english/information/downloadfiles/PressRelease/080620KANSEI.pdf

Ministry of Health. Labour and Welfare. (2014a). *Heisei25nen shougaishakoyoujokyo no shuukeikekka* [Aggregate results of the 2013 disability employment situation]. Retrieved from http://www.mhlw.go.jp/stf/houdou/0000029691.html

Ministry of Health. Labour and Welfare. (2014b). *Heisei25nendo shougaishakoyoujittaichosakekka* [(Actual) Conditions of employment of persons with disabilities survey result in fiscal year 2013]. Retrieved from http://www.mhlw.go.jp/stf/houdou/0000068921.html

Ministry of Health. Labour and Welfare. (2015). *Shougaisha no koyo no sokushintou nikansuru horitsu* [Act for the promotion of employment of persons with disabilities]. Retrieved from http://law.e-gov.go.jp/htmldata/S35/S35HO123.html

Minsky, M. (1975). A framework for representing knowledge. In P. H. Winston (Ed.), *The psychology of computer vision*. McGraw-Hill.

Minsky, M. (1988). *The society of mind*. Touchstone Books.

Mishima, Y. (1963). *Gogo no eiko* [The sailor who fell from grace with the sea]. Tokyo: Kodansha.

Mita, M. (1965). *Gendainihon no seishinkouzou* [Mental structure of Japan]. Tokyo, Japan: Koubundo.

Mizoguchi, R. (2005). *Ontoroji kogaku* [Ontology engineering]. Tokyo: Ohmsha.

Mlot, S. (2015). *Apple adds diverse emojis to OS X, iOS Betas*. Retrieved from http://www.pcmag.com/article2/0,2817,2477318,00.asp

Monaco, J. (1977). *How to read a film: the art technology, language, history and theory of film and media*. New York, NY: Oxford University Press.

Montfort, N. (2006). Natural language generation and narrative variation in interactive fiction. In *Proceedings of Computational Aesthetics: Artificial Intelligence Approaches to Beauty and Happiness:Papers from the 2006 AAAI Workshop* (pp. 45-52). Menlo Park, CA: AAAI Press.

Montfort, N. (2007). *Generating narrative variation in interactive fiction* (Doctoral dissertation). Available from ProQuest. (AAI3271851)

Montfort, N. (2007). *Generating narrative variation in interactive fiction.* (Doctoral dissertation). University of Pennsylvania, Philadelphia, PA.

Morgan, A. (2000). *What is narrative therapy?* Adelaire, Australia: Dulwich Center Publication.

Mori, A. (2010). *Takechi Tetsuji toiu geijutsu–Amarini kontenporarii na* [Arts of Takechi Tetsuji: Very contemporary]. Tokyo, Japan: Shinyosha.

Morita, H. (2006). Literary hyper-text conversion: Applications of comuter aided text analysis. In *Proceedings of the 19th Congress of the International Association of Empirical Aesthetics* (pp. 401-405). Avignon, France: Academic Press.

Mosteller, F., & Wallace, D. L. (1963). Inference in an authorship problem: A comparative study of discrimination methods applied to the authorship of the disputed Federalist Papers. *Journal of the American Statistical Association, 58*(302), 275–309.

Mothersbaugh, D. L., Huhmann, B. A., & Franke, G. R. (2002). Combinatory and separative effects of rhetorical figures on consumers' effort and focus in ad processing. *The Journal of Consumer Research, 28*(4), 589–602. doi:10.1086/338211

Mueller, E. T. (2007). Understanding goal-based stories through model finding and planning. In *Intelligent Narrative Technologies: Papers from the 2007 AAAI Fall Symposium, Technical Report* (FS-07-05, pp. 95-101), Arlington, Virginia.

Mueller, E. T. (1990). *Daydreaming in humans and machines*. Ablex.

Mukoyama, K., Shinohara, K., Kanai, A., & Ogata, T. (2002). Rhetorical analysis and automatic editing of the film. In *Proceedings of 17th Congress of the International Association of Empirical Aesthetics* (pp. 571-574). Takarazuka, Japan: Academic Press.

Murakami, M., & Imanishi, Y. (1999). Quatitative analysis of auxiliary verb of The Tale of Genji. *Journal of Information Processing, 40*(3), 774–782.

Murch, W. (2001). *In the blink of an eye: A perspective on film editing* (2nd ed.). Los Angeles, CA: Silman-James Press.

Murray, J. H. (1998). *Hamlet on the holodeck*. New York, NY: Free Press.

Murray, M. (2015). Narrative psychology. In J. A. Smith (Ed.), *Qualitative Psychology* (3rd ed., pp. 85–106). London, UK: SAGE.

Naito, Y., & Kanai, A. (2012a). The narrative structure of nostalgia cognition and film. In *Proceedings of the International Conference on Cognitive Science'12*. Sapporo, Japan: Academic Press.

Naito, Y., & Kanai, A. (2012b). Nostalgia and film creation. In *Proceeding of the 26th Annual Conference of the Japanese Society for Artificial Intelligence, 2012*, (1N1-OS-1a-2). Yamaguchi, Japan: Academic Press.

Nakagawa, N., Asao, Y., & Nagaya, N. (2008). Information structure and intonation of right-dislocation sentences in Japanese. Kyoto University Linguistic Research, 27, 1-22.

Nakamura, T. (2006). *Kabuki no kindai-Sakka to sakuhin* [The modern age of kabuki: authors and works]. Tokyo, Japan: Iwanami Shoten.

Nakano, T., Yamamoto, Y., Kitajo, K., Takahashi, T., & Kitazawa, S. (2009). Synchronization of spontaneous eyeblinks while viewing video stories. In *Proceedings of the Royal Society of London B: Biological Sciences*. doi:10.1098/rspb.2009.0828

Nakano, T., Kato, M., Morito, Y., Itoi, S., & Kitazawa, S. (2013). Blink-related momentary activation of the default mode network while viewing videos. *Proceedings of the National Academy of Sciences of the United States of America, 110*(2), 702–706. doi:10.1073/pnas.1214804110 PMID:23267078

Nakano, T., Kato, N., & Kitazawa, S. (2011). Lack of eyeblink entrainments in autism spectrum disorders. *Neuropsychologia, 49*(9), 2784–2790. doi:10.1016/j.neuropsychologia.2011.06.007 PMID:21699907

Nakano, T., & Kitazawa, S. (2010). Eyeblink entrainment at breakpoints of speech. *Experimental Brain Research, 205*(4), 577–581. doi:10.1007/s00221-010-2387-z PMID:20700731

Nakashima, M., & Ogata, T. (2006). Narrative generation system and intertextuality: A consideration on the concept and prototype systems. In *Proceedings of the 20th Annual Conference of the Japanese Society for Artificial Intelligence* (2E2-2). Tokyo, Japan: Academic Press.

Nakashima, H. (2006). Constructive informatics and AI. *Transactions of the Japanese Society for Artificial Intelligence, 21*(6), 502–513. doi:10.1527/tjsai.21.502

National institute of vocational rehabilitation. (2011). *Empirical Research for Effective Cooperation of Supports for Independent Life and Work of Persons with disabilities*. Chiba, Japan: National Institute of Vocational Rehabilitation.

Natsume, S. (2007). *Bungaku ron (I, II)* [Literary theory]. Iwanami Shoten. (Original work published 1907)

Néda, Z., Ravasz, E., Brechet, Y., Vicsek, T., & Barabási, A. L. (2000). Self-organizing processes: The sound of many hands clapping. *Nature, 403*(6772), 849–850. doi:10.1038/35002660 PMID:10706271

Newell, A., & Simon, H. A. (1972). *Human problem solving*. Prentice Hall.

Nikolejeva, M. (2012). Reading other people's minds through word. *Children's Literature in Education*, *43*(3), 273–291. doi:10.1007/s10583-012-9163-6

Nishioka, H. (2014). *Kyoiku ni ikasu digital storytelling* [*Digital storytelling on education*]. Tokyo, Japan: Tokyo Tosho Shuppan.

Nishiyama, Y. (2003). *Nihongo meishiku-no imiron-to-goyouron* [The semantics and pragmatics of noun phrases in Japanese]. Tokyo, Japan: Hituzi Publishing.

Niwango. (n.d.). *Niconico*. Retrieved from http://www.nicovideo.jp/

Noguchi, Y. (Ed.). (2005). Naratibu no rinshoshakaigaku [Clinical sociology of narrative]. Tokyo, Japan: Keiso shobo.

Noguchi, Y. (Ed.). (2009). Naratibu apurochi [Narrative approach]. Tokyo, Japan: Keiso shobo.

Noma, T., Kai, K., Nakamura, J., & Okada, N. (1992). Translating from natural language story to computer animation. In *Proceedings of First Singapore International Conference on Intelligent Systems 92* (pp. 475-480). Singapore: Academic Press.

Nomura, J. (2008). *Japanese postposing*. (Unpublished doctoral dissertation). University of Hawaii, Manoa, HI.

Nomura, R. (2012). The Rakugo-learning environment: An alternative epistemology. In *Proceedings of The Macrotheme Conference on Education and Training 2012, 44*. Espace Vocation Paris Haussaman Saint-Lazare, Paris, France.

Nomura, R., Hino, K., Shimazu, M., Liang, Y., & Okada, T. (2015a). Emotionally excited eyeblink-rate variability predicts an experience of transportation into the narrative world. *Frontiers in Psychology*, *6*(477). doi:10.3389/fpsyg.2015.00447 PMID:26029123

Nomura, R., Liang, Y., & Okada, T. (2015b). Interaction among audience facilitate eyeblink synchronization. *PLoS ONE*, *10*(10), e0140774. doi:10.1371/journal.pone.0140774 PMID:26479405

Nomura, R., & Okada, T. (2014). Spontaneous synchronization of eyeblinks during story-telling performance. *Cognitive Studies: Bulletin of the Japanese Cognitive Science Society*, *21*(2), 226–244.

Nouchi, M. (2008). Shitsudokushou no "katari" o kikukoto. [Listening to the "talk" of dyslexia] In Y. Yamada (Ed.), *Jinsei to yamai no katari* [Narrative of the life and the illness] (pp. 51–78). Tokyo, Japan: University of Tokyo Press.

Nozomi, K. (2014). *Inou battle wa nichijou kei no naka de* [Battles using special skills in usual scenes]. Tokyo, Japan: SB Creative.

O'Donnell, B. (1966). Stephen Crane's the O'Ruddy: A problem in authorship discrimination. In Leed (Ed.), The Computer and Literary Style (pp. 107-115). Kent, OH: Kent State University Press.

Oatley, K. (1994). A taxonomy of the emotions of the literary response and a theory of identification in fictional narrative. *Poetics*, *9*(23), 53–74.

Oda, J. (2007). Re-reinvestigation of Raimundus Lullus on creativity. *Proceedings of Language Sense Engineering Research Group in Japanese Artificial Intelligence Society*, *26*, 47–51.

Oe, K. (1979). *Dojidai ge-mu* [The game of contemporaneity]. Tokyo: Shinchosha.

Ogata, T. (1995). *Narrative generation: An approach based on techniques and strategies for narrative.* (Ph.D thesis). The University of Tokyo, Tokyo, Japan.

Ogata, T. (1998). A proposal of computational narratology. *PSJ SIG Notes Computer and Humanities Abstract* No. 041 - 008.

Ogata, T. (1999). Proposal of computational narratology. In *Proceedings of IPSJ SIG Computers and the Humanities* (pp. 53-60). Academic Press.

Ogata, T. (2002). Expanded literary theory: Cognitive/computational expansion of literary theories and narratology. In *Proceedings of 17th Congress of the International Association of Empirical Aesthetics* (pp. 163-166). Osaka, Japan: Academic Press.

Ogata, T. (2002). Expanded literary theory: Cognitive/computational expansion of literary theories and narratology. In *Proceedings of 17th Congress of the International Association of Empirical Aesthetics* (pp. 163-166). Takarazuka, Japan: Academic Press.

Ogata, T. (2004). A computational approach to literary and narrative production: Toward computational narratology. In *Proceedings of 18th Congress of the International Association of Empirical Aesthetics* (pp. 509-516). Lisbon, Portugal: Academic Press.

Ogata, T. (2004a). A computational approach to literary and narrative production: Toward computational narratology. In *Proceedings of 18th Congress of the International Association of Empirical Aesthetics* (pp. 509-516). Lisbon, Portugal: Academic Press.

Ogata, T. (2004b). Toward the consistent simulation of narrative discourse based on narratology. In *Proceedings of the Ninth International Symposium on Artificial Life and Robotics* (*Vol. 2*, pp. 579-584). Oita, Japan: Academic Press.

Ogata, T. (2014). Expanded literary theory for automatic narrative generation. In *Proceedings of Joint 7th International Conference on Soft Computing and Intelligent Systems and 15th International Symposium on Advanced Intelligent Systems* (pp. 1558-1563). Kitakyushu, Japan: Academic Press.

Ogata, T., & Hosaka, Y. (2004). Transformation of story in the story generation system based on narratology. In *Proceedings of the Ninth International Symposium on Artificial Life and Robotics* (*Vol. 2*, pp. 593-596). Lisbon, Portugal: Academic Press.

Ogata, T., & Terano, T. (1991). Explanation-based narrative generation using semiotic theory. In *Proceedings of Natural Language Processing Pacific Rim Symposium* (pp. 321-328). Singapore: Academic Press.

Ogata, T., & Terano, T. (1991). Explanation-based narrative generation using semiotic theory. In *Proceedings of Natural Language Processing Pacific Rim Symposium 1991* (pp. 321-328). Academic Press.

Ogata, T., & Terano, T. (1992). Plot generation and expansion in explanation-based narrative generator. In *Proceedings of First Singapore International Conference on Intelligent Systems* (pp. 549-554). Singapore: Academic Press.

Ogata, T., & Yamakage, S. (2004). A computational mechanism of the "distance" in narrative: A trial in the expansion of literary theory. In *Proceedings of the 8th World Multiconference on Systemics, Cybernetics and Informatics* (pp. 179-184). Orlando, FL: Academic Press.

Ogata, T., & Yazawa, K. (1999). Bakhtin literary theory and structure of novels as artificial society simulation. In *Proceedings of the 2nd International Conference on Cognitive Science and the 16th Annual Meeting of the Japanese Cognitive Science Society Joint Conference* (pp. 950-953). Tokyo, Japan: Academic Press.

Ogata, T., Hori, K., & Ohsuga, S. (1994). Towards narrative text generation based on narrative techniques and strategies. In Proceedings of International Federation for Information and Documentation (pp. 296-300). Saitama, Japan: Academic Press.

Ogata, T., Tachibana, S., & Tomite, S. (2009). Animated movie generation from narrative conceptual representation and the automatic camerawork: Analysis and simulation of "Tokyo Story." In *Proceedings of the 26th Annual Meeting of the Japanese Cognitive Science Society* (P2-32). Yokohama, Japan: Academic Press.

Ogata, K., Sato, S., & Komatani, K. (2014). Automatic generation of very short stories by imitation and substitution. In *Proceedings of the 28th Annual Conference of the Japanese Society for Artificial Intelligence (JSAI'14).* Ehime, Japan: The Japanese Society for Artificial Intelligence.

Ogata, T. (1999). An attempt for systematization of narrative discourse theory from the viewpoint of narrative generation system. *Proceedings of IPSJ SIG Computers and the Humanities, 99*(85), 31–38.

Ogata, T. (2007). To the rhetoric of story from Propp: Centering around the rhetoric of de-composition and recomposition. *Cognitive Studies, 14*(4), 532–558.

Ogata, T. (2007). To the rhetoric of story from Propp: Centering around the rhetoric of de-composition and re-composition. *Cognitive Studies, 14*(4), 532–558.

Ogata, T. (2010). "Monogatari seisei sisutemu" no haikei oyobi monogatari to bungaku no aida. [Backgrounds of the "narrative generation system" and "relations between narrative and literature"] In T. Ogata & A. Kanai (Eds.), *Monogatariron no jouhougaku josetsu: monogatari seisei no shisou to gijutsu wo megutte* [An introduction to the informatics of narratology: about the thought and technologies of narrative generation] (pp. 186–258). Tokyo, Japan: Gakubunsha.

Ogata, T. (2010). Monogatari seisei sisutemu no taikyoku-teki kekkou-Monogatari no gijutsu to keiei heno jo. [The macro architecture of a narrative generation system: An introduction to narrative technology and management] In T. Ogata & A. Kanai (Eds.), *Monogatariron no johogaku josetsu-Monogatari seisei no shiso to gijutsu wo megutte* [An introduction to the informatics of narratology: About the thoughts and technologies of narrative generation] (pp. 259–340). Tokyo, Japan: Gakubunsha.

Ogata, T. (2011). Narrative generation system as the practice of "informatics of narratology.". *Journal of Japan Society for Fazzy Theory and Intelligent Informatics, 23*(5), 14–24.

Ogata, T. (2011). Narrative generation system as the practice of "informatics of narratology.". *Journal of Japan Society for Fuzzy Theory and Intelligent Informatics, 23*(5), 676–685.

Ogata, T. (2015). Building conceptual dictionaries for an integrated narrative generation system. *Journal of Robotics. Networking and Artificial Life, 1*(4), 270–284. doi:10.2991/jrnal.2015.1.4.6

Ogata, T., Hori, K., & Ohsuga, S. (1995). A basic framework of narrative generation system as creative interface. In Y. Anzai, K. Ogawa, & H. Mori (Eds.), *Symbiosis of human and artifact (20A)* (pp. 679–684). Elsevier. doi:10.1016/S0921-2647(06)80107-3

Ogata, T., Hori, K., & Ohsuga, S. (1996a). A basic framework for narrative conceptual structure generation based on narrative techniques and strategies. *Journal of the Japanese Society for Artificial Intelligence, 11*(1), 148–159.

Ogata, T., Hori, K., & Ohsuga, S. (1996b). An analysis of narrative structure and generation process for narrative generation system. *Cognitive Studies, 3*(1), 72–109.

Ogata, T., & Kanai, A. (2010). *An introduction to informatics of narratology: Towards the thoughts and technologies of narrative generation.* Tokyo, Japan: Gakubunsha.

Ogata, T., & Kanai, A. (2010). *Monogatariron no jouhougaku jyosetsu* [An introduction of informatics of narratology: on thought and technology of narrative generation 1]. Tokyo, Japan: Gakubunsha.

Ogata, T., & Kanai, A. (2010). *Monogatariron no jyohogaku jyosetsu: Monogatariseisei no shiso to gijyutsu wo megutte* [An introduction to informatics of narratology: Towards the thoughts and technologies of narrative generation]. Tokyo, Japan: Gakubun-sha.

Ogata, T., & Ono, J. (2013). Designing narrative interface with a function of narrative generation. In *Proceeding of the 2013 International Conference on Cyberworlds* (pp. 214-221). Yokohama, Japan. doi:10.1109/CW.2013.74

Ogata, T., Watanabe, K., Hori, K., & Ohsuga, S. (1995). A basic framework of the application of narrative generation system for integrated support of marketing/advertisement. *Journal of the Japan Society for Management Information, 4*(1), 19–42.

Ogata, T., Watanabe, K., Hori, K., & Ohsuga, S. (1995). Monogatari seisei shisutemu niyoru koukoku sousaku shien wo mokuteki toshita terebi komahsharu no kouzou bunseki[Structural analysis of television commercials to support advertising creation using a narrative generation system]. *Journal of Advertising Science*, *30*, 1–22.

Ogawa, Y. (2011). A cognitive-affective mechanism concerning enjoyment of a television drama: Verification and consideration of paradoxical enjoyment by empathy for the characters. *Cognitive Studies*, *18*(1), 79–99.

Ogawa, Y., & Kanai, A. (2013). Rhetoric of biopic and viewer's reconsideration: A verification that how TARO's enjoyment and YUMEJI's irrational cutting cause an effect in concept reconsideration. *Cognitive Studies*, *20*(2), 224–248.

Ohara, K. H., Fujii, S., Saito, H., Ishizaki, S., Ohori, T., & Suzuki, R. (2003). *The Japanese FrameNet project: a preliminary report.* Poster presented at the Pacific Association for Computational Linguistics, Halifax, Canada.

Ohkura, S. (Photographs) (2001). Kabuki today: the art and tradition. Tokyo, Japan: Kodansha International.

Oikawa, H., & Ogata, T. (2012). On the narrative generation as a mutual cognition mechanism among characters. In *Proceedings of the 29th Annual Meeting of the Japanese Cognitive Science Society* (pp. 540-549). Sendai, Japan: Academic Press.

Okada, N., & Endo, T. (1992). Story generation based on dynamics of the mind. *Computational Intelligence*, *8*(1), 123–160. doi:10.1111/j.1467-8640.1992.tb00341.x

Okawa, H., & Honda, T. (2014). Shuroushienryouiki no esuesutiunei ni hituyonagijutsu: tekisutomaininguhou o mochiite [Techniques necessary for the SST administration in employment support domain: Using the text mining method]. In *Proceedings of SST Promotion Association 19th Annual Scientific Meeting* (p.62). Sendai, Japan: Academic Press.

Oliver, M. B. (1993). Exploring the paradox of the enjoyment of sad films. *Human Communication Research*, *19*(3), 315–342. doi:10.1111/j.1468-2958.1993.tb00304.x

Oliver, M. B. (2007). Appreciation as audience response: The case of tragic, poignant, and touching entertainment. In A. Bartsch, J. Eder, & K. Fahlenbrach (Eds.), *Audiovisuelle Emotionen* (pp. 207–219). Köln, Germany: Halem.

Oliver, M. B. (2008). Tender affective states as predictors of entertainment preference. *Journal of Communication*, *58*(1), 40–U14. doi:10.1111/j.1460-2466.2007.00373.x

Oliver, M. B., Weaver, J. B. III, & Sargent, S. L. (2000). An examination of factors related to sex differences in enjoyment of sad films. *Journal of Broadcasting & Electronic Media*, *44*(2), 282–300. doi:10.1207/s15506878jobem4402_8

Ono, J., & Ogata, T. (2013). A framework of the inter-textual knowledge acquisition and creation mechanism for an integrated narrative generation system. In *Proceedings of Forum on Information Technology 2013* (*Vol.2*, pp. 201-204). Tottori, Japan: Academic Press.

Onodera, K., Akimoto, T., & Ogata, T. (2012). A state-event transformation mechanism for generating micro structures of story in an integrated narrative generation system. In *Proceedings of the 34th Annual Conference of the Cognitive Science Society* (pp. 2150-2155). Sapporo, Japan: Academic Press.

Ono, T. (2006). Postpredicate-elements in Japanese conversation. In T. Vance & K. Jones (Eds.), *Japanese/Korean Linguistics 14* (pp. 381–391). Stanford, CA: Center for the Study of Language and Information.

Ontañón, S., & Zho, J. (2011). The SAM algorithm for analogy-based story generation. In *Proceedings of the 7th AAAI Conference of Artificial Intelligence and Interactive Digital Entertainment* (pp. 67-71). Academic Press.

Orwin, M., Howes, C., & Kempson, R. (2013). *Language, music and interaction*. London, UK: College Publications.

Otsuka, H., Inui, T., & Okumura, M. (2007). *Opinion mining engine*. Tokyo, Japan: Corona Publishing.

Palmer, M. (2009). SemLink: linking PropBank, VerbNet and FrameNet. In *Proceedings of the Generative Lexicon Conference*. Pisa, Italy: Academic Press.

Palmer, M., Gildea, D., & Kingsbury, P. (2005). The proposition bank: An annotated corpus of semantic roles. *Computational Linguistics*, *31*(1), 71–106. doi:10.1162/0891201053630264

Peinado, F., & Gervás, P. (2005). Creativity issues in plot generation. In *Workshop on Computational Creativity, Working Notes, 19th International Joint Conference on A.I.* (pp. 45-52), Scotland, UK: Academic Press.

Peinado, F., & Gervás, P. (2005). Creativity issues in plot generation. In *Workshop on Computational Creativity, Working Notes, 19th International Joint Conference on A.I.* (pp. 45-52). Edinburgh, UK: Academic Press.

Peinado, F., & Gervás, P. (2006). Evaluation of automatic generation of basic stories. *New Generation Computing*, *24*(3), 289–302. doi:10.1007/BF03037336

Pemberton, L. (1989). A modular approach to story generation. In *Proceedings of the Fourth Conference on European Chapter of the Association for Computational Linguistics* (pp. 217-224), Manchester, UK. doi:10.3115/976815.976845

Pérez y Pérez, R., & Sharples, M. (2001). MEXICA: A computer model of a cognitive account of creative writing. *Journal of Experimental & Theoretical Artificial Intelligence*, *13*(2), 119–139. doi:10.1080/09528130010029820

Pérez, R. (1999). *A computer model of creativity of writing*. (Ph.D. Thesis). The University of Sussex, Brighton, UK.

Pérez, X. (2001). *La suspense cinematografica*. Roma: Editori Riuniti.

Phillips, B. J. (1997). Thinking into it: Consumer interpretation of complex advertising images. *Journal of Advertising*, *26*(2), 77–87. doi:10.1080/00913367.1997.10673524

Potts, C. (2005). *The logic of conventional implicatures*. Oxford, UK: Oxford University Press.

Prince, G. (1982). *Narratology*. Walter de Gruhter. doi:10.1515/9783110838626

Prince, G. (2003). *A dictionary of narratology* (Revised ed.). University of Nebraska Press.

Propp, V. (1928). *The morphology of the fairy tale*. Leningrad, USSR: Academia.

Propp, V. Y. (1968). *Morphology of the folktale* (L. Scott, Trans.). Austin, TX: University of Texas Press. (Original work published 1928)

Purver, M., Gregoromichelaki, E., Meyer-Viol, W., & Cann, R. (2010). Splitting the 'I's and crossing the 'you's. In P. Łupkowski & M. Purver (Eds.), *Aspects of semantics and pragmatics of dialogue* (pp. 43–50). Poznań, Poland: Polish Society for Cognitive Science.

Purver, M., Hough, J., & Gregoromichelaki, E. (2014). Dialogue and compound contributions. In A. Stent & S. Bangalore (Eds.), *Natural language generation in interactive systems* (pp. 63–92). Cambridge, UK: Cambridge University Press. doi:10.1017/CBO9780511844492.004

Quesenbery, W., & Brooks, K. (2010). *Storytelling for user experience: Crafting stories for better design.* New York, NY: Rosenfeld Media.

Quillian, M. (1968). Semantic memory. In M. Minsky (Ed.), *Semantic information processing* (pp. 227–270). Cambridge, MA: MIT Press.

Rabkin, E. S. (1973). Narrative suspense: "When Slim Turned Sideways". New York: Ann Arbor.

Raney, A. A. (2002). Moral judgment as a predictor of enjoyment of crime drama. *Media Psychology*, *4*(4), 305–322. doi:10.1207/S1532785XMEP0404_01

Raney, A. A. (2004). Expanding disposition theory: Reconsidering character liking, moral evaluations, and enjoyment. *Communication Theory*, *14*(4), 348–369. doi:10.1111/j.1468-2885.2004.tb00319.x

Raney, A. A. (2005). Punishing media criminals and moral judgment: The impact on enjoyment. *Media Psychology*, *7*(2), 145–163. doi:10.1207/S1532785XMEP0702_2

Raney, A. A., & Bryant, J. (2002). Moral judgment and crime drama: An integrated theory of enjoyment. *Journal of Communication*, *52*(2), 402–415. doi:10.1111/j.1460-2466.2002.tb02552.x

Reiter, E., & Dale, R. (2006). *Building natural language generation systems: Studies in natural language processing.* London: Cambridge University Press.

Riedl, M. O., & Bulitko, V. (2013). Interactive narrative: An intelligent systems approach. *AI Magazine*, *34*(1), 67–77.

Riedl, M. O., & Young, R. M. (2006). From linear story generation to branching story graphs. *IEEE Computer Graphics and Applications*, *26*(3), 23–31. doi:10.1109/MCG.2006.56 PMID:16711214

Riedl, M. O., & Young, R. M. (2010). Narrative planning: Balancing plot and character. *Journal of Artificial Intelligence Research*, *39*, 217–267.

Riedl, M., Saretto, C. J., & Young, R. M. (2003). Managing interaction between users and agents in a multi-agent storytelling environment. In *Proceedings of the Second International Joint Conference on Autonomous Agents and Multiagent Systems* (pp. 741-748). Melbourne, Australia. doi:10.1145/860575.860694

Riesbeck, C. K., & Schank, R. C. (1989). *Inside case-based reasoning.* Lawrence Erlbaum.

Ritchie, G. (2005). Computational mechanisms for pun generation. In *Proceedings of the 10th European Natural Language Generation Workshop* (pp. 125-132). Academic Press.

Ritchie, G. (2008). Uninformed resource creation for humour simulation. In *Proceedings of the 5th International Joint Workshop on Computational Creativity* (pp. 147-150). Academic Press.

Ritchie, G., Manurung, R., Pain, H., Waller, A., Black, R., & O'Mara, D. (2007). A practical application of computational humour. In *Proceedings of the 4th International Joint Conference on Computational Creativity* (pp. 91-98). Academic Press.

Ritchie, G. (2009). Can computers create humor? *AI Magazine*, *30*(3), 71–81.

Rizzolatti, G., Fogassi, L., & Gallese, V. (2001). Neurophysiological mechanism underlying the understanding and imitation of action. *Nature Reviews. Neuroscience*, *2*(9), 661–669. doi:10.1038/35090060 PMID:11533734

Romesburg, H. C. (1984). *Cluster analysis for researchers.* Belmont, CA: Lifetime Learning Publications.

Rooney, R., Benson, C., & Hennessy, E. (2012). The apparent reality of movies and emotional arousal: A study using physiological and self-report measures. *Poetics*, *40*(5), 405–422. doi:10.1016/j.poetic.2012.07.004

Rowe, J. P., McQuiggan, S. W., Robison, J. L., Marcey, D. R., & Lester, J. C. (2009). STORYEVAL: An empirical evaluation framework for narrative generation. In *Intelligent Narrative Technologies II: Papers from the 2009 AAAI Spring Symposium, Technical Report* (SS-09-06, pp. 103-110), Palo alto, California.

Rumelhart, D. E. (1975). Notes on a schema for stories. In D. G. Bobrow & A. Collins (Eds.), *Representation and understanding: Studies in cognitive science*. Academic Press. doi:10.1016/B978-0-12-108550-6.50013-6

Ryan, M. L. (2011). The interactive onion: layers of user participation in digital narrative texts. In B. Thomas & R. E. Page (Eds.). *New narratives: Stories and storytelling in the digital age*. Retrieved from http://0-eds.a.ebscohost.com.opac.bilgi.edu.tr/eds/ebookviewer/ebook/bmxlYmtfXzQ3NzE2NF9fQU41?sid=f26ccbf4-cbc8-4e3f-8bf9-227e9654122b@sessionmgr4002&vid=3&format=EB&rid=3

Ryan, M. L. (1991). *Possible worlds, artificial intelligence, and narrative theory*. Bloomington, IN: Indiana University Press.

Ryan, M.-L., & Thon, J.-N. (Eds.). (2014). *Storyworlds across media*. University of Nebraska Press.

Rzepka, R., & Araki, K. (2015). Haiku generator that reads blogs and illustrates them with sounds and images. *Proceedings of, IJCAI2015*, 2496–2502.

Sackett, D. L., Richardson, W. S., Straus, S. E., Rosenberg, W., & Haynes, R. B. (1997). *Evidence-based MEDICINE: how to practice and teach EBM*. London, UK: Churchill Livingstone.

Sag, I., Wasow, T., & Bender, E. (2003). *Syntactic theory* (2nd ed.). Stanford, CA: Center for the Study of Language and Information.

Saiki, S. (2008). Shounigan no kodomo no toubyoutaiken. [Narrative based medicine and clinical intellect? Narrative of a pediatric cancer patient] In Y. Yamada (Ed.), *Jinsei to yamai no katari* [Narrative of life and illness]. (pp. 103–132). Tokyo, Japan: University of Tokyo Press.

Saito, Y., & Ogata, T. (1998). On the computational modeling of Freud's dream theory. In *Proceedings of the 12rd Annual Conference of the Japanese Society for Artificial Intelligence* (pp. 706-706). Tokyo, Japan: Academic Press.

Saito, S. (2003). Naratibubeisudomedisun to rinshochi. [Narrative based medicine and clinical intellect] In Y. Yamada (Ed.), *Jinsei to yamai no katari* [Narrative of the life and the illness] (pp. 133–163). Tokyo, Japan: University of Tokyo Press.

Sakai, S., Inagaki, Y., Higuchi, K., & Kato, H. (2011). Jidouyougoshisetunai niokeru kodomokanbouryoku no naiyou no bunseki[Analysis of contents and correspondence of violence among children in a child nursing home]. *Child Abuse & Neglect*, *13*, 115–124.

Sakuma, T., & Ogata, T. (2005). Story generation support system used the story theory of Propp. In *Proceedings of the 19th Annual Conference of the Japanese Society for Artificial Intelligence* (3D3-04). Kitakyushu, Japan: Academic Press.

Sakuyama, F. (2012). Hito, kankyo, kankei oyobi joukyou otoushitekangaeru sosharuwaku no shouten[The focus of social work from a person, environment, relationships, and situation perspective]. *Japanese Journal of Social Welfare*, *53*(1), 79–90.

Satio, M. (1985). *Some asymmetries in Japanese and their theoretical implications*. (Unpublished doctoral dissertation). MIT, Cambridge, MA.

Sato, S., Iwata, K., Furukawa, S., Matsuda, Y., Hatsuse, N., & Ikebuchi, E. (2014). The effects of the combination of cognitive training and supported employment on improving clinical and working outcomes for people with schizophrenia in Japan. *Clinical Practice and Epidemiology in Mental Health, 10*(1), 18–27. doi:10.2174/1745017901410010018 PMID:24600481

Schank, R. C. (1979). Interestingness: Controlling inferences. *Artificial Intelligence, 12*(3), 273–297. doi:10.1016/0004-3702(79)90009-2

Schank, R. C. (1982). *Dynamic memory: A theory of learning in computers and people*. Cambridge, UK: Cambridge University Press.

Schank, R. C. (1986). *Explanation patterns: understanding mechanically and creativity*. Lawrence Erlbaum.

Schank, R. C. (1990). *Tell me a story*. Scribners.

Schank, R. C. (1990). *Tell me a story: Narrative and intelligence*. Chicago, IL: Northwestern University Press.

Schank, R. C., & Abelson, R. P. (1977). *Scripts, plans, goals, and understanding: An inquiry into human knowledge structures*. Lawrence Erlbaum.

Schank, R. C., & Riesbeck, C. K. (1981). *Inside computer understanding*. Lawrence Erlbaum.

Schank, R., & Abelson, R. (1977). *Scripts, plans, goals, and understanding. Erlbaum*. Hillsdale, NJ: Psychology Press.

Schwartz, P. (1991). *The art of the long view: Scenario planning-protecting your company against an uncertain world.* London, UK: Century Business.

Scott, L. M. (1994). Images in advertising: The need for a theory of visual rhetoric. *The Journal of Consumer Research, 21*(2), 252–272. doi:10.1086/209396

Seino, K., & Haruna, Y. (2015a). Chiiki niokeru kenriyougo toshiteno shuroushien noarikatanikansuru kenkyuu [The study on employment support as advocacy in the region]. In *Proceedings of Kanto Branch, Japanese Society for the Study of Social Welfare 2014 Annual Meeting*. Tokyo, Japan: Academic Press.

Seino, K., Haruna, Y., & Ishizaki, S. (2015b). Analysis using text mining for the narrative told about work of persons with disabilities. In *Proceedings of the Japanese Cognitive Science Society 32rd Annual Meeting*. Chiba, Japan: Academic Press.

Seino, K., & Haruna, Y. (2014). Hokeniryo, fukushi, kyouikubunya niokeru shougaisha no shuuroushien no genjo [The current state of employment support of disabled persons in the field of education and medicine and welfare]. In *Proceedings of Vocational Rehabilitation Society 42rd Annual Meeting*. Iwate, Japan.

Seraku, T. (2013). *Clefts, relatives, and language dynamics*. (Unpublished doctoral dissertation). University of Oxford, Oxford, UK.

Seraku, T. (2015, October). *A Dynamic Syntax modelling of postposing in Japanese narratives*. Paper presented at the 29th Pacific Asia Conference on Language, Information and Computation, Shanghai, China.

Seraku, T., & Ohtani, A. (2015, October). *The* wh-*licensing in Japanese right dislocations*. Paper presented at Colloque de Syntaxe et Sémantique à Paris 2015, Paris, France.

Seraku, T. (2015). Nihongo-no kouchibun [Postposed sentences in Japanese]. *Journal of the Society of Japanese Language and Literature. Japanology, 70*, 71–96.

Sharma, M., Ontañón, S., Mehta, M., & Ram, A. (2007). Drama management evaluation for interactive fiction games. In *Intelligent Narrative Technologies: Papers from the 2007 AAAI Fall Symposium, Technical Report* (FS-07-05, pp. 138-145), Arlington, Virginia.

Sharples, M. (1996). An account of writing as creative design. In C. M. Levy & S. Ransdell (Eds.), *The science of writing: Theories, methods, individual difference and applications* (pp. 127–148). Lawrence Erlbaum.

Shibuya, Y., Morita, Y., Fukuda, H., Ueda, K., & Sasaki, M. (2012). Asynchronous relation between body action and breathing in bunraku: Uniqueness of manner of breathing in Japanese traditional performing arts. *Cognitive Studies, 19*(3), 337–364.

Shimazu, M., & Nomura, R. (2015). *Development of automated measuring and analyzing system for eyeblinks of viewing audience.* Oral presented and communicative demonstrated at Interaction 2015 the 19th symposium of Information Processing Society of Japan.

Shimp, T. A. (1976). Methods of commercial presentation employed by national television advertisers. *Journal of Advertising, 5*(4), 30–36. doi:10.1080/00913367.1976.10672661

Shklovsky, V. (1965). Art as technique. In *Russian formalist criticism: Four essays* (L. T. Lemon & M. J. Reis, Trans. & Eds.). Lincoln, NE: University of Nebraska Press. (Original work published 1917)

Shklovsky, V. (1990). *Theory of prose* (B. Sher, Trans.). Dalkey Archive Press.

Shojima, S. (2008). Multilayered contexts in which narrative is generated and interpreted: Toward the next narrative based inquiry. *Kyoto University Research Studies in Education, 54*, 138–151.

Si, M. (2010). *Thespian: a decision-theoretic framework for interactive narratives.* (Ph.D thesis). Faculty of the USC Graduate School, University of Southern California, Los Angeles, CA.

Singh, P., Barry, B., & Liu, H. (2004). Teaching machines about everyday life. *BT Technology Journal, 22*(4), 227–240. doi:10.1023/B:BTTJ.0000047601.53388.74

Smith, S., & Bates, J. (1989). Towards a theory of narrative for interactive fiction. *Technical Report CMU-CS-89-121.* Pittsburgh: Carnegie Melllon University.

Sono, S. (2012a). *Kibô no Kuni* [The Land of Hope]. Tokyo, Japan: Little More.

Sono, S. (2012b). Kibô no Kuni - Mada owatteinai genpatsu no mondai[The Land of Hope -Problem of the nuclear disaster which has not been yet over]. *Tsukuru, 42*(8), 128–133.

Sono, S., & Oshima, A. (2015). Interview: Ore ha itan jya-nai[Interview: I am not a heretic]. *Bungakukai, 69*(11), 26–41.

Sono, S., & Sato, Y. (2012, October). Kibô no Kuni long interview - Sono Sion, genpatsu wo egaku[The Land of Hope long interview - Sion Sono depict a nuclear disaster]. *Kinema Junpo, 1622*, 87–91.

Stathakopoulos, V., Theodorakis, I. G., & Mastoridou, E. (2008). Visual and verbal rhetoric in advertising: The case of 'resonance'. *International Journal of Advertising, 27*(4), 629–657. doi:10.2501/S0265048708080177

Steinmetz, K. (2014, July28). Not just a smiley face. The emoji boom is changing the way we communicate. *Time.*

Stern, B. B. (1992). Historical and personal nostalgia in advertising text: The fin de siècle effect. *Journal of Advertising, 21*(4), 11–22. doi:10.1080/00913367.1992.10673382

Stern, J. A., Walrath, L. C., & Goldstein, R. (1984). The endogenous eyeblink. *Psychophysiology, 21*(1), 22–33. doi:10.1111/j.1469-8986.1984.tb02312.x PMID:6701241

Stewart, D. W., & Furse, D. H. (1986). *Effective television advertising: A study of 1000 commercials.* Lexington, MA: Lexington Books.

Stockwell, P. (2002). *Cognitive poetics: An introduction.* Routledge.

Strogatz, S., Abrams, D., McRobie, A., Eckhardt, B., & Ott, E. (2005). Theoretical mechanics: Crowd synchrony on the millennium bridge. *Nature*, *438*(7064), 43–44. doi:10.1038/438043a PMID:16267545

Study Group of Written Japanese Grammar. (2009). *Contemporary Japanese grammar 2: Syntax and Voice*. Tokyo, Japan: Kurosio Publishers.

Sumi, Y., Sakamoto, R., Nakao, K., Mase, K., & Kunifuji, S. (2002). Change of individual experiences and interests in comics style. *IPSJ Journal*, *43*(12), 3582–3595.

Sundermeier, B. A., Van den Broek, P., & Zwaan, R. A. (2005). Causal coherence and the availability of locations and objects during narrative comprehension. *Memory & Cognition*, *33*(3), 462–470. doi:10.3758/BF03193063 PMID:16156181

Suwa, H. (1991). *Kabuki no houhou* [Methods of kabuki]. Tokyo, Japan: Bensei Shuppan.

Swanson, R., & Gordon, A. S. (2012). Say Anything: Using textual case-based reasoning to enable open-domain interactive storytelling. *ACM Transactions on Interactive Intelligent Systems, 2*(3), Article 16.

Swartjes, I. (2010). *Whose story is it anyway? How improve informs agency and authorship of emergent narrative.* (Ph.D thesis). University of Twente, Enschede, Netherlands.

Szilas, N. (2010). Requirements for computational models of interactive narrative. In *Computational Models of Narrative: Papers from the 2010 AAAI Fall Symposium, Technical Reports* (FS-10-04, pp. 62-68), Arlington, Virginia.

Szilas, N. (2015). Towards narrative-based knowledge representation in cognitive systems. In *Proceedings of 6th Workshop on Computational Models of Narrative* (pp. 133-141). Academic Press.

Tada, H., Omori, Y., Hirokawa, K., Ohira, H., & Tomonaga, M. (2013). Eye-blink behaviors in 71 species of primates. *PLoS ONE*, *8*(5), e66018. doi:10.1371/journal.pone.0066018 PMID:23741522

Tagaki, M. (2012). Sosharuwaku niokeru ebidensu toha nanika [What is the evidence in the social work?]. In Japanese Society for the Study of Social Welfare (Ed.), Taironshakaifukushigaku [Discussion social welfare studies] (pp. 124-144). Tokyo, Japan: Chuohoki Publishing.

Tagaki, M. (2008). Experiences of people with acquired long-term physical disability: Life stories of persons with spinal cord injuries in japan. *Qualitative Psychology Nexus*, *7*, 51–79.

Tagaki, M. (2009). A mixed method of qualitative analysis and text mining of qualitative data in a municipal action plan for a disabled policy. *Journal of Social Problems*, *58*, 71–86.

Taguchi, A. (2003). *Kabuki to ningyou joururi* [Kabuki and ningyo-joruri]. Tokyo, Japan: Yoshikawa-kobunkan.

Tajima, M., Okada, Y., Nakamura, S., Otowa, K., Numa, H., Ono, H., & Akiyama, T. (2010). Effect examination of group cognitive-behavioral therapy for people taking a leave of absence due to depression. *Japanese Journal of Psychiatric Treatment*, *25*(10), 1374–1378.

Takami, K. (1995). *Kinouteki koubunron-niyoru Nichi-Eigo hikaku* [Japanese-English comparisons in functional syntax]. Tokyo, Japan: Kuroshio Publishers.

Takano, Y. (2014). A comparative approach to Japanese postposing. In M. Saito (Ed.), *Japanese syntax in comparative perspective* (pp. 139–180). Oxford, UK: Oxford University Press. doi:10.1093/acprof:oso/9780199945207.003.0006

Takeuchi, K., Inui, K., Takeuchi, N., & Fujita, A. (2010). A thesaurus of predicate-argument structure for Japanese verbs to deal with granularity of verb meanings. In *Proceedings of the 8th Workshop on Asian Language Resources* (pp. 1-8). Beijing, China: Academic Press.

Takeuchi, K., Ishihara, Y., & Takeuchi, N. (2014). Discussion on semantic structure of nouns from the view of predicate argument structure thesaurus. In *Proceedings of the 28th Annual Conference of the Japanese Society for Artificial Intelligence* (2I5-OS-08b-1). Matsuyama, Japan: Academic Press.

Takeuchi, K., Ueno, M., & Takeuchi, N. (2015) Annotating semantic role information to Japanese balanced corpus. In *Proceedings of MAPLEX 2015*. Tendo, Japan: Academic Press.

Takeuchi, K., Tsuchiyama, S., Moriya, M., Moriyasu, Y., & Satoh, K. (2011). Verb sense disambiguation based on thesaurus of predicate-argument structure. In *Proceedings of International Conference on Knowledge Engineering and Ontology Development* (pp. 208-213). Setúbal, Portugal: Science and Technology Publications.

Takita, K. (2014). Pseudo-right dislocation, the bare-topic construction, and hanging topic constructions. *Lingua*, *140*, 137–157. doi:10.1016/j.lingua.2013.12.010

Takiura, M. (2002). Kotoba asobi ha nani wo tsutaeruka?—Jakobson no shiteki kinou to Gris no kaiwa riorn wo baikai to shite[Wordplay and communication—from the viewpoint of poetic function by Jakobson and conversation theory by Gris]. *Nihongo Kagaku*, *11*, 79–96.

Tanaka, H. (2001). Right-dislocation as scrambling. *Journal of Linguistics*, *37*(03), 551–579. doi:10.1017/S0022226701001049

Tanaka, H. (2011). A-kitekuchuraru ko-dingu. [Architectural coding]. In Y. Karasawa, H. Tanaka, C. Dominick, R. Fujimura, & S. Matsukawa (Eds.), *Sekkei no sekkei* [Design of design] (pp. 53–110). Tokyo, Japan: INAX Publishing.

Tanaka, H., & Kizu, M. (2007). Island insensitive constructions in Japanese. *York Papers in Linguistics*, *2*, 219–234.

Tanaka, T., Toyama, F., Miyamichi, J., & Shoji, K. (2010). Detection and classification of speech balloons in comic images. *The Journal of The Institute of Image Information and Television Engineers*, *64*(12), 1933–1939. doi:10.3169/itej.64.1933

Tapiero, I., van den Broek, P., & Quintana, M. P. (2002). The mental representation of narrative texts as networks: The role of necessity and sufficiency in the detection of different types of causal relations. *Discourse Processes*, *34*(3), 237–258. doi:10.1207/S15326950DP3403_1

Tarasti, E. (1994). *A theory of musical semiotics*. Bloomington, IN: Indiana University Press.

Tashiro, T., Ito, T., Yoshida, S., & Tashiro, K. (2013). Trial of the integrated reinstatement support program on residual symptoms in remitted depression patients: To deal with pathologic variety. *Japanese Journal of Psychiatric Treatment*, *28*(6), 805–814.

Thaler, M. (1987). *Jokes, riddles and activities*. Modern Publishing.

Thawonmas, R., Oda, K., & Shuda, T. (2009). Camerawork editor for automatic comic generation from game log. In NICOGRAPH International 2009 (V-3).

Theodorakis, I. G., Koritos, C., & Stathakopoulos, V. (2015). Rhetorical maneuvers in a controversial tide: Assessing the boundaries of advertising rhetoric. *Journal of Advertising*, *44*(1), 14–24. doi:10.1080/00913367.2014.930679

Thorndyke, P. W. (1977). Cognitive structures in comprehension and memory of narrative discourse. *Cognitive Psychology*, *9*(1), 77–110. doi:10.1016/0010-0285(77)90005-6

Todorov, T. (2001). Structural analysis of narrative. In V. B. Leich (Ed.), The Norton anthology of theory and criticism (pp. 2099-2016). Norton.

Tokosumi, A. (2007). *Computational theories of mind: New edition*. Tokyo, Japan: Tokyo University Press.

Trabasso, T., & Wiley, J. (2005). Goal plans of action and inferences during comprehension of narratives. *Discourse Processes*, *39*(2&3), 129–164. doi:10.1080/0163853X.2005.9651677

Tsuchida, T., Aoyagi, E., & Ito, N. (1996). *Gendaibungakuriron* [Contemporary literature theory]. Tokyo, Japan: Shinyosha.

Tsuchihashi, S., & Ogata, T. (2009). Toward the narrative generation by quotations and anagram. In *Proceedings of the 23rd Annual Conference of the Japanese Society for Artificial Intelligence* (1J1-OS2-2). Takamatsu, Japan: Academic Press.

Tsuchiyama, G., & Murakami, M. (2014). A quantitative analysis on the formation of the third part of "The Tale of Genji", *Computer and Humanities Symposium Essays*, 2014(3), 213-220.

Tsuzuki, A. (1975). Shitsumonshicyosa no igi. [The significance of the questionnaire] In M. Arima & E. Murakami (Eds.), *Shinrigakukenkyuhou 9* [Psychology Research Methods 9]. Tokyo, Japan: University of Tokyo Press.

Turner, S. R. (1994). *The creative process: A computer model of storytelling and creativity*. NJ: Lawrence Erlbaum.

Tynyanov, Y. (1982). Bungaku no sinka. [Evolution of literature]. In *Rosia forumarizumu bungaku ronshuu 2* [A collection of literary essays in Russian formalism 2] (T. Kodaira, Trans.) (pp. 104–130). Tokyo, Japan: Serika Shobo. (Original work published 1929)

Ueda, K., & Ogata, T. (2004). A computational modeling of perspective and voice in the narrative rhetoric. In *Proceedings of 18th Congress of the International Association of Empirical Aesthetics* (pp. 480-486). Lisbon, Portugal: Academic Press.

Ueno, M., Mori, N., & Matsumoto, K. (2014). *2-scene comic creating system based on the distribution of picture state transition. Advances in Intelligent Systems and Computing* (Vol. 290, pp. 459–467). New York, NY: Springer, International Publishing.

United Nations Enable. (2007). *Convention on the rights of persons with disabilities*. Retrieved from http://www.un.org/esa/socdev/enable/rights/convtexte.htm

Utsumi, A., Nakamura, K., & Sakamoto, M. (2012). Effects of discourse goals on the process of metaphor production. In *Proceedings of the 34th Annnual Meeting of the Cognitive Science Society* (pp. 2475-2480). Sapporo, Japan: Academic Press.

Van der Heijden, K. (1996). *Scenarios*. Chichester, UK: John Wiley & Sons.

van der Werf, F., Brassinga, P., Reits, D., Aramideh, M., & Ongerboer de Visser, B. (2003). Eyelid movements: Behavioral studies of blinking in humans under different stimulus conditions. *Journal of Neurophysiology*, *89*(5), 2784–2796. doi:10.1152/jn.00557.2002 PMID:12612018

van Laer, T., De Ruyter, K., Visconti, L. M., & Wetzels, M. (2014). The extended transportation-imagery model: A meta-analysis of the antecedents and consequences of consumers' narrative transportation. *The Journal of Consumer Research*, *40*(5), 797–817. doi:10.1086/673383

Vendler, Z. (1967). *Linguistics in philosophy*. Ithaca, NY: Cornell University Press.

Victor, J. D., & Purpura, K. P. (1997). Metric-space analysis of spike trains: Theory, algorithms and application. *Network (Bristol, England)*, *8*(2), 127–164. doi:10.1088/0954-898X_8_2_003

Visch, V. T., & Tan, E. S. (2009). Categorizing moving objects into film genres: The effect of animacy attribution, emotional response, and the deviation from non-fiction. *Cognition*, *110*(2), 265–272. doi:10.1016/j.cognition.2008.10.018 PMID:19118823

Vorderer, P., Klimmt, C., & Ritterfeld, U. (2004). Enjoyment: At the heart of media entertainment. *Communication Theory*, *14*(4), 388–408. doi:10.1111/j.1468-2885.2004.tb00321.x

Vuokila-Oikkonen, P., Janhonen, S., & Vaisanen, L. (2004). "Shared-rhythm cooperation" in cooperative team meetings in acute psychiatric inpatient care. *Journal of Psychiatric and Mental Health Nursing*, *11*(2), 129–140. doi:10.1111/j.1365-2850.2003.00679.x PMID:15009487

Wade, W. (2012). *Scenario planning: A field guide to the future*. Hoboken, NJ: John Wiley & Sons.

Walther, J. B., Loh, T., & Granka, L. (2005). Let me count the ways: The interchange of verbal and nonverbal cues in computer-mediated and face-to-face affinity. *Journal of Language and Social Psychology*, *24*(1), 36–65. doi:10.1177/0261927X04273036

Watanabe, N. (2012). *Nihon shosetsu gijutsu shi* [A history of techniques in Japanese novels]. Tokyo, Japan: Shinchosha.

Watanabe, T. (1989). *Kabuki–Kajo naru kigo no mori* [Kabuki: The forest of excessive signs]. Tokyo, Japan: Shinyosha.

Watanabe, T. (2009). *Kabuki no mikata* [Kabuki's viewpoints]. Tokyo, Japan: Kadokawa Gakugei Shuppan.

Watanabe, T. (2012). *Watashi no kabuki henreki–Aru gekihyo-ka no kokuhaku* [My kabuki wandering: A confession by a drama critic]. Tokyo, Japan: Engeki Shuppansha.

Whitaker, R. (1970). *The language of film*. Englewood Cliffs, NJ: Prentice-Hall, Inc.

White, H. (1980). The value of narrativity in the representation of reality. W. J. T. Mitchell (Ed.), On narrative. Chicago: The University of Chicago Press.

White, M., & Epston, D. (1990). *Narrative means to therapeutic ends*. New York, NY: W. W. Norton & Company.

Whitman, J. (2000). Right dislocation in English and Japanese. In K. Takami et al. (Eds.), *Syntactic and functional explorations in honor of Susumu Kuno* (pp. 445–470). Tokyo, Japan: Kuroshio Publishers.

Winograd, T. (1972). *Understanding natural language*. New York, NY: Academic Press.

Winograd, T. (1983). *Syntax*. Boston, MA: Addison-Wesley Publishing.

Wittgenstein, L. (1921). *Tractatus Logico-Philosophicus*. Retrieved from http://www.gutenberg.org/files/5740/5740-pdf.pdf

Wittgenstein, L. (1986). *Philosophical investigations*. Oxford, UK: Blackwell Publishing.

Wolf, W. (2011). Narratology and media(lity): The transmedial expansion of a literary discipline and possible consequences. In G. Olson (Ed.), *Current trends in narratology* (pp. 145–180). doi:10.1515/9783110255003.145

World Health Organization. (2001). International classification of functioning, disability and health: ICF. Geneva, Swiss Confederation: World Health Organization.

Wu, Y. (2005). *The dynamic syntax of left and right dislocation*. (Unpublished doctoral dissertation). University of Edinburgh, Edinburgh, UK.

Yaeda, J., Fujikawa, M., Wakabayashi, I., Ozawa, A., Ishihara, M., Nishimura, S., & Iwanaga, K. (2012). Shokugyourihabiriteshon no ebidensu towa nanika?[What is the evidence of vocational rehabilitation?]. *Japanese Journal of Vocational Rehabilitation*, *25*(1), 24–26.

Yaeda, J., Ozawa, A., & Wakabayashi, I. (2013). Shokugyourihabiritesyhon to shougaishakoyoubunya niokeru kenkyuudoukou[Research trends in vocational rehabilitation and employment of persons with disabilities policy]. *Japanese Journal of Rehabilitation*, *156*, 22–33.

Yamabe, S. (2012). Sosharuwaku niokeru ebidensu tohananika: Purorogu [What is the evidence in the social work?: Prologue]. In Japanese Society for the Study of Social Welfare (Ed.), Taironshakaihukushigaku [Discussion social welfare studies] (pp. 85-87). Tokyo, Japan: Chuohoki Publishing.

Yamada, E. (2013). *Taini sutorizu* [Tiny stories]. Tokyo, Japan: Bungei Shunju.

Yamada, Y. (2007a). Shitsutekikenkyuu niokeru taiwatekimoderukouseihou[Interactive model construction method in qualitative research]. *Japanese Journal of Qualitative Psychology*, *6*, 174–194.

Yamada, Y. (2007b). *Shitsutekishinrigaku no houhou: Katari o kiku* [Method of qualitative psychology: Listening to narrative]. Tokyo, Japan: Shinyousha.

Yamaha. (n.d.). *What is VOCALOID*. Retrieved from http://www.vocaloid.com/en/about/

Yamamoto, S. (2006). *Zusetsu Rakugo-no rekishi* [The history Rakugo with illustrations]. Tokyo, Japan: Kawade Shobo Shinsha.

Yamanaka, A. (2008). *Utterance interpretation, group-defining practices and linguistic meaning*. (Unpublished doctoral dissertation). King's College London, London, UK.

Yamoto, T. (1974). *Bungakugijyuturon* [Literature technique theory]. Tokyo, Japan: Kenkyusha.

Yasuda, S. (1970). *Shakaichousa no keikaku to kaiseki* [Planning and analysis of social research]. Tokyo, Japan: University of Tokyo Press.

Yasumoto, B. (1957). Uji Jujo no sakusha: Bunsho sinrigaku ni yoru sakusya suitei[The author of Uji Jujo: Inferring the author through stylometry]. *Japanese Psychological Review*, *2*(1), 147–156.

Yasumoto, B. (1977). Gendai no buntai kenkyu[Stylometric research in recent years] [the Japanese language]. *Nihongo*, *10*, 395–423.

Yoshida, S. (2002). *Saigo-no-musuko* [The last son]. Tokyo, Japan: Bungei Shunju.

Yoshihara, M., & Imura, O. (2008). Psychological aspects in parents of muscular dystrophy patients: Based on analysis of the free description in questionnaires. *The Japanese Journal of Rehabilitation Psychology*, *35*(1), 49–60.

Yoshimoto, T. (1968). *Kyodo genso ron* [The theory of communal fantasy]. Tokyo, Japan: Kawade Shobo Shinsha.

Yuda, Y. (Ed.) (1965). Bunraku joruri shuu [A selection of bunraku and joruri works]. Tokyo, Japan: Iwanami Shoten.

Zhang, Y., Ono, J., & Ogata, T. (2011). An advertising rhetorical mechanism for single event combined with conceptual dictionary in narrative generation system. In *Proceedings of 7th International Conference on Natural Language Processing and Knowledge Engineering* (pp. 340-343). Tokushima, Japan. doi:10.1109/NLPKE.2011.6138221

Zhang, Y., Ono, J., & Ogata, T. (2012). Single event and scenario generation based on advertising rhetorical techniques using the conceptual dictionary in narrative generation system. In *Proceedings of the Fourth IEEE International Conference on Digital Game and Intelligent Toy Enhanced Learning* (pp. 162-164). Takamatsu, Japan. doi:10.1109/DIGITEL.2012.46

Zillmann, D. (1998). Does tragic drama have redeeming value? *Siegener Periodikum für Internationale Literaturwissenschaft*, *16*, 1–11.

Zunshine, L. (2014). Theory of mind as a pedagogical tool. *Interdisciplinary Literary Studies*, *16*(1), 89–105. doi:10.5325/intelitestud.16.1.0089

Zwaan, R. A., & Radvansky, G. A. (1998). Situation models in language comprehension and memory. *Psychological Bulletin*, *123*(2), 162–185. doi:10.1037/0033-2909.123.2.162 PMID:9522683

# About the Contributors

**Takashi Ogata**, after receiving his bachelor of social science in Waseda University in 1983, he received his M.S. in Tsukuba University in 1992 and his Ph.D. in the University of Tokyo in 1995. He has industrial experience since 1983 at software development companies. Having experienced Associate Professor of the Faculty of Engineering at Yamanashi University since 1997, he is Professor of the Faculty of Software and Information Science at Iwate Prefectural University since 2005. His major research interests include artificial intelligence, cognitive science, natural language processing, narratology and literary theories, an interdisciplinary approach to the development of narrative generation systems based on AI and narratology, and the application to narrative creation and business. He is a member of the Japanese Society for Artificial Intelligence, the Japanese Cognitive Science Society (committee), and the Japanese Association for Natural Language Processing. He is also a main manager of Literature, Cognition and Computer research group at the JCSS. He received JSAI best paper award (1996), best paper award of Japan Academy of Advertising (1996), and other academic awards.

**Taisuke Akimoto** is a postdoctoral researcher in the Graduate School of Informatics and Engineering, the University of Electro-Communications, Japan. He received his Ph.D. from Iwate Prefectural University in 2014. His research interests include Artificial Intelligence, Informatics, Cognitive Science, etc. Especially, he interests automatic narrative generation system and its applications. He is a member of the Japanese Society for Artificial Intelligence, Japanese Cognitive Science Society, and the Association for Natural Language Processing in Japan.

* * *

**Akinori Abe** received an M.E. and Doctor of Engineering (PhD) from the University of Tokyo in 1988 and 1991 respectively. His main research interests are abduction, analogical reasoning, data mining, Chance Discovery and language sense processing (rather emotional aspects of language processing). He worked in NTT Communication Science Laboratories from 1991 to 2000, NTT MSC (Malaysia) from 2000 to 2002, and ATR from 2002 to 2009. He also worked as an associate professor of IREIIMS, Tokyo Women's Medical Univ. and a visiting associate professor of Kobe Univ. Graduate School (Cooperation Course). In 2009 he returned to NTT Communication Science Laboratories. Then he moved to Faculty of Letters, Chiba University in April 2012. Since then he is a full professor of Chiba University.

**Stefano Calabrese** is Professor of Text Semiotic at the University of Modena and Regggio Emilia. Latest Publications: Anatomia del Best Seller (Best Seller Anatomy), Roma, Laterza, 2015; The Immersive Novel (with S. Uboldi), International Journal of Language and Literature, 1,3, (in press); Retorica e Neuroscienze Cognitive (Rhetoric and Cognitive Neuroscience), Carocci, Roma, 2013.

**Kiyohito Fukuda** is a doctor's course student in the department of Computer Science and Intelligent Systems at Osaka Prefecture University. He received his B.S. and M.S. degrees in engineering from Osaka Prefecture University in 2013 and 2015 respectively. His research interests include natural language processing, and artificial intelligence.

**Tüge T. Gülşen** holds the degrees of BA in Foreign Languages Education (Middle East Technical University), MA in Learning and Teaching of English and Literacy (Institute of Education, University of London), MA in Cultural Studies (Istanbul Bilgi University). She is currently a PhD candidate in Communication Studies in Istanbul Bilgi University. She is an EAP instructor and has been teaching academic skills and contributing to the curriculum and material design in Istanbul Bilgi University since 2001.

**Yuichiro Haruna** received a B.S., a M.S., and a Ph.D. in Health Sciences from the University of Tokyo, Japan. He began work at the NIVR in 1994, has been a principal investigator at the NIVR and a member of the National Expert Committee on Intractable Diseases Policy since 2012. He has been a lecturer of the Faculy of Medicine, the University of Tokyo since 1999.

**Akihito Kanai** was born in Yokohama, Japan, in 1972. He received his B.A. and M.A. degrees from the University of Tokyo in 1995 and 1997, respectively, and his Ph.D. degree in Engineering from Yamanashi University in 2004. In 2004, as a Lecturer, he joined the Department of Media and Communication Studies, Faculty of Social Sciences, Hosei University, where he became an Associate Professor in 2006, and a Professor in 2014. His current research interests include film cognition, film rhetoric, film narrative, and computational film composition.

**Yoji Kawamura** (M.B.A., Tsukuba University; B.S., Tokyo Institute of Technology) is professor of business administration at Kindai University. His majoring is modeling the various social (include business, advertising) phenomena based on the modeling of consumer and the system building for simulation. His published research has appeared in journals (in Japan) as Journal of Advertising Science, Japan Marketing Journal, Cognitive Studies, IPSJ Journal. He was received the 2005 Research Article Award given by Japan Academy of Advertising.

**Naoki Mori** 1997- Department of Computer and Systems Sciences, College of Engineering, Osaka Prefecture University. 1999- Ph.D in engineering from Kyoto University Main Works: evolutionary computation, multi-agent system, kansei engineering Membership in Academic Societies: The Institute of Systems, Control and Information Engineers (ISCIE) The Society of Instrument and Control Engineers (SICE) Japan Association of Simulation and Gaming (JASAG) The Institute of Electrical Engineers of Japan (IEEJ) The Association for Natural Language Processing (NLP).

**Ryota Nomura** was received the Ph. D. in Psychology from Kyushu University, Fukuoka, Japan, in 2008. He is now an assistant professor of the University of Tokyo. His research interest includes expertise in performing arts and epistemology in education.

**Yukiko Ogawa** holds a Ph.D. degree in Arts and Sciences from the University of Tsukuba, Japan, and teaches at Hosei University in Tokyo. Her research focuses on the areas of film studies by means of cognitive approaches including much interests in aesthetics, philosophy, narratology and psychology. Her specific interest on questions is enjoyment as one of the cognitive effects from various films.

**Akira Ohtani** works in computational and theoretical linguistics, the implementation of grammar development systems and the application of highly lexicalized, non-derivational generative grammar theories to the Japanese language. He received a Ph.D. in language and culture from Osaka University in 1999, and a Ph.D. in engineering from Nara Institute of Science and Technology in 2005, writing dissertations on designing an HPSG parser for Japanese grammatical constructions and on its extension with semantic and pragmatic constraints. He was an assistant professor at Osaka University and, in 2000, accepted a position as a lecturer at Osaka Gakuin University where he is now an associate professor. From 2007 to 2009 he was a visiting researcher at the University of Edinburgh, where he studied automatic induction of a CCG grammar for Japanese. He is currently working on a Dynamic Syntax modelling of postposing in Japanese.

**Takeshi Okada** is a professor of educational psychology at the University of Tokyo. He conducts psychological studies on artistic creativity and its educational implications.

**Tohru Seraku** received his DPhil in Comparative Philology and General Linguistics from the University of Oxford in 2014. From January to July in 2014, he was a teaching fellow at SOAS (University of London), teaching Japanese linguistics to both undergraduate and graduate students. Since September 2014, he has been an assistant professor at the Department of Japanese Interpretation and Translation at Hankuk University of Foreign Studies in Korea, where he teaches Japanese linguistics and the Japanese language. He writes and presents widely on issues of theoretical linguistics (syntax, semantics, pragmatics) as well as formal grammar, with the principal target language of his research being contemporary Japanese.

**Yoko Takeda** received her Ph.D. in Business Administration at Keio Business School. She is a professor at Graduate School of Environment and Information Sciences, Yokohama National University, Japan. Her research interest is related to impacts of information technologies on organization and innovation processes. She has published research papers at national and international journals, conference proceedings and books.

**Koichi Takeuchi** is Senior Assistant Professor of the Graduate School of Natural Science and Technology, Okayama University, Japan. He is the conductor of the free thesaurus with predicate-argument structure for Japanese predicates, which is accessible from the Public Internet. He is the conductor of ASA: The program of analyzing predicate-argument structure for Japanese texts.

**Gen Tsuchiyama** holds a PhD in Culture and Information Science from Doshisha University, and is currently Assistant Professor (non-tenured researcher) at Doshisha University. His research interests include stylometry, text mining, statistics, and digital humanities.

**Sara Uboldi** is PhD Humanities. Her research interests are: Narratology and Cognitive Neuroscience, Cognitive Poetics, Storytelling and Cultural Heritage. Latest Publication: Fiaba e Neuroscience Cognitive (Fairy Tales and Cognitive Neuroscience), Milano, Ledizioni, 2014 - The immersive Novel (with S. Calabrese), International Journal of Language and Literature, Vol. 3, n. 1 (in press).

**Miki Ueno** has been an assistant professor at Toyohashi University of Technology since 2015 and received her M.S and Ph.D. degrees of engineering from Osaka Prefecture University in 2012 and 2015 respectively. Her research interests are kansei engineering and human agent interaction. She is a member of JSAI, ISCIE and SICE.

# Index

## O



## P



## Q



## R



## S



## T



## U



## V



## W

## Receive Free Lifetime E-Access or Free Hardcover*

Purchase a print book or e-book through the IGI Global Online Bookstore and receive the alternate version for free! Shipping fees apply.

**www.igi-global.com**

# Recommended Reference Books

**Take 20% Off through the IGI Global Online Bookstore****

ISBN: 978-1-4666-6042-7
© 2014; 1,727 pp.
**Take 20% Off:* $1,756**

ISBN: 978-1-4666-6571-2
© 2015; 927 pp.
**Take 20% Off:* $404**

ISBN: 978-1-4666-5170-8
© 2014; 592 pp.
**Take 20% Off:* $304**

ISBN: 978-1-4666-7401-1
© 2015; 362 pp.
**Take 20% Off:* $156**

ISBN: 978-1-4666-4916-3
© 2014; 398 pp.
**Take 20% Off:* $164**

ISBN: 978-1-4666-5003-9
© 2014; 580 pp.
**Take 20% Off:* $152**

*IGI Global now offers the option to purchase hardcover, e-access, or hardcover + e-access for one price! You choose the format that best suits your needs. This offer is only valid on purchases made directly through IGI Global's Online Bookstore and not intended for use by book distributors or wholesalers. Shipping fees will be applied for hardcover purchases during checkout if this option is selected. E-Access will remain available for the lifetime of the publication and will only allow access to the edition purchased. Free Lifetime E-Access is only available to individuals and single institutions that purchase printed publications directly through IGI Global. Sharing the Free Lifetime E-Access is prohibited and will result in the termination of e-access. **20% discount cannot be combined with any other offer. Only valid on purchases made directly through IGI Global's Online Bookstore and not intended for use by book distributors or wholesalers. Not applicable on databases.

Publishing Progressive Information Science and Technology Research Since 1988

IGI Global — Disseminator of Knowledge

www.igi-global.com | Sign up at www.igi-global.com/newsletters | facebook.com/igiglobal | twitter.com/igiglobal

www.ingramcontent.com/pod-product-compliance
Lightning Source LLC
LaVergne TN
LVHW060354300926
849162LV00006B/1261